Worlds of History

A Comparative Reader

Volume One: To 1550

Second Edition

Kevin Reilly
Raritan Valley College

Bedford/St. Martin's
Boston • New York

To My Teachers: Eugene Meehan, Traian Stoianovich, Donald Weinstein, and to the memory of Warren Susman

For Bedford/St. Martin's

Publisher for History: Patricia A. Rossi
Director of Development for History: Jane Knetzger
Developmental Editor: Elizabeth Harrison
Editorial Assistant: Carina Schoenberger
Assistant Editor, Publishing Services: Maria Burwell
Production Supervisor: Jennifer Wetzel
Senior Marketing Manager: Jenna Bookin Barry
Project Management: Books By Design, Inc.
Cover Design: Billy Boardman
Cover Art: Painted wooden stele of the singer of Amon (playing the harp before the deity Horus), 950–730 B.C.E. 22nd Dynasty (Libyan). Louvre, Paris, France. © Giraudon/Art Resource, NY. *Harp player* (King David?); detail of painting. Klaus Synagogue, Prague, Czech Republic. © Scala/Art Resource, NY.
Composition: Pine Tree Composition, Inc.
Printing and Binding: Haddon Craftsmen, an RR Donnelley & Sons Company

President: Joan E. Feinberg
Editorial Director: Denise B. Wydra
Director of Marketing: Karen Melton Soeltz
Director of Editing, Design, and Production: Marcia Cohen
Manager, Publishing Services: Emily Berleth

Library of Congress Catalog Card Number: 2003110548

Copyright © 2004 by Bedford/St. Martin's

All rights reserved. No part of this book may be reproduced, stored in a retrieval system, or transmitted in any form or by any means, electronic, mechanical, photocopying, recording, or otherwise, except as may be expressly permitted by the applicable copyright statutes or in writing by the Publisher.

Manufactured in the United States of America.

9 8 7 6 5 4
f e d c b a

For information, write: Bedford/St. Martin's, 75 Arlington Street, Boston, MA 02116   (617-399-4000)

ISBN: 0-312-40201-5 (Volume 1)
       0-312-40202-3 (Volume 2)

Acknowledgments

Acknowledgments and copyrights are continued at the back of the book on pages 506-10, which constitute an extension of the copyright page.

Preface

Teaching introductory world history to college students for thirty-five years has helped me appreciate three enduring truths that provide the framework for this book. The first is that any introductory history course must begin with the students, as they sit before us in their remarkable diversity. The second is that history embraces all, the entire past, the whole world. The third is that students need to learn to think historically, critically, and independently, and that the subject matter of history can teach them how. With these goals in mind, I have constructed chapters in *Worlds of History* that pique student interest, teach broad trends and comparative experiences, and develop what today we call "critical thinking skills" and the Romans used to call "habits of mind."

The primary and secondary source selections in both volumes of this reader address the question, "What specific topics can imbue a general understanding of world history while helping students develop critical thinking skills?" The reader's format helps students (and instructors) make sense of the overwhelming richness and complexity of world history. First, the reader has a **topical organization** that is also chronological, with each chapter focusing on an engaging topic within a particular time period. I am convinced that students are generally more interested in topics than eras, and that an appreciation of period and process can be taught by concentrating on topics. Into these topical chapters I've woven a **comparative approach**, examining two or more cultures at a time. In some chapters students can trace parallel developments in separate regions, such as the rise of cities in China, Italy, and Egypt in Volume One, or Chinese and European expansion in the fifteenth and sixteenth centuries in Volume Two. In other cases students examine the enduring effects of contact and exchange between cultures, as in Volume One's chapter on the First Crusade in the eleventh century or Volume Two's chapter on the European colonization of Burma, the Philippines, and Nigeria in the nineteenth and twentieth centuries.

A wealth of **pedagogical tools** helps students unlock the readings and extend their critical thinking skills. Each chapter begins with "Historical Context," an introduction to the chapter's topic that sets the stage for directed comparisons among the readings. A separate "**Thinking Historically**" section follows, exploring a particular critical thinking skill—reading primary and secondary sources or distinguishing causes of change—that ties to the chapter's selections. These skills increase in difficulty with each chapter so that a student's capacity to manipulate knowledge—to analyze, synthesize, and interpret—builds one step at a time.

"Reflections," a section that summarizes or extends the chapter's lessons, concludes each chapter.

Each volume's fourteen chapters should correspond to general survey texts and to most instructors' syllabi. Understanding that some variation might exist, I have included a correlation chart in the new **online instructor's resource manual** that matches each reading in this text with related chapters in sixteen of the most widely used survey texts. The manual, available at **bedfordstmartins.com/reilly**, also highlights teaching strategies, provides the rationale for the selection and organization of the readings, and includes information about ancillary resources, including films and Internet sites.

NEW TO THIS EDITION

While I am continually testing selections in my own classroom, I appreciate input from readers and adopters and I want to thank them for their many suggestions. Having incorporated some of this feedback, I think those who have used the first edition will find this edition tighter, more interesting, and even more accessible to students. In response to numerous requests, I have added new chapters on gender and women's history in each volume. In Volume One, a chapter on women in the Classical world compares women's lives in India, China, and Rome, enabling students to draw comparisons from classic primary texts. In Volume Two, students read about gender and the family in early modern societies from China to Spanish America, building and evaluating theory as they juxtapose one society with another.

New scholarship has pointed the way to revising other chapters. In Volume One, a chapter on the expansion of Christianity and Buddhism has been broadened to include recent work on the importance of trade along the Silk Road and the expansion of Islam. The last chapter in Volume Two, on globalization, is almost entirely new, benefiting from recent scholarship and post-9/11 interpretations. In other cases, I have added readings of classical scholarship that suddenly give a chapter the focus I have always sought: Fernand Braudel on cities in Volume One and Benedict Anderson on nationalism in Volume Two.

Some of the best new materials in this edition are the illustrations and maps that Bedford/St. Martin's has enabled me to add. In this revision I've introduced brand-new geographic reference maps to many of the chapters' "Historical Context" sections. Not to be "read" as sources themselves, these maps are simply meant to give students a geographic point of reference for readings that span the globe. For example, in Chapter 5 of Volume One, I've provided straightforward maps of the expanding Chinese and Roman empires discussed in the chapter. In Volume Two's chapter on

World War I, I've included a map showing the Allied and Central Powers, as well as the Western Front. As one of my reviewers put it, "Simple maps simply work better"; this has been the inspiration for the new map program.

To emphasize the importance of using nonwritten materials in historical analysis, both volumes now include more visual sources, such as prehistoric Venus statues in Volume One and a global warming cartogram in Volume Two. In some cases, these visuals stand alone to advance the lesson of the chapter: historic Chinese maps of Zheng He's expeditions in Volume Two, for instance. In other cases they are tied to a specific selection and help students better understand the reading, like the graphs depicting the rate of conversion to Islam in medieval Iran in Volume One.

I am not a believer in change for its own sake; when I have a successful way of teaching a subject, I am not disposed to jettison it for something new. Consequently, many of my most satisfying changes are incremental: a better translation of a document or the addition of a newly discovered source. In some cases I have been able to further edit a useful source, retaining its muscle, but providing room for a precious new find. I begin each round of revision with the conviction that the book is already as good as it can get. And I end each round with the surprising discovery that it is much better than it was.

ACKNOWLEDGMENTS

A book like this cannot be written without the help and advice, even if sometimes unheeded, of a vast army of colleagues and professionals. I count myself enormously fortunate to have met and known such a large group of gifted and generous scholars and teachers in my years with the World History Association. Among them, I would like to thank those who were reviewers and questionnaire respondents for this book: Robin Anderson, Arkansas State University; Pierre Asselin, Kapiolani Community College; Martin E. Berger, Youngstown State University; Donna Bohanan, Auburn University; Andrew Clark, University of North Carolina at Wilmington; Franklin M. Doeringer, Lawrence University; S. Ross Doughty, Ursinus College; E. Thomas Ewing, Virginia Polytechnic; Christopher Guthrie, Tarleton State University; Carla Hay, Marquette University; Susan Hult, Houston Community College; Norman Love, El Paso Community College; Justin D. Murphy, Howard Payne University; Patrick Patterson, Honolulu Community College; and Rachel Stocking, Southern Illinois University.

Other friends and colleagues contributed selections, suggestions, and advice for the book in other ways. Among them I would like to thank the following: Michael Adas, Rutgers University; Jerry Bentley, University of

Hawaii; David Berry, Essex County Community College; Catherine Clay, Shippensburg University; Roger Cranse, Norwich University; Philip Curtin, Johns Hopkins University; Ross Dunn, San Diego State University; Martin Gilbert, North Georgia College; Steve Gosch, University of Wisconsin at Eau Claire; Gregory Guzman, Bradley University; Brock Haussamen, Raritan Valley College; Sarah Hughes, Shippensburg University; Allen Howard, Rutgers University; Karen Jolly, University of Hawaii; Maghan Keita, Villanova University; Pat Manning, Northeastern University; William H. McNeill, University of Chicago; John Mears, Southern Methodist University; Gyan Prakash, Princeton University; Heidi Roupp, Aspen High School; Richard Rosen, Drexel University; Robert Rosen, University of California at Los Angeles; John Russell-Wood, Johns Hopkins University; Lynda Shaffer, Tufts University; Anthony Snyder, Brookdale Community College; Leften Stavrianos, University of California at San Diego; Robert Stayer; Peter Stearns, George Mason University; Robert Tignor, Princeton University; Mary Evelyn Tucker, Bucknell University; John Voll, Georgetown University; and Judith Zinsser, Miami University.

I also want to thank the people at Bedford/St. Martin's, especially Joan Feinberg, Denise Wydra, Patricia Rossi, Jane Knetzger, Elizabeth Harrison, Emily Berleth, Nancy Benjamin, Jenna Bookin Barry, Donna Dennison, and Billy Boardman.

While writing this book, memories of my own introduction to history and critical thinking have come flooding back to me. I was blessed at Rutgers in the 1960s with teachers I still aspire to emulate. Eugene Meehan taught me that learning could be both hard work and fun. Traian Stoianovich, who introduced me to the work of his own teacher, Fernand Braudel, demonstrated a vision of history that was boundless, and demanded only originality from this graduate student. Donald Weinstein taught me to listen to students as if they were Stradivarii. And Warren Susman filled a room with more life than I ever knew existed. I dedicate this book to them.

Finally, I want to thank my own institution, Raritan Valley College, for nurturing my career, allowing me to teach whatever I wanted, and entrusting me with some of the best students one could encounter anywhere. I could not ask for anything more. Except, of course, a loving wife like Pearl.

Introduction

You have here fourteen lessons in world history, each of which deals with a particular historical period from human origins to the 1500s. (A companion volume covers the last five hundred years.) Some of the topics are narrow and specific, covering events such as the First Crusade and the Mongols in detail, while others are broad and general, such as technology and ecology and cities.

As you learn about historical periods and topics, you also will be coached to think systematically. The "Thinking Historically" passages in each chapter encourage habits of mind that I associate with my own study of history. They are not necessarily intended to turn you into historians but, rather, to give you skills that will help you in all of your college courses and throughout your life. For example, the first chapter leads you to become more perceptive about time, the passage of time, measuring time, the time between events—all of which are useful throughout life. Similarly, a number of chapters help you in various ways to distinguish between fact and opinion, clearly an ability as necessary at work, on a jury, in the voting booth, and in discussions with friends as it is in the study of history.

World history is nothing less than everything ever done or imagined, so we cannot possibly cover it all. In his famous novel *Ulysses*, James Joyce imagines the thoughts and actions of a few friends on a single day in Dublin, June 16, 1904. The book runs almost a thousand pages. Obviously, there were many more than a few people in Dublin on that particular day, countless other cities in the world, and infinitely more days than that one particular day in world history. So we are forced to choose places and times.

In this volume our choices include some particular days, like the day in 1519 that Cortés and Montezuma met, but our attention will be directed mainly toward much longer periods. And while we will visit particular places like Mexico City in 1519, typically we will study more than one place at a time by using a comparative approach.

Comparisons can be enormously useful in studying world history. When we compare London and Cairo, Greece and India, Rome and China, Christians and Buddhists, and Spaniards and Aztecs, we learn about the general and the specific at the same time. My hope is that by comparing some of the various *worlds* of history, an understanding of world history will emerge.

Contents

3. Identity in Caste and Territorial Societies

Greece and India, 1000–300 B.C.E.   *69*

Ancient Greece and India developed with different ideas of society. Does who we are depend on where we are or who we know? While finding out, we explore the relationship between facts and opinions, sources and interpretations.

4. Women in Classical Societies

India, China, and Rome, 500 B.C.E.–500 C.E.   *107*

Classical societies were largely patriarchal, but the experiences of women varied greatly both within and between the cultures of India, China, and Rome. Reading classic texts often reveals more than their authors imagined.

5. Empire and Officialdom: Bureaucracy, Law, and Individuality

China and Rome, 300 B.C.E.–300 C.E.   *139*

Two thousand years ago the Chinese Han dynasty and the Roman Empire spanned Eurasia. But they governed their vast realms according to different principles and with different personnel. What does the experience of individuals tell us about the history of empires?

6. Tribal to Universal Religion

Hindu-Buddhist and Judeo-Christian Traditions, 1000 B.C.E.–100 C.E. *173*

Two religious traditions transformed themselves into universal religions at about the same time in two different parts of Asia as each became part of a more connected world. Their holy books reveal the changes as well as the desire to hold on to the tried and true.

HISTORICAL CONTEXT   *173*

THINKING HISTORICALLY
Detecting Change in Primary Sources   *174*

Reflections   *200*

7. Encounters and Conversions: Monks and Merchants

Expansion of Salvation Religions, 400 B.C.E.–1000 C.E.   *202*

Christianity, Buddhism, and later, Islam, spread far across Eurasia often along the same routes in the first thousand years of the Common Era. To understand their success, we explore the evolution of religions in a larger context.

HISTORICAL CONTEXT   *202*

THINKING HISTORICALLY
Studying Religion in Historic Context   *203*

MAP 7.1 The Silk Road   *204*

8. Medieval Civilizations

European, Islamic, and Chinese Societies, 600–1300 C.E.   *238*

Three great civilizations spanned Eurasia between 500 and 1500. Of the three, China and Islam were the strongest, Europe the weakest. But their differences can be best understood by looking separately at the social structure, economy, politics, and culture of each.

9. Love and Marriage

Medieval Societies and Cultures, 1000–1200 C.E.   *280*

Love and marriage make the world go 'round today, but not a thousand years ago. Love meant different things in Europe, India, Japan, and Africa, and we use cultural comparisons to find out more.

10. The First Crusade

Muslims, Christians, and Jews during the First Crusade, 1095–1102 C.E.   315

The First Crusade initiated a centuries-long struggle and dialogue between Christians and Muslims that would have a lasting impact on both. Wars are windows on cultures, but they also make moving narratives. Using the selections here, put together your own version of the story.

HISTORICAL CONTEXT   315

THINKING HISTORICALLY
Analyzing and Writing Narrative   316

11. Ecology, Technology, and Science

Europe, Asia, and Africa, 500–1500 C.E.   349

The most important changes since the Middle Ages have been technological. Did these changes originate in Europe or South Asia? In comparing two interpretations, can images offer clues?

HISTORICAL CONTEXT   349

12. "Barbarians" and Mongols

Mongol Eurasia, 1200–1350 C.E.   *386*

In the thirteenth century, the Mongols created the largest empire the world had ever known. Did they bring peace, as they claimed, or unrelieved terror, as those they conquered complained? How do you judge the past?

13. On Cities

European, Chinese, and Islamic Cities, 1000–1550 C.E.   *426*

Has global urbanization made us more alike or different? You evaluate two theories about urban history as you wander through some of the great cities of medieval Europe, China, and the Islamic world.

14. The Spanish Conquest of Mexico
Mexico and "The Indies," 1500–1550 C.E.   465

The meeting of Cortéz and Montezuma was fraught with peril for both. Similarly driven, they understood almost nothing of each other. Eyewitnesses on both sides recounted the inevitable conflict. Later generations reinterpreted it for their own times. What does it mean today?

Prehistory and the Origins of Patriarchy

Gathering, Agricultural, and Urban Societies, 20,000–3000 B.C.E.

HISTORICAL CONTEXT

Men control more of the world's income, wealth, and resources; enjoy more opportunities, freedoms, and positions of power; and exercise greater control over the bodies, wishes, and lives of others than do women. In most of the world, men dominate, parents prefer sons to daughters, and most people—even women—associate maleness with strength, energy, reason, science, and the important public sphere. A system of male rule—"patriarchy"—seems as old as humanity itself. But is it? This chapter will ask if patriarchy is natural or historical. If patriarchy did not always exist, did it have a historical beginning, middle, and, therefore, potentially a historical end? If patriarchy had human causes, can humans also create a more equal world?

The selections in this chapter span the three types of societies known to human history: hunting and gathering (the earliest human lifestyle), agricultural and pastoral (beginning about ten thousand years ago), and urban (beginning about five thousand years ago). Thus, we can speak of the agricultural revolution (8000 B.C.E.) and the urban revolution (3000 B.C.E.) as two of the most important changes in human history. These events drastically transformed the way people earned a living and led to increased populations, greater productivity, and radically changed lifestyles. Each of these stages of human development brought to the fore unique methods of working, living, and thinking.

How did the lives of men and women change with these revolutions? How did the relationships between men and women change? As people settled in agricultural villages, and later in cities, economic and social differences between groups became more marked. Did differences between the sexes increase as well? Did men and women have relatively equal power before the development of agriculture and the rise of cities? Did patriarchy originate as part of the transition from agricultural to urban society, or did men always have more power?

THINKING HISTORICALLY
Thinking about History in Stages

To answer these questions, one must think of early human history in broad periods or stages. History does not develop in neat compartments, however, one clearly distinguished from the other. Historians must organize and analyze disparate events and developments that occur over time in order to make sense of them. This chapter follows a widely accepted division of early history into the hunting-gathering, agricultural/pastoral, and urban stages. You might reflect on how this system of structuring the past makes history more intelligible; you might also consider the shortcomings of such a system. What challenges to the idea of historical stages do the readings in the chapter pose? On balance, does organizing history into stages make it easier or more difficult to understand complex changes, such as evolving gender roles?

1

NATALIE ANGIER

Furs for Evening, But Cloth Was the Stone Age Standby

The female "Venus" statues discussed in the following article date back over 20,000 years and are the earliest sculptures of humans. Archaeologists have long considered them symbols of fertility, given their exaggerated depiction of the female anatomy. As *New York Times* science writer Natalie Angier reports, some archaeologists have recently begun to reinterpret these "Venuses," emphasizing the de-

Natalie Angier, "Furs for Evening, But Cloth Was the Stone Age Standby," *New York Times*, December 15, 1999, p. F1.

tailed clothing and reconsidering what these costumes might reveal about the role of women in hunting and gathering societies. What conclusions do archaeologists draw from these new interpretations? What conclusions might you draw from these statues about the roles of women and their relative status in prehistoric society?

Thinking Historically

Grouping prehistory into the hunting-gathering, agricultural/pastoral, and urban stages emphasizes how early people sustained themselves. Archaeologists and historians also divide prehistory into eras defined by the tools that humans developed. They also call the age of hunters and gatherers the Old Stone Age, or Paleolithic era, because of the rough stone tools and arrow points that humans fashioned in this period. The age of agriculture is called the New Stone Age, or Neolithic era, because of the use of more sophisticated stone tools. The urban age is often called the Bronze Age because city people began to smelt tin and copper to make bronze tools. Angier's article asks us to reconsider the importance of these designations by highlighting what Dr. Elizabeth Wayland Barber has termed "the string revolution." What is the string revolution, and what was its significance? According to Angier, how might the string revolution prompt us to reconsider stages of prehistory?

Ah, the poor Stone Age woman of our kitschy imagination. When she isn't getting bonked over the head with a club and dragged across the cave floor by her matted hair, she's hunched over a fire, poking at a roasting mammoth thigh while her husband retreats to his cave studio to immortalize the mammoth hunt in fresco. Or she's Raquel Welch, saber-toothed sex kitten, or Wilma Flintstone, the original Soccer Mom. But whatever her form, her garb is the same: some sort of animal pelt, cut nasty, brutish, and short.

Now, according to three anthropologists, it is time to toss such hidebound clichés of Paleolithic woman on the midden heap of prehistory. In a new analysis of the renowned "Venus" figurines, the hand-size statuettes of female bodies carved from 27,000 to 20,000 years ago, the researchers have found evidence that the women of the so-called upper Paleolithic era were far more accomplished, economically powerful, and sartorially gifted than previously believed.

As the researchers see it, subtle but intricate details on a number of the figurines offer the most compelling evidence yet that Paleolithic women had already mastered a revolutionary skill long thought to have arisen much later in human history: the ability to weave plant fibers into cloth, rope, nets, and baskets.

And with a flair for textile production came a novel approach to adorning and flaunting the human form. Far from being restricted to a wardrobe of what Dr. Olga Soffer, one of the researchers, calls "smelly animal hides," Paleolithic people knew how to create fine fabrics that very likely resembled linen. They designed string skirts, slung low on the hips or belted up on the waist, which artfully revealed at least as much as they concealed. They wove elaborate caps and snoods for the head, and bandeaux for the chest—a series of straps that amounted to a cupless brassiere. [See Figure 1.1.]

"Some of the textiles they had must have been incredibly fine, comparable to something from Donna Karan or Calvin Klein," said Dr. Soffer, an archaeologist with the University of Illinois in Urbana-Champaign.

Archaeologists and anthropologists have long been fascinated by the Venus figurines and have theorized endlessly about their origin and purpose. But nearly all of that speculation has centered on the exaggerated body parts of some of the figurines: the huge breasts, the bulging thighs and bellies, the well-defined vulvas. Hence, researchers have suggested that the figurines were fertility fetishes, or prehistoric erotica, or gynecology primers.

"Because they have emotionally charged thingies like breasts and buttocks, the Venus figurines have been the subject of more spilled ink

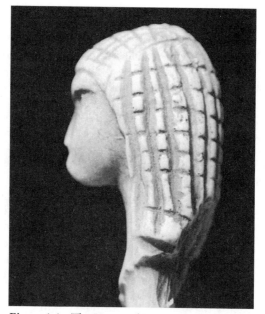

Figure 1.1   The Venus of Brassempouy, France.
Source: Steve Holland, University of Illinois.

than anything I know of," Dr. Soffer said. "There are as many opinions on them as there are people in the field."

In their new report, which will be published in the spring in the journal *Current Anthropology*, Dr. Soffer and her colleagues, Dr. James M. Adovasio and Dr. David C. Hyland of the Mercyhurst Archaeological Institute at Mercyhurst College in Erie, Pa., point out that voluptuous body parts notwithstanding, a number of the figurines are shown wearing items of clothing. And when they zeroed in on the details of those carved garments, the researchers saw proof of considerable textile craftsmanship, an intimate knowledge of how fabric is woven.

"Scholars have been looking at these things for years, but unfortunately, their minds have been elsewhere," Dr. Adovasio said. "Most of them didn't recognize the clothing as clothing. If they noticed anything at all, they misinterpreted what they saw, writing off the bandeaux, for example, as tattoos or body art." [See Figure 1.2.]

Scrutinizing the famed Venus of Willendorf, for example, which was discovered in lower Austria in 1908, the researchers paid particular attention to the statuette's head. The Venus has no face to speak of, but detailed coils surround its scalp. Most scholars have interpreted the

Figure 1.2 The Venus of Kostenki (Russia), wearing a woven bandeau.

Source: Bill Wiegand, University of Illinois.

coils as a kind of paleo-coiffure, but Dr. Adovasio, an authority on textiles and basketry, recognized the plaiting as what he called a "radially sewn piece of headgear with vertical stem stitches."

Willendorf's haberdashery "might have looked like one of those woven hats you see on Jamaicans on the streets of New York," he said, adding, "These were cool things."

On the Venus of Lespugue, an approximately 25,000-year-old figurine from southwestern France, the anthropologists noticed a "remarkable" degree of detail lavished on the rendering of a string skirt, with the tightness and angle of each individual twist of the fibers carefully delineated. The skirt is attached to a low-slung hip belt and tapers in the back to a tail, the edges of its hem deliberately frayed. [See Figure 1.3.]

"That skirt is to die for," said Dr. Soffer, who, before she turned to archaeology, was in the fashion business. "Though maybe it's an acquired taste."

Figure 1.3   The Venus of Lespugue,
with a low-slung cloth
skirt.
Source: Steve Holland, University of Illinois.

To get an idea of what such an outfit might have looked like, she said, imagine a hula dancer wrapping a 1930s-style beaded curtain around her waist. "We're not talking protection from the elements here," Dr. Soffer said. "This would have been ritual wear, if it was worn at all, a way of communicating with higher powers."

Other anthropologists point out that string skirts, which appear in Bronze-Age artifacts and are mentioned by Homer, may have been worn at the equivalent of a debutantes' ball, to advertise a girl's coming of age. In some parts of Eastern Europe, the skirts still survive as lacy elements of folk costumes.

The researchers presented their results earlier this month at a meeting on the importance of perishables in prehistory that was held at the University of Florida in Gainesville. "One of the most common reactions we heard was, 'How could we have missed that stuff all these years?'" Dr. Adovasio said.

Dr. Margaret W. Conkey, a professor of anthropology at the University of California at Berkeley, and co-editor, with Joan Gero, of *Engendering Archaeology* (Blackwell Publishers, 1991) said, "They're helping us to look at old materials in new ways, to which I say bravo!"

Not all scholars had been blinded by the Venusian morphology. Dr. Elizabeth Wayland Barber, a professor of archaeology and linguistics at Occidental College in Los Angeles, included in her 1991 volume *Prehistoric Textiles* a chapter arguing that some Venus figurines were wearing string skirts. The recent work from Dr. Soffer and her colleagues extends and amplifies on Dr. Barber's original observations.

The new work also underscores the often neglected importance of what Dr. Barber has termed the "string revolution." Archaeologists have long emphasized the invention of stone and metal tools in furthering the evolution of human culture. Even the names given to various periods in human history and prehistory are based on heavyweight tools: the word *Paleolithic*—the period extending from about 750,000 years ago to 15,000 years ago—essentially means "Old Stone Age." And duly thudding and clanking after the Paleolithic period were the Mesolithic and Neolithic, or Middle and New Stone Age, the Bronze Age, the Iron Age, the Industrial Age.

But at least as central to the course of human affairs as the invention of stone tools was the realization that plant products could be exploited for purposes other than eating. The fact that some of the Venus figurines are shown wearing string skirts, said Dr. Barber, "means that the people who made them must also have known how to make twisted string."

With the invention of string and the power to weave, people could construct elaborate yet lightweight containers in which to carry, store, and cook food. They could fashion baby slings to secure an infant snugly against its mother's body, thereby freeing up the woman to work and wander. They could braid nets, the better to catch prey animals without the risk of hand-to-tooth combat. They could lash together wooden logs or planks to build a boat.

"The string revolution was a profound event in human history," Dr. Adovasio said. "When people started to fool around with plants and plant byproducts, that opened vast new avenues of human progress."

In the new report, the researchers argue that women are likely to have been the primary weavers and textile experts of prehistory, and may have even initiated the string revolution in the first place—although men undoubtedly did their share of weaving when it came to making hunting and fishing nets, for example. They base that conclusion on modern crosscultural studies, which have found that women constitute the great bulk of the world's weavers, basketry makers, and all-round mistresses of plant goods.

But while vast changes in manufacturing took the luster off the textile business long ago, with the result that such "women's work" is now accorded low status and sweatshop wages, the researchers argue that weaving and other forms of fiber craft once commanded great prestige. By their estimate, the detailing of the stitches shown on some of the Venus figurines was intended to flaunt the value and beauty of the original spinsters' skills. Why else would anybody have bothered etching the stitchery in a permanent medium, if not to boast, whoa! Check out these wefts!

"It's made immortal in stone," Dr. Soffer said. "You don't carve something like this unless it's very important."

The detailing of the Venusian garb also raises the intriguing possibility that the famed little sculptures, which rank right up there with the Lascaux cave paintings in the pantheon of Western art, were hewn by women—moonlighting seamstresses, to be precise. "It's always assumed that the carvers were men, a bunch of guys sitting around making their zaftig Barbie dolls," Dr. Soffer said. "But maybe that wasn't the case, or not always the case. With some of these figurines, the person carving them clearly knew weaving. So either that person was a weaver herself, or he was living with her. He's got an adviser."

Durable though the Venus figurines are, Dr. Adovasio and his co-workers are far more interested in what their carved detailing says about the role of perishables in prehistory. "The vast bulk of what humans made was made in media that hasn't survived," Dr. Adovasio said. Experts estimate the ratio of perishable objects to durable objects generated in the average culture is about 20 to 1.

"We're reconstructing the past based on 5 percent of what was used," Dr. Soffer said.

Because many of the items that have endured over the millennia are things like arrowheads and spear points, archaeologists studying the Paleolithic era have generally focused on the ways and means of that noble savage, a.k.a. Man the Hunter, to the exclusion of other members of the tribe.

"To this day, in Paleolithic studies we hear about Man the Hunter doing such boldly wonderful things as thrusting spears into woolly mammoths, or battling it out with other men," Dr. Adovasio said. "We've emphasized the activities of a small segment of the population—healthy young men—at the total absence of females, old people of either sex, and children. We've glorified one aspect of Paleolithic life ways at the expense of all the other things that made that life way successful."

Textiles are particularly fleeting. The oldest examples of fabric yet discovered are some carbonate-encrusted swatches from France that are about 18,000 years old, while pieces of cordage and string dating back 19,000 years have been unearthed in the Near East, many thousands of years after the string and textile revolution began.

In an effort to study ancient textiles in the absence of textiles, Dr. Soffer, Dr. Adovasio, and Dr. Hyland have sought indirect signs of textile manufacture. They have pored over thousands of ancient fragments of fired and unfired clay, and have found impressions of early textiles on a number of them, the oldest dating to 29,000 B.C.E. But the researchers believe that textile manufacture far predates this time period, for the sophistication of the stitchery rules out its being, as Dr. Soffer put it, "what you take home from Crafts 101." Dr. Adovasio estimates that weaving and cord-making probably goes back to the year 40,000 B.C.E. "at a minimum," and possibly much further.

Long before people had settled down into towns with domesticated plants and animals, then, while they were still foragers and wanderers, they had, in a sense, tamed nature. The likeliest sort of plants from which they extracted fibers were nettles. "Nettle in folk tales and mythology is said to have magic properties," Dr. Soffer said. "In one story by the Brothers Grimm, a girl whose two brothers have been turned into swans has to weave them nettle shirts by midnight to make them human again." The nettles stung her fingers, but she kept on weaving.

But what didn't make it into Grimms' was that when the girl was done with the shirts, she took out a chisel, and carved herself a Venus figurine.

2

MARJORIE SHOSTAK

From *Nisa: The Life and Words of a !Kung Woman*

Marjorie Shostak, a writer and photographer, interviewed Nisa, a woman of the hunting-gathering !Kung people of the Kalahari Desert of Southern Africa. (The exclamation point at the beginning of !Kung indicates one of the clicking sounds used in their language.) From these interviews, which took place between 1969 and 1971, Shostak compiled Nisa's story in Nisa's own words.

As you read Nisa's account of her early adulthood, consider how it is similar to, and how it is different from, that of a young woman growing up today in modern society. If Nisa is typical of women in her world, do !Kung women have more or less authority, prestige, or power than women in your own society?

Finally, what does Nisa's story tell us about women in hunting-gathering societies?

Thinking Historically

Keep in mind that Nisa exists in the late twentieth century. When we think of stages of history, we are abstracting the human past in a way that vastly oversimplifies what happened but allows us to draw important conclusions. We know hunting and gathering did not end ten thousand years ago when agriculture first began. Hunters and gatherers still live in the world today—in places like the Arctic, the Amazon, and the Kalahari. That is why we use Nisa's account, which we are lucky to have. We have no vivid first-person accounts from those ancient hunters and gatherers—writing was not invented until the first cities developed five thousand years ago. So we generalize from Nisa's experience because we know that in some ways her life is like that of our hunting-gathering ancestors. But there are ways in which it is not. At the very least, the hunters and gatherers in the world today have been pushed by farmers and city people into the most remote parts of the globe—like the Kalahari desert.

Using a contemporary of ours, like Nisa, as a kind of representative of our most distant ancestors is clearly a strange thing to do. Why does it work? What precautions should we take?

Marjorie Shostak, *Nisa: The Life and Words of a !Kung Woman* (Cambridge: Harvard University Press, 1981), 51, 56–59, 61–62, 89–90, 132–38.

One time, my father went hunting with some other men and they took dogs with them. First they saw a baby wildebeest and killed it. Then, they went after the mother wildebeest and killed that too. They also killed a warthog.

As they were coming back, I saw them and shouted out, "Ho, ho, Daddy's bringing home meat! Daddy's coming home with meat!" My mother said, "You're talking nonsense. Your father hasn't even come home yet." Then she turned to where I was looking and said, "Eh-hey, daughter! Your father certainly has killed something. He *is* coming with meat."

I remember another time when my father's younger brother traveled from far away to come and live with us. The day before he arrived he killed an eland. He left it in the bush and continued on to our village. When he arrived, only mother and I were there. He greeted us and asked where his brother was. Mother said, "Eh, he went to look at some tracks he had seen near a porcupine hole. He'll be back when the sun sets." We sat together the rest of the day. When the sun was low in the sky, my father came back. My uncle said, "Yesterday, as I was coming here, there was an eland—perhaps it was just a small one—but I spent a long time tracking it and finally killed it in the thicket beyond the dry water pan. Why don't we get the meat and bring it back to the village?" We packed some things, left others hanging in the trees, and went to where the eland had died. It was a huge animal with plenty of fat. We lived there while they skinned the animal and the meat into strips to dry. A few days later we started home, the men carrying the meat on sticks and the women carrying it in their karosses.

At first my mother carried me on her shoulder. After a long way, she set me down and I started to cry. She was angry, "You're a big girl. You know how to walk." It was true that I was fairly big by then, but I still wanted to be carried. My older brother said, "Stop yelling at her, she's already crying," and he picked me up and carried me. After a long time walking, he also put me down. Eventually, we arrived back at the village.

We lived, eating meat; lived and lived. Then, it was finished. . . .

When adults talked to me, I listened. When I was still a young girl with no breasts, they told me that when a young woman grows up, her parents give her a husband and she continues to grow up next to him.

When they first talked to me about it, I said, "What kind of thing am I that I should take a husband? When I grow up, I won't marry. I'll just lie by myself. If I married, what would I be doing it for?"

My father said, "You don't know what you're saying. I, I am your father and am old; your mother is old, too. When you marry, you will gather food and give it to your husband to eat. He also will do things for you. If you refuse, who will give you food? Who will give you things to wear?"

I said, "There's no question about it, I won't take a husband. Why should I? As I am now, I'm still a child and won't marry." I said to my mother, "You say you have a man for me to marry? Why don't you take him and set him beside Daddy? You marry him and let them be co-husbands. What have I done that you're telling me I should marry?"

My mother said, "Nonsense. When I tell you I'm going to give you a husband, why do you say you want me to marry him? Why are you talking to me like this?"

I said, "Because I'm only a child. When I grow up and you tell me to take a husband, I'll agree. But I haven't passed through my child-hood yet and I won't marry!" . . .

When I still had no breasts, when my genitals still weren't devel-oped, when my chest was without anything on it, that was when a man named Bo came from a distant area and people started talking about marriage. Was I not almost a young woman?

One day, my parents and his parents began building our marriage hut. The day we were married, they carried me to it and set me down inside. I cried and cried and cried. Later, I ran back to my parents' hut, lay down beside my little brother, and slept, a deep sleep like death.

The next night, Nukha, an older woman, took me into the hut and stayed with me. She lay down between Bo and myself, because young girls who are still children are afraid of their husbands. So, it is our cus-tom for an older woman to come into the young girl's hut to teach her not to be afraid. The woman is supposed to help the girl learn to like her husband. Once the couple is living nicely together and getting along, the older woman leaves them beside each other.

That's what Nukha was supposed to do. Even the people who saw her come into the hut with me thought she would lay me down and that once I fell asleep, she would leave and go home to her husband.

But Nukha had within her clever deceit. My heart refused Bo be-cause I was a child, but Nukha, she liked him. That was why, when she laid me down in the hut with my husband, she was also laying me down with her lover. She put me in front and Bo was behind. We stayed like that for a very long time. As soon as I was asleep, they started to make love. But as Bo made love to Nukha, they knocked into me. I kept waking up as they bumped me, again and again.

I thought, "I'm just a child. I don't understand about such things. What are people doing when they move around like that? How come Nukha took me into my marriage hut and laid me down beside my hus-band, but when I started to cry, she changed places with me and lay down next to him? Is he hers? How come he belongs to her yet Mommy and Daddy said I should marry him?"

I lay there, thinking my thoughts. Before dawn broke, Nukha got up and went back to her husband. I lay there, sleeping, and when it started getting light, I went back to my mother's hut.

The next night, when darkness sat, Nukha came for me again. I cried, "He's your man! Yesterday you took me and brought me inside the hut, but after we all lay there, he was with you! Why are you now bringing me to someone who is yours?" She said, "That's not true, he's not mine. He's *your* husband. Now, go to your hut and sit there. Later, we'll lie down."

She brought me to the hut, but once inside, I cried and cried and cried. I was still crying when Nukha lay down with us. After we had been lying there for a very long time, Bo started to make love to her again. I thought, "What is this? What am I? Am I supposed to watch this? Don't they see me? Do they think I'm only a baby?" Later, I got up and told them I had to urinate. I passed by them and went to lie down in mother's hut and stayed there until morning broke.

That day, I went gathering with my mother and father. As we were collecting mongongo nuts and klaru roots, my mother said, "Nisa, as you are, you're already a young woman. Yet, when you go into your marriage hut to lie down, you get up, come back, and lie down with me. Do you think I have married you? No, I'm the one who gave birth to you. Now, take this man as your husband, this strong man who will get food, for you and for me to eat. Is your father the only one who can find food? A husband kills things and gives them to you; a husband works on things that become your things; a husband gets meat that is food for you to eat. Now, you have a husband, Bo; he has married you."

I said, "Mommy, let me stay with you. When night sits, let me sleep next to you. What have you done to me that I'm only a child, yet the first husband you give me belongs to Nukha?" My mother said, "Why are you saying that? Nukha's husband is not your husband. Her husband sits elsewhere, in another hut."

I said, "Well . . . the other night when she took me and put me into the hut, she laid me down in front of her; Bo slept behind. But later, they woke me up, moving around the way they did. It was the same last night. Again, I slept in front and Bo behind and again, they kept bumping into me. I'm not sure exactly what they were doing, but that's why tonight, when night sits, I want to stay with you and sleep next to you. Don't take me over there again."

My mother said, "Yo! My daughter! They were moving about?" I said. "Mm. They woke me while I was sleeping. That's why I got up and came back to you." She said, "Yo! How horny that Bo is! He's screwing Nukha! You are going to leave that man, that's the only thing I will agree to now."

My father said, "I don't like what you've told us. You're only a child, Nisa, and adults are the ones responsible for arranging your marriage. But when an adult gives a husband and that husband makes love to someone else, then that adult hasn't done well. I understand what you have told us and I say that Bo has deceived me. Therefore, when Nukha comes for you tonight, I will refuse to let you go. I will say, 'My daughter won't go into her marriage hut because you, Nukha, you have already taken him for a husband.' "

We continued to talk on our way back. When we arrived at the village, I sat down with my parents. Bo walked over to our marriage hut, then Nukha went over to him. I sat and watched as they talked. I thought, "Those two, they were screwing! That's why they kept bumping into me!"

I sat with Mother and Father while we ate. When evening came, Nukha walked over to us. "Nisa, come, let me take you to your hut." I said, "I won't go." She said, "Get up. Let me take you over there. It's your hut. How come you're already married but today you won't make your hut your home?"

That's when my mother, drinking anger, went over to Nukha and said, "As I'm standing here, I want you to tell me something. Nisa is a child who fears her husband. Yet, when you took her to her hut, you and her husband had sex together. Don't you know her husband should be trying to help bring her up? But that isn't something either of you are thinking about!"

Nukha didn't say anything, but the fire in my mother's words burned. My mother began to yell, cursing her, "Horny, that's what you are! You're no longer going to take Nisa to her husband. And, if you ever have sex with him again, I'll crack your face open. You horny woman! You'd screw your own father!"

That's when my father said, "No, don't do all the talking. You're a woman yet, how come you didn't ask me? I am a man and I will do the talking now. You, you just listen to what I say. Nisa is my child. I also gave birth to her. Now, you are are a woman and will be quiet because I am a man."

Then he said, "Nukha, I'm going to tell you something. I am Gau and today I'm going to pull my talk from inside myself and give it to you. We came together here for this marriage, but now something very bad has happened, something I do not agree to at all. Nisa is no longer going to go from here, where I am sitting, to that hut over there, that hut which you have already made your own. She is no longer going to look for anything for herself near that hut."

He continued, "Because, when I agree to give a man to my daughter, then he is only for my daughter. Nisa is a child and her husband isn't there for two to share. So go, take that man, he's already yours. Today my daughter will sit with me; she will sit here and sleep here. Tomorrow I will take her and we will move away. What you have already done to this marriage is the way it will remain."

Nukha didn't say anything. She left and went to the hut without me. Bo said, "Where's Nisa? Why are you empty, returning here alone?" Nukha said, "Nisa's father refused to let her go. She told him that you had made love to me and that's what he just now told me. I don't know what to do about this, but I won't go back to their hut again." Bo said, "I have no use for that kind of talk. Get the girl and come back with her." She said, "I'm not going to Gau's hut. We're finished with that talk now. And when I say I'm finished, I'm saying I won't go back there again."

She left and walked over to her own hut. When her husband saw her, he said, "So, you and Bo are lovers! Nisa said that when you took her to Bo, the two of you . . . how exactly *did* Bo reward you for your help?" But Nukha said, "No, I don't like Bo and he's not my lover. Nisa is just a child and it is just a child's talk she is talking."

Bo walked over to us. He tried to talk but my father said, "You, be quiet. I'm the one who's going to talk about this." So Bo didn't say anything more, and my father talked until it was finished.

The next morning, very early, my father, mother, and aunt packed our things and we all left. We slept in the mongongo groves that night and traveled on until we reached another water hole where we continued to live.

We lived and lived and nothing more happened for a while. After a long time had passed, Bo strung together some trade beads made of wood, put them into a sack with food, and traveled the long distance to the water hole where we were living.

It was late afternoon; the sun had almost left the sky. I had been out gathering with my mother, and we were coming back from the bush. We arrived in the village and my mother saw them, "Eh-hey, Bo's over there. What's he doing here? I long ago refused him. I didn't ask him to come back. I wonder what he thinks he's going to take away from here?"

We put down our gatherings and sat. We greeted Bo and his relatives — his mother, his aunt, Nukha, and Nukha's mother. Bo's mother said, "We have come because we want to take Nisa back with us." Bo said, "I'm again asking for your child. I want to take her back with me."

My father said, "No, I only just took her from you. That was the end. I won't take her and then give her again. Maybe you didn't hear me the first time? I already told you that I refused. Bo is Nukha's husband and my daughter won't be with him again. An adult woman does not make love to the man who marries Nisa."

Then he said, "Today, Nisa will just continue to live with us. Some day, another man will come and marry her. If she stays healthy and her eyes stand strong, if God doesn't kill her and she doesn't die, if God stands beside her and helps, then we will find another man to give to her."

That night, when darkness set, we all slept. I slept beside mother. When morning broke, Bo took Nukha, her mother, and the others and they left. I stayed behind. They were gone, finally gone.

We continued to stay at that water hole, eating things, doing things, and just living. No one talked further about giving me another husband, and we just lived and lived and lived.

3

ELISE BOULDING

Women and the Agricultural Revolution

Because women were the foragers or gatherers in hunting-gathering societies (while men were normally the hunters), women probably developed agriculture. The earliest form of agriculture was horticulture, a simple process of planting seeds with a digging stick and tending the plants in a garden. Elise Boulding imagines how the planting of wild einkorn, a wheatlike grain of the ancient Middle East, must have transformed the lives of men and women about ten thousand years ago. How might this early agriculture or horticulture have contributed to women's power or prestige?

Thinking Historically

Boulding draws a distinction between the early horticultural stage of agriculture and the later agriculture that depended on animal-drawn plows. How did this later stage of agriculture change the roles of men and women?

Is agriculture one stage for the history of women, or are there two stages? How does our idea of stages of history depend on what we are studying?

Elise Boulding, *The Underside of History: A View of Women Through Time* (Boulder, CO: Westview Press, 1976), 114–17, 118–19.

There is some disagreement about whether the domestication of animals or plants came first. In fact, both were probably happening at the same time. There is evidence from campfire remains as long ago as 20,000 B.C.E. that women had discovered the food value of einkorn, a kind of wild wheat that grows all through the fertile crescent.[1] An enterprising Oklahoma agronomist, Professor Jack Harlan of the University of Oklahoma, noticed several years ago, on an expedition to eastern Turkey, how thick these stands of wild einkorn grew. He tried harvesting some, and once he had resorted to a nine-thousand-year-old flint sickle blade set in a new wooden handle (he tried to use his bare hands first, with disastrous results), he was able to come away with an excellent harvest. After weighing what he had reaped, he estimated that a single good stand of einkorn would feed a family for a whole year. He also found that the grains had 50 percent more protein than the wheat we use now in North America for bread flour. Einkorn grains are found everywhere on the ancient home-base sites of the fertile crescent, either as roasted hulls in cooking hearths, or as imprints in the mud-and-straw walls of the earliest preagriculture huts.

It would be inevitable that grains from sheaves of einkorn carried in from a distant field would drop in well-trodden soil just outside the home base, or perhaps in a nearby pile of refuse. When the band returned the following year to this campsite—perhaps a favorite one, since not all campsites were revisited—there would be a fine stand of einkorn waiting for them right at their doorstep. We might say that the plants taught the women how to cultivate them. Planting, however, was quite a step beyond just leaving some stalks at the site where they were picked, to seed themselves for the next year. There was less reason for deliberate planting as long as bands were primarily nomadic and there was plenty of game to follow. But in time there was a premium on campsites that would have abundant grain and fruit and nuts nearby, and then there was a point in scattering extra grain on the ground near the campsite for the next year. Because of the construction of the seed, einkorn easily plants itself, so it was a good plant for initiating humans into agriculture.

Gradually, bands lengthened their stays at their more productive home bases, harvesting what had been "planted" more or less intentionally, and letting the few sheep they had raised from infancy graze on nearby hills. One year there would be such a fine stand of wheat at their favorite home base, and so many sheep ambling about, that a band would decide just to stay for a while, not to move on that year.

If any one band of nomads could have anticipated what lay in store for humankind as a result of that fateful decision (made separately by

---

[1]The Tigris-Euphrates river valley, so called because it forms a crescent of highly fertile land between the Persian Gulf and the uplands near the Mediterranean Sea. [Ed.]

thousands of little bands over the next ten thousand years), would they after all have moved on? While it may have been a relief not to be on the move, they in fact exchanged a life of relative ease, with enough to eat and few possessions, for a life of hard work, enough to eat, and economic surplus. As [archeologist V. Gordon] Childe says, "a mild acquisitiveness could now take its place among human desires."

Successful nomads have a much easier life than do farmers. Among the !Kung bushmen today, the men hunt about four days a week and the women only need to work two-and-a-half days at gathering to feed their families amply for a week. (At that, meat is a luxury item, and most of the nourishment comes from nuts and roots.) The rest of their time is leisure, to be enjoyed in visiting, creating and carrying out rituals, and just "being."

The First Settlements

For better or worse, the women and the men settled down. They settled in the caves of Belt and Hotu to a prosperous life of farming and herding on the Caspian. They settled in Eynan, Jericho, Jarmo, Beidha, Catal Huyuk, Hacilar, Arpachiyah, and Kherokitia in Cyprus, and in uncounted villages that no archaeologist's shovel has touched. These places were home-base sites first, some going back thousands of years. By 10,000 B.C.E. Eynan had fifty houses, small stone domes, seven meters in diameter, around a central area with storage pits. This was probably preagricultural, still a hunting and gathering band, but a settled one. The village covered two thousand square meters. Each hut had a hearth, and child and infant burials were found under some of the floors. Three successive layers of fifty stone houses have been found at the same site, so it must have been a remarkably stable site for a settlement.

What was life like, once bands settled down? This was almost from the start a woman's world. She would mark out the fields for planting, because she knew where the grain grew best, and would probably work in the fields together with the other women of the band. There would not be separate fields at first, but as the former nomads shifted from each sleeping in individual huts to building houses for family groups of mother, father, and children, a separate family feeling must have developed and women may have divided the fields by family groups.

Their fire-hardened pointed digging sticks, formerly used in gathering, now became a multipurpose implement for planting and cultivating the soil. At harvest time everyone, including the children, would help bring in the grain. The women also continued to gather fruit and nuts, again with the help of the children. The children watched the sheep and goats, but the women did the milking and cheese making. Ethnologists who have studied both foraging and agricultural societies comment on the change in the way of life for children that comes with agriculture. Whereas in foraging societies they have no responsibilities beyond feeding themselves and learning the hunting and foraging skills they will need, and therefore they have much leisure, it is very common in agricultural societies to put children to work at the age of three, chasing birds from the food plots. Older children watch the animals, and keep them out of the planted areas.

The agriculture practiced by these first women farmers and their children, producing enough food for subsistence only, must be distinguished from that agriculture which developed out of subsistence farming and which produced surpluses and fed nonfarming populations in towns. The first type is commonly called horticulture and is carried out with hand tools only. The second is agriculture proper, and involves intensive cultivation with the use of plow and (where necessary) irrigation. In areas like the hilly flanks of the fertile crescent in the Middle East, horticulture moved fairly rapidly into agriculture as it spread to the fertile plains. As we shall see, trading centers grew into towns and cities needing food from the countryside. Women and children could not unaided produce the necessary surpluses, and by the time the digging stick had turned into an animal-drawn plow, they were no longer the primary workers of the fields.

The simpler form of farming continued in areas where the soil was less fertile, and particularly in the tropical forest areas of Africa. Here soils were quickly exhausted, and each year the village women would enlist the men in helping to clear new fields which were then burned over in the slash-and-burn pattern which helped reconstitute the soils for planting again. The slash-and-burn pattern of horticulture has continued into this century, since it is a highly adaptive technique for meager tropical soils. Where the simple horticultural methods continued to be used, women continued as the primary farmers, always with their children as helpers. In a few of these societies women continued also in the positions of power; these are usually the tribes labeled by ethnologists as matrilocal. Not many tribes have survived into the twentieth century with a matrilocal pattern, however, though traces of matrilineal descent reckoning are not infrequent.

The first women farmers in the Zagreb foothills were very busy. Not only did they tend the fields and do the other chores mentioned above, they also probably built the round stone or mud-brick houses in the first villages. The frequency with which women construct shelters in foraging societies has already been cited.

Women also began to spend more time on making tools and containers. No longer needing to hold the family possessions down to what they could carry, women could luxuriate in being able to choose larger and heavier grinding stones that crushed grain more efficiently. They could make containers to hold food stores that would never have to go on the road. They ground fine stone bowls, made rough baskets, and in the process of lining their baskets with mud accidentally discovered that a mudlined basket placed in the hearth would come out hardened—the first pottery. [Archaeologist] Sonja Cole suggests that pottery was invented in Khartoum in Africa about 8000 B.C.E., spreading northwest to the Mediterranean, but the same process probably happened over and over again as people became more sedentary.

The evidence from food remains in these early villages, 10,000 to 6000 B.C.E., indicates that men were still hunting, to supplement the agriculture and modest domestic herds. This means that they were not around very much. When they were, they probably shared in some of the home-base tasks.

Evidence from some of the earliest village layouts suggests that adults lived in individual huts, women keeping the children with them. Marriage agreements apparently did not at first entail shared living quarters. As the agricultural productivity of the women increased, and the shift was made to dwellings for family units, husband-wife interaction probably became more frequent and family living patterns more complex.

With the accumulation of property, decisions about how it was to be allocated had to be made. The nature of these agreements is hardly to be found in the archaeological record, so we must extrapolate from what we know of the "purest" matrilineal tribes of the recent past.

The senior woman of a family and her daughters and sons formed the property-holding unit for the family. The senior woman's *brother* would be the administrator of the properties. His power, whether over property or in political decision making, would be derivative from his status as brother (usually but not always the oldest) to the senior woman in a family. This role of the brother, so important in present-day matrilineal societies, may not have been very important in the period we are now considering, between 12,000 and 8000 B.C.E.

4

GERDA LERNER

The Urban Revolution:
Origins of Patriarchy

Often called "the rise of civilization," the urban revolution ushered in many changes five thousand years ago. The city societies or city-states that developed in Mesopotamia, Egypt, and the Indus River Valley after 3000 B.C.E. gave rise to the first kings, temples, priests, and social classes, as well as to writing, laws, metallurgy, warfare, markets, and private property. With the city-state came patriarchy, the assertion of male power, and the subordination of women—the signs of which were clear in Sumer and Mesopotamia. Assemblies of men or kings ruled both cities. Mesopotamian law codes favored men: Women could be divorced, punished, or sold into slavery for adultery, while men could not. Laws also required that women wear veils, restricted women's freedom of movement, and treated women as the property of fathers or husbands.

People in ancient Egypt worshiped their kings as gods. Cities worshiped Sky Father Gods. One Egyptian myth of creation describes the great god Ra emerging from the waters of Nun and creating the Egyptian universe from his own body. A Mesopotamian creation story, the *Enuma Elish,* recounts a primordial battle between the male god Marduk and the mother goddess Tiamat: Marduk splits Tiamat's heart with his arrow and then cracks her dead body in half like a shellfish, her hollowed-out form becoming heaven and earth.

In this selection from modern historian Gerda Lerner's *The Creation of Patriarchy,* the author gives considerable attention to the way in which religious ideas changed as city-based states replaced the world of small Neolithic villages. At the beginning of the selection, Lerner notes the impact of urban social classes and patriarchy. Because cities legislated the rule of the rich and powerful classes above the poor and slaves, there were periods in which some women—the wives and daughters of wealthy and powerful men—benefited at the expense of other women. Eventually, though, city law curtailed the freedom of all women, rich and poor. Despite these restrictions, some women continued to play a role in popular religion. What was that role? How important do you think it was?

Gerda Lerner, *The Creation of Patriarchy* (Oxford: Oxford University Press, 1986), 141–45.

What do you think of the author's comparison of Ishtar and the Virgin Mary? Does this comparison suggest that Christianity was more patriarchal? Do we live in a patriarchy today? What would suggest a modern patriarchy? What would suggest its absence?

Thinking Historically

Any stage theory of history depends on a series of broad generalizations. We might distinguish two here. First, Lerner suggests that cities, archaic states, kings, gods, militarism, and patriarchy are all related, that they appeared at about the same time as part of the same process of change. Notice how Lerner links some of these elements, one to the other. Which of these couplings are persuasive?

Second, notice the absence of specific dates in this selection. The kinds of evidence Lerner uses here cannot be dated very precisely. She uses phrases like "the first half of the third millennium B.C.," which would mean between 3000 and 2500 B.C.E. When would you date the origins of patriarchy? Notice the time lag between the imposition of patriarchial laws and the slower process of replacing goddesses with gods. How does Lerner account for this time lag?

Do you think religion would be slower to change than law or social custom? Could the worship of Ishtar have been representative of an earlier, more agricultural, religious tradition?

. . . In Mesopotamian societies the institutionalization of patriarchy created sharply defined boundaries between women of different classes, although the development of the new gender definitions and of the customs associated with them proceeded unevenly. The state, during the process of the establishment of written law codes, increased the property rights of upper-class women, while it circumscribed their sexual rights and finally totally eroded them. The lifelong dependency of women on fathers and husbands became so firmly established in law and custom as to be considered "natural" and god-given. In the case of lower-class women, their labor power served either their families or those who owned their families' services. Their sexual and reproductive capacities were commodified, traded, leased, or sold in the interest of male family members. Women of all classes had traditionally been excluded from military power and were, by the turn of the first millennium B.C., excluded from formal education, insofar as it had become institutionalized.

Yet, even then, powerful women in powerful roles lived on in cultic service, in religious representation, and in symbols. There was a considerable time lag between the subordination of women in patriarchal society and the declassing of the goddesses. As we trace below changes in the position of male and female god figures in the pantheon of the gods in a period of over a thousand years, we should keep in mind that the power of the goddesses and their priestesses in daily life and in popular religion continued in force, even as the supreme goddesses were dethroned. It is remarkable that in societies which had subordinated women economically, educationally, and legally, the spiritual and metaphysical power of goddesses remained active and strong.

We have some indication of what practical religion was like from archaeological artifacts and from temple hymns and prayers. In Mesopotamian societies the feeding of and service to the gods was considered essential to the survival of the community. This service was performed by male and female temple servants. For important decisions of state, in warfare, and for important personal decisions one would consult an oracle or a diviner, who might be either a man or a woman. In personal distress, sickness, or misfortune the afflicted person would seek the help of his or her household-god and, if this was of no avail, would appeal to any one of a number of gods or goddesses who had particular qualities needed to cure the affliction. If the appeal were to a goddess, the sick person also required the intercession and good services of a priestess of the particular goddess. There were, of course, also male gods who could benefit one in case of illness, and these would usually be served by a male priest.

For example, in Babylonia a sick man or woman would approach the Ishtar temple in a spirit of humility on the assumption that the sickness was a result of his or her transgression. The petitioner would bring appropriate offerings: food, a young animal for sacrifice, oil, and wine. For the goddess Ishtar such offerings quite frequently included images of a vulva, the symbol of her fertility, fashioned out of precious lapis lazuli stone. The afflicted person would prostrate himself before the priestess and recite some appropriate hymns and prayers. A typical prayer contained the following lines:

> Gracious Ishtar, who rules over the universe,
> Heroic Ishtar, who creates humankind,
> who walks before the cattle, who loves the shepherd . . .
> You give justice to the distressed, the suffering you give
>   them justice.
> Without you the river will not open,
> the river which brings us life will not be closed,
> without you the canal will not open,
> the canal from which the scattered drink,
> will not be closed . . . Ishtar, merciful lady . . .
> hear me and grant me mercy.

Mesopotamian men or women, in distress or sickness, humbled themselves before a goddess-figure and her priestly servant. In words reflecting the attitude of slave toward master, they praised and worshiped the goddess's power. Thus, another hymn to Ishtar addresses her as "mistress of the battle field, who pulls down the mountains"; "Majestic one, lioness among the gods, who conquers the angry gods, strongest among rulers, who leads kings by the lead; you who open the wombs of women . . . mighty Ishtar, how great is your strength!" Heaping praise upon praise, the petitioner continued:

> Where you cast your glance, the dead awaken, the sick arise;
> The bewildered, beholding your face, find the right way.
> I appeal to you, miserable and distraught,
> tortured by pain, your servant,
> be merciful and hear my prayer! . . .
> I await you, my mistress; my soul turns toward you.
> I beseech you: Relieve my plight.
> Absolve me of my guilt, my wickedness, my sin,
> forget my misdeeds, accept my plea!

We should note that the petitioners regarded the goddess as all-powerful. In the symbol of the goddess's vulva, fashioned of precious stone and offered up in her praise, they celebrated the sacredness of female sexuality and its mysterious life-giving force, which included the power to heal. And in the very prayers appealing to the goddess's mercy, they praised her as mistress of the battlefield, more powerful than kings, more powerful than other gods. Their prayers to the gods similarly extolled the god's virtues and listed his powers in superlatives. My point here is that men and women offering such prayers when in distress must have thought of women, just as they thought of men, as capable of metaphysical power and as potential mediators between the gods and human beings. That is a mental image quite different from that of Christians, for example, who in a later time would pray to the Virgin Mary to intercede with God in their behalf. The power of the Virgin lies in her ability to appeal to God's mercy; it derives from her motherhood and the miracle of her immaculate conception. She has no power for herself, and the very sources of her power to intercede separate her irrevocably from other women. The goddess Ishtar and other goddesses like her had power in their own right. It was the kind of power men had, derived from military exploits and the ability to impose her will on the gods or to influence them. And yet Ishtar was female, endowed with a sexuality like that of ordinary women. One cannot help but wonder at the contradiction between the power of the goddesses and the increasing societal constraints upon the lives of most women in Ancient Mesopotamia.

Unlike the changes in the social and economic status of women, which have received only tangential and scattered attention in Ancient Mesopotamian studies, the transition from polytheism to monotheism and its attendant shift in emphasis from powerful goddesses to a single male god have been the subject of a vast literature. The topic has been approached from the vantage point of theology, archaeology, anthropology, and literature. Historical and artistic artifacts have been interpreted with the tools of their respective disciplines; linguistic and philosophical studies have added to the richness of interpretation. With Freud and Jung and Erich Fromm, psychiatry and psychology have been added as analytic tools, focusing our attention on myth, symbols, and archetypes. And recently a number of feminist scholars from various disciplines have discussed the period and the subject from yet another vantage point, one which is critical of patriarchal assumptions.

Such a richness and diversity of sources and interpretations makes it impossible to discuss and critique them all within the confines of this volume. I will therefore focus, as I have done throughout, on a few analytic questions and discuss in detail a few models which, I believe, illustrate larger patterns.

Methodologically, the most problematic question is the relation between changes in society and changes in religious beliefs and myths. The archaeologist, art historian, and historian can record, document, and observe such changes, but their causes and their meaning cannot be given with any kind of certainty. Different systems of interpretation offer varying answers, none of which is totally satisfying. In the present case it seems to me most important to record and survey the historical evidence and to offer a coherent explanation, which I admit is somewhat speculative. So are all the other explanations including, above all, the patriarchal tradition.

I am assuming that Mesopotamian religion responded to and reflected social conditions in the various societies. Mental constructs cannot be created from a void; they always reflect events and concepts of historic human beings in society. Thus, the existence of an assembly of the gods in "The Epic of Gilgamesh" has been interpreted as indicating the existence of village assemblies in pre-state Mesopotamian society. Similarly, the explanation in the Sumerian Atrahasis myth that the gods created men in order that men might serve them and relieve them of hard work can be regarded as a reflection of social conditions in the Sumerian city-states of the first half of the third millennium B.C.E., in which large numbers of people worked on irrigation projects and in agricultural labor centered on the temples. The relation between myth and reality is not usually that direct, but we can assume that no people could invent the concept of an assembly of the gods if they had not at some time experienced and known a like institution on earth. While we cannot say with certainty that certain political and economic changes "caused" changes in religious beliefs and myths, we cannot help but notice a pattern in the changes of religious beliefs in a number of societies, following upon or concurrent with certain societal changes.

My thesis is that, just as the development of plow agriculture, coinciding with increasing militarism, brought major changes in kinship and in gender relations, so did the development of strong kingships and of archaic states bring changes in religious beliefs and symbols. The observable pattern is: first, the demotion of the Mother-Goddess figure and the ascendance and later dominance of her male consort/son; then his merging with a storm-god into a male Creator-God, who heads the pantheon of gods and goddesses. Wherever such changes occur, the power of creation and of fertility is transfered from the Goddess to the God.

REFLECTIONS

A historical stage is a specific example of a larger process that historians call *periodization*. Dividing history into periods is one way historians make the past comprehensible. Without periodization, history would be a vast, unwieldly continuum, lacking points of reference, form, intelligibility, and meaning.

One of the earliest forms of historical periodization—years of reign—was a natural system of record keeping in the ancient cities dominated by kings. Each kingdom had its own list of kings, and each marked the current date by numbering the years of the king's reign. Some ancient societies periodized their history according to the years of rule of local officials or priesthoods. In the ancient Roman Republic, time was figured according to the terms of the elected consuls. The ancient Greeks used four-year periods called Olympiads, beginning with the first Olympic games in 776 B.C.E.

The ancient Greeks did not use "B.C." or "B.C.E.," of course. The periodization of world history into B.C. ("before Christ") and A.D. (*anno Domini*, "the Year of Our Lord" or "after Christ") did not come until the sixth century A.D., when a Christian monk named Dionysius Exiguus hit upon a way to center Christ as the major turning point in history. We use a variant of this system in this text, when designating events "B.C.E." for "before the common era" or "C.E." for "of the common era." This translation of "B.C." and "A.D." avoids the Christian bias of the older system but preserves its simplicity. A common dating system can be used worldwide to delineate time and coordinate different dynastic calendars.

All systems of periodization implicitly claim to designate important transitions in the past. The periodization of Dionysius inscribed the Christian belief that Christ's life, death, and resurrection fundamentally changed world history: Because Christ died to atone for the sins of humankind, only those who lived after Christ's sacrifice could be saved when they died. Few other systems of periodization made such a sweeping claim, though, of course, most people today—even many non-Christians—use it because of its convenience. Muslims count the years from a year one A.H. (*anno Hegire*, designating the year of the prophet Muhammad's escape from Mecca to Medina) in 622 A.D. of the Christian calendar, and Jews date the years from a Biblical year one.

Millennia, centuries, and decades are useful periods for societies that count in tens and (after the spread of Indian numerals) use the zero. While such multiples are only mathematical, some historians use them for rough periodization, to distinguish between the 1950s and the 1960s or between the eighteenth and nineteenth centuries, for example, as if there were a genuine and important transition between one period and the other. Sometimes historians "stretch" the boundaries of centuries or decades in order to account for earlier or later changes. For example, some historians speak of "the long nineteenth century," embracing the period from the French Revolution in 1789 to the First World War in 1914, on the grounds that peoples' lives were transformed in 1789 rather than in 1800 and in 1914 rather than in 1900. Similarly, the "sixties," as a term for American society and culture during the Vietnam War era, often means the period from about 1963 to about 1975, since civil rights and antiwar activity became significant a few years after the beginning of the decade and the war continued until 1975.

Characterizing and defining a decade or century in chronological terms is only one method of periodization, however. Processes can also be periodized. In this chapter we have periodized world history by process. All of world history can be divided into three periods—hunting-gathering, agricultural/pastoral, and urban. These are overlapping and continuing periods, and we can date only the beginning of the agricultural/pastoral and the urban periods, at about ten thousand and five thousand years ago, respectively. None of these periods has ended, as there are still hunters and gatherers and many farmers and pastoralists in the world. Still, the periodization is useful, because both the agricultural/pastoral revolution and the urban revolution brought about widespread and permanent changes.

We have also tried to locate patriarchy in a historical period, suggesting that it was a product of the urban revolution. We have not attempted to periodize changes in patriarchy over the course of the last five thousand years, but we could investigate this as well. Many people would say that patriarchy has been declining in recent decades. Is this a valid view, or is it a view specific to North America? If patriarchy is a product of cities and if the world is becoming more urban, can patriarchy be declining globally? What forces do you see bringing a decline or end to patriarchy?

To periodize something like the history of patriarchy would require a good deal of knowledge about the history of male and female relations over the course of the last five thousand years. That is a tall order for anyone. But you can get a sense of how the historian goes about periodizing and a feeling for its value if you periodize something you know a lot about. You might start, for instance, with your own life. Think of the most important change or changes in your life. How have these changes divided your life into certain periods? Outline your autobiography by marking these periods as parts or chapters of the story of your life so far. As you review these periods of your life, recognize how periodization must be grounded in reality. Defining these periods may help you understand yourself better.

To gain a sense of how periodization is imposed on reality, imagine how a parent or good friend would periodize your life. How would you periodize your life ten or twenty years from now? How would you have done it five years ago?

2

The Urban Revolution and "Civilization"

Mesopotamia and Egypt, 3500–1000 B.C.E.

HISTORICAL CONTEXT

The urban revolution that began approximately five thousand years ago produced a vast complex of new inventions, institutions, and ideas in cities that dominated surrounding farms and pastures. The first selection in this chapter surveys the wide range of innovations in these earliest civilizations.

The term "civilization" has to be used cautiously. Especially when the idea of civilization is used as a part of a stage theory of human history, we tend to assume that technological advancement means moral advancement. For instance, one hundred years ago scholars described ancient history as the progression from "savagery" to "barbarism" to "civilization."

It would be a shame to throw out the word "civilization" because it has been written more often with an axe than with a pen. The fact remains that the ancient cities created new ways of life for better or worse that were radically different from the world of agricultural villages. If we discard the word "civilization" as too overburdened with prejudice, we will have to find another one to describe that complex of changes. The term "civilization" comes from the Latin root word for city, *civitas,* from which we also get *civic, civilian,* and *citizen.* But, as the first reading argues, cities also created social classes, institutionalized inequalities, and calls to arms; most civilizations created soldiers as well as civilians.

The earliest cities, the small city-states on the Tigris and Euphrates in ancient Sumer, included King Gilgamesh's Uruk, which is recounted

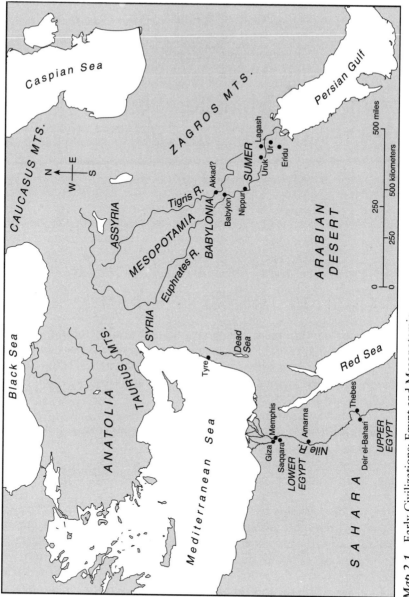

Map 2.1 Early Civilizations: Egypt and Mesopotamia.

in the second reading. Later cities, like Hammurabi's Babylon, united Sumerian city-states and upriver pastoral kingdoms into giant empires. The third reading presents excerpts from Hammurabi's law code (see Map 2.1).

The ancient Egyptian empire depended less on cities than on the power of the king or pharaoh, but life along the Nile was magnified in the pharaoh's residence city and in his future home in the City of the Dead.

As you read these selections, consider the overall transformation of the urban revolution in both Mesopotamia and Egypt. Note also the differences between Mesopotamian and Egyptian civilizations.

THINKING HISTORICALLY
Distinguishing Primary and Secondary Sources

For some historians, the "age of cities" is the beginning of history because cities invented writing. The period before city building and the creation of writing systems thus is often called "prehistory."

Our knowledge of ancient cities is enormously enhanced by ancient writings. We call these writings primary sources. These would include literature, law codes, inscriptions, indeed virtually anything from the time and place being studied. Secondary sources differ: They are written after the fact. History books or historical interpretations are secondary sources. They are secondary in that they rely on primary sources for information. Historians read, study, and interpret primary sources to compose secondary sources. In this chapter you will read two secondary sources and three primary sources to help you learn ways to discern sources and extrapolate information from them.

KEVIN REILLY

Cities and Civilization

This selection from a college textbook is an obvious secondary source. You know it is a secondary source because it was written long after the events described by a modern historian—me.

From my perspective, this selection does two things. First, it explores the wide range of changes brought about by the urban revolution, from particulars like writing and money and metallurgy to abstractions like social class, visual acuity, and anonymity. After you read the selection, you might make a list of all of the inventions and new phenomena of cities. You will likely be surprised by the great number of ideas, institutions, and activities that originated in the first cities. You might also find it interesting to place pluses and minuses next to the items on your list to help you determine whether "civilization" (city life) was, on balance, beneficial or harmful.

Second, the selection compares the "civilizations" of Mesopotamia and Egypt. According to the selection, what are the chief differences between Mesopotamian and Egyptian civilization? What accounts for these differences?

Thinking Historically

To get a feel for the differences between a primary source and a secondary source, try to determine what primary sources might lead to some of these interpretations. Choose a sentence or two that appears specific enough to be based on a primary source. What kind of source could lead to such an interpretation? Conversely, find interpretations in this selection that *could not* possibly derive from a primary source and ask yourself, why not?

Kevin Reilly, *The West and the World: A History of Civilization,* 2nd ed. (New York: Harper & Row, 1989), 48–54, 56, 58, 60.

The Urban Revolution: Civilization and Class

The full-scale urban revolution occurred not in the rain-watered lands that first turned some villages into cities, but in the potentially more productive river valleys of Mesopotamia around 3500 B.C.E. Situated along the Tigris and Euphrates rivers, large villages like Eridu, Erech, Lagash, Kish, and later Ur and Babylon built irrigation systems that increased farm production enormously. Settlements like these were able to support five thousand, even ten thousand people, and still allow something like 10 percent of the inhabitants to work full-time at non-farming occupations.

A change of this scale was a revolution, certainly the most important revolution in human living since the invention of agriculture five thousand years earlier. The urban revolution was prepared by a whole series of technological inventions in agricultural society. Between 6000 and 3000 B.C.E. people not only learned how to harness the power of oxen and the wind with the plow, the wheeled cart, and the sailboat; they also discovered the physical properties of metals, learned how to smelt copper and bronze, and began to work out a calendar based on the movements of the sun. River valleys like those of the Tigris and Euphrates were muddy swamps that had to be drained and irrigated to take advantage of the rich soil deposits. The dry land had literally to be built by teams of organized workers.

Therefore, cities required an organizational revolution that was every bit as important as the technological one. This was accomplished under the direction of the new class of rulers and managers—probably from the grasslands—who often treated the emerging cities as a conquered province. The work of irrigation itself allowed the rulers ample opportunity to coerce the inhabitants of these new cities. Rain knows no social distinctions. Irrigated water must be controlled and channeled.

It is no wonder then that the first cities gave us our first kings and our first class societies. In Mesopotamia, along the Nile of Egypt, in China, and later in Middle America the king is usually described as the founder of cities. These kings were able to endow their control with religious sanction. In Egypt and America the king was god. In Mesopotamia a new class of priests carried out the needs of the king's religion of control.

In some cities the new priesthood would appoint the king. In others, the priests were merely his lieutenants. When they were most loyal, their religion served to deify the king. The teachings of the new class of Mesopotamian priests, for instance, were that their god had created the people solely to work for the king and make his life easier. But even when the priesthood attempted to wrest some of the king's power from him, the priests taught the people to accept the divided society, which benefited king and priesthood as providers of a natural god-given order. The priesthood, after all, was responsible for measuring time, bounding space, and predicting seasonal events. The mastery of people was easy for those who controlled time and space.

The priesthood was only one of the new classes that insured the respectability of the warrior-chieftain turned king. Other palace intellectuals—scribes (or writers), doctors, magicians, and diviners—also struggled to maintain the king's prestige and manage his kingdom. This new class was rewarded, as were the priests, with leisure, status, and magnificent buildings, all of which further exalted the majesty of the king and his city.

Beneath the king, the priesthood, and the new class of intellectuals-managers was another new class charged with maintaining the king's law and order. Soldiers and police were also inventions of the first cities. Like the surrounding city wall, the king's military guard served a double function: it provided defense from outside attack and an obstacle to internal rebellion.

That these were the most important classes of city society can be seen from the physical remains of the first cities. The archeologist's spade has uncovered the monumental buildings of these classes in virtually all of the first cities. The palace, the temple, and the citadel (or fort) are, indeed, the monuments that distinguish cities from villages. Further, the size of these buildings and the permanency of their construction (compared with the small, cheaply built homes of the farmers) attest to the fundamental class divisions of city society.

Civilization: Security and Variety

The most obvious achievements of the first civilizations are the monuments—the pyramids, temples, palaces, statues, and treasures—that were created for the new ruling class of kings, nobles, priests, and their officials. But civilized life is much more than the capacity to create monuments.

Civilized life is secure life. At the most basic level this means security from the sudden destruction that village communities might suffer. Civilized life gives the feeling of permanence. It offers regularity, stability, order, even routine. Plans can be made. Expectations can be realized. People can be expected to act predictably, according to the rules.

The first cities were able to attain stability with walls that shielded the inhabitants from nomads and armies, with the first codes of law that defined human relationships, with police and officials who enforced the laws, and with institutions that functioned beyond the lives of their particular members. City life offered considerably more permanence and security than village life.

Civilization involves more than security, however. A city that provided only order would be more like a prison than a civilization. The first cities provided something that the best-ordered villages lacked. They provided far greater variety: more races and ethnic groups were speaking more languages, engaged in more occupations, and living a greater variety of lifestyles. The abundance of choice, the opportunities for new sensations, new experiences, knowledge—these have always been the appeals of city life. The opportunities for growth and enrichment were far greater than the possibilities of plow and pasture life.

Security plus variety equals creativity. At least the possibility of a more creative, expressive life was available in the protected, semipermanent city enclosures that drew, like magnets, foreign traders and diplomats, new ideas about gods and nature, strange foods and customs, and the magicians, ministers, and mercenaries of the king's court. Civilization is the enriched life that this dynamic urban setting permitted and the human creativity and opportunity that it encouraged. At the very least, cities made even the most common slave think and feel a greater range of things than the tightly knit, clannish agricultural village allowed. That was (and still is) the root of innovation and creativity—of civilization itself.

The variety of people and the complexity of city life required new and more general means of communication. The villager knew everyone personally. Cities brought together people who often did not even speak the same language. Not only law codes but written language itself became a way to bridge the many gaps of human variety. Cities invented writing so that strangers could communicate, and so that those communications could become permanent—remembered publicly, officially recorded. [Writer and philosopher Ralph Waldo] Emerson was right when he said that the city lives by memory, but it was the official memory that enabled the city to carry on its business or religion beyond the lifetime of the village elders. Written symbols that everyone could recognize became the basis of laws, invention, education, taxes, accounting, contracts, and obligations. In short, writing and records made it possible for each generation to begin on the shoulders of its ancestors. Village life and knowledge often seemed to start from scratch. Thus, cities cultivated not only memory and the past, but hope and the future as well. City civilizations invented not only history and record keeping but also prophecy and social planning.

Writing was one city invention that made more general communication possible. Money was another. Money made it possible to deal with anyone just as an agreed-upon public language did. Unnecessary in the village climate of mutual obligations, money was essential in the city society of strangers. Such general media of communication as writing and money vastly increased the number of things that could be said and thought, bought and sold. As a consequence, city life was more impersonal than village life, but also more dynamic and more exciting.

The "Eye" and "I"

[Communication theorist] Marshall McLuhan has written that "civilization gave the barbarian an eye for an ear." We might add that civilization also gave an "I" for an "us." City life made the "eye" and the "I" more important than they had been in the village. The invention of writing made knowledge more visual. The eye had to be trained to recognize the minute differences in letters and words. Eyes took in a greater abundance of detail: laws, prices, the strange cloak of the foreigner, the odd type of shoes made by the new craftsworker from who-knows-where, the colors of the fruit and vegetable market, and elaborate painting in the temple, as well as the written word. In the village one learned by listening. In the city seeing was believing. In the new city courts of law an "eyewitness account" was believed to be more reliable than "hearsay evidence." In some villages even today, the heard and the spoken are thought more reliable than the written and the seen. In the city, even spoken language took on the uniformity and absence of emotion that is unavoidable in the written word. Perhaps emotions themselves became less violent. "Civilized" is always used to mean emotional restraint, control of the more violent passions, and a greater understanding, even tolerance, of the different and foreign.

Perhaps empathy (the capacity to put yourself in someone else's shoes) increased in cities — so full of so many different others that had to be understood. When a Turkish villager was recently asked, "What would you do if you were president of your country?" he stammered: "My God! How can you ask such a thing? How can I . . . I cannot . . . president of Turkey . . . master of the whole world?" He was completely unable to imagine himself as president. It was as removed from his experience as if he were master of the world. Similarly, a Lebanese villager who was asked what he would do if he were editor of a newspaper accused the interviewer of ridiculing him, and frantically waved the interviewer on to another question. Such a life was beyond his comprehension. It was too foreign to imagine. The very variety of city life must have increased the capacity of the lowest commoner to imagine, empathize, sympathize, and criticize.

The oral culture of the village reinforced the accepted by saying and singing it almost monotonously. The elders, the storytellers, and the minstrels must have had prodigious memories. But their stories changed only gradually and slightly. The spoken word was sacred. To say it differently was to change the truth. The written culture of cities taught "point of *view*." An urban individual did not have to remember everything. That was done permanently on paper. Knowledge became a recognition of different interpretations and the capacity to look up things. The awareness of variety meant the possibility of criticism, analysis, and an ever-newer synthesis. It is no wonder that the technical and scientific knowledge of cities increased at a geometric rate compared with the knowledge of villages. The multiplication of knowledge was implicit in the city's demand to recognize difference and variety. Civilization has come to mean that ever-expanding body of knowledge and skill. Its finest achievements have been that knowledge, its writing, and its visual art. The city and civilization (like the child) are to be seen and not heard.

It may seem strange to say that the impersonal life of cities contributed greatly to the development of personality—the "I" as well as the "eye." Village life was in a sense much more personal. Everything was taken personally. Villagers deal with each other not as "the blacksmith," "the baker," "that guy who owes me a goat," or "that no-good bum." They do not even "deal" with each other. They know each other by name and family. They love, hate, support, and murder each other because of who they are, because of personal feelings, because of personal and family responsibility. They have full, varied relationships with each member of the village. They do not merely buy salt from this person, talk about the weather with this other person, and discuss personal matters with only this other person. They share too much with each other to divide up their relationships in that way.

City life is a life of separated, partial relationships. In a city you do not know about the butcher's life, wife, kids, and problems. You do not care. You are in a hurry. You have too many other things to do. You might discuss the weather—but while he's cutting. You came to buy meat. Many urban relationships are like that. There are many business, trading, or "dealing" relationships because there are simply too many people to know them all as relatives.

The impersonality of city life is a shame in a way. (It makes it easier to get mugged by someone who does not even hate you.) But the luxurious variety of impersonal relationships (at least some of the time) provides the freedom for the individual personality to emerge. Maybe that is why people have often dreamed of leaving family and friends (usually for a city) in the hope of "finding themselves." Certainly, the camaraderie and community of village life had a darker side of surveillance and conformity. When everything was known about everyone, it was difficult for the individual to find his or her individuality. Family ties and village custom were often obstacles to asserting self-identity. The city offered its inhabitants a huge variety of possible relationships and personal identities. The urban inhabitant was freer than his village cousin to choose friends, lovers, associates, occupation, housing, and lifestyle. The city was full of choices that the village could not afford or condone. The village probably provided more security in being like everyone else and doing what was expected. But the city provided the variety of possibilities that could allow the individual to follow the "inner self" and cultivate inner gardens.

The class divisions of city society made it difficult for commoners to achieve an effective or creative individuality. But the wealthy and powerful—especially the king—were able to develop models of individuality and personality that were revolutionary. No one before had ever achieved such a sense of the self, and the model of the king's power and freedom became a goal for the rest of the society. The luxury, leisure, and opportunity of the king was a revolutionary force. In contrast to a village elder, the king could do whatever he wanted. Recognizing that, more and more city inhabitants asked, "Why can't we?" City revolutions have continually extended class privilege and opportunities ever since.

Once a society has achieved a level of abundance, once it can offer the technological means, the educational opportunities, the creative outlets necessary for everyone to lead meaningful, happy, healthy lives, then classes may be a hindrance. Class divisions were, however, a definite stimulus to productivity and creativity in the early city civilizations. The democratic villagers preferred stability to improvement. As a result, their horizons were severely limited. They died early, lived precipitously, and suffered without much hope. The rulers of the first cities discovered the possibilities of leisure, creation, and the good life. They invented heaven and utopia—first for themselves. Only very gradually has the invention of civilization, of human potential, sifted down to those beneath the ruling class. In many cases, luxury, leisure, freedom, and opportunity are still the monopolies of the elite. But once the powerful have exploited the poor enough to establish their own paradise on earth and their own immortality after death, the poor also have broader horizons and plans.

Mesopotamian and Egyptian Civilizations: A Tale of Two Rivers

Experts disagree as to whether Mesopotamian or Egyptian civilization is older. Mesopotamian influence in Egypt was considerable enough to suggest slightly earlier origins, but both had evolved distinct civilizations by 3000 B.C.E. Indeed, the difference between the two civilizations attests to the existence of multiple routes to civilized life. In both cases, river valleys provided the necessary water and silt for an agricultural surplus large enough to support classes of specialists who did not have to farm. But the differing nature of the rivers had much to do with the different types of civilization that evolved.

The Egyptians were blessed with the easier and more reliable of the two rivers. The Nile overflowed its banks predictably every year on the parched ground in the summer after August 15, well after the harvest had been gathered, depositing its rich sediment, and withdrawing by early October, leaving little salt or marsh, in time for the sowing of winter crops. Later sowings for summer crops required only simple canals that tapped the river upstream and the natural drainage of the Nile Valley. Further, transportation on the Nile was simplified by the fact that the prevailing winds blew from the north, while the river flowed from the south, making navigation a matter of using sails upstream and dispensing with them coming downstream.

The Euphrates offered none of these advantages as it cut its way through Mesopotamia. The Euphrates flowed high above the flood plain (unlike the neighboring Tigris) so that its waters could be used, but it flooded suddenly and without warning in the late spring, after the summer crops had been sown and before the winter crops could be harvested. Thus, the flooding of the Euphrates offered no natural irrigation. Its waters were needed at other times, and its flooding was destructive. Canals were necessary to drain off water for irrigation when the river was low, and these canals had to be adequately blocked, and the banks reinforced, when the river flooded. Further, since the Euphrates was not as easily navigable as the Nile, the main canals had to serve as major transportation arteries as well.

In Mesopotamia the flood was the enemy. The Mesopotamian deities who ruled the waters, Nin-Girsu and Tiamat, were feared. The forces of nature were often evil. Life was a struggle. In Egypt, on the other hand, life was viewed as a cooperation with nature. Even the Egyptian god of the flood, Hapi, was a helpful deity, who provided the people's daily bread. Egyptian priests and philosophers were much more at ease with their world than were their Mesopotamian counterparts. And, partly because of their different experiences with their rivers, the Mesopotamians developed a civilization based on cities, while the Egyptians did not. From the first Sumerian city-states on the lower Euphrates to the later northern Mesopotamian capital of Babylon, civilization was the product and expression of city life. Egyptian civilization, in contrast, was the creation of the pharaoh's court rather than of cities. Beyond the court, which was moved from one location to another, Egypt remained a country of peasant villages.

A prime reason for Egypt's lack of urbanization was the ease of farming on the banks of the Nile. Canal irrigation was a relatively simple process that did not demand much organization. Small market towns were sufficient for the needs of the countryside. They housed artisans, shopkeepers, the priests of the local temple, and the agents of the pharaoh, but they never swelled with a large middle class and never developed large-scale industry or commerce.

In Sumer, and later in Mesopotamia, the enormous task of fighting the Euphrates required a complex social organization with immediate local needs. Only communal labor could build and maintain the network of subsidiary canals for irrigation and drainage. Constant supervision was necessary to keep the canals free of silt, to remove salt deposits, to maintain the riverbanks at flood-time, and to prevent any farmer from monopolizing the water in periods of drought. Life on the Euphrates required cooperative work and responsibility that never ceased. It encouraged absolute, administrative control over an area larger than the village, and it fostered participation and loyalty to an irrigated area smaller than the imperial state. The city-state was the political answer to the economic problems of Sumer and Mesopotamia.

The religious practices in the Euphrates Valley reflected and supported city organization. Residents of each local area worshiped the local god while recognizing the existence of other local gods in a larger Sumerian, and eventually Mesopotamian, pantheon of gods. The priests of the local temple supervised canal work, the collection of taxes, and the storage of written records, as well as the proper maintenance of religious rituals. Thus, religious loyalty reinforced civic loyalty. Peasant and middle-class Sumerians thought of themselves as citizens of their particular city, worshipers of their particular city god, subjects of their particular god's earthly representative, but not as Sumerian nationals. By contrast, the Egyptian peasant was always an Egyptian, a subject of the pharaoh, but never a citizen.

The local, civic orientation of Mesopotamian cities can be seen in the physical structure of the capital city of Sumer, the city of Ur. Like other cities on the Euphrates, Ur was surrounded by a wall. It was dominated by the temple of Nannar, the moon-god who owned the city, and the palace complex beneath the temple. The residential areas were situated outside of the sacred Temenos, or temple compound, but within the walls, between the river and the main canal. The well-excavated remains of Ur of the seventeenth century B.C.E. show a residential street plan that looks like many Middle Eastern cities of today. A highly congested area of winding alleys and broad streets sheltered one- and two-story houses of merchants, shopkeepers, tradespeople, and occasional priests and scribes that suggest a large, relatively prosperous middle class. Most houses were built around a central courtyard that offered shade throughout the day, with mud-brick, often even plastered, outside walls that protected a number of interior rooms from the sun and the eyes of the tax inspector. The remains of seventeenth-century Ur show both the variety and the density of modern city life. There are specialized districts throughout the city. Certain trades have their special quarters: a bakers' square, probably special areas for the dyers, tanners, potters, and metalworkers. But life is mixed together as well. Subsidiary gods have temples outside the Temenos. Small and large houses are jumbled next to each other. There seems to be a slum area near the Temenos, but there are small houses for workers, tenant farmers, and the poor throughout the city. And no shop or urban professional is more than a short walking distance away. The entire size of the walled city was an oval that extended three-quarters of a mile long and a half a mile wide.

A well-excavated Egyptian city from roughly the same period (the fourteenth century B.C.E.) offers some striking contrasts. Akhetaton, or Tell el Amarna, Pharaoh Akhenaton's capital on the Nile, was not enclosed by walls or canals. It merely straggled down the eastern bank of the Nile for five miles and faded into the desert. Without the need for extensive irrigation or protection, Tell el Amarna shows little of the crowded, vital density of Ur. Its layout lacks any sense of urgency. The North Palace of the pharaoh is a mile and a half north of the temple complex and offices, which are three and a half miles from the official pleasure garden. The palaces of the court nobility and the large residences of the court's officials front one of the two main roads that parallel the river, or they are situated at random. There is plenty of physical space (and social space) between these and the bunched villages of workers' houses. The remains suggest very little in the way of a middle class or a merchant or professional class beyond the pharaoh's specialists and retainers. Life for the wealthy was, judging from the housing, more luxurious than at Ur, but for the majority of the population, city life was less rich. In many ways, the pharaoh's court at Tell el Amarna was not a city at all.

6

From *The Epic of Gilgamesh*

The Epic of Gilgamesh is the earliest story written in any language. It also serves as a primary source for the study of ancient Mesopotamia—the land between the two great rivers, the Tigris and Euphrates.

Gilgamesh was an ancient king of Sumer, who lived about 2700 B.C.E. Since *The Epic* comes from a thousand years later, we can assume Sumerians kept telling this tale about King Gilgamesh for some time before it was written down. In Sumer, writing was initially used

The Epic of Gilgamesh, trans. N. K. Sanders (London: Penguin Books, 1972), 61–69, 108–13.

by temple priests to keep track of property and taxes. Soon, however, writing was used to preserve stories and to celebrate kings.

The more you know about the Sumerian people, the more information you will be able to mine from your source. In the previous secondary selection, you read some historical background that will help you make sense of this story. Look in *The Epic* for evidence of the urban revolution discussed in the previous selection. What is the meaning of the story of the taming of Enkidu by the harlot? Does Enkidu also tame Gilgamesh? What two worlds do Enkidu and Gilgamesh represent?

Do the authors or listeners of *The Epic* think city life is better than life in the country? According to *The Epic*, what are the advantages of the city? What problems does it have?

What does the story of the flood tell you about life in ancient Mesopotamia? Would you expect the ancient Egyptians to tell a similar story?

Thinking Historically

Reading a primary source differs markedly from reading a secondary source. Primary sources were not written with you or me in mind. It is safe to say that the author of *The Epic of Gilgamesh* never even imagined our existence. For this reason, primary sources are a bit difficult to access. Reading a primary source usually requires some intensive work. You have to keep asking yourself, why was this story told? How would a story like this help or teach people at that time? That is, you must put yourself in the shoes of the original teller and listener.

Primary sources offer us a piece of the past. No historian is in your way explaining things. With your unique perspective, you have an advantage over the intended audience: You can ask questions about the source that the author and original audience never imagined or, possibly, would not have dared ask.

Ask a question for which this primary source can provide an answer, then find the answer.

Prologue: Gilgamesh King in Uruk

I will proclaim to the world the deeds of Gilgamesh. This was the man to whom all things were known; this was the king who knew the countries of the world. He was wise, he saw mysteries and knew secret things, he brought us a tale of the days before the flood. He went on a long journey, was weary, worn-out with labor; returning he rested, he engraved on a stone the whole story.

When the gods created Gilgamesh they gave him a perfect body. Shamash the glorious sun endowed him with beauty, Adad the god of the storm endowed him with courage, the great gods made his beauty perfect, surpassing all others, terrifying like a great wild bull. Two thirds they made him god and one third man.

In Uruk he built walls, a great rampart, and the temple of blessed Eanna for the god of the firmament Anu, and for Ishtar the goddess of love. Look at it still today: the outer wall where the cornice runs, it shines with the brilliance of copper; and the inner wall, it has no equal. Touch the threshold; it is ancient. Approach Eanna the dwelling of Ishtar, our lady of love and war, the like of which no latter-day king, no man alive can equal. Climb upon the wall of Uruk; walk along it, I say; regard the foundation terrace and examine the masonry; is it not burnt brick and good? The seven sages laid the foundations.

The Coming of Enkidu

Gilgamesh went abroad in the world, but he met with none who could withstand his arms till he came to Uruk. But the men of Uruk muttered in their houses, "Gilgamesh sounds the tocsin for his amusement, his arrogance has no bounds by day or night. No son is left with his father, for Gilgamesh takes from all, even the children; yet the king should be a shepherd to his people. His lust leaves no virgin to her lover, neither the warrior's daughter nor the wife of the noble; yet this is the shepherd of the city, wise, comely, and resolute."

The gods heard their lament, the gods of heaven cried to the Lord of Uruk, to Anu the god of Uruk: "A goddess made him, strong as a savage bull, none can withstand his arms. No son is left with his father, for Gilgamesh takes them all; and is this the king, the shepherd of his people? His lust leaves no virgin to her lover, neither the warrior's daughter nor the wife of the noble." When Anu had heard their lamentation the gods cried to Aruru, the goddess of creation, "You made him, O Aruru, now create his equal; let it be as like him as his own reflection, his second self, stormy head for stormy heart. Let them contend together and leave Uruk in quiet."

So the goddess conceived an image in her mind, and it was of the stuff of Anu of the firmament. She dipped her hands in water and pinched off clay, she let it fall in the wilderness, and noble Enkidu was created. There was virtue in him of the god of war, of Ninurta himself. His body was rough; he had long hair like a woman's; it waved like the hair of Nisaba, the goddess of corn. His body was covered with matted hair like Samuqan's, the god of cattle. He was innocent of mankind; he knew nothing of cultivated land.

Enkidu ate grass in the hills with the gazelle and lurked with wild beasts at the water-holes; he had joy of the water with the herds of wild game. But there was a trapper who met him one day face to face at the drinking-hole, for the wild game had entered his territory. On three days he met him face to face, and the trapper was frozen with fear. He went back to his house with the game that he had caught, and he was dumb, benumbed with terror. His face was altered like that of one who has made a long journey. With awe in his heart he spoke to his father: "Father, there is a man, unlike any other, who comes down from the hills. He is the strongest in the world, he is like an immortal from heaven. He ranges over the hills with wild beasts and eats grass; he ranges through your land and comes down to the wells. I am afraid and dare not go near him. He fills in the pits which I dig and tears up my traps set for the game; he helps the beasts to escape and now they slip through my fingers."

His father opened his mouth and said to the trapper, "My son, in Uruk lives Gilgamesh; no one has ever prevailed against him, he is strong as a star from heaven. Go to Uruk, find Gilgamesh, extol the strength of this wild man. Ask him to give you a harlot, a wanton from the temple of love; return with her, and let her woman's power overpower this man. When next he comes down to drink at the wells she will be there, stripped naked; and when he sees her beckoning he will embrace her, and then the wild beasts will reject him."

So the trapper set out on his journey to Uruk and addressed himself to Gilgamesh saying, "A man unlike any other is roaming now in the pastures; he is as strong as a star from heaven and I am afraid to approach him. He helps the wild game to escape; he fills in my pits and pulls up my traps." Gilgamesh said, "Trapper, go back, take with you a harlot, a child of pleasure. At the drinking-hole she will strip, and when he sees her beckoning he will embrace her and the game of the wilderness will surely reject him."

Now the trapper returned, taking the harlot with him. After a three days' journey they came to the drinking-hole, and there they sat down; the harlot and the trapper sat facing one another and waited for the game to come. For the first day and for the second day the two sat waiting, but on the third day the herds came; they came down to drink and Enkidu was with them. The small wild creatures of the plains were glad of the water, and Enkidu with them, who ate grass with the gazelle and was born in the hills; and she saw him; the savage man, come from far-off in the hills. The trapper spoke to her: "There he is. Now, woman, make your breasts bare, have no shame, do not delay but welcome his love. Let him see you naked, let him possess your body. When he comes near uncover yourself and lie with him; teach him, the savage man, your woman's art, for when he murmurs love to you the wild beasts that shared his life in the hills will reject him."

She was not ashamed to take him, she made herself naked and welcomed his eagerness; as he lay on her murmuring love she taught him the woman's art. For six days and seven nights they lay together, for

Enkidu had forgotten his home in the hills; but when he was satisfied he went back to the wild beasts. Then, when the gazelle saw him, they bolted away; when the wild creatures saw him they fled. Enkidu would have followed, but his body was bound as though with a cord, his knees gave way when he started to run, his swiftness was gone. And now the wild creatures had all fled away; Enkidu was grown weak, for wisdom was in him, and the thoughts of a man were in his heart. So he returned and sat down at the woman's feet, and listened intently to what she said. "You are wise, Enkidu, and now you have become like a god. Why do you want to run wild with the beasts in the hills? Come with me. I will take you to strong-walled Uruk, to the blessed temple of Ishtar and of Anu, of love and of heaven: there Gilgamesh lives, who is very strong, and like a wild bull he lords it over men."

When she had spoken Enkidu was pleased; he longed for a comrade, for one who would understand his heart. "Come, woman, and take me to that holy temple, to the house of Anu and of Ishtar, and to the place where Gilgamesh lords it over people. I will challenge him boldly, I will cry out aloud in Uruk, 'I am the strongest here, I have come to change the old order, I am he who was born in the hills, I am he who is strongest of all.'"

She said, "Let us go, and let him see your face. I know very well where Gilgamesh is in great Uruk. O Enkidu, there all the people are dressed in their gorgeous robes, every day is holiday, the young men and the girls are wonderful to see. How sweet they smell! All the great ones are roused from their beds. O Enkidu, you who love life, I will show you Gilgamesh, a man of many moods; you shall look at him well in his radiant manhood. His body is perfect in strength and maturity; he never rests by night or day. He is stronger than you, so leave your boasting. Shamash the glorious sun has given favors to Gilgamesh, and Anu of the heavens, and Enlil, and Ea the wise has given him deep understanding. I tell you, even before you have left the wilderness, Gilgamesh will know in his dreams that you are coming."

Now Gilgamesh got up to tell his dream to his mother, Ninsun, one of the wise gods. "Mother, last night I had a dream. I was full of joy, the young heroes were round me and I walked through the night under the stars of the firmament, and one, a meteor of the stuff of Anu, fell down from heaven. I tried to lift it but it proved too heavy. All the people of Uruk came round to see it, the common people jostled and the nobles thronged to kiss its feet; and to me its attraction was like the love of woman. They helped me, I braced my forehead and I raised it with thongs and brought it to you, and you yourself pronounced it my brother."

Then Ninsun, who is well-beloved and wise, said to Gilgamesh, "This star of heaven which descended like a meteor from the sky; which you tried to lift, but found too heavy, when you tried to move it it would not budge, and so you brought it to my feet; I made it for you, a goad and spur, and you were drawn as though to a woman. This is the strong comrade, the one who brings help to his friend in his need. He is the strongest of wild creatures, the stuff of Anu; born in the grasslands and the wild hills reared him; when you see him you will be glad; you will love him as a woman and he will never forsake you. This is the meaning of the dream."

Gilgamesh said, "Mother, I dreamed a second dream. In the streets of strong-walled Uruk there lay an axe; the shape of it was strange and the people thronged round. I saw it and was glad. I bent down, deeply drawn towards it; I loved it like a woman and wore it at my side." Ninsun answered, "That axe, which you saw, which drew you so powerfully like love of a woman, that is the comrade whom I give you, and he will come in his strength like one of the host of heaven. He is the brave companion who rescues his friend in necessity." Gilgamesh said to his mother, "A friend, a counsellor has come to me from Enlil, and now I shall befriend and counsel him." So Gilgamesh told his dreams; and the harlot retold them to Enkidu.

And now she said to Enkidu, "When I look at you you have become like a god. Why do you yearn to run wild again with the beasts in the hills? Get up from the ground, the bed of a shepherd." He listened to her words with care. It was good advice that she gave. She divided her clothing in two and with the one half she clothed him and with the other herself; and holding his hand she led him like a child to the sheepfolds, into the shepherds' tents. There all the shepherds crowded round to see him, they put down bread in front of him, but Enkidu could only suck the milk of wild animals. He fumbled and gaped, at a loss what to do or how he should eat the bread and drink the strong wine. Then the woman said, "Enkidu, eat bread, it is the staff of life; drink the wine, it is the custom of the land." So he ate till he was full and drank strong wine, seven goblets. He became merry, his heart exulted and his face shone. He rubbed down the matted hair of his body and anointed himself with oil. Enkidu had become a man; but when he had put on man's clothing he appeared like a bridegroom. He took arms to hunt the lion so that the shepherds could rest at night. He caught wolves and lions and the herdsmen lay down in peace; for Enkidu was their watchman, that strong man who had no rival.

He was merry living with the shepherds, till one day lifting his eyes he saw a man approaching. He said to the harlot, "Woman, fetch that man here. Why has he come? I wish to know his name." She went and called the man saying, "Sir, where are you going on this weary journey?" The man answered, saying to Enkidu, "Gilgamesh has gone into the marriage-house and shut out the people. He does strange things in Uruk, the city of great streets. At the roll of the drum work begins for the men, and work for the women. Gilgamesh the king is about to celebrate marriage with the Queen of Love, and he still demands to be first with the bride, the king to be first and the husband to follow, for that was ordained by the gods from his birth, from the time the umbilical cord was cut. But now the drums roll for the choice of the bride and the city groans." At these words Enkidu turned white in the face. "I will go to the place where Gilgamesh lords it over the people, I will challenge him boldly, and I will cry aloud in Uruk, 'I have come to change the old order, for I am the strongest here.'"

Now Enkidu strode in front and the woman followed behind. He entered Uruk, that great market, and all the folk thronged round him where he stood in the street in strong-walled Uruk. The people jostled; speaking of him they said, "He is the spit of Gilgamesh." "He is shorter." "He is bigger of bone." "This is the one who was reared on the milk of wild beasts. His is the greatest strength." The men rejoiced: "Now Gilgamesh has met his match. This great one, this hero whose beauty is like a god, he is a match even for Gilgamesh."

In Uruk the bridal bed was made, fit for the goddess of love. The bride waited for the bridegroom, but in the night Gilgamesh got up and came to the house. Then Enkidu stepped out, he stood in the street and blocked the way. Mighty Gilgamesh came on and Enkidu met him at the gate. He put out his foot and prevented Gilgamesh from entering the house, so they grappled, holding each other like bulls. They broke the doorposts and the walls shook, they snorted like bulls locked together. They shattered the doorposts and the walls shook. Gilgamesh bent his knee with his foot planted on the ground and with a turn Enkidu was thrown. Then immediately his fury died. When Enkidu was thrown he said to Gilgamesh, "There is not another like you in the world. Ninsun, who is as strong as a wild ox in the byre, she was the mother who bore you, and now you are raised above all men, and Enlil has given you the kingship, for your strength surpasses the strength of men." So Enkidu and Gilgamesh embraced and their friendship was sealed.

The Story of the Flood

"You know the city Shurrupak, it stands on the banks of Euphrates? That city grew old and the gods that were in it were old. There was Anu, lord of the firmament, their father, and warrior Enlil their counsellor, Ninurta the helper, and Ennugi watcher over canals; and with them also was Ea. In those days the world teemed, the people multiplied, the world bellowed like a wild bull, and the great god was aroused by the clamour. Enlil heard the clamour and he said to the gods in council, 'The uproar of mankind is intolerable and sleep is no longer possible by reason of the babel.' So the gods agreed to exterminate mankind. Enlil did this, but Ea because of his oath warned me in a dream. He whispered their words to my house of reeds, 'Reed-house, reed-house! Wall, O wall, hearken reed-house, wall reflect; O man of Shurrupak, son of Ubara-Tutu; tear down your house and build a boat, abandon possessions and look for life, despise worldly goods and save your soul alive. Tear down your house, I say, and build a boat. These are the measurements of the barque as you shall build her: let her beam equal her length, let her deck be roofed like the vault that covers the abyss; then take up into the boat the seed of all living creatures.'

"When I had understood I said to my lord, 'Behold, what you have commanded I will honour and perform, but how shall I answer the people, the city, the elders?' The Ea opened his mouth and said to me, his servant, 'Tell them this: I have learnt that Enlil is wrathful against me, I dare no longer walk in his land nor live in his city; I will go down to the Gulf to dwell with Ea my lord. But on you he will rain down abundance, rare fish and shy wild-fowl, a rich harvest-tide. In the evening the rider of the storm will bring you wheat in torrents.'

"In the first light of dawn all my household gathered round me, the children brought pitch and the men whatever was necessary. On the fifth day I laid the keel and the ribs, then I made fast the planking. The ground-space was one acre, each side of the deck measured one hundred and twenty cubits, making a square. I built six decks below, seven in all, I divided them into nine sections with bulkheads between. I drove in wedges where needed, I saw to the punt-poles, and laid in supplies. The carriers brought oil in baskets, I poured pitch into the furnace and asphalt and oil; more oil was consumed in caulking, and more again the master of the boat took into his stores. I slaughtered bullocks for the people and every day I killed sheep. I gave the shipwrights wine to drink as though it were river water, raw wine and red wine and oil and white wine. There was feasting then as there is at the time of the New Year's festival; I myself anointed my head. On the seventh day the boat was complete.

"Then was the launching full of difficulty; there was shifting of ballast above and below till two thirds was submerged. I loaded into her all that I had of gold and of living things, my family, my kin, the beast of the field both wild and tame, and all the craftsmen. I sent them on board, for the time that Shamash had ordained was already fulfilled when he said 'In the evening, when the rider of the storm sends down the destroying rain, enter the boat and batten her down.' The time was fulfilled, the evening came, the rider of the storm sent down the rain. I looked out at the weather and it was terrible, so I too boarded the boat and battened her down. All was now complete, the battening and the caulking; so I handed the tiller to Puzur-Amurri the steersman, with the navigation and the care of the whole boat.

"With the first light of dawn a black cloud came from the horizon; it thundered within where Adad, lord of the storm was riding. In front over hill and plain Shullat and Hanish, heralds of the storm, led on. Then the gods of the abyss rose up; Nergal pulled out the dams of the nether waters, Ninurta the war-lord threw down the dykes, and the seven judges of hell, the Annunaki, raised their torches, lighting the land with their livid flame. A stupor of despair went up to heaven when the god of the storm turned daylight to darkness, when he smashed the land like a cup. One whole day the tempest raged, gathering fury as it went, it poured over the people like the tides of battle; a man could not see his brother nor the people be seen from heaven. Even the gods were terrified at the flood, they fled to the highest heaven, the firmament of Anu; they crouched against the walls, cowering like curs. Then Ishtar the sweet-voiced Queen of Heaven cried out like a woman in travail: 'Alas the days of old are turned to dust because I commanded evil; why did I command this evil in the council of all the gods? I commanded wars to destroy the people, but are they not my people, for I brought them forth? Now like the spawn of fish they float in the ocean.' The great gods of heaven and of hell wept, they covered their mouths.

"For six days and six nights the winds blew, torrent and tempest and flood overwhelmed the world, tempest and flood raged together like warring hosts. When the seventh day dawned the storm from the south subsided, the sea grew calm, the flood was stilled; I looked at the face of the world and there was silence, all mankind was turned to clay. The surface of the sea stretched as flat as a roof-top; I opened a hatch and the light fell on my face. Then I bowed low, I sat down and I wept, the tears streamed down my face, for on every side was the waste of water. I looked for land in vain, but fourteen leagues distant there appeared a mountain, and there the boat grounded; on the mountain of Nisir the boat held fast, she held fast and did not budge. One day she held, and a second day on the mountain of Nisir she held fast and did not budge. A third day, and a fourth day she held fast on the mountain and did not budge; a fifth day and a sixth day she held fast on the mountain. When the seventh day dawned I loosed a dove and let her go. She flew away, but finding no resting-place she returned. Then I loosed a swallow, and she flew away but finding no resting-place she returned. I loosed a raven, she saw that the waters had retreated, she ate, she flew around, she cawed, and she did not come back. Then I threw everything open to the four winds, I made a sacrifice and poured out a libation on the mountain top. Seven and again seven cauldrons I set up on their stands, I heaped up wood and cane and cedar and myrtle. When the gods smelled the sweet savour, they gathered like flies over the sacrifice. Then, at last, Ishtar also came, she lifted her necklace with the jewels of heaven that once Anu had made to please her. 'O you gods here present, by the lapis lazuli round my neck I shall remember these days as I remember the jewels of my throat; these last days I shall not forget. Let all the gods gather round the sacrifice, except Enlil. He shall not approach this offering, for without reflection he brought the flood; he consigned my people to destruction.'

"When Enlil had come, when he saw the boat, he was wrath and swelled with anger at the gods, the host of heaven, 'Has any of these mortals escaped? Not one was to have survived the destruction.' Then the god of the wells and canals Ninurta opened his mouth and said to the warrior Enlil, 'Who is there of the gods that devise without Ea? It is Ea alone who knows all things.' Then Ea opened his mouth and spoke to warrior Enlil, 'Wisest of gods, hero Enlil, how could you so senselessly bring down the flood?

> Lay upon the sinner his sin,
> Lay upon the transgressor his transgression,
> Punish him a little when he breaks loose,
> Do not drive him too hard or he perishes;
> Would that a lion had ravaged mankind
> Rather than the flood,
> Would that a wolf had ravaged mankind
> Rather than the flood,
> Would that famine had wasted the world
> Rather than the flood,
> Would that pestilence had wasted mankind
> Rather than the flood.

It was not I that revealed the secret of the gods; the wise man learned it in a dream. Now take your counsel what shall be done with him.'

"Then Enlil went up into the boat, he took me by the hand and my wife and made us enter the boat and kneel down on either side, he standing between us. He touched our foreheads to bless us saying, 'In time past Utnapishtim was a mortal man; henceforth he and his wife shall live in the distance at the mouth of the rivers.' Thus it was that the gods took me and placed me here to live in the distance, at the mouth of the rivers."

7

From Hammurabi's Code

King Hammurabi of Babylon conquered the entire area of Meso-potamia (including Sumer) between 1793 and 1750 B.C.E. His law code provides us with a rare insight into the daily life of ancient urban society.

Law codes give us an idea of a people's sense of justice and notions of proper punishment. This selection includes only parts of Hammurabi's Code, so we cannot conclude that if something is not mentioned here it was not a matter of legal concern. We can, however, deduce much about Babylonian society from the laws mentioned in this essay.

What do these laws tell us about class divisions or social distinctions in Babylonian society? What can we learn from these laws about the roles of women and men? Which laws or punishments seem unusual today? What does that difference suggest to you about ancient Babylon compared to modern society?

Thinking Historically

As a primary source, law codes are extremely useful. They zero in on a society's main concerns, revealing minutiae of daily life in great detail. But, for a number of reasons, law codes cannot be viewed as a precise reflection of society.

We cannot assume, for instance, that all of Hammurabi's laws were strictly followed or enforced, nor can we assume that for our own society. If there was a law against something, we can safely assume that some people obeyed it and some people did not. (That is, if no one engaged in the behavior, there would be no need for the law.) Therefore, law codes suggest a broad range of behaviors in a society.

While laws tell us something about the concerns of the society that produces them, we cannot presume that all members of society share the same concerns. Recall that, especially in ancient society, laws were written by the literate, powerful few. What evidence do you see of the upper-class "patrician" composition of Babylonian law in this code?

Finally, if an ancient law seems similar to our own, we cannot assume that the law reflects motives, intents, or goals similar to our own laws. Laws must be considered within the context of the society in which they were created. Notice, for instance, the laws in Hammurabi's Code that may seem, by our standards, intended to protect women. On closer examination, what appears to be their goal?

"Hammurabi's Code," from C. H. Johns, *Babylonian and Assyrian Laws, Contracts and Letters* [Library of Ancient Inscriptions] (New York: Charles Scribner's Sons, 1904), 33–35.

Theft

6. If a man has stolen goods from a temple, or house, he shall be put to death; and he that has received the stolen property from him shall be put to death.

8. If a patrician has stolen ox, sheep, ass, pig, or goat, whether from a temple, or a house, he shall pay thirtyfold. If he be a plebeian, he shall return tenfold. If the thief cannot pay, he shall be put to death.

14. If a man has stolen a child, he shall be put to death.

15. If a man has induced either a male or female slave from the house of a patrician, or plebeian, to leave the city, he shall be put to death.

21. If a man has broken into a house he shall be killed before the breach and buried there.

22. If a man has committed highway robbery and has been caught, that man shall be put to death.

23. If the highwayman has not been caught, the man that has been robbed shall state on oath what he has lost and the city or district governor in whose territory or district the robbery took place shall restore to him what he has lost.

Family

128. If a man has taken a wife and has not executed a marriage-contract, that woman is not a wife.

129. If a man's wife be caught lying with another, they shall be strangled and cast into the water. If the wife's husband would save his wife, the king can save his servant.

130. If a man has ravished another's betrothed wife, who is a virgin, while still living in her father's house, and has been caught in the act, that man shall be put to death; the woman shall go free.

131. If a man's wife has been accused by her husband, and has not been caught lying with another, she shall swear her innocence, and return to her house.

138. If a man has divorced his wife, who has not borne him children, he shall pay over to her as much money as was given for her bride-price and the marriage-portion which she brought from her father's house, and so shall divorce her.

139. If there was no bride-price, he shall give her one mina of silver, as a price of divorce.

140. If he be a plebeian, he shall give her one-third of a mina of silver.

148. If a man has married a wife and a disease has seized her, if he is determined to marry a second wife, he shall marry her. He shall not divorce the wife whom the disease has seized. In the home they made together she shall dwell, and he shall maintain her as long as she lives.

149. If that woman was not pleased to stay in her husband's house, he shall pay over to her the marriage-portion which she brought from her father's house, and she shall go away.

153. If a man's wife, for the sake of another, has caused her husband to be killed, that woman shall be impaled.

154. If a man has committed incest with his daughter, that man shall be banished from the city.

155. If a man has betrothed a maiden to his son and his son has known her, and afterward the man has lain in her bosom, and been caught, that man shall be strangled and she shall be cast into the water.

156. If a man has betrothed a maiden to his son, and his son has not known her, and that man has lain in her bosom, he shall pay her half a mina of silver, and shall pay over to her whatever she brought from her father's house, and the husband of her choice shall marry her.

186. If a man has taken a young child to be his son, and after he has taken him, the child discovers his own parents, he shall return to his father's house.

188, 189. If a craftsman has taken a child to bring up and has taught him his handicraft, he shall not be reclaimed. If he has not taught him his handicraft that foster child shall return to his father's house.

Assault

195. If a son has struck his father, his hands shall be cut off.

196. If a man has knocked out the eye of a patrician, his eye shall be knocked out.

197. If he has broken the limb of a patrician, his limb shall be broken.

198. If he has knocked out the eye of a plebeian or has broken the limb of a plebeian's servant, he shall pay one mina of silver.

199. If he has knocked out the eye of a patrician's servant, or broken the limb of a patrician's servant, he shall pay half his value.

200. If a patrician has knocked out the tooth of a man that is his equal, his tooth shall be knocked out.

201. If he has knocked out the tooth of a plebeian, he shall pay one-third of a mina of silver.

Liability

229. If a builder has built a house for a man, and has not made his work sound, and the house he built has fallen, and caused the death of its owner, that builder shall be put to death.

230. If it is the owner's son that is killed, the builder's son shall be put to death.

231. If it is the slave of the owner that is killed, the builder shall give slave for slave to the owner of the house.

232. If he has caused the loss of goods, he shall render back whatever he has destroyed. Moreover, because he did not make sound the house he built, and it fell, at his own cost he shall rebuild the house that fell.

237. If a man has hired a boat and a boatman, and loaded it with corn, wool, oil, or dates, or whatever it be, and the boatman has been careless, and sunk the boat, or lost what is in it, the boatman shall restore the boat which he sank, and whatever he lost that was in it.

238. If a boatman has sunk a man's boat, and has floated it again, he shall pay half its value in silver.

251. If a man's ox be a gorer, and has revealed its evil propensity as a gorer, and he has not blunted its horn, or shut up the ox, and then that ox has gored a free man, and caused his death, the owner shall pay half a mina of silver.

252. If it be a slave that has been killed, he shall pay one-third of a mina of silver.

ZAHI HAWASS

Love and Marriage in Ancient Egypt

With the urban revolution, people unrelated to each other began living together in large, organized communities. To do so peaceably they needed not only laws (like Hammurabi's Code) to punish unacceptable behavior but also a body of common values to regulate social practices and relationships. Marriage was one of the most important of these relationships, because it formed the core bond of the society — the family — and affected other important aspects of social life such as inheritance and the performing of funerary rites. In the following selection, Hawass, a modern archaeologist and historian, draws from a

Zahi Hawass, *Silent Images: Women in Pharaonic Egypt* (New York: Harry N. Abrams, Inc., 2000), 72–81.

number of primary sources to create a portrait of love and marriage in ancient Egypt, and to illuminate the ideals and laws that might have shaped them. How does Hawass's description of Egyptian civilization compare to the primary sources from Mesopotamia? Do you see any signs in this selection that Egypt was a happier civilization than Mesopotamia? What signs of patriarchy do you see in ancient Egypt? What powers did Egyptian women enjoy? How would you compare the lives of Egyptian women with the lives of women living in other ancient civilizations?

Thinking Historically

Notice how the author refers to ancient primary sources, and how he uses them. How do these primary sources enhance or limit the author's account of ancient Egypt? What kinds of sources are unavailable to the historian, either because the Egyptians were not inclined to create them or because the sources have been lost over the years? What kinds of primary sources are most readily available to historians, again either because of Egyptian interest or preservation? How might the nature of our sources affect our view of Egyptian history?

Like many traditional cultures, the nucleus of ancient Egyptian society was the family. As modern psychiatrists have discovered, the Egyptians knew that a stable and happy family produces secure and contented children, children who would realize their full potential as adults and contribute positively to their society. Hence marriage, as the fundamental basis of the family, was very highly regarded and universally practiced. Indeed, through their role in establishing and maintaining the family and through the care of children, tomorrow's adults, Egyptian women can rightly be said to have contributed to those areas of Egyptian culture—literature, mathematics, technology, and so on—which were apparently monopolized by men.

Early marriage was desirable and universal and its aim was to establish a family. Children were all important, especially a son who would carry out the funerary rituals for his parents. From the books of instructions which were written in the Old Kingdom and later, we can get an idea of how the ancient Egyptians themselves viewed marriage, with the proviso that these compositions were always authored by men and addressed to other men, usually the pupil of the writer. Nowhere do we have comparable texts written by or for women. This source then, though useful, may well be biased.

Most marriages seem to have been within the same social stratum and no doubt this helped to keep property and professions within the family. One well-documented example from the sixth century gives an account of how a priest of Amun-Re in the Fayoum was asked by a young relative from Thebes for a priestly appointment in the Fayoum as well as for his daughter in marriage. Both requests were eventually conceded. We have no idea if the young lady in question had any say in the matter.

Other records suggest that the father was involved in his daughter's marriage arrangements. For example, Ankhsheshonq advises his son to "take a wise man for your daughter and not a rich man," implying that the father had the final say in the choice of bridegroom. The scribe Any wrote for his son:

"Take a wife while you're young,
That she make a son for you;
She should bear for you while you're youthful,
It is proper to make people."

Another later text recommends marrying at the age of twenty, again, in order to have a son while young. Low life expectancy was obviously one factor to recommend this practice, but the desire to avoid illicit unions, and in particular, illegitimate children was very strong. Most responsible fathers would therefore see that their daughters were married soon after puberty, probably at an age of between twelve and fourteen. Until marriage, girls lived with their parents, but were certainly not all confined to the house. Girls from low-income families helped with the household chores, which included fetching water from the river or well, taking the animals to graze, running errands, helping with the harvest, and so on, giving them ample opportunity to review the local talent when prospecting for a future spouse. The middle- and upper-class women were probably more confined, and their contacts with the opposite sex were more likely to have been restricted to their extended family. As in modern rural Egypt, the first cousin marriage was very popular in antiquity, but other close-kin marriages such as uncles and nieces were tolerated then, although they would not be now. Brother and sister unions were usually restricted to the royal family, although isolated cases of marriage between half brother and sister have been demonstrated from records of common people.

Young men probably married somewhat later in their early 20s, at least amongst the educated classes, when their careers were well enough advanced to set up their own household. The educated ones were less tied to the parental home as their careers could take them further afield, even abroad, and their field of choice in theory was therefore much wider, although family approval was still needed.

We are lucky that a rich body of love poetry has survived, written on papyrus and pottery and now preserved in Turin, London, and Cairo. These are literary compositions rather than spontaneous poetry, and they present an ideal which may have been removed from reality, but which nevertheless must lie within social conventions of the time. They present a rather different picture from that obtained from wisdom literature or other records, and are probably the closest we will get to an idea of the preliminaries to marriage.

In these poems, lovers address each other as "brother" and "sister"; used loosely as terms of endearment rather than implying family kinship. They convey the idea that young men and women had the opportunity to meet and fall in love, and indicate that, as long as they could get family approval, they had some degree of choice in their future partner. Young girls as well as men are able to speak openly of their feelings, and one famous cycle of songs from the Chester Beatty Papyrus takes the form of stanzas sung alternately by male and female singers. It starts with a description of the woman's beauty:

"Shining bright, fair of skin,
Lovely the look of her eyes.
Sweet the speech of her lips . . .
Upright neck, shining breast
Hair true lapis lazuli;
Heavy thighs, narrow waist,
Her legs parade her beauty;
With graceful steps she treads the ground,
Captures my heart by her movements."

In the next stanza, the young girl admits that she also is smitten: "My brother torments my heart with his voice, He makes sickness take hold of me." Further on, she complains that she cannot control her heart: "My heart flutters hastily, When I think of my love of you"; and describes all the symptoms of lovesickness, ending in despair; "My heart, do not flutter!"

The young man is suffering likewise:
"Seven days since I saw my sister;
And sickness invaded me . . .
When the physicians come to me,
My heart rejects their remedies;
My sister is better than all prescriptions . . .
The sight of her makes me well!"

In another song cycle, the lover complains that his girl is playing hard to get: "How well she knows to cast the noose, And yet not pay the cattle tax!" And elsewhere, he has to resort to a ruse to see her:

"I shall lie down at home,
And pretend to be ill;
Then enter the neighbors to see me,
Then comes my sister with them."

The goddess Hathor; the "Golden One," was the Mistress of Love and Beauty and the protector of lovers, able to aid and abet them:

"I praise the Golden [One],
I worship her majesty,
I extol the Lady of Heaven;
I give adoration to Hathor . . .
I called to her; she heard my plea
She sent my mistress to me."

The ancient Egyptians were also sensitive to the beauty of nature: gardens, the river Nile, trees, and birds were evoked in the love poems. "I belong to you like this plot of ground, That I planted with flowers. And sweet-smelling herbs." Or, more explicitly:

"The voice of the dove is calling,
It says: 'It's day! Where are you?'
O bird, stop scolding me!
I found my brother on his bed,
My heart was overjoyed:
Each said: 'I shall not leave you,
My hand is in your hand:
You and I shall wander,
In all the places fair.'"

This and other similar examples imply a certain freedom for young people before marriage but we have no means of knowing whether this was normal or exceptional, although it does seem to apply to girls as well as young men.

In practice, one suspects that most marriages were arranged between families who knew each other or who were related. Records show that it was normal for a young man to approach the father for permission to marry his daughter. But the girl, although perhaps not free to marry without permission, could certainly try persuasion, especially to win her mother's agreement:

"He knows not my wish to embrace him,
Or he would write to my mother . . .
Come to me that I see your beauty,
Father: Mother will rejoice!
My people will hail you all together,
They will hail you. O my brother!"

Clearly, if these poems are indicative of the normal expression of feelings of young people they had some say in the choice of partner; although the final outcome needed family support. The emphasis on mutual love and respect between husband and wife expressed elsewhere was an ideal to aspire to. It may have discouraged forced marriages, but no evidence either way has survived. Not every romance can have had a happy ending, however, and there must have been many unrequited love affairs:

> "I made my brother's love my sole concern,
> About him my heart is not silent;
> It sends me a fleet-footed messenger
> Who comes and goes to tell me:
> 'He deceives you, in other words,
> He found another woman,
> She is dazzling to his eyes.'"

Apart from poetry, we have little material about the preliminaries to marriage. Scenes in the tombs do not apparently touch on this side of life, but only depict the outcome, with husband and wife participating together or separately in a variety of activities. Even the marriage ceremony, if they had one, is never shown; in fact, nothing has survived to tell us exactly what happened at a wedding. One of the ancient Egyptian terms for marriage—"to establish a household"—has been taken by some scholars to indicate that the setting-up of an independent house and cohabiting was the sole significant act, without any legal or religious ceremony. But although there are no texts which mention marriage formalities, legal documents clearly show that married men and women had well-defined responsibilities towards each other and their married status must have been formally acknowledged to distinguish them from unmarried people.

Another term for marriage was "to take as wife," which implies some formal procedure. This may have been only a spoken declaration or oath by the man alone or with the bride's father in the presence of witnesses, probably family members. In some cases, the bride's father bestowed some of his property on his daughter. Items she might bring with her into the marriage would be domestic equipment, textiles, and sometimes a donkey, the chief means of transport. There is also mention in some documents of the husband's gift to the wife of items of jewelry or commodities.

We have no record of a religious ceremony to mark the occasion, but considering the religious nature of the society, it is likely that some of the protective deities, particularly the goddess Hathor, were invoked to ensure a happy outcome. After a celebration, probably involving dancing, singing, feasting, and story-telling, the bride would be conveyed to the bridegroom's house in the evening.

Contracts defining property rights within the marriage are first mentioned in the New Kingdom, but the earliest examples which actually survive date from the Third Intermediate Period. Some of these are between husband and father-in-law, and record the material rights of the wife, sometimes even specifying the amount of food and clothing her husband should provide annually, and what would happen in the event of divorce. These are not marriage contracts per se, as some of the couples named seem to have been married some time and already have children, but rather economic statements of the rights of each partner: In the case of divorce the wife usually received one third of the joint property as well as whatever she brought with her. By the Late Period, it was stated that the wife as well as the husband had the right to initiate divorce, a right which shocked the misogynist Greeks of that time!

A married woman was expected to be chaste and not have affairs outside the marriage. This was obviously so that the husband could be sure of the paternity of her children; maternity can never be in doubt, but the father's role is less visible. Usually the marriages were monogamous, although the king was expected to have many wives. In fact there were no legal or social constraints on a man taking more than one wife if he could afford it. Even so, it seems that most marriages were monogamous, perhaps influenced by the ideal example of the divine couple, Isis and Osiris. The high incidence of death in childbirth, however, meant that a man could have more than one wife during his lifetime. Scenes in tomb paintings which show more than one wife record consecutive marriages after the death of a spouse, rather than concurrent wives.

Amongst the records from Deir al-Madina, the village which housed the artisans and scribes who built and decorated the royal tombs, are fragments of a register of the occupants of each house. The owner is listed, with his parental affiliation, then his wife and her affiliation, if he is married, and their children. None of the surviving fragments lists more than one wife, although if the modern system applied that each wife should have her own house, polygamy would not show up in this type of register. Nevertheless, in other records of the New Kingdom we have two examples of men with two wives each. One of these identifies herself as "I am one of four wives, two being dead and another still alive." By the Late Period contracts do not suggest that a man could take a second wife without divorcing the first.

Women were only allowed one husband, although again, death or divorce might mean more than one partner over a lifetime. She was also expected to be faithful to her husband. Men might have been more free to have sexual relations with women other than their own wives, but affairs with married women were greatly criticized and generally not tolerated by society. Several cases are known from Deir al-Madina where individuals are accused of affairs with married women. For example, in an attempt to remove an especially unsavoury character named Paneb from his office of chief workman, he was accused, amongst other charges, of sexual relations with several married women. Another Deir al-Madina workman complained to the court that his wife was having an affair with one Merysekhmet. Rather than divorcing his wife, the workman tried to stop the liaison. Merysekhmet swore an oath in court that he would not see her again, but then resumed his liaison; the next time, it was his own father who took him to court in an attempt to stop him. Clearly his behavior was not approved of by his family or by his community.

Another text tells of a married man, Nesamenemipet, who had been having an affair with a woman for eight months. Both the woman (who does not seem to be married) and the man aroused social criticism because he had been visiting her regularly without first divorcing his own wife. He was told to swear an oath in court with his wife, presumably to divorce her, so that his relations with the other woman could be regularized. The indignation that this affair aroused suggests that responsibilities towards the marriage partner were taken seriously, and that social pressure could be exerted to ensure conformity.

There are some hints that adultery, in theory at least, was punishable by death. In The Instructions of Ptahhotep the advice is given:

"If you want friendship to endure
In the house you enter
As master, brother or friend,
In what ever place you enter,
Beware of approaching the women!
Unhappy is the place where it is done,
Unwelcome is he who intrudes upon them . . .
A short moment like a dream,
Then death comes from having known them."

Some of the stories such as The Tale of the Two Brothers also indicate that death could be the punishment for adultery, but in practice, divorce was more likely. If the husband was the offender, then he was legally obliged to compensate his wife adequately. That meant returning everything she had brought with her, as well as relinquishing a third of their joint property and whatever had been put aside for the children. No wonder Nesamenemipet was reluctant to divorce his wife despite his affair with the other woman! If, on the other hand, the wife was at fault, she received no financial compensation.

Divorce was not uncommon, and seems, like marriage, to have been a private affair, unless it was contested, in which case the partners might be subjected to an embarrassing interrogation before the local council of elders. The usual grounds for divorce were adultery, barrenness, the wish to marry someone else, or simply incompatibility. Both parties could remarry. The property contracts which detail a woman's share of joint property in the case of divorce were safeguards so that she was not left destitute, or a burden on her father's household to which she would presumably return. They also must have been a deterrent to a hasty repudiation of a spouse.

Despite all this, the ancient Egyptians had an idealistic view of marriage, as shown by the advice given in the wisdom literature (always, of course, from the man's point of view) which advises on conjugal harmony and respect. In The Instructions of Ptahhotep, the author counsels his "son" (i.e., pupil) to care for his wife;

"When you prosper and found your house,
And love your wife with ardor,
Fill her belly, clothe her back,
Ointment soothes her body,
Gladden her heart as long as you live,
She is a fertile field for her lord."

But he also cannot resist adding: "Keep her from power, restrain her, Her eye is her storm when she gazes, Thus will you make her stay in your house." What we lack to balance this male-oriented picture are the instructions of the women, but these, if they existed, must have been oral and have not survived.

At a later date the scribe Any says: "It is a joy when your hand is with her, there are many who don't know this." Indeed, statues and tomb paintings illustrate the close relationship of the ideal conjugal partnership by showing the couple hand in hand or with the wife's arm around her husband's shoulders.

9

THE INSTRUCTIONS OF PTAHHOTEP

This primary document from Egyptian Middle Kingdom (1976–1793 B.C.E.) is a typical example of an Egyptian genre that archaeologists call wisdom literature. Egyptians used these writings, often presented as letters from father to son, to teach personal morality, business procedures, social behavior, and public service. The existence of these documents testifies to the importance of written language in establishing and sustaining cultural norms in urban societies.

Charles F. Horne, *The Sacred Books and Early Literature of the East* (New York: Parke, Austin & Lipscomb, 1978), 62–70.

In this selection, Ptahhotep, the aged vizier, or royal advisor, to the Pharaoh, addresses the next generation of Egyptians. The instructions that he gives, based on "the sayings of the former days," range from honoring the god Ptah and respecting the Pharaoh to debating politely in court, behaving modestly, avoiding temptation, maintaining good humor, and loving one's wife. What do you think of Ptahhotep's instructions? What do they tell you about Egyptian civilization?

Thinking Historically

Notice that Zahi Hawass used two parts of this primary source document in the preceding selection, but that the wording is slightly different. There are two reasons for this disparity. First, the Egyptian hieroglyphics can be translated differently. Second, there are different versions of the original document. In studying ancient history, historians often have to reconstruct the most reliable document before translating it. How significant is the difference between the renderings of Ptahhotep's instructions on loving one's wife at the end of each of these readings? If Zahi Hawass used the wording contained in this selection, could he have described Egyptian married life as he did? What does that tell you about the relationship between primary and secondary sources?

Precepts of the Prefect, the Lord Ptahhotep, under the Majesty of the King of the South and North, Assa, Living Eternally Forever

. . . Who will cause me to have authority to speak, that I may declare to him the words of those who have heard the counsels of former days? And the counsels heard of the gods, who will give me authority to declare them? Cause that it be so and that evil be removed from those that are enlightened; send the double . . . The majesty of this god says: Instruct him in the sayings of former days. It is this which constitutes the merit of the children of the great. All that which makes the soul equal penetrates him who hears it, and that which it says produces no satiety.

Beginning of the arrangement of the good sayings, spoken by the noble lord, the divine father, beloved of Ptah, the son of the king, the first-born of his race, the prefect and feudal lord Ptahhotep, so as to instruct the ignorant in the knowledge of the arguments of the good sayings. It is profitable for him who hears them, it is a loss to him who shall transgress them. He says to his son:

Be not arrogant because of that which you know; deal with the ignorant as with the learned; for the barriers of art are not closed, no artist being in possession of the perfection to which he should aspire.

But good words are more difficult to find than the emerald, for it is by slaves that that is discovered among the rocks of pegmatite.

If you find a disputant while he is hot, and if he is superior to you in ability, lower the hands, bend the back, do not get into a passion with him. As he will not let you destroy his words, it is utterly wrong to interrupt him; that proclaims that you are incapable of keeping yourself calm, when you are contradicted. If then you have to do with a disputant while he is hot, imitate one who does not stir. You have the advantage over him if you keep silence when he is uttering evil words. "The better of the two is he who is impassive," say the bystanders, and you are right in the opinion of the great.

If you find a disputant while he is hot, do not despise him because you are not of the same opinion. Be not angry against him when he is wrong; away with such a thing. He fights against himself; require him not further to flatter your feelings. Do not amuse yourself with the spectacle which you have before you; it is odious, it is mean, it is the part of a despicable soul so to do. As soon as you let yourself be moved by your feelings, combat this desire as a thing that is reproved by the great.

If you have, as leader, to decide on the conduct of a great number of men, seek the most perfect manner of doing so that your own conduct may be without reproach. Justice is great, invariable, and assured; it has not been disturbed since the age of Ptah. To throw obstacles in the way of the laws is to open the way before violence. Shall that which is below gain the upper hand, if the unjust does not attain to the place of justice? Even he who says: I take for myself, of my own free-will; but says not: I take by virtue of my authority. The limitations of justice are invariable; such is the instruction which every man receives from his father.

Inspire not men with fear, else Ptah will fight against you in the same manner. If any one asserts that he lives by such means, Ptah will take away the bread from his mouth; if any one asserts that he enriches himself thereby, Ptah says: I may take those riches to myself. If any one asserts that he beats others, Ptah will end by reducing him to impotence. Let no one inspire men with fear; this is the will of Ptah. Let one provide sustenance for them in the lap of peace; it will then be that they will freely give what has been torn from them by terror.

If you are among the persons seated at meat in the house of a greater man than yourself, take that which he gives you, bowing to the ground. Regard that which is placed before you, but point not at it; regard it not frequently; he is a blameworthy person who departs from this rule. Speak not to the great man more than he requires, for one knows not what may be displeasing to him. Speak when he invites you and your worth will be pleasing. As for the great man who has plenty of means of existence, his conduct is as he himself wishes. He does that which pleases him; if he desires to repose, he realizes his intention. The great man stretching forth his hand does that to which other men do not attain. But as the means of existence are under the will of Ptah, one can not rebel against it.

If you are one of those who bring the messages of one great man to another, conform yourself exactly to that wherewith he has charged you; perform for him the commission as he has enjoined you. Beware of altering in speaking the offensive words which one great person addresses to another; he who perverts the trustfulness of his way, in order to repeat only what produces pleasure in the words of every man, great or small, is a detestable person.

If you are a farmer, gather the crops in the field which the great Ptah has given you, do not boast in the house of your neighbors; it is better to make oneself dreaded by one's deeds. As for him who, master of his own way of acting, being all-powerful, seizes the goods of others like a crocodile in the midst even of watchment, his children are an object of malediction, of scorn, and of hatred on account of it, while his father is grievously distressed, and as for the mother who has borne him, happy is another rather than herself. But a man becomes a god when he is chief of a tribe which has confidence in following him.

If you abase yourself in obeying a superior, your conduct is entirely good before Ptah. Knowing who you ought to obey and who you ought to command, do not lift up your heart against him. As you know that in him is authority, be respectful toward him as belonging to him. Wealth comes only at Ptah's own good-will, and his caprice only is the law. . . .

Be active during the time of your existence, do no more than is commanded. Do not spoil the time of your activity; he is a blameworthy person who makes a bad use of his moments. Do not lose the daily opportunity of increasing that which your house possesses. Activity produces riches, and riches do not endure when it slackens.

If you are a wise man, bring up a son who shall be pleasing to Ptah. If he conforms his conduct to your way and occupies himself with your affairs as is right, do to him all the good you can; he is your son, a person attached to you whom your own self has begotten. Separate not your heart from him. . . . But if he conducts himself ill and transgresses your wish, if he rejects all counsel, if his mouth goes according to the evil word, strike him on the mouth in return. Give orders without hesitation to those who do wrong, to him whose temper is turbulent; and he will not deviate from the straight path, and there will be no obstacle to interrupt the way. . . .

If you are with people who display for you an extreme affection, saying: "Aspiration of my heart, aspiration of my heart, where there is no remedy! That which is said in your heart, let it be realized by springing up spontaneously. Sovereign master, I give myself to your opinion. Your name is approved without speaking. Your body is full of vigor, your face is above your neighbors." If then you are accustomed to this excess of flattery, and there be an obstacle to you in your desires, then your impulse is to obey your passion. But he who . . . according to his caprice, his soul is . . . , his body is. . . . While the man who is master of his soul is superior to those whom Ptah has loaded with his gifts; the man who obeys his passion is under the power of his wife.

Declare your line of conduct without reticence; give your opinion in the council of your lord; while there are people who turn back upon their own words when they speak, so as not to offend him who has put forward a statement, and answer not in this fashion: "He is the great man who will recognize the error of another; and when he shall raise his voice to oppose the other about it he will keep silence after what I have said."

If you are a leader, setting forward your plans according to that which you decide, perform perfect actions which posterity may remember, without letting the words prevail with you which multiply flattery, which excite pride and produce vanity.

If you are a leader of peace, listen to the discourse of the petitioner. Be not abrupt with him; that would trouble him. Say not to him: "You have already recounted this." Indulgence will encourage him to accomplish the object of his coming. As for being abrupt with the complainant because he described what passed when the injury was done, instead of complaining of the injury itself let it not be! The way to obtain a clear explanation is to listen with kindness.

If you desire to excite respect within the house you enter, for example the house of a superior, a friend, or any person of consideration, in short everywhere where you enter, keep yourself from making advances to a woman, for there is nothing good in so doing. There is no prudence in taking part in it, and thousands of men destroy themselves in order to enjoy a moment, brief as a dream, while they gain death, so as to know it. It is a villainous intention, that of a man who thus excites himself; if he goes on to carry it out, his mind abandons him. For as for him who is without repugnance for such an act, there is no good sense at all in him.

If you desire that your conduct should be good and preserved from all evil, keep yourself from every attack of bad humor. It is a fatal malady which leads to discord, and there is no longer any existence for him who gives way to it. For it introduces discord between fathers and mothers, as well as between brothers and sisters; it causes the wife and the husband to hate each other; it contains all kinds of wickedness, it embodies all kinds of wrong. When a man has established his just equilibrium and walks in this path, there where he makes his dwelling, there is no room for bad humor.

Be not of an irritable temper as regards that which happens at your side; grumble not over your own affairs. Be not of an irritable temper in regard to your neighbors; better is a compliment to that which displeases than rudeness. It is wrong to get into a passion with one's neighbors, to be no longer master of one's words. When there is only a little irritation, one creates for oneself an affliction for the time when one will again be cool.

If you are wise, look after your house; love your wife without alloy. Fill her stomach, clothe her back; these are the cares to be bestowed on her person. Caress her, fulfill her desires during the time of her existence; it is a kindness which does honor to its possessor. Be not brutal; tact will influence her better than violence; her . . . behold to what she aspires, at what she aims, what she regards. It is that which fixes her in your house; if you repel her, it is an abyss. Open your arms for her, respond to her arms; call her, display to her your love. . . .

REFLECTIONS

To focus our subject in a brief chapter we have examined Mesopotamia and Egypt almost exclusively. This enabled us to observe the beginnings of the urban revolution in Mesopotamia and one of the most spectacular and best preserved of ancient civilizations in Egypt. The city-states of Mesopotamia and the territorial state of Egypt were the two extremes of ancient civilization. City-states packed most people tightly within their walls. Eighty percent of Mesopotamians lived within city walls by 2800 B.C.E. By contrast, less than 10 percent of Egyptians lived in cities—if we can call their unwalled settlements, palace compounds, and pyramid construction sites "cities" at all. The lesser role of cities in Egypt has led some historians to drop the term "urban revolution" for "the rise of civilization." Other historians, objecting to the moralistic implications of the term "civilization," prefer "the rise of complex societies." "Complex" is not a very precise term, but it would refer to the appearance of social classes, the mixing of different populations, a multilayered governmental structure with rulers, officials, and ordinary people, and numerous specialists who are not full-time farmers or herders. More specifically, we might include kings, priests, writing, wheels, monumental building, markets, and money.

If we broaden our view, however, to include the "complex societies" of South Asia, China, and the Americas, cities—even city-states—pop up like mushrooms after a spring rain. Along the Indus River in Pakistan dozens of small and midsize cities formed independent clones of Harappa and Mohenjodaro. These numerous cities seem to have enjoyed the independence of city-states since there is no evidence of kings, soldiers, or warfare along the Indus. Instead of being bound to a territorial sovereign, these cities and dozens of others in what is today Iran, Afghanistan, India, and surrounding areas communicated and traded with each other in a web of economic interactions. A recent discovery of objects traded from Mesopotamia and Arabia to India reveals an international or "intercultural style" of design that mixed iconic images of what were previously presumed to be entirely separate civilizations.

Territorial states, more like Egypt than Mesopotamia, integrated the Yellow River valley of northern China and the settlements of the high Andes in South America, but they also constructed large cities as administrative and spiritual centers. In Mexico, early civilizations were centered in cities: the Zapotec at Monte Alban, the Toltec at Teotihuacan, the Aztec at Tenochtitlan, and the Mayan at numerous ceremonial and residential centers. Cities defined the complex societies of the Americas more than wheels (used only for toys) and writing, which remained highly pictorial in Mexico, and, in the Andes, a matter of reading colored strings.

Thus, a larger lens raises more questions than we have allowed in our brief examination of Mesopotamia and Egypt. How important were such "urban inventions" as kings, soldiers, warfare, wheels, and writing if they did not exist everywhere cities were created? Further, how important were cities in the creation of the complex lives we have lived for the last five thousand years? These are questions worth raising even if we still answer on reflection, "very important, indeed."

Identity in Caste and Territorial Societies

Greece and India, 1000–300 B.C.E.

HISTORICAL CONTEXT

Both India and Greece developed ancient city-based civilizations within a thousand years of the urban revolution. In India that civilization was concentrated on the Indus River valley in what is today Pakistan. In Greece the Minoan civilization on the island of Crete was followed by the Mycenaean civilization on the mainland. But both ancient Indian and ancient Greek civilizations had disappeared when new peoples from the grasslands of Eurasia settled in both areas between 1500 and 1000 B.C.E. Called by later generations the Aryans in India and the Dorians in Greece, these pastoral peoples arrived with horses, different customs, and new technologies. The Aryans came with chariots (as had the early Mycenaeans), while the Dorians, somewhat later, brought iron tools and weapons.

Despite the similar origins of the newcomers and the similar urban experience of the lands in which they settled, Aryan India and Dorian Greece developed in significantly different ways. As William H. McNeill writes in the first selection, by the year 500 B.C.E. Indian and Greek civilizations had found entirely different ways of organizing and administering their societies. And these differences had profound effects on the subsequent history of Indian and European society.

THINKING HISTORICALLY
Interpreting Primary Sources
in Light of a Secondary Source

In Chapter 2, we distinguished between primary and secondary sources. Similarly, we begin here with a secondary source, or an interpretation. We then turn, as we did in the last chapter, to a series of primary sources. But while the last chapter focused on recognizing and distinguishing primary from secondary sources, here we concentrate on the relationship of the primary sources to the secondary interpretation — how one affects our reading of the other.

In this chapter, the primary sources were chosen to illustrate points made in the introductory interpretation. This provides an opportunity to understand the interpretation in some detail and with some degree of subtlety. The primary sources do not give you enough material to argue that McNeill is right or wrong, but you will be able to flesh out some of the meaning of his interpretation. You might also reflect more generally on the relationship of sources and interpretations. You will be asked how particular sources support or even contradict the interpretation. You will consider the relevance of sources for other interpretations, and you will imagine what sort of sources you might seek for evidence.

$$10$$

WILLIAM H. McNEILL

Greek and Indian Civilization

William H. McNeill is one of the leading world historians in the United States. In this selection from his college textbook *A World History*, he compares the different ways in which Indian and Greek civilizations of the classical age (by around 500 B.C.E.) organized themselves. He distinguishes between Indian *caste* and Greek *territorial sovereignty*. These concepts are complex but useful to distinguish between two of the basic ways societies organize and identify them-

---

William H. McNeill, *A World History*, 2nd ed. (New York: Oxford University Press, 1971), 78–83, 88, 90, 95, 99–100.

selves. As you read, try to define what each term means. McNeill argues that caste and territorial sovereignty had enormously different effects on the subsequent development of Indian and European society. What were some of these different effects?

Thinking Historically

As you read this secondary source or historical interpretation, consider what sort of primary sources might have led McNeill to this view or support his interpretation. Notice especially that in the first half of the selection, McNeill mentions specific ancient Indian writings: These are obvious primary sources for his interpretation. Not having read McNeill's primary sources, can you imagine what in them would lead to this interpretation?

Less of McNeill's interpretation of Greece is included in this selection and, consequently, there is no mention of primary sources. In this chapter, you will read a number of Greek primary sources, but at this point can you speculate about what types of sources would demonstrate the Greek idea of territorial sovereignty?

Keep in mind that caste and territorial sovereignty are modern terms not known or used by the ancients; therefore, you will not find them in the primary sources that follow. What words might the ancient Indians or Greeks have used to denote these concepts?

Caste

A modern caste is a group of persons who will eat with one another and intermarry, while excluding others from these two intimacies. In addition, members of any particular caste must bear some distinguishing mark, so that everyone will know who belongs and who does not belong to it. Definite rules for how to behave in the presence of members of other castes also become necessary in situations where such contacts are frequent. When an entire society comes to be organized on these principles, any group of strangers or intruders automatically becomes another caste, for the exclusive habits of the rest of the population inevitably thrust the newcomers in upon themselves when it comes to eating and marrying. A large caste may easily break into smaller groupings as a result of some dispute, or through mere geographical separation over a period of time. New castes can form around new occupations. Wanderers and displaced individuals who find a new niche in society are automatically compelled to eat together and marry one another by the caste-bound habits of their neighbors.

How or when Indian society came to be organized along these lines remains unclear. Perhaps the Indus civilization itself was built upon something like the caste principle. Or perhaps the antipathy between Aryan invaders and the dark-skinned people whom they attacked lay at the root of the caste system of later India. But whatever the origins of caste, three features of Indian thought and feeling were mobilized to sustain the caste principle in later times. One of these was the idea of ceremonial purity. Fear of contaminating oneself by contact with a member of a lower, "unclean" caste gave Brahmans and others near the top of the pyramid strong reasons for limiting their association with low-caste persons.

From the other end of the scale, too, the poor and humble had strong reasons for clinging to caste. All but the most miserable and marginal could look down upon somebody, a not unimportant psychological feature of the system. In addition, the humbler castes were often groups that had only recently emerged from primitive forest life. They naturally sought to maintain their peculiar customs and habits, even in the context of urban or mixed village life, where men of different backgrounds and different castes lived side by side. Other civilized societies usually persuaded or compelled newcomers to surrender their peculiar ways, and assimilated them in the course of a few generations to the civilized population as a whole. In India, on the contrary, such groups were able to retain their separate identities indefinitely by preserving their own peculiar customs within the caste framework, generation after generation.

The third factor sustaining the caste principle was theoretical: the doctrine of reincarnation and of "varna." The latter declared that all men were naturally divided into four castes: the Brahmans who prayed, the Kshatriyas who fought, the Vaisyas who worked, and the Sudras who performed unclean tasks. Official doctrine classified the first three castes as Aryan, the last as non-Aryan, and put much stress on caste rank, from Brahmans at the top to Sudras at the bottom. Reality never corresponded even remotely to this theory. There were hundreds if not thousands of castes in India, rather than the four recognized in Brahmanical teaching. But apparent injustices and anomalies disappeared when the doctrine of reincarnation was combined with the doctrine of varna. The idea of reincarnation, indeed, gave logical explanation and justification to the system by explaining caste as a divinely established institution, hereditary from father to son, and designed to reward and punish souls for their actions in former lives. This undoubtedly helped to stabilize the confused reality. A man of unblemished life, born into the lowest caste, could hope for rebirth higher up the ladder. Conversely, a man of high caste who failed to conform to proper standards could expect rebirth in a lower caste. A man even risked reincarnation as a worm or beetle, if his misbehavior deserved such a punishment.

Clearly, the caste system as observed today did not exist in ancient India. Yet modern castes are the outgrowth of patterns of social organization that are as old as the oldest records. Early Buddhist stories, for instance, reveal many episodes turning upon caste distinctions, and passages in the *Rig Veda* and other ancient writings imply caste-like practices and attitudes. By 500 B.C.E. we can at least be sure that the seeds from which the modern caste organization of society grew had already sprouted luxuriantly on Indian soil.

Caste lessened the significance of political, territorial administration. Everyone identified himself first and foremost with his caste. But a caste ordinarily lacked both definite internal administration and distinct territorial boundaries. Instead, members of a particular caste mingled with men of other castes, observing the necessary precautions to prevent contamination of one by the other. No king or ruler could command the undivided loyalty of people who felt themselves to belong to a caste rather than to a state. Indeed, to all ordinary caste members, rulers, officials, soldiers, and tax collectors were likely to seem mere troublesome outsiders, to be neglected whenever possible and obeyed only as far as necessary. The fragile character of most Indian states resulted in large part from this fact. A striking absence of information about war and government is characteristic of all early Indian history; and this, too, presumably reflects Indian peoples' characteristic emotional disengagement from the state and from politics. . . .

The Vedas and Brahmanas

Our knowledge of Aryan religion derives from the Vedas. The Vedas, used as handbooks of religious ritual, consist of songs that were recited aloud during sacrifices, together with other passages instructing the priests what to do during the ceremony. In course of time, the language of the Vedas became more or less unintelligible, even to priests. A great effort was thereupon made to preserve details of accent and pronunciation, by insisting on exact memorization of texts from master to pupil across the generations. Every jot and tittle of the inherited verses was felt to matter, since a misplaced line or mispronounced word could nullify a whole sacrifice and might even provoke divine displeasure.

Preoccupation with correctness of detail speedily shifted emphasis from the gods of the Aryan pantheon to the act of worship and invocation itself. Aryan priests may also have learned about magical powers claimed by priests of the Indus civilization. At any rate, some Brahmans began to argue that by performing rituals correctly they could actually compel the gods to grant what was asked of them. Indeed, proper sacrifice and invocation created the world of gods and men

anew, and stabilized afresh the critical relation between natural and su-
pernatural reality. In such a view, the importance and personalities of
the separate gods shrank to triviality, while the power and skill of the
priesthood was greatly magnified. These extravagent priestly claims
were freely put forward in texts called Brahmanas. These were cast
in the form of commentaries on the Vedas, purportedly explaining
what the older texts really meant, but often changing meanings in the
process.

The Upanishads and Mysticism

Priestly claims to exercise authority over gods and men were never
widely accepted in ancient India. Chiefs and warriors might be a bit
wary of priestly magic, but they were not eager to cede to the priests
the primacy claimed by the Brahmanas. Humbler ranks of society also
objected to priestly presumption. This is proved by the fact that a rival
type of piety took hold in India and soon came to constitute the most
distinctive element in the whole religious tradition of the land. Another
body of oral literature, the Upanishads, constitutes our evidence of this
religious development. The Upanishads are not systematic treatises nor
do they agree in all details. Yet they do express a general consensus on
important points.

First of all, the Upanishads conceive the end of religious life in a
radically new way. Instead of seeking riches, health, and long life, a
wise and holy man strives merely to escape the endless round of rebirth. Success allows his soul to dissolve into the All from whence it
had come, triumphantly transcending the suffering, pain, and imperfec-
tion of existence.

In the second place, holiness and release from the cycle of rebirths
were attained not by obedience to priests nor by observance of ceremonies. The truly holy man had no need of intermediaries and, for
that matter, no need of gods. Instead, by a process of self-discipline,
meditation, asceticism, and withdrawal from the ordinary concerns of
daily life, the successful religious athlete might attain a mystic vision of
Truth — a vision which left the seer purged and happy. The nature
and content of the mystic vision could never be expressed in words. It
revealed Truth by achieving an identity between the individual soul
and the Soul of the universe. Such an experience, surpassing human
understanding and ordinary language, constituted a foretaste of the ultimate bliss of self-annihilation in the All, which was the final goal of
wise and holy life. . . .

While India worked its way toward the definition of a new and distinctive civilization on one flank of the ancient Middle East, on its
other flank another new civilization was also emerging: the Greek. The

principal stages of early Greek history closely resemble what we know or can surmise about Indian development. But the end product differed fundamentally. The Greeks put political organization into territorial states above all other bases of human association, and attempted to explain the world and man not in terms of mystic illumination but through laws of nature. Thus despite a similar start, when fierce "tamers of horses" — like those of whom Homer[1] later sang — overran priest-led agricultural societies, the Indian and Greek styles of civilization diverged strikingly by 500 B.C.E. . . .

The self-governing city-states created by Greeks on the coast of Asia Minor had . . . great . . . importance in world history. For by inventing the city-state or *polis* (hence our word "politics"), the Greeks of Ionia established the prototype from which the whole Western world derived its penchant for political organization into territorially defined sovereign units, i.e., into states. The supremacy of territoriality over all other forms of human association is neither natural nor inevitable, as the Indian caste principle may remind us. . . .

Dominance of the Polis in Greek Culture

So powerful and compelling was the psychological pull of the polis that almost every aspect of Greek cultural activity was speedily caught up in and — as it were — digested by the new master institution of Greek civilization. Religion, art, literature, philosophy, took shape or acquired a new accent through their relationship with the all-engulfing object of the citizens' affection. . . .

Despite the general success of the polis ordering of things, a few individuals fretted over the logical inconsistencies of Greek religion and traditional world view. As trade developed, opportunities to learn about the wisdom of the East multiplied. Inquiring Greeks soon discovered that among the priestly experts of the Middle East there was no agreement about such fundamental questions as how the world was created or why the planets periodically checked their forward movement through the heavens and went backward for a while before resuming their former motion. It was in Ionia that men first confronted this sort of question systematically enough to bother recording their views. These, the first philosophers, sought to explain the phenomena of the world by imaginative exercise of their power of reason. Finding conflicting and unsupported stories about the gods to be unsatisfactory, they took the drastic step of omitting the gods entirely, and boldly substituted natural law instead as the ruling force of the universe. To be sure, the Ionian philosophers did not agree among themselves when

---

[1] Greek poet c. 800 B.C.E.; author of *The Iliad* and *The Odyssey*. [Ed.]

they sought to describe how the laws of nature worked, and their naive efforts to explain an ever wider range of phenomena did not meet with much success.

Nevertheless, their attempts at using speculative reason to explain the nature of things marked a major turning point in human intellectual development. The Ionian concept of a universe ruled not by the whim of some divine personality but by an impersonal and unchangeable law has never since been forgotten. Throughout the subsequent history of European and Middle Eastern thought, this distinctively Greek view of the nature of things stood in persistent and fruitful tension with the older, Middle Eastern theistic explanation of the universe. Particular thinkers, reluctant to abandon either position entirely, have sought to reconcile the omnipotence of the divine will with the unchangeability of natural law by means of the most various arguments. Since, however, the two views are as logically incompatible with one another as were the myths from which the Ionian philosophers started, no formulation or reconciliation ever attained lasting and universal consent. Men always had to start over again to reshape for themselves a more satisfactory metaphysic and theology. Here, therefore, lay a growing point for all subsequent European thought which has not yet been exhausted.

Indeed, the recent successes of natural science seem to have vindicated the Ionian concept of natural law in ways and with a complexity that would have utterly amazed Thales (d. c. 546 B.C.E.) or any of his successors, who merely voiced what turned out to be amazingly lucky guesses. How did they do it? It seems plausible to suggest that the Ionians hit upon the notion of natural law by simply projecting the tight little world of the polis upon the universe. For it was a fact that the polis was regulated by law, not by the personal will or whim of a ruler. If such invisible abstractions could govern human behavior and confine it to certain roughly predictable paths of action, why could not similar laws control the natural world? To such a question, it appears, the Ionians gave an affirmative answer, and in doing so gave a distinctive cast to all subsequent Greek and European thought.

Limitations of the Polis

It would be a mistake to leave the impression that all facets of Greek life fitted smoothly and easily into the polis frame. The busy public world left scant room for the inwardness of personal experience. Striving for purification, for salvation, for holiness, which found such ample expression in the Indian cultural setting, was almost excluded. Yet the Greeks were not immune from such impulses. Through the ancient mystery religions, as well as through such an association as the "Order" founded by Pythagoras, the famous mathematician and mystic (d. c. 507 B.C.E.), they sought to meet these needs. But when such efforts took organized form, a fundamental incompatibility between the claims of the polis to the unqualified loyalty of every citizen and the pursuit of personal holiness quickly became apparent. This was illustrated by the stormy history of the Pythagorean Order. Either the organized seekers after holiness captured the polis, as happened for a while in the city of Croton in southern Italy, or the magistrates of the polis persecuted the Order, as happened in Pythagoras' old age. There seemed no workable ground of compromise in this, the earliest recorded instance of conflict between church and state in Western history.

The fundamental difference between Greek and Indian institutions as shaped by about 500 B.C.E. was made apparent by this episode. The loose federation of cultures allowed by the caste principle in India experienced no difficulty at all in accommodating organized seekers after holiness such as the communities of Buddhist monks. By contrast, the exclusive claim upon the citizens' time, effort, and affection which had been staked out by the Greek polis allowed no sort of corporate rival.

Enormous energies were tapped by the polis. A wider segment of the total population was engaged in cultural and political action than had been possible in any earlier civilized society, and the brilliant flowering of classical Greek civilization was the consequence. Yet the very intensity of the political tie excluded ranges of activity and sensitivity that were not compatible with a territorial organization of human groupings, and sowed seeds of civil strife between the Greek cities which soon proved disastrous. But every achievement involves a surrender of alternatives: it is merely that the Greek achievement, by its very magnitude, casts an unusually clear light upon what it also excluded.

11

From the Rig-Veda:
Sacrifice as Creation

As McNeill discusses in the previous selection, the Vedas are the writings of the ancient Brahman priests in India. They cover a wide variety of religious subjects and concerns: ritual, sacrifice, hymns, healing, incantations, allegories, philosophy, and the problems of everyday life. In general, the earliest Vedas (like the Rig-Veda) focus more on

---

"Rig Veda," 10.90, in *Sources of Indian Tradition*, 2nd ed., ed. and rev. Ainslie T. Embree (New York: Columbia University Press, 1988), 18–19.

the specifics of ritual and sacrifice, reflecting the needs and instructions of the priests during the Aryan conquest. The last of the Vedas (like the Upanishads) are more philosophical and speculative.

This selection is from the Rig-Veda. What happened when Purusha was sacrificed? What is the meaning of this first sacrifice? How does this story support the role of priests?

Thinking Historically

Consider how this primary source supports the division of Indian society into castes, as McNeill discusses in the previous selection. The castes are mentioned in only one paragraph. What are the four castes mentioned in that paragraph? Notice the alternate name for one of them. In addition to the names of the castes, what information does this paragraph provide concerning the functions and relative importance of each caste?

Reread the paragraph prior to the one mentioning castes and notice how the naming of the castes fits into the larger point of this story about the sacrifice of Purusha. How does this story suggest that the people who wrote the Rig-Veda thought the division of society into four castes was pretty basic? Can you deduce from this source which of the four castes was most likely the originator of the story? Does this support anything else that McNeill said in his interpretation?

Thousand-headed Purusha, thousand-eyed, thousand-footed — he, having pervaded the earth on all sides, still extends ten fingers beyond it.

Purusha alone is all this — whatever has been and whatever is going to be. Further, he is the lord of immortality and also of what grows on account of food.

Such is his greatness; greater, indeed, than this is Purusha. All creatures constitute but one-quarter of him, his three-quarters are the immortal in the heaven.

With his three-quarters did Purusha rise up; one-quarter of him again remains here. With it did he variously spread out on all sides over what eats and what eats not.

From him was Virāj born, from Virāj the evolved Purusha. He, being born, projected himself behind the earth as also before it.

When the gods performed the sacrifice with Purusha as the oblation, then the spring was its clarified butter, the summer the sacrificial fuel, and the autumn the oblation.

The sacrificial victim, namely, Purusha, born at the very beginning, they sprinkled with sacred water upon the sacrificial grass. With him as oblation, the gods performed the sacrifice, and also the Sādhyas [a class of semidivine beings] and the rishis [ancient seers].

From that wholly offered sacrificial oblation were born the verses [*rc*] and the sacred chants; from it were born the meters [*chandas*]; the sacrificial formula was born from it.

From it horses were born and also those animals who have double rows [i.e., upper and lower] of teeth; cows were born from it, from it were born goats and sheep.

When they divided Purusha, in how many different portions did they arrange him? What became of his mouth, what of his two arms? What were his two thighs and his two feet called?

His mouth became the brāhman; his two arms were made into the rajanya; his two thighs the vaishyas; from his two feet the shūdra was born.

The moon was born from the mind, from the eye the sun was born; from the mouth Indra and Agni, from the breath [*prāna*] the wind [*vāyu*] was born.

From the navel was the atmosphere created, from the head the heaven issued forth; from the two feet was born the earth and the quarters (the cardinal directions) from the ear. Thus did they fashion the worlds.

Seven were the enclosing sticks in this sacrifice, thrice seven were the fire-sticks made when the gods, performing the sacrifice, bound down Purusha, the sacrificial victim.

With this sacrificial oblation did the gods offer the sacrifice. These were the first norms [*dharma*] of sacrifice. These greatnesses reached to the sky wherein live the ancient Sādhyas and gods.

12

From the Upanishads:
Karma and Reincarnation

The idea of karma (cause and effect, appropriate consequences) appears in the earliest Upanishads. Karma meant: "As you sow, so shall you reap." Good karma would be enhanced; bad karma would lead to more bad karma. The universe was a system of complete justice in which all people got what they deserved. The idea that the soul might

Brihad Aranyaka, IV:4:5–6, in *The Thirteen Principle Upanishads*, ed. and trans. R. E. Hume (Bombay: Oxford University Press, 1954), 140–41. *Chandogya*, V:10:7, in Hume, quoted in *The Hindu Tradition: Readings in Oriental Thought*, ed. Ainslee T. Embree (New York: Vintage, 1966, copyright renewed 1994), 62–63.

be reborn in another body may have been an even older idea, but in the Upanishads it combined easily with the idea of karma. That a good soul was reborn in a higher life, or a bad soul in a lower, was perhaps a more material, less subtle, version of the justice of karma. The idea of reincarnation, or the transmigration of souls, united justice with caste.

What effect would these ideas have on people? In what ways would these ideas aid people in gaining a sense of power over their lives? How might these ideas be tools of control? What does "morality" mean in this tradition?

Thinking Historically

How does the idea of karma presented in this primary source support McNeill's interpretation of the importance of the caste system in India? Would the idea of reincarnation make caste organization stronger or weaker?

According as one acts, according as one conducts himself, so does he become. The doer of good becomes good. The doer of evil becomes evil. One becomes virtuous by virtuous action, bad by bad action.

But people say: "A person is made not of acts, but of desires only." In reply to this I say: As is his desire, such is his resolve; as is his resolve, such the action he performs; what action (*karma*) he performs, that he procures for himself.

On this point there is this verse: —

Where one's mind is attached — the inner self
Goes thereto with action, being attached to it alone.

   Obtaining the end of his action,
   Whatever he does in this world,
   He comes again from that world
   To this world of action.

— So the man who desires.

Now the man who does not desire. — He who is without desire, who is freed from desire, whose desire is satisfied, whose desire is the Soul — his breaths do not depart. Being very Brahman, he goes to Brahman.

Accordingly, those who are of pleasant conduct here — the prospect is, indeed, that they will enter a pleasant womb, either the womb of a Brahman, or the womb of a Kshatriya, or the womb of a Vaishya. But those who are of stinking conduct here — the prospect is, indeed, that they will enter a stinking womb, either the womb of a dog, or the womb of a swine, or the womb of an outcaste (*candāla*).

13

From the Upanishads:
Brahman and Atman

In this selection *Brahman* does not refer to priests or to a specific god. Brahman is all divinity, and all is Brahman. Even the individual soul or *atman* can be one with the universal Brahman. How would ideas like these challenge the caste system?

Thinking Historically

McNeill suggests that the Upanishads expressed a religious vision that challenged the religion of priests, sacrifice, and caste. How does this selection from the Upanishads support that interpretation?

Great is the Gayatri, the most sacred verse of the Vedas; but how much greater is the Infinity of Brahman! A quarter of his being is this whole vast universe: the other three quarters are his heaven of Immortality. (3.12.5)

There is a Light that shines beyond all things on earth, beyond us all, beyond the heavens, beyond the highest, the very highest heavens. This is the Light that shines in our heart. (3.13.7)

All this universe is in the truth Brahman. He is the beginning and end and life of all. As such, in silence, give unto him adoration.

Man in truth is made of faith. As his faith is in this life, so he becomes in the beyond: with faith and vision let him work.

There is a Spirit that is mind and life, light and truth and vast spaces. He contains all works and desires and all perfumes and all tastes. He enfolds the whole universe, and in silence is loving to all.

This is the Spirit that is in my heart, smaller than a grain of rice, or a grain of barley, or a grain of mustard-seed, or a grain of canary-seed, or the kernel of a grain of canary-seed. This is the Spirit that is in my heart, greater than the earth, greater than the sky, greater than heaven itself, greater than all these worlds.

He contains all works and desires and all perfumes and all tastes. He enfolds the whole universe and in silence is loving to all. This is the Spirit that is in my heart, this is Brahman.

Chandogya Upanishad, in *The Upanishads*, trans. Juan Mascaro (Harmondsworth: Penguin Press, 1965), 113–14.

To him I shall come when I go beyond this life. And to him will come he who has faith and doubts not. Thus said Sandilya, thus said Sandilya. (3.14)

14

From the *Bhagavad Gita*: Caste and Self

The *Bhagavad Gita* is the best-known work in Hindu religious literature. It is part of a larger epic called the *Mahabharata,* a story of two feuding families that may have had its origins in the Aryan invasion of 1500 B.C.E. The *Bhagavad Gita* is a philosophical interlude that interrupts the story just before the great battle between the two families. It poses some fundamental questions about the nature of life, death, and proper religious behavior. It begins as the leader of one of the battling armies, Arjuna, asks why he should fight his friends and relatives on the other side. The answer comes from none other than the god Krishna, who has taken the form of Arjuna's charioteer.

What is Krishna's answer? What will happen to the people Arjuna kills? What will happen to Arjuna? What would happen to Arjuna if he refused to fight the battle? What does this selection tell you about Hindu ideas of life, death, and the self?

Thinking Historically

In some ways this work reconciles the conflict in the Upanishads between caste and *atman.* Performing the *dharma,* or duty, of caste is seen as a liberating act. Would the acceptance of this story support or challenge the caste system? Does this primary source support McNeill's interpretation of Indian society?

Lord Krishna

You grieve for those beyond grief,
and you speak words of insight;

Bhagavad Gita, trans. Barbara Stoler Miller (New York: Bantam Books, 1986), 31–34, 52, 86–87.

but learned men do not grieve
for the dead or the living.

Never have I not existed,
nor you, nor these kings;
and never in the future
shall we cease to exist.

Just as the embodied self
enters childhood, youth, and old age,
so does it enter another body;
this does not confound a steadfast man.

Contacts with matter make us feel
heat and cold, pleasure and pain.
Arjuna, you must learn to endure
fleeting things — they come and go!

When these cannot torment a man,
when suffering and joy are equal
for him and he has courage,
he is fit for immortality.

Nothing of nonbeing comes to be,
nor does being cease to exist;
the boundary between these two
is seen by men who see reality.

Indestructible is the presence
that pervades all this;
no one can destroy
this unchanging reality.

Our bodies are known to end,
but the embodied self is enduring,
indestructible, and immeasurable;
therefore, Arjuna, fight the battle!

He who thinks this self a killer
and he who thinks it killed,
both fail to understand;
it does not kill, nor is it killed.

It is not born,
it does not die;
having been,
it will never not be;
unborn, enduring,
constant, and primordial,
it is not killed
when the body is killed.

Arjuna, when a man knows the self
to be indestructible, enduring, unborn,
unchanging, how does he kill
or cause anyone to kill?

As a man discards
worn-out clothes
to put on new
and different ones,
so the embodied self
discards
its worn-out bodies
to take on other new ones.

Weapons do not cut it,
fire does not burn it,
waters do not wet it,
wind does not wither it.

It cannot be cut or burned;
it cannot be wet or withered;
it is enduring, all-pervasive,
fixed, immovable, and timeless.

It is called unmanifest,
inconceivable, and immutable;
since you know that to be so,
you should not grieve!

If you think of its birth
and death as ever-recurring,
then too, Great Warrior,
you have no cause to grieve!

Death is certain for anyone born,
and birth is certain for the dead;
since the cycle is inevitable,
you have no cause to grieve!

Creatures are unmanifest in origin,
manifest in the midst of life,
and unmanifest again in the end.
Since this is so, why do you lament!

Rarely someone
sees it,
rarely another
speaks it,
rarely anyone

hears it —
even hearing it,
no one really knows it.

The self embodied in the body
of every being is indestructible;
you have no cause to grieve
for all these creatures, Arjuna!

Look to your own duty;
do not tremble before it;
nothing is better for a warrior
than a battle of sacred duty.

The doors of heaven open
for warriors who rejoice
to have a battle like this
thrust on them by chance.

If you fail to wage this war
of sacred duty,
you will abandon your own duty
and fame only to gain evil.

People will tell
of your undying shame,
and for a man of honor
shame is worse than death.

> In this next passage from the *Bhagavad Gita*, Krishna reveals a deeper
> meaning to his message to Arjuna. Not only must Arjuna act like a war-
> rior because that is his caste, but he must also act without regard to the
> consequences of his action. What does Krishna seem to mean by this?
> How does one do "nothing at all even when he engages in action"?

Abandoning attachment to fruits
of action, always content, independent,
he does nothing at all
even when he engages in action.

He incurs no guilt if he has no hope,
restrains his thought and himself,
abandons possessions,
and performs actions with his body only.

Content with whatever comes by chance,
beyond dualities, free from envy,
impartial to failure and success,
he is not bound even when he acts.

When a man is unattached and free,
his reason deep in knowledge,
acting only in sacrifice,
his action is wholly dissolved.

When devoted men sacrifice
to other deities with faith,
they sacrifice to me, Arjuna,
however aberrant the rites.

I am the enjoyer
and the lord of all sacrifices;
they do not know me in reality,
and so they fail.

Votaries of the gods go to the gods,
ancestor-worshippers go to the ancestors,
those who propitiate ghosts go to them,
and my worshippers go to me.

The leaf or flower or fruit or water
that he offers with devotion,
I take from the man of self-restraint
in response to his devotion.

Whatever you do — what you take,
what you offer, what you give,
what penances you perform —
do as an offering to me, Arjuna!

You will be freed from the bonds of action,
from the fruit of fortune and misfortune;
armed with the discipline of renunciation,
your self liberated, you will join me.

I am impartial to all creatures,
and no one is hateful or dear to me;
but men devoted to me are in me,
and I am within them.

If he is devoted solely to me,
even a violent criminal
must be deemed a man of virtue,
for his resolve is right.

His spirit quickens to sacred duty,
and he finds eternal peace;
Arjuna, know that no one
devoted to me is lost.

If they rely on me, Arjuna,
women, commoners, men of low rank,
even men born in the womb of evil,
reach the highest way.

How easy it is then for holy priests
and devoted royal sages —
in this transient world of sorrow,
devote yourself to me!

Keep me in your mind and devotion,
sacrifice to me, bow to me,
discipline yourself toward me,
and you will reach me!

$$15$$

ARISTOTLE

From *The Athenian Constitution*: Territorial Sovereignty

The process of establishing political authority based on the territorial state was not achieved at one particular moment in history. Much of Greek history (indeed much of world history since the Greeks) witnessed the struggle of territorial authority over family, blood, and kinship ties.

The process of replacing kinship and tribal alliances with a territorial "politics of place" can, however, be seen in the constitutional reforms attributed to the Athenian noble Cleisthenes in 508 B.C.E. Cleisthenes was not a democrat; his reform of Athenian politics was probably intended to win popular support for himself in his struggle with other noble families. But the inadvertent results of his reforms were to establish the necessary basis for democracy: a territorial state in which commoners as citizens had a stake in government. A description of those reforms is contained in a document called "The Athenian

---

Aristotle, "The Athenian Constitution," in *Aristotle, Politics, and the Athenian Constitution,* trans. John Warrington (London: David Campbell Publishers, 1959).

Constitution," discovered in Egypt only a hundred years ago and thought to have been written by the philosopher Aristotle (384–322 B.C.E.) around 330 B.C.E.

Modern scholars doubt that Cleisthenes created the *demes* (local neighborhoods) that were the basis of his reforms. Some existed earlier. But by making the *demes* the root of political organization, he undoubtedly undercut the power of dominant families. As *demes* were given real authority, power shifted from relatives to residents. Also, as Cleisthenes expanded the number of citizens, the *deme* structure became more "*deme*-ocratic."

Notice how the constitutional reform combined a sense of local, residential identity with citizenship in a larger city-state by tying city, country, and coastal *demes* together in each new "tribe." Why were these new tribes less "tribal" than the old ones? What would be the modern equivalent of these new tribes? Was democracy possible without a shift from kinship to territorial or civic identity? Was it inevitable?

Thinking Historically

Territorial sovereignty is something we take for granted. It means the law of the land. Regardless of the beliefs of our parents or ancestors, we obey the law of the territory. In the United States, we are bound to observe the law of the nation and the law of the state and municipal ordinances. We do not take our own family law with us when we move from one town or state or country to another. When we go to Japan, we are bound by Japanese law, even if we are not Japanese. In the modern world, sovereignty, ultimate authority, is tied to territory. Because this is so obvious to us in modern society, it is difficult to imagine that this was not always the case.

Historians have to acknowledge that things they and their societies take for granted may not have always existed; rather, they have developed throughout history. McNeill's interpretation of the essential difference between India and Greece makes such a leap. Many people have pointed out the unique Athenian invention of democracy. But McNeill recognized that the Athenians invented democracy because they had already invented something more fundamental — territorial sovereignty, politics, government, citizenship. How does "The Athenian Constitution" support McNeill's interpretation?

The overthrow of the Peisistratid tyranny left the city split into two actions under Isagoras and Cleisthenes respectively. The former, a son of Tisander, had supported the tyrants; the latter was an Alcmaeonid. Cleisthenes, defeated in the political clubs, won over the people by offering citizen rights to the masses. Thereupon Isagoras, who had fallen behind in the race for power, once more invoked the help of his friend

Cleomenes and persuaded him to exorcise the pollution; that is, to expel the Alcmaeonidae, who were believed still to be accursed. Cleisthenes accordingly withdrew from Attica with a small band of adherents, while Cleomenes proceeded to drive out seven hundred Athenian families. The Spartan next attempted to dissolve the Council and to set up Isagoras with three hundred of his supporters as the sovereign authority. The Council, however, resisted; the populace flew to arms; and Cleomenes with Isagoras and all their forces took refuge in the Acropolis, to which the people laid siege and blockaded them for two days. On the third day it was agreed that Cleomenes and his followers should withdraw. Cleisthenes and his fellow exiles were recalled.

The people were now in control, and Cleisthenes, their leader, was recognized as head of the popular party. This was not surprising; for the Alcmaeonidae were largely responsible for the overthrow of the tyrants, with whom they had been in conflict during most of their rule.

... The people, therefore, had every grounds for confidence in Cleisthenes. Accordingly, three years after the destruction of the tyranny, in the archonship of Isagoras, he used his influence as leader of the popular party to carry out a number of reforms. (A) He divided the population into ten tribes instead of the old four. His purpose here was to intermix the members of the tribes so that more persons might have civic rights; and hence the advice "not to notice the tribes," which was tendered to those who would examine the lists of the clans. (B) He increased the membership of the Council from 400 to 500, each tribe now contributing fifty instead of one hundred as before. His reason for not organizing the people into *twelve* tribes was to avoid the necessity of using the existing division into trittyes, which would have meant failing to regroup the population on a satisfactory basis. (C) He divided the country into thirty portions — ten urban and suburban, ten coastal, and ten inland — each containing a certain number of demes. These portions he called trittyes, and assigned three of them by lot to each tribe in such a way that each should have one portion in each of the three localities just mentioned. Furthermore, those who lived in any given deme were to be reckoned fellow demesmen. This arrangement was intended to protect new citizens from being shown up as such by the habitual use of family names. Men were to be officially described by the names of their demes; and it is thus that Athenians still speak of one another. Demes had now supplanted the old naucraries,[1] and Cleisthenes therefore appointed Demarchs whose duties were identical with those of the former Naucrari. He named some of the demes from their localities, and others from their supposed founders; for certain areas no longer corresponded to named localities. On the other hand, he

---

[1] Forty-eight subdivisions of the old four tribes, each responsible for one galley of the Athenian navy. [Ed.]

allowed everyone to retain his family and clan and religious rites according to ancestral custom. He also gave the ten tribes names which the Delphic oracle had chosen out of one hundred selected national heroes.

16

THUCYDIDES

The Funeral Oration of Pericles

The most famous statement of Greek loyalty to the city-state is the following account of the funeral speech of the Athenian statesman Pericles in the classic *History of the Peloponnesian War* by the ancient historian Thucydides. The speech eulogized the Athenian soldiers who had died in the war against Sparta in 431 B.C.E.

Notice the high value placed on loyalty to Athens and service to the state. Here is the origin of patriotism. Pericles also insists that Athens is a democratic city-state. He praises Athenian freedom as well as public service. Could there be a conflict between personal freedom and public service? If so, how would Pericles resolve such a conflict? You might also notice that Pericles is praising Athenian citizen-soldiers who died defending not their home but the empire. Could there be a conflict between Athenian democracy and the ambitious empire?

Thinking Historically

Are the sentiments that Pericles expresses a consequence of territorial sovereignty? Could such sentiments be expressed in defense of caste? Notice how Pericles speaks of ancestors, family, and parents. Do his words suggest any potential conflict between family ties and loyalty to the state? How is Pericles able to convince his audience of the priority of the state over kinship ties? How does this primary source provide evidence for McNeill's interpretation?

The History of Thucydides, Book II, trans. Benjamin Jowett (New York: Tandy-Thomas, 1909).

Most of those who have spoken here before me have commended the lawgiver who added this oration to our other funeral customs; it seemed to them a worthy thing that such an honour should be given at their burial to the dead who have fallen on the field of battle. But I should have preferred that, when men's deeds have been brave, they should be honoured in deed only, and with such an honour as this public funeral, which you are now witnessing. Then the reputation of many would not have been imperilled on the eloquence or want of eloquence of one, and their virtues believed or not as he spoke well or ill. For it is difficult to say neither too little nor too much; and even moderation is apt not to give the impression of truthfulness. The friend of the dead who knows the facts is likely to think that the words of the speaker fall short of his knowledge and of his wishes; another who is not so well informed, when he hears of anything which surpasses his own powers, will be envious and will suspect exaggeration. Mankind are tolerant of the praises of others as long as each hearer thinks that he can do as well or nearly as well himself, but, when the speaker rises above him, jealousy is aroused and he begins to be incredulous. However, since our ancestors have set the seal of their approval upon the practice, I must obey, and to the utmost of my power shall endeavour to satisfy the wishes and beliefs of all who hear me.

I will speak first of our ancestors, for it is right and seemly that now, when we are lamenting the dead, a tribute should be paid to their memory. There has never been a time when they did not inhabit this land, which by their valour they have handed down from generation to generation, and we have received from them a free state. But if they were worthy of praise, still more were our fathers, who added to their inheritance, and after many a struggle transmitted to us their sons this great empire. And we ourselves assembled here today, who are still most of us in the vigour of life, have carried the work of improvement further, and have richly endowed our city with all things, so that she is sufficient for herself both in peace and war. Of the military exploits by which our various possessions were acquired, or of the energy with which we or our fathers drove back the tide of war, Hellenic or Barbarian [non-Greek], I will not speak: for the tale would be long and is familiar to you. But before I praise the dead, I should like to point out by what principles of action we rose to power, and under what institutions and through what manner of life our empire became great. For I conceive that such thoughts are not unsuited to the occasion, and that this numerous assembly of citizens and strangers may profitably listen to them.

Our form of government does not enter into rivalry with the institutions of others. We do not copy our neighbours, but are an example to them. It is true that we are called a democracy, for the administration is in the hands of the many and not of the few. But while the law secures equal justice to all alike in their private disputes, the claim of excellence is also recognised; and when a citizen is in any way distinguished, he is preferred to the public service, not as a matter of privilege, but as the reward of merit. Neither is poverty a bar, but a man may benefit his country whatever be the obscurity of his condition. There is no exclusiveness in our public life, and in our private intercourse we are not suspicious of one another, nor angry with our neighbour if he does what he likes; we do not put on sour looks at him which, though harmless, are not pleasant. While we are thus unconstrained in our private intercourse, a spirit of reverence pervades our public acts; we are prevented from doing wrong by respect for the authorities and for the laws, having an especial regard to those which are ordained for the protection of the injured as well as to those unwritten laws which bring upon the transgressor of them the reprobation of the general sentiment.

And we have not forgotten to provide for our weary spirits many relaxations from toil; we have regular games and sacrifices throughout the year; our homes are beautiful and elegant; and the delight which we daily feel in all these things helps to banish melancholy. Because of the greatness of our city the fruits of the whole earth flow in upon us; so that we enjoy the goods of other countries as freely as of our own.

Then, again, our military training is in many respects superior to that of our adversaries. Our city is thrown open to the world, and we never expel a foreigner or prevent him from seeing or learning anything of which the secret if revealed to an enemy might profit him. We rely not upon management or trickery, but upon our own hearts and hands. And in the matter of education, whereas they from early youth are always undergoing laborious exercises which are to make them brave, we live at ease, and yet are equally ready to face the perils which they face. And here is the proof. The Lacedaemonians come into Attica not by themselves, but with their whole confederacy following; we go alone into a neighbour's country; and although our opponents are fighting for their homes and we on a foreign soil, we have seldom any difficulty in overcoming them. Our enemies have never yet felt our united strength; the care of a navy divides our attention, and on land we are obliged to send our own citizens everywhere. But they, if they meet and defeat a part of our army, are as proud as if they had routed us all, and when defeated they pretend to have been vanquished by us all.

If then we prefer to meet danger with a light heart but without laborious training, and with a courage which is gained by habit and not enforced by law, are we not greatly the gainers? Since we do not anticipate the pain, although, when the hour comes, we can be as brave as those who never allow themselves to rest; and thus too our city is equally admirable in peace and in war. For we are lovers of the beautiful, yet simple in our tastes, and we cultivate the mind without loss of manliness. Wealth we employ, not for talk and ostentation, but when there is a real use for it. To avow poverty with us is no disgrace; the true disgrace is in doing nothing to avoid it. An Athenian citizen does not neglect the state because he takes care of his own household; and even those of us who are engaged in business have a very fair idea of politics. We alone regard a man who takes no interest in public affairs, not as a harmless, but as a useless character; and if few of us are originators, we are all sound judges of policy. The great impediment to action is, in our opinion, not discussion, but the want of that knowledge which is gained by discussion preparatory to action. For we have a peculiar power of thinking before we act and of acting too, whereas other men are courageous from ignorance but hesitate upon reflection. And they are surely to be esteemed the bravest spirits who, having the clearest sense both of the pains and pleasures of life, do not on that account shrink from danger. In doing good, again, we are unlike others; we make our friends by conferring, not by receiving favours. Now he who confers a favour is the firmer friend, because he would fain by kindness keep alive the memory of an obligation; but the recipient is colder in his feelings, because he knows that in requiting another's generosity he will not be winning gratitude but only paying a debt. We alone do good to our neighbours, not upon a calculation of interest, but in the confidence of freedom and in a frank and fearless spirit.

To sum up: I say that Athens is the school of Hellas, and that the individual Athenian in his own person seems to have the power of adapting himself to the most varied forms of action with the utmost versatility and grace. This is no passing and idle word, but truth and fact; and the assertion is verified by the position to which these qualities have raised the state. For in the hour of trial Athens alone among her contemporaries is superior to the report of her. No enemy who comes against her is indignant at the reverses which he sustains at the hands of such a city; no subject complains that his masters are unworthy of him. And we shall assuredly not be without witnesses; there are mighty monuments of our power which will make us the wonder of this and of succeeding ages; we shall not need the praises of Homer or of any other panegyrist whose poetry may please for the moment, although his representation of the facts will not bear the light of day. For we have compelled every land and every sea to open a path for our valour, and have everywhere planted eternal memorials of our friendship and of our enmity. Such is the city of whose sake these men nobly fought and died; they could not bear the thought that she might be taken from them; and every one of us who survive should gladly toil on her behalf.

I have dwelt upon the greatness of Athens because I want to show you that we are contending for a higher prize than those who enjoy none of these privileges, and to establish by manifest proof the merit of these men whom I am now commemorating. Their loftiest praise has been already spoken. For in magnifying the city I have magnified them, and men like them whose virtues made her glorious. And of how few Hellenes can it be said as of them, that their deeds when weighed in the balance have been found equal to their fame! Methinks that a death such as theirs has been given the true measure of a man's worth; it may be the first revelation of his virtues, but is at any rate their final seal. For even those who come short in other ways may justly plead the valour with which they have fought for their country; they have blotted out the evil with the good, and have benefited the state more by their public services than they have injured her by their private actions. None of these men were enervated by wealth or hesitated to resign for pleasures of life, none of them put off the evil day in the hope, natural to poverty, that a man, though poor, may one day become rich. But, deeming that the punishment of their enemies was sweeter than any of these things, and that they could fall in no nobler cause, they determined at the hazard of their lives to be honourably avenged, and to leave the rest. They resigned to hope their unknown chance of happiness; but in the fact of death they resolved to rely upon themselves alone. And when the moment came they were minded to resist and suffer, rather than to fly and save their lives; they ran away from the word of dishonour, but on the battlefield their feet stood fast, and in an instant, at the height of their fortune, they passed away from the scene, not of their fear, but of their glory.

Such was the end of these men; they were worthy of Athens, and the living need not desire to have a more heroic spirit, although they may pray for a less fatal issue. The value of such a spirit is not to be expressed in words. Any one can discourse to you forever about the advantages of a brave defence, which you know already. But instead of listening to him I would have you day by day fix your eyes upon the greatness of Athens, until you become filled with the love of her; and when you are impressed by the spectacle of her glory, reflect that this empire has been acquired by men who knew their duty and had the courage to do it, who in the hour of conflict had the fear of dishonour always present to them, and who, if ever they failed in an enterprise, would not allow their virtues to be lost to their country, but freely gave their lives to her as the fairest offering which they could present at her feast. The sacrifice which they collectively made was individually repaid to them; for they received again each one of himself a praise which grows not old, and the noblest of all sepulchres — I speak not of that in which their remains are laid, but of that in which their glory survives, and is proclaimed always and on every fitting occasion both in word and deed. For the whole earth is the sepulchre of famous men; not only are they commemorated by columns and inscriptions in their own country, but in foreign lands there dwells also an unwritten memorial of them, graven not on stone but in the hearts of men. Make them your examples, and, esteeming courage to be freedom and freedom to be happiness, do not weigh too nicely the perils of war. The unfortunate who has no hope of a change for the better has less reason to throw away his life than the prosperous who, if he survives, is always liable to a change for the worse, and to whom any accidental fall makes the most serious difference. To a man of spirit, cowardice and disaster coming together are far more bitter than death striking him unperceived at a time when he is full of courage and animated by the general hope.

Wherefore I do not now commiserate the parents of the dead who stand here; I would rather comfort them. You know that your life has been passed amid manifold vicissitudes; and that they may be deemed fortunate who have gained most honour, whether an honourable death like theirs, or an honourable sorrow like yours, and whose days have been so ordered that the term of their happiness is likewise the term of their life. I know how hard it is to make you feel this, when the good fortune of others will too often remind you of the gladness which once lightened your hearts. And sorrow is felt at the want of those blessings, not which a man never knew, but which were a part of his life before they were taken from him. Some of you are of an age at which they may hope to have other children, and they ought to bear their sorrow better; not only will the children who may hereafter be born make them forget their own lost ones, but the city will be doubly a gainer. She will not be left desolate, and she will be safer. For a man's counsel cannot have equal weight or worth, when he alone has no children to risk in the general danger. To those of you who have passed their prime, I say: Congratulate yourselves that you have been happy during the greater part of your days; remember that your life of sorrow will not last long, and be comforted by the glory of those who are gone. For the love of honour alone is ever young, and not riches, as some say, but honour is the delight of men when they are old and useless.

To you who are the sons and brothers of the departed, I see that the struggle to emulate them will be an arduous one. For all men praise the dead, and, however pre-eminent your virtue may be, hardly will you be thought, I do not say to equal, but even to approach them. The living have their rivals and detractors, but when a man is out of the way, the honour and good-will which he receives is unalloyed. And, if I am to speak of womanly virtues to those of you who will henceforth be widows, let me sum them up in one short admonition: To a woman not to show more weakness than is natural to her sex is a great glory, and not to be talked about for good or for evil among men.

I have paid the required tribute, in obedience to the law, making use of such fitting words as I had. The tribute of deeds has been paid in part; for the dead have been honourably interred, and it remains only that their children should be maintained at the public charge until they are grown up; this is the solid prize with which, as with a garland, Athens crowns her sons living and dead, after a struggle like theirs. For where the rewards of virtue are greatest, there the noblest citizens are enlisted in the service of the state. And now, when you have duly lamented, everyone his own dead, you may depart.

17

PLATO

From *The Republic*

This selection is from one of the world's most famous books of philosophy. Two events dominated the early life of Plato (428–348 B.C.E.), turning him away from the public life he was expected to lead. Plato was born in the shadow of the Peloponnesian War, which ended with the defeat of Athens in his twenty-third year. The postwar governments, especially the democracy that condemned his teacher Socrates in 399 B.C.E., turned him away from the political arena to a life of contemplation.

Plato's philosophical books, called dialogues because of the way they develop ideas from discussion and debate, follow Plato's teacher Socrates around the city-state of Athens. Often they begin, like *The Republic,* with a view of Socrates and other Athenian citizens enjoying the public spaces and festivals of the city. Notice in this introduction how territorial sovereignty creates public places and public activities.

Thinking Historically

Plato was neither a democrat nor politically active. Nevertheless, his life and his philosophy exemplify a commitment to the world of what McNeill calls "territorial sovereignty."

A primary source can support a particular viewpoint by espousing it, as Plato espouses the benefits of living in a territorial state or thinking about government. But a source can also provide clues about the society from which it comes. What clues in Plato's text show that his life and the lives of the people around him are shaped by the city-state?

Plato, *The Republic of Plato,* trans. F. M. Cornford (London: Oxford University Press, 1941), 2–3, 177–79, 227–35.

Chapter 1

SOCRATES. I walked down to the Piraeus yesterday with Glaucon, the son of Ariston, to make my prayers to the goddess. As this was the first celebration of her festival, I wished also to see how the ceremony would be conducted. The Thracians, I thought, made as fine a show in the procession as our own people, though they did well enough. The prayers and the spectacle were over, and we were leaving to go back to the city, when from some way off Polemarchus, the son of Cephalus, caught sight of us starting homewards and sent his slave running to ask us to wait for him. The boy caught my garment from behind and gave me the message.

I turned around and asked where his master was.

There, he answered; coming up behind. Please wait.

Very well, said Glaucon; we will.

A minute later Polemarchus joined us, with Glaucon's brother, Adeimantus, and Niceratus, the son of Nicias, and some others who must have been at the procession.

Socrates, said Polemarchus, I do believe you are starting back to town and leaving us.

You have guessed right, I answered.

Well, he said, you see what a large party we are?

I do.

Unless you are more than a match for us, then, you must stay here.

Isn't there another alternative? said I; we might convince you that you must let us go.

How will you convince us, if we refuse to listen?

We cannot, said Glaucon.

Well, we shall refuse; make up your minds to that.

Here Adeimantus interposed: Don't you even know that in the evening there is going to be a torch-race on horseback in honour of the goddess?

On horseback! I exclaimed; that is something new. How will they do it? Are the riders going to race with torches and hand them on to one another?

Just so, said Polemarchus. Besides, there will be a festival lasting all night, which will be worth seeing. We will go out after dinner and look on. We shall find plenty of young men there and we can have a talk. So please stay, and don't disappoint us.

It looks as if we had better stay, said Glaucon.

Well, said I, if you think so, we will.

Accordingly, we went home with Polemarchus.

At the home of Polemarchus, the participants meet a number of other old friends. After the usual greetings and gossip, the discussion begins in response to Socrates' question, what is justice?

Each of the participants poses an idea of justice that Socrates challenges. Then Socrates outlines an ideal state that would be based on absolute justice. In the following selection he is asked how this ideal could ever come about.

Aside from the specifics of Socrates' argument, notice the way in which public issues, for Socrates, are passionate personal concerns.

Chapter 18

But really, Socrates, Glaucon continued, if you are allowed to go on like this, I am afraid you will forget all about the question you thrust aside some time ago; whether a society so constituted can ever come into existence, and if so, how. No doubt, if it did exist, all manner of good things would come about. I can even add some that you have passed over. Men who acknowledged one another as fathers, sons, or brothers and always used those names among themselves would never desert one another; so they would fight with unequalled bravery. And if their womenfolk went out with them to war, either in the ranks or drawn up in the rear to intimidate the enemy and act as a reserve in case of need, I am sure all this would make them invincible. At home, too, I can see many advantages you have not mentioned. But, since I admit that our commonwealth would have all these merits and any number more, if once it came into existence, you need not describe it in further detail. All we have now to do is to convince ourselves that it can be brought into being and how.

This is a very sudden onslaught, said I; you have no mercy on my shilly-shallying. Perhaps you do not realize that, after I have barely escaped the first two waves, the third, which you are now bringing down upon me, is the most formidable of all. When you have seen what it is like and heard my reply, you will be ready to excuse the very natural fears which made me shrink from putting forward such a paradox for discussion.

The more you talk like that, he said, the less we shall be willing to let you off from telling us how this constitution can come into existence; so you had better waste no more time.

Well, said I, let me begin by reminding you that what brought us to this point was our inquiry into the nature of justice and injustice.

True; but what of that?

Merely this: suppose we do find out what justice is, are we going to demand that a man who is just shall have a character which exactly corresponds in every respect to the ideal of justice? Or shall we be satisfied if he comes as near to the ideal as possible and has in him a larger measure of that quality than the rest of the world?

That will satisfy me.

If so, when we set out to discover the essential nature of justice and injustice and what a perfectly just and a perfectly unjust man would be like, supposing them to exist, our purpose was to use them as ideal patterns: we were to observe the degree of happiness or unhappiness that each exhibited, and to draw the necessary inference that our own destiny would be like that of the one we most resembled. We did not set out to show that these ideals could exist in fact.

That is true.

Then suppose a painter had drawn an ideally beautiful figure complete to the last touch, would you think any the worse of him, if he could not show that a person as beautiful as that could exist?

No, I should not.

Well, we have been constructing in discourse the pattern of an ideal state. Is our theory any the worse, if we cannot prove it possible that a state so organized should be actually founded?

Surely not.

That, then, is the truth of the matter. But if, for your satisfaction, I am to do my best to show under what conditions our ideal would have the best chance of being realized, I must ask you once more to admit that the same principle applies here. Can theory ever be fully realized in practice? Is it not in the nature of things that action should come less close to truth than thought? People may not think so; but do you agree or not?

I do.

Then you must not insist upon my showing that this construction we have traced in thought could be reproduced in fact down to the last detail. You must admit that we shall have found a way to meet your demand for realization, if we can discover how a state might be constituted in the closest accordance with our description. Will not that content you? It would be enough for me.

And for me too.

Then our next attempt, it seems, must be to point out what defect in the working of existing states prevents them from being so organized, and what is the least change that would effect a transformation into this type of government — a single change if possible, or perhaps two; at any rate let us make the changes as few and insignificant as may be.

By all means.

Well, there is one change which, as I believe we can show, would bring about this revolution — not a small change, certainly, nor an easy one, but possible.

What is it?

I have now to confront what we called the third and greatest wave. But I must state my paradox, even though the wave should break in laughter over my head and drown me in ignominy. Now mark what I am going to say.

Go on.

Unless either philosophers become kings in their countries or those who are now called kings and rulers come to be sufficiently inspired with a genuine desire for wisdom; unless, that is to say, political power and philosophy meet together, while the many natures who now go their several ways in the one or the other direction are forcibly debarred from doing so, there can be no rest from troubles, my dear Glaucon, for states, nor yet, as I believe, for all mankind; nor can this commonwealth which we have imagined ever till then see the light of day and grow to its full stature. This it was that I have so long hung back from saying; I knew what a paradox it would be, because it is hard to see that there is no other way of happiness either for the state or for the individual.

Socrates, exclaimed Glaucon, after delivering yourself of such a pronouncement as that, you must expect a whole multitude of by no means contemptible assailants to fling off their coats, snatch up the handiest weapon, and make a rush at you, breathing fire and slaughter. If you cannot find arguments to beat them off and make your escape, you will learn what it means to be the target of scorn and derision.

Well, it was you who got me into this trouble.

Yes, and a good thing too. However, I will not leave you in the lurch. You shall have my friendly encouragement for what it is worth; and perhaps you may find me more complaisant than some would be in answering your questions. With such backing you must try to convince the unbelievers.

I will, now that I have such a powerful ally.

In arguing that philosophers should be kings, Plato (or Socrates) was parting ways with the democratic tradition of Athens. Like other conservative Athenians, he seems to have believed that democracy degenerated into mob rule. The root of this antidemocratic philosophy was the belief that the mass of people was horribly ignorant and only the rare philosopher had true understanding. Plato expressed this idea in one of the most famous passages in the history of philosophy: the parable of the cave.

Next, said I, here is a parable to illustrate the degrees in which our nature may be enlightened or unenlightened. Imagine the condition of men living in a sort of cavernous chamber underground, with an entrance open to the light and a long passage all down the cave. Here they have been from childhood, chained by the leg and also by the neck, so that they cannot move and can see only what is in front of them, because the chains will not let them turn their heads. At some distance higher up is the light of a fire burning behind them; and between the prisoners and the fire is a track with a parapet built along it, like the screen at a puppet-show, which hides the performers while they show their puppets over the top.

I see, said he.

Now behind this parapet imagine persons carrying along various artificial objects, including figures of men and animals in wood or stone or other materials, which project above the parapet. Naturally, some of these persons will be talking, others silent.

It is a strange picture, he said, and a strange sort of prisoners.

Like ourselves, I replied; for in the first place prisoners so confined would have seen nothing of themselves or of one another, except the shadows thrown by the firelight on the wall of the Cave facing them, would they?

Not if all their lives they had been prevented from moving their heads.

And they would have seen as little of the objects carried past.

Of course.

Now, if they could talk to one another, would they not suppose that their words referred only to those passing shadows which they saw?

Necessarily.

And suppose their prison had an echo from the wall facing them? When one of the people crossing behind them spoke, they could only suppose that the sound came from the shadow passing before their eyes.

No doubt.

In every way, then, such prisoners would recognize as reality nothing but the shadows of those artificial objects.

Inevitably.

Now consider what would happen if their release from the chains and the healing of their unwisdom should come about in this way. Suppose one of them was set free and forced suddenly to stand up, turn his head, and walk with eyes lifted to the light; all these movements would be painful, and he would be too dazzled to make out the objects whose shadows he had been used to see. What do you think he would say, if someone told him that what he had formerly seen was meaningless illusion, but now, being somewhat nearer to reality and turned towards more real objects, he was getting a truer view? Suppose further that he were shown the various objects being carried by and were made to say, in reply to questions, what each of them was. Would he not be perplexed and believe the objects now shown him to be not so real as what he formerly saw?

Yes, not nearly so real.

And if he were forced to look at the firelight itself, would not his eyes ache, so that he would try to escape and turn back to the things which he could see distinctly, convinced that they really were clearer than these other objects now being shown to him?

Yes.

And suppose someone were to drag him away forcibly up the steep and rugged ascent and not let him go until he had hauled him out into the sunlight, would he not suffer pain and vexation at such treatment, and, when he had come out into the light, find his eyes so full of its radiance that he could not see a single one of the things that he was now told were real?

Certainly he would not see them all at once.

He would need, then, to grow accustomed before he could see things in that upper world. At first it would be easiest to make out shadows, and then the images of men and things reflected in water, and later on the things themselves. After that, it would be easier to watch the heavenly bodies and the sky itself by night, looking at the light of the moon and stars rather than the Sun and the Sun's light in the daytime.

Yes, surely.

Last of all, he would be able to look at the Sun and contemplate its nature, not as it appears when reflected in water or any alien medium, but as it is in itself in its own domain.

No doubt.

And now he would begin to draw the conclusion that it is the Sun that produces the seasons and the course of the year and controls everything in the visible world, and moreover is in a way the cause of all that he and his companions used to see.

Clearly he would come at last to that conclusion.

Then if he called to mind his fellow prisoners and what passed for wisdom in his former dwelling-place, he would surely think himself happy in the change and be sorry for them. They may have had a practice of honouring and commending one another, with prizes for the man who had the keenest eye for the passing shadows and the best memory for the order in which they followed or accompanied one another, so that he could make a good guess as to which was going to come next. Would our released prisoner be likely to covet those prizes or to envy the men exalted to honour and power in the Cave? Would he not feel like Homer's Achilles, that he would far sooner "be on earth as a hired servant in the house of a landless man" or endure anything rather than go back to his old beliefs and live in the old way?

Yes, he would prefer any fate to such a life.

Now imagine what would happen if he went down again to take his former seat in the Cave. Coming suddenly out of the sunlight, his eyes would be filled with darkness. He might be required once more to deliver his opinion on those shadows, in competition with the prisoners who had never been released, while his eyesight was still dim and unsteady; and it might take some time to become used to the darkness. They would laugh at him and say that he had gone up only to come back with his sight ruined; it was worth no one's while even to attempt the ascent. If they could lay hands on the man who was trying to set them free and lead them up, they would kill him.

Yes, they would.

Every feature in this parable, my dear Glaucon, is meant to fit our earlier analysis. The prison dwelling corresponds to the region revealed to us through the sense of sight, and the firelight within it to the power of the Sun. The ascent to see the things in the upper world you may take as standing for the upward journey of the soul into the region of the intelligible; then you will be in possession of what I surmise, since that is what you wish to be told. Heaven knows whether it is true; but this, at any rate, is how it appears to me. In the world of knowledge, the last thing to be perceived and only with great difficulty is the essential Form of Goodness. Once it is perceived, the conclusion must follow that, for all things, this is the cause of whatever is right and good; in the visible world it gives birth to light and to the lord of light, while it is itself sovereign in the intelligible world and the parent of intelligence and truth. Without having had a vision of this Form no one can act with wisdom, either in his own life or in matters of state.

So far as I can understand, I share your belief.

Then you may also agree that it is no wonder if those who have reached their height are reluctant to manage the affairs of men. Their souls long to spend all their time in that upper world — naturally enough, if here once more our parable holds true. Nor, again, is it at all strange that one who comes from the contemplation of divine things to the miseries of human life should appear awkward and ridiculous when, with eyes still dazed and not yet accustomed to the darkness, he is compelled, in a law court or elsewhere, to dispute about the shadows of justice or the images that cast those shadows, and to wrangle over the notions of what is right in the minds of men who have never beheld Justice itself.

It is not at all strange.

No; a sensible man will remember that the eyes may be confused in two ways — by a change from light to darkness or from darkness to light; and he will recognize that the same thing happens to the soul. When he sees it troubled and unable to discern anything clearly, instead of laughing thoughtlessly, he will ask whether, coming from a brighter existence, its unaccustomed vision is obscured by the darkness, in which case he will think its condition enviable and its life a happy one; or whether, emerging from the depths of ignorance, it is dazzled by excess of light. If so, he will rather feel sorry for it; or, if he were inclined to laugh, that would be less ridiculous than to laugh at the soul which has come down from the light.

That is a fair statement.

If this is true, then, we must conclude that education is not what it is said to be by some, who profess to put knowledge into a soul which does not possess it, as if they could put sight into blind eyes. On the contrary, our own account signifies that the soul of every man does possess the power of learning the truth and the organ to see it with; and that, just as one might have to turn the whole body round in order that the eye should see light instead of darkness, so the entire soul must be turned away from this changing world, until its eye can bear to contemplate reality and that supreme splendour which we have called the Good. Hence there may well be an art whose aim would be to effect this very thing, the conversion of the soul, in the readiest way; not to put the power of sight into the soul's eye, which already has it, but to ensure that, instead of looking in the wrong direction, it is turned the way it ought to be.

Yes, it may well be so.

It looks, then, as though wisdom were different from those ordinary virtues, as they are called, which are not far removed from bodily qualities, in that they can be produced by habituation and exercise in a soul which has not possessed them from the first. Wisdom, it seems, is certainly the virtue of some diviner faculty, which never loses its power, though its use for good or harm depends on the direction towards which it is turned. You must have noticed in dishonest men with a reputation for sagacity the shrewd glance of a narrow intelligence piercing the objects to which it is directed. There is nothing wrong with their power of vision, but it has been forced into the service of evil, so that the keener its sight, the more harm it works.

Quite true.

And yet if the growth of a nature like this had been pruned from earliest childhood, cleared of those clinging overgrowths which come of gluttony and all luxurious pleasure and, like leaden weights charged with affinity to this mortal world, hang upon the soul, bending its vision downwards; if, freed from these, the soul were turned round towards true reality, then this same power in these very men would see the truth as keenly as the objects it is turned to now.

Yes, very likely.

Is it not also likely, or indeed certain after what has been said, that a state can never be properly governed either by the uneducated who know nothing of truth or by men who are allowed to spend all their days in the pursuit of culture? The ignorant have no single mark before their eyes at which they must aim in all the conduct of their own lives and of affairs of state; and the others will not engage in action if they can help it, dreaming that, while still alive, they have been translated to the Islands of the Blest.

Quite true.

It is for us, then, as founders of a commonwealth, to bring compulsion to bear on the noblest natures. They must be made to climb the ascent to the vision of Goodness, which we called the highest object of knowledge; and, when they have looked upon it long enough, they must not be allowed, as they now are, to remain on the heights, refusing to come down again to the prisoners or to take any part in their labours and rewards, however much or little these may be worth.

Shall we not be doing them an injustice, if we force on them a worse life than they might have?

You have forgotten again, my friend, that the law is not concerned to make any one class specially happy, but to ensure the welfare of the commonwealth as a whole. By persuasion or constraint it will unite the citizens in harmony, making them share whatever benefits each class can contribute to the common good; and its purpose in forming men of that spirit was not that each should be left to go his own way, but that they should be instrumental in binding the community into one.

True, I had forgotten.

You will see, then, Glaucon, that there will be no real injustice in compelling our philosophers to watch over and care for the other citizens. We can fairly tell them that their compeers in other states may quite reasonably refuse to collaborate: there they have sprung up, like a self-sown plant, in despite of their country's institutions; no one has fostered their growth, and they cannot be expected to show gratitude for a care they have never received. "But," we shall say, "it is not so with you. We have brought you into existence for your country's sake as well as for your own, to be like leaders and king-bees in a hive; you have been better and more thoroughly educated than those others and hence you are more capable of playing your part both as men of thought and as men of action. You must go down, then, each in his turn, to live with the rest and let your eyes grow accustomed to the darkness. You will then see a thousand times better than those who live there always; you will recognize every image for what it is and know what it represents, because you have seen justice, beauty, and goodness in their reality; and so you and we shall find life in our commonwealth no mere dream, as it is in most existing states, where men live fighting one another about shadows and quarrelling for power, as if that were a great prize; whereas in truth government can be at its best and free from dissension only where the destined rulers are least desirous of holding office."

Quite true.

Then will our pupils refuse to listen and to take their turns at sharing in the work of the community, though they may live together for most of their time in a purer air?

No; it is a fair demand, and they are fair-minded men. No doubt, unlike any ruler of the present day, they will think of holding power as an unavoidable necessity.

Yes, my friend; for the truth is that you can have a well-governed society only if you can discover for your future rulers a better way of life than being in office; then only will power be in the hands of men who are rich, not in gold, but in the wealth that brings happiness, a good and wise life. All goes wrong when, starved for lack of anything good in their own lives, men turn to public affairs hoping to snatch from thence the happiness they hunger for. They set about fighting for power, and this internecine conflict ruins them and their country. The life of true philosophy is the only one that looks down upon offices of state; and access to power must be confined to men who are not in love with it; otherwise rivals will start fighting. So whom else can you compel to undertake the guardianship of the commonwealth, if not those who, besides understanding best the principles of government, enjoy a nobler life than the politician's and look for rewards of a different kind?

There is indeed no other choice.

REFLECTIONS

While Plato opposed democracy, he did not oppose territorial sovereignty or its effects, such as personal involvement in public policy and politics. You might reread Plato and underline the sections where participation in politics is assumed to be a proper activity. This assumption was widespread in ancient Greece, but it hardly existed in India.

Compare Plato's investigation of politics with Arjuna's in the *Bhagavad Gita.* Can you imagine Arjuna asking any of the questions that Plato asked? You might try to imagine a conversation between Plato and Arjuna. How accurately would they understand each other's assumptions? Would Plato's distrust of democracy elicit some sympathy from Arjuna?

We might expect democrats like Aristotle, Thucydides, and Pericles to be even more at odds with the caste-based politics of the *Bhagavad Gita.* Nevertheless, they might find some points of agreement as well. Both Pericles and the author of the *Bhagavad Gita,* for instance, approve of killing and dying, but they do so for very different reasons. Define those reasons. What do they tell us about the differences between their two societies?

Women in Classical Societies

India, China, and Rome
500 B.C.E.–500 C.E.

HISTORICAL CONTEXT

The period between 500 B.C.E. and 500 C.E. is called the Classical era because it witnessed the development of many great works of literature, philosophy, and religion that continue to influence the civilizations that conceived them. The teachings of Confucius and Lao Tze in China, the epic poems *The Mahabharata* and *The Ramayana* in India, Greek philosophy and natural science, Roman literature, the writings of Persian Zoroastrianism, the Judaic and Christian Bible, and many of the sacred texts of Hinduism and Buddhism are all examples of classic works from this period. Studying these works can tell us about both the age-old societies in which they originated and the modern societies that they have helped to shape.

In Chapter 1, we focused on patriarchy and the evolving relationship between men and women during the prehistoric period. In the following selections we revisit this theme in primary classic sources from India, China, and Rome, and in modern secondary sources that analyze these classics. We examine conventional attitudes toward women, what shaped these attitudes, and instances in which women flouted convention. What sources of power did women have in these societies? How might these classic works influence both men and women today?

THINKING HISTORICALLY
Using Classic Texts as Primary Sources

Classic texts are obvious and frequently chosen primary sources. The historian can assume that a culture's great classic texts, having survived the test of time, reflect important and widely held beliefs. But there are qualifications to these assumptions. Like Christians reading the Bible, people may have different interpretations of a text. Some may interpret it literally, whereas others may find only symbolic meaning in its message. Some, especially the illiterate, might draw their ideas from oral versions, which introduce new interpretations and meanings. Classics generally evolve over time, sometimes with the aid of different authors. Finally, texts are rarely neutral; those that come to dominate a culture often serve the interests of the ruling group. In short, classic texts are heavily weighted in meanings that may not be readily apparent to the historian. Other primary sources—pottery shards, laundry lists, notes to the baby-sitter—lack the deep cultural resonance of the classics, but they are pristine by comparison. We can be reasonably sure that they were not created with an eye on posterity and that no one has worked them over in order to gain a desired effect. Such sources may be less representative but more reliable. As you read the primary sources in this chapter, consider the question of reliability and representation. As you read the secondary sources, notice how the historians use classic texts in their histories, in particular, how they reinterpret these texts or seek to challenge their relevance.

18

R. K. NARAYAN

From *The Ramayana*

The Ramayana is a classic Indian epic that originated as an oral tradition between 1500 and 400 B.C.E., and was first recorded in the first century C.E. by the poet Valmiki. The poem celebrates the virtues of Prince Rama and his wife Sita, who eventually came to be worshiped as deities in the Hindu pantheon. Exiled from his father's kingdom,

R. K. Narayan, *The Ramayana* (Harmondsworth: Penguin Books, 1977), 20–22, 161–64.

Rama goes to live in the forest, and Sita, a dutiful and devoted wife, follows him. Sita is abducted by Ravana, an evil king who holds her prisoner in his kingdom. Rama eventually defeats Ravana with the help of the god Hanuman and brings his beloved Sita back to his own kingdom, which he rightfully regains. But before Rama can fully accept Sita as his queen, she must prove that she has remained loyal to him during her captivity.

There are innumerable versions and variations on this basic story, which is divided into distinct episodes, two of which you will read here. The first selection, the story of Ahalya and Gautama, serves as a prologue to the main tale of Rama and Sita, and focuses on female loyalty. We skip over the main body of the epic and pick up at the end of the story in the second selection, in which Sita proves her fidelity to Rama. The assurance of a wife's loyalty to her husband was (and still is) an important requirement in patriarchal societies in which men preserve their family lines by ensuring the legitimacy of their sons. In Hindu society Rama and Sita are celebrated as heroic figures to this day because they fulfill their *dharma*, or their duty, in the face of adversity. In classical Hindu society this was one of the most important ideals one could strive for, and it still informs Indian society today. What examples of the pursuit of *dharma* did you see in the previous chapter? How might the concept of fulfilling one's *dharma* reinforce patriarchy? Conversely, how might it empower both men and women?

Thinking Historically

Over the centuries, Indians have read and listened to numerous versions of the story of Rama and Sita. The one excerpted here, by the modern Indian novelist R. K. Narayan, is based on an eleventh-century C.E. version. Narayan writes in the introduction: "Everyone of whatever age, outlook, education, or station in life knows the essential part of the epic and adores the main figures in it—Rama and Sita." Using the epic to understand the ideas and behavior of women and men in the Classical era is difficult, given the two thousand years that separate us. Nevertheless, what does *The Ramayana* suggest about the classical Indian roles of men and women? What other primary sources can you imagine using to understand classical Indian men and women? What sorts of primary sources might be more reliable than this one?

While passing over slightly raised ground beside the walls of the fort, Rama noticed a shapeless slab of stone, half buried vertically in the ground; when he brushed past, the dust of his feet fell on it, and transformed it, that very instant, into a beautiful woman. As the woman did obeisance and stood aside respectfully, Viswamithra introduced her to

Rama. "If you have heard of Sage Gautama, whose curse resulted in great Indra's body being studded with a thousand eyes, all over . . . This lady was his wife, and her name is Ahalya." And he told Rama her story.

Ahalya's Story

Brahma once created, out of the ingredients of absolute beauty, a woman, and she was called Ahalya (which in the Sanskrit language means non-imperfection). God Indra, being the highest god among the gods, was attracted by her beauty and was convinced that he alone was worthy of claiming her hand. Brahma, noticing the conceit and presump-tuousness of Indra, ignored him, sought out Sage Gautama, and left him in charge of the girl. She grew up in his custody, and when the time came the sage took her back to Brahma and handed her over to him.

Brahma appreciated Gautama's purity of mind and heart (never once had any carnal thought crossed his mind), and said, "Marry her, she is fit to be your wife, or rather you alone deserve to be her hus-band." Accordingly, she was married, blessed by Brahma and other gods. Having spent her childhood with Gautama, Ahalya knew his needs and so proved a perfect wife, and they lived happily.

Indra, however, never got over his infatuation for Ahalya, and often came in different guises near to Gautama's *ashram,* waiting for every chance to gaze and feast on Ahalya's form and figure; he also watched the habits of the sage and noticed that the sage left his ashram at the dawn of each day and was away for a couple of hours at the river for his bath and prayers. Unable to bear the pangs of love any more, Indra decided to attain the woman of his heart by subterfuge. One day, hardly able to wait for the sage to leave at his usual hour, Indra as-sumed the voice of a rooster, and woke up the sage, who, thinking that the morning had come, left for the river. Now Indra assumed the sage's form, entered the hut, and made love to Ahalya. She surrendered her-self, but at some stage realized that the man enjoying her was an im-poster; but she could do nothing about it. Gautama came back at this moment, having intuitively felt that something was wrong, and sur-prised the couple in bed. Ahalya stood aside filled with shame and re-morse; Indra assumed the form of a cat (the most facile animal form for sneaking in or out) and tried to slip away. The sage looked from the cat to the woman and was not to be deceived. He arrested the cat where he was with these words:

"Cat, I know you; your obsession with the female is your undoing. May your body be covered with a thousand female marks, so that in all the worlds, people may understand what really goes on in your mind all the time." Hardly had these words left his lips when every inch of Indra's body displayed the female organ. There could be no greater shame for the proud and self-preening Indra.

After Indra slunk away, back to his world, Gautama looked at his wife and said, "You have sinned with your body. May that body harden into a shapeless piece of granite, just where you are. . . . " Now in desperation Ahalya implored, "A grave mistake has been committed. It is in the nature of noble souls to forgive the errors of lesser beings. Please . . . I am already feeling a weight creeping up my feet. Do something . . . please help me. . . . "

Now the sage felt sorry for her and said, "Your redemption will come when the son of Dasaratha, Rama, passes this way at some future date. . . . "

"When? Where?" she essayed to question, desperately, but before the words could leave her lips she had become a piece of stone.

Indra's predicament became a joke in all the worlds at first, but later proved noticeably tragic. He stayed in darkness and seclusion and could never appear before men or women. This caused much concern to all the gods, as his multifarious duties in various worlds remained suspended, and they went in a body to Brahma and requested him to intercede with Gautama. By this time, the sage's resentment had vanished. And he said in response to Brahma's appeal, "May the thousand additions to Indra's features become eyes." Indra thereafter came to be known as the "thousand-eyed god."

Viswamithra concluded the story and addressed Rama. "O great one, you are born to restore righteousness and virtue to mankind and eliminate all evil. At our yagna, I saw the power of your arms, and now I see the greatness of the touch of your feet."

Rama said to Ahalya, "May you seek and join your revered husband, and live in his service again. Let not your heart be burdened with what is past and gone."

On their way to Mithila, they stopped to rest at Gautama's hermitage, and Viswamithra told the sage, "Your wife is restored to her normal form, by the touch of Rama's feet. Go and take her back, her heart is purified through the ordeal she has undergone." All this accomplished, they moved on, leaving behind the scented groves and forest, and approached the battlemented gates of Mithila City.

Conclusion

After the death of Ravana, Rama sent Hanuman as his emissary to fetch Sita. Sita was overjoyed. She had been in a state of mourning all along, completely neglectful of her dress and appearance, and she immediately rose to go out and meet Rama as she was. But Hanuman explained that it was Rama's express wish that she should dress and decorate herself before coming to his presence.

A large crowd pressed around Rama. When Sita eagerly arrived, after her months of loneliness and suffering, she was received by her husband in full view of a vast public. She felt awkward but accepted this with resignation. But what she could not understand was why her lord seemed preoccupied and moody and cold. However, she prostrated herself at his feet, and then stood a little away from him, sensing some strange barrier between herself and him.

Rama remained brooding for a while and suddenly said, "My task is done. I have now freed you. I have fulfilled my mission. All this effort has been not to attain personal satisfaction for you or me. It was to vindicate the honour of the Ikshvahu race and to honour our ancestors' codes and values. After all this, I must tell you that it is not customary to admit back to the normal married fold a woman who has resided all alone in a stranger's house. There can be no question of our living together again. I leave you free to go where you please and to choose any place to live in. I do not restrict you in any manner."

On hearing this, Sita broke down. "My trials are not ended yet," she cried. "I thought with your victory all our troubles were at an end . . . ! So be it." She beckoned to Lakshmana and ordered, "Light a fire at once, on this very spot."

Lakshmana hesitated and looked at his brother, wondering whether he would countermand the order. But Rama seemed passive and acquiescent. Lakshmana, ever the most unquestioning deputy, gathered faggots and got ready a roaring pyre within a short time. The entire crowd watched the proceedings, stunned by the turn of events. The flames rose to the height of a tree; still Rama made no comment. He watched. Sita approached the fire, prostrated herself before it, and said, "O Agni, great god of fire, be my witness." She jumped into the fire.

From the heart of the flame rose the god of fire, bearing Sita, and presented her to Rama with words of blessing. Rama, now satisfied that he had established his wife's integrity in the presence of the world, welcomed Sita back to his arms.

Rama explained that he had to adopt this trial in order to demonstrate Sita's purity beyond a shadow of a doubt to the whole world. This seemed a rather strange inconsistency on the part of one who had brought back to life and restored to her husband a person like Ahalya, who had avowedly committed a moral lapse; and then there was Sugreeva's wife, who had been forced to live with Vali, and whom Rama commended as worthy of being taken back by Sugreeva after Vali's death. In Sita's case Ravana, in spite of repeated and desperate attempts, could not approach her. She had remained inviolable. And the fiery quality of her essential being burnt out the god of fire himself, as he had admitted after Sita's ordeal. Under these circumstances, it was very strange that Rama should have spoken harshly as he had done at the first sight of Sita, and subjected her to a dreadful trial.

The gods, who had watched this in suspense, were now profoundly relieved but also had an uneasy feeling that Rama had, perhaps, lost sight of his own identity. Again and again this seemed to happen. Rama displayed the tribulations and the limitations of the human frame and it was necessary from time to time to remind him of his divinity. Now Brahma, the Creator, came forward to speak and addressed Rama thus: "Of the Trinity, I am the Creator. Shiva is the Destroyer and Vishnu is the Protector. All three of us derive our existence from the Supreme God and we are subject to dissolution and rebirth. But the Supreme God who creates us is without a beginning or an end. There is neither birth nor growth nor death for the Supreme God. He is the origin of everything and in him everything is assimilated at the end. That God is yourself, and Sita at your side now is a part of that Divinity. Please remember that this is your real identity and let not the fear and doubts that assail an ordinary mortal ever move you. You are beyond everything; and we are all blessed indeed to be in your presence."

19

From the *Devi-Mahatmya*

The *Devi-Mahatmya* is part of a collection of classical Indian texts called the Puranas, which include stories of the gods and devotional hymns intended to make the holy Vedas more accessible to a general audience. First recorded around 600 C.E., the *Devi-Mahatmya* tells the story of the Great Goddess, recounting her accomplishments and singing her praise. There are innumerable gods and goddesses in the Hindu pantheon, but in this poem the Goddess is worshipped as a supreme being, even superior to the main Hindu gods Brahma (the Creator), Vishnu (the Preserver), and Shiva (the Destroyer), and is said to embody all three. The *Devi-Mahatmya* is the main devotional text for those who worship the Goddess, and it is still recited by her followers today.

The epic consists of three episodes in which the Goddess defeats a number of demons and restores order to the universe. In the first episode, from which both of the excerpts here are drawn, the gods have been waging a battle against demons for hundreds of years. Defeated, they appeal to Brahma, Vishnu, and Shiva for assistance, who in turn conjure the Goddess. Upon calling her forth, the gods praise her, which is where our first selection (lines 1.56–1.63) begins. In the

Thomas B. Coburn, *Encountering the Goddess: A Translation of the Devi-Mahatmya and a Study of Its Interpretation* (Albany: State University of New York Press, 1991), 37, 48–51.

second selection (lines 4.1–4.26), the Goddess has defeated the demons, and the gods, lying prostrate, express their gratitude. What qualities do the gods attribute to the Goddess? Note how she is portrayed as both kind and loving and angry and vengeful. Compare the portrayal of the Goddess to the portrayal of Sita in *The Ramayana*. How do they differ? Which epic presents a more empowering ideal for women? Do you think the *Devi-Mahatmya* threatens patriarchy in Indian society?

Thinking Historically

Like *The Ramayana*, the Puranas were widely read and recited. The *Devi-Mahatmya* was, and still is, recited as part of a Hindu ritual dedicated to the Goddess. Reciting prayers or hymns, like performing rituals, gives the words a timeless quality, freezing their meaning in time. On the other hand, stories like *The Ramayana* lead themselves to updating, as was our version by R. K. Narayan, the modern novelist. How might this difference affect the way people understand the contemporary relevance of these two works?

You are she; you are Sāvitrī (the Gāyatrī *mantra*); you are the Goddess, the supreme mother.

1.56   By you is everything supported, by you is the world created;
By you is it protected, O Goddess, and you always consume (it) at the end (of time).

1.57   At (its) emanation you have the form of creation; in (its) protection (you have) the form of steadiness;
Likewise at the end of this world (you have) the form of destruction, O you who consist of the world!

1.58   You are the great knowledge (*mahāvidyā*), the great illusion (*mahāmāyā*), the great insight (*mahāmedhā*), the great memory,
And the great delusion, the great Goddess (*mahādevī*), the great demoness (*mahāsurī*).

1.59   You are the primordial material (*prakṛti*) of everything, manifesting the triad of constituent strands,
The night of destruction, the great night, and the terrible night of delusion.

1.60   You are śrī,[1] you are the queen, you modesty, you intelligence, characterized by knowing;
Modesty, well-being, contentment, too, tranquility and forebearance are you.

1.61   Terrible with your sword and spear, likewise with cudgel and discus,

[1]Wealth, good luck, or fortune. [Ed.]

With conch and bow, having arrows, sling, and iron mace as weapons,

1.62   Gentle, more gentle than other gentle ones, exceedingly beautiful,
You are superior to the high and low, the supreme queen.

1.63   Whatever and wherever anything exists, whether it be real or unreal, O you who have everything as your very soul,
Of all that, you are the power (*śakti*); how then can you be adequately praised?

4.1   When the exceedingly brave (and) wicked (Mahiṣa)[2] and the army of the enemies of the gods were slain by the Goddess, throngs of gods, led by Indra,[3]
Praised her with their voices, their necks and shoulders bowed in reverence, their bodies made beautiful by shuddering in ecstacy.

4.2   "To the Goddess by whom this world was spread out through her own power, whose body is comprised of the powers of all the hosts of gods,
To Ambikā,[4] worthy of worship by all gods and great seers, are we bowed down in devotion; may she bring about auspicious things for us.

4.3   May she whose peerless splendor and might the blessed Viṣṇu, Brahmā, and Śiva cannot describe,[5]
May she, Caṇḍikā,[6] fix her mind on the protection of the entire world, and on the destruction of the fear of evil.

4.4   May she who is Śrī herself in the abodes of those who do good, Alakṣmī[7] (in the abodes) of those whose soul is wicked, intelligence in the hearts of the wise,
Faith (in the hearts) of the good, modesty (in the heart of) one of good birth, to you who are she are we bowed down: protect the universe, O Goddess!

4.5   How can we describe this unthinkable form of yours? Or your abundant, surpassing valor which destroys Asuras?[8]
Or such deeds as (you do) in battles among all the throngs of Asuras and gods, O Goddess?

4.6   (You are) the cause of all the worlds; although possessed of the three qualities (*guṇas*), by faults you are not known; (you are) unfathomable even by Hari, Hara, and the other gods.

---

[2]The buffalo demon that the Goddess has just defeated. [Ed.]
[3]The Vedic god of fire. [Ed.]
[4]Dear Mother. [Ed.]
[5]The three main Hindu gods. [Ed.]
[6]Another name for the Goddess. [Ed.]
[7]Bad fortune. [Ed.]
[8]Demons. [Ed.]

(You are) the resort of all, (you are) this entire world that is composed of parts, for you are the supreme, original, untransformed Prakṛti.[9]

4.7   By means of whose utterance, every deity attains satisfaction at all sacrifices, O Goddess,

You are Svāhā,[10] and, (as) the cause of satisfaction of the multitude of Manes, you are proclaimed by men to be Svadhā.[11]

4.8   You who are the cause of release and of inconceivable austerities, your name is repeated by sages, who hold the essence of truth because they have restrained their senses,

Intent upon *mokṣa*[12] with all faults shed: you are this blessed, supreme knowledge, O Goddess.

4.9   Having sound as your very soul, the resting-place of the utterly pure *Ṛg* and *Yajur* (hymns) and of the *Samans,* delightfully recited with the *Udgītha,*[13]

The Goddess (are you), the blessed triple (Veda), acting for the existence and production of all worlds, the supreme destroyer of pain.

4.10   O Goddess, you are insight, knowing the essence of all scripture, you are Durgā,[14] a vessel upon the ocean of life (that is so) hard to cross, devoid of attachments. . . .

4.11   Slightly smiling, spotless, like the orb of the full moon, as pleasing as the luster of the finest gold (is your face).

Wondrous it is that when the Asura Mahiṣa saw (this) face, he suddenly struck it, his anger aroused.

4.12   But, O Goddess, the fact that Mahiṣa, having seen (your face) angry, terrible with knitted brows, in hue like the rising moon, did not immediately

Give up his life is exceedingly wondrous — for who can live, having seen Death enraged?

4.13   O Goddess, may you, the supreme one, be gracious to life; enraged, you (can) destroy (whole) families in a trice.

This is now known, since the extensive power of the Asura Mahiṣa has been brought to an end.

4.14   Honored are they among nations, riches are theirs, honors are theirs, and their portion of *dharma* does not fail,

Fortunate are they, with devoted children, servants, and wives, on whom you, the gracious one, always bestow good fortune.

---

[9]Primordial material of which the universe is made. [Ed.]

[10]A ritual exclamation such as "Praise be!" [Ed.]

[11]Similar to Svāhā. [Ed.]

[12]A state of spiritual liberation. [Ed.]

[13]*Samans* and *Udgitha* are also Vedic hymns. [Ed.]

[14]Another name for the Goddess. [Ed.]

4.15   O Goddess, a virtuous man always attentively performs all righteous actions on a daily basis,

And then he goes to heaven by your grace: are you not thus the
bestower of rewards on the three worlds, O Goddess?

4.16   O Durgā, (when) called to mind, you take away fear from every
creature; (when) called to mind by the healthy, you bestow an exceedingly
pure mind.

O you who destroy poverty, misery, and fear, who other than you
is always tender-minded, in order to work benefits for all?

4.17   Since these (foes) are slain, the world attains happiness; although
they have committed (enough) sin to remain in hell for a long time,

It is with the thought—'Having met death in battle, may they go
to heaven'—that you assuredly slay (our) enemies, O Goddess.

4.18   Having, in fact, seen them, why do you not (immediately) reduce
all the Asuras to ashes, since you hurl your weapon at enemies?

'Let even enemies, purified by (my) weapons, attain (heavenly)
worlds'—such is your most gracious intent even toward those who are
hostile.

4.19   Although the eyes of the Asuras were not destroyed by the terrible
flashings of the light-mass of your sword, or by the abundant luster of
your spearpoint,

While they looked at your face, which was like a portion of the
radiant moon, that very thing happened (i.e., their eyes were destroyed).

4.20   Your disposition, O Goddess, calms the activity of evildoers, and
this incomprehensible form (of yours) is unequalled by others,

And (your) valor slays those who have robbed the gods of their
prowess: thus was compassion shown by you even towards enemies.

4.21   With what may this prowess of yours be compared? Where is there
(such a) form, exceedingly charming (yet) striking fear into enemies?

Compassion in mind and severity in battle are seen in you, O
Goddess, who bestow boons even upon the triple world.

4.22   This whole world was rescued by you, through the destruction
of (its) enemies; having slain (them) at the peak of battle,

The hosts of enemies were led to heaven by you, and our fear,
arising from the frenzied foes of the gods, was dispelled: Hail to you!

4.23   With (your) spear protect us, O Goddess! And with (your) sword
protect (us), O Ambikā!

Protect us with the sound of (your) bell, and with the twang of
your bowstring!

4.24   In the east protect (us) and in the west, O Candikā; protect (us)
in the south

By the wielding of your spear, likewise in the north, O queen.

4.25   With your gentle forms that roam about in the triple world,
And with the exceedingly terrible ones, protect us, and also the earth.

4.26   And with the weapons, O Ambikā, sword, and spear, and club,
and the rest,
Which lie in your sprout(-like) hands, protect (us) on every side."

20

BAN ZHAO

Lessons for Women

Just as the epic poem *The Ramayana* created ideals for men and women in India, the teachings of Confucius provided the Chinese and other Asian peoples with ideals of private and public conduct. Confucius' teachings emphasized the importance of filial piety, or the duty of children to serve and obey their parents, as well as to exercise restraint and treat others as one would like to be treated (see selection 25 for excerpts from Confucius' *Analects*). Ban Zhao (45–116 C.E.) was the leading female Confucian scholar of classical China. Born into a literary family and educated by her mother, she was married at the age of fourteen. After her husband's death she finished writing her brother's history of the Han dynasty and served as imperial historian to Emperor Han Hedi (r. 88–105 C.E.) and as an advisor to the Empress-Dowager Deng.

Ban Zhao is best remembered, however, for her *Lessons for Women,* which she wrote to fill a gap in Confucian literature. With their emphasis on the responsibilities of the son to the father and on the moral example of a good ruler, the writings of Confucius (561–479 B.C.E.) virtually ignored women. Ban Zhao sought to rectify that oversight by applying Confucian principles to the moral instruction of women. Although she states that the *Lessons* were intended for her own daughters, she clearly had a larger audience in mind. In what ways would Ban Zhao's *Lessons* support Chinese patriarchy? In what ways might they challenge the patriarchy or make it less oppressive for women? What similarities are there between the Confucian ideal of filial piety and the Hindu concept of *dharma?*

Pan Chao: Foremost Woman Scholar of China, trans. Nancy Lee Swann (New York: Century Co., 1932), 82–90.

Thinking Historically

This is one of the great classic Chinese texts, one that was read repeat-edly to generations of young women. Unlike many other Confucian texts, including those attributed to Confucius himself but of uncertain authorship, the author and time and circumstances of writing are clearly known. Therefore, we do not have to wonder, as we did with *The Ramayana,* whether women learned a different version of this text. We might still ask, however, what the text meant to them.

We cannot know how a Chinese woman of the Classical era would have responded to this text unless we know her expectations, and thus the degree to which the text departs from what she expected. To the modern ear, much of the text sounds unabashedly patriarchal. Why?

In the context of Chinese culture of the period, however, Ban Zhao might have been something of a feminist (as the author of the follow-ing selection argues). Try to find elements of this text that women of the Chinese classical age might have thought feminist. What other pri-mary sources would you like to have in order to understand how close Ban Zhao's *Lessons* were to the expectations of the time?

I, the unworthy writer, am unsophisticated, unenlightened, and by na-ture unintelligent, but I am fortunate both to have received not a little favor from my scholarly Father, and to have had a cultured mother and instructresses upon whom to rely for a literary education as well as for training in good manners. More than forty years have passed since at the age of fourteen I took up the dustpan and the broom in the Cao family.[1] During this time with trembling heart I feared constantly that I might disgrace my parents, and that I might multiply difficulties for both the women and the men of my husband's family. Day and night I was distressed in heart, but I labored without confessing weariness. Now and hereafter, however, I know how to escape from such fears.

Being careless, and by nature stupid, I taught and trained my chil-dren without system. Consequently I fear that my son Gu may bring disgrace upon the Imperial Dynasty by whose Holy Grace he has un-precedentedly received the extraordinary privilege of wearing the Gold and the Purple, a privilege for the attainment of which by my son, I a humble subject never even hoped. Nevertheless, now that he is a man and able to plan his own life, I need not again have concern for him. But I do grieve that you, my daughters, just now at the age for mar-riage, have not at this time had gradual training and advice; that you still have not learned the proper customs for married women. I fear that by failure in good manners in other families you will humiliate both your ancestors and your clan. I am now seriously ill, life is uncertain.

[1] Her husband's family. [Ed.]

As I have thought of you all in so untrained a state, I have been uneasy many a time for you. At hours of leisure I have composed . . . these instructions under the title, "Lessons for Women." In order that you may have something wherewith to benefit your persons, I wish every one of you, my daughters each to write out a copy for yourself.

From this time on every one of you strive to practice these lessons.

Humility

On the third day after the birth of a girl the ancients observed three customs: first to place the baby below the bed; second to give her a potsherd[2] with which to play; and third to announce her birth to her ancestors by an offering. Now to lay the baby below the bed plainly indicated that she is lowly and weak, and should regard it as her primary duty to humble herself before others. To give her potsherds with which to play indubitably signified that she should practice labor and consider it her primary duty to be industrious. To announce her birth before her ancestors clearly meant that she ought to esteem as her primary duty the continuation of the observance of worship in the home.

These three ancient customs epitomize woman's ordinary way of life and the teachings of the traditional ceremonial rites and regulations. Let a woman modestly yield to others; let her respect others; let her put others first, herself last. Should she do something good, let her not mention it; should she do something bad let her not deny it. Let her bear disgrace; let her even endure when others speak or do evil to her. Always let her seem to tremble and to fear. When a woman follows such maxims as these then she may be said to humble herself before others.

Let a woman retire late to bed, but rise early to duties; let her not dread tasks by day or by night. Let her not refuse to perform domestic duties whether easy or difficult. That which must be done, let her finish completely, tidily, and systematically. When a woman follows such rules as these, then she may be said to be industrious.

Let a woman be correct in manner and upright in character in order to serve her husband. Let her live in purity and quietness of spirit, and attend to her own affairs. Let her love not gossip and silly laughter. Let her cleanse and purify and arrange in order the wine and the food for the offerings to the ancestors. When a woman observes such principles as these, then she may be said to continue ancestral worship.

No woman who observes these three fundamentals of life has ever had a bad reputation or has fallen into disgrace. If a woman fails to observe them, how can her name be honored; how can she but bring disgrace upon herself?

[2]A piece of broken pottery. [Ed.]

Husband and Wife

The Way of husband and wife is intimately connected with Yin and Yang and relates the individual to gods and ancestors. Truly it is the great principle of Heaven and Earth, and the great basis of human relationships. Therefore the "Rites"[3] honor union of man and woman; and in the "Book of Poetry"[4] the "First Ode" manifests the principle of marriage. For these reasons the relationship cannot but be an important one.

If a husband be unworthy, then he possesses nothing by which to control his wife. If a wife be unworthy, then she possesses nothing with which to serve her husband. If a husband does not control his wife, then the rules of conduct manifesting his authority are abandoned and broken. If a wife does not serve her husband, then the proper relationship between men and women and the natural order of things are neglected and destroyed. As a matter of fact the purpose of these two[5] is the same.

Now examine the gentlemen of the present age. They only know that wives must be controlled, and that the husband's rules of conduct manifesting his authority must be established. They therefore teach their boys to read books and study histories. But they do not in the least understand that husbands and masters must also be served, and that the proper relationship and the rites should be maintained. Yet only to teach men and not to teach women—is that not ignoring the essential relation between them? According to the "Rites," it is the rule to begin to teach children to read at the age of eight years, and by the age of fifteen years they ought then to be ready for cultural training. Only why should it not be that girls' education as well as boys' be according to this principle?

Respect and Caution

As Yin and Yang are not of the same nature, so man and woman have different characteristics. The distinctive quality of the Yang is rigidity; the function of the Yin is yielding. Man is honored for strength; a woman is beautiful on account of her gentleness. Hence there arose the common saying: "A man though born like a wolf may, it is feared, become a weak monstrosity; a woman though born like a mouse may, it is feared, become a tiger."

Now for self-culture nothing equals respect for others. To counteract firmness nothing equals compliance. Consequently it can be said that the Way of respect and acquiescence is woman's most important

[3]*The Classic of Rites.* [Ed.]
[4]*The Classic of Odes.* [Ed.]
[5]The controlling of women by men, and the serving of men by women. [Ed.]

principle of conduct. So respect may be defined as nothing other than holding on to that which is permanent; and acquiescence nothing other than being liberal and generous. Those who are steadfast in devotion know that they should stay in their proper places; those who are liberal and generous esteem others, and honor and serve them.

If husband and wife have the habit of staying together, never leaving one another, and following each other around within the limited space of their own rooms, then they will lust after and take liberties with one another. From such action improper language will arise between the two. This kind of discussion may lead to licentiousness. But of licentiousness will be born a heart of disrespect to the husband. Such a result comes from not knowing that one should stay in one's proper place.

Furthermore, affairs may be either crooked or straight; words may be either right or wrong. Straightforwardness cannot but lead to quarreling; crookedness cannot but lead to accusation. If there are really accusations and quarrels, then undoubtedly there will be angry affairs. Such a result comes from not esteeming others, and not honoring and serving them.

If wives suppress not contempt for husbands, then it follows that such wives rebuke and scold their husbands. If husbands stop not short of anger, then they are certain to beat their wives. The correct relationship between husband and wife is based upon harmony and intimacy, and conjugal love is grounded in proper union. Should actual blows be dealt, how could matrimonial relationship be preserved? Should sharp words be spoken, how could conjugal love exist? If love and proper relationship both be destroyed, then husband and wife are divided.

Womanly Qualifications

A woman ought to have four qualifications: (1) womanly virtue; (2) womanly words; (3) womanly bearing; and (4) womanly work. Now what is called womanly virtue need not be brilliant ability, exceptionally different from others. Womanly words need be neither clever in debate nor keen in conversation. Womanly appearance requires neither a pretty nor a perfect face and form. Womanly work need not be work done more skillfully than that of others.

To guard carefully her chastity; to control circumspectly her behavior; in every motion to exhibit modesty; and to model each act on the best usage, this is womanly virtue.

To choose her words with care; to avoid vulgar language; to speak at appropriate times; and not to weary others with much conversation, may be called the characteristics of womanly words.

To wash and scrub filth away; to keep clothes and ornaments fresh and clean; to wash the head and bathe the body regularly, and to keep the person free from disgraceful filth, may be called the characteristics of womanly bearing.

With whole-hearted devotion to sew and to weave; to love not gossip and silly laughter; in cleanliness and order to prepare the wine and food for serving guests, may be called the characteristics of womanly work.

These four qualifications characterize the greatest virtue of a woman. No woman can afford to be without them. In fact they are very easy to possess if a woman only treasures them in her heart. The ancients had a saying: "Is love afar off? If I desire love, then love is at hand!" So can it be said of these qualifications.

Implicit Obedience

Whenever the mother-in-law says, "Do not do that," and if what she says is right, unquestionably the daughter-in-law obeys. Whenever the mother-in-law says, "Do that," even if what she says is wrong, still the daughter-in-law submits unfailingly to the command. Let a woman not act contrary to the wishes and the opinions of parents-in-law about right and wrong; let her not dispute with them what is straight and what is crooked. Such docility may be called obedience which sacrifices personal opinion. Therefore the ancient book, "A Pattern for Women," says: "If a daughter-in-law who follows the wishes of her parents-in-law is like an echo and shadow, how could she not be praised?"

21

ROXANN PRAZNIAK

Ban Zhao and the End of Chinese Feudalism

In the following essay, Roxann Prazniak, a modern historian of China, argues that Ban Zhao's work was actually a feminist departure from the increasingly patriarchal practices of the Chinese Classical era. Prazniak contends that Ban Zhao subverted the patriarchal bias of Confucianism by stressing the husband/wife relationship at the

Roxann Prazniak, *Dialogues across Civilizations* (Boulder: Westview Press, 1996), 32–33, 37–39, 40–41, 43–44.

expense of the father/son bond. By Prazniak's account, Chinese feudalism (before the unification of the Chinese state in 221 B.C.E.) allowed women from powerful families and clans a considerable range of authority. But as China became unified into a territorial state, and then an empire under the Han dynasty, relationships between male subjects, as heads of patriarchal families, took precedence over clan and tribal ties. The teachings of Confucius became official state policy, Prazniak suggests, because they served the interests of the new world of male officials and subjects. What do you think of her argument?

Thinking Historically

If Prazniak is correct, then Ban Zhao was actually undermining the classic Confucian texts at the same time she pretended to invoke and apply them. Why might she have done this? What might have been the results? In our own day, some people invoke classic texts for conservative purposes. But can you think of a case in which an individual or group uses a classic text for its conservative authority while interpreting it in a way that will bring change from the old ways? Do people invoke the Bible or "the founding fathers" to return to older ways or to bring about the changes they desire?

In Early Han China the rulers of the newly established dynastic order sought to transform the territories and leaders of the former feudal states into a unified administration in which political authority would be achieved not by birthright but by a civil service examination system. The state ideology deriving from Kong Zi's[1] political philosophy was recognized at this time as a viable set of principles around which to restructure society beyond feudalism. Under central government auspices the classics of the Zhou period (*The Book of Changes, The Book of Songs, The Book of History, The Book of Rites, The Spring and Autumn Annals*) were edited and compiled with commentaries to constitute orthodox classical scholarship, which would gradually become the basis for the examination system and entry into political office. Although the definition of proper male/female relations varied, sometimes significantly in tone, from one period, region, and social class to another, the patriarchal framework was evident from the Zhou period (1122–256 B.C.E.) forward. *The Book of Rites* stipulated that "the observance of propriety commenced with a careful attention to the relations between husband and wife. They built the mansion and its apart-

---

[1]Kong Zi, meaning Master Kong, or Konfuzi, was Latinized as Confucius by Christian missionaries long after his death.

ments, distinguishing between exterior and interior parts. The men occupied the exterior; the women the interior. The mansion was deep, and the doors were strong, guarded by porter and gateman. The men did not enter the interior; the women did not come out into the exterior."

The Book of Songs, which mentioned women and their social roles in a generally positive tone, also emphasized this separation of spheres:

> Our lord's lady hard at work
> Sees to the dishes, so many,
> Needed for guests, for strangers.
> Healths and pledges go the round,
> Every custom and rite is observed,
> Every smile, every word is in place.

Women were to be responsible for preparing food that was central to ceremonial gatherings and, of course, for bringing sons and grandsons into the family. In contrast to the frequent presence of women in *The Book of Songs,* the *Analects* attributed to Kong Zi contained only a rare reference to social norms regarding women, and it was the *Analects* that increasingly became an interpretive guide to the classical texts. Through social practice, adherence to the more restrictive aspects of women's subordination within the family and political life became the means by which women found security. Common wisdom increasingly held that women followed their fathers before marriage, their husbands after marriage, and the sons in widowhood. . . .

Of the five relationships that structured social life (ruler/subject, father/son, elder brother/younger brother, husband/wife, and friend/friend), the only one involving women was the relationship of husband to wife. Among the family relationships, it was the only one not based on blood ties. Mother/son, mother/daughter, and father/daughter were among the blood relations devalued by omission. Ban Zhao wrote at a time when feudal family relations still allowed greater freedom of mobility and choice of activities to women than would progressively be the case under Chinese social practice. The feudal principle of status by birthright could elevate the status of women in a way that the five relationships could not. A princess, for example, could have superior status to her husband and his family. "Because a princess was superior in status to her husband and his family members, there was a tendency to reverse the usual pattern of wife-subordinate-to-husband. Hsun Shuang complained about this, saying in a memorial that the domination of a princess over her husband was contrary to the universal principle of *yin-yang.*"

The family relationship most stressed by the emerging state ideology based on principles attributed to Kong Zi was the father/son bond. Ban Zhao obliquely challenged this ranking when she argued that "The

Way of husband and wife is intimately connected with *Yin* and *Yang,* and relates the individual to gods and ancestors. Truly it is the great principle of Heaven and Earth, and the great basis of human relationships." In effect Ban implicitly elevated the husband/wife relationship above the others. In doing so, she gave more importance to the woman's role in society since all other specified relations excluded women. Neither Kong Zi's philosophy nor Chinese social practice in the course of its evolution intended such a subversive reading of the classical texts. To the extent that Ban's work was upheld as a standard for women, this reading was itself subverted.

Ban also specified the nature of the marriage bond:

> The correct relationship between husband and wife is based upon harmony and intimacy, and (conjugal) love is grounded in proper union. Should actual blows be dealt, how could matrimonial relationship be preserved? Should sharp words be spoken, how could (conjugal) love exist? If love and proper relationship both be destroyed, then husband and wife are divided.

Ban Zhao's emphasis on love and intimacy underlined the primacy of the husband/wife relationship. In Ban Zhao's view a woman sought the love of her parents-in-law through proper conduct in order to gain the love of her husband. The intimate relationship with the husband was the core of the woman's life. Ban Zhao quoted an ancient text to this effect: " 'To obtain the love of one man is the crown of a woman's life; to lose the love of one man is to miss the aim in woman's life.' For these reasons a woman cannot but seek to win her husband's heart."

It was through the role of wife, not mother or daughter-in-law, that Ban Zhao defined a woman's highest virtue. Tension among these female roles remained characteristic of Chinese family life. Contrary to Ban's suggestion, Chinese social practice evolved to empower the role of the mother-in-law. Increasingly, the dominant pattern would be for the son's mother to intercede between husband and wife at cost to the marriage bond. Within the extended Chinese family, it became most common for female authority within the family to reside in the mother-in-law's generation rather than the daughter's. Ban Zhao argued for the kind of female status that came from a mutually respectful relationship with the husband. The worthiness of the husband and wife as individuals was evident, according to Ban Zhao, not so much in the husband's ability to establish authority over his wife but in his ability to allow his wife to serve him. Here Ban Zhao was critical of the men of her times:

> Now examine the gentlemen of the present age. They only know that wives must be controlled, and that the husband's rules of conduct manifesting his authority must be established. They therefore teach their boys to read books and (study) histories. But they do not in the

least understand that husbands and masters must (also) be served, and the proper relationship and the rites should be maintained.

The proper relationship between husband and wife was not simply male domination and female subservience but the refinement and ritual of serving and being served—an interaction of mutual spiritual nourishment in which the female was actor and the male was appreciatively understanding of the wife's efforts. In matters beyond the family circle, Ban envisioned women as public figures. "When *she goes outside her own home,* let her not be conspicuous in dress and manners." A woman should not attract attention to herself, according to Ban, but contrary to the confinement of upper-class women in families that aspired to scholar-bureaucratic status after the Song dynasty (960–1279), Ban's guidelines for women did not encourage female seclusion. They also did not propose that women become scholars or public leaders. . . .

Attitudes toward Education: Women and Reason

According to the writings of Ban Zhao . . . women should be educated to cultivate their qualities of intelligence, moderation, and gentleness. Ban Zhao argued forthrightly for equal treatment of boys and girls in education. This is one of the most far reaching critiques in her *Lessons for Women:*

> Yet only to teach men and not to teach women,—is that not ignoring the essential relation between them? According to the "Rites," it is the rule to begin to teach children to read at the age of eight years, and by the age of fifteen years they ought then to be ready for cultural training. Only why should it not be (that girls' education as well as boys' be) according to this principle?

Even though some scholarly families had the luxury to educate a talented daughter, equal educational opportunity for boys and girls never became a social principle, and daughters were never allowed formally to participate in public life. Although a popular saying from the Ming dynasty (1368–1644) held that "lack of talent is a virtue in women," throughout most of China's history some degree of women's education, especially in the upper classes, was deemed valuable for social and family purposes. An educated daughter and wife was an asset to a household that prided itself on a genteel status. In fact, Ban Zhao's *Lessons for Women* was a part of a discourse on women's education that continued throughout the evolution of Chinese society and the accompanying shifts in social relations in general and women's roles in particular. On the subject of the basic qualities to which women should be educated, Ban Zhao wrote:

Man is honored for strength; a woman is beautiful on account of her gentleness. . . . The Way of respect and acquiescence is woman's most important principle of conduct. So respect may be defined as nothing other than holding on to that which is permanent; and acquiescence nothing other than being liberal and generous. Those who are steadfast in devotion know that they should stay in their proper places; those who are liberal and generous esteem others, and honor and serve (them).

$$\boxed{22}$$

LIVY

Women Demonstrate against the Oppian Law

In 215 B.C.E., after suffering a disastrous defeat by Hannibal of Carthage in the Second Punic War, Rome desperately needed to raise money to replenish its armies. Roman citizens met the emergency with various taxes and sacrifices. Among these was the Oppian law, which prohibited women from buying certain luxury goods and limited the amount of gold they could possess, passing the remainder on to the state. Because so many men had been killed in battle, wives and daughters had acquired unprecedented wealth through inheritance, which is why the law specifically targeted women. The state also wanted to ensure that women did not engage in ostentatious displays of wealth during this grim time.

Twenty years later, the crisis a dim memory, Roman women demonstrated to bring an end to the Oppian law. The moment of confrontation in 195 B.C.E. offers a window into gender relations in the Roman republic. Livy (64 or 59 B.C.E.–17 C.E.), a Roman historian writing at the beginning of the first century C.E., provides us with the following account of the women's protest. What does the debate tell you about the relative power and position of women in this period? Do the women seem to be more or less powerful than the women of classical India or China? Do you think the repeal of the Oppian law was a step toward women's liberation in Rome?

Maureen B. Fant, trans., in Mary R. Lefkowitz and Maureen B. Fant, *Women's Lives in Greece and Rome,* 2nd ed. (Baltimore: The Johns Hopkins Press, 1982), 143–47.

Thinking Historically

Livy was writing about events almost two hundred years before his time, so although we read him as a primary source from ancient Rome, he was a secondary source in his own age. Inevitably the concerns of his age—civil war, the rise and fall of Julius Caesar, the ascendancy of Caesar's nephew Octavian as Emperor Augustus, and replacement of the republic by the empire—colored his view of history. Livy is said to have been apolitical but nostalgic for the republic, which he thought to be an age of greater morality and social cohesion. Do you see any signs of such an attitude here? Do you think Livy's sympathies were with the supporters or opponents of the Oppian law?

We do not know Livy's sources for the speeches of Cato and Lucius Valerius, but the speeches may have been drawn from earlier histories including Cato's own *Origines*. Notice how these two speakers, Cato the conservative and Valerius the reformer, treat their own classical past. Which speaker presents the Oppian law as a classic? Which argues that the Oppian law is a departure from traditional practice? Which sees the women's demonstration as a shocking breakdown of the traditional moral order? Which sees women's political participation as part of a long tradition of republican Rome? How do these attitudes toward the past bolster the speakers' arguments? How is Valerius's treatment of the past like Ban Zhao's in her *Lessons for Women*?

Among the troubles of great wars, either scarcely over or yet to come, something intervened which, while it can be told briefly, stirred up enough excitement to become a great battle. Marcus Fundanius and Lucius Valerius, the tribunes of the people, brought a motion to repeal the Oppian law before the people. Gaius Oppius had carried this law as tribune at the height of the Punic War, during the consulship of Quintus Fabius and Tiberius Sempronius. The law said that no woman might own more than half an ounce of gold nor wear a multicoloured dress nor ride in a carriage in the city or in a town within a mile of it, unless there was a religious festival. The tribunes, Marcus and Publius Junius Brutus, were in favour of the Oppian law and said that they would not allow its repeal. Many noble men came forward hoping to persuade or dissuade them; a crowd of men, both supporters and opponents, filled the Capitoline Hill. The matrons, whom neither counsel nor shame nor their husbands' orders could keep at home, blockaded every street in the city and every entrance to the Forum. As the men came down to the Forum, the matrons besought them to let them, too, have back the luxuries they had enjoyed before, giving as their reason that the republic was thriving and that everyone's private wealth was increasing with every day. This crowd of women was growing daily, for now they were even gathering from the towns and villages. Before long they dared go up and solicit the consuls, praetors, and other magistrates; but one of the consuls could not be moved in the least, Marcus Porcius Cato, who spoke in favour of the law:

"If each man of us, fellow citizens, had established that the right and authority of the husband should be held over the mother of his own family, we should have less difficulty with women in general; now, at home our freedom is conquered by female fury, here in the Forum it is bruised and trampled upon, and, because we have not contained the individuals, we fear the lot . . .

"Indeed, I blushed when, a short while ago, I walked through the midst of a band of women. Had not respect for the dignity and modesty of certain ones (not them all!) restrained me (so they would not be seen being scolded by a consul), I should have said, "What kind of behaviour is this? Running around in public, blocking streets, and speaking to other women's husbands! Could you not have asked your own husbands the same thing at home? Are you more charming in public with others' husbands than at home with your own? And yet, it is not fitting even at home (if modesty were to keep married women within the bounds of their rights) for you to concern yourselves with what laws are passed or repealed here." Our ancestors did not want women to conduct any—not even private—business without a guardian; they wanted them to be under the authority of parents, brothers, or husbands; we (the gods help us!) even now let them snatch at the government and meddle in the Forum and our assemblies. What are they doing now on the streets and crossroads, if they are not persuading the tribunes to vote for repeal? Give the reins to their unbridled nature and this unmastered creature, and hope that they will put limits on their own freedom; unless you do something yourselves, this is the least of the things imposed upon them either by custom or by law which they endure with hurt feelings. They want freedom, nay licence (if we are to speak the truth), in all things.

"If they are victorious now, what will they not attempt? . . . As soon as they begin to be your equals, they will have become your superiors . . .

"What honest excuse is offered, pray, for this womanish rebellion? 'That we might shine with gold and purple,' says one of them, 'that we might ride through the city in coaches on holidays and working-days, as though triumphant over the conquered law and the votes which we captured by tearing them from you; that there should be no limit to our expenses and our luxury.' . . .

"The woman who can spend her own money will do so; the one who cannot will ask her husband. Pity that husband—the one who gives in and the one who stands firm! What he refuses, he will see given by another man. Now they publicly solicit other women's husbands, and, what is worse, they ask for a law and votes, and certain men give them what they want. You there, you, are easily moved about things which concern yourself, your estate, and your children; once the law no longer limits your wife's spending, you will never do it by yourself. Fellow citizens, do not imagine that the state which existed before the law was passed will return. A dishonest man is safer never accused than acquitted, and luxury, left alone, would have been more acceptable than it will be now, as when wild animals are first chafed by their chains and then released. I vote that the Oppian law should not, in the smallest measure, be repealed; whatever course you take, may all the gods make you happy with it."

After this, when the tribunes of the people, who had declared that they would oppose the motion to repeal, had added a few remarks along the same lines, Lucius Valerius spoke on behalf of the motion which he himself had brought:

"[Cato] used up more words castigating the women than he did opposing the motion, and he left in some uncertainty whether the women had done the deeds which he reproached on their own or at our instigation. I shall defend the motion, not ourselves, against whom the consul has hurled this charge, more for the words than for the reality of the accusation. He has called this assemblage 'secession' and sometimes 'womanish rebellion,' because the matrons have publicly asked you, in peacetime when the state is happy and prosperous, to repeal a law passed against them during the straits of war . . .

"What, may I ask, are the women doing that is new, having gathered and come forth publicly in a case which concerns them directly? Have they never appeared in public before this? Allow me to unroll your own *Origines* before you. Listen to how often they have done so—always for the public good. From the very beginning—the reign of Romulus—when the Capitoline had been taken by the Sabines and there was fighting in the middle of the Forum, was not the battle halted by the women's intervention between the two lines? How about this? After the kings had been expelled, when the Volscian legions and their general, Marcius Coriolanus, had pitched camp at the fifth milestone, did not the matrons turn away the forces which would have buried the city? When Rome was in the hands of the Gauls, who ransomed it? Indeed the matrons agreed unanimously to turn their gold over to the public need. Not to go too far back in history, in the most recent war, when we needed funds, did not the widows' money assist the treasury? And when new gods were summoned to bring their power to our difficulties, was it not all the matrons who went to the sea to meet the Idaean Mother? You say these cases are different. I am not here to say they are the same; it is enough to prove that nothing new has been done. Indeed, as no one is amazed that they acted in situations affecting men and women alike, why should we wonder that they have taken action in a case which concerns themselves? What, after all, have they done? We have proud ears indeed, if, while masters do not scorn the appeals of slaves, we are angry when honourable women ask something of us . . .

"Who then does not know that this is a recent law, passed twenty years ago? Since our matrons lived for so long by the highest standards of behaviour without any law, what risk is there that, once it is repealed, they will yield to luxury? For if the law were an old one, or if it had been passed to restrain feminine licence, there might be reason to fear that repeal would incite them. The times themselves will show you why the law was passed. Hannibal was in Italy, victorious at Cannae. Already he held Tarentum, Arpi, and Capua. He seemed on the verge of moving against Rome. Our allies had gone over to him. We had no reserve troops, no allies at sea to protect the fleet, no funds in the treasury. Slaves were being bought and armed, on condition that the price be paid their owners when the war was over. The contractors had declared that they would provide, on that same day of payment (after the war), the grain and other supplies the needs of war demanded. We were giving our slaves as rowers at our own expense, in proportion to our property rating. We were giving all our gold and silver for public use, as the senators had done first. Widows and children were donating their funds to the treasury. We were ordered to keep at home no more than a certain amount of wrought and stamped gold and silver. At a time like that were the matrons so taken up with luxury and fancy trappings that the Oppian law was needed to restrain them, when, since the rites of Ceres had been suspended because all the women were in mourning, the senate ordered mourning limited to thirty days? To whom is it not clear that poverty and misfortune were the authors of that law of yours, since all private wealth had to be turned over to public use, and that it was to remain in effect only as long as the reason for its writing did? . . .

"Shall it be our wives alone to whom the fruits of peace and tranquility of the state do not come? . . . Shall we forbid only women to wear purple? When you, a man, may use purple on your clothes, will you not allow the mother of your family to have a purple cloak, and will your horse be more beautifully saddled than your wife is garbed? . . .

"[Cato] has said that, if none of them had anything, there would be no rivalry among individual women. By Hercules! All are unhappy and indignant when they see the finery denied them permitted to the wives of the Latin allies, when they see them adorned with gold and purple, when those other women ride through the city and they follow on foot, as though the power belonged to the other women's cities, not to their own. This could wound the spirits of men; what do you think it could do to the spirits of women, whom even little things disturb? They cannot partake of magistracies, priesthoods, triumphs, badges of office, gifts, or spoils of war; elegance, finery and beautiful clothes are women's badges, in these they find joy and take pride, this our forebears called the women's world. When they are in mourning, what, other than purple and gold, do they take off? What do they put on again when they have completed the period of mourning? What do they add for public prayer and thanksgiving other than still greater ornament? Of course, if you repeal the Oppian law, you will not have the power to prohibit that which the law now forbids; daughters, wives, even some men's sisters will be less under your authority—never, while her men are well, is a woman's slavery cast off; and even they hate the freedom created by widowhood and orphanage. They prefer their adornment to be subject to your judgment, not the law's; and you ought to hold them in marital power and guardianship, not slavery; you should prefer to be called fathers and husbands to masters. The consul just now used odious terms when he said 'womanish rebellion' and 'secession.' For there is danger—he would have us believe—that they will seize the Sacred Hill as once the angry plebeians did, or the Aventine. It is for the weaker sex to submit to whatever you advise. The more power you possess, all the more moderately should you exercise your authority."

When these speeches for and against the law had been made, a considerably larger crowd of women poured forth in public the next day; as a single body they besieged the doors of the Brutuses, who were vetoing their colleagues' motion, and they did not stop until the tribunes took back their veto. After that there was no doubt but that all the tribes would repeal the law. Twenty years after it was passed, the law was repealed.

┌─────┐
│ 23 │
└─────┘

J. P. V. D. BALSDON

From *Roman Women*

J. P. V. D. Balsdon (1901–1977) was one of the great Roman historians of the twentieth century. In this selection from his book *Roman Women,* he placed the repeal of the Oppian law in the larger context of the changing status of Roman women. Balsdon argues that Roman women became freer and more powerful over the life of the Roman republic. When does Balsdon think these changes occurred? What

J. P. V. D. Balsdon, *Roman Women: Their History and Habits* (New York: Barnes and Noble, 1962), 32–37, 45–47.

sources does he point to as evidence of such changes? What do Roman complaints about morality have to do with the changing status of women? How did the role of women in the Roman republic differ from the role of women in classical India or China?

Thinking Historically

Notice how Balsdon uses Livy's history as a classic primary source for his history of the debate over the repeal of the Oppian law. If you were using Livy's history as a primary source, what parts would you quote to show the debate between Cato and Valerius? What accounts for the difference between your choices and Balsdon's? Instead of quoting Livy, write a few paragraphs that summarize the debate. When do direct quotes make better history than summaries?

From 200 B.C.E. onwards the history of current events was being written by contemporary Roman historians; and though their works have not survived, they were available to Livy and other writers whose books we ourselves can read. At last our feet are — very nearly — on firm ground.

Among the historians who wrote towards the middle of the second century B.C.E. and whose work has perished, was that self-confident and boorish embodiment of austere moral rectitude, the elder Cato. It was his view, and the view of other Roman historians too, that they lived in a period of increasing moral decline. Opinions differed only as to the moment at which the rot set in. Some traced its origins to the relief and relaxation which followed the defeat of Hannibal in 202 B.C.E., the end of the anxious years of the second Punic war. Others thought the defeat of Macedon in the third Macedonian war at the battle of Pydna in 168 to be the critical moment, since the victorious armies on their return infected Roman Italy with a taste for the art and civilized luxury of the Greek-speaking world. Others were to think that 146 was the vital date, for then Carthage was utterly destroyed and Rome was left without a rival in the Mediterranean world whose power she needed any longer to fear.

The increasing emancipation and self-assertion of women was symptomatic, and in 195 B.C.E. a tremendous issue was made in the Senate of the repeal of the Oppian law. Passed twenty years earlier under the critical stress of war, it appeared to women and to those who shared their views to have lost its *raison d'être*. Women even went as far as to behave like early twentieth-century suffragettes — to demonstrate publicly in the streets at the time of the debate. This in itself was enough to persuade the recalcitrant Cato, consul in this year, to believe that, as a matter of principle, a firm stand should be made. He was the man who once said bitterly, "All men rule their wives, we rule all men—and who rules us? Our wives." Livy gives the text of the long and pompous speech which he made.

Cato's History (*Origines*) included the period of his own career and in it he is known to have inserted the texts of his own public speeches; so, as Cato's History was used by the historians on whom Livy depended, and indeed read by Livy himself, it might be hoped that in Livy we could read the speech which Cato actually made in the Senate in 195 [B.C.E.]; and scholars of repute have argued that this is indeed the case. On the whole, however, the view prevails that this is not a genuine speech, but is the invention either of Livy or of the historian (probably Valerius Antias) on whom he depended. But if it is fiction, it is good fiction, for the speech is one which, however deplorably, Cato would have been happy to have composed. So, with a few adaptations, would many an eminent Victorian. . . .

For good or ill, the liberal view prevailed. Valerius Maximus, writing more than two centuries later at the time of the emperor Tiberius, looked back on this as a black day in the history of Rome: "The end of the second Punic war . . . encouraged a looser way of living—when married women did not shrink from blockading the tribunes M. and P. Junius Grutus in their houses because they were prepared to veto the abrogation of the Oppian law. . . . They succeeded, and the law which had been continuously effective for twenty years was rescinded. This was because the men of the period had no conception of the extravagance to which women's indomitable passion for novelty in fashion would lead or of the extremes to which their brazenness would go, once it had succeeded in trampling on the laws. Had they been able to foresee the sort of fashions which would appeal to women, hardly a day passing without the invention of some further expensive novelty, they would have set their faces firmly against the devastating spread of extravagance at the moment of its introduction. But why speak of women? Lacking strong mental powers and being denied the opportunity of more serious interests, they are naturally driven to concentrate their attention on creating more and more startling effects in their appearance. What of men? . . . "

At no time did Roman women live in the semi-oriental seclusion in which women lived in Greece. The wife was mistress of the household—*materfamilias domina;* and shared with her husband responsibility for the supervision of the religious cult of the family. In early Rome, if she was loving and obedient to her husband, a good Hausfrau and an attentive mother, she led by Roman standards—as by the later standards of the Victorian age—a full and complete life. She had no legal personality. As a girl she had lived in absolute subjection to her father; as a married woman she lived in absolute subjection to her husband, as inseparably bound to him as his own daughter. Women should have been blissfully contented with their lot: so the elder Cato and his like would have assured you.

That they were not all content is clear from the fact that by the third century B.C.E. the old forms of marriage which bound them in subjection to their husbands had generally given place to a free form of marriage in which the wife remained in the power of her father, and after she was twenty-five years old, subject only to formal supervision by her guardian (*tutor*), she retained possession of her own property and was able with no trouble at all to free herself by divorce from her husband. The period in which the change occurred is one on which, in a matter of this sort, we have next to no evidence at all. By the last fifty years of the Republic, when we have plenty of contemporary evidence—for good or ill—in the smart, corrupt society of Rome itself, the New Woman has arrived. Her interests lie outside the four walls of her home. In politics she is a power in her own right. She is, perhaps, the center of notorious public scandal. She may have no more sinister ambition than to escape from domesticity into the world of cultured and clever Bohemianism. Or she may wish nothing more than to share her husband's—or her son's—public interests and to help him in his public career.

At the same time—subject, of course, to the greater independence which they enjoyed under the system of free marriage—the majority of married women even in the higher social class were probably still contented—or forced to content themselves—with the duties and responsibilities of domestic life. This was certainly true of society in the country towns of Italy; and it was true, too, of many a woman whose husband played a prominent part in politics in Rome. More than nine hundred of Cicero's letters survive, including twenty-four to his wife Terentia, but there is nothing in them to suggest that she shared his literary or political confidences; she evidently tolerated him for the egotist that he was and, until in the end he became obsessed with the idea that she was stealing his money and he divorced her, she kept a home for him. Her cross-grained sister-in-law, difficult wife of a difficult husband (Cicero's brother Quintus) nursed her grievances or, more often, embarrassed other people by expressing them; but the marriage survived more than twenty years before breaking up.

When the Greek historian Polybius lived in Rome in the middle of the second century B.C.E., among all the dignified formalities of public life, few ceremonies impressed him more strongly than the ceremonial of a statesman's funeral, the parading of the death-masks of his distinguished ancestors, and the funeral oration in which his public achievement was commemorated. It would probably have surprised him greatly to know that within half a century it would be conceded that a woman might be entitled, on her death, to such public recognition. It was in 102 B.C.E. that the first public funeral oration was pronounced in honour of a woman. This was spoken by the consul Q. Lutatius Catulus, in memory of his mother Popilia. The precedent was followed and in the last period of the Republic more than one distinguished woman was publicly honoured at her death. The most famous speech of all was that delivered in honour of Julia, the widow of Marius, by her nephew Julius Caesar, in 68 B.C.E. It started in this remarkable fashion: "My aunt Julia was descended on her mother's side from Kings, on her father's from Gods. Her mother was a Marcia, and the Marcii Reges go back to Ancus Marcius; our own family, the Julii, traces its descent from Venus. She combined, therefore, the sanctity of Kings and the holiness of Gods, who have Kings for their servants."

We can be certain that if, instead of invading Britain in 54 B.C.E., Caesar had been in Rome when his mother Aurelia died, he would have delivered an even more remarkable oration in her memory. For his father had died when he was young, and she had played a notable part in her son's upbringing, and was closely attached to him as he laid the foundations of his career.

REFLECTIONS

Twenty-five years ago the historian Joan Kelly ignited the study of women's history with an essay that asked: "Was there a Renaissance for women?" Questioning whether the great eras in men's history were also great eras for women, she found that men's achievements often came at the expense of women. We have seen how the urban revolution fit this pattern. The rise of cities, the creation of territorial states, the invention of writing, and the development of complex societies, all beginning about 5,000 years ago, accompanied the development of patriarchal institutions and ideas. Similarly, the rise of classical cultures, cities, and states about 2,500 years ago seems to have cemented patriarchy. Our study of the transition from feudalism to state society in China and the suppression of women in early Greco-Roman city-states supports the idea that patriarchy gained strength in the beginning of the classical age. But did it continue unabated? Was it universal? J. P. V. D. Balsdon argued that the later Roman republic was less patriarchal than the early republic. Other historians have concurred and found the Roman Empire even less restrictive for women than its republican predecessor. To see whether a similar process occurred in India and China, you might want to contrast the Former Han period (206 B.C.E.–25 C.E.) with the Later Han (25–220 C.E.) in China, the Mauryan era (321–183 B.C.E.) with the Gupta period (320–550 C.E.) in India.

Different cultures, classical or otherwise, do not develop in lockstep with each other, however. In addition to underlining the strengthening of patriarchy, our comparisons in this chapter suggest differences and variations between and within cultures. Understanding the ways in which processes like state building have subjugated women in general is useful, but it is also important to recognize the variations and contradictions that might exist as we examine one culture or compare two cultures. Our selection from the *Devi-Mahatmya* is an example of a classic text celebrating female power that evolved in a patriarchal society — a striking contradiction.

Women's lives varied considerably in the classical world. Roman and Greek women were affected differently by the rise of the state. The establishment of civil society in fifth-century Greece certainly undermined the power of familial clans and tribes, and with them the prestige and power of well-connected women. Most city-states confined women to the domestic sphere while male citizens controlled the public business of government. Nevertheless, the women of Sparta were less cloistered than the women of Athens, and the women of Rome enjoyed greater use of the public outdoors than most of their Greek sisters. And, as Balsdon reminds us, Romans could place even the highest civic honors at the feet of their wives, mothers, and aunts.

Empire and Officialdom: Bureaucracy, Law, and Individuality

China and Rome, 300 B.C.E.–300 C.E.

HISTORICAL CONTEXT

Between 200 B.C.E. and 200 C.E., both China and Rome conquered expansive territories that made them the two leading empires of the world. China was unified by the Qin (Ch'in) dynasty, from which its name derives, around 221 B.C.E. Its successor, the Han dynasty (202 B.C.E.–220 C.E.) expanded China's boundaries almost to the point where they are today (see Map 5.1). Similarly, between 264 B.C.E. and 117 C.E. Rome expanded from a modest territory that included most of modern Italy to one that spanned across almost all of Europe: England and Portugal to the west, Western Asia from Turkey to Iran, and the entire region surrounding the Mediterranean Sea, including North Africa and Egypt (see Map 5.2). In this four-hundred-year period each of these empires controlled between one and a half and two million square miles and about sixty million people.

To control such large areas, the Chinese and Romans adopted practices that were in some ways similar and in other ways quite different. Chinese governance was more centralized and more bureaucratic than Roman. Chinese bureaucracy meant even-handed, professional administration as well as red tape. Roman rule relied more on law, the army, and private regional administrators who sometimes were more intent on personal gain than justice.

Empires are steamrollers: They crush idiosyncrasy. In governing extensive territories and millions of people, bureaucratic and legal considerations often outweigh individual needs. Empires need standard measures, uniform decisions, predictable outcomes, and individual compliance. At

139

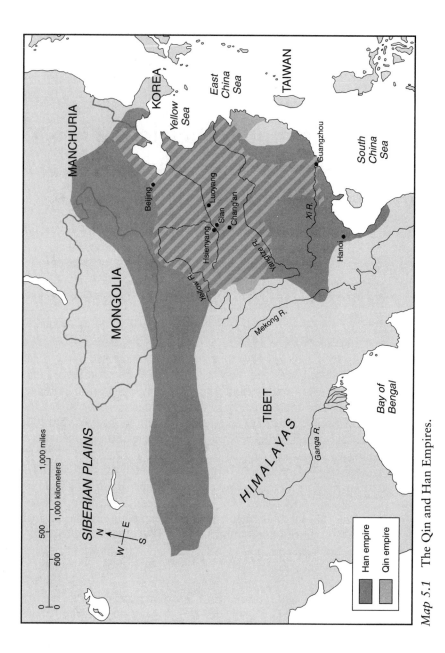

Map 5.1 The Qin and Han Empires.

140

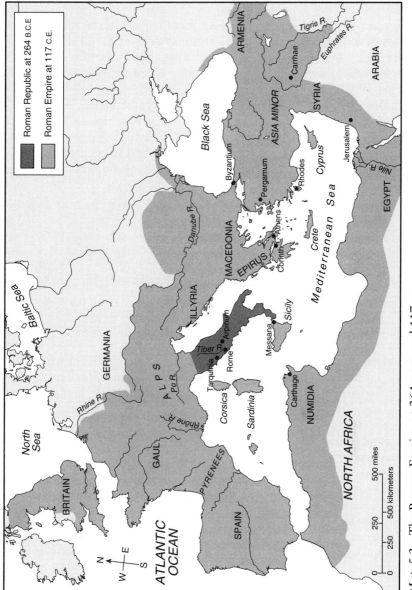

Map 5.2 The Roman Empire, at 264 B.C.E. and 117 C.E.

the same time, large numbers of people can prosper under a government that keeps the peace or makes decisions that are responsible, reliable, and fair. Some individuals have lives or fortunes enhanced by the forces an empire can command—for example, a merchant who can transport goods unmolested over thousands of miles, a provincial governor who rules with the backing of an emperor-god.

In this chapter, we compare Chinese and Roman styles of imperial rule. We ask how each style affected the way in which officials governed and the experiences of people under their rule. We try to understand both the ideals and realities of Chinese and Roman administration: what they hoped to accomplish and what they did accomplish.

THINKING HISTORICALLY
Relating the Individual and History

People have long debated the role of the individual in history. To what extent are historical events shaped by particular individuals? To what extent are individuals shaped by historical forces? Although these are philosophical questions that are not easy to resolve, they are also questions that create practical problems for readers and writers of history. In trying to understand such enormous historical phenomena as the ancient Chinese and Roman empires, how much attention should we pay to the lives, thoughts, and actions of individuals? Surely some individuals—emperors, at least—deserve more attention than others. But how about advisors, especially the grand theorists and philosophers who influenced emperors and others? And how about the people on the ground—the actual administrators of the emperor's imperial policy? And what about the average people: the soldiers, merchants, and farmers? If they are not important in their individuality, they are certainly important as examples of types or classes of people, and we must read individual histories—even their letters and autobiographies—to understand them.

In addition, the contrast we have already suggested between the Chinese and Roman empires calls for another distinction. Is the study of individuals more valuable or necessary in understanding some societies rather than others? If, for instance, the Chinese emperor was more powerful than the Roman emperor, does a biography of the Chinese emperor tell us more about China than a biography of the Roman emperor would tell us about Rome? These are some of the questions we raise in this chapter.

VALERIE HANSEN

The Creation of the Chinese Empire

Hansen, a modern historian of China, explains how the king of Qin province first unified the various states of China into an empire in 221 B.C.E., and how the Han dynasty, which ruled from 202 B.C.E. to 220 C.E., then reformed that empire. As she explains, the military conquest of the other warring states was only the first step in the creation of an empire. By what means was the ruler of Qin able to create a single China? How did the Han dynasty establish its rule over rival royal and noble families? Why was the undermining of noble families so important? What sorts of farmers and soldiers did both Qin and Han emperors seek to create?

Thinking Historically

Hansen mentions a number of influential individuals in her history of the creation of the Chinese empire, not all of whom were emperors. One individual she mentions is Shang Yang, or Lord Shang, a legalist philosopher and early prime minister of Qin in 359 B.C.E. How were the legalist policies of Shang Yang instrumental in setting the state of Qin on the path to empire? Were Shang Yang's policies unique, or did they represent common ideas of the period? How similar were the policies of King Zheng, who became the first Qin emperor? Did Liu Bang, the first Han emperor, reverse or continue these policies? What common problems did all of these emperors have, and how were their solutions similar? To what extent was the creation of the Chinese empire the creation of the legalists? To what extent is the history of China during this period a series of emperors' biographies?

In 221 B.C.E., the Warring States period came to a sudden end when the kingdom of Qin defeated all its competitor kingdoms and unified the empire—roughly two-thirds of the area of modern China—for the first time. The Qin ruler then crowned himself China's first emperor. Indeed, the English word for China (which came via Latin and Sanskrit) derives from the name of the uniting dynasty, the Qin. The Qin

Valerie Hansen, *The Open Empire: A History of China to 1600* (New York: W. W. Norton, 2000), 97, 99–104, 112–15.

were able to conquer their rivals not because of any new technologies but because they found a new way to organize their state. To draw a modern analogy, one could say that the armies of the regional kingdoms all fought with the same hardware—crossbows, bronze weapons, and armor—but that the Qin had the advantage of new software—namely a bureaucracy organized on the basis of merit. The Qin founder followed the teachings of Legalist ministers who advocated the abolition of all privileges of the nobility.

In twentieth-century America, the word *bureaucracy* carries largely negative connotations of inefficiency. In third-century B.C.E. China, however, bureaucracy provided a new form of government far more efficient than the aristocratic rule of the Warring States period. The Qin ruler used this new type of government to build a powerful fighting machine. The state created by the Qin survived for a mere fourteen years, but its immediate successor, the Han dynasty, ruled China for the next four hundred years. Although the Han founders denounced the rule of the Qin as brutal, the Han dynasty took over many Qin-dynasty organizational techniques. One of the greatest challenges for the modern analyst is to assess the accomplishments of the Qin dynasty without being blinded by overly critical Han-dynasty sources. . . .

With the founding of the empire, Chinese society assumed the contours it would retain for the next two thousand years. During the Warring States period, social commentators envisioned a society of two classes: the privileged aristocracy and the laboring masses. But after 221 B.C.E., observers ranked society into four groups: scholars, peasants, artisans, and merchants. (A convenient way to remember this ranking is by the first letter of each group: SPAM.) This ranking reflected Legalist prejudices in favor of producers, namely peasants and artisans, over merchants, whom they felt manufactured nothing and so contributed little of value to the economy. Of course, merchants had much more money and much more freedom than did peasants, and most cultivators would have gladly switched places with any merchant. . . .

The Legalist State

The philosophers of the Warring States, most notably Xunzi, had remarked on the unusual strength and Legalist policies of the state of Qin at the turn of the third century B.C.E. In an age that prized eloquence, the Legalist thinker Han Fei (280–233 B.C.E.) stuttered, so he wrote directly to his ruler about his philosophy of government. In doing so, he became the first thinker to record his own ideas—unlike earlier thinkers whose students compiled their teachings after their deaths, often in a question-and-answer format. Han Fei envisioned the role of the ruler in much the same terms as *The Way and Integrity Classic*. The ruler was to remain detached from the everyday business of government; if he applied an unbending standard to judge his officials and his people, his kingdom would become stronger than its rivals.

Although the Chinese term for Legalist, *fajia*, literally means "law experts," Legalist thinkers did not advocate rule of law in the modern Western sense. They did not believe in a law that could be used to challenge their rule. Instead, they believed in a law that treated all men equally. Only the systematic application of the law, Legalists felt, could control people, whose essential nature was evil.

The Architect of Qin Success: Shang Yang's Reforms

In 359 B.C.E., a powerful prime minister named Shang Yang initiated a series of reforms to build a strong Legalist state. These are described in a book bearing the name *The Book of Lord Shang*, which was written after his death. Since the seventh century B.C.E., the Qin kingdom had occupied the former homeland the Zhou dynasty abandoned when it moved to Luoyang, but it did not rise up above its rivals until Shang Yang's term in office. His policies strengthened the fiscal basis of the Qin state, enabling it to finance a fighting force far stronger than that of any other contemporary state.

Legalist teachings differed from all other Warring States–period philosophies in their disdain for the past, voiced in this passage from *The Book of Lord Shang:*

> Former generations did not follow the same doctrines, so what antiquity should one imitate? The emperors and kings did not copy one another, so what rites should one follow? ... As rites and laws were fixed in accordance with what was opportune, regulations and orders were all expedient, and weapons, armor, implements, and equipment were all practical.

This skepticism about the past allowed Legalists to reject all that the Confucians valued, especially ritual, which Legalists viewed as a series of expensive and pointless ceremonies.

Sima Qian's *Records of the Grand Historian* gives a detailed description of the measures Shang Yang took to reorganize the Qin state: "He commanded that the people be divided into tens and fives." The registration of individual households marked the culmination of a trend taking place in other kingdoms of the Warring States period. By abolishing all intermediaries between cultivators and the state, the Legalists extended the earlier attempts of Warring States–period rulers to establish a direct link between subject and ruler.

As part of this reform, Minister Shang established population registers to record who lived together in different households.

He commanded that . . . they supervise each other and be mutually liable. Anyone who failed to report criminal activity would be chopped in two at the waist, while those who reported it would receive the same reward as that for obtaining the head of an enemy.

The registers listed the members of groups of five and ten who bore mutual responsibility should anyone in their group commit a crime. Once a man reached sixteen or seventeen years of age and a height of 1.5 meters (5 feet), he was obliged to perform military service, fulfill his labor obligations, and pay taxes on his land. Because the Legalists drew no distinction between the army and society, they expected all men to serve in the army.

Minister Shang is credited with establishing private ownership of land. In fact, land continued to be viewed as the property of the ruler, but the link between land ownership and military service provided people with a stronger claim to the land than when they had worked on estates in earlier ages. The institution of the population registers marked a sharp break with the past, with officials keeping detailed records of their subjects for the first time. These registers shaped popular consciousness as well, because many people thought the gods kept a set of parallel registers on which they recorded each person's allotted life span.

"Any family that had more than two adult males who did not divide the household would pay a double military tax," continued Historian Sima Qian. This clause documents the deep antipathy of the Legalists toward cherished Confucian beliefs. Where Confucians advocated that sons live together in harmony with their parents, Legalists required that an extended family break apart into separate households, a trend that may have been occurring anyway.

"Those who had achievements in the army would receive an increase in rank in proportion to their accomplishments." This simple statement represented a startling departure from past practice. The entire population of the Qin state was divided into twenty different ranks, each with its own perquisites in the form of permitted clothing, land, slaves, or housing. All hereditary titles—even those of the royal family—were dropped in favor of this new ranking based strictly on performance. The Legalists did not subscribe to the Confucian belief that only gentlemen should serve as officials or even that one should reward virtue. They felt instead that strict standards of personal achievement should replace subjective judgment and hereditary privilege. In the army, for example, soldiers gained promotions strictly on the basis of how many severed heads they submitted. Those who submitted more heads rose faster than those who submitted fewer heads. "Those who devoted themselves to the fundamental enterprises and through their farming and weaving contributed much grain and cloth would be freed from tax and corvee." Here, the historian Sima Qian summarizes the economic thinking of the Legalists. Because all farmers also served as soldiers, the agricultural sector provided the lifeblood of the state. The farmer-soldiers of the Qin staffed the Qin armies, completed all the public works, and produced the food for everyone in the state. Anyone who did not produce food must, then, play a less important role in society. This rigid blueprint of the economy minimized the importance of merchants and scholars.

"He collected the small district towns together into large counties and established officials for them." Minister Shang Yang divided society into a series of interlocking units, the smallest of which was the groups of five or ten households. These units formed larger units of counties (*xian*), which provided the population with the services of local government. County officials organized the army, carried out public works, collected taxes, and administered justice. The Qin state reached up from the county to the center, and it reached down to the very lowest unit of land, an individual's fields.

"For the fields he opened up the footpaths and set up boundaries." Although the meaning of "opened up" is not clear, it is likely that the Qin eliminated the grid paths through agricultural land. Later historians thought these reforms made the sale of land possible. "He equalized the military levies and land tax and standardized the measures of capacity, weight, and length," continues Sima. The standardizing impulse extended to different measures of weight and length, which varied from place to place.

The Qin first implemented these measures within their own borders, but in 316 B.C.E., the Qin state began a series of conquests that accelerated under the leadership of young King Zheng (259–210 B.C.E.), who came to the throne in 246 B.C.E. at the age of thirteen. In 237 B.C.E., when the king turned twenty-two, he took power into his own hands and led his kingdom through fifteen years of all-out war that culminated in the unification of China in 221 B.C.E.

China's First Emperor

. . . As part of his effort to unify China, the Qin ruler required that the six defeated kings move to his capital accompanied by the noble families of their kingdoms. The title he took, *Shi Huangdi*, literally meant First August Emperor. *Di* ("emperor," "highest deity") contrasted with the word *wang* ("king") that earlier regional rulers, including the founders of the Zhou, had used to refer to themselves.

Once he had assumed his new title, the Qin emperor implemented various policies to shore up his power. He toured his empire five times between 220 and 210 B.C.E., in an effort to show himself to his people and to make offerings to the spirits. In line with Shang Yang's teachings, the First August Emperor emphasized farming as the mainstay of the economy. He unified all measures and imposed a standard currency on the empire. A circular coin with a square in the middle replaced the different monies of the Warring States period, which had taken the shape of knives, shovels, or shells. This new currency had the advantage that it could be threaded together to form strings, which became the major unit of accounting in subsequent periods. In addition to implementing a unified system of units for length and volume, the new dynasty also specified a national standard gauge for vehicles so that roads could be a uniform width and carts could travel freely throughout the empire.

After unifying the empire, the Qin divided all the territory under its control into regional units called commanderies (the initial thirty-six were increased to forty-two), and the commanderies were further subdivided into counties. The administrative structure of the commanderies replicated that of the central government. Governmental functions were divided into three: civil matters having to do with taxation and the registration of the population, military affairs, and the supervision of governmental officials. The top officials in the central government were the chancellor, who headed the bureaucracy; the imperial secretary, who drafted the emperor's orders; and the grand commandant, who was in charge of the military. Similarly, each commandery had three main officials; first, the administrator who collected taxes, updated population registers, and heard legal disputes; next, an oversight official who ensured that the administrator followed all imperial regulations and laws; finally, a commandant who recruited and trained the militia. The law of avoidance, which held that no official could serve in his home area, was already in effect at the time, but clerks were recruited locally.

Perhaps the most striking standardization was that of the script. Scribes in earlier centuries had used Large Seal script to write, and many regional variants of the same character had come into use in the years of the coexisting Warring States. The Qin reformers introduced a new, simpler script called Small Seal script, and they discouraged the use of different variants for the same character. (The Small Seal script they used was largely abandoned in the succeeding dynasty, when it was replaced by the characters in use today.) Because the Qin forbade any writing in regional or popular variants, the rulers ensured that linguistic unity would continue even when the empire was no longer unified. Chinese characters continued to be used without significant change until the introduction of simplified characters after 1949. . . .

The Founding of the Han Dynasty

The absence of peasant uprisings during his reign suggests that the Qin emperor must have enjoyed a measure of popularity with his subjects. As soon as he died and his unpopular second son succeeded him, many of the former regional states broke away once again. The rebels may initially have hoped to restore the emperor's first son to power while leaving the Qin dynasty in place. As the situation at court deteriorated, the rebels, who included both bona fide peasants and low-ranking officials, began to denounce the cruelty of the Qin and to call for the founding of a new dynasty. The rebel who would defeat all his rivals to become the founder of the Han, Liu Bang (reigned 206–195 B.C.E.) was one of only two emperors born into a commoner family. (The other founded the Ming dynasty.) The Grand Historian Sima Qian describes him as a man whose oafish ways antagonized everyone he met, but also as a man whom local innkeepers allowed to drink for free since their receipts unaccountably went up whenever he was around. During the years of the Qin, he passed an examination and won a low-level appointment as a neighborhood head who supervised one thousand households.

As he sought to increase his popular support, Liu Bang attacked the Qin for its brutal laws. When his forces won the decisive battle and entered the Qin capital, he proclaimed an agreement with the assembled leaders of the community:

> You elders have long suffered under the harsh laws of Qin. . . . I make an agreement with you that the law shall consist of only three sections: He who kills others shall die; he who harms others or steals from them shall incur appropriate punishment. For the rest, all other Qin laws should be abolished.

So Liu Bang pledged, but in fact he retained most of the Qin laws. His service as a neighborhood head gave him some experience with the Qin legal system, whose careful procedures must have impressed him. Sima Qian described the early Han legal reforms saying, "When Han arose it lopped off the harsh corners of the Qin code and retreated to an easy roundness, whittled away the embellishments and achieved simplicity." As his comment suggests, the early Han rulers modified rather than eliminated the Qin legal system. They allowed those who had been found guilty to pay fines rather than be subject to stipulated punishments, the most gruesome of which they canceled.

One major departure from Qin policies concerned the treatment of the nobility. Where the Qin emperor had required all the nobility of the vanquished kingdoms to reside in his capital, the Han founder created a new nobility. He gave nine of his brothers and sons the title of king and the lands necessary to sustain them, and named one hundred fifty of his most important followers to the rank of marquis. Two-thirds of his territory remained in the hands of his sons and other relatives. Only one-third of his empire, the crucial western half containing the capital, remained under direct administration. We should remember that the core of the Han-dynasty empire lay in the region around Changan, or the modern city of Xian in the province of Shaanxi, while the coastal areas and much of south China remained backwaters largely populated by non-Chinese peoples.

As with their Qin predecessors, the Han-dynasty government at both the central and local levels had three major divisions: one branch supervised the collection of taxes, one the army, and the third, government officials. The central authorities presided over some one hundred commanderies, which were in turn divided into fifteen hundred counties. Local authorities were in charge of registering the population, collecting taxes, maintaining waterways, and dispensing justice. Local officials also recommended literate men of good character for government positions.

After Liu Bang had defeated his rivals and assumed the title of emperor, he asked prominent Confucians to design new rituals for his court. He hoped to create an aura around himself that would discourage his former drinking companions from being too familiar. Although occasionally willing to take the advice of ritual specialists, the future emperor did not slavishly follow all of Confucius's teachings. At one point in the struggle to gain power, his main rival Xiang Yu (233–202 B.C.E.) captured Liu Bang's father and threatened to boil him alive unless the son surrendered. Liu Bang replied that because he and Xiang Yu had taken an oath of brotherhood, his father was also Xiang Yu's father. As he put it, "My father is your father too. If you insist on boiling your own father, I hope you will be kind enough to send me a cup of the soup." Shockingly to Confucians, he did not allow familial ties, even the all-important bond between parent and child, to interfere with his ambition to rule the empire. (Xiang Yu subsequently adhered to the terms of his oath and freed the father.) . . .

25

CONFUCIUS

From *The Analects*

Confucius (551–479 B.C.E.), China's most renowned thinker, was an independent teacher and advisor in the feudal period that preceded the founding of the Qin empire. His teachings came to form the bedrock of Chinese culture and have greatly influenced the cultures of Japan, Korea, Vietnam, and Southeast Asia. Confucius' ideas, however, were not always universally known or accepted. In fact, as you read in the

---

The Analects of Confucius, trans. Arthur Waley (London: George Allen & Unwin, 1958).

previous selection, the Qin Legalists, who were instrumental in the establishment of the first Chinese empire, harshly criticized Confucian ideas and considered them subversive to the emperor's rule. The Han dynasty, however, once firmly established, embraced Confucianism. In 140 B.C.E. the Han emperor Wu created a Confucian academy and selected imperial administrators based partly on exams that tested their knowledge of the Confucian classics. Eventually, Confucianism became the state religion under the Han.

From this brief selection of writings attributed to Confucius, how would you characterize his philosophy? Why were the Qin Legalists dissatisfied with Confucian philosophy, and why did the Han embrace it? Why might Confucian philosophy not appeal to the builders of an empire but appeal to those securely in power?

Thinking Historically

Judging from the number of times he is quoted, taught, read, or referred to, Confucius is widely considered to be the most influential individual in all of Chinese history. Many of the Confucian classics, however, were actually written by later followers. The most authentic record of Confucius' thoughts is *The Analects,* but these teachings were not recorded by Confucius but collected by his students after his death. Therefore it is difficult to know exactly what to attribute to Confucius and what to attribute to his followers. If we discovered an autobiography of Confucius or a store of his letters, would our new knowledge of the individual change our estimate of his influence? Is he important as an individual or for the legacy of teachings that he left?

On the Gentleman

IV, 16 The Master said, "A gentleman takes as much trouble to discover what is right as lesser men take to discover what will pay."

VI, 25 The Master said, "A gentleman who is widely versed in letters and at the same time knows how to submit his learning to the restraints of ritual is not likely, I think, to go far wrong."

VIII, 2 . . . The Master said, "When gentlemen deal generously with their own kin, the common people are incited to Goodness. When old dependents are not discarded, the common people will not be fickle."

IX, 13 The Master wanted to settle among the Nine Wild Tribes of the East. Someone said, "I am afraid you would find it hard to put up with their lack of refinement." The Master said, "Were a true gentleman to settle among them there would soon be no trouble about lack of refinement."

XII, 16 The Master said, "The gentleman calls attention to the good points in others; he does not call attention to their defects. The small man does just the reverse of this."

XV, 18 The Master said, "A gentleman is distressed by his own lack of capacity; he is never distressed at the failure of others to recognize his merits."

XV, 20 The Master said, "The demands that a gentleman makes are upon himself; those that a small man makes are upon others."

XV, 21 The Master said, "A gentleman is proud, but not quarrelsome, allies himself with individuals, but not with parties."

On Filial Piety

II, 5 Meng I Tzu asked about the treatment of parents. The Master said, "Never disobey!" When Fan Ch'ih was driving his carriage for him, the Master said, "Meng asked me about the treatment of parents and I said, 'Never disobey!'" Fan Ch'ih said, "In what sense did you mean it?" The Master said, "While they are alive, serve them according to ritual. When they die, bury them according to ritual and sacrifice to them according to ritual."

II, 7 Tzu-yu asked about the treatment of parents. The Master said, "'Filial sons' nowadays are people who see to it that their parents get enough to eat. But even dogs and horses are cared for to that extent. If there is no feeling of respect, wherein lies the difference?"

On Government by Moral Force

I, 5 The Master said, "A country of a thousand war-chariots cannot be administered unless the ruler attends strictly to business, punctually observes his promises, is economical in expenditure, shows affection toward his subjects in general, and uses the labour of the peasantry only at the proper times of year."

II, 3 The Master said, "Govern the people by regulations, keep order among them by chastisements, and they will flee from you, and lose all self-respect. Govern them by moral force, keep order among them by ritual and they will keep their self-respect and come to you of their own accord."

XII, 11 Duke Ching of Ch'i asked Master K'ung about government. Master K'ung replied saying, "Let the prince be a prince, the minister a minister, the father a father and the son a son." The Duke said, "How true! For indeed when the prince is not a prince, the minister not a minister, the father not a father, the son not a son, one may have a dish of millet in front of one and yet not know if one will live to eat it."

XII, 19 Chi L'ang-tzu asked Master K'ung about government, saying, "Suppose I were to slay those who have not the Way in order to help on those who have the Way, what would you think of it?" Master K'ung replied saying, "You are there to rule, not to slay. If you desire what is good, the people will at once be good. The essence of the gentleman is that of wind; the essence of small people is that of grass. And when a wind passes over the grass, it cannot choose but bend."

XIII, 6 The Master said, "If the ruler himself is upright, all will go well even though he does not give orders. But if he himself is not upright, even though he gives orders, they will not be obeyed."

XIII, 10 The Master said, "If only someone were to make use of me, even for a single year, I could do a great deal; and in three years I could finish off the whole work."

XIII, 11 The Master said, "'Only if the right sort of people had charge of a country for a hundred years would it become really possible to stop cruelty and do away with slaughter.' How true the saying is!"

On Public Opinion

II, 19 Duke Ai asked, "What can I do in order to get the support of the common people?" Master K'ung replied, "If you 'raise up the straight and set them on top of the crooked,' the commoners will support you. But if you raise the crooked and set them on top of the straight, the commoners will not support you."

II, 20 Chi L'ang-tzu asked whether there were any form of encouragement by which he could induce the common people to be respectful and loyal. The Master said, "Approach them with dignity, and they will respect you. Show piety towards your parents and kindness toward your children, and they will be loyal to you. Promote those who are worthy, train those who are incompetent; that is the best form of encouragement."

XII, 7 Tzu-kung asked about government. The Master said, "Sufficient food, sufficient weapons, and the confidence of the common people." Tzu-kung said, "Suppose you had no choice but to dispense with one of these three, which would you forgo?" The Master said, "Weapons." Tzu-kung said, "Suppose you were forced to dispense with one of the two that were left, which would you forgo?" The Master said, "Food. For from of old death has been the lot of all men; but a people that no longer trusts its rulers is lost indeed."

26

SIMA QIAN

The Annals of Qin

This section is taken from one of the great ancient histories of China. Sima Qian (145–86 B.C.E.), like generations of Simas before him, was Grand Historian of China. Usually, the official historians flattered the emperor, but Sima Qian had the courage to criticize his own emperor, Wudi, who had Sima Qian castrated for treason. In this selection he writes of the First Emperor, beginning with the period shortly after unification.

What evidence do you see of bureaucratic organization before the First Emperor? Why does the First Emperor want to centralize authority? What kind of power do the various officials mentioned exercise? To what extent are the changes that the First Emperor decrees his own ideas? To what extent were these changes probably routine for earlier kings of Qin or kings of other Chinese states? How does the king of Qin distinguish himself from the king of Zhou, the previous dynasty?

Thinking Historically

Ancient historians relied on biography more than modern historians do. An important goal of history in the ancient world was to retell the stories of famous men as object lessons of proper or improper behavior. What object lesson do you think Sima Qian is trying to make? What lesson do you take from the story?

. . . Chief Minister Wang Wan, Imperial Secretary Feng Jie, Superintendent of Trials Li Si, and others all said: "In days of old the territory of the Five Emperors was 1,000 li[1] square, and beyond this was the territory of the feudal princes and of the barbarians. Some of the feudal princes came to court and some did not, for the Son of Heaven was unable to exercise control. Now Your Majesty has raised a righteous army to punish the oppressors and bring peace and order to all under Heaven, so that everywhere within the seas has become our provinces and districts and the laws and ordinances have as a result become unified. This is something which has never once existed from remote antiq-

[1]One li is about a third of a mile. [Ed.]

Sima Qian, *Historical Records*, trans. Raymond Dawson (Oxford: Oxford University Press, 1994), 63–68.

uity onwards, and which the Five Emperors did not attain. Your servants have carefully discussed this with the scholars of broad learning and, as in antiquity there was the Heavenly August, the Earthly August, and the Supreme August, and the Supreme August was the most highly honoured, so your servants, risking death, submit a venerable title, and propose that the King should become "the Supreme August." His commands should be "edicts," his orders should be "decrees," and the Son of Heaven should refer to himself as "the mysterious one." The King said: "Omit the word 'supreme' and write 'august' and pick out the title of 'emperor' used from remote antiquity, so that the title will be 'August Emperor.' The rest shall be as you suggest." And an edict was issued saying that it should be done. King Zhuangxiang was to be posthumously honoured as "the Supreme August on High."

The following edict was issued: "We have heard that in high antiquity there were titles but no posthumous names. In middle antiquity there were titles, but when people died they were provided with posthumous names in accordance with their conduct. If this is so, then it is a case of the son passing judgement on the father and the subject passing judgement on the ruler. This is quite pointless, and We will not adopt this practice in such matters. Henceforward the law on posthumous names is abolished. We are the First August Emperor and later generations will be numbered in accordance with this system, Second Generation, Third Generation, right down to Ten Thousandth Generation,[2] and this tradition will continue without end."

To continue the succession of the Five Powers[3] the First Emperor considered that, as Zhou had got the Power of Fire and Qin was replacing the Zhou power, it should adopt what fire does not overcome, so it was precisely at this moment that the Power of Water started. The beginning of the year was changed, and the court celebrations all started at the beginning of the tenth month. In all garments, flags, and pennants, black was made predominant. And as far as number was concerned they took six as the basis of calculation, so that tallies and law caps were 6 inches, carriages were 6 feet wide, 6 feet equalled a "pace," and imperial carriages had six horses. The Yellow River was renamed "the Powerful Water" to inaugurate the Power of Water. Repression was intensive and matters were all decided by the law, for only through harsh treatment

---

[2]One of the most ironic moments in history, since Second Generation had been on the throne for only a few years when the whole edifice came tumbling down.

[3]According to this theory, the Five Powers (sometimes known as Five Elements, but in the Chinese *wu de*, using the *de*, which is often translated as "virtue") were each in turn associated with a new dynasty. . . . There was much speculation concerning this doctrine, and differences of opinion as to which power should be associated with which historical period. There was also an elaborate system of correspondences between powers, colours, numbers, and so on. The colour black and number six, which are referred to in the text, were associated with the Power of Water.

and the abandonment of humanness, kindness, harmony, and righteousness could he accord with the destiny of the Five Powers. And so the law was made rigorous, and for a long time no amnesty was declared.

The Chief Minister Wang Wan and others said: "The states are newly defeated and the territories of Yan, Qi, and Chu are distant, so if we do not establish kings for them there will be no means of bringing order to them. We beg to set up your sons in authority, but it is up to the Supreme One alone to favour us with his agreement." The First Emperor handed down their suggestion to the ministers, and they all thought this would be expedient. But the Superintendent of Trials Li Si advised: "Only after an extremely large number of sons and younger brothers and people of the same surname had been enfeoffed by King Wen and King Wu did they win the adherence of the distant, and then they attacked and smote each other and behaved like enemies. And when the feudal states wrought vengeance on each other more and more, the Zhou Son of Heaven was incapable of preventing them. Now all within the seas has been unified thanks to Your Majesty's divine power, and everywhere has been turned into provinces and districts. And if your sons and the successful officials are richly rewarded from the public revenues, that will be quite sufficient to secure easy control. If there is no dissension throughout the Empire, then this is the technique for securing tranquility. To establish feudal states would not be expedient." The First Emperor said: "It is because of the existence of marquises and kings that all under Heaven has shared in suffering from unceasing hostilities. When, thanks to the ancestral temples, all under Heaven has for the first time been brought to order, if states are reintroduced, this will mean the establishment of armies, and it would surely be difficult to seek peace in those places. The advice of the Superintendent of Trials is right."

So the Empire was divided into thirty-six provinces, and a governor and army commander and an inspector were established for each. The people were renamed "the black-headed people," and there were great celebrations. The weapons from all under Heaven were gathered in and collected together at Xianyang and were melted down to make bells and stands and twelve statues of men made of metal, each 1,000 piculs in weight,[4] to be set up in the courts and palaces. All weights and measures were placed under a unified system, and the axle length of carriages was standardized. For writings they standardized the characters.[5]

The land to the east stretched as far as the sea and Chaoxian, to the west as far as Lintao and Qiangzhong, to the south as far as the land

---

[4]A huge weight, since a picul is what a man can carry.

[5]In this version of the reforms the text speaks of the standardization of the script rather than of bureaucratic practice. The standardization of the axle length of carriages may appear bizarre or possibly a concession to numerology, but it may have seemed prudent to have wheel-ruts a standard size, especially in [the soft soil of] loess country.

where the doors face north, and in the north they constructed defences along the Yellow River to form the frontier, and along the Yin Mountains as far as Liaodong. One hundred and twenty thousand powerful and wealthy households from all under Heaven were transferred to Xian-yang. All the temples together with Zhangtai and Shanglin were to the south of the Wei. Every time Qin destroyed a feudal state, a replica of its palaces and mansions was produced and it was created on the slope north of Xianyang, overlooking the Wei to the south, while eastwards from Yongmen as far as the Jing and Wei there was a series of mansions, connecting walkways, and pavilions. The beautiful women, bells, and drums[6] which they had obtained from the various states were installed there to fill them.

In the twenty-seventh year the First Emperor toured Longxi and Beidi, went out via Jitou Mountain and passed Huizhong. Then he built the Xin palace south of the Wei, and subsequently it was renamed the Temple of the Apex, to represent the Apex of Heaven. From the Temple of the Apex a roadway went through to Mount Li, and the front hall of the Ganquan palace was built, and they built a walled roadway from Xianyang to connect with it. This year one degree of promotion was bestowed and express roads were constructed.

In the twenty-eighth year the First Emperor travelled eastwards through his provinces and districts and ascended Mount Zouyi. He set up a stone tablet, and after discussion with the various Confucian scholars of Lu an inscription was carved on the stone extolling the virtue of Qin. They also discussed the matter of the *feng* and *shan* sacrifices[7] and the sacrifices to mountains and rivers. So next he ascended Mount Tai, set up a stone tablet, and made the *feng* sacrifice. As he descended and there was a violent onset of wind and rain, he rested under a tree, which was consequently enfeoffed as fifth-rank grandee.[8] He made the *shan* sacrifice at Liangfu. The stone tablet that he had set up was inscribed with the following words:

> When the August Emperor came to the throne, he created regulations and made the laws intelligent, and his subjects cherished his instructions.
>
> In the twenty-sixth year of his rule, he for the first time unified all under Heaven, and there were none who did not submit.
>
> In person he made tours of the black-headed people in distant places, climbed this Mount Tai, and gazed all around at the eastern limits.

---

[6]Possession of harems and the means of providing musical entertainment were the prizes of conquest which symbolized the unification. This is a clear statement of the commonly expressed view that the main purpose of political power was to ensure that one enjoyed all the pleasures of life.

[7]Important sacrifices performed by emperors when they felt their authority was secure.

[8]A ranking of nobility. [Ed.]

His servants who were in attendance concentrated on following his footsteps, looked upon his deeds as the foundation and source of their own conduct, and reverently celebrated his achievements and virtue.

As the Way of good government circulates, all creation obtains its proper place, and everything has its laws and patterns.

His great righteousness shines forth with its blessings, to be handed down to later generations, and they are to receive it with compliance and not make changes in it.

The August Emperor is personally sage, and has brought peace to all under Heaven, and has been tireless in government.

Rising early and retiring late, he has instituted long-lasting benefits, and has brought especial glory to instructions and precepts.

His maxims and rules spread all around, and far and near everything has been properly organized, and everyone receives the benefits of his sagely ambitions.

Noble and base have been divided off and made clear, and men and women conform in accordance with propriety, and carefully fulfil their duties.

Private and public are made manifest and distinguished, and nothing is not pure and clean, for the benefit of our heirs and successors.

His influence will last to all eternity, and the decrees he bequeaths will be revered, and his grave admonitions will be inherited for ever. . . .

27

NICHOLAS PURCELL

Rome: The Arts of Government

Rome took a different path to the empire than China. In China, the state of Qin formed a unified state by suppressing the independent power of local kings, princes, and nobility. In other words, the First Emperor and the emperors of the Han dynasty brought an end to feudalism.

Nicholas Purcell, "The Arts of Government," in *The Oxford History of the Classical World: The Roman World*, ed. John Boardman, Jasper Griffin, and Oswyn Murray (Oxford: Oxford University Press, 1988), 154, 155, 156, 170–74, 175–77.

Conversely, before Rome became an empire, it was a *republic*: a unified state, not a series of competing feudal powers. The Roman republic inherited Greek ideas of territorial sovereignty and popular government. But as Roman military power spread beyond Italy, a republican form of government became more and more untenable. Governors had to be sent to conquered provinces, soldiers had to be recruited, and taxes had to be collected from non-Romans. The authority of popular institutions of government was eclipsed first by the aristocratic senate and then by warring generals, the dictator Caesar (47–44 B.C.E.), and finally Octavian, Caesar's nephew and adopted successor, who after 27 B.C.E. declared himself Augustus (Revered) and Imperator (Emperor).

Thus, for at least one hundred years before Rome officially became an empire, it governed vast territories of conquered and allied peoples. The way in which it ruled these subjects after Augustus had been honed by generations of provincial governors and did not change significantly.

Purcell, a modern historian, argues that Roman procedures for administering the empire were developed piecemeal to fit the circumstances. Instead of a trained professional bureaucracy, the Romans relied on law and the military to keep order and peace. The power of the central government, and of the emperor, was as great as that of the Chinese emperor, but Roman indirect rule relied more on local officials, independent politicians, and private contractors.

What is the evidence for Roman administration being less bureaucratic than that of China? Was the Roman Empire less centralized than China or merely less bureaucratic? What were the advantages and disadvantages of Roman administration compared to that of the Chinese empire?

Thinking Historically

This is an institutional history, a history of Roman government. As such, the personal stories of individual administrators offer relevant information, but there is no need to tell their life stories. Indeed, unlike emperors, there are simply too many officials to attempt to recount the details of their lives.

Notice how few proper names are included in these pages. If Rome were less bureaucratic, would we need to know more, or fewer, individual stories? What if Rome were more bureaucratic?

... "And it came to pass in those days, that there went out a decree from Caesar Augustus, that all the world should be enrolled to be taxed" (Luke 2:1). The evangelist wants to emphasize the centrality in world history of the coming of the Messiah, and accordingly links the birth of Christ to the moment when the power of Rome seemed at its most universal. For him, as often for us, the power of Rome is most potently expressed by reference to its administrative activity. St. Luke, however, was wrong. We know now that no such decree commanded a universal registration of the Roman world, at this time or any other; he exaggerated Roman omnipotence on the basis of the experience of a single province. It remains extremely easy for us too to misunderstand the scope, practice, and effects of Rome's governmental procedures. We mistake patterns of decision-making for policies and take hierarchical sequences of posts for career-structures. When we find the taking of minutes or the accumulation of archives, we immediately see a bureaucracy. Virtuosity in the public service is confused with professionalism. Recent work has been able to show well how far Rome's administration failed, or could be corrupted or subverted, or simply had no effect but oppression on thousands of provincials. There have been fewer examinations of the way in which the arts of government at which the Romans thought themselves that they excelled actually worked— imposing civilization and peace, leniency to the defeated, and war to the last with the proud (Virgil, *Aeneid* 6. 852–3)....

Roman theories of government were not elaborate; the practice too was simple. Two broad categories cover almost all the activities of Roman rule: settling disputes between communities or individuals, and assembling men, goods, or money—jurisdiction and exaction. Antiquity recognized three main types of authority: magistrate, soldier, and master of a household; and all governmental activity in the Roman Empire can be linked with one of these. The first, deriving from the Greek city, covers both the immemorial officers of the city-state which Rome had been and the magistrates of the hundreds of essentially self-governing cities which made up nearly all the Roman Empire. In a *polis* magistrates ran the military; at Rome the usual citizen militia became under the Empire a permanent, institutionally separate army, whose officers played an ever greater part in government culminating in the militarization of the third century. Finally, in a slave-owning society the type of authority exercised within the household was naturally recognizably different, and also came to be of considerable importance in government.... [I]t was always through activities which we would hesitate to call governmental that Roman rule was most effectively maintained: through the involvement of the upper classes in public religion, spectacles, impressive patronage of architecture, philosophy, literature, painting; and in civil benefactions all over the Empire. The civilizing and beneficial effects of this should be remembered as we move on to find the actual administrative and executive structure of the Empire erratic and illiberal.

Rome had from the earliest times enjoyed very close contacts with the Greek world, and had, like most ancient cities, a tripartite political structure of magistrates, council (the Senate), and popular assembly. The importance of the last for our purpose is that its early power produced the uniquely Roman and constitutionally vital concept of *im-*

perium. The Roman people conferred upon its chosen magistrates the right to command it and the sanctions against disobedience—ever more strictly circumscribed—of corporal and capital punishment of its members. . . .

This is why Rome long retained the habit of dealing with her subjects with the respect deserved by the free, and why Roman rule so long remained indirect. To the end of antiquity most of the cities of the Empire and their territories were ruled by local magistrates many of whose domestic executive actions were taken as if they were independent; indeed they often needed to be reminded that there were limits to the licence they were allowed. Similarly Rome also long tolerated local kings and dynasts, and the survival of these dependent kingdoms and free cities contributed much to the fuzzy informality of the power structure of the Empire before the age of the Antonines.[1] . . .

The search for bureaucracy in the Roman world is vain. . . .

28

PLUTARCH

Cicero

Plutarch (46–120 C.E.) was one of the ancient world's most famous biographers. Cicero (106–43 B.C.E.) was a Roman statesman, considered Rome's greatest orator. In this selection Plutarch relates Cicero's early career as a Roman official in Sicily from 75 B.C.E. to 70 B.C.E.

Why would a Roman like Cicero take an official position in a place like Sicily? How would he expect it to advance his career? By Plutarch's account, was Cicero a good public official? What seems to be Cicero's source of power and authority: his office, his family, or his friends?

Thinking Historically

At the beginning of his work, Plutarch notes that he aims to write biography, not history. He picks and chooses incidents from his subjects' lives that best reveal their moral outlooks and inner thoughts, even if in doing so he must ignore their historical significance. How

---

[1]96–192 C.E., period of Roman imperial peace and prosperity; emperors included Trajan (r. 98–117), Hadrian (r. 117–138), and Marcus Aurelius (r. 161–180). [Ed.]

Plutarch, *Fall of the Roman Republic*, trans. Rex Warner (London: Penguin, 1958), 316–19.

does Plutarch give the reader a feeling for Cicero's inner life? How does a biography of Cicero help us to understand the administration of the Roman Empire?

...He was appointed quaestor[1] at a time when there was a shortage of grain: Sicily was the province allotted to him, and at first he made himself unpopular with the Sicilians by forcing them to send grain to Rome. Later, however, when they had had experience of his careful management of affairs, his justice, and his kindly nature, they honoured him more than any governor they had ever had. It happened too that a number of young men from Rome, all from well-known and distinguished families, came up for trial before the praetor[2] in charge of Sicily on charges of indiscipline or cowardice in the war. Cicero undertook their defence and did it brilliantly, securing their acquittal. Afterwards, when he was on his way to Rome and, as the result of these successes, was feeling particularly proud of himself, he had, as he informs us, an amusing experience. In Campania he happened to meet a well-known man and one whom he considered a friend of his. Imagining that he had filled the whole of Rome with the fame and glory of his achievements, he asked this man: "What are people in Rome saying about what I've done? What do they think of it?" To which the reply was: "But, Cicero, you must tell me where you've been all this time." At the moment, he tells us, he was thoroughly discouraged by this. He saw that all the news about him had been swallowed up in the city like a drop of water in the ocean with no visible effect at all on his reputation. But afterwards he thought things over and saw that this glory for which he was contending was something infinite, that there was no fixed point at which one could say "now I have arrived"; and so he introduced some moderation into his ambitious thoughts. It remains true, however, that throughout his life he was always far too fond of praise and too concerned about what people thought of him; and this very often had a disturbing effect on policies of his which were in themselves excellent.

Now that he was beginning to go in for politics more seriously he came to the conclusion that it was a disgraceful thing that, while a craftsman who uses inanimate tools and inanimate materials still knows what each of these is called, where it can be found, and what it can do, the statesman, who uses men as his instruments for public action, should be slack and indifferent where knowledge of his fellow-citizens is concerned. He therefore trained himself not only to memorize names, but also to know in what part of the city every important

---

[1]A specialist financial official. [Ed.]

[2]Roman official concerned with jurisdiction (law and administration); originally military; magistrates. [Ed.]

person lived, where he had his country houses, who were his friends and who his neighbours. And so, whatever road in Italy Cicero happened to be travelling on, it was easy for him to name and to point out the estates and villas of his friends. His fortune was sufficient for his expenses, but was still small, so that people were surprised and admired him when he took no fees or gifts for his services as an advocate— particularly so at the time when he took on the case for the prosecution against Verres.[3] Verres had been, as praetor, governor of Sicily and was prosecuted by the Sicilians for his numerous misdeeds. Cicero secured his conviction not by the speech he made but, in a sense, by the speech which he did not make. For the praetors in charge of the courts in Rome were doing what they could for Verres and by various methods of postponement had had the case adjourned until the last possible day on which it could be heard. It therefore seemed obvious to them that, since one day wouldn't be long enough for the speeches of the advocates, the trial could not possibly be concluded. But Cicero stood up and said that there was no need of speeches; he merely called his witnesses and examined them and then asked the jury to cast their votes. There are still on record, however, a number of witty sayings of his in connection with this trial. For instance, when an ex-slave called Caecilius, who was suspected of Jewish practices, wanted to push himself forward instead of the Sicilian witnesses and to make a speech against Verres himself Cicero said: "What has a Jew got to do with a pig?"— "verres" being the Roman word for a castrated boar. And when Verres attacked Cicero and said that he was not a robust character, Cicero replied: "Surely this is the sort of language you ought to be using to your sons at home"; Verres having a grown-up son who had the reputation of being little better than a male prostitute. Then there was the remark he made to the orator Hortensius. Hortensius had not dared to speak for Verres at the trial proper, but when it came to the assessment of the fine he was induced to appear for him and received in reward a sphinx made of ivory. In the course of his speech Cicero made some oblique reference to him, and Hortensius interjected: "I am afraid I am not an expert at solving riddles"; to which Cicero replied: "Really? In spite of having the sphinx in your house?"

When Verres was convicted Cicero assessed the fine at 750,000 denarii, and because of this was suspected of having been bribed to make the fine a low one. However, the Sicilians were certainly grateful to him and when he was aedile[4] they sent him all sorts of livestock and farm produce from their islands. He used this generosity of theirs only in order to lower the prices of food in Rome, making no profit out of it for himself.

---

[3]A corrupt governor in Sicily in 74–71 B.C.E.
[4]A municipal officer in Rome concerned with buildings, police, and public welfare. [Ed.]

He had a fine country estate at Arpinum, a farm near Naples, and another near Pompeii, none of them very large. The dowry of his wife Terentia came to 100,000 denarii, and he also received a legacy which brought him 90,000. This was enough to enable him to live in easy circumstances, though on a modest scale, with the Greek and Roman men of letters with whom he associated. He rarely, if ever, had a regular meal before sunset, not so much because he was too busy as because he suffered from a weak digestion. He was indeed very particular and even fussy about his health in general and used to have massages at regular intervals and go for a fixed number of walks. By looking after himself in this way he managed to maintain a state of health which was free from illness and strong enough to support much hard work and many calls upon his energy. The house that used to belong to his father he made over to his brother and lived himself near the Palatine hill, so that those who came to visit him in the morning should not have the trouble of a long walk. And the visitors who came to his house every day were no fewer than those who went to call on Crassus because of his wealth or on Pompey because of his power in the army, these two being the greatest and most sought-after men in Rome. Pompey, in fact, used himself to call on Cicero, and owed much of his power and reputation to Cicero's help in politics. . . .

$$\boxed{29}$$

CICERO

Letter on Provincial Government

In 60 B.C.E. Cicero wrote the following letter to his brother Quintus, governor of the Roman province of Asia. Informing Quintus that he would have to serve a third year as governor, Cicero uses the occasion to praise his brother's character and administration and to reflect on Roman government of the provinces. One problem Cicero refers to is working with the *publicani,* a class of businessmen who were under contract to carry out various economic activities, including the collection of taxes, customs, and port duties. As Purcell pointed out in selec-

M. Tullius Cicero, *Letters,* ed. Evelyn Shuckburgh, B.C. 60. coss., Q. Caecilius Metellus Celer, L. Afranius. Editions and translations: Latin (ed. L. C. Purser); English (ed. Evelyn Shuckburgh).

tion 27, there was no Roman bureaucracy; senators appointed governors and a limited number of political officials, but much of the daily work of governance was carried out by the *publicani*. The *publicani's* power over taxation and other economic matters was a constant source of irritation to the people of the provinces, and Roman governors often were called upon to mediate disputes.

According to Cicero, what made for an ideal provincial administrator? What were the obstacles to attaining this ideal? How was Roman provincial administration different from Chinese provincial administration? How were the problems that Cicero faced different from those of a Chinese provincial governor?

Thinking Historically

What does Cicero's letter tell you about Roman imperial administration? What signs do you see in this letter that Cicero's ideals were not universally carried out by Roman provincial governors or other administrators? What importance does Cicero place on the character of the individual and his ability to shape those he governs?

For what trouble is it to govern those over whom you are set, if you do but govern yourself? That may be a great and difficult task to others, and indeed it is most difficult: to you it has always been the easiest thing in the world, and indeed ought to be so, for your natural disposition is such that, even without discipline, it appears capable of self-control; whereas a discipline has, in fact, been applied that might educate the most faulty of characters. But while you resist, as you do, money, pleasure, and every kind of desire yourself, there will, I am to be told, be a risk of your not being able to suppress some fraudulent banker or some rather over-extortionate tax-collector! For as to the Greeks, they will think, as they behold the innocence of your life, that one of the heroes of their history, or a demigod from heaven, has come down into the province. And this I say, not to induce you to act thus, but to make you glad that you are acting or have acted so. It is a splendid thing to have been three years in supreme power in Asia without allowing statue, picture, plate, napery, slave, anyone's good looks, or any offer of money — all of which are plentiful in your province — to cause you to swerve from the most absolute honesty and purity of life. What can be imagined so striking or so desirable as that a virtue, a command over the passions, a self-control such as yours, are not remaining in darkness and obscurity, but have been set in the broad daylight of Asia, before the eyes of a famous province, and in the hearing of all nations and peoples? That the inhabitants are not being ruined by your progresses, drained by your charges, agitated by your approach? That there is the liveliest joy, public and private, wheresoever you come, the city regarding you as a protector and not a tyrant, the private house as a guest and not a plunderer? . . .

And indeed, Plato, the fountain-head of genius and learning, thought that states would only be happy when scholars and philosophers began being their rulers, or when those who were their rulers had devoted all their attention to learning and philosophy. It was plainly this union of power and philosophy that in his opinion might prove the salvation of states. And this perhaps has at length fallen to the fortune of the whole empire: certainly it has in the present instance to your province, to have a man in supreme power in it, who has from boyhood spent the chief part of his zeal and time in imbibing the principles of philosophy, virtue, and humanity. Wherefore be careful that this third year, which has been added to your labor, may be thought a prolongation of prosperity to Asia. And since Asia was more fortunate in retaining you than I was in my endeavor to bring you back, see that my regret is softened by the exultation of the province. For if you have displayed the very greatest activity in earning honors such as, I think, have never been paid to anyone else, much greater ought your activity to be in preserving these honors. What I for my part think of honors of that kind I have told you in previous letters. I have always regarded them, if given indiscriminately, as of little value, if paid from interested motives, as worthless: if, however, as in this case, they are tributes to solid services on your part, I hold you bound to take much pains in preserving them. Since, then, you are exercising supreme power and official authority in cities, in which you have before your eyes the consecration and apotheosis of your virtues, in all decisions, decrees, and official acts consider what you owe to those warm opinions entertained of you, to those verdicts on your character, to those honors which have been rendered you. And what you owe will be to consult for the interests of all, to remedy men's misfortunes, to provide for their safety, to resolve that you will be both called and believed to be the "father of Asia."

However, to such a resolution and deliberate policy on your part the great obstacle are the *publicani:* for, if we oppose them, we shall alienate from ourselves and from the Republic an order which has done us most excellent service, and which has been brought into sympathy with the Republic by our means; if, on the other hand, we comply with them in every case, we shall allow the complete ruin of those whose interests, to say nothing of their preservation, we are bound to consult. This is the one difficulty, if we look the thing fairly in the face, in your whole government. For disinterested conduct on one's own part, the suppression of all inordinate desires, the keeping a check upon one's staff, courtesy in hearing causes, in listening to and admitting suitor—all this is rather a question of credit than of difficulty: for it does not depend on any special exertion, but rather on a mental resolve and inclination. But how much bitterness of feeling is caused to allies by that question of the *publicani* we have had reason to know in the case of citizens who, when recently urging the removal of the port-dues in Italy, did not complain so much of the dues themselves, as of certain extortionate conduct on the part of the collectors. Wherefore, after hearing the grievances of citizens in Italy, I can comprehend what happens to allies in distant lands. To conduct oneself in this matter in such a way as to satisfy the *publicani* especially when contracts have been undertaken at a loss, and yet to preserve the allies from ruin, seems to demand a virtue with something divine in it, I mean a virtue like yours. To begin with, that they are subject to tax at all, which is their greatest grievance, ought not to be thought so by the Greeks, because they were so subject by their own laws without the Roman government. Again, they cannot despise the word *publicanus,* for they have been unable to pay the assessment according to Sulla's poll-tax without the aid of the publican. But that Greek *publicani* are not more considerate in exacting the payment of taxes than our own may be gathered from the fact that the Caunii, and all the islands assigned to the Rhodians by Sulla, recently appealed to the protection of the senate, and petitioned to be allowed to pay their tax to us rather than to the Rhodians. Wherefore neither ought those to revolt at the name of a *publicanus* who have always been subject to tax, nor those to despise it who have been unable to make up the tribute by themselves, nor those to refuse his services who have asked for them. At the same time let Asia reflect on this, that if she were not under our government, there is no calamity of foreign war or internal strife from which she would be free. And since that government cannot possibly be maintained without taxes, she should be content to purchase perpetual peace and tranquility at the price of a certain proportion of her products.

But if they will fairly reconcile themselves to the existence and name of publican, all the rest may be made to appear to them in a less offensive light by your skill and prudence. They may, in making their bargains with the *publicani* not have regard so much to the exact conditions laid down by the censors as to the convenience of settling the business and freeing themselves from further trouble. You also may do, what you have done splendidly and are still doing, namely, dwell on the high position of the *publicani,* and on your obligations to that order, in such a way as—putting out of the question all considerations of your *imperium* and the power of your official authority and dignity—to reconcile the *Greeks* with the *publicani;* and to beg of those, whom you have served eminently well, and who owe you everything, to suffer you by their compliance to maintain and preserve the bonds which unite us with the *publicani.* But why do I address these exhortations to you, who are not only capable of carrying them out of your own accord without anyone's instruction, but have already to a great extent thoroughly done so? For the most respectable and important companies do not cease offering me thanks daily, and this is all the more gratifying to me because the *Greeks* do the same. Now it is an achievement of great difficulty to unite in feeling things which are opposite in interests, aims, and, I had almost said, in their very nature. But I have not written all this to instruct you—for your wisdom requires no man's instruction—but it has been a pleasure to me while writing to set down your virtues, though I have run to greater length in this letter than I could have wished, or than I thought I should.

30

PAUL VEYNE

The Roman Empire:
Where Public Life Was Private

Veyne, a modern historian, argues that corruption was always an intrinsic part of Roman politics, but that the exploitation of the provinces increased toward the end of the Republican era. Cicero's ideal of moral leadership, expressed in the previous selection, was widely ignored in his own day when *publicani* were barred from politics and senators did not openly engage in commerce. Corruption only increased when the barriers between business and government came down as *publicani* and senators traded places and stock tips. Senators always took a personal interest in public affairs, but under the empire they lost sight of the boundaries of public trust and responsibility. What does Veyne mean by "evergetism"? Were there advantages to this Roman style of individual, entrepreneurial government? What were the disadvantages?

Thinking Historically

What are some of the implications of Veyne's argument for those who study the history of the Roman Empire? If public life was private, do we learn more about the Roman Empire by studying the biographies

---

A History of Private Life, Volume 1: From Pagan Rome to Byzantium, ed. Paul Veyne (Cambridge: Harvard University Press, 1987), 95, 96, 98–100, 104–8.

of the important notables than by studying the history of the Roman constitution or its institutions? Or are the lives of these individuals similar enough that the historian can generalize about them as a class with definable backgrounds, aspirations, policies, and effects? What is Veyne's answer to this question?

Roman nobles had a keen sense of the authority and majesty of their Empire, but nothing like our notion of public service. They made no clear distinction between public functions and private rank, or between public finances and personal wealth. The grandeur of Rome was the collective property of the governing class and the ruling group of senators. Similarly, the thousands of autonomous cities that formed the fabric of the Empire were controlled by local notables.

In these cities, as in Rome, legitimate power was in the hands of the governing elite, which stood out by its opulence. The elite had the exclusive right to judge whether or not a particular family was worthy of membership. Legal criteria such as election or wealth of some specified amount were fictions, necessary conditions perhaps, but not at all sufficient. If wealth had been the real criterion, thousands of landowners might have contended for every seat in the Senate. The real method of selection was cooptation. The Senate was a club, and club members decided whether or not a man had the social profile necessary for membership, whether or not he could add to the prestige of the group. Senators did not select new members directly, however; this chore was left to innumerable clientage networks. Public offices were treated as though they were private dignities, access to which depended on private contacts. . . .

Even the least important public positions (*militia*), such as apparitor or clerk of the courts, were sold by their incumbents to aspiring candidates, because every position carried with it a guaranteed income in the form of bribes. A new officeholder was supposed to pay a substantial gratuity (*sportula*) to his superior. In the Late Empire even the highest dignitaries, appointed by the emperor, paid such a gratuity to the imperial treasury. From the very beginning of the Empire, every dignity bestowed by the emperor, from consul to mere captain, imposed upon the person honored the moral duty to make a bequest to his benefactor, the emperor. Failure to fulfill this duty meant running the risk of having one's will set aside for ingratitude and one's estate confiscated by the imperial treasury. And, since every nomination was made on the recommendation of "patrons" with court connections, these recommendations (*suffragia*) were sold or, in any case, paid for. If the patron did not keep his word, the victim did not hesitate to complain to the courts. Courtiers (*proxenetae*) specialized in buying and selling recommendations and clientage (*amicitiae*), though their profession was denounced as disreputable.

Public officials paid themselves. The troops that patrolled the countryside and were responsible for rural administration forced the towns and villages under their jurisdiction to vote them gratuities (*stephanos*). Every official had his palm greased before taking the slightest action. But, because it was important not to skin the animals one fleeced, an official schedule of bribes was eventually established and posted in every office. Suppliants were careful to bring gifts whenever they visited a functionary or high dignitary. The gift was a tangible symbol of the superiority of rulers over ruled.

In addition to bribery, high mandarins practiced extortion. After the Roman conquest of Great Britain, the military administration forced the conquered tribes to take the grain they paid as tax to remote public storehouses and then took bribes for granting permission to use storehouses located closer to home. Demanding payment of illegal taxes was big business among provincial governors, who bought the silence of imperial inspectors and split the profits with their department heads. The central government allowed these abuses to continue, content to receive its due. To pillage the provinces of which one was governor, Cicero said, was the "senatorial way to get rich." A good example was Verres, who ran his province, Sicily, with an iron fist and conducted a bloody reign of terror.

The notion that the government of a province was like a private economic enterprise persisted, albeit on a less spectacular scale, as long as the Empire. It was no secret. Erotic poets waited impatiently for the husbands of their beloved paramours to leave town for a year to make their fortunes in the provinces. The poets professed to live for love alone and to care nothing for career or wealth (the two being interchangeable). Officials enriched themselves in part at public expense. One governor was paid colossal sums for costs incurred in the course of his mission; he never rendered an accounting. Under the Republic, these costs accounted for the bulk of the state budget. Apart from extortion, moreover, the governor engaged in business. In the first century B.C. Italian traders took over the economy of the Greek Orient with the help of governors sent to the region, who profited from their complicity. Roman governors backed Roman merchants because of corruption, not "economic imperialism." . . .

The Romans were in the habit of transforming generalized relations into personal ones, ritualizing them in the process. The younger generation divided itself into a thousand clienteles and went every morning to hail its patrons.

In return for his protection, the patron took pleasure in the knowledge that his peers' protégés did not outnumber his own. The circulation of political elites depended on personal connections. Oral promises, if not kept, resulted in charges of ingratitude. Patrons deluded themselves into thinking that they advanced the careers of young men out of pure friendship. They liked to give advice about careers. (Cicero adopts a condescending tone toward young Trebatius that he does not allow himself with other correspondents.) They wrote innumerable letters of recommendation, which, though usually quite devoid of content, became almost a distinctive literary genre. The essential thing was to inform one's peers of the name of some protégé. Each patron trusted his peers and used his influence in their behalf, as they used theirs in his. Some aspirants were no doubt omitted when recommendations were made. Only those likely to win the approval of the governing class could be recommended; otherwise the patron risked forfeiting his credibility. And credibility was everything. The man with many protégés and many places to distribute was hailed every morning by a small mob. By contrast, the man who turned his back on public life was abandoned: "He will have no more entourage, no escort for his sedan chair, no visitors in his antechamber." Neither in law nor in custom was there a clear dividing line between public life and private life. Certain philosophers urged such a division, but that was all. "Leave your clients, then, and come dine peacefully with me," said the wise Horace to a friend. . . .

"Engaging in political life," which meant simply "holding public office," was not a specialized activity. It was something that any man worthy of the name, and member of the governing class, was expected to do — an ideal of private behavior. To be deprived of access to public office and hence to the city's political life was to be less than a man, a person of no account. . . .

The individual who held public office paid dearly for his lifetime of honor. The lack of distinction between public and private funds was not a one-way affair. The curious institution of public benefaction by government officials has been called "evergetism." Any man named praetor or consul was expected to spend billions from his own pocket to pay for public spectacles, plays, chariot races at the Circus, and even ruinous gladiatorial battles in the Colosseum, to amuse the people of Rome. Afterward the newly appointed official went to the provinces to replenish his coffers. Such was the lot of families included in the senatorial aristocracy — one family out of every ten or twenty thousand. . . .

REFLECTIONS

The legacies of empire in both Rome and China have been considerable. While the Roman Empire was overrun by successive waves of nomadic peoples from the fourth to the eighth centuries, the eventual Christianization of those peoples in Europe was accompanied by the introduction of the Roman language (Latin), the refurbishing of Roman roads, and the revival of Roman law and legal principles. Latin-based languages and Roman-based law are employed today not only in Europe but in regions throughout the world. You might check a world language map to discover the number of countries in which a Latin-based language is spoken.

The most obvious legacy of the Chinese Empire is its continuation, with only brief interruptions, down to the twentieth century. The unique longevity of the Chinese Empire can be attributed to its strikingly early development of bureaucracy.

In his book *The Origins of Statecraft in China,* noted historian Herrlee G. Creel argues that the later European adoption of bureaucracies and civil service examinations were not just reinventions of the same wheel. Such European innovations in the seventeenth and eighteenth centuries, he argues, were based explicitly on Chinese models.

Thus, although they no longer exist today, both the Roman and Chinese empires had a lasting impact and continue to shape our cultures, legal systems, and governments.

Tribal to Universal Religion

Hindu-Buddhist and Judeo-Christian
Traditions, 1000 B.C.E.–100 C.E.

HISTORICAL CONTEXT

From 1000 B.C.E. to 100 C.E. two major religious traditions, one centered in the Middle East and the other in northern India, split into at least four major religious traditions, so large that today they are embraced by a majority of the inhabitants of the world. Each of the two original traditions, Hinduism and Judaism, were in 1000 B.C.E. highly restricted in membership. Neither sought converts but instead ministered to members of their own tribe and castes. This chapter explores how these two essentially inward-looking religions created universal religions, open to all. It is a story not only of the emergence of Christianity and Buddhism but also of the development of modern Judaic and Hindu religions, often called Rabbinical Judaism and devotional Hinduism.

Remarkably, both of these traditions moved from tribal to universal religions; even more remarkable are the common elements, given their different routes along that path. While Hinduism cultivated a psychological approach to spiritual enlightenment out of a priestly religion of obligation, Judaism developed an abiding faith in historical providence from a disastrous history.

As you read the selections in this chapter, notice over the course of the first millennium B.C.E. how both core religions created new faiths and the reform of the old. Notice also the fundamentally different ways these two great religious traditions changed. Finally, observe how the later offspring religions, Buddhism and Christianity, preached ideas that were already current, but not dominant, in the "parental" traditions.

THINKING HISTORICALLY
Detecting Change in Primary Sources

Understanding how religions change or evolve is especially difficult because of the tendency of religious adherents to emphasize the timelessness of their truths. Fortunately, religious commitment and belief does not require a denial of historical change. Indeed, many adherents have found strength in all manifestations of the sacred—the specific and historical as well as the universal and eternal.

Whether motives are primarily religious or secular, however, the historical study of religion offers a useful window on understanding large-scale changes in human behavior. Since religions tend to conserve, repeat, and enshrine, change is more gradual than in many other aspects of human thought and behavior: fashion, say, or technology. Thus, when religions develop radically new ideas or institutions, we can learn much about human resistance and innovation by studying the circumstances.

Because religions typically prefer conservation over innovation, changes are often grafted on to old formulations. Historians who want to understand when and how change occurred must sometimes discover and unmask new ideas and ways of doing things that have been assimilated into the tradition. We will ask you to look for signs of this process of adapting and updating religious ideas.

$$\boxed{31}$$

Svetasvatara Upanishad

In Chapter 3 selections from the Hindu Vedas and Upanishads help introduce some basic ideas in Hinduism: the belief that animals and human castes were created out of the primal sacrifice of the god Purusha in the Vedas, the complementary ideas of karma and reincarnation in the Upanishads, and, lastly, the identification of Brahman and *atman* (self and God) also in the Upanishads.

Svetasvatara Upanishad in *The Upanishads: The Breath of the Eternal*, trans. Swami Prabhavananda and Frederick Manchester (Hollywood: The Vedanta Society of Southern California, 1948; New York: Mentor Books, 1957), 118–21.

We might look at the same selections again to understand the changing nature of Hinduism from the earliest Vedas to the latest Upanishads. For example, we see in selection 11 the interest of the Aryan invaders of India in defining and justifying caste differences and the supremacy of the Brahman priests as masters of sacrifice, prayers, rituals, and sacred hymns.

The authors of the Upanishads were less interested in sacrifice and priestly rituals and more absorbed by philosophical questions. Thus, selection 12 on karma and reincarnation spells out the idea of justice and a philosophy of nature that reflects the interests of a later settled society. Finally, selection 13 on the identity of Brahman and *atman* reflects an even more meditative Upanishad that virtually ignores the role of priests. This meditative tradition may have existed in early Hinduism, but there is far more evidence of its expression in the Upanishads (after 800 B.C.E.) than in the earlier Vedas.

The *Svetasvatara* Upanishad selection included here reflects an additional step along the path from the religion of priests, sacrifice, and caste obligation to individualized spirituality. Here the idea of the transmigration of souls from one body to another in an endless cycle of reincarnations — an idea that developed after the Vedas — is challenged by the idea that the individual who seeks Brahman might break out of the wheel of life. How would this idea of escaping reincarnation diminish the power of Brahman priests? How does it minimize the importance of caste and karma?

Thinking Historically

Recognizing changes in the Hindu tradition is more difficult than in the Judaic tradition. The literature of Judaism is full of historical references: names of historical figures and even dates. Hindu sacred literature, as you can tell from this brief introduction, shows virtually no interest in historical names and dates. Because time in India was conceived as cyclical, rather than linear, and the cycles of the Indian time scheme were immense, determining the exact time an event occurred was less important in Hindu thought than understanding its eternal meaning.

Consequently, our analysis of the changes in Hinduism is more logical than chronological. We can therefore speak of a long-term historical process even though we cannot date each step.

The oldest of the thirteen universally recognized Upanishads, all of which were composed between 800 and 400 B.C.E., are the Brihadaranyaka (from which selection 12 on karma and reincarnation is taken) and the Chandogya (from which selection 13 on *atman* and Brahman is taken). The *Svetasvatara* is one of the last of the thirteen, composed closer to 400 B.C.E. What is the idea of time suggested by this Upanishad?

This vast universe is a wheel. Upon it are all creatures that are subject to birth, death, and rebirth. Round and round it turns, and never stops. It is the wheel of Brahman. As long as the individual self thinks it is separate from Brahman, it revolves upon the wheel in bondage to the laws of birth, death, and rebirth. But when through the grace of Brahman it realizes its identity with him, it revolves upon the wheel no longer. It achieves immortality.

He who is realized by transcending the world of cause and effect, in deep contemplation, is expressly declared by the scriptures to be the Supreme Brahman. He is the substance, all else the shadow. He is the imperishable. The knowers of Brahman know him as the one reality behind all that seems. For this reason they are devoted to him. Absorbed in him, they attain freedom from the wheel of birth, death, and rebirth.

The Lord supports this universe, which is made up of the perishable and the imperishable, the manifest and the unmanifest. The individual soul, forgetful of the Lord, attaches itself to pleasure and thus is bound. When it comes to the Lord, it is freed from all its fetters.

Mind and matter, master and servant — both have existed from beginningless time. The Maya which unites them has also existed from beginningless time. When all three — mind, matter, and Maya — are known as one with Brahman, then is it realized that the Self is infinite and has no part in action. Then is it revealed that the Self is all.

Matter is perishable. The Lord, the destroyer of ignorance, is imperishable, immortal. He is the one God, the Lord of the perishable and of all souls. By meditating on him, by uniting oneself with him, by identifying oneself with him, one ceases to be ignorant.

Know God, and all fetters will be loosed. Ignorance will vanish. Birth, death, and rebirth will be no more. Meditate upon him and transcend physical consciousness. Thus will you reach union with the lord of the universe. Thus will you become identified with him who is One without a second. In him all your desires will find fulfillment.

The truth is that you are always united with the Lord. But you must *know* this. Nothing further is there to know. Meditate, and you will realize that mind, matter, and Maya (the power which unites mind and matter) are but three aspects of Brahman, the one reality.

Fire, though present in the firesticks, is not perceived until one stick is rubbed against another. The Self is like that fire: it is realized in the body by meditation on the sacred syllable OM.[1]

Let your body be the stick that is rubbed, the sacred syllable OM the stick that is rubbed against it. Thus shall you realize God, who is hidden within the body as fire is hidden within the wood.

---

[1] Sacred symbol for God and the sound chanted in meditation. [Ed.]

Like oil in sesame seeds, butter in cream, water in the river bed, fire in tinder, the Self dwells within the soul. Realize him through truthfulness and meditation.

Like butter in cream is the Self in everything. Knowledge of the Self is gained through meditation. The Self is Brahman. By Brahman is all ignorance destroyed.

To realize God, first control the outgoing senses and harness the mind. Then meditate upon the light in the heart of the fire — meditate, that is, upon pure consciousness as distinct from the ordinary consciousness of the intellect. Thus the Self, the Inner Reality, may be seen behind physical appearance.

Control your mind so that the Ultimate Reality, the self-luminous Lord, may be revealed. Strive earnestly for eternal bliss.

With the help of the mind and the intellect, keep the senses from attaching themselves to objects of pleasure. They will then be purified by the light of the Inner Reality, and that light will be revealed.

The wise control their minds, and unite their hearts with the infinite, the omniscient, the all-pervading Lord. Only discriminating souls practice spiritual disciplines. Great is the glory of the self-luminous being, the Inner Reality.

Hear, all ye children of immortal bliss, also ye gods who dwell in the high heavens: Follow only in the footsteps of the illumined ones, and by continuous meditation merge both mind and intellect in the eternal Brahman. The glorious Lord will be revealed to you.

Control the vital force. Set fire to the Self within by the practice of meditation. Be drunk with the wine of divine love. Thus shall you reach perfection.

Be devoted to the eternal Brahman. Unite the light within you with the light of Brahman. Thus will the source of ignorance be destroyed, and you will rise above karma.

Sit upright, holding the chest, throat, and head erect. Turn the senses and the mind inward to the lotus of the heart. Meditate on Brahman with the help of the syllable OM. Cross the fearful currents of the ocean of worldliness by means of the raft of Brahman — the sacred syllable OM.

With earnest effort hold the senses in check. Controlling the breath, regulate the vital activities. As a charioteer holds back his restive horses, so does a persevering aspirant hold back his mind.

Retire to a solitary place, such as a mountain cave or a sacred spot. The place must be protected from the wind and rain, and it must have a smooth, clean floor, free from pebbles and dust. It must not be damp, and it must be free from disturbing noises. It must be pleasing to the eye and quieting to the mind. Seated there, practice meditation and other spiritual exercises.

As you practice meditation, you may see in vision forms resembling snow, crystals, smoke, fire, lightning, fireflies, the sun, the moon. These are signs that you are on your way to the revelation of Brahman.

As you become absorbed in meditation, you will realize that the Self is separate from the body and for this reason will not be affected by disease, old age, or death.

32

Buddhism: Gotama's Discovery

Gotama Siddhartha (c. 563–483 B.C.E.), known to history as the Buddha, was the son of a Hindu Kshatriya prince in northern India. This selection tells a traditional story about his youth. Because his father was warned by "Brahman soothsayers" that young Gotama would leave his home to live among the seekers in the forest, his father kept the boy distracted in the palace, the sufferings of people outside hidden from him. This selection begins when the prince or *raja* finally agrees to let Gotama tour outside the palace.

What does Gotama discover? What seems to be the meaning of these discoveries for him? How is his subsequent thought or behavior similar to that of other Hindus in the era? How is the message of this story similar to the lessons of the Upanishads, especially the *Svetasvatara* Upanishad?

Thinking Historically

None of the stories we have of the Buddha was written during his lifetime. For some four hundred years, stories of the Buddha were passed by word of mouth before they were put into writing. Can you see any signs in this story that it was memorized and told orally? When the stories were finally written, some were no doubt more faithful to the Buddha's actual words and experience than others. What elements in this story would most likely reflect the historical experience of Gotama? What parts of the story would most likely be added later by people who worshiped the Buddha?

"The Life of Gotama the Buddha," trans. E. H. Brewster, in Clarence H. Hamilton, *Buddhism* (1926; reprint, New York: Routledge, 1952).

Now the young lord Gotama, when many days had passed by, bade his charioteer make ready the state carriages, saying: "Get ready the carriages, good charioteer, and let us go through the park to inspect the pleasaunce." "Yes, my lord," replied the charioteer, and harnessed the state carriages and sent word to Gotama: "The carriages are ready, my lord; do now what you deem fit." Then Gotama mounted a state carriage and drove out in state into the park.

Now the young lord saw, as he was driving to the park, an aged man as bent as a roof gable, decrepit, leaning on a staff, tottering as he walked, afflicted and long past his prime. And seeing him Gotama said: "That man, good charioteer, what has he done, that his hair is not like that of other men, nor his body?"

"He is what is called an aged man, my lord."

"But why is he called aged?"

"He is called aged, my lord, because he has not much longer to live."

"But then, good charioteer, am I too subject to old age, one who has not got past old age?"

"You, my lord, and we too, we all are of a kind to grow old; we have not got past old age."

"Why then, good charioteer, enough of the park for today. Drive me back hence to my rooms."

"Yea, my lord," answered the charioteer, and drove him back. And he, going to his rooms, sat brooding sorrowful and depressed, thinking, "Shame then verily be upon this thing called birth, since to one born old age shows itself like that!"

Thereupon the rāja sent for the charioteer and asked him: "Well, good charioteer, did the boy take pleasure in the park? Was he pleased with it?"

"No, my lord, he was not."

"What then did he see on his drive?"

(And the Charioteer told the rāja all.)

Then the rāja thought thus: We must not have Gotama declining to rule. We must not have him going forth from the house into the homeless state. We must not let what the brāhman soothsayers spoke of come true.

So, that these things might not come to pass, he let the youth be still more surrounded by sensuous pleasures. And thus Gotama continued to live amidst the pleasures of sense.

Now after many days had passed by, the young lord again bade his charioteer make ready and drove forth as once before. . . .

And Gotama saw, as he was driving to the park, a sick man, suffering and very ill, fallen and weltering in his own water, by some being lifted up, by others being dressed. Seeing this, Gotama asked: "That man, good charioteer, what has he done that his eyes are not like others' eyes, nor his voice like the voice of other men?"

"He is what is called ill, my lord."

"But what is meant by ill?"

"It means, my lord, that he will hardly recover from his illness."

"But am I too, then, good charioteer, subject to fall ill; have I not got out of reach of illness?"

"You, my lord, and we too, we are all subject to fall ill; we have not got beyond the reach of illness."

"Why then, good charioteer, enough of the park for today. Drive me back hence to my rooms." "Yea, my lord," answered the charioteer, and drove him back. And he, going to his rooms, sat brooding sorrowful and depressed, thinking: Shame then verily be upon this thing called birth, since to one born decay shows itself like that, disease shows itself like that.

Thereupon the rāja sent for the charioteer and asked him: "Well, good charioteer, did the young lord take pleasure in the park and was he pleased with it?"

"No, my lord, he was not."

"What did he see then on his drive?"

(And the charioteer told the rāja all.)

Then the rāja thought thus: We must not have Gotama declining to rule; we must not have him going forth from the house to the homeless state; we must not let what the brāhman soothsayers spoke of come true.

So, that these things might not come to pass, he let the young man be still more abundantly surrounded by sensuous pleasures. And thus Gotama continued to live amidst the pleasures of sense.

Now once again, after many days . . . the young lord Gotama . . . drove forth.

And he saw, as he was driving to the park, a great concourse of people clad in garments of different colours constructing a funeral pyre. And seeing this he asked his charioteer: "Why now are all those people come together in garments of different colours, and making that pile?"

"It is because someone, my lord, has ended his days."

"Then drive the carriage close to him who has ended his days."

"Yea, my lord," answered the charioteer, and did so. And Gotama saw the corpse of him who had ended his days and asked: "What, good charioteer, is ending one's days?"

"It means, my lord, that neither mother, nor father, nor other kinsfolk will now see him, nor will he see them."

"But am I too then subject to death, have I not got beyond reach of death? Will neither the rāja, nor the ranee, nor any other of my kin see me more, or shall I again see them?"

"You, my lord, and we too, we are all subject to death; we have not passed beyond the reach of death. Neither the rāja, nor the ranee, nor any other of your kin will see you any more, nor will you see them."

"Why then, good charioteer, enough of the park for today. Drive me back hence to my rooms."

"Yea, my lord," replied the charioteer, and drove him back.

And he, going to his rooms, sat brooding sorrowful and depressed, thinking: Shame verily be upon this thing called birth, since to one born the decay of life, since disease, since death shows itself like that!

Thereupon the rāja questioned the charioteer as before and as before let Gotama be still more surrounded by sensuous enjoyment. And thus he continued to live amidst the pleasures of sense.

Now once again, after many days . . . the lord Gotama . . . drove forth.

And he saw, as he was driving to the park, a shaven-headed man, a recluse, wearing the yellow robe. And seeing him he asked the charioteer, "That man, good charioteer, what has he done that his head is unlike other men's heads and his clothes too are unlike those of others?"

"That is what they call a recluse, because, my lord, he is one who has gone forth."

"What is that, 'to have gone forth'?"

"To have gone forth, my lord, means being thorough in the religious life, thorough in the peaceful life, thorough in good action, thorough in meritorious conduct, thorough in harmlessness, thorough in kindness to all creatures."

"Excellent indeed, friend charioteer, is what they call a recluse, since so thorough is his conduct in all those respects, wherefore drive me up to that forthgone man."

"Yea, my lord," replied the charioteer and drove up to the recluse. Then Gotama addressed him, saying, "You master, what have you done that your head is not as other men's heads, nor your clothes as those of other men?"

"I, my lord, am one who has gone forth."

"What, master, does that mean?"

"It means, my lord, being thorough in the religious life, thorough in the peaceful life, thorough in good actions, thorough in meritorious conduct, thorough in harmlessness, thorough in kindness to all creatures."

"Excellently indeed, master, are you said to have gone forth since so thorough is your conduct in all those respects." Then the lord Gotama bade his charioteer, saying: "Come then, good charioteer, do you take the carriage and drive it back hence to my rooms. But I will even here cut off my hair, and don the yellow robe, and go forth from the house into the homeless state."

"Yea, my lord," replied the charioteer, and drove back. But the prince Gotama, there and then cutting off his hair and donning the yellow robe, went forth from the house into the homeless state.

Now at Kapilavatthu, the rāja's seat, a great number of persons, some eighty-four thousand souls, heard of what prince Gotama had done and thought: Surely this is no ordinary religious rule, this is no common going forth, in that prince Gotama himself has had his head shaved and has donned the yellow robe and has gone forth from the house into the homeless state. If prince Gotama has done this, why then should not we also? And they all had their heads shaved and donned the yellow robes; and in imitation of the Bodhisat [Buddha] they went forth from the house into the homeless state. So the Bodhisat went forth from the house into the homeless state. So the Bodhisat went up on his rounds through the villages, towns and cities accompanied by that multitude.

Now there arose in the mind of Gotama the Bodhisat, when he was meditating in seclusion, this thought: That indeed is not suitable for me that I should live beset. 'Twere better were I to dwell alone, far from the crowd.

So after a time he dwelt alone, away from the crowd. Those eighty-four thousand recluses went one way, and the Bodhisat went another way.

Now there arose in the mind of Gotama the Bodhisat, when he had gone to his place and was meditating in seclusion, this thought: Verily, this world had fallen upon trouble — one is born, and grows old, and dies, and falls from one state, and springs up in another. And from the suffering, moreover, no one knows of any way to escape, even from decay and death. O, when shall a way of escape from this suffering be made known — from decay and from death?

33

The Buddha's First Sermon

This is said to be the Buddha's first sermon, delivered shortly after he achieved enlightenment. It contains the essence of Buddhist thought: the four noble truths, the eightfold path, and the middle way. The middle way is the course between the extremes of the pursuit of pleasure and the pursuit of pain. It is defined by an eightfold path, eight steps to a peaceful mind. The four noble truths might be summarized as the following:

1. Life is sorrow.
2. Sorrow is the result of selfish desire.

The Buddhist Tradition in India, China and Japan, ed. William Theodore de Bary (New York: Random House, 1969), 16–17.

3. Selfish desire can be destroyed.
4. It can be destroyed by following the eightfold path.

What do these ideas mean? What was considered the value of a "middle way"? In what ways did the eightfold path offer a spiritual discipline? What answers did the four noble truths provide?

Thinking Historically

How is the tone and style of this selection different from "Gotama's Discovery"? Would these events occur before or after the "discovery"? Nevertheless, why is it likely that this story was created earlier than the previous one and is probably closer to the actual words and experience of the Buddha?

Thus I have heard. Once the Lord was at Vrānasī, at the deer park called Iwipatana. There he addressed the five monks:

There are two ends not to be served by a wanderer. What are these two? The pursuit of desires and of the pleasure which springs from desire, which is base, common, leading to rebirth, ignoble, and unprofitable; and the pursuit of pain and hardship, which is grievous, ignoble, and unprofitable. The Middle Way of the Tathāgata avoids both these ends. It is enlightened, it brings clear vision, it makes for wisdom, and leads to peace, insight, enlightenment, and Nirvāna. What is the Middle Way? . . . It is the Noble Eightfold Path — Right Views, Right Resolve, Right Speech, Right Conduct, Right Livelihood, Right Effort, Right Mindfulness, and Right Concentration. This is the Middle Way. . . .

And this is the Noble Truth of Sorrow. Birth is sorrow, age is sorrow, disease is sorrow, death is sorrow; contact with the unpleasant is sorrow, separation from the pleasant is sorrow, every wish unfulfilled is sorrow — in short all the five components of individuality are sorrow.

And this is the Noble Truth of the Arising of Sorrow. It arises from craving, which leads to rebirth, which brings delight and passion, and seeks pleasure now here, now there — the craving for sensual pleasure, the craving for continued life, the craving for power.

And this is the Noble Truth of the Stopping of Sorrow. It is the complete stopping of that craving, so that no passion remains, leaving it, being emancipated from it, being released from it, giving no place to it.

And this is the Noble Truth of the Way which Leads to the Stopping of Sorrow. It is the Noble Eightfold Path — Right Views, Right Resolve, Right Speech, Right Conduct, Right Livelihood, Right Effort, Right Mindfulness, and Right Concentration.

$\boxed{34}$

Buddhism and Caste

This story, part of the Buddhist canon that was written between one and four hundred years after his death, tells of a confrontation between the Buddha and Brahmans, members of the Hindu priestly caste. This encounter would have been common. Why would it be important? How would you expect most Brahmans to react to the Buddha's opposition to caste? Would some Brahmans be persuaded by the Buddha's arguments? How and why would the appeal of Buddhism be more universal than Hinduism?

Thinking Historically

Notice the mention of Greece and the dialogue style of this selection. If, as some scholars have suggested, there may be Greek influence here, which Greek writer would they be referring to? How might this Greek influence help us find an approximate date for this writing?

Once when the Lord was staying at Sāvatthī there were five hundred brāhmans from various countries in the city . . . and they thought: "This ascetic Gautama preaches that all four classes are pure. Who can refute him?"

At that time there was a young brāhman named Assalāyana in the city . . . a youth of sixteen, thoroughly versed in the Vedas . . . and in all brāhmanic learning. "He can do it!" thought the brāhmans, and so they asked him to try; but he answered, "The ascetic Gautama teaches a doctrine of his own, and such teachers are hard to refute. I can't do it!" They asked him a second time . . . and again he refused; and they asked him a third time, pointing out that he ought not to admit defeat without giving battle. This time he agreed, and so, surrounded by a crowd of brāhmans, he went to the Lord, and, after greeting him, sat down and said:

"Brāhmans maintain that only they are the highest class, and the others are below them. They are white, the others black; only they are pure, and not the others. Only they are the true sons of Brahmā, born

---

The Buddhist Tradition in India, China and Japan, ed. William Theodore de Bary (New York: Random House, 1969), 49–51.

from his mouth, born of Brahmā, creations of Brahmā, heirs of Brahmā. Now what does the worthy Gautama say to that?"

"Do the brāhmans really maintain this, Assalāyana, when they're born of women just like anyone else, of brāhman women who have their periods and conceive, give birth and nurse their children, just like any other women?"

"For all you say, this is what they think. . . . "

"Have you ever heard that in the lands of the Greeks and Kambojas and other peoples on the borders there are only two classes, masters and slaves, and a master can become a slave and vice versa?"

"Yes, I've heard so."

"And what strength or support does that fact give to the brāhmans' claim?"

"Nevertheless, that is what they think."

"Again if a man is a murderer, a thief, or an adulterer, or commits other grave sins, when his body breaks up on death does he pass on to purgatory if he's a kshatriya,[1] vaishya,[2] or shūdra,[3] but not if he's a brāhman?"

"No, Gautama. In such a case the same fate is in store for all men, whatever their class."

"And if he avoids grave sin, will he go to heaven if he's a brāhman, but not if he's a man of the lower classes?"

"No, Gautama. In such a case the same reward awaits all men, whatever their class."

"And is a brāhman capable of developing a mind of love without hate or ill-will, but not a man of the other classes?"

"No, Gautama. All four classes are capable of doing so."

"Can only a brāhman go down to a river and wash away dust and dirt, and not men of the other classes?"

"No, Gautama, all four classes can."

"Now suppose a king were to gather together a hundred men of different classes and to order the brāhmans and kshatriyas to take kindling wood of sāl, pine, lotus, or sandal, and light fires, while the low-class folk did the same with common wood. What do you think would happen? Would the fires of the high-born men blaze up brightly . . . and those of the humble fail?"

"No, Gautama. It would be alike with high and lowly. . . . Every fire would blaze with the same bright flame." . . .

"Suppose there are two young brāhman brothers, one a scholar and the other uneducated. Which of them would be served first at memorial feasts, festivals, and sacrifices, or when entertained as guests?"

[1] Warrior. [Ed.]

[2] Free peasant, artisan, or producer. [Ed.]

[3] Serf. [Ed.]

"The scholar, of course; for what great benefit would accrue from entertaining the uneducated one?"

"But suppose the scholar is ill-behaved and wicked, while the uneducated one is well-behaved and virtuous?"

"Then the uneducated one would be served first, for what great benefit would accrue from entertaining an ill-behaved and wicked man?"

"First, Assalāyana, you based your claim on birth, then you gave up birth for learning, and finally you have come round to my way of thinking, that all four classes are equally pure!"

At this Assalāyana sat silent . . . his shoulders hunched, his eyes cast down, thoughtful in mind, and with no answer at hand.

$$35$$

The Bible:
History, Laws, and Psalms

Just as the caste-based Hinduism of ancient Aryan tribes gave rise to universal Buddhism after 500 B.C.E., so did the Judaism of the tribe of Abraham give birth to universalist Christianity. Judaism was already an ancient religion by the time of Jesus. It traced its roots back (perhaps two thousand years) to Abraham himself who, according to tradition, made a contract (or covenant) with God to worship him and him alone. This God promised Abraham and his descendants prosperity and many heirs. In return Abraham and his male descendants would be circumcised as a sign of their loyalty.

This commitment to one god, and one god only, was to mark the ancient Jews as unique. No other people in the ancient world were monotheistic. The people of Mesopotamia, Egypt, India, and the Mediterranean accepted various ancestral and natural gods. Only the Egyptians for a brief moment (around 1300 B.C.E.) preached the singularity of god, in this case the sun god Aton, but that was soon renounced. Since such a belief was unusual, the descendants of Abraham had difficulty accepting it. In their wanderings throughout the

---

Gen. 1:1–2:25, 17:1–17:14; Exod. 19:1–20:18; Lev. 1:1–1:9; Ps. 23:1–23:6; Amos 5:21–5:24. All biblical selections are from the King James Version.

land of the Tigris and Euphrates Rivers, from Abraham's native Ur to Egypt, the Jews came into contact with many different religious beliefs; some were even tempted by foreign gods. However, by around 1300 B.C.E., Abraham's descendants escaped Egyptian domination, crossed the Red Sea, and with the help of Moses renewed their covenant with God in the Ten Commandments. Even then, stories were told of Jews who worshiped the Golden Calf and other idols and of the displeasure of the God of Abraham. "I am a jealous God," he told his people. "Thou shall not take other gods before you." In fact, seven hundred years later, the prophet Jeremiah (628–526 B.C.E.) chastised the people for worshiping Baal as well as Yahweh, the God of Abraham.

Such is the story told in the books of the Bible, written after the Jews settled in Jerusalem and the surrounding area sometime after 1000 B.C.E. They wrote of their history since the time of Abraham, even their version of the ages before the patriarch, stretching back to the beginning of the world. And in the heady days of Jewish kingdoms, Kings Saul, David, and Solomon ruled large parts of what is today Israel, Palestine, and Jordan by about 900 B.C.E. The book we know as the Bible included these histories, the laws of the two Jewish kingdoms Judah and Israel, and various other writings (songs, psalms, and philosophy).

As you read these first selections from the Bible (Genesis, Exodus, Leviticus, and Psalms), note how they are similar to, and different from, the Vedas and Upanishads of Hinduism. How, for instance, is the story of the beginning of the world different from the sacrifice of Purusha? Why is an understanding of history more important to the Jews than it was to the Hindus? Compare the role of morality in the religion of Jews and Hindus. In what sense is the morality of Judaism universal and that of Hinduism caste based? How is the Judaic emphasis on morality also different from Buddhist ideas?

Thinking Historically

Since the books of the Hebrew Bible were composed over a long period of time, from about 900 B.C.E. to about 165 B.C.E., we might expect to see changes in emphasis, especially since this period was such a tumultuous one in Jewish history. The immediate descendants of Abraham were a nomadic pastoral people — shepherds, Psalm 23 reminds us, though this beautiful psalm attributed to King David was written in an urban, monarchal stage of Jewish history. Leviticus, too, echoes an earlier pastoral life where animal sacrifice, and the worship by shepherds generally, was still practiced.

When did morality replace sacrifice as the sign of respect to the God of Abraham? Was it around 1300 B.C.E., the traditional date for the reception by Moses of the Ten Commandments? Or is the existence of Leviticus, perhaps five hundred years later, a sign that sacrifice was still practiced? The sentiments of Amos (783–743 B.C.E.) suggest a later rejection not only of animal sacrifice but also of moral obedience that was not truly felt.

When did monotheism (the belief in one god) become unequivocal, unquestioned? Since this was a new idea, there must have been a time when it wasn't held. Some scholars see signs of an earlier polytheism (belief in many gods) in the book of Genesis itself. Certainly the beginning of Genesis is no-nonsense monotheism, majestically so: "In the beginning God created the heaven and the earth." But scholars have pointed out that this opening precedes another story of origin beginning at Chapter 2, Verse 4, that not only tells the story over again, but does so without the intense declarative monotheism. They date this document at about 850 B.C.E. and the section from 1:1 to 2:3 at about 650 B.C.E. What evidence do you see in this second, older Genesis (after 2:4) of remnants of an older polytheism?

Finally, notice there is no heaven here — no afterlife. God promised Abraham land and prosperity. Even today, a belief in personal immortality is more accepted by Christians than Jews. Still, we will explore the development of that idea in Judaism in the second century B.C.E.

Genesis

Chapter 1

1 In the beginning God created the heaven and the earth. 2 And the earth was without form, and void; and darkness was upon the face of the deep. And the Spirit of God moved upon the face of the waters. 3 And God said, Let there be light: and there was light. 4 And God saw the light, and it was good: and God divided the light from the darkness. 5 And God called the light Day, and the darkness he called Night. And the evening and the morning were the first day.

6 And God said, Let there be a firmament in the midst of the waters, and let it divide the waters. 7 And God made the firmament, and divided the waters which were under the firmament from the waters which were above the firmament: and it was so. 8 And God called the firmament Heaven. And the evening and the morning were the second day.

9 And God said, Let the waters under the heaven be gathered together unto one place, and let the dry land appear: and it was so. 10 And God called the dry land Earth; and the gathering together of the water called he Seas: and God saw it was good. 11 And God said, Let the earth

bring forth grass, the herb yielding seed, and the fruit tree yielding fruit after his kind, whose seed is in itself, upon the earth: and it was so. 12 And the earth brought forth grass, and herb yielding seed after his kind, and the tree yielding fruit, whose seed was in itself, after his kind: and God saw it was good. 13 And the evening and the morning were the third day.

14 And God said, Let there be lights in the firmament of the heaven to divide the day from the night; and let them be for signs, and for seasons, and for days, and years: 15 And let them be for lights in the firmament of the heaven to give light upon the earth: and it was so. 16 And God made two great lights; the greater light to rule the day, and the lesser light to rule the night: he made the stars also. 17 And God set them in the firmament of the heaven to give light upon the earth, 18 And to rule over the day and over the night, and to divide the light from the darkness: and God saw that it was good. 19 And the evening and the morning were the fourth day.

20 And God said, Let the waters bring forth abundantly the moving creatures that hath life, and fowl that may fly above the earth in the open firmament of heaven. 21 And God created great whales, and every living creature that moveth, which the waters brought forth abundantly, after their kind, and every winged fowl after his kind: and God saw that it was good. 22 And God blessed them, saying, Be fruitful, and multiply, and fill the waters in the seas, and let fowl multiply in the earth. 23 And the evening and the morning were the fifth day.

24 And God said, Let the earth bring forth the living creature after his kind, cattle, and creeping thing, and beast of the earth after his kind: and it was so. 25 And God made the beast of the earth after his kind, and cattle after their kind, and every thing that creepeth upon the earth after his kind: and God saw that it was good.

26 And God said, Let us make man in our image, after our likeness: and let them have dominion over the fish of the sea, and over the fowl of the air, and over the cattle, and over all the earth, and over every creeping thing that creepeth upon the earth. 27 So God created man in his own image, in the image of God created he him: male and female created he them. 28 And God blessed them, and God said unto them, Be fruitful, and multiply, and replenish the earth, and subdue it: and have dominion over the fish of the sea, and over the fowl of the air, and over every living thing that moveth upon the earth.

29 And God said, Behold, I have given you every herb bearing seed, which is upon the face of all the earth, and every tree, in which is the fruit of a tree yielding seed; to you it shall be for meat. 30 And to every beast of the earth, and to every fowl of the air, and to every thing that creepeth upon the earth, wherein there is life, I have given every green herb for meat: and it was so. 31 And God saw every thing that he had made, and, behold, it was very good. And the evening and the morning were the sixth day.

Chapter 2

1 Thus the heavens and the earth were finished, and all the host of them. 2 And on the seventh day God ended his work which he had made; and he rested on the seventh day from all his work which he had made. 3 And God blessed the seventh day, and sanctified it: because that in it he had rested from all this work which God created and made.

4 These are the generations of the heavens and of the earth when they were created, in the day that the Lord God made the earth and the heavens. 5 And every plant of the field before it was in the earth, and every herb of the field before it grew: for the Lord God had not caused it to rain upon the earth, and there was not a man to till the ground. 6 But there went up a mist from the earth, and watered the whole face of the ground. 7 And the Lord God formed man of the dust of the ground, and breathed into his nostrils the breath of life; and man became a living soul.

8 And the Lord God planted a garden eastward in Eden; and there he put the man whom he had formed. 9 And out of the ground made the Lord God to grow every tree that is pleasant to the sight, and good for food; and the tree of life also in the midst of the garden, and the tree of knowledge of good and evil. 10 And a river went out of Eden to water the garden; and from thence it was parted, and became into four heads. 11 The name of the first is Pison: that is it which compasseth the whole land of Havilah, where there is gold; 12 And the gold of the land is good: there is bdellium and the onyx stone. 13 And the name of the second river is Gihon: the same is it that compasseth the whole land of Ethiopia. 14 And the name of the third river is Hiddekel: that is it which goeth toward the east of Assyria. And the fourth river is Euphrates. 15 And the Lord God took the man, and put him into the garden of Eden to dress it and to keep it. 16 And the Lord God commanded the man, saying, Of every tree of the garden thou mayest freely eat: 17 But of the tree of the knowledge of good and evil, thou shalt not eat of it: for in the day that thou eatest thereof thou shalt surely die.

18 And the Lord God said, It is not good that the man should be alone; I will make him a help meet for him. 19 And out of the ground the Lord God formed every beast of the field, and every fowl of the air; and brought them unto Adam to see what he would call them: and whatsoever Adam called every living creature, that was the name thereof. 20 And Adam gave names to all cattle, and to the fowl of the air, and to every beast of the field; but for Adam there was not found a help meet for him. 21 And the Lord God caused a deep sleep to fall upon Adam, and he slept; and he took one of his ribs, and closed up the flesh instead thereof. 22 And the rib, which the Lord God had taken from man, made he a woman, and brought her unto the man. 23 And Adam said, This is now bone of my bones, and flesh of my flesh: she shall be called Woman, because she was taken out of man. 24 There-

fore shall a man leave his father and his mother, and shall cleave unto his wife: and they shall be one flesh. 25 And they were both naked, the man and his wife, and were not ashamed.

Chapter 17

1 And when Abram was ninety years old and nine, the Lord appeared to Abram, and said unto him, I am the Almighty God; walk before me, and be thou perfect. 2 And I will make my covenant between me and thee, and will multiply thee exceedingly. 3 And Abram fell on his face: and God talked with him, saying, 4 As for me, behold, my covenant is with thee, and thou shalt be a father of many nations. 5 Neither shall thy name any more be called Abram, but thy name shall be Abraham; for a father of many nations I have made thee. 6 And I will make thee exceeding fruitful, and I will make nations of thee, and kings shall come out of thee. 7 And I will establish my covenant between me and thee and thy seed after thee in their generations, for an everlasting covenant, to be a God unto thee and to thy seed after thee. 8 And I will give unto thee, and to thy seed after thee, the land wherein thou art a stranger, all the land of Canaan, for an everlasting possession; and I will be their God. 9 And God said unto Abraham. Thou shalt keep my covenant therefore, thou, and thy seed after thee in their generations.

10 This is my covenant, which he shall keep, between me and you and thy seed after thee; Every man child among you shall be circumcised.

11 And ye shall circumcise the flesh of your foreskin; and it shall be a token of the covenant betwixt me and you. 12 And he that is eight days old shall be circumcised among you, every man child in your generations, he that is born in the house, or bought with money of any stranger, which is not of thy seed. 13 He that is born in thy house, and he that is bought with thy money, must needs be circumcised: and my covenant shall be in your flesh for an everlasting covenant. 14 And the uncircumcised man child whose flesh of his foreskin is not circumcised, that soul shall be cut off from his people; he hath broken my covenant.

Exodus

Chapter 19

1 In the third month, when the children of Israel were gone forth out of the land of Egypt, the same day came they into the wilderness of Sinai.

2 For they were departed from Rephidim, and were come to the desert of Sinai, and had pitched in the wilderness; and there Israel camped before the mount. 3 And Moses went up unto God, and the

Lord called unto him out of the mountain, saying, Thus shalt thou say to the house of Jacob, and tell the children of Israel; 4 Ye have seen what I did unto the Egyptians, and how I bare you on eagles' wings, and brought you unto myself. 5 Now therefore, if ye will obey my voice indeed, and keep my covenant, then ye shall be a peculiar treasure unto me above all people: for all the earth is mine: 6 And ye shall be unto me a kingdom of priests, and a holy nation. These are the words which thou shalt speak unto the children of Israel.

7 And Moses came and called for the elders of the people, and laid before their faces all these words which the Lord commanded him. 8 And all the people answered together, and said, All that the Lord hath spoken we will do. And Moses returned the words of the people unto the Lord. 9 And the Lord said unto Moses, Lo, I come unto thee in a thick cloud, that the people may hear when I speak with thee, and believe thee for ever. And Moses told the words of the people unto the Lord.

Chapter 20

1 And God spake all these words, saying,

2 I am the Lord thy God, which have brought thee out of the land of Egypt, out of the house of bondage. 3 Thou shalt have no other gods before me.

4 Thou shalt not make unto thee any graven image, or any likeness of any thing that is in heaven above, or that is in the earth beneath, or that is in the water under the earth: 5 Thou shalt not bow down thyself to them, nor serve them: for I the Lord thy God am a jealous God, visiting the iniquity of the fathers upon the children unto the third and fourth generation of them that hate me; 6 And showing mercy unto thousands of them that love me, and keep my commandments.

7 Thou shalt not take the name of the Lord thy God in vain: for the Lord will not hold him guiltless that taketh his name in vain.

8 Remember the sabbath day, to keep it holy. 9 Six days shalt thou labor, and do all thy work: 10 But the seventh day is the sabbath of the Lord thy God: in it thou shalt not do any work, thou, nor thy son, nor thy daughter, nor thy manservant, nor thy maidservant, nor thy cattle, nor thy stranger that is within thy gates: 11 For in six days the Lord made heaven and earth, the sea, and all that in them is, and rested the seventh day: wherefore the Lord blessed the sabbath day, and hallowed it.

12 Honor thy father and thy mother: that thy days may be long upon the land which the Lord thy God giveth thee.

13 Thou shalt not kill.

14 Thou shalt not commit adultery.

15 Thou shalt not steal.

16 Thou shalt not bear false witness against thy neighbor.

17 Thou shalt not covet thy neighbor's house; thou shalt not covet thy neighbor's wife, nor his manservant, nor his maidservant, nor his ox, nor his ass, nor any thing that is thy neighbor's.

18 And all the people saw the thunderings, and the lightnings, and the noise of the trumpet, and the mountain smoking: and when the people saw it, they removed, and stood afar off.

Leviticus

Chapter 1

1 And the Lord called unto Moses, and spake unto him out of the tabernacle of the congregation, saying, 2 Speak unto the children of Israel, and say unto them, If any man of you bring an offering unto the Lord, ye shall bring your offering of the cattle, even of the herd, and of the flock.

3 If his offering be a burnt sacrifice of the herd, let him offer a male without blemish: he shall offer it of his own voluntary will at the door of the tabernacle of the congregation before the Lord. 4 And he shall put his hand upon the head of the burnt offering; and it shall be accepted for him to make atonement for him. 5 And he shall kill the bullock before the Lord: and the priests, Aaron's sons, shall bring the blood, and sprinkle the blood round about upon the altar that is by the door of the tabernacle of the congregation. 6 And he shall flay the burnt offering, and cut it into his pieces. 7 And the sons of Aaron the priest shall put fire upon the altar, and lay the wood in order upon the fire: 8 And the priests, Aaron's sons, shall lay the parts, the head, and the fat, in order upon the wood that is on the fire which is upon the altar: 9 But his inwards and his legs shall he wash in water: and the priest shall burn all on the altar, to be a burnt sacrifice, an offering made by fire, of a sweet savor unto the Lord.

Psalm 23

1 The Lord is my shepherd; I shall not want.

2 He maketh me to lie down in green pastures: He leadeth me beside the still waters.

3 He restoreth my soul: He leadeth me in the paths of righteousness for his name's sake.

4 Yea, though I walk through the valley of the shadow of death, I will fear no evil: for thou art with me; Thy rod and thy staff they comfort me.

5 Thou preparest a table before me in the presence of mine enemies: Thou anointest my head with oil; my cup runneth over.

6 Surely goodness and mercy shall follow me all the days of my life:
And I will dwell in the house of the Lord for ever.

Amos

Chapter 5

21 I hate, I despise your feast days, and I will not delight in your solemn
assemblies.

22 Though you offer me burnt offerings and your meat offerings, I
will not accept them: neither will I regard the peace offerings of your
fat beasts.

23 Take thou away from me the noise of thy songs; for I will not
hear the melody of thy viols.

24 But let judgment run down as waters, and righteousness as a
mighty stream.

36

The Hebrew Bible: Prophets and Apocalypse

The golden days of Jewish kings were not to last. Powerful empires
rose up to challenge and dominate the Jews: the Assyrians in 800
B.C.E., the Babylonians around 600 B.C.E., then the Medes, the Persians, the armies of Alexander the Great, his successor states — ruled
by his generals and their descendants — and then the Romans after 64
B.C.E. The Babylonians were among the worst of the invaders. They
conquered Jerusalem, destroyed the temple, and brought Jews as
hostages to Babylon. In 538 B.C.E. Cyrus, king of the Persians, allowed
Jews to return to Jerusalem and even rebuild the temple. But the Jews
never regained their kingdom or independence (except for brief periods), and the Greek Seleucid rulers after Alexander proved to be intolerant of non-Greek forms of worship.

Ironically, it was during this period of conquest and dispersal that
Judaism began to develop the elements of a universal religion. The
Babylonian destruction of the temple and population transfer made

---

Dan. 12:1–12:13 King James.

the religion of Yahweh less dependent on place. Virtually all religions of the ancient world were bound to a particular place, usually the sacred temple where the god was thought to reside. Judaism remained a religion of the descendants of Abraham and his son Israel, and the period after 600 B.C.E. was one of intense cultivation of that identity. But much of the Hebrew Bible was composed in exile, as a way of recalling a common history, reaffirming a common identity, predicting a common future. The prophets foresaw a brighter future or explained how the violation of the covenant had brought God's wrath on the people. In exile in Babylon, the Psalms mourned the loss of Jerusalem. "By the rivers of Babylon. . . . we wept. . . . How shall we sing the Lord's song in a strange land?" Psalms 137:1–4. But in Babylon, the children of Israel found their God transcended worldly boundaries. "I am the Lord and there is none else. I form the light and create darkness," Isaiah (550–539 B.C.E.) wrote.

One of the great prophets of the exile and the postexile period was Daniel, described as one of the young men who was brought to Babylon by Nebuchadnezzar, conqueror of Jerusalem in 586 B.C.E. The Book of Daniel begins by recounting that conquest. In Babylon Nebuchadnezzar asked Daniel to reveal the meaning of a dream. Daniel told the king that a dream in which a large statue with a gold head, silver chest, bronze thighs, iron legs, and feet of clay is destroyed is a symbol of Nebuchadnezzar's golden kingdom and future kingdoms that will come after him. But, Daniel reveals, the destruction of the statue means that after the kings of clay, the world itself will come to an end.

Daniel is the first to foretell this apocalyptic end to history and the first to envision personal immortality. Previous prophets had predicted a new independent kingdom of Judah or they had predicted God's punishment of his people, but Daniel prophesied that God would come down to reign on earth forever, judging the living and the dead for all eternity. These ideas — an end to history, the Last Judgment, the Kingdom of God, eternal life or damnation — became more important later in Christianity than in Judaism, where these notions never entered the mainstream. But their appearance in Daniel shows the way in which Judaic ideas became more universal over the course of the first millennium B.C.E. Why would Daniel's ideas open the Judaic tradition to non-Jews or people not descended from Abraham? How would Daniel's prophecy affect his contemporaries? How would it affect you?

Thinking Historically

When did the idea of an afterlife enter Judaism? To answer this question we have to date the Book of Daniel, which is a bit more complex than it would seem. As mentioned, the book is presented as the prophecy of a Daniel who was taken from Jerusalem to Babylon around 586 B.C.E. If there was such a Daniel and he was a prophet, the version we have shows signs of continual updating. In the initial prophecy for Nebuchadnezzar and in similar instances reported throughout the Book of Daniel, the author predicts the string of empires that determined the fate of the Jews from the Babylonian to the Median to the Persian to the Greek under Alexander to the Seleucid (Alexander's successors). This is the meaning of the gold, silver, bronze, iron, clay sequence. In each case, the prophecy is vague (and sometimes inaccurate) when referring to the Babylonian period but very specific and exact about the period of iron and clay (the Seleucids). When Daniel speaks of the signs of the last days, his veiled references clearly refer to events during the reign of the Seleucid ruler Antiochus IV. He distinctly sees the desecration of the temple by Antiochus as the key event that will bring about God's eternal kingdom. Antiochus, who ruled from 175 to 163 B.C.E., pressured the Jews to accept Greek gods. In 168 B.C.E. he polluted the temple by slaughtering pigs on the altar and then erecting a statue of the Greek god Zeus — the event that Daniel predicts will bring on God's last judgment.

What would be the purpose of putting this prophecy in the writings of someone who had lived hundreds of years earlier? How does the age of Daniel's message give it added impact? When and why would the author of the Book of Daniel have predicted that the end of the world would occur 1290 days after an event in 168 B.C.E.? When and why would he have written "blessed are those who wait 1335 days"?

Daniel

Chapter 12

1 And at that time shall Michael stand up, the great prince which standeth for the children of thy people: and there shall be a time of trouble, such as never was since there was a nation even to that same time: and at that time thy people shall be delivered, every one that shall be found written in the book. 2 And many of them that sleep in the dust of the earth shall awake, some to everlasting life, and some to shame and everlasting contempt. 3 And they that be wise shall shine as the brightness of the firmament; and they that turn many to righteousness, as the stars forever and ever. 4 But thou, O Daniel, shut up the words, and seal the book, even to the time of the end: many shall run to and fro, and knowledge shall be increased.

5 Then I Daniel looked, and, behold, there stood other two, the one on this side of the bank of the river, and the other on that side of the bank of the river. 6 And one said to the man clothed in linen, which was upon the waters of the river, How long shall it be to the end of these wonders? 7 And I heard the man clothed in linen, which was upon the waters of the river, when he held up his right hand and his left hand unto heaven, and swore by him that liveth for ever, that it shall be for a time, times, and a half; and when he shall have accomplished to scatter the power of the holy people, all of these things shall be finished.

8 And I heard, but I understood not: then said I, O my Lord, what shall be the end of these things? 9 And he said, Go thy way, Daniel: for the words are closed up and sealed till the time of the end. 10 Many shall be purified, and made white, and tried; but the wicked shall do wickedly: and none of the wicked shall understand; but the wise shall understand.

11 And from the time that the daily sacrifice shall be taken away, and the abomination that maketh desolate set up, there shall be a thousand two hundred and ninety days. 12 Blessed is he that waiteth, and cometh to the thousand three hundred and five and thirty days. 13 But go thou thy way till the end be: for thou shalt rest, and stand in thy lot at the end of the days.

37

Christianity:
Jesus according to Matthew

The related ideas first enunciated in Daniel — the coming end of the world or the Kingdom of God, the Last Judgment, individual immortality or life after death — were to become central to the branch of Judaism that produced Christianity. Along with Judaic monotheism and the insistence of the prophets (like Amos) on internalized morality, the idea of personal responsibility and eternal salvation or damnation gave Christianity an appeal that would eventually reach far beyond the children of Abraham.

Matt. 24:1–24:41 King James.

In this selection from the Gospel of Matthew, the evangelist re-counts Jesus speaking of the apocalypse. There is a note of urgency here. Jesus tells his listeners that when they "see the abomination of desolation," they shall flee. Like Daniel, Jesus speaks of the signs that the end is at hand. He then tells his listeners "this generation shall not pass till all these things be fulfilled." (24:34)

In the same chapter, sometimes in the same paragraph, however, Matthew recounts Jesus telling his listeners that there is plenty of time before the end. There will be wars and rumors of wars, famines, earthquakes, false prophets. "And this gospel of the kingdom shall be preached in all the world for a witness unto all nations; and then shall the end come" (24:14).

What accounts for this apparent contradiction? If you were in the audience listening to Jesus, what idea would motivate you more — the fact that the end of the world is rapidly approaching or that it is gen-erations away? If you were taking notes for the daily newspaper, which message would get the headline? If you were writing a history of Jesus for future generations, which message would you emphasize?

Thinking Historically

Matthew was writing about forty years after Jesus died. If he had been among those who heard Jesus speak, he took a long time to write it down. It is more likely that the author of this gospel is a second-generation evangelist, drawing on an earlier source, now lost. He may have had access to an earlier eyewitness account, or to a collection of sayings of Jesus. If he did have an earlier source, how would we deter-mine what was in it?

We know that Matthew updated the words of Jesus for the benefit of those Christians living after 70 C.E. Notice, for example, Matthew's reference to Daniel in 24:15: Jesus tells his listeners that when they see the abomination of the temple of which Daniel spoke, they should flee into the mountains to prepare for the end. But we know today that Daniel was speaking of the desecration of the temple by Antiochus IV in 168 B.C.E. Matthew, unaware of the historical context of Daniel and writing after the Roman destruction of the temple in 70 C.E., be-lieved that Roman destruction was the event Daniel was predicting. So Matthew updates the message of Jesus for future generations by in-cluding the temple desecration for the readers of his gospel ("whoso readeth, let him understand"). This is one of the ways we know that Matthew was written after 70 C.E. Jesus would not have referred to an event which was for his audience forty years into the future, and ex-pect his audience to understand his reference. So we know that Matthew added material that would update the message of Jesus for future generations. The question is how much did Matthew add to or alter Jesus' message? Which parts of this selection would most likely have been updated by Matthew? Which quotations of Jesus were apt to need updating?

Matthew

Chapter 24

1 And Jesus went out, and departed from the temple: and his disciples came to him for to show him the buildings of the temple. 2 And Jesus said unto them, See ye not all these things? verily I say unto You, There shall not be left here one stone upon another, that shall not be thrown down. 3 And as he sat upon the Mount of Olives, the disciples came unto him privately, saying, Tell us, when shall these things be? and what shall be the sign of thy coming, and of the end of the world? 4 And Jesus answered and said unto them, Take heed that no man deceive you. 5 For many shall come in my name, saying, I am Christ; and shall deceive many. 6 And ye shall hear of wars and rumors of wars: see that ye be not troubled: for all these things must come to pass, but the end is not yet. 7 For nation shall rise against nation, and kingdom against kingdom: and there shall be famines, and pestilences, and earthquakes, in divers places. 8 All these are the beginning of sorrows. 9 Then shall they deliver you up to be afflicted, and shall kill you: and ye shall be hated of all nations for my name's sake. 10 And then shall many be offended, and shall betray one another, and shall hate one another. 11 And many false prophets shall rise, and shall deceive many. 12 And because iniquity shall abound, the love of many shall wax cold. 13 But he that shall endure unto the end, the same shall be saved. 14 And this gospel of the kingdom shall be preached in all the world for a witness unto all nations; and then shall the end come.

15 When ye therefore shall see the abomination of desolation, spoken of by Daniel the prophet, stand in the holy place (whoso readeth, let him understand), 16 Then let them which be in Judea flee into the mountains: 17 Let him which is on the housetop not come down to take any thing out of his house: 18 Neither let him which is in the field return back to take his clothes. 19 And woe unto them that are with child, and to them that give suck in those days! 20 But pray ye that your flight be not in the winter, neither on the sabbath day: 21 For then shall be great tribulation, such as was not since the beginning of the world to this time, no, nor ever shall be. 22 And except those days should be shortened, there should no flesh be saved: but for the elect's sake those days shall be shortened. 23 Then if any man shall say unto you, Lo, here is Christ, or there; believe it not. 24 For there shall arise

false Christs, and false prophets, and shall show great signs and wonders; insomuch that, if it were possible, they shall deceive the very elect. 25 Behold, I have told you before. 26 Wherefore if they shall say unto you, Behold, he is in the desert; go not forth: behold he is in the secret chambers; believe it not. 27 For as the lightning cometh out of the east, and shineth even unto the west; so shall also the coming of the Son of man be. 28 For wheresoever the carcass is, there will the eagles be gathered together.

29 Immediately after the tribulation of those days shall the sun be darkened, and the moon shall not give her light, and the stars shall fall from heaven, and the powers of the heavens shall be shaken: 30 And then shall appear the sign of the Son of man in heaven: and then shall all the tribes of the earth mourn, and they shall see the Son of man coming in the clouds of heaven with power and great glory. 31 And he shall send his angels with a great sound of a trumpet, and they shall gather together his elect from the four winds, from one end of heaven to the other. 32 Now learn a parable of the fig tree; When his branch is yet tender, and putteth forth leaves, ye know that summer is nigh: 33 So likewise ye, when ye shall see all these things, know that it is near, even at the doors. 34 Verily I say unto you, This generation shall not pass, till all these things be fulfilled. 35 Heaven and earth shall pass away, but my words shall not pass away.

36 But of that day and hour knoweth no man, no, not the angels of heaven, but my Father only. 37 But as the days of Noe [Noah] were, so shall also the coming of the Son of man be. 38 For as in the days that were before the flood they were eating and drinking, marrying and giving in marriage, until the day that Noe entered into the ark, 39 And knew not until the flood came, and took them all away; so shall also the coming of the Son of man be. 40 Then shall two be in the field; the one shall be taken, and the other left. 41 Two women shall be grinding at the mill; the one shall be taken, and the other left.

REFLECTIONS

We have seen how Hinduism produced Buddhism and how Judaism generated Christianity, but neither Hinduism nor Judaism ended two thousand years ago. In fact, both "parental" religions underwent profound changes as well. Both became more universal, less dependent on particular places or people, and less limited to caste, region, or tribe.

We saw in the Upanishads how, around 500 B.C.E., Hinduism became almost monotheistic in its worship of Brahman. Similarly, about three hundred years later, Hindu devotional cults that centered on two of the other deities of the Hindu pantheon (Vishnu — especially in his incarnation as Krishna — and Shiva) developed. Reread the last eight stanzas of selection 14 from the *Bhagavad Gita* (written about 200 B.C.E.) to see how the worship of Vishnu/Krishna became enormously appealing to masses of Indian people.

At about the time of Jesus, Judaism also underwent a transformation that has continued until this day. A process that began with the destruction of the first temple and the captivity in Babylon in the sixth century B.C.E. — the development of a Judaism independent of a particular temple or place — was revived after the Romans destroyed the second temple in 70 C.E. The Roman conquest created a much greater diaspora (migration or dispersal) of Jews throughout the world than what the Babylonian conquest had spawned. Among new exiles throughout the world, Judaism became a religion of rabbis (teachers) rather than of temple priests. So great was this transformation of Judaism that one might argue, with Alan Segal in *Rebecca's Children,* that "the time of Jesus marks the birth of not one but two great religions in the West, Judaism and Christianity. . . . So great is the contrast between previous Jewish religious systems and rabbinism."[1]

And yet neither Judaism nor Hinduism became missionary religions; neither sought converts aggressively. Christianity and Buddhism did, however, and that is the subject of the next chapter.

[1] Alan F. Segal, *Rebecca's Children: Judaism and Christianity in the Roman World* (Cambridge: Harvard University Press, 1986), 1.

7

Encounters and Conversions:
Monks and Merchants

Expansion of Salvation Religions,
400 B.C.E.–1000 C.E.

HISTORICAL CONTEXT

From their beginnings, Buddhism and Christianity were less tribal and more universal than their parental religions, Judaism and Hinduism, because they offered universal salvation to their followers. The teachings of Jesus and the Buddha emphasized personal religious experience over the dictates of caste, ancestry, and formal law, making their ideas more likely to spread beyond their cultures of origin. Both religions, however, had relatively small followings at the deaths of their founders. How, then, did they win millions of converts within the next few hundred years? Similarly, how did Islam, founded in 622 C.E., spread from the Arabian peninsula to embrace the Berbers of North Africa, the Visigoths of Spain, Syrians, Persians, Turks, Central Asians, Indians, and even the western Chinese by 750 C.E.? What was happening throughout Eurasia that explained these successes? In this chapter we explore how both an array of powerful and charismatic individuals—religious figures, political leaders, and even merchants and traders—and specific economic, political, and social conditions helped to broaden the appeal of the salvation religions and find larger audiences for their gospels.

Religious thinkers loosened the new religions from their parental ties, often changing them as they spread them. St. Paul almost single-handedly separated Jesus from his Jewish roots, presenting him as the Son of God who was sacrificed for the sins of humankind, not just the Jewish people. Similarly, Mahayana Buddhists taught that Buddha was more than a teacher and spiritual guide whom one could imitate;

he was a savior, responsive to prayer and worship. Sufi shaykhs spread Islam in remote rural areas by incorporating local beliefs and practices into Islamic teachings.

Religious leaders weren't the only ones spreading faith; merchants and traders also played a crucial role. The spread of universal faiths and common cultures over great distances owed much to the roads and maritime transport of the Roman and Chinese empires, as well as the Persian, central Asian, and Indian states in between. But it was also a product of the Silk Road, or roads, that connected China with Rome after 100 B.C.E. (see Map 7.1, p. 204). The expansion of the great religious traditions was the work of merchants as well as monks; gods traveled in camel caravans, and holy images were carried on rolls of silk.

Contact alone, however, is not enough to explain why people converted to Christianity, Buddhism, and Islam. The appeals to salvation beyond this world testified to difficult times. Nomadic pastoral peoples undermined the stability of empires that had become riddled by public debt and class antagonisms. Cities closed as crop yields fell and diseases became endemic. Populations declined from 200–800 C.E., and did not reach earlier levels again until about 1000 C.E. in Europe and China. People sought spiritual reassurance as well as economic alliances that would protect them in uncertain times. When those in power adopted new religions, it often benefited others to follow their lead, securing a network of influence for new religious movements.

In the following selections, we examine the many ways in which Buddhism, Christianity, and Islam spread, the obstacles they faced, and the political, economic, and spiritual factors that influenced their growth.

THINKING HISTORICALLY
Studying Religion in Historic Context

In the previous chapter we looked for evidence of change in primary religious documents. In this chapter we take the historical study of religion a step further by examining how religions developed in the larger historical context of political, economic, and social change. Religions evolve not only according to an inner theological dynamic but also in response to changes within the broader society. Our study of the expansion of Buddhism, Christianity, and Islam provides a particularly useful set of questions about the relationship of religion to other historical forces. When we ask how these great salvation religions spread, we must consider how religious ideas are different from other ideas. How are such ideas affected by political, social, and economic forces, and how are these forces affected by religious ideas?

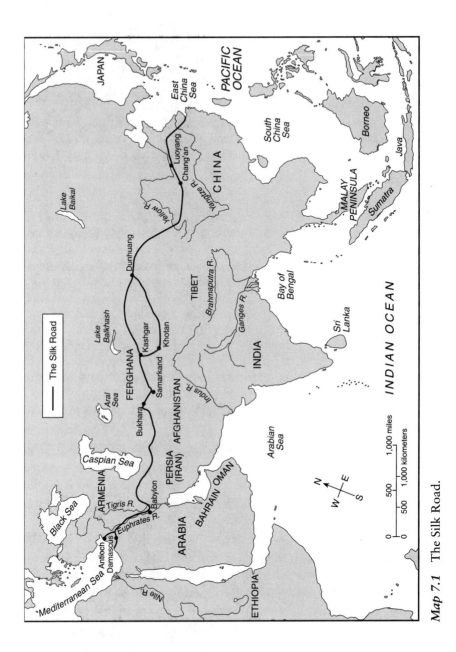

Map 7.1 The Silk Road.

JERRY H. BENTLEY

The Spread of World Religions

In this selection, modern historian Jerry Bentley examines a range of cultural and religious encounters that occurred across Eurasia in the period between 400 B.C.E. and 400 C.E. He first explores the spread of Buddhism from India northward to China and southward to Southeast Asia, highlighting the importance of merchants and trade in seeding new conversions. According to Bentley, what accounted for the initial resistance to Buddhism in China and the resounding success of Indian ideas and faiths in Southeast Asia? What relationships developed between religious and political leaders that aided the spread of Buddhism? Where do you see instances of cultural exchange?

Bentley then examines the spread of Christianity throughout the Roman Empire, from its rocky start as a faction of rebellious Jews to its eventual legalization under the emperor Constantine in 313 C.E. What specific developments does Bentley highlight to explain Christianity's success? What similarities and differences were there between the way Buddhism and Christianity spread?

Thinking Historically

In addition to describing *how* cultures and religions spread throughout Eurasia during this period, Bentley also asks *why*. What makes a people convert to a "foreign" religion? In trying to answer this question, he distinguishes three patterns of religious conversion. One he calls "voluntary association," the choice one people make to accept another group's religion largely for the benefits of associating with them. The second type of conversion is syncretism, or assimilation, the blending of old and new religious practices that usually occurs gradually over the course of generations. The third pattern is conversion by pressure, when people are forced by political, economic, or social pressure to accept a new religion. Obviously, these categories overlap, and it is often difficult to tell whether a conversion is voluntary or coerced. Which of these patterns best describes the spread of Christianity and Buddhism? How useful do you find these categories? Can you think of other patterns of religious conversion?

Jerry H. Bentley, *Old World Encounters: Cross-Cultural Contacts and Exchanges in Pre-Modern Times* (Oxford: Oxford University Press, 1993), 47–53, 60–64.

. . . Buddhism benefited enormously from the commercial traffic that crossed the silk roads. Once it arrived on the trade routes, Buddhism found its way very quickly indeed to distant lands. Merchants proved to be an efficient vector of the Buddhist faith, as they established diaspora communities in the string of oasis towns—Merv, Bukhara, Samarkand, Kashgar, Khotan, Kuqa, Turpan, Dunhuang—that served as lifeline of the silk roads through central Asia. The oases depended heavily on trade for their economic survival, and they quickly accommodated the needs and interests of the merchants whom they hosted. They became centers of high literacy and culture; they organized markets and arranged for lodging, care of animals, and storage of merchandise; and they allowed their guests to build monasteries and bring large contingents of Buddhist monks and copyists into their communities. Before too long—perhaps as early as the first or even the second century B.C.E.—the oasis dwellers themselves converted to Buddhism.

Thus a process of conversion through voluntary association with well-organized foreigners underwrote the first major expansion of Buddhism outside India. Buddhist merchants linked the oases to a large and cosmopolitan world, and the oases became enormously wealthy by providing useful services for the merchants. It is not at all surprising that inhabitants of the small oasis communities would gradually incline toward the beliefs and values of the numerous Buddhist merchants who traveled the silk roads and enriched the oases.

Once established in oasis communities, Buddhism had the potential to spread both to nomadic peoples on the steppes of central Asia and even to China, a land of long-settled civilization with its own long-established cultural traditions. Buddhism realized this potential only partially, however, and only in gradual fashion. As a faith foreign to China and generally despised by Chinese during its early centuries there, Buddhism had a certain attraction for nomadic peoples who themselves had quite difficult relations with the Chinese. In other words, Buddhism exercised a kind of countercultural appeal to nomads who loathed the Chinese, but who also desired and even depended upon trade with China. Yet many nomadic peoples found it difficult to accept Buddhism; they did not have traditions of literacy to accommodate Buddhist moral and theological teachings, and their mobility made it impossible to maintain fixed monastic communities. As a result, many nomadic peoples held to their native shamanist cults, and others turned to Manichaeism[1] or Nestorian Christianity.[2] Meanwhile, some

---

[1]Third-century Persian religion; belief that the body is trapped in darkness searching for the light. [Ed.]

[2]Fifth-century Syrian faith that spread to India, central Asia, and China; belief in the human nature of Jesus. [Ed.]

of those who adopted Buddhism did so at a very late date. Among the Mongols, for example, Buddhism did not become a popular faith until the sixteenth century. When nomadic peoples became involved in commerce, however, or when they established themselves as rulers of settled lands that they conquered, they frequently adopted Buddhism through a process of conversion through voluntary association. These patterns were quite prominent in central Asia and northern China during the era of the ancient silk roads.

The career of the monk and missionary Fotudeng especially helps to illuminate the voluntary conversion of nomadic peoples to Buddhism. Fotudeng probably came from Kuqa, an oasis town on the Silk Road in modern Xinjiang. He became a priest at an early age, traveled through central Asia, visited Kashmir, and set out to do missionary work in northern China during the early fourth century. He went to Dunhuang in order to improve his Chinese, then continued on to Luoyang about the year 310. There he caught the attention of Shi Le, the ruler of the nomadic Jie people (western allies of the Xiongnu), who controlled most of northern China during the fourth century. Fotudeng realized early on that he would not get very far with Shi Le by lecturing him on fine points of Buddhist philosophy, but he had a reputation for working miracles, which he used to the advantage of his mission. He dazzled Shi Le by producing bright blue lotus blossoms from his monk's begging bowl and by looking into his palm to see the reflection of distant events. Among his more utilitarian talents were rainmaking, healing, and prophecy. Fotudeng helped Shi Le plan military campaigns by foreseeing the outcome and devising clever strategies to ensure success. As a result of his miraculous talents, Fotudeng won widespread fame, and people from distant regions worshipped him. When he died about the year 345, he reportedly had ten thousand disciples and the erection of 893 temples to his credit.

Thus did a process of voluntary conversion help to establish Buddhism in northern China. The nomadic Jie settled in northern China and became deeply engaged in the political and economic affairs of a large and complex world. Fotudeng represented the culture of that larger world and brought talents useful for Jie rulers as they entered its life. He parlayed his personal relationship with Shi Le into official approval for his efforts to spread Buddhist values and even to found Buddhist institutions in northern China. Hence, his work not only illuminates the voluntary conversion of nomadic peoples but also helps to explain the early presence of the Buddhist faith in China.

The establishment of Buddhism in China was an even more difficult and gradual affair than its spread among nomadic peoples. Indeed, it required half a millennium for Buddhism to attract a large popular following in China. There as in Persia, the foreign faith could not immediately attract many followers away from indigenous cultural traditions, in this case principally Confucianism and Daoism. Even in its early years in China, Buddhism encountered determined resistance from Confucian and Daoist quarters. Representatives of the native Chinese traditions charged that Buddhism detracted from the authority of the state, that monasteries were unproductive and useless drags on the economy, that Buddhism itself was a barbarian faith inferior to Chinese traditions, and that the monastic life violated the natural order of society and disrupted family life. Not surprisingly, then, during its early centuries in China, Buddhism remained largely the faith of foreigners: merchants, ambassadors, refugees, hostages, and missionaries. During the second century C.E., for example, the Buddhist monastery at Luoyang included among its inhabitants two Parthians, two Sogdians, three Indians, and three Scythians, but no known Chinese. During its early years in China, then, Buddhism seems to have served principally as a cultural resource for trade diaspora communities.

As an alien cultural tradition that did not resonate in China, Buddhism could easily have experienced the same fate there that it did in Persia: It could have survived in the quarters inhabited by foreign merchants as an expatriate faith, perhaps even for centuries, without attracting much interest from the larger host community. The explanation for Buddhism's remarkable spread as a popular faith in east Asia begins with the voluntary conversion of elites, which enabled the foreign tradition to gain a foothold in Chinese society. In the north, where Buddhism first established its presence in China, voluntary conversion reflected the political interests of ruling elites. In most cases they were nomads, such as the Jie whom Fotudeng served so well, or the Toba rulers of the Northern Wei dynasty (386–534). After an initial period of tension and uncertain relations, it dawned on both Buddhists and rulers that an alliance could serve the interests of both parties. Buddhist monasteries provided ideological and economic support for established ruling houses: They recognized the legitimacy of the Jie and Toba rule; they facilitated long-distance trade, which figured prominently in the local economy; and they served as a conduit for the importation of exotic and luxury goods that symbolized the special status of the ruling elites. Meanwhile, the dynasties patronized the Buddhists in return, participated in their rituals, and protected the interests of their monasteries.

Like the oasis dwellers of central Asia, then, the ruling elites of northern China made common cause with representatives of a foreign cultural tradition who had extensive political and commercial links in the larger world. This sort of voluntary conversion was the only way by which Buddhism could find a place in Chinese society. Buddhists entered China in numbers too small to bring about a massive social transformation by way of pressure or assimilation. Only by winning the favor and protection of elites could the early Buddhists ensure their survival in China. As it happened, when missionaries found ways to communicate their message effectively to native Chinese and thus to bring a process of syncretism to their aid, their faith brought about a large-scale social conversion in China—but this development took place well after the era of the ancient silk roads. . . .

Meanwhile, as Buddhism found tentative footing in China, both Buddhism and Hinduism attracted the attention of elites and won converts in southeast Asia. As in China, the carriers of Indian cultural traditions were mostly merchants. During the late centuries B.C.E., Indian traders began to sail the seas and visit the coastal towns of southeast Asia. Even during those remote centuries, there was considerable incentive for merchants to embark upon long and often dangerous voyages. According to an ancient Gujarati story, for example, men who went to Java never returned—but if by chance they did return, they brought with them wealth enough to provide for seven generations. By the early centuries C.E., southeast Asian mariners themselves traveled to India as well as to other southeast Asian sites. The resulting networks of trade and communication invigorated not only the economic but also the political and cultural life of southeast Asia.

Among the principal beneficiaries of early trade between India and southeast Asia were the political and cultural traditions of India. Merchants from the subcontinent established diaspora communities, into which they invited Hindu and Buddhist authorities. Local chiefs controlled commerce at the trading sites they ruled, and they quickly became introduced to the larger world of the Indian Ocean. The ruler of an important trading site was no longer a "frog under a coconut shell," as the Malay proverb has it, but, rather, a cultural and commercial broker of some moment. Trade and external alliances enabled local rulers to organize states on a larger scale than ever before in southeast Asia. The first of these well represented in historical sources—though by no means the only early state in southeast Asia—was Funan, founded along the Mekong River in the first century C.E. Through its main port, Oc Eo, Funan carried on trade with China, Malaya, Indonesia, India, Persia, and indirectly with Mediterranean lands. By the end of the second century, similar trading states had appeared in the Malay peninsula and Champa (southern Vietnam).

Indian influence ran so deep in these states that they and their successors for a millennium and more are commonly referred to as the "Indianized states of southeast Asia." Indian traditions manifested their influence in many different ways. In a land previously governed by charismatic individuals of great personal influence, for example, rulers adopted Indian notions of divine kingship. They associated themselves with the cults of Siva, Visnu, or the Buddha, and they claimed both foreign and divine authority to legitimize their rule. They built walled cities with temples at the center, and they introduced Indian music and ceremonies into court rituals. They brought in Hindu and Buddhist advisers, who reinforced the sense of divinely sanctioned rule. They took Sanskrit names and titles for themselves, and they used Sanskrit as the language of law and bureaucracy. Indian influence was so extensive, in fact, that an earlier generation of historians suggested that vast armadas of Indians had colonized southeast Asia—a view now regarded as complete fiction. More recent explanations of the Indianization process place more emphasis on southeast Asian elites who for their own purposes associated themselves as closely as possible with the Hindu and Buddhist traditions. They certainly found no lack of willing and talented tutors; the quality of Sanskrit literature produced in southeast Asia argues for the presence there of many sophisticated and well-educated representatives of Indian cultural traditions. But high interest in foreign traditions on the part of southeast Asian elites drove the process of Indianization.

By no means did indigenous cultures fade away or disappear. During the early years after their arrival in southeast Asia, Indian traditions worked their influence mostly at the courts of ruling elites, and not much beyond. Over a longer term, however, Indian and native traditions combined to fashion syncretic cultural configurations and to bring about social conversion on a large scale. . . . In any case, though, the voluntary conversion of local elites to Hinduism and Buddhism decisively shaped the cultural development of southeast Asia.

· · ·

Of all the religions that established themselves in the Roman empire, however, none succeeded on such a large scale or over such a long term as Christianity. Its early experience thus calls for some discussion.

Christianity had many things in common with other religions that became widely popular in the Roman empire. It offered an explanation of the world and the cosmic order, one that endowed history with a sense of purpose and human life with meaning. It addressed the needs and interests of individuals by holding out the prospect of personal immortality, salvation, and perpetual enjoyment of a paradisiacal existence. It established high standards of ethics and morality, well suited to the needs of a complex, interdependent, and cosmopolitan world where peoples of different races and religions intermingled on a systematic basis. It was a religion of the cities, efficiently disseminated throughout the empire along established routes of trade and communication. It welcomed into its ranks the untutored and unsophisticated as well as the more privileged classes. It even shared with the other religions several of its ritual elements, such as baptism and the community meal. In many ways, then, early Christianity reflected the larger cultural world of the early Roman empire.

During its first three centuries, Christianity developed under a serious political handicap. The earliest Christians were associated with parties of rebellious Jews who resisted Roman administration in Palestine. Later Christians, even gentiles, refused to honor the Roman emperor and state in the fashion deemed appropriate by imperial authorities. As a result, Christians endured not only social contempt and scorn but also organized campaigns of persecution. Meanwhile, the Roman state generously patronized many of the empire's pagan cults: in exchange for public honor and recognition, the emperors and other important political figures provided financial sponsorship for rituals, festivals, and other pagan activities.

Nevertheless, Christianity benefited from the work of zealous missionaries who were able to persuade individuals and small groups that the Christians' god possessed awesome and unique powers. They communicated this message most effectively among the popular masses by acquiring a reputation for the working of miracles—healing illnesses, casting out demons, bestowing blessings on the faithful—that demonstrated the powers at their god's disposal. Ramsay MacMullen has recently argued, in fact, that fear of pain and punishment, desire for blessings, and belief in miracles were the principal inducements that attracted pagans to Christianity in the period before the conversion of Constantine about the year 312 c.e.

A bit of information survives on one of the more effective of the early Christian missionaries, Gregory the Wonderworker, and it illustrates the importance of miracles for the building of the early Christian community. Gregory had studied with the great Origen,[3] and he wrote several formal theological treatises. For present purposes, though, his significance arises from his work in the Roman province of Pontus (north central Anatolia) during the 240s. Early accounts of his mission record one miracle after another. Gregory's prayers prevented a pagan deity from exercising his powers, but upon request Gregory summoned the deity to his pagan temple, thus demonstrating his superior authority; as a result, the caretaker of the temple converted to Christianity. On several occasions individuals interrupted Gregory's public teaching; each time, Gregory exorcized a demon from the offensive party, provoking widespread amazement and winning converts in the process. Gregory moved boulders, diverted a river in flood, and dried up an inconveniently located lake. By the end of his campaign, Gregory had brought almost every soul of the town of Neocaesarea into the ranks of the Christians, and surrounding communities soon joined the bandwagon. As in the case of Fotudeng in north China, Gregory's reputation as a miracle worker seized the attention of his audiences and helped him to promote his faith among pagans.

Did the conversions brought about by Christian miracle workers represent cases of conversion through voluntary association? To some extent, this interpretation seems plausible, in that converts voluntarily adopted Christianity as the cultural alternative that best reflected the

---

[3]Biblical scholar and Christian theologian, c. 185–254. [Ed.]

realities of the larger world—for example by offering access to powers not available to others. A reputation for the ability to work miracles helped missionaries to dramatize the benefits and blessings that Christianity promised to individuals and suggested that Christianity possessed an unusually effective capacity to explain and control the world. In other ways, however, the winning of early Christian converts differed from the more common pattern of conversion through voluntary association. Converts came from all ranks of society, not just those of merchants, rulers, and others who had extensive dealings with representatives from the larger world. Moreover, until the conversion of the emperor Constantine and the legalization of Christianity, there were some powerful disincentives to conversion, so that potential converts to the new faith had to weigh heavy political, social, and economic risks against the personal and spiritual benefits offered by Christianity.

On balance, then, it seems to me that the category of conversion through voluntary association helps at least in a limited way to explain the early spread of Christianity in the Mediterranean basin. From the viewpoint of Roman society as a whole, however, rather than that of individual citizens, early conversion to Christianity benefited especially from two additional developments that accompanied the process of conversion through voluntary association. In the first place, until the fourth century, Christianity spread largely through a process of syncretism. In the second place, following the conversion of Constantine, Christianity gained state sponsorship, and a process of conversion by political, social, and economic pressure consolidated the new faith as a securely institutionalized church. Both of these developments warrant some attention.

The decline of long-established pagan cults afforded an opportunity for Christianity to extend its influence by way of syncretism. Beginning in the third century, the pagan cults suffered progressively more difficult financial problems as the Roman economy went into serious decline. The Roman state could no longer afford to support the cults on the generous basis of centuries past. Wealthy individuals continued to provide a great deal of aid, but their sponsorship was more erratic and precarious than that of the state.

As the pagan cults failed to provide for the needs and interests of their followers, Christianity offered a meaningful alternative that was the more acceptable for its resemblance to the cults. In their rituals and their assumptions about the natural world, the early Christians very much reflected the larger culture of the late Roman empire. Like devotees of the pagan cults, they offered their sacraments as great mysteries, and there were pagan analogues to many of their rituals, such as the intonation of divine language, the use of special garments and paraphernalia, and even the observance of ceremonies like baptism and a community meal open only to initiates. Christians appropriated the power and authority associated with pagan heroes by emphasizing the virtues of a saint or martyr with similar attributes. Eventually, Christians even baptized pagan philosophy and festivals, which served as new links between pagan and Christian cultures: St. Augustine transformed Neoplatonism into a powerful Christian philosophy, and the birthdate of the unconquered pagan sun god became Christmas, the birthdate also of Jesus. Thus from a very early date, Christianity appealed to Mediterranean peoples partly because of its syncretic capacity: It came in familiar dress, and it dealt with many of the same concerns addressed by the pagan cults.

The conversion of Constantine amplified the effects of syncretism by inaugurating a process of officially sponsored conversion that ultimately resulted in the cultural transformation of the entire Roman empire. Constantine favored Christians from the moment that he consolidated his hold on the imperial throne. In the year 313 he issued his famous edict of toleration, which for the first time recognized Christianity as a legal religion in the Roman empire. At some indeterminate point, Constantine himself converted to Christianity. Constantine's personal example of course did not lead to immediate Christianization of the Roman empire, or even of the army that the emperor directly supervised. In several ways, though, it brought long-term changes that favored the Christians' efforts. It brought immediate material benefits, as Constantine and his successors underwrote the construction of churches and showered Christians with financial support. It also brought an intangible but nonetheless important social benefit: Christianity gained more public respect than it had ever previously enjoyed. As a result, ambitious and reputable individuals of increasing prominence joined Christian ranks—especially because Christians received preferential consideration for high imperial posts. Finally, the legalization of their religion allowed Christians to promote their faith more publicly and more aggressively than ever before. From its earliest days, the Christian community had produced combative and confrontational spokesmen. After Constantine's edict of toleration allowed Christians to promote their faith publicly, they relentlessly attacked the pagan cults, sometimes sparking episodes of personal violence, forcible conversion of individuals, and destruction of pagan temples and images.

State sponsorship provided Christianity with the material and political support required to bring about social conversion on a large scale. Christianity quickly became the official and only legally tolerated religion of the Roman empire: Already by the late fourth century, the emperors had begun to prohibit observance of pagan cults. By no means, however, did the various pagan religions forfeit their claims to cultural allegiance. Pagan spokesmen resisted efforts to destroy their cults, and thanks to syncretism, their values and rituals to some extent survived in Christian dress. Nevertheless, by the late fourth century, Christianity had won a cultural and institutional initiative over paganism that it would never relinquish. . . .

39

Pliny Consults the Emperor Trajan

The inhabitants of an average city of the ancient Mediterranean worshiped dozens of gods, though usually one was thought to be a special guardian of the populace, a protector of the state, an embodiment of its territorial sovereignty. Cities of the Roman Empire added deities and cults from conquered and distant territories, creating a bewildering array. General tolerance prevailed. No one cared which gods an individual worshiped. Only Rome, as the capital of the empire, might require worship of a state god, including, at times, the emperor himself. But aside from this matter of loyalty to the state, one's religious convictions were one's own affair.

Christians ran afoul of the law and practice not only by refusing the demonstration of loyalty to the state but also by aggressively denying the validity of all other gods—an attitude the Romans defined as atheism, which, though not illegal, was distasteful to many.

Like the Jews, Christians were alternately persecuted and ignored. Roman oppression broke out when Nero blamed Christians for the great fire in Rome in 64 C.E. but then abated under the moderate rule of Trajan.

A brief correspondence between Pliny, serving as governor of Bithynia (in modern Turkey), and the Emperor Trajan from about the year 111 C.E. has survived, throwing light on official Roman policy toward Christians of that era. What does Pliny's letter to Trajan tell you about official Roman policy? What do you think of Trajan's answer?

Thinking Historically

Pliny is enforcing policy while at the same time he is personally repelled by the Christians. Try to distinguish these elements in Pliny's mind. What does he see as their legal guilt, and what does he find personally repelling? How do you explain Pliny's confusion about whether he should punish former Christians? What does Pliny know about the Christians?

Pliny mentions that some of the accused Christians admitted that they had been Christians but were no longer. Do you think some Christians left the religion under Roman pressure or persecution, or do you think they just said they had?

Pliny, Letters 10:96–97, from *Pliny Secundus: Letters and Panegyricus*, Loeb Classical Library, vol. II, trans. Betty Radice (Cambridge: Harvard University Press, 1959), 285, 287, 289, 291, 293.

Pliny to the Emperor Trajan

It is my custom to refer all my difficulties to you, Sir, for no one is better able to resolve my doubts and to inform my ignorance.

I have never been present at an examination of Christians. Consequently, I do not know the nature or the extent of the punishments usually meted out to them, nor the grounds for starting an investigation and how far it should be pressed. Nor am I at all sure whether any distinction should be made between them on the grounds of age, or if young people and adults should be treated alike; whether a pardon ought to be granted to anyone retracting his beliefs, or if he has once professed Christianity, he shall gain nothing by renouncing it; and whether it is the mere name of Christian which is punishable, even if innocent of crime, or rather the crimes associated with the name.

For the moment this is the line I have taken with all persons brought before me on the charge of being Christians. I have asked them in person if they are Christians, and if they admit it, I repeat the question a second and third time, with a warning of the punishment awaiting them. If they persist, I order them to be led away for execution; for, whatever the nature of their admission, I am convinced that their stubbornness and unshakeable obstinacy ought not to go unpunished. There have been others similarly fanatical who are Roman citizens. I have entered them on the list of persons to be sent to Rome for trial.

Now that I have begun to deal with this problem, as so often happens, the charges are becoming more widespread and increasing in variety. An anonymous pamphlet has been circulated which contains the names of a number of accused persons. Among these I considered that I should dismiss any who denied that they were or ever had been Christians when they had repeated after me a formula of invocation to the gods and had made offerings of wine and incense to your statue (which I had ordered to be brought into court for this purpose along with the images of the gods), and furthermore had reviled the name of Christ: none of which things, I understand, any genuine Christian can be induced to do.

Others, whose names were given to me by an informer, first admitted the charge and then denied it; they said that they had ceased to be Christians two or more years previously, and some of them even twenty years ago. They all did reverence to your statue and the images of the gods in the same way as the others, and reviled the name of Christ. They also declared that the sum total of their guilt or error amounted to no more than this: they had met regularly before dawn on a fixed day to chant verses alternately among themselves in honour of Christ as if to a god, and also to bind themselves by oath, not for any criminal purpose, but to abstain from theft, robbery and adultery, to commit no breach of trust and not to deny a deposit when called upon to restore it. After this ceremony it had been their custom to disperse and reassemble later to take food of an ordinary, harmless kind; but they had in fact given up this practice since my edict, issued on your instructions, which banned all political societies. This made me decide it was all the more necessary to extract the truth by torture from two slave-women, whom they call deaconesses. I found nothing but a degenerate sort of cult carried to extravagant lengths.

I have therefore postponed any further examination and hastened to consult you. The question seems to me to be worthy of your consideration, especially in view of the number of persons endangered; for a great many individuals of every age and class, both men and women, are being brought to trial, and this is likely to continue. It is not only the towns, but villages and rural districts too which are infected through contact with this wretched cult. I think though that it is still possible for it to be checked and directed to better ends, for there is no doubt that people have begun to throng the temples which had been almost entirely deserted for a long time; the sacred rites which had been allowed to lapse are being performed again, and flesh of sacrificial victims is on sale everywhere, though up till recently scarcely anyone could be found to buy it. It is easy to infer from this that a great many people could be reformed if they were given an opportunity to repent.

Trajan to Pliny

You have followed the right course of procedure, my dear Pliny, in your examination of the cases of persons charged with being Christians, for it is impossible to lay down a general rule to a fixed formula. These people must not be hunted out; if they are brought before you and the charge against them is proved, they must be punished, but in the case of anyone who denies that he is a Christian, and makes it clear that he is not by offering prayers to our gods, he is to be pardoned as a result of his repentance however suspect his past conduct may be. But pamphlets circulated anonymously must play no part in any accusation. They create the worst sort of precedent and are quite out of keeping with the spirit of our age.

40

EUSEBIUS

From *Life of Constantine*

If Christianity were persecuted by Roman officials and emperors, and if Christians were despised by the thoughtful and powerful elite of Roman society, how then did Christianity ever succeed? As the historian Ramsay MacMullen put it: "How did it ever happen that the church could grow at such a rate, so as actually to predominate in occasional little towns or districts by the turn of the second century [100 C.E.] and, by the turn of the fourth [300 C.E.], to have attained a population of, let us say, five million [in an empire of about 60 million]?"[1]

Part of the answer lies in the location of these Christians. They were more concentrated in urban than rural areas (the Latin word *pagan* meant "rural" before it meant "unchristian") and managed to gain significant advocates among the powerful elite.

No more powerful spokesman could be found than a Roman emperor, and so a short answer to the question of how Christianity succeeded must be "the Emperor Constantine" (288–337 C.E.). The emperor's historian Eusebius (260–339 C.E.) recognized both the importance of the emperor and the role of the empire in the success of Christianity in winning the Roman Empire:

> At the same time one universal power, the Roman Empire arose and flourished, while the enduring and implacable hatred of nation against nation was now removed; and as the knowledge of one god and one way of religion and salvation, even the doctrine of Christ, was made known to all mankind; so at the same time the entire dominion of the Roman Empire being invested in a single sovereign, profound peace reigned throughout the world. And thus, by the express appointment of the same God, two roots of blessing, the Roman Empire and the doctrine of Christian piety, sprang up together for the benefit of men.[2]

[1]Ramsay MacMullen, *Christianizing the Roman Empire*, A.D. 100–400 (New Haven: Yale University Press, 1984), 32. [Ed.]

[2]Eusebius, *Oration in Praise of Constantine*, xv, 4. [Ed.]

The Library of Nicene and Post-Nicene Fathers, ed. P. Schaff and H. Wace, vol. I, *Church History, Life of Constantine, Oration in Praise of Constantine* (New York: The Christian Literature Company, 1890), 489–91.

Eusebius wanted to believe that the victory of Christianity was implicit from the beginning of the Roman Empire. In his *History of the Church*, for instance, he says that at the time of the trial of Jesus, Pontius Pilate convinced the Emperor Tiberius to deify Jesus, but the Roman Senate prevented it. Further, Eusebius argues that Roman persecution of Christians was rare rather than frequent: Nero and Domitian the exceptions, Trajan more the rule.

Eusebius may have been more accurate in the broad sense. Universal religion and universal empire did go together, but the empire and Christianity were three hundred years old before the union occurred.

In his *Life of Constantine*, Eusebius, who knew the emperor, tells a story that must have circulated at the time to explain Constantine's support of Christianity (granting toleration to Christians and restoring Church lands as well as personal declarations of faith).

What do you think of Eusebius's explanation for Constantine's acceptance of Christianity? What does Constantine's reasoning say about how people of his day chose their religious beliefs and loyalties? How would the conversion of the emperor encourage others to become Christians? What, if anything, might have slowed the advance of Christianity after 312 C.E.?

Thinking Historically

This story helps us to understand what Romans and Christians knew of each other in 312 C.E. Specifically, what did Constantine seem to know about Christianity before he converted? How might you expect his conversion to change his behavior?

Being convinced, however, that he needed some more powerful aid than his military forces could afford him,[3] on account of the wicked and magical enchantments which were so diligently practiced by the tyrant [Maxentius], he sought Divine assistance, deeming the possession of arms and a numerous soldiery of secondary importance, but believing the cooperating power of Deity invincible and not to be shaken. He considered, therefore, on what God he might rely for protection and assistance. While engaged in this enquiry, the thought occurred to him, that, of the many emperors who had preceded him, those who had rested their hopes in a multitude of gods, and served them with sacrifices and offerings, had in the first place been deceived by flattering predictions, and oracles which promised them all prosperity,

---

[3]In 312 C.E., Constantine, who ruled Gaul and Britain, was about to invade Italy and try to gain the throne of the western empire by defeating Maxentius, who ruled Rome.

and at last had met with an unhappy end, while not one of their gods had stood by to warn them of the impending wrath of heaven; while one alone who had pursued an entirely opposite course, who had condemned their error, and honored the Supreme God during his whole life, had found him to be the Saviour and Protector of his empire, and the Giver of every good thing. Reflecting on this, and well weighing the fact that they who had trusted in many gods had also fallen by manifold forms of death, without leaving behind them either family or offspring, stock, name, or memorial among men: while the God of his father had given to him, on the other hand, manifestations of his power and very many tokens: and considering farther that those who had already taken arms against the tyrant, and had marched to the battle-field under the protection of a multitude of gods, had met with a dishonorable end (for one of them had shamefully retreated from the contest without a blow, and the other, being slain in the midst of his own troops, became, as it were, the mere sport of death); reviewing, I say, all these considerations, he judged it to be folly indeed to join in the idle worship of those who were no gods, and after such convincing evidence, to err from the truth; and therefore felt it incumbent on him to honor his father's God alone.

Accordingly he called on Him with earnest prayer and supplications that he would reveal to him who He was, and stretch forth His right hand to help him in his present difficulties. And while he was thus praying with fervent entreaty, a most marvelous sign appeared to him from heaven, the account of which it might have been hard to believe had it been related by any other person. But since the victorious emperor himself long afterwards declared it to the writer of this history, when he was honored with his acquaintance and society, and confirmed his statement by an oath, who could hesitate to accredit the relation, especially since the testimony of after-time has established its truth? He said that about noon, when the day was already beginning to decline, he saw with his own eyes the trophy of a cross of light in the heavens, above the sun, and bearing the inscription, CONQUER BY THIS. At this sight he himself was struck with amazement, and his whole army also, which followed him on this expedition, and witnessed the miracle.

He said, moreover, that he doubted within himself what the import of this apparition could be. And while he continued to ponder and reason on its meaning, night suddenly came on; then in his sleep the Christ of God appeared to him with the same sign which he had seen in the heavens, and commanded him to make a likeness of that sign which he had seen in the heavens, and to use it as a safeguard in all engagements with his enemies.

At the dawn of day he arose, and communicated the marvel to his friends: and then, calling together the workers in gold and precious stones, he sat in the midst of them, and described to them the figure of the sign he had seen, bidding them represent it in gold and precious stones. And this representation I myself have had an opportunity of seeing.

Now it was made in the following manner. A long spear, overlaid with gold, formed the figure of the cross by means of a transverse bar laid over it. On the top of the whole was fixed a wreath of gold and precious stones; and within this, the symbol of the Saviour's name, two letters indicating the name of Christ by means of its initial characters, the letter P being intersected by X in its centre; and these letters the emperor was in the habit of wearing on his helmet at a later period. From the cross-bar of the spear was suspended a cloth, a royal piece, covered with a profuse embroidery of most brilliant precious stones; and which, being also richly interlaced with gold, presented an indescribable degree of beauty to the beholder. This banner was of a square form, and the upright staff, whose lower section was of great length, bore a golden half-length portrait of the pious emperor and his children on its upper part, beneath the trophy of the cross, and immediately above the embroidered banner.

The emperor constantly made use of this sign of salvation as a safeguard against every adverse and hostile power, and commanded that others similar to it should be carried at the head of all his armies.

These things were done shortly afterwards. But at the time above specified, being struck with amazement at the extraordinary vision, and resolving to worship no other God save Him who had appeared to him, he sent for those who were acquainted with the mysteries of His doctrines, and enquired who that God was, and what was intended by the sign of the vision he had seen.

They affirmed that He was God, the only begotten Son of the one and only God: that the sign which had appeared was the symbol of immortality, and the trophy of that victory over death which He had gained in time past when sojourning on earth. They taught him also the causes of His advent, and explained to him the true account of His incarnation. Thus he was instructed in these matters, and was impressed with wonder at the divine manifestation which had been presented to his sight. Comparing, therefore, the heavenly vision with the interpretation given, he found his judgment confirmed; and, in the persuasion that the knowledge of these things had been imparted to him by Divine teaching, he determined thenceforth to devote himself to the reading of the inspired writings.

41

Buddhism in China:
From *The Disposition of Error*

The Disposition of Error is a Buddhist guide for converting the Chinese. While the author and date are uncertain, this kind of tract was common under the Southern Dynasties (420–589 C.E.). The author uses a frequently asked questions (FAQ) format that enables us to see what the Chinese—mainly Confucian—objections were to Buddhism, as well as what they considered good Buddhist answers.

What were the main Chinese objections to Buddhism? Why were Buddhist ideas of death such a stumbling block for Chinese Confucians? Were Confucian ideas about care of the body and hair only superficial concerns, or did they reflect basic differences between Confucianism and Buddhism?

Thinking Historically

How does Mou Tzu, the Buddhist monk, answer Confucian objections with quotes from the Confucian classics? How does he use the ideas of Lao Tzu or Taoism to answer the objections? Would this be a good guide to answering the objections of Chinese Taoists?

Why Is Buddhism Not Mentioned in the Chinese Classics?

The questioner said: If the way of the Buddha is the greatest and most venerable of ways, why did Yao, Shun, the Duke of Chou, and Confucius not practice it? In the seven Classics one sees no mention of it. You, sir, are fond of the *Book of Odes* and the *Book of History,* and you take pleasure in rites and music. Why, then, do you love the way of the Buddha and rejoice in outlandish arts? Can they exceed the Classics and commentaries and beautify the accomplishments of the sages? Permit me the liberty, sir, of advising you to reject them.

Mou Tzu said: All written works need not necessarily be the words of Confucius, and all medicine does not necessarily consist of the formulae of [the famous physician] P'ien-ch'üeh. What accords with principle is to be followed, what heals the sick is good. The gentleman-scholar draws widely on all forms of good, and thereby benefits his

---

Hung-ming Chi, in Taishō daizōkyō, LII, 1–7, quoted in William Theodore de Bary, ed., *The Buddhist Tradition in India, China and Japan* (New York: Random House, 1969), 132–37.

character. Tzu-kung [a disciple of Confucius] said, "Did the Master have a permanent teacher?" Yao served Yin Shou, Shun served Wu-ch'eng, the Duke of Chou learned from Lü Wang, and Confucius learned from Lao Tzu. And none of these teachers is mentioned in the seven Classics. Although these four teachers were sages, to compare them to the Buddha would be like comparing a white deer to a unicorn, or a swallow to a phoenix. Yao, Shun, the Duke of Chou, and Confucius learned even from such teachers as these. How much less, then, may one reject the Buddha, whose distinguishing marks are extraordinary and whose superhuman powers know no bounds! How may one reject him and refuse to learn from him? The records and teachings of the Five Classics do not contain everything. Even if the Buddha is not mentioned in them, what occasion is there for suspicion?

Why Do Buddhist Monks
Do Injury to Their Bodies?

The questioner said: The *Classic of Filial Piety* says, "Our torso, limbs, hair, and skin we receive from our fathers and mothers. We dare not do them injury." When Tseng Tzu was about to die, he bared his hands and feet.[1] But now the monks shave their heads. How this violates the sayings of the sages and is out of keeping with the way of the filially pious! . . .

Mou Tzu said: . . . Confucius has said, "He with whom one may follow a course is not necessarily he with whom one may weigh its merits." This is what is meant by doing what is best at the time. Furthermore, the *Classic of Filial Piety* says, "The kings of yore possessed the ultimate virtue and the essential Way." T'ai-po cut his hair short and tattooed his body, thus following of his own accord the customs of Wu and Yüeh and going against the spirit of the "torso, limbs, hair, and skin" passage.[2] And yet Confucius praised him, saying that his might well be called the ultimate virtue.

Why Do Monks Not Marry?

The questioner said: Now of felicities there is none greater than the continuation of one's line, of unfilial conduct there is none worse than childlessness. The monks forsake wife and children, reject property and wealth. Some do not marry all their lives. How opposed this conduct is to felicity and filial piety! . . .

---

[1]To show he had preserved them intact from all harm.

[2]Uncle of King Wen of the Chou who retired to the barbarian land of Wu and cut his hair and tattooed his body in barbarian fashion, thus yielding his claim to the throne to King Wen.

Mou Tzu said: . . . Wives, children, and property are the luxuries of the world, but simple living and inaction are the wonders of the Way. Lao Tzu has said, "Of reputation and life, which is dearer? Of life and property, which is worth more?" . . . Hsü Yu and Ch'ao-fu dwelt in a tree. Po I and Shu Ch'i starved in Shou-yang, but Confucius praised their worth, saying, "They sought to act in accordance with humanity and they succeeded in acting so." One does not hear of their being ill-spoken of because they were childless and propertyless. The monk practices the Way and substitutes that for the pleasures of disporting himself in the world. He accumulates goodness and wisdom in exchange for the joys of wife and children.

Death and Rebirth

The questioner said: The Buddhists say that after a man dies he will be reborn. I do not believe in the truth of these words. . . .

Mou Tzu said: . . . The spirit never perishes. Only the body decays. The body is like the roots and leaves of the five grains, the spirit is like the seeds and kernels of the five grains. When the roots and leaves come forth they inevitably die. But do the seeds and kernels perish? Only the body of one who has achieved the Way perishes. . . .

Someone said: If one follows the Way one dies. If one does not follow the Way one dies. What difference is there?

Mou Tzu said: You are the sort of person who, having not a single day of goodness, yet seeks a lifetime of fame. If one has the Way, even if one dies one's soul goes to an abode of happiness. If one does not have the Way, when one is dead one's soul suffers misfortune.

Why Should a Chinese Allow Himself to Be Influenced by Indian Ways?

The questioner said: Confucius said, "The barbarians with a ruler are not so good as the Chinese without one." Mencius criticized Ch'en Hsiang for rejecting his own education to adopt the ways of [the foreign teacher] Hsü Hsing, saying, "I have heard of using what is Chinese to change what is barbarian, but I have never heard of using what is barbarian to change what is Chinese." You, sir, at the age of twenty learned the way of Yao, Shun, Confucius, and the Duke of Chou. But now you have rejected them, and instead have taken up the arts of the barbarians. Is this not a great error?

Mou Tzu said: . . . What Confucius said was meant to rectify the way of the world, and what Mencius said was meant to deplore one-sidedness. Of old, when Confucius was thinking of taking residence among the nine barbarian nations, he said, "If a gentleman-scholar dwells in their midst, what baseness can there be among them?" . . . The Commentary says, "The north polar star is in the center of heaven and to the north of man." From this one can see that the land of China is not necessarily situated under the center of heaven. According to the Buddhist scriptures, above, below, and all around, all beings containing blood belong to the Buddha-clan. Therefore I revere and study these scriptures. Why should I reject the Way of Yao, Shun, Confucius, and the Duke of Chou? Gold and jade do not harm each other, crystal and amber do not cheapen each other. You say that another is in error when it is you yourself who err.

Why Must a Monk Renounce Worldly Pleasures?

The questioner said: Of those who live in the world, there is none who does not love wealth and position and hate poverty and baseness, none who does not enjoy pleasure and idleness and shrink from labor and fatigue. . . . But now the monks wear red cloth, they eat one meal a day, they bottle up the six emotions, and thus they live out their lives. What value is there in such an existence?

Mou Tzu said: Wealth and rank are what man desires, but if he cannot obtain them in a moral way, he should not enjoy them. Poverty and meanness are what man hates, but if he can only avoid them by departing from the Way, he should not avoid them. Lao Tzu has said, "The five colors make men's eyes blind, the five sounds make men's ears deaf, the five flavors dull the palate, chasing about and hunting make men's minds mad, possessions difficult to acquire bring men's conduct to an impasse. The sage acts for his belly, not for his eyes." Can these words possibly be vain? Liu-hsia Hui would not exchange his way of life for the rank of the three highest princes of the realm. Tuan-kan Mu would not exchange his for the wealth of Prince Wen of Wei. . . . All of them followed their ideas, and cared for nothing more. Is there no value in such an existence?

Why Does Mou Tzu Support His Contentions from Secular Rather Than Buddhist Literature?

The questioner said: You, sir, say that the scriptures are like the rivers and the sea, their phrases like brocade and embroidery. Why, then, do you not draw on the Buddhist scriptures to answer my question? Why instead do you refer to the books of *Odes* and *History,* joining together things that are different to make them appear the same?

Mou Tzu said: . . . I have quoted those things, sir, which I knew you would understand. Had I preached the words of the Buddhist scriptures or discussed the essence of non-action, it would have been like speaking to a blind man of the five colors or playing the five sounds to a deaf man.

Does Buddhism Have No Recipe for Immortality?

The questioner said: The Taoists say that Yao, Shun, the Duke of Chou, and Confucius and his seventy-two disciples did not die, but became immortals. The Buddhists say that men must all die, and that none can escape. What does this mean?

Mou Tzu said: Talk of immortality is superstitious and unfounded; it is not the word of the sages. Lao Tzu says, "Even Heaven and earth cannot be eternal. How much the less can man!" Confucius says, "The wise man leaves the world, but humanity and filial piety last forever." I have observed the six arts and examined the commentaries and records. According to them, Yao died, Shun had his [death place at] Mount Ts'ang-wu, Yü has his tomb on K'uai-chi, Po I and Shu Ch'i have their grave in Shou-yang. King Wen died before he could chastise Chou, King Wu died without waiting for King Ch'eng to grow up. We read of the Duke of Chou that he was reburied, and of Confucius that [shortly before his death] he dreamed of two pillars. [As for the disciples of Confucius], Po-yü died before his father, of Tzu Lu it is said that his flesh was chopped up and pickled.

┌───────┐
│ 42   │
└───────┘

RICHARD C. FOLTZ

The Islamization of the Silk Road

In the following selection Foltz, a modern historian of religion, explores the early history of Islam and its spread east of the Mediterranean. Placing the rise of Islam solidly within the Arab traditions of trading and raiding, Foltz distinguishes between the initial development

Richard C. Foltz, *Religions of the Silk Road: Overland Trade and Cultural Exchange from Antiquity to the Fifteenth Century* (New York: St. Martin's Press, 1999), 89–93, 95–97.

of unified Arab rule and the subsequent spread of Islamic religious culture. He argues that the "convert or die" idea that pervades the history of Islam is largely mythic and that early Muslim rulers actually discouraged conversion. According to Foltz, what role did economics play in early Muslim expansion? How did Islam spread so widely and so quickly, and what was the nature of this early growth? How did non-Arabs who converted to Islam change it?

Thinking Historically

There is evidence here for all three patterns of conversion discussed by Bentley in selection 38: voluntary association, syncretism, and pressure. What examples of each can you find in Foltz's discussion of the expansion of Islam? What economic and political forces does Foltz emphasize? What roles did individuals play in the conversion process? According to Bentley and Foltz, what similarities were there between the spread of Buddhism, Christianity, and Islam?

No religious tradition in world history favored trade as much as did Islam. The Prophet Muhammad himself was a businessman by profession. While in his twenties he became employed by a wealthy merchant woman of Mecca, Khadija, and made his reputation by successfully carrying out a trade mission to Syria; Khadija married him soon after.

Sometime around 610 of the common era, Muhammad, who liked to spend time alone meditating in the mountains outside Mecca, began hearing voices during the course of these retreats. At first he began to doubt his own sanity, but Khadija persuaded him that these voices might be divine in nature and should be listened to. Gradually Muhammad came to believe he was receiving revelations from God, calling upon him to "rise and warn" his fellow Meccans that the time had come to mend their ways.

Mecca was a desert town with little to subsist on apart from its trade. Successful merchants must have been its wealthiest inhabitants. Many of the revelations Muhammad received dealt with social injustice, which was clearly a problem in Mecca at that time. His message found a growing audience of sympathetic ears, while it increasingly alienated the social classes who were the target of his criticism. Before long certain powerful residents of Mecca were making life difficult for Muhammad and his followers.

In 622 the citizens of Yathrib, a town some two hundred twenty miles to the north of Mecca, were involved in factional disputes they could not resolve. Hearing of Muhammad's reputation for fairness and piety, they invited him to come and arbitrate. He accepted. Sending most of his followers ahead of him, the Prophet of Islam put his affairs in order and finally left his hometown, an event known to Muslims as the *hijra*, or migration, which marks the beginning of the Islamic calendar.

Once in Yathrib, the Muslims were not only no longer persecuted, they enjoyed special status. From their new power base they launched raids (Ar. *Razzia*) on Meccan-bound caravans, at the same time enriching their own treasury while inflicting damage on their former persecutors. After several battles with the Meccans, the Muslims were able to negotiate the right to return to Mecca for the traditional Arabian pilgrimage to the sacred *ka' ba* stone; by 628 Mecca was under Muslim control.

Raiding caravans was an established part of the economic life of Arabia. The only rule was that one couldn't raid clan members or groups with whom one had made a nonaggression pact. With the successes of the Muslims growing from year to year, eventually all the tribes of the Arabian peninsula sent emissaries to Muhammad in order to seek such pacts. Their professions of loyalty were described by later Muslim writers as "submission," which in Arabic is *islam*. Small wonder that these sources, and the non-Muslim histories based on them, interpret this as meaning all the Arabian tribes had accepted the new religion.

Understanding this term "submission" in its more restricted literal sense, however, more easily explains what happened upon the Prophet's death in 632: Most of the Arabian tribes rebelled. Later Muslim sources refer to these as rebellions of "apostasy." A simpler interpretation would be that the rebel parties simply saw their nonaggression pacts as having been rendered null and void by the Prophet's passing.

The Muslims immediately chose a successor, or caliph (from Middle Pers. *Khalifa*), Abu Bakr, under whose leadership the various Arab tribes were forced to resubmit. Since the Arabian economy required the component of raiding, and since according to the nonaggression pacts no one in Arabia could legitimately be raided, the Muslims were forced to launch forays beyond the Arabian peninsula into Byzantine and Persian territory. Their successes in defeating the armies of both empires probably surprised many of the Muslims as much as it did their imperial enemies.

It is important to recognize the economic aspect of Muslim expansion, driven by the ancient Arabian tradition of raiding. While in hindsight both Muslims and non-Muslims have read into this early expansion a large element of religious zeal, the Arab armies of the time were simply doing what they were naturally acculturated to do, what the economic conditions of their homeland had always constrained them to do. What had changed was that, for the first time, all the Arab groups of the peninsula had excluded for themselves the possibility of raiding other Arab groups. They were forced, therefore, to raid elsewhere. Their new religious self-concept may indeed have inspired them by giving divine meaning to their increasing successes, but other factors were at work as well.

Iranians, in the form of Medes, Achemenians, Parthians, and Sasanians, had been vying with Athenian, Seleucid, and Roman Greeks for hegemony in western Asia for over a millennium. By the seventh century both the Sasanian Persian and Byzantine Greek empires were exhausted and decadent. Neither treated their subject peoples in Mesopotamia, Syria, or Egypt with anything that could be called benevolence. In many locations townspeople threw open the gates to the Arabs and welcomed them as liberators. The Muslims were, in fact, no more foreign in most of the lands they conquered than had been the previous rulers, and at first they were less exploitative.

By the 660s, however, the ruling Arab family, the Umayyads, had set themselves up in Damascus in very much the mold of the Byzantine governors they had dislodged. Throughout the subsequent decades non-Muslims came to chafe under the new regime. Many Arab Muslims, furthermore, resented the imperial manner and "un-Islamic" lifestyles of the Umayyads, many of whom had taken to drinking and debauchery in the best Roman tradition.

But the group which was to bring about the Umayyads' downfall and, in doing so, forever change the very nature of Islam as a cultural tradition was the non-Arabs who chose to adopt the Islamic religion.

Initially and throughout the Umayyad period, the Arabs had seen Islam as a religion belonging to them; their subjects, likewise, referred to Islam as "the Arab religion" (*al-din al-'arab*). The Qur'an enjoined Muslims to spread Muslim *rule* throughout the world but laid down no requirement to spread the faith itself. The original impulse of holy war (*jihad*) was that no Muslim should be constrained to live under the rule of infidels. Once a given locality agreed to submit to Muslim authority and pay the poll tax (*jizya*) levied on protected communities (*dhimmis*, usually "peoples of the Book," i.e., Christians and Jews), there was no further need for coercion on either side.

In fact, Arab Muslims had strong reasons *not* to want non-Arabs to join the faith, since conversion directly affected both their sources of income and the spread of its distribution among Muslims. Conversely, there were numerous reasons why non-Muslims might wish to join the ruling group, which could most obviously be symbolized by adopting their faith. Despite some apparent resistance from the Arab elite, by the early eighth century non-Arab converts were probably beginning to outnumber Arab Muslims.

Islam had attempted to eliminate class and racial distinctions, but even during the Prophet's lifetime this goal was never met. Early converts and their descendants often felt entitled to greater status and privilege than later converts, and members of aristocratic families never forgot who came from humble ones. Tribal and clan loyalties affected government appointments and led to rivalries.

Often these rivalries developed power bases in garrison towns where particular factions were dominant. Local governors, therefore, usually had more or less personal armies at their ready disposal. In areas where the Arabs were quartered among non-Arab majority populations, there was increasing pressure from converts to be treated on equal footing with Arab Muslims.

The problem was that a non-Arab, even after converting to Islam, had no tribal affiliation which could provide him an identity within Arab society. A solution to this was devised whereby an Arab Muslim could take a non-Arab convert under his wing as a "client" (*mawla*), making the convert a sort of honorary tribal member. Of course, such clients were at the mercy of the individual who sponsored them.

Over time this inequality between Arab and non-Arab Muslims became a major pretext for various parties disaffected with Umayyad rule. Not surprisingly it was in eastern Iran, at the fringes of Umayyad power, that a rebel movement capable of overthrowing the central government and completely reshaping Muslim society took place.

In addition to complaints about the un-Islamic character of the Umayyad elite and the inequalities between Arab and non-Arab Muslims, the anti-Umayyad movement could draw on the issue of the very legitimacy of Umayyad rule. The first Umayyad caliph, Mu'awiya, had assumed power by refusing to recognize the selection of the Prophet's nephew and son-in-law, Ali, as fourth caliph. A significant minority of Muslims felt that leadership should be sought in charismatic authority passed down through the Prophet's line. For the "partisans of Ali" (*shi' at Ali*), the Umayyads (and indeed the first three caliphs) had been usurpers from the outset.

All of these antigovernment impulses came together in the so-called Abbasid revolution of 749 to 751, in which a Khurasan-based Muslim army rallied behind an Iranian general, Abu Muslim, in the name of an Arab descendant of the Prophet's uncle Abbas. The rebels succeeded in wresting power from the Umayyads, moved the capital to Mesopotamia, and began setting up a new Islamic administration on the Sasanian imperial model. The new ministers and functionaries were overwhelmingly Iranian, often recent converts from Zoroastrianism or Christianity or, in the case of the influential Barmak family from Balkh, from Buddhism. In 762 the Caliph Mansur built a new capital at Baghdad (Pers. "given by God") and commented that this would put Muslims in touch "with lands as far off as China."

. . .

Islam and Trade in the Eastern Lands

As with any case of mass cultural conversion, the Islamization of Central Asia was a complex process which occurred on more than one level. The first, and most visible, level was the spread of political power. It is worth noting that the spread of a particular religion's rule is not identical with the spread of faith, although historians have often written as if it were.

Muslim rule over the western half of the Silk Road came fairly early and was established, albeit through a period of false starts and occasional reversals, by the mid-eighth century. Muslims thereafter controlled much of trans-Asian trade, which became the second major factor in the Islamization of Central Asian culture. Gradually a third factor, the influence of charismatic Muslim preachers, entered into the process.

The reality of Muslim rule could no longer be reasonably ignored once the numerous eighth-century attempts to rally behind local, non-Islamic religious figures had all failed. Politics was therefore an initial influence encouraging Central Asians to abandon their native cultural traditions and join the growing world culture of Islamic civilization. It appears, however, that only local rulers, especially those who had raised arms against the Muslims, were ever subjected to the convert-or-die alternative that has so long been the stereotype characterizing the spread of Islam. Other people, at least at first, would have embraced the faith of their new rulers for other reasons, in certain cases no doubt spiritual ones.

One of the most commonly cited incentives to religio-cultural conversion is the pursuit of patronage. Anyone directly dependent on the government for his livelihood might sense advantages in joining the cultural group of his patrons and accepting the norms and values of that ruling group. To a large extent, converts to Islam do appear to have held onto their preconquest positions, and being a Muslim increased one's chances of attaining a new or better one.

A second and probably greater influence affecting Islamization was the Muslim domination of commercial activity. A businessman could feel that becoming a Muslim would facilitate contacts and cooperation with other Muslim businessmen both at home and abroad; he would also benefit from favorable conditions extended by Muslim officials and from the Islamic laws governing commerce.

The presence of Muslim rule and the increasing Muslim dominance of trade meant that Islamization came first in the urban areas along the Silk Road and only in later centuries spread to the countryside. The gradual Islamization of the nomadic Turkic peoples of Central and Inner Asia was at first directly tied to their increasing participation in the oasis-based Silk Road trade in the tenth century, accelerated by the political activities of three Turkic Muslim dynasties—the Qarakhanids, the Ghaznavids, and the Seljuks—and supplemented by the proselytizing efforts of Muslim missionaries.

The third major factor accounting for the Islamization of the Silk Road, which follows those of politics and economics, is assimilation.

Whatever the reasons for one's converting to Islam, Islamization occurs most profoundly (and irrevocably) among the succeeding generation, since the convert's children in principle will be raised within the father's new community, not his original one. Furthermore, although a Muslim man may marry a non-Muslim woman, Islamic law requires that the children of a mixed marriage be raised as Muslims. However, . . . it may be safe to assume that aspects of pre-Islamic local religion survived through transmission by non-Muslim wives of Muslims.

Central Asians of the countryside, being less directly affected by the factors just described, held onto their Iranian (usually agriculturalist) or Turkic (usually pastoral nomadic) native religious traditions longer than did their urban counterparts. Gradually, though, the same influences were felt throughout the rural areas. An additional and even more significant Islamicizing influence especially on the pastoral peoples came through the activities of Sufi shaykhs, who took it upon themselves to spread Islam to the remotest areas. Their influence stemmed largely from their personal charisma, which often made them the authoritative sources for the religion even above and beyond the Qur'an, *hadith* (stories about the prophet), or Islamic law.

It was the shaykh's own personal interpretations of the Islamic message that formed the basis of the faith as the pastoral folk heard it. Often these personal interpretations were accommodating towards pre-existing local beliefs and practices, leading to the development of "popular" expressions of Islam which could deviate significantly from the normative tradition emanating from the cities. In some ways local religion in Central Asia, whether of the Iranian or Turkic variety, never really disappeared. Rather, it acquired Islamic meanings, interpretations, and appearances.

43

RICHARD W. BULLIET

Religious Conversion
and the Spread of Innovation

The previous selections in this chapter illustrate that there are many reasons why people converted to the new salvation religions. The author of the following selection, an historian of Islam specializing in Iran and Central Asia, offers a simpler explanation. Bulliet argues that Persians in medieval Iran converted to Islam at the same statistical rate that any group of people would adopt any innovation. What theories of Islamic expansion does this refute? What was the pace of Iranian conversions to Islam? What implications does Bulliet's argument have for explaining the spread of Islam and other religions?

Thinking Historically

Bulliet speaks of "social conversion" as a process by which groups, not individuals, adopt new religions. Like Bentley and Foltz, Bulliet largely ignores the role of individual choice in making these decisions. In effect, he suggests that it does not matter whether one is spreading a new religion or selling a high-definition television; people will respond at the same pace. Are one's personal ideas and beliefs irrelevant in choosing a religion? Should the historian ignore the role of individuals in accounting for why religions change, develop, and grow?

Cassius Clay became Muhammad Ali, Lew Alcindor became Karim Abdul-Jabbar. Change of name has accompanied adoption of the Islamic faith since the Arab conquests first spread Muhammad's message into non-Arab lands in the seventh century. Change of name also leaves its trace in a person's genealogy. If you meet a man named Muhammad who says his grandfather was named Robert, you reasonably assume that the family's conversion to Islam has taken place sometime in the last three generations—either with Muhammad himself, or with his father, or possibly even with grandfather Robert, since Robert might be a baptismal name that was changed to a Muslim name later in life at the time of conversion.

Richard W. Bulliet, "Religious Conversion and the Spread of Innovation," excerpted from *Conversion to Islam in the Medieval Period* (Cambridge: Harvard University Press, 1979) by "Fathom: The Source for Online Learning" at http://www.fathom.com.

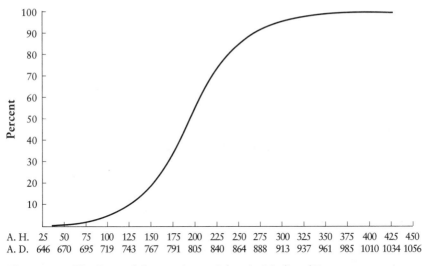

Figure 7.1   The Rate of Conversion to Islam in Medieval Iran.

Hundreds of Iranian genealogies dating to the first four centuries of Islam, approximately 650–1050, reveal the telltale pattern of conversion. They begin with a Persian name and then continue for one to seven generations with Arabic names. Assuming that the first Arabic name in the genealogy marks the generation of conversion, and further assuming a standard length for a generation, it is possible to make a rough estimate of when each of these ancestors decided to start identifying with the ruling stratum of Muslim Arabs. When these rough dates are then laid against a time scale, the following curve results (Figure 7.1).

The long, shallow S shape marks the growth of the Muslim community in Iran and indicates that the conversion wave took three to four centuries to complete. It started slowly, it gained momentum toward the middle, and it tapered off slowly.

Most obviously, this curve of Muslim community growth refutes the worn-out view that the Arab invaders forced the people they conquered to convert. More important, it links religious conversion—in this case Islam—to a more general phenomenon. Medieval Iranians adopted Islam according to the same pattern that has time and time again been shown to describe the adoption of technological innovations in modern times. Deep-well drilling, hybrid corn, kindergartens, and countless other innovations have spread according to a shallow S-shaped curve. Its proper name is a logistic curve.

Disguised behind the logistic curve is another curve, the familiar bell-shaped curve of random distribution. If you slice the area beneath the bell curve into time divisions and add the area in each slice to the cumulative total of the preceding slices, the result is a logistic curve. Both curves reflect random probability.

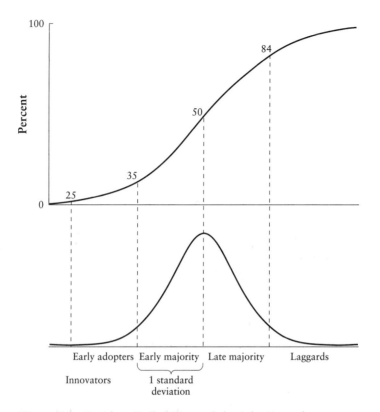

Figure 7.2   Random Probability and the Adoption of
Innovation: The Logistic and the Bell-shaped Curve.

This element of randomness invites analysis of adoption curves by statistical methods. Probability indicates that 64 percent of all adopters will opt for the new thing, idea, or process within one standard deviation (SD) to either side of the midpoint of the curve. They form the "early majority" and the "late majority," depending on which side of the curve they are. The "early adopter" category takes in the 13.5 percent who fall two SD to the left of the mean, and the "innovators" are the 2.5 percent who are three SD to the left of the mean. Adopters who fall two or more SD to the right of the mean can be called "laggards." (See Figure 7.2.)

Dividing adopters, or in our case religious converts, into probability groups according to where they fall on the curve invites further questions. Take high-definition television (HDTV). Specialists in technological innovation ask: What prompts "innovators" to adopt HDTV when it is still so new and untested that many people haven't even heard of it? Who is most likely to follow these "innovators" and become "early adopters"? What kind of people—the "early majority" and "late majority"—will wait to adopt until they see that everyone else is going along with the trend and are assured that HDTV is truly the wave of the future? Who will be the recalcitrant "laggards" who swear they will never change? By constructing social profiles for people in these statistical categories, HDTV manufacturers are able to plan marketing campaigns with much more precision than general mass advertising would permit.

Obviously, religious or ideological change differs from technological innovation. The advantages of the latter are usually self-evident. Hybrid corn produces higher yields; HDTV looks better; CDs don't scratch. People who change religion in hopes of going to heaven, however, don't find out whether they made the right choice until they die. Yet there is usually more than the theology of salvation behind a person's decision to terminate his or her association with one religious group and associate instead with another. We can call this sort of change in association "social conversion" to distinguish it from a deep change in spiritual feeling, on the one hand, or an unwitting ritual occurrence, such as infant baptism, on the other.

Following this line of analysis, the universally asked question "Why did so-and-so convert?" evokes a wide variety of answers. If you ask the first person in a community who shaves his head, dons saffron robes and chants "Hare Rama! Hare Krishna!" on the street why he has chosen to change his social identity as a religious person, you will almost certainly get a different answer than you will get from someone in the middle of the curve, who is joining the movement in company with a mass of other people, or from the last few holdouts who take to wearing saffron robes only after almost everyone else has adopted them. Stereotypical statements like "New converts are zealots" or "Iranians (Africans, African-Americans, Indonesians) converted to Islam (Christianity, Buddhism, Mormonism) because the doctrine of (fill in the blank) appealed to them (fit their culture)" are almost certainly incorrect when applied to the totality of a conversion movement.

Is it impossible, then, to determine how and why a religion makes headway in a given society? In strictly doctrinal terms, it may well be impossible, since most people do not change religion on the basis of careful and comparative study of texts. But other elements can be analyzed. How does the religion organize for dissemination of information? What are the material benefits of conversion? What are the penalties for leaving one's current community? To what degree does conversion compel one to abandon customary practices? How does conversion affect social or legal status?

Mysteries may always remain, however. One of the most (if not the most) common goads to adoption of something new is personal contact with someone you trust who has already adopted it. This process is modeled in advertising mini-dramas when an actor playing a pharmacist or doctor, persons a potential adopter is assumed to respect, holds up a box of something and says he uses it and you should, too; or when an actress portraying a mother asks her daughter-in-law how she gets her sheets so white and is told to use a new detergent. Every viewer sees the artifice in these dramas, but they nevertheless prime viewers to respond positively when someone they actually do trust or admire recommends a new product.

Ironically, in the early stages of religious conversion the person the potential convert knows best and is most willing to follow is rarely an authority on the religion in question. What this "role model" actually knows about the new faith, particularly in pre-modern or nonliterate societies, may be incomplete, or even dead wrong. The person who thinks he or she is adopting a specific new faith, therefore, may actually be converting to a highly distorted version of that faith. Hence the overall perception that a particular faith is growing in a given time and place often disguises a reality in which the faith may indeed be growing numerically, but growing also in diversity of ritual, confusion of doctrine, and contamination by local custom. Rather than being unfortunate aberrations, such divergences from orthodox doctrine and practice are an inevitable part of the conversion process I have been describing.

This is not to say, however, that all religions grow in the same way, or that any given religion grows in the same way in every social or historical situation. The S-shaped curve of technological innovation may work for medieval Iran, but it may not apply everywhere. Since we are in a period when historians are applying themselves as never before to studying the growth of religious traditions, many careful studies will have to be completed before a general theory of conversion can be attempted. The technological innovation model is helpful, nevertheless, in cautioning against simple-minded and stereotypical explanations of religious change and in suggesting that mass religious change is a dynamic process in which the explanations that seem to work for one phase of the process may not apply for the process as a whole.

REFLECTIONS

What does it mean if, as Bulliet suggests, people convert to a religion at about the same pace as they decide to buy high-definition televisions? In the case of the spread of Islam, it may tell us that people were not forced to become Muslims, challenging the misconception that Islam expanded only at sword point. Does it mean, however, that people converted to Islam with as much enthusiasm as they would bring to the electronics store? Theorizing about the behavior of whole societies is different from knowing how and why an individual acts. We can chart religious conversion like income growth or any other social process only when we ignore the emotional and intellectual ferment of individuals and concentrate instead on large-scale behavioral similarities.

The relationship between individual religious ideas, faith, or belief, on the one hand, and religious social identity, membership, or behavior, on the other hand, is difficult to understand. Inevitably our own religious experiences and cultural background affect our understanding of others'. If we have strong beliefs, we expect intelligent, sensitive people to have similar beliefs. If they do not, we expect them to be easily persuaded when exposed to ideas that we find compelling. This may be a particularly American expectation. American culture, even in its secular forms, is a product of the Protestant reformation and Christian efforts to create a "city on a hill," as a beacon to the world.

Belief has always meant a lot to Christians. Ever since St. Paul organized a church based purely on faith—all you have to do is believe, he said—the particulars of belief have splintered Christianity into a thousand sects. But most religions did not evolve this way. Even other religions that have scriptural authorities—Judaism, Islam, Buddhism, Hinduism, to a certain extent—have devoted less attention to defining doctrine and rooting out heretics than they have to regulating daily life within the larger society. Among them only Islam displays a similar zeal to convert nonbelievers (and Foltz questions to what extent this has been overemphasized) but there is no set of doctrines, no credo, required of the Muslim besides the profession of faith in God and his Prophet. The schism of Islam between Sunnis and Shi'ites is deep, but it is historical and communal rather than intellectual or doctrinal. Jews, Buddhists, and Hindus do not evangelize and would be hard-pressed to answer if asked by potential recruits what to believe. For most people throughout the history of the world, religion was defined by birth; beliefs came later. It may be a particularly Christian concept to think of religion as belief rather than behavior.

It may also be a modern concept. The modern individual, religious or secular, increasingly asserts the self with ideas—personal ideas—rather than kinship, community, or membership. Foltz reminds us how little ideas mattered in the early spread of Islam. Bentley's categories of conversion say the same: People did not "convert" to ideas; they took sides and formed beneficial alliances. Of course most people, then and now, do not choose but are born into religions. To be raised in a religion demands more association and action than thought. Yet modern society prizes individual thought. Modern missionaries, secular as well as religious, find combustible tinder in new generations taught to think for themselves. It may be we, not the generation of the Buddha, St. Paul, or the Prophet Muhammad, who must shape behavior to belief.

8

Medieval Civilizations

European, Islamic, and Chinese Societies, 600–1300 C.E.

HISTORICAL CONTEXT

In the centuries after 200 C.E., an influx of nomadic peoples from the grasslands of Eurasia into the Roman and Han Chinese Empires brought an end to the classical civilizations. In their wake, three distinct civilizations developed: European Christian, Islamic (after 622 C.E.), and Chinese. Of the three, the Chinese was most like its preceding classical civilization; in some ways the Sui dynasty (589–618) revived the institutions of the Han. The greatest change occurred in Western Europe, especially the former urban areas of the Roman Empire, some of which virtually disappeared. The area from Byzantium to the Indus River was radically transformed by the rise of Islam, but a foreign observer might have been struck more by the continuity of urban growth and material progress than by the change of faith in Western Asia from the classical to Muslim period.

In any case, these three worlds of Eurasia in the Middle Ages were vastly different from each other. The goal of this chapter is to explore some of those differences.

THINKING HISTORICALLY
Distinguishing Social, Economic, Political, and Cultural Aspects

Comparing civilizations is a daunting undertaking; there are so many variables one must keep in mind. Consequently, when historians compare civilizations, or any social system, they first break them down into parts. Most commonly, historians distinguish between the political, economic, social, and cultural features of a system. The political refers to how a society or civilization is governed, the economic to how it supports itself, the social to how it organizes population groups, including families, and the cultural to how it explains and represents itself, including its religion.

In this chapter, you are asked to be systematic in distinguishing among these features for each of the three main civilizations. We will break them down to compare each part — for example, European and Chinese politics, Muslim and Chinese culture — but also to see how the parts of each civilization make a whole: for example, how Chinese politics and Chinese culture fit together.

44

Feudalism: An Oath of Homage and Fealty

This primary source is from France, selected to illustrate one of the important institutions of Europe in the Middle Ages: feudalism. This document details the mutual obligation between a feudal lord and his vassal. In this case, the feudal lord is a religious institution, the monastery of St. Mary of Grasse. Acting for the monastery and its lands is the abbot, Leo. The vassal who holds the properties of the monastery as a fief, and in return pledges homage and fealty, is Bernard Atton, viscount of Carcassonne. The year is 1110.

What exactly does the viscount of Carcassonne promise to do? What is Leo the abbot's responsibility on behalf of the monastery? How new or old does this agreement appear to be? What else does this document tell you about the relationship of lords and vassals in European feudalism?

Thinking Historically

Using the distinctions suggested in the chapter introduction, how would you characterize this agreement? In short, is it an economic, political, social, or cultural agreement? Because it obviously has more

"Charter of Homage and Fealty of the Viscount of Carcassone, 1110," in D. C. Munro, *Translations and Reprints from the Original Sources of European History*, vol. IV, bk. 3 (Philadelphia: University of Pennsylvania Press, 1897), 18–20.

than one of these elements, how might you argue for each of the four characterizations?

What would be the closest equivalent to this sort of agreement today? Would you characterize the modern equivalent as economic, political, social, or cultural?

In the name of the Lord, I, Bernard Atton, Viscount of Carcassonne, in the presence of my sons, Roger and Trencavel, and of Peter Roger of Barbazan, and William Hugo, and Raymond Mantellini, and Peter de Vietry, nobles, and of many other honorable men, who had come to the monastery of St. Mary of Grasse, to the honor of the festival of the august St. Mary; since lord Leo, abbot of the said monastery, has asked me, in the presence of all those above mentioned, to acknowledge to him the fealty and homage for the castles, manors, and places which the patrons, my ancestors, held from him and his predecessors and from the said monastery as a fief, and which I ought to hold as they held, I have made to the lord abbot Leo acknowledgment and homage as I ought to do.

Therefore, let all present and to come know that I the said Bernard Atton, lord and viscount of Carcassonne, acknowledge verily to thee my lord Leo, by the grace of God, abbot of St. Mary of Grasse, and to thy successors that I hold and ought to hold as a fief, in Carcassonne, the following: . . . Moreover, I acknowledge that I hold from thee and from the said monastery as a fief the castle of Termes in Narbonne; and in Minerve the castle of Ventaion, and the manors of Cassanolles, and of Ferral and Aiohars; and in Le Rogès, the little village of Longville; for each and all of which I make homage and fealty with hands and with mouth to thee my said lord abbot Leo and to thy successors, and I swear upon these four gospels of God that I will always be a faithful vassal to thee and to thy successors and to St. Mary of Grasse in all things in which a vassal is required to be faithful to his lord, and I will defend thee, my lord, and all thy successors, and the said monastery and the monks present and to come and the castles and manors and all your men and their possessions against all malefactors and invaders, at my request and that of my successors at my own cost; and I will give to thee power over all the castles and manors above described, in peace and in war, whenever they shall be claimed by thee or by thy successors.

Moreover I acknowledge that, as a recognition of the above fiefs, I and my successors ought to come to the said monastery, at our own expense, as often as a new abbot shall have been made, and there do homage and return to him the power over all the fiefs described above. And when the abbot shall mount his horse I and my heirs, viscounts of

Carcassonne, and our successors ought to hold the stirrup for the honor of the dominion of St. Mary of Grasse; and to him and all who come with him, to as many as two hundred beasts, we should make the abbot's purveyance in the borough of St. Michael of Carcassonne, the first time he enters Carcassonne, with the best fish and meat and with eggs and cheese, honorably according to his will, and pay the expense of the shoeing of the horses, and for straw and fodder as the season shall require.

And if I or my sons or their successors do not observe to thee or to thy successors each and all the things declared above, and should come against these things, we wish that all the aforesaid fiefs should by that very fact be handed over to thee and to the said monastery of St. Mary of Grasse and to thy successors.

I, therefore, the aforesaid lord Leo, by the grace of God, abbot of St. Mary of Grasse, receive thy homage and fealty for all the fiefs of castles and manors and places which are described above; in the way and with the agreements and understandings written above; and likewise I concede to thee and thy heirs and their successors, the viscounts of Carcassonne, all the castles and manors and places aforesaid, as a fief, along with this present charter, divided through the alphabet. And I promise to thee and thy heirs and successors, viscounts of Carcassonne, under the religion of my order, that I will be good and faithful lord concerning all those things described above.

Moreover, I, the aforesaid viscount, acknowledge that the little villages of [twelve are listed] with the farmhouse of Mathus and the chateaux of Villalauro and Claromont, with the little villages of St. Stephen of Surlac, and of Upper and Lower Agrifolio, ought to belong to the said monastery, and whoever holds anything there holds from the same monastery, as we have seen and have heard read in the privileges and charters of the monastery, and as was there written.

Made in the year of the Incarnation of the Lord 1110, in the reign of Louis. Seal of [the witnesses named in paragraph one, Bernard Atton and abbot Leo] who has accepted this acknowledgment of the homage of the said viscount.

And I, the monk John, have written this charter at the command of the said lord Bernard Atton, viscount of Carcassonne and of his sons, on the day and year given above, in the presence and witness of all those named above.

45

Manorialism: Duties of a Villein

Manorialism is another term used to describe medieval European civilization. It concerns the life around the manor houses that were the centers of life in the countryside. Manors were owned by feudal lords whose income derived, at least in good part, from the work of free peasants and dependent serfs *(villeins)*.

This document, from England in 1307, delineates the duties required of a villein, John of Cayworth, to the lord of the manor, Battle Abbey. What duties does the abbey require of John of Cayworth? What does he get in return? In what ways is this document similar to the previous one? In what ways is it different?

Thinking Historically

How is the social status of John of Cayworth different from that of Bernard Atton in the previous selection? What would you imagine about the differences in their economic welfare?

What would be the modern equivalent of this document? Would you call that modern equivalent economic, political, social, or cultural? Which word best characterizes this document?

They say that John of Cayworth holds one house and thirty acres of land, and he owes 2 s.[1] a year at Easter and Michaelmas, and he owes one cock and two hens at Christmas worth 4 s.

And he ought to harrow for two days at the sowing at Lent with one man and his own horse and harrow, the value of the work is 4 d.;[2] and he receives from the lord on each day three meals worth 3 d.; and the lord will thus lose 1 d.; and so this harrowing is worth nothing to the service of the lord.

And he ought to carry the manure of the lord for two days with one cart using his own two oxen, the work to value 8 s., and he receives from the lord three meals of the above value each day; and so the work is worth 3 d. clear.

---

[1] Shilling, a British measure of money traditionally worth ⅟₂₀ of a pound (now ⅟₁₀). [Ed.]

[2] Pence, smallest measure of British currency traditionally worth ⅟₁₂ of a shilling (now ⅟₁₀). "d" comes from Roman *denarius*. [Ed.]

"Services Due from a Villein, 1307," ed. S. R. Scargill-Bird, Customals of Battle Abbey (The Camden Society, 1887), 19–23.

And he should find one man for two days to mow the meadow of the lord, who can mow an estimated one acre and a half: the value of mowing one acre is 6 *d.*; and the total is 9 *d.*; and he receives for each day three meals of the above value, and thus the mowing is worth 4 *d.* clear.

And he ought to collect and carry that same hay which he has mowed, the value of the work is 3 *d.* And he has from the lord two meals to one man worth 1½ *d.*; thus the work is worth 1½ *d.* clear.

And he ought to carry the hay of the lord for one day with one cart and three animals of his own, the price of the work is 6 *d.*; and he has from the lord three meals worth 2½ *d.*; and thus the work has a value of 3½ *d.* clear.

And he ought to carry in the autumn beans or oats for two days with one cart and three of his own animals, the price of the work is 12 *d.*; and he has from the lord three meals of the above price for each day, and thus the work is worth 7 *d.* clear.

And he ought to carry wood from the woods of the lord to the manor house for two days in summer with one cart and three of his own animals, the price of the work is 9 *d.*; and he receives from the lord for each day three meals of the above price. And so the work is worth 4 *d.* clear.

And he ought to find one man for two days to cut heath, the price of the work is 4 [*d.*]; and he will have three meals for each day of the above price; and so the lord loses if he receives the work 1 *d.*; and thus that cutting is worth nothing to the work of the lord.

And he ought to carry the heath that he has cut, the price of the work is 5 *d.*; and he receives from the lord three meals of the price of 2½ *d.*; and thus the work is worth 2½ *d.* clear.

And he ought to carry to Battle [Abbey] two times in the summer half a load of grain each time, the price of the work is 4 *d.*; and he will receive in the manor each time one meal worth 2 *d.*; and thus the work is worth 2 *d.* clear.

The sum of the rents, with the price of the chickens is 2 *s.* 4 *d.*; the sum of the value of the work is 2 *s.* 3½ *d.*; owed from the said John per year. . . .

And it must be noted that all the aforesaid villeins may not marry their daughters nor have their sons tonsured, nor can they cut down timber growing on the lands they hold, without the personal approval of the bailiff or servant of the lord, and then for building and no other purpose.

And after the death of any one of the aforesaid villeins the lord will have as a heriot the best animal that he had; if, however, he had no living beast, the lord will have no heriot, as they say.

The sons or daughters of the aforesaid villeins will give to enter the tenement after the death of their ancestors as much as they gave in rent per year.

46

From the Magna Carta

The Magna Carta was a contract between King John of England and his nobles (or "liegemen") in which the king agreed to recognize certain rights and liberties of the nobility. In return the nobles accepted certain obligations to the king. What were some of these rights and obligations? Can you tell from these provisions what some of the nobles' complaints had been? Did the signing of this agreement in 1215 improve the position of the common people, women, or foreigners? What does the document tell you about English society in the early thirteenth century?

Thinking Historically

This is obviously a political document, as it details the mutual obligations of King John and his nobles, the barons. But in addition to political matters, it covers a number of issues that might be considered economic, social, and cultural. Which items would you characterize as falling into one of those categories?

What does the Magna Carta have in common with the other European documents on feudalism and manorialism? What does this commonality tell you about European society in the Middle Ages?

John, by the grace of God, King of England, Lord of Ireland, Duke of Normandy and Aquitaine, and Count of Anjou: To the Archbishops, Bishops, Abbots, Earls, Barons, Justiciaries, Foresters, Sheriffs, Reeves, Ministers, and all Bailiffs and others, his faithful subjects, Greeting. Know ye that in the presence of God, and for the health of Our soul, and the souls of Our ancestors and heirs, to the honor of God, and the exaltation of Holy Church, and amendment of Our Kingdom, by the advice of Our reverend Fathers, Stephen, Archbishop of Canterbury, Primate of all England, and Cardinal of the Holy Roman Church; Henry, Archbishop of Dublin; William of London, Peter of Winchester, Jocelin of Bath and Glastonbury, Hugh of Lincoln, Walter of Worcester, William of Coventry, and Benedict of Rochester, Bishops; Master Pandulph, the Pope's subdeacon and familiar; Brother Aymeric,

---

"Magna Carta," trans. E. P. Cheney, in D. C. Munro, ed., *Translations and Reprints from the Original Sources of European History*, vol. I, bk. 6 (Philadelphia: University of Pennsylvania Press, 1897), 6–15, passim.

Master of the Knights of the Temple in England; and the noble persons, William Marshal, Earl of Pembroke; William, Earl of Salisbury; William, Earl of Warren; William, Earl of Arundel; Alan de Galloway, Constable of Scotland; Warin Fitz-Gerald, Peter Fitz-Herbert, Hubert de Burgh, Seneschal of Poitou, Hugh de Neville, Matthew Fitz-Herbert, Thomas Basset, Alan Basset, Philip Daubeny, Robert de Roppelay, John Marshal, John Fitz-Hugh, and others, Our liegemen:

1. We have, in the first place, granted to God, and by this Our present Charter confirmed for Us and Our heirs forever — That the English Church shall be free and enjoy her rights in their integrity and her liberties untouched. And that We will this so to be observed appears from the fact that We of Our own free will, before the outbreak of the dissensions between Us and Our barons, granted, confirmed, and procured to be confirmed by Pope Innocent III the freedom of elections, which if considered most important and necessary to the English Church, which Charter We will both keep Ourself and will it to be kept with good faith by Our heirs forever. We have also granted to all the free men of Our kingdom, for Us and Our heirs forever, all the liberties underwritten, to have and to hold to them and their heirs of Us and Our heirs.

2. If any of Our earls, barons, or others who hold of Us in chief by knight's service shall die, and at the time of his death his heir shall be of full age and owe a relief[1] he shall have his inheritance by ancient relief; to wit, the heir or heirs of an earl of an entire earl's barony, £100; the heir or heirs of a baron of an entire barony, £100; the heir or heirs of a knight of an entire knight's fee, 100s. at the most; and he that owes less shall give less, according to the ancient custom of fees.

3. If, however, any such heir shall be under age and in ward, he shall, when he comes of age, have his inheritance without relief or fine.

4. The guardian of the land of any heir thus under age shall take therefrom only reasonable issues, customs, and services, without destruction or waste of men or property; and if We shall have committed the wardship of any such land to the sheriff or any other person answerable to Us for the issues thereof, and he commit destruction or waste, We will take an amends from him, and the land shall be committed to two lawful and discreet men of that fee, who shall be answerable for the issues to Us or to whomsoever We shall have assigned them. And if We shall give or sell the wardship of any such land to anyone, and he commit destruction or waste upon it, he shall lose the wardship, which shall be committed to two lawful and discreet men of that fee, who shall, in like manner, be answerable unto Us as has been aforesaid.

---

[1] A form of tax. [Ed.]

5. The guardian, so long as he shall have the custody of the land, shall keep up and maintain the houses, parks, fishponds, pools, mills, and other things pertaining thereto, out of the issues of the same, and shall restore the whole to the heir when he comes of age, stocked with ploughs and tillage, according as the season may require and the issues of the land can reasonably bear.

6. Heirs shall be married without loss of station, and the marriage shall be made known to the heir's nearest of kin before it be contracted.

7. A widow, after the death of her husband, shall immediately and without difficulty have her marriage portion and inheritance. She shall not give anything for her marriage portion, dower, or inheritance which she and her husband held on the day of his death, and she may remain in her husband's house for forty days after his death, within which time her dower shall be assigned to her.

8. No widow shall be compelled to marry so long as she has a mind to live without a husband, provided, however, that she give security that she will not marry without Our assent, if she holds of Us, or that of the lord of whom she holds, if she holds of another.

9. Neither We nor Our bailiffs shall seize any land or rent for any debt so long as the debtor's chattels are sufficient to discharge the same; nor shall the debtor's sureties be distrained so long as the debtor is able to pay the debt. If the debtor fails to pay, not having the means to pay, then the sureties shall answer the debt, and, if they desire, they shall hold the debtor's lands and rents until they have received satisfaction of the debt which they have paid for him, unless the debtor can show that he has discharged his obligation to them.

10. If anyone who has borrowed from the Jews any sum of money, great or small, dies before the debt has been paid, the heir shall pay no interest on the debt so long as he remains under age, of whomsoever he may hold. If the debt shall fall into Our hands, We will take only the principal sum named in the bond. . . .

12. No scutage[2] or aid shall be imposed in Our kingdom unless by common counsel thereof, except to ransom Our person, make Our eldest son a knight, and once to marry Our eldest daughter, and for these only a reasonable aid shall be levied. So shall it be with regard to aids from the City of London.

13. The City of London shall have all her ancient liberties and free customs, both by land and water. Moreover, We will and grant that all other cities, boroughs, towns, and ports shall have their liberties and free customs.

14. For obtaining the common counsel of the kingdom concerning the assessment of aids (other than in the three cases aforesaid) or of

---

[2] A payment in place of a personal service. [Ed.]

scutage, We will cause to be summoned, severally by Our letters, the archbishops, bishops, abbots, earls, and great barons; We will also cause to be summoned, generally, by Our sheriffs and bailiffs, all those who hold lands directly of Us, to meet on a fixed day, but with at least forty days' notice, and at a fixed place. In all letters of such summons We will explain the cause thereof. The summons being thus made, the business shall proceed on the day appointed, according to the advice of those who shall be present, even though not all the persons summoned have come.

15. We will not in the future grant permission to any man to levy an aid upon his free men, except to ransom his person, make his eldest son a knight, and once to marry his eldest daughter, and on each of these occasions only a reasonable aid shall be levied.

16. No man shall be compelled to perform more service for a knight's fee or other free tenement than is due therefrom.

17. Common Pleas shall not follow Our Court, but shall be held in some certain place. . . .

20. A free man shall be amerced[3] for a small fault only according to the measure thereof, and for a great crime according to its magnitude, saving his position; and in like manner a merchant saving his trade, and a villein[4] saving his tillage, if they should fall under Our mercy. None of these amercements shall be imposed except by the oath of honest men of the neighborhood.

21. Earls and barons shall be amerced only by their peers, and only in proportion to the measure of the offense.

22. No amercement shall be imposed upon a clerk's[5] lay property, except after the manner of the other persons aforesaid, and without regard to the value of his ecclesiastical benefice.

23. No village or person shall be compelled to build bridges over rivers except those bound by ancient custom and law to do so. . . .

28. No constable or other of Our bailiffs shall take corn or other chattels of any man without immediate payment, unless the seller voluntarily consents to postponement of payment.

29. No constable shall compel any knight to give money in lieu of castle-guard when the knight is willing to perform it in person or (if reasonable cause prevents him from performing it himself) by some other fit man. Further, if We lead or send him into military service, he shall be quit of castle-guard for the time he shall remain in service by Our command.

---

[3] Fined. [Ed.]
[4] Serf. [Ed.]
[5] Clergyman. [Ed.]

30. No sheriff or other of Our bailiffs, or any other man, shall take the horses or carts of any free man for carriage without the owner's consent.

31. Neither We nor Our bailiffs will take another man's wood for Our castles or for any other purpose without the owner's consent. . . .

35. There shall be one measure of wine throughout Our kingdom, and one of ale, and one measure of corn, to wit, the London quarter, and one breadth of dyed cloth, russets, and haberjets[6] to wit, two cells within the selvages. As with measure so shall it also be with weights. . . .

38. In the future no bailiff shall upon his own unsupported accusation put any man to trial without producing credible witnesses to the truth of the accusation.

39. No free man shall be taken, imprisoned, disseised,[7] outlawed, banished, or in any way destroyed, nor will We proceed against or prosecute him, except by the lawful judgment of his peers and by the law of the land.

40. To no one will We sell, to none will We deny or delay, right or justice.

41. All merchants shall have safe conduct to go and come out of and into England, and to stay in and travel through England by land and water for purposes of buying and selling, free of illegal tolls, in accordance with ancient and just customs, except, in time of war, such merchants as are of a country at war with Us. If any such be found in Our dominion at the outbreak of war, they shall be attached, without injury to their persons or goods, until it be known to Us or Our Chief Justiciary how Our merchants are being treated in the country at war with Us, and if Our merchants be safe there, then theirs shall be safe with Us.

42. In the future it shall be lawful (except for a short period in time of war, for the common benefit of the realm) for anyone to leave and return to Our kingdom safely and securely by land and water, saving his fealty to Us. Excepted are those who have been imprisoned or outlawed according to the law of the land, people of the country at war with Us, and merchants, who shall be dealt with as aforesaid. . . .

52. If anyone has been disseised or deprived by Us, without the legal judgment of his peers, of lands, castles, liberties, or rights, We will immediately restore the same, and if any dispute shall arise thereupon, the matter shall be decided by judgment of the twenty-five barons men-

---

[6] Types of cloth. [Ed.]
[7] Dispossessed. [Ed.]

tioned below in the clause for securing the peace. With regard to all those things, however, of which any man was disseised or deprived, without legal judgment of his peers, by King Henry Our Father or Our Brother King Richard, and which remain in Our warranty, We shall have respite during the term commonly allowed to the Crusaders, except as to those matters on which a plea had arisen, or an inquisition had been taken by Our command, prior to Our taking the Cross. Immediately after Our return from Our pilgrimage, or if by chance We should remain behind from it, We will at once do full justice.

47

From the Koran

The Koran is the founding document of Islamic civilization. Muslims believe that the Koran is the word of God, revealed to Muhammad, an illiterate caravan trader, beginning around his fortieth year (610 C.E.) and continuing until his death (632). Muhammad had been influenced by the monotheism of Jews and Christians in Arabia, finding their beliefs preferable to the polytheism of most Arab tribes. But the Koran (literally the "recitation" of Muhammad) was understood by the early Muslims (including those who wrote it down in later years) as a fresh revelation from God to the last of his prophets, bringing a conclusion to revelations that had come for thousands of years to prophets that included Abraham, Moses, and Jesus.

The rich, subtle, and evocative Arabic of the Koran is said to be virtually untranslatable. Its accessibility to non-Muslims is made even more difficult by the way in which it is organized: generally later, longer sections first, followed by earlier shorter ones. Nevertheless, some sense of the power and sweep of the book can be inferred.

Early sections, from the period before 622 when Muhammad left Mecca for Medina, display the power of the call to worship only God. The first selection, roman numeral C, called "The Coursers" (or "The Chargers") — one of the early Meccan surahs (or chapters) — captures the passion of those years. What appears to be the message of this surah?

The Glorious Koran, trans. Muhammad Marmaduke Pickthall (Mecca: Muslim World League, 1977), 27–30, 75–76, 727.

While some were converted to Islam by words like these, others, especially among the ruling elite of Mecca, were threatened by them. To preserve the pilgrimage trade at their pagan shrine, the ka'bah in Mecca, the elite of the city conspired to kill Muhammad. But Muhammad and his Meccan followers were saved by a call from members of two feuding tribes in the more northerly city of Medina who had heard Muhammad preach and asked him to come and bring peace. Muhammad's migration to Medina in 622 marks year 1 in the Muslim calendar, the year when the rule of God was instituted on earth.

The surahs that come from this last decade of Muhammad's life reflect the role of the prophet as lawgiver. The selection from "The Cow" (surah II) discusses some of the ways in which a devout Muslim was expected to behave. What are these requirements? What is the impact of such rules?

Finally, the selection from "Women" (surah IV) shows how detailed the instructions of the Koran became as Muhammad administered a city that was to become an empire and a civilization. What kind of ideas about government and politics would likely develop among those who believed Muhammad revealed the words of God?

Thinking Historically

While the Koran is a religious (i.e., cultural) product, it contains passages about politics, economics, and society as well as culture. Find passages from the following selection that deal with each of these four aspects of life.

What sort of social life is suggested by surah C? What kind of social life or society is evoked in "The Cow" and "Women"? What accounts for the different images of social life in these surahs? In what ways are either of these societies different from those depicted in the documents from medieval Europe?

Surah C: The Coursers

In the name of Allah, the Beneficent, the Merciful.
1. By the snorting coursers,
2. Striking sparks of fire
3. And scouring to the raid at dawn.
4. Then, therewith, with their trail of dust,
5. Cleaving, as one, the centre (of the foe),
6. Lo! man is an ingrate unto his Lord
7. And lo! he is a witness unto that;
8. And lo! in the love of wealth he is violent.
9. Knoweth he not that, when the contents of the graves are poured forth
10. And the secrets of the breasts are made known,

11. On that day will their Lord be perfectly informed concerning them.

Surah II: The Cow

177. It is not righteousness that ye turn your faces to the East and the West; but righteous is he who believeth in Allah and the Last Day and the angels and the Scripture and the Prophets; and giveth his wealth, for love of Him, to kinsfolk and to orphans and the needy and the wayfarer and to those who ask, and to set slaves free; and observeth proper worship and payeth the poor-due. And those who keep their treaty when they make one, and the patient in tribulation and adversity and time of stress. Such are they who are sincere. Such are the Godfearing.

178. O ye who believe! Retaliation is prescribed for you in the matter of the murdered; the freeman for the freeman, and the slave for the slave, and the female for the female. And for him who is forgiven somewhat by his (injured) brother, prosecution according to usage and payment unto him in kindness. This is an alleviation and a mercy from your Lord. He who transgresseth after this will have a painful doom.

179. And there is life for you in retaliation, O men of understanding, that ye may ward off (evil).

180. It is prescribed for you, when one of you approacheth death, if he leave wealth, that he bequeath unto parents and near relatives in kindness. (This is) a duty for all those who ward off (evil).

181. And whoso changeth (the will) after he hath heard it — the sin thereof is only upon those who change it. Lo! Allah is Hearer, Knower.

182. But he who feareth from a testator some unjust or sinful clause, and maketh peace between the parties, (it shall be) no sin for him. Lo! Allah is Forgiving, Merciful.

183. O ye who believe! Fasting is prescribed for you, even as it was prescribed for those before you, that ye may ward off (evil);

184. (Fast) a certain number of days; and (for) him who is sick among you, or on a journey, (the same) number of other days; and for those who can afford it there is a ransom: the feeding of a man in need — But whoso doth good of his own accord, it is better for him: and that ye fast is better for you if ye did but know —

185. The month of Ramadān in which was revealed the Qur'ān, a guidance for mankind, and clear proofs of the guidance, and the Criterion (of right and wrong). And whosoever of you is present, let him fast the month, and whosoever of you is sick or on a journey, (let him fast the same) number of other days. Allah desireth for you ease; He desireth not hardship for you; and (He desireth) that ye should complete the period, and that ye should magnify Allah for having guided you, and that peradventure ye may be thankful.

186. And when My servants question thee concerning Me, then surely I am nigh. I answer the prayer of the suppliant when he crieth unto Me. So let them hear My call and let them trust in Me, in order that they may be led aright.

187. It is made lawful for you to go unto your wives on the night of the fast. They are raiment for you and ye are raiment for them. Allah is aware that ye were deceiving yourselves in this respect and He hath turned in mercy toward you and relieved you. So hold intercourse with them and seek that which Allah hath ordained for you, and eat and drink until the white thread becometh distinct to you from the black thread of the dawn. Then strictly observe the fast till nightfall and touch them not, but be at your devotions in the mosques. These are the limits imposed by Allah, so approach them not. Thus Allah expoundeth His revelations to mankind that they may ward off (evil).

188. And eat not up your property among yourselves in vanity, nor seek by it to gain the hearing of the judges that ye may knowingly devour a portion of the property of others wrongfully.

189. They ask thee, (O Muhammad), of new moons. Say: They are fixed seasons for mankind and for the pilgrimage. It is not righteousness that ye go to houses by the backs thereof (as do the idolaters at certain seasons), but the righteous man is he who wardeth off (evil). So go to houses by the gates thereof, and observe your duty to Allah, that ye may be successful.

190. Fight in the way of Allah against those who fight against you, but begin not hostilities. Lo! Allah loveth not aggressors.

191. And slay them wherever ye find them, and drive them out of the places whence they drove you out, for persecution is worse than slaughter. And fight not with them at the Inviolable Place of Worship until they first attack you there, but if they attack you (there) then slay them. Such is the reward of disbelievers.

192. But if they desist, then lo! Allah is Forgiving, Merciful.

193. And fight them until persecution is no more, and religion is for Allah. But if they desist, then let there be no hostility except against wrongdoers.

194. The forbidden month for the forbidden month, and forbidden things in retaliation. And one who attacketh you, attack him in like manner as he attacked you. Observe your duty to Allah, and know that Allah is with those who ward off (evil).

195. Spend your wealth for the cause of Allah, and be not cast by your own hands to ruin; and do good. Lo! Allah loveth the beneficent.

196. Perform the pilgrimage and the visit (to Mecca) for Allah. And if ye are prevented, then send such gifts as can be obtained with ease, and shave not your heads until the gifts have reached their destination. And whoever among you is sick or hath an ailment of the head must pay a ransom of fasting or almsgiving or offering. And when ye are in

safety, then whosoever contenteth himself with the Visit for the Pilgrimage (shall give) such gifts as can be had with ease. And whosoever cannot find (such gifts), then a fast of three days, while on the pilgrimage, and of seven when ye have returned; that is, ten in all. That is for him whose folk are not present at the Inviolable Place of Worship. Observe your duty to Allah, and know that Allah is severe in punishment.

197. The pilgrimage is (in) the well-known months, and whoever is minded to perform the pilgrimage therein (let him remember that) there is (to be) no lewdness nor abuse nor angry conversation on the pilgrimage. And whatsoever good ye do Allah knoweth it. So make provision for yourselves (hereafter); for the best provision is to ward off evil. Therefore keep your duty unto Me, O men of understanding.

198. It is no sin for you that ye seek the bounty of your Lord (by trading). But, when ye press on in the multitude from "Arafāt," remember Allah by the sacred monument. Remember Him as He hath guided you, although before ye were of those astray.

199. Then hasten onward from the place whence the multitude hasteneth onward, and ask forgiveness of Allah. Lo! Allah is Forgiving, Merciful.

200. And when ye have completed your devotions, then remember Allah as ye remember your fathers or with a more lively remembrance. But of mankind is he who saith: "Our Lord! Give unto us in the world," and he hath no portion in the Hereafter.

Surah IV: Women

11. Allah chargeth you concerning (the provision for) your children: to the male the equivalent of the portion of two females, and if there be women more than two, then theirs is two-thirds of the inheritance, and if there be one (only) then the half. And to his parents a sixth of the inheritance if he have a son; and if he have no son and his parents are his heirs, then to his mother appertaineth the third; and if he have brethren, then to his mother appertaineth the sixth, after any legacy he may have bequeathed, or debt (hath been paid). Your parent or your children: Ye know not which of them is nearer unto you in usefulness. It is an injunction from Allah. Lo! Allah is Knower, Wise.

12. And unto you belongeth a half of that which your wives leave, if they have no child; but if they have a child then unto you the fourth of that which they leave, after any legacy they may have bequeathed, or debt (they may have contracted, hath been paid). And unto them belongeth the fourth of that which ye leave if ye have no child, but if ye have a child then the eighth of that which ye leave, after any legacy ye may have bequeathed, or debt (ye may have contracted, hath been paid). And if a man or a woman have a distant heir (having left neither

parent nor child), and he (or she) have a brother or a sister (only on the mother's side) then to each of them twain (the brother and the sister) the sixth, and if they be more than two, then they shall be sharers in the third, after any legacy that may have been bequeathed or debt (contracted) not injuring (the heirs by willing away more than a third of the heritage) hath been paid. A commandment from Allah. Allah is Knower, Indulgent.

13. These are the limits (imposed by) Allah. Whoso obeyeth Allah and His messenger, He will make him enter Gardens underneath which rivers flow, where such will dwell for ever. That will be the great success.

14. And whoso disobeyeth Allah and His messenger and transgresseth His limits, He will make him enter Fire, where such will dwell for ever; his will be a shameful doom.

15. As for those of your women who are guilty of lewdness, call to witness four of you against them. And if they testify (to the truth of the allegation) then confine them to the houses until death take them or (until) Allah appoint for them a way (through new legislation).

16. And as for the two of you who are guilty thereof, punish them both. And if they repent and improve, then let them be. Lo! Allah is Relenting, Merciful.

48

Sayings Ascribed to the Prophet

To understand how Muhammad governed and what he preached, Muslims also consult the *hadiths,* or "sayings," attributed to the Prophet. While the sayings have nothing like the force of the Koran, the words of God, they provide valuable insight and guidance. What likely effect would the sayings included here have on a devout Muslim?

Thinking Historically

Most of these sayings deal with religion and government. What attitude toward politics do they express? If this selection was all you had to construct a Muslim idea of government, what would it be? How

---

Al-Muttaqi, *Kanz al'Ummal,* quoted in *Islam from the Prophet Muhammad to the Capture of Constantinople,* ed. and trans. Bernard Lewis, vol. I (New York: Harper, 1974), 150–51.

are these political ideas different from those in medieval Europe? What accounts for the differences?

I charge the Caliph[1] after me to fear God, and I commend the community of the Muslims to him, to respect the great among them and have pity on the small, to honor the learned among them, not to strike them and humiliate them, not to oppress them and drive them to unbelief, not to close his doors to them and allow the strong to devour the weak.

The Imams[2] are of Quraysh;[3] the godly among them rulers of the godly, and the wicked among them rulers of the wicked. If Quraysh gives a crop-nosed Ethiopian slave authority over you, hear him and obey him as long as he does not force any of you to choose between his Islam and his neck. And if he does force anyone to choose between his Islam and his neck, let him offer his neck.

Hear and obey, even if a shaggy-headed black slave is appointed over you.

Whosoever shall try to divide my community, strike off his head.

If allegiance is sworn to two Caliphs, kill the other.

He who sees in his ruler something he disapproves should be patient, for if anyone separates himself from the community, even by a span, and dies, he dies the death of a pagan.

Obey your rulers, whatever happens. If their commands accord with the revelation I brought you, they will be rewarded for it, and you will be rewarded for obeying them; if their commands are not in accord with what I brought you, they are responsible and you are absolved. When you meet God, you will say, "Lord God! No evil." And He will say, "No evil!" And you will say, "Lord God! Thou didst send us Prophets, and we obeyed them by Thy leave; and Thou didst appoint over us Caliphs, and we obeyed them by Thy leave; and Thou didst place over us rulers, and we obeyed them for Thy sake." And He will say, "You speak truth. They are responsible, and you are absolved."

If you have rulers over you who ordain prayer and the alms tax and the Holy War for God, then God forbids you to revile them and allows you to pray behind them.

If anyone comes out against my community when they are united and seeks to divide them, kill him, whoever he may be.

---

1 Successor to the prophet; supreme authority. [Ed.]

2 A leader, especially in prayer; clergyman. [Ed.]

3 An aristocratic trading clan of Mecca; hostile to Muhammad, but after his death regained prominence. That religious leaders come from Quraysh was agreed after victory of Meccan faction in 661. [Ed.]

He who dies without an Imam dies the death of a pagan, and he who throws off his obedience will have no defense on the Day of Judgment.

Do not revile the Sultan, for he is God's shadow on God's earth. Obedience is the duty of the Muslim man, whether he like it or not, as long as he is not ordered to commit a sin. If he is ordered to commit a sin, he does not have to obey.

The nearer a man is to government, the further he is from God; the more followers he has, the more devils; the greater his wealth, the more exacting his reckoning.

He who commends a Sultan in what God condemns has left the religion of God.

J. J. SAUNDERS
Civilization of Medieval Islam

In this selection the author, a modern historian, suggests answers to three important questions. First, he asks why the Arab invasions of the seventh century brought about a cultural flowering while the German invasions of Western Europe in the fifth century had the opposite effect. What, in other words, were the causes of this rise of Arabic civilization? Next, he asks about the nature of that civilization. What were its notable features? Finally, he asks about its decline after the thirteenth century. How was such a vigorous civilization overcome by the previously backward West?

What are the author's answers to these questions? Which answers do you find most convincing? Why?

Thinking Historically

While it is not the author's intention to distinguish political, social, economic, and cultural matters in this essay, he provides enough detail to enable you to discuss each of these categories for Muslim (or, as he would prefer, Arabic) civilization. Write your own characterizations

J. J. Saunders, *A History of Medieval Islam* (London: Routledge, 1978).

of these four facets for this civilization, then compare them to your characterizations of the politics, society, economics, and culture of medieval Western Europe. Overall, how would you distinguish Muslim or Arabic civilization from Western European in the Middle Ages?

For some centuries (roughly between A.D. 800 and 1200) the lands conquered by the Arabs were the soil from which grew and blossomed one of the most brilliant civilizations in the history of humanity. To give it a suitable name is a matter of some difficulty. It has been variously styled Arab, Muslim, Islamic, and Arabic. The first is clearly a misnomer, implying as it does that this culture was created or dominated by men of Arab race, which was by no means the case; the second and third define it too narrowly in religious terms, whereas many of its most distinguished figures were Christians, Jews, or pagans, and not Muslims at all. "Arabic" seems open to the least objection, since it draws attention to the fact that the literature of this particular civilization was written almost wholly in the Arabic language and acquired its characteristic unity largely from this circumstance.

The causes of the rise and fall of civilizations are often hidden from us, and the questions which start to mind are more easily framed than answered. Why were the German invasions of Western Europe in the fifth century followed by a long "dark age" of barbarism and ignorance, while the Arab invasions of the seventh century were followed by a general rise in the cultural level of the countries affected by them? So startling a contrast demands explanation, which must take the form of showing that certain conditions favourable to the growth of the arts and sciences were present in one case and absent in the other.

1. The Arab conquests politically unified a huge segment of the globe from Spain to India, a unity which remained unbroken until the fall of the Omayyads in 750. The disappearance of so many dividing frontiers, above all the one which had so long separated Rome and Persia, was a useful preliminary to the building of a new civilization.

2. As the Arabs overran one country after another, they carried their language with them. But that language possessed a unique status: to every Muslim it was not just one form of human speech among others, but the vehicle through which God had chosen to deliver his final revelation to men. Arabic was "God's tongue," and as such enjoyed a prestige which Latin and Greek and Hebrew had never known. The Koran could not, must not be translated: the believer must hear and understand and if possible read the divine book in the original, even though Arabic were not his mother tongue. To study, illustrate, and elucidate the text became a pious duty: the earliest branch of science developed by Muslims was Arabic philology, traditionally founded at

Basra in the late Omayyad age. The further Islam spread among non-Arabs, the further a knowledge of Arabic spread with it. A century or so after the conquests even Christians, Jews, and Zoroastrians within the Caliphate found it convenient to speak and write Arabic. Thus to political unity was added the widespread use of a common language, which immensely facilitated the exchange of ideas.

3. The first conquests of the Arabs were made in lands which had been the home of settled, urban civilizations for thousands of years; that is, the river valleys of the Nile and the Tigris-Euphrates. The fighting here was relatively brief (Syria was conquered in six or seven years, Egypt and Iraq in two or three), and the physical destruction was light. The native population was akin to the Arabs in race and speech, and stood aside from a struggle which was essentially between the invaders and the Byzantine or Sassanid[1] ruling class. The local officials often stayed at their posts, and administrative continuity, at least at the lower levels, remained unbroken. From motives of policy, the Caliphs cultivated friendly relations with the Jacobite and Nestorian Christians, who constituted the bulk of the people, and who during the long period of Roman rule had learnt a good deal of the science and philosophy of the Greeks. This learning, translated into Syriac, a Semitic tongue closely related to Arabic, was at the disposal of the newcomers, who were impressed by the rich and ancient culture of the region, and it was this region, and not Arabia proper, which was the birthplace of the Arabic civilization.

4. Once invasion and resettlement were over, the lands brought under the sovereignty of the Caliphs enjoyed immunity from serious external attack for three or four centuries. There was plenty of fighting on the frontiers and many internal revolts and disturbances, but no prolonged and ruinous barbarian assaults such as the Latin Christian West had to endure from the Vikings and Magyars. Under the shield of the *Pax Islamica,* which may be compared with the Augustan and Antonine Peace of the early Roman Empire, the arts and sciences rose to a new and flourishing life. Not until about 1050 did this peace begin to break down: Islam was then exposed to a series of attacks from the nomads of the steppes and deserts, culminating in the dreadful Mongol explosion of the thirteenth century.

5. The creation of the vast Arab Empire, besides levelling barriers and abolishing frontiers, brought into existence a great free-trade area, promoted safe and rapid travel, and gave a tremendous stimulus to commerce. During these four centuries (800–1200) international trade was more vigorous than at any time since the heyday of imperial Rome. Merchants from the Caliphate were found in places as far apart as

---

[1] Persian dynasty ruling just before the Arab invasion. [Ed.]

Senegal and Canton. The hoards of Arabic coins dug up in Scandinavia reveal the brisk exchange of goods between Northern Europe and the cities of Iraq and Persia via the great rivers of Russia. The negro lands south of the Sahara were drawn into the stream of world commerce. The ancient Silk Road through the oases of Central Asia which carried the products of China to the West had never been so frequented. Cities expanded, fortunes were made, a wealthy middle-class of traders, shippers, bankers, manufacturers, and professional men came into being, and a rich and sophisticated society gave increasing employment and patronage to scholars, artists, teachers, physicians, and craftsmen.

6. The pursuit of knowledge was quickened by the use of paper and the so-called "Arabic" numerals. Neither originated in the Islamic world, but both were widely employed there by the ninth century. The manufacture of paper from hemp, rags, and tree-bark seems to have been invented in China about A.D. 100, but it remained unknown outside that country until some Chinese prisoners of war skilled in the art were brought to Samarkand in 751. In 793 a paper manufactory was set up in Baghdad; by 900 the commodity was being produced in Egypt, and by 950 in Spain. The Arabic numerals, despite their name, are probably Hindu, and may have reached Islam through the translation of the *Siddhanta,* a Sanskrit astronomical treatise, made by order of the Caliph Mansur in 773. The oldest Muslim documents employing these signs date from 870–890: the zero is represented by a dot, as has always been the case in Arabic. These innovations multiplied books and facilitated calculation, and the rich scientific literature of the next few centuries undoubtedly owes much to them.

Such are of the possible causes of the rise of the Arabic civilization. To attempt a detailed description and analysis of that civilization would be impossible, but certain notable features or peculiarities of it may be considered: —

1. It was not specifically Muslim. Islam provided it with a framework and a universal language, but its only creations which possess a definitely Muslim character are Arabic grammar, law, and theology. All else came from non-Muslim sources, even Arabic poetry and belles-lettres, which were based on a literary tradition going back to pre-Islamic times, the "days of ignorance" of the sixth century.

2. The biggest single influence which helped to shape it was Greek science and philosophy, but this reached it indirectly, chiefly through the medium of Syriac. Of course, the great days of Hellenism were long over by the time of the Arab conquests: Greek science went out with Ptolemy in the second century, and the noble line of Greek thinkers ended when Justinian closed the schools of Athens in 529. But if nothing new was being created or discovered, the work of preserving and transmitting what had already been accomplished went on among the

Byzantine Greeks and their Syriac-speaking pupils in Syria, Egypt, and Iraq, and when the Arabs broke into these lands most of the leading works of Greek medicine and metaphysics had been translated into Syriac by scholars of the Oriental Christian communities. Established in an educated society, the invaders grew ashamed of their ignorance, and the Caliphs encouraged learned Christians and Jews to turn these books into the dominant language of the Empire. This translating went on for some two centuries (800–1000), at the close of which educated Muslims could read the masters of Hellenic thought in Arabic versions of Syriac translations of the Greek originals.

3. As the Syriac-speaking Christians spread through the Islamic world a knowledge of Greek thought, so the Persians introduced to it much of the lore of Sanskrit India. Hindu influences had travelled west in late Sassanid times: the game of chess and Sanskrit medical writings are said to have reached Ctesiphon in the reign of Khusrau Nushirvan. When the Abbasids moved the metropolis of Islam to Iraq, Persian scholars were given every facility to pursue this quest. At the command of Mansur, Fazari translated the *Siddhanta;* Ibn al-Mukaffa turned into Arabic the famous *Fables of Bidpai,* an Indian collection of animal stories which has gone round the world; and the celebrated mathematician al-Khwarizmi, from whose name the European word "algorism" (the old term for arithmetic) was derived, founded the science of algebra (Arabic *al-jabr,* a restoring, literally, setting a bone) on the basis of Hindu mathematical achievement. Translation from Sanskrit into Arabic went on till the time of the great Persian scientist al-Biruni (973–1048), who among numerous learned works left an admirable sociological description of India. The double and simultaneous impact of Greece and India provided a powerful stimulus to the building of the Arabic civilization.

4. The center of Arabic intellectual life was long fixed in Iraq, the ancient home of culture, "a palimpsest (as it has been styled) on which every civilization from the time of the Sumerians had left its trace." A meeting-place of Hellenic and Iranian culture, it had been the heart of the old Persian monarchy and was the seat of the Caliphate from 750 to 1258. Baghdad became a greater Ctesiphon, the capital not simply of a State but of a world civilization. Perhaps in no other region of its size could such an extraordinary variety of belief and speech have been found. Jews and Zoroastrians, Nestorian, Monophysite and Greek Orthodox Christians, Gnostics and Manichaeans, the pagans of Harran, and the strange baptist sect of the Mandeans, all mingled in the same province. In the Arab camp settlements of Basra and Kufa the Muslims first found leisure to devote themselves to things of the mind: here was inaugurated the study of Arabic philology and Islamic law. In Baghdad the Caliph Ma'mun, the son of a Persian mother, founded and endowed as a centre of research the Bait al-Hikma, or House of Wisdom, which was at once a library, an observatory, and a scientific academy.

Men of many races and faiths contributed to the fame of Baghdad as a home of scholarship, and Arabic civilization never recovered from the sack of the city by the Mongols in 1258.

5. The culture of medieval Islam was multiracial. Arabs, Syrians, Jews, Persians, Turks, Egyptians, Berbers, Spaniards, all contributed to it. One of its leading philosophers, al-Kindi, was an Arab of the tribe of Kinda (as his name implies); al-Farabi, a Neo-Platonist and commentator on Aristotle, a Turk from Transoxiana; Ibn Sina or Avicenna, perhaps the finest scientific thinker of Islam, a Persian from Bukhara; and Ibn Rushd, best known under his Europeanized name Averroës, a Spanish Moor from Cordova. A remarkable feature of Arabic philosophical literature is that much of it was written by Jews. As the Jewish religion, like the Christian, was a tolerated one among Muslims, Jews were found settled in almost all the great cities of Islam, where they learnt to write Arabic and to share in the vigorous intellectual life around them. In Spain they acted as mediators between the Muslim and Christian Spanish culture, helping Christian scholars to translate Arabic works into Latin and so making them available to the then backward West. Spain was also the birthplace of Maimonides, "the second Moses," perhaps the acutest Jewish thinker before Spinoza, who was born in Cordova in 1135 and died in Cairo in 1204, and whose *Guide for the Perplexed,* a bold attempt to reconcile reason and religious faith, finds readers to this day.

6. By far the biggest share in the construction of the Arabic civilization was taken by the Persians, a people whose recorded history was already more than a thousand years old when the Arabs broke into their land, and who found in their cultural superiority compensation for their political servitude. Persia has been described as "the principal channel irrigating the somewhat arid field of Islam with the rich alluvial flood of ancient culture": Sufism was virtually a Persian creation, and the Persian al-Ghazali was the greatest of Muslim theologians. In secular learning the Persians were predominant. "If knowledge were attached to the ends of the sky, some amongst the Persians would have reached it," was a traditional saying. Among the famous men of the age sprung from this gifted race were Razi (Rhazes), the great physician who first distinguished smallpox from measles; Tabari (died 923), the Arabic Livy, whose *Annals of Apostles and Kings* provided us with our chief source of information on early Muslim history; Ibn Sina, whose medical writings instructed the world for centuries; Biruni, a many-sided genius whose fame now rests chiefly on his description of medieval India; Omar Khayyám (died 1123), more celebrated in the East for his mathematical achievements than for his poetry; Shahrastani (died 1153), whose *Book of Religion and Sects* is really a pioneering study in comparative religion; Nasir al-Din al-Tusi (died 1274), a distinguished astronomer who collected valuable data at his observatory at Maragha in Azerbaijan; and Rashid al-Din Fadl Allad (died 1318),

author of the first world history worthy of that name. If to these scholars and scientists we add the poets (Firdawsi, Sa'di, Rumi, etc.), who shone luster on their country's literature, the picture is even brighter.

7. The core of the scientific studies of medieval Islam was medicine. Socially, the medical profession had always stood high in the East: whereas in the Greco-Roman world doctors were often freed slaves, in Persia and Babylonia they could rise to be the prime ministers of kings. At the time of the Arab conquests the classical medicine of Hippocrates and Galen was being studied by Egyptian Greeks in Alexandria and Nestorian Christians at Jundi-Shapur, in southwest Persia. The Caliphs employed graduates of these schools as their personal physicians: members of one Nestorian family, the Bakht-yashu (a name meaning "happiness of Jesus") served in this capacity at the court of Baghdad for several generations. Nestorian medical professors translated most of Galen and other authorities into Arabic, and by 900 the science of medicine was being assiduously cultivated by Muslims all over Islam. Razi was the first of their faith to acquire world fame through his vast medical encyclopedia, the *Hawi* (best known under its Latin title *Continens*), which was filled with long extracts from Greek and Hindu writers and displayed a knowledge of chemistry most unusual in that age. A similar work by Ibn Sina, the *Canon,* attained even greater celebrity and was treated for centuries as a kind of medical Bible. The branch of medicine most successively investigated was ophthalmology, eye diseases being sadly common in the East, and the *Optics* of Ibn al-Haitham, court physician to the Fatimids in Cairo where he died in 1039, remained the standard authority on its subject till early modern times, being studied with profit by the astronomer Kepler in the seventeenth century. It was through the medical schools that many of the natural sciences found their way into Muslim education, the curricula including instruction in physics, chemistry, and botany as well as in anatomy and pathology, and it was in this field that the Arabic writers made their greatest contribution to human knowledge. They added substantially to the achievement of the Greeks in the theory and art of healing disease; they founded hospitals and invented new drugs, and they filled libraries of books with detailed and accurate clinical observations. Their long superiority is proved by the fact that most of the Arabic works translated into Latin in the twelfth and thirteenth centuries were medical writings and that these were among the first to be printed at the time of the Renaissance. Razi, Ibn Sina, and Ibn al-Haitham in their Latinized form continued to be "set books" in the medical schools of Europe till as late as the mid-seventeenth century.

8. Like all civilizations, the Arabic was highly selective in its borrowings from outside. Human societies take over only those elements which seem well suited to fill a conscious gap, and disregard those which conflict with their fundamental values; thus in modern times Russia has appropriated the science rather than the humanism of the

West, and China has borrowed Marxism and rejected almost all else of European origin. Islam drew extensively on Hindu mathematics and medicine, but took small notice of Hindu philosophy, which being the reflection of a polytheistic society and of belief in the world as *maya* or illusion, was wholly repugnant to the teachings of the Koran. It helped itself to a good deal of Greek (chiefly Aristotelian) logic and metaphysics, in order to clothe its religious doctrines in a form more acceptable to a sophisticated society and enable it to defend them against philosophically trained opponents, but though it knew Aristotle's *Poetics* and *Rhetoric,* it ignored the Greek poets, dramatists, and historians as spokesmen of a pagan past it had no desire to investigate. In architecture it was ready to use Byzantine and Persian models, but painting and sculpture were virtually banned because the Prophet [Mohammed] was alleged to have pronounced representational art a temptation to idolatry. Of classical Latin literature it knew nothing: The only Latin work ever translated into Arabic is said to have been the *History* of Orosius.

That the Arabic culture was merely imitative, that it copied and transmitted what it learnt at secondhand from the Greeks, and lacked the ability to strike out on independent lines of its own, is a judgment no longer accepted. It certainly borrowed freely from the Greeks — so did the West later — but what it built on these foundations was truly original and creative, and one of the great achievements of the human spirit. For more than four hundred years the most fruitful work in mathematics astronomy, botany, chemistry, medicine, history, and geography was produced in the world of Islam by Muslims and Christians, Jews and Zoroastrians, pagans and Manichaeans. Neither the collapse of the Caliphate nor the Isma'ilian schism checked the process, for the local dynasties which sprang up on the ruins of the old Arab Empire competed with one another to attract scholars and artists to their courts, and the possession of a common language far outweighed the loss of political unity. Yet this brilliant culture, which shone so brightly in contrast to the darkness of the Latin West and the stagnation of Byzantium, began to fade from the thirteenth century onwards. Arabic philosophy was dead by 1200, Arabic science by 1500. The nations of Western Europe, once sunk in barbarism, caught up and overtook the peoples of Islam. How did this come about? The question has hardly yet received a complete and satisfactory answer, but some tentative suggestions may be offered: —

1. The collapse of the *Pax Islamica*[2] after about 1050. The end of the long peace was marked by wave after wave of nomadic invasion,

---

2 *Pax Islamica,* by analogy to the *Pax Romana,* refers to widespread peace created by Muslim societies from Morocco to India.

the Banu-Hilal in North Africa, the Turkomans and Seljuks in Western Asia, and the mighty Mongol devastations which inflicted such irreparable damage on so many Muslim lands between 1220 and 1260. Cities were sacked and burnt, wealth dissipated, libraries destroyed, and teachers dispersed. The loss to culture in the fall of Baghdad alone is incalculable. The Christian West escaped all this, since after the Northmen and Magyars had been tamed and converted around 1000, it had nothing more to fear from barbarian attack, and the Mongols never got farther west than Hungary and Silesia.

2. The decay of city life and economic prosperity. The Arabic civilization was essentially urban, and its material basis was the vigorous commercial activity which once covered an area extending as far as Scandinavia, China, and the Sudan. This activity was much diminished when nomad raids and invasions threatened the security of the caravan routes. From the eleventh century onwards the volume of international trade contracted, urban wealth declined, and social and economic conditions in the Muslim world underwent drastic change. Princes, finding their revenues falling, were obliged to pay their civil and military officers out of the rents and produce of landed estates: hence the growth of the *ikta* system, which has been compared, rather loosely, to Western feudalism. Owing presumably to the prevalence of slavery, which assured a plentiful supply of labor, there was no stimulus to technological progress and invention, which might have provided some compensation for the loss of distant markets. Nor did the cities of Islam ever develop self-governing institutions or combine in defense of their interests like the Lombard League or the Hansa in contemporary Europe: It was not that civic patriotism was wholly lacking (Arabic literature contains many town histories and biographical dictionaries of famous citizens), but that in this society the primary loyalty of a man was to his religious community, and in cities where Muslims, Christians, and Jews lived together in separate quarters, it was not easy for the inhabitants to feel and act as a united body. Thus the middle classes (merchants, traders, shippers, shopkeepers, and craftsmen) had little defense when the economic basis of their position weakened, and the decline of the town was almost certainly related to the falling off of intellectual capacity and output.

3. The loss of linguistic and cultural unity. In the days of its widest expansion, Arabic was written and understood wherever Islam prevailed, but its intellectual monopoly was threatened and finally broken by the revival of Persian in the lands east of the Tigris. The fall of the Sassanid Empire reduced the native tongue to the level of Anglo-Saxon in England after the Norman conquest, but under the Abbasids it began to reemerge in an altered form, its vocabulary swollen with Arabic words and the old Pahlawi script replaced by the Arabic. With the rise

of native dynasties after the disintegration of the Caliphate, Persia experienced a literary renaissance; the Samanids and Ghaznavids in particular were generous patrons of poets and scholars, and Firdawsi's great epic, the *Shah-nama,* or Book of Kings, finished in 1010, gave the new Persian a position in world literature it has never since lost. Fewer and fewer Persians wrote in Arabic, though the sacred language of the Koran continued to be used for works of theology, law, and devotion. When the Turks entered Islam *en masse* with the Seljuks, it was the Persianized provinces that they first occupied, and it was on Persian officials that they relied for the administration of their Empire. Deeply affected in consequence by Persian culture, the Turks carried it with them westwards into Asia Minor and eastwards into northern India: By contrast, they set little store by Arabic, except for purely religious purposes. The Mongol invasions, the fall of Baghdad and the destruction of the Caliphate dealt a fatal blow to Arabic in eastern Islam, where in the field of secular learning and literature it was steadily overshadowed by Persian and Turkish. Never again was the Muslim world to be dominated by a single language.

4. Probably the biggest factor was the strongly religious character of Islam itself and the absence of a vigorous pre-Islamic secular tradition. Behind Christian Europe lay the science and rationalism of classical Greece: behind Islam lay nothing save the cultural poverty of "the days of ignorance." The Muslims did, as we have seen, borrow a good deal from Greece, but in a limited and indirect fashion: the Greek past never *belonged* to them in the sense in which it did to Christendom, and there was never a joyous acceptance or recovery of it as took place in the West at the time of the Renaissance. The spirit of Islam was not rational in the Greek sense of the term, in that God is beyond reason and his ordering of the universe is to be accepted rather than explained. True knowledge is that of God and his Law, and the Law embraces all human activity: secular learning for its own sake is to be strongly discouraged, and intellectual pursuits are permissible only insofar as they further a deeper piety and understanding of religious truth. Such an attitude was implicit in Islamic thinking from the onset, but it became explicit only at a later stage, largely in consequence of the reaction against the Isma'ilian heresy and of a fuller realization of the dangers to orthodoxy lurking in Greek philosophy. The shift in outlook became noticeable in the Seljuk age. The great Ghazali devoted his life to the defense of Koranic truth against what he regarded as the insidious encroachments of unbelief. Islamic dogma was linked with Sufi mysticism. Muslim education was geared to the new orthodoxy by the founding of *madrasas,* where the religious sciences alone received intensive study. The Shari'a came to dominate Muslim life as the Torah had dominated post-exilic Judaism. The door was closed against further borrowings

from outside: Philosophy was repudiated as a danger to the Faith, because it was alleged to deny a personal God, creation *ex nihilo,* and the resurrection of the body. The attempt of Ibn Rushd (Averroës) in Spain to answer Ghazali and defend the pursuit of secular science fell on deaf ears and exposed him to the charge of teaching atheism. How far the reaction went can be seen from the attitude of Ibn Khaldun (1337–1406), often regarded as Islam's profoundest thinker, who dismissed all knowledge unconnected with religion as useless. Plato (he says) admitted that no certainty about God could be attained by the reason: why then waste our time on such futile inquiries? Truth is to be sought only in divine revelation. The profane sciences, which had always operated on the fringe and had never been free from the suspicion of impiety, were largely and quietly dropped as "un-Muslim."

50

ICHISADA MIYAZAKI

The Chinese Civil Service Exam System

The Chinese civil service examination system originated fourteen hundred years ago, making it the first in the world. As a device for ensuring government by the brightest young men, regardless of class or social standing, it may also be viewed as one of the world's earliest democratic systems. It was not perfect. Like democratic systems in the West only two hundred years ago, it excluded women. The system also put enormous pressure on young boys of ambitious families.

This selection consists of two passages from a book by a noted modern Japanese historian of China. The first passage concerns the elaborate early preparations for the exams.

What did young boys have to learn? In what ways was their education different from your own? What effects did the examination system have on the goals and values of young people?

Ichisada Miyazaki, *China's Examination Hell,* trans. Conrad Schirokauer (New York: Weatherhill, 1976), 13–17, 111–16, passim.

Thinking Historically

The Chinese examination system was primarily a political system, a way for the emperor to rule most effectively, employing the most talented administrators. In what sense did this system make China more "democratic" than the political systems of Western Europe or the Muslim world? In what sense was it less so? Did it become more or less democratic over the course of Chinese history? How did its purpose change from the Tang to the Sung dynasty?

Like any political system, the civil service system had a major impact on other aspects of life, social, economic, and cultural. How did it affect Chinese society, families, class differences, boys and girls? What were the economic effects of the system? How did it change Chinese cultural values, ideas, and education?

Judging from this essay and your readings about Western Europe and the Islamic world, what was the single most important difference between Chinese and Western European civilizations? Between Chinese and Muslim civilization?

Preparing for the Examinations

Competition for a chance to take the civil service examinations began, if we may be allowed to exaggerate only a little, even before birth. On the back of many a woman's copper mirror the five-character formula "Five Sons Pass the Examinations" expressed her heart's desire to bear five successful sons. Girls, since they could not take the examinations and become officials but merely ran up dowry expenses, were no asset to a family; a man who had no sons was considered to be childless. People said that thieves warned each other not to enter a household with five or more girls because there would be nothing to steal in it. The luckless parents of girls hoped to make up for such misfortune in the generation of their grandchildren by sending their daughters into marriage equipped with those auspicious mirrors.

Prenatal care began as soon as a woman was known to be pregnant. She had to be very careful then, because her conduct was thought to have an influence on the unborn child, and everything she did had to be right. She had to sit erect, with her seat and pillows arranged in exactly the proper way, to sleep without carelessly pillowing her head on an arm, to abstain from strange foods, and so on. She had to be careful to avoid unpleasant colors, and she spent her leisure listening to poetry and the classics being read aloud. These preparations were thought to lead to the birth of an unusually gifted boy.

If, indeed, a boy was born the whole family rejoiced, but if a girl arrived everyone was dejected. On the third day after her birth it was the custom to place a girl on the floor beneath her bed, and to make her grasp a tile and a pebble so that even then she would begin to form a lifelong habit of submission and an acquaintance with hardship. In contrast, in early times when a boy was born arrows were shot from an exorcising bow in the four directions of the compass and straight up and down. In later times, when literary accomplishments had become more important than the martial arts, this practice was replaced by the custom of scattering coins for servants and others to pick up as gifts. Frequently the words "First-place Graduate" were cast on those coins, to signify the highest dreams of the family and indeed of the entire clan.

It was thought best for a boy to start upon his studies as early as possible. From the very beginning he was instructed almost entirely in the classics, since mathematics could be left to merchants, while science and technology were relegated to the working class. A potential grand official must study the Four Books, the Five Classics, and other Confucian works, and, further, he must know how to compose poems and write essays. For the most part, questions in civil service examinations did not go beyond these areas of competence.

When he was just a little more than three years old, a boy's education began at home, under the supervision of his mother or some other suitable person. Even at this early stage the child's home environment exerted a great effect upon his development. In cultivated families, where books were stacked high against the walls, the baby sitter taught the boy his first characters while playing. As far as possible these were characters written with only a few strokes.

First a character was written in outline with red ink on a single sheet of paper. Then the boy was made to fill it in with black ink. Finally he himself had to write each character. At this stage there was no special need for him to know the meanings of the characters.

After he had learned in this way to hold the brush and to write a number of characters, he usually started on the *Primer of One Thousand Characters*. This is a poem that begins:

Heaven is dark, earth is yellow,
The universe vast and boundless . . .

It consists of a total of two hundred and fifty lines, and since no character is repeated, it provided the student with a foundation of a thousand basic ideograms.

Upon completing the *Primer,* a very bright boy, who could memorize one thing after another without difficulty, would go on to a history text called *Meng Ch'iu (The Beginner's Search)* and then proceed to the Four Books and the Five Classics normally studied in school. If rumors of such a prodigy reached the capital, a special "tough examination" was held, but often such a precocious boy merely served as a plaything for adults and did not accomplish much in later life. Youth examinations were popular during the Sung dynasty, but declined and finally were eliminated when people realized how much harm they did to the boys.

Formal education began at about seven years of age (or eight, counting in Chinese style). Boys from families that could afford the expense were sent to a temple, village, communal, or private school staffed by former officials who had lost their positions, or by old scholars who had repeatedly failed the examinations as the years slipped by. Sons of rich men and powerful officials often were taught at home by a family tutor in an elegant small room located in a detached building, which stood in a courtyard planted with trees and shrubs, in order to create an atmosphere conducive to study.

A class usually consisted of eight or nine students. Instruction centered on the Four Books, beginning with the *Analects,* and the process of learning was almost entirely a matter of sheer memorization. With their books open before them, the students would parrot the teacher, phrase by phrase, as he read out the text. Inattentive students, or those who amused themselves by playing with toys hidden in their sleeves, would be scolded by the teacher or hit on the palms and thighs with his fan-shaped "warning ruler." The high regard for discipline was reflected in the saying, "If education is not strict, it shows that the teacher is lazy."

Students who had learned how to read a passage would return to their seats and review what they had just been taught. After reciting it a hundred times, fifty times while looking at the book and fifty with the book face down, even the least gifted would have memorized it. At first the boys were given twenty to thirty characters a day, but as they became more experienced they memorized one, two, or several hundred each day. In order not to force a student beyond his capacity, a boy who could memorize four hundred characters would be assigned no more than two hundred. Otherwise he might become so distressed as to end by detesting his studies.

Along with the literary curriculum, the boys were taught proper conduct, such as when to use honorific terms, how to bow to superiors and to equals, and so forth — although from a modern point of view their training in deportment may seem somewhat defective, as is suggested by the incident concerning a high-ranking Chinese diplomat in the late Ch'ing dynasty who startled Westerners by blowing his nose with his fingers at a public ceremony.

It was usual for a boy to enter school at the age of eight and to complete the general classical education at fifteen. The heart of the curriculum was the classics. If we count the number of characters in the classics that the boys were required to learn by heart, we get the following figures:

Analects	11,705
Mencius	34,685
Book of Changes	24,107
Book of Documents	25,700
Book of Poetry	39,234
Book of Rites	99,010
Tso Chuan	196,845

The total number of characters a student had to learn, then, was 431,286.

The *Great Learning* and the *Doctrine of the Mean,* which together with the *Analects* and the *Mencius* constitute the Four Books, are not counted separately, since they are included in the *Book of Rites.* And, of course, those were not 431,286 *different* characters: Most of the ideographs would have been used many times in the several texts. Even so, the task of having to memorize textual material amounting to more than 400,000 characters is enough to make one reel. They required exactly six years of memorizing, at the rate of two hundred characters a day.

After the students had memorized a book, they read commentaries, which often were several times the length of the original text, and practiced answering questions involving passages selected as examination topics. On top of all this, other classical, historical, and literary works had to be scanned, and some literary works had to be examined carefully, since the students were required to write poems and essays modeled upon them. Anyone not very vigorous mentally might well become sick of it all halfway through the course.

Moreover, the boys were at an age when the urge to play is strongest, and they suffered bitterly when they were confined all day in a classroom as though under detention. Parents and teachers, therefore, supported a lad, urging him on to "become a great man!" From ancient times, many poems were composed on the theme, "If you study while young, you will get ahead." The Sung emperor Chen-tsung wrote such a one:

> To enrich your family, no need to buy good land:
> Books hold a thousand measures of grain.
> For an easy life, no need to build a mansion:
> In books are found houses of gold.
> Going out, be not vexed at absence of followers:
> In books, carriages and horses form a crowd.
> Marrying, be not vexed by lack of a good go-between:
> In books there are girls and faces of jade.
> A boy who wants to become a somebody
> Devotes himself to the classics, faces the window, and reads.

In later times this poem was criticized because it tempted students with the promise of beautiful women and riches, but that was the very reason it was effective.

Nonetheless, in all times and places students find shortcuts to learning. Despite repeated official and private injunctions to study the Four Books and Five Classics honestly, rapid-study methods were devised with the sole purpose of preparing candidates for the examinations. Because not very many places in the classics were suitable as subjects for examination questions, similar passages and problems were often repeated. Aware of this, publishers compiled collections of examination answers, and a candidate who, relying on these compilations, guessed successfully during the course of his own examinations could obtain a good rating without having worked very hard. But if he guessed wrong he faced unmitigated disaster because, unprepared, he would have submitted so bad a paper that the officials could only shake their heads and fail him. Reports from perturbed officials caused the government to issue frequent prohibitions of the publication of such collections of model answers, but since it was a profitable business with a steady demand, ways of issuing them surreptitiously were arranged, and time and again the prohibitions rapidly became mere empty formalities.

An Evaluation of the Examination System

Did the examination system serve a useful purpose? . . .

The purpose of instituting the examinations, some fourteen hundred years ago under the Sui rulers, was to strike a blow against government by the hereditary aristocracy, which had prevailed until then, and to establish in its place an imperial autocracy. The period of disunion lasting from the third to the sixth century was the golden age of the Chinese aristocracy: during that time it controlled political offices in central and local governments. . . .

The important point in China, as in Japan, was that the power of the aristocracy seriously constrained the emperor's power to appoint officials. He could not employ men simply on the basis of their ability, since any imperial initiative to depart from the traditional personnel policy evoked a sharp counterattack from the aristocratic officials. This was the situation when the Sui emperor, exploiting the fact that he had reestablished order and that his authority was at its height, ended the power of the aristocracy to become officials merely by virtue of family status. He achieved this revolution when he enacted the examination system (and provided that only its graduates were to be considered qualified to hold government office), kept at hand a reserve of such officials, and made it a rule to use only them to fill vacancies in central and local government as they occurred. This was the origin of the examination system.

The Sui dynasty was soon replaced by the T'ang, which for the most part continued the policies of its predecessor. Actually, as the T'ang was in the process of winning control over China, a new group of aristocrats appeared who hoped to transmit their privileges to their descendants. To deal with this problem the emperor used the examination system and favored its *chin-shih*[1] trying to place them in important posts so that he could run the government as he wished. The consequence was strife between the aristocrats and the *chin-shih*, with the contest gradually turning in favor of the latter. Since those who gained office simply through their parentage were not highly regarded, either by the imperial government or by society at large, career-minded aristocrats, too, seem to have found it necessary to enter officialdom through the examination system. Their acceptance of this hard fact meant a real defeat for the aristocracy.

The T'ang can be regarded as a period of transition from the aristocratic government inherited from the time of the Six Dynasties to the purely bureaucratic government of future regimes. The examination system made a large contribution to what was certainly a great advance for China's society, and in this respect its immense significance in Chinese history cannot be denied. Furthermore, that change was begun fourteen hundred years ago, at about the time when in Europe the feudal system had scarcely been formed. In comparison, the examination system was immeasurably progressive, containing as it did a superb idea the equal of which could not be found anywhere else in the world at that time.

This is not to say that the T'ang examination system was without defects. First, the number of those who passed through it was extremely small. In part this was an inevitable result of the limited diffusion of China's literary culture at a time when printing had not yet become practical and hand-copied books were still both rare and expensive, thus restricting the number of men able to pursue scholarly studies. Furthermore, because the historical and economic roots of the new bureaucratic system were still shallow, matters did not always go smoothly and sometimes there were harsh factional conflicts among officials. The development of those conflicts indicates that they were caused by the examination system itself and constituted a second serious defect.

As has been indicated, a master-disciple relationship between the examiner and the men he passed was established, much like that between a political leader and his henchmen, while the men who passed

---

[1] Highest degree winner. [Ed.]

the examination in the same year considered one another as classmates and helped one another forever after. When such combinations became too strong, factions were born.

These two defects of the examination system were eliminated during the Sung regime. For one thing, the number of men who were granted degrees suddenly rose, indicating a similar rise in the number of candidates. This was made possible by the increase in productive power and the consequent accumulation of wealth, which was the underlying reason that Chinese society changed so greatly from the T'ang period to the Sung. A new class appeared in China, comparable to the bourgeoisie in early modern Europe. In China this newly risen class concentrated hard on scholarship, and with the custom of this group, publishers prospered mightily. The classic books of Buddhism and Confucianism were printed; the collected writings of contemporaries and their discourses and essays on current topics were published; and the government issued an official gazette, so that in a sense China entered upon an age of mass communications. As a result learning was so widespread that candidates for the examinations came from virtually every part of the land, and the government could freely pick the best among them to form a reserve of officials.

In the Sung dynasty the system of conducting the examinations every three years was established. Since about three hundred men were selected each time, the government obtained an average of one hundred men a year who were qualified for the highest government positions. Thus the most important positions in government were occupied by *chin-shih,* and no longer were there conflicts between men who differed in their preparatory backgrounds, such as those between *chin-shih* and non–*chin-shih* that had arisen in the T'ang period.

Another improvement made during the Sung period was the establishment of the palace examination as the apex of the normal examination sequence. Under the T'ang emperors the conduct of the examinations was completely entrusted to officials, but this does not mean that emperors neglected them, because they were held by imperial order. It even happened that Empress Wu (r. 684–705) herself conducted the examinations in an attempt to win popularity. . . .

The position of the emperor in the political system changed greatly from T'ang times to Sung. No longer did the emperor consult on matters of high state policy with two or three great ministers deep in the interior of the palace, far removed from actual administrators. Now he was an autocrat, directly supervising all important departments of government and giving instructions about every aspect of government. Even minor matters of personnel needed imperial sanction. Now the emperor resembled the pivot of a fan, without which the various ribs of government would fall apart and be scattered. The creation of the palace examination as the final examination, given directly under the emperor's personal supervision, went hand in hand with this change in his function in the nation's political machinery and was a necessary step in the strengthening of imperial autocracy.

Thus, the examination system changed, along with Chinese society as a whole. Created to meet an essential need, it changed in response to that society's demand. It was most effective in those early stages when, first in the T'ang period, it was used by the emperor to suppress the power of the aristocracy, and then later, in the Sung period, when the cooperation of young officials with the *chin-shih* was essential for the establishment of imperial autocracy. Therefore, in the early Sung years *chin-shih* enjoyed very rapid promotion; this was especially true of the first-place *chin-shih*, not a few of whom rose to the position of chief councilor in fewer than ten years.

51

LIU TSUNG-YUAN

Camel Kuo the Gardener

Liu Tsung-yuan (773–819) was one of the great writers of the T'ang dynasty (618–907). He was especially loved for his scenes of nature, a topic he uses here for an allegory about government. What is the message of the allegory?

Thinking Historically

Are the ideas of government expressed here more like those of Confucius or Lao Tzu? How do you think Liu Tsung-yuan felt about the civil service system? Can we assume that Chinese government was practiced as the author desired, or that it was not?

How does this view of government differ from that of Western European or Muslim societies? In what sense is it more typically Chinese?

Liu Tsung-yuan, "Camel Kuo the Gardener," in *Anthology of Chinese Literature,* ed. and trans. Cyril Birch (New York: Grove Press, 1965), 258–59.

Whatever name Camel Kuo may have had to begin with is not known. But he was a hunchback and walked in his bumpy way with his face to the ground, very like a camel, and so that was what the country folk called him. When Camel Kuo heard them he said, "Excellent. Just the right name for me." — And he forthwith discarded his real name and himself adopted "Camel" also.

He lived at Feng-lo, to the west of Ch'ang-an. Camel was a grower of trees by profession; and all the great and wealthy residents of Ch'ang-an who planted trees for their enjoyment or lived off the sale of their fruit would compete for the favour of his services. It was a matter of observation that when Camel Kuo had planted a tree, even though it was uprooted from elsewhere, there was never a one but lived, and grew strong and glossy, and fruited early and abundantly. Other growers, however they spied on him and tried to imitate his methods, never could achieve his success.

Once, when questioned on the point, Camel replied: "I cannot make a tree live for ever or flourish. What I *can* do is comply with the nature of the tree so that it takes the way of its kind. When a tree is planted its roots should have room to breathe, its base should be firmed, the soil it is in should be old, and the fence around it should be close. When you have it this way, then you must neither disturb it nor worry about it, but go away and not come back. If you care for it like this when you plant it, and neglect it like this *after* you have planted it, then its nature will be fulfilled and it will take the way of its kind. And so all *I* do is avoid harming its growth — I have no power to make it grow; I avoid hindering the fruiting — I have no power to bring it forward or make it more abundant.

"With other growers it is not the same. They coil up the roots and they use fresh soil. They firm the base either too much or not enough. Or if they manage to avoid these faults, then they dote too fondly and worry too anxiously. They inspect the tree every morning and cosset it every night; they cannot walk away from it without turning back for another look. The worst of them will even scrape off the bark to see if it is still living, or shake the roots to test whether they are holding fast. And with all this the tree gets further every day from what a tree should be. This is not mothering but smothering, not affection but affliction. This is why they cannot rival my results: what other skill can I claim?"

"Would it be possible to apply this philosophy of yours to the art of government?" asked the questioner.

"My only art is the growing of trees," said Camel Kuo in answer. "Government is not my business. But living here in the country I have seen officials who go to a lot of trouble issuing orders as though they were deeply concerned for the people; yet all they achieve is an increase of misfortune. Morning and evening runners come yelling, 'Orders from the government: plough at once! Sow right away! Harvest inspection! Spin your silk! Weave your cloth! Raise your children! Feed your livestock!' Drums roll for assembly, blocks are struck to summon us. And we the common people miss our meals to receive the officials and still cannot find the time: how then can we expect to prosper our livelihood and find peace in our lives? This is why we are sick and weary; and in this state of affairs I suppose there may be some resemblance to my profession?"

"Wonderful!" was the delighted cry of the man who had questioned him. "The art I sought was of cultivating trees; the art I found was of cultivating men. Let this be passed on as a lesson to all in office!"

52

Rules for the Fan Lineage's Charitable Estate

From the time of the Sung dynasty (960–1279), many wealthy Chinese families formed charitable trusts for their descendants. One of the first men to set up such a trust was Fan Zhongyan (989–1052), an important political official.

This selection presents the rules that Fan set down for the way in which his descendants would share the income from his estate. What activities did the lineage support? What other activities would have been left to individual families? Why would lineages be more common among wealthy than poor families?

Thinking Historically

Lineage was both a social and economic organization. What impact would these lineages have on Chinese social life? Would they strengthen or weaken Chinese families? How might they effect Chinese economic life?

How did lineages make Chinese society different from that of Western Europe? Were there similar social institutions in Islamic society? Is there a modern equivalent?

Fan Zhongyan, *Fan Wengzheng gong ji*, in *Chinese Civilization: A Sourcebook*, 2nd ed., ed. and trans. Patricia Buckley Ebrey (New York: The Free Press, 1993), 155–56.

1. One pint of rice per day may be granted for each person whom a branch has certified to be one of its members. (These quantities refer to polished rice. If hulled rice is used, the amount should be increased proportionately.)

2. Children of both sexes over five years of age are counted in the total.

3. Female servants may receive rice if they have borne children by men in the lineage and the children are over fifteen or they themselves are over fifty.

4. One bolt of silk for winter clothing may be granted for each individual, except children between five and ten years of age who may receive half a bolt.

5. Each branch may receive a rice ration for a single slave, but not any silk.

6. Every birth, marriage, death, or other change in the number of lineage members must immediately be recorded.

7. Each branch should make a list of those entitled to grain rations. At the end of the month the manager should examine these requests. He must not make any prior arrangements or exceed the stipulated monthly rations. The manager should also keep his own register in which he records the quantity due each branch based on the number of its members. If the manager spends money wastefully or makes advance payments to anyone, the branches have the authority to require him to pay an indemnity.

8. For the expenses of marrying a daughter, thirty strings of cash may be granted, unless the marriage is a second one, in which case twenty strings may be granted.

9. For the expenses of taking a first wife, twenty strings may be granted (but nothing for a second wife).

10. Lineage members who become officials may receive the regular rice and silk grants and the special grants for weddings and funerals if they are living at home awaiting a post, awaiting selection, or mourning their parents. They may also receive the grants if they leave their families at home while they serve in Sichuan, Gwangdong, or Fujien, or for any other good reason.

11. For the expenses of mourning and funerals in the various branches, if the deceased is a senior member, when mourning begins, a grant of ten strings of cash may be made, and a further fifteen at the time of the burial. For more junior members, the figures are five and ten strings respectively. In the case of low-ranking members or youths under nineteen, seven strings for both expenses; for those under fifteen, three strings; for those under ten, two strings. No grant should be made for children who die before seven, or slaves or servants.

12. If any relatives through marriage living in the district face dire need or unexpected difficulties, the branches should jointly determine

the facts and discuss ways to provide assistance from the income of the charitable estate.

13. A stock of rice should be stored by the charitable estate from year to year. The monthly rations and the grants of silk for winter clothing should start with the tenth month of 1050. Thereafter, during each year with a good harvest, two years' worth of grain rations should be hulled and stored. If a year of dearth occurs, no grants should be made except for the rice rations. Any surplus over and above the two years' reserve should be used first for funeral and mourning expenses, then marriage expenses. If there is still a remainder, winter clothes may be issued. However, if the surplus is not very large, the priorities should be discussed, and the amount available divided up and granted in equitable proportions. If grants cannot be made to all entitled to them, they should be made first to those who have suffered bereavement, next to those with weddings. In cases where more than one death has occurred at the same time, senior members take precedence over junior ones. Where the relative seniority of those concerned is the same, the grant should be made on the basis of which death or burial took place first. If, after paying out the rations and the allowances for marriages and burials, a surplus still remains, it must not be sold off, but hulled and put into storage for use as rations for three or more years. If there is a danger that the stored grain might go bad, it may be sold off and replaced with fresh rice after the autumn harvest. All members of the branches of the lineage will carefully comply with the above rules.

> Tenth month, 1050. Academician of the Zizheng Hall, Vice-president of the Board of Rites, and Prefect of Hangzhou, Fan. Sealed.

REFLECTIONS

To pull together and compare some of the characterizations you made from the selections in this chapter, make a chart: Write the names of the three civilizations — European, Islamic, and Chinese — across the top of the page, and the categories social, economic, political, and cultural down the left margin, allowing a quarter page for each. Try to fill in as many of the blocks as you can. You might use more than one characterization for each. For instance, in the box for social aspects of European civilization you would, no doubt, write "feudalism." You might also write "nobles," "monasteries," "fealty and homage," "vassals defend," and "sons inherit status." Or your style of observing and characterizing might lead you to such notes as "churches can be landlords," "lots of witnesses," and "they were very formal." All of these descriptions are correct: Just make sure your comments are about society, social behavior, social relationships, social organization, or various social elements — class, family, men and women, population, and age. Repeat this exercise with the other three categories. These are by no means exclusive, but try not to use the same words in describing, say, a social and an economic aspect.

After you have filled in as many of the blanks as you can, you can make comparisons in a number of interesting ways. (You have already done some of this, but here you can be more systematic.) First, compare how one category, say society, is different in Europe and Islam, or Europe and China, or China and Islam. You might, for example, say that European society was less centralized than Chinese or Islamic society or that the extended family was more important in China.

After doing the same for economics, politics, and culture, notice how the four categories of any civilization fit together. How does the type of society in medieval Europe, for instance, "fit" medieval Europe's economy? This interaction is what constitutes a civilization. See if you used a word repetitively in characterizing each of the four aspects of a particular civilization. Then try to categorize the civilization as a whole.

Now you are ready to compare each of these civilizations to another one. These characterizations may be general, or they may be qualified and later modified, but at the very least you now have a general starting point for more in-depth analysis of these three great civilizations in future chapters.

9

Love and Marriage

Medieval Societies and Cultures,
1000–1200 C.E.

HISTORICAL CONTEXT

Love and marriage, love and marriage,
Go together like a horse and carriage.
This I tell ya, brother,
You can't have one without the other.[1]

Despite the lyrics of the song, love and marriage had little to do with each other throughout most of human history. Parents arranged marriages with their own economic needs foremost. Few people had the time to cultivate the idea of romantic love. One group who did, the ancient Greeks, wrote of love as a sickness; its symptoms were sweaty palms, palpitating heart, blushing complexion, and stammering speech. Marriage cured the disease, ending all symptoms, returning the couple to the steady sanity of daily life. But the idea of love as affliction, accident, or attack (symbolized by the random shot of Cupid's arrow) was evidently too enticing to disappear with the end of the classical world. Cultivated in the religious poetry of the Islamic world, ideas of fevered emotional dedication revived in Europe in the Middle Ages. How unusual was this European idea of courtly love?

---

[1] Written by Sammy Cahn and Jimmy Van Heusen.

THINKING HISTORICALLY
Analyzing Cultural Differences

From a biological perspective humans everywhere are alike. We all share the same basic genetic makeup, despite superficial variations in appearance. Yet our cultures—the sets of ideas and learned behaviors that a group of people embrace and pass on to future generations—make us different. Cultural differences often invite rough generalizations that encompass ethnic groups: for example, the French eat cheese and drink wine, whereas the Japanese eat rice and drink tea. Such comparisons are subject to heated debate when they pass judgement on a group of people. Generalizations can easily verge on becoming stereotypes, but because there clearly are cultural differences among humans, the attempt to describe and classify those differences cannot be ignored.

In this chapter we explore the concept of romantic love in various cultures. The classic debate on this subject is whether romantic love was a product of Western European culture. No one has ever argued, at least legitimately, that only Europeans knew love. Rather, some propose that Europeans developed a unique concept of love, variously called romantic, courtly, or chivalric, that had a profound impact on the development of Western and other societies.

We ask whether different societies have different kinds of love (the idea, the feeling, or the behavior). How culturally variable are our emotions? If they vary, do they vary by nation, by region, by "culture" or "civilization"? What role do technology, modernity, social structure, and wealth play? We ask whether love is natural or learned, and to the extent it may be cultural, what the different cultures of love are.

53

KEVIN REILLY

Love in Medieval Europe, India, and Japan

The following selection begins with the classic argument that romantic love was a product of medieval Europe, originating in the troubadour tradition of southern France around the twelfth century. The story of Ulrich von Lichtenstein, although probably not typical, details all the facets of the new idea of love, as well as the courts of chivalry that developed its code of behavior. What, according to this interpretation, are the elements of romantic love? How is it similar to, or different from, other kinds of love? How does it relate to sex and marriage? How is the medieval Indian tradition of *bhakti* different from European romantic love? How were medieval Hindu ideas of sex different from Christian ideas of sex? How was the Heian Japanese idea of love different from European romantic love? How was it similar?

Thinking Historically

Every culture encompasses a wide variety of ideas and behavior at any one time, making it difficult to argue that a certain idea or behavior defines the culture as a whole. Nevertheless, if there were no commonalities, no widely agreed upon form, there could be no culture. One way to understand what makes one culture different from another, is to discount the extreme behavior at the fringes and focus on what most people think or do. But another way to reach such an understanding is to compare the extremes of one culture with the extremes of another, with the assumption that the extremists of any culture will magnify the culture's main trait. You might think of Ulrich von Lichtenstein as an extreme example of medieval European ideas of romantic love. A question to ask after you read about other societies is: Could there have been an Ulrich elsewhere? Could medieval India or Japan have produced an Ulrich? If not, why not?

Notice also that this selection highlights particular social classes as well as particular cultures. How do cultures and classes interact to form the ideal of romantic love in Europe and something both similar and different in Japan?

Kevin Reilly, *The West and the World,* 3rd edition (Princeton, N.J.: Markus Wiener, 1997), 279–80, 282–83, 287–92.

In the Service of Woman

In the twelfth century the courtly love tradition of the troubadours traveled north into France and Germany, and it became a guide to behavior for many young knights.

We are lucky to have the autobiography of one of these romantic knights, a minor noble who was born in Austria about 1200. His name was Ulrich von Lichtenstein, and he called his autobiography, appropriately enough, *In the Service of Woman*.[1]

At an early age Ulrich learned that the greatest honor and happiness for a knight lay in the service of a beautiful and noble woman. He seems to have realized, at least subconsciously, that true love had to be full of obstacles and frustrations in order to be spiritually ennobling. So at the age of twelve Ulrich chose as the love of his life a princess. She was a perfect choice: Far above him socially, she was also older than Ulrich and already married. Ulrich managed to become a page in her court so that he could see her and touch the same things that she touched. Sometimes he was even able to steal away to his room with the very water that she had just washed her hands in, and he would secretly drink it.

By the age of seventeen Ulrich had become a knight and took to the countryside to joust the tournaments wearing the lady's colors. Finally after a number of victories, Ulrich gained the courage to ask his niece to call on the lady and tell her that he wanted to be a distant, respectful admirer. The princess would have none of it. She told Ulrich's niece that she was repulsed by Ulrich's mere presence, that he was low class and ugly—especially with that harelip of his. On hearing her reply Ulrich was overjoyed that she had noticed him. He went to have his harelip removed, recuperated for six weeks, and wrote a song to the princess. When the lady heard of this she finally consented to let Ulrich attend a riding party she was having, suggesting even that he might exchange a word with her if the opportunity arose. Ulrich had his chance. He was next to her horse as she was about to dismount, but he was so tongue-tied that he couldn't say a word. The princess thought him such a boor that she pulled out a lock of his hair as she got off her horse.

Ulrich returned to the field for the next three years. Finally the lady allowed him to joust in her name, but she wouldn't part with as much as a ribbon for him to carry. He sent her passionate letters and songs that he had composed. She answered with insults and derision. In one letter the princess derided Ulrich for implying that he had lost a finger while fighting for her when he had actually only wounded it slightly. Ulrich responded by having a friend hack off the finger and send it to

---

[1] Paraphrased from Morton Hunt, *The Natural History of Love* (New York: Knopf, 1959), 132–139. Quotations indicate Hunt's words. [Ed.]

the lady in a green velvet case. The princess was evidently so impressed with the power that she had over Ulrich that she sent back a message that she would look at it every day—a message that Ulrich received as he had the others," "on his knees, with bowed head and folded hands."

More determined than ever to win his lady's love, Ulrich devised a plan for a spectacular series of jousts, in which he challenged all comers on a five-week trip. He broke eight lances a day in the service of his princess. After such a showing, the princess sent word that Ulrich might at last visit her, but that he was to come disguised as a leper and sit with the other lepers who would be there begging. The princess passed him, said nothing, and let him sleep that night out in the rain. The following day she sent a message to Ulrich that he could climb a rope to her bedroom window. There she told him that she would grant no favors until he waded across the lake; then she dropped the rope so that he fell into the stinking moat.

Finally, after all of this, the princess said that she would grant Ulrich her love if he went on a Crusade in her name. When she learned that he was making preparations to go, she called it off and offered her love. After almost fifteen years Ulrich had proved himself to the princess.

What was the love that she offered? Ulrich doesn't say, but it probably consisted of kisses, an embrace, and possibly even a certain amount of fondling. Possibly more, but probably not. That was not the point. Ulrich had not spent fifteen years for sex. In fact, Ulrich had not spent fifteen years to win. The quest is what kept him going. His real reward was in the suffering and yearning. Within two years Ulrich was after another perfect lady.

Oh yes. We forgot one thing. Ulrich mentions that in the middle of his spectacular five-week joust, he stopped off for three days to visit the wife and kids. He was married? He was married. He speaks of his wife with a certain amount of affection. She was evidently quite good at managing the estate and bringing up the children. But what were these mundane talents next to the raptures of serving the ideal woman? Love was certainly not a part of the "details of crops, and cattle, fleas and fireplaces, serfs and swamp drainage." In fact, Ulrich might expect that his wife would be proud of him if she knew what he was up to. The love of the princess should make Ulrich so much more noble and esteemed in his wife's eyes.

Courtly Love

The behavior of Ulrich von Lichtenstein reflected in exaggerated form a new idea of love in the West. Historians have called it "courtly love" because it developed in the courts of Europe, where noble ladies and knights of "quality" came together. For the first time since the Greeks a man could idealize a woman, but only if he minimized her sexuality. The evidence is overwhelming that these spiritual affairs would ideally never be consummated.

It is difficult for us to understand how these mature lords and ladies could torture themselves with passionate oaths, feats of endurance, fainting spells when they heard their lover's name or voice, in short the whole repertoire of romance, and then refrain from actually consummating that love. Why did they insist on an ideal of "pure love" that allowed even naked embraces but drew the line at intercourse, which they called "false love"? No doubt the Christian antipathy for sex was part of the problem. Earlier Christian monks had practiced a similar type of *agape*, Christianity had always taught that there was a world of difference between love and lust. The tendency of these Christian men to think of their ladies as replicas of the Virgin Mother also made sex inappropriate, if not outright incestuous.

But these lords and ladies were also making a statement about their "class" or good breeding. They were saying (as did Sigmund Freud almost a thousand years later) that civilized people repress their animal lust. They were distinguishing themselves from the crude peasants and soldiers around them who knew only fornication and whoring and raping. They were cultivating their emotions and their sensitivity, and priding themselves on their self-control. They were privileged (as members of the upper class) to know that human beings were capable of loyalty and love and enjoying beauty without behaving like animals. They were telling each other that they were refined, that they had "class." . . .

Further, despite the new romanticized view of the woman (maybe because of it), wives were just as excluded as they had always been. Noble, uplifting love, genuine romantic love, could not be felt for someone who swept the floor any more than it could be felt *by* someone whose life was preoccupied with such trivia. The lords and one of their special ladies, Marie, the countess of Champagne, issued the following declaration in 1174:

> We declare and we hold as firmly established that love cannot exert its power between two people who are married to each other. For lovers give each other everything freely, under no compulsion of necessity, but married people are in duty bound to give in to each other's desires and deny themselves to each other in nothing.[2]

---

[2]Andreas, *Tractatus de Amore*, 1:6, 7th Dialogue. Quoted in Hunt, 143–44. [Ed.]

The Court of Love

The proclamation was one of many that were made by the "courts of love" that these lords and ladies established in order to settle lovers' quarrels—and to decide for themselves the specifics of the new morality....

No one did more to formulate these rules than Andreas Capellanus. Andreas not only summarized the numerous cases that came before the court, but he used these decisions to write a manual of polite, courtly love. He called his influential book *A Treatise on Love and Its Remedy*, a title that indicated his debt to Sappho and the Greek romantic idea of love as a sickness. Andreas, however, did not think that he was advocating a "romantic" idea of love. The word was not even used in his day. He considered himself to be a modern twelfth-century Ovid—merely updating the Roman's *Art of Love*. He called himself Andreas the Lover and, like Ovid, considered himself an expert on all aspects of love.

But Andreas only used the same word as Ovid. The similarity ended there. The "aspects" of love that Andreas taught concerned the loyalty of the lovers, courteous behavior, the spiritual benefits of "pure love," the importance of gentleness, the subservience of the man to his lover, and the duties of courtship. There is none of Ovid's preoccupation with the techniques of seduction. Andreas is not talking about sex. In fact, he clearly advises against consummating the relationship.

Ovid made fun of infatuation and silly emotional behavior, but urged his readers to imitate such sickness in order to get the woman in bed. Andreas valued the passionate emotional attachment that Ovid mocked. Sincerity and honesty were too important to Andreas to dream of trickery, deceit, or pretense. Love, for Andreas, was too noble an emotion, too worthy a pursuit, to be put on like a mask. In short, the Roman had been after sexual gratification; the Christian wanted to refine lives and cleanse souls. They both called it love, but Andreas never seemed to realize that they were not talking the same language.

A Medieval Indian Alternative: Mystical Eroticism

Sometimes the best way to understand our own traditions is to study those of a different culture. It is difficult, for instance, for us to see Christian sexual morality as unusual because it has shaped our culture to such a great extent.

There have been alternatives, however. One of the most remarkable was the Indian ecstatic religion of the Middle Ages. Here the erotic played a central role, not as temptation to be shunned but as a source of salvation. Most medieval temple sculpture was erotic. The temples at Khajuraho and Orissa are full of sexual imagery: sensuous nudes and embracing couples. The temple architecture itself suggests fertility and reproduction. The temple sculptures, like the popular story *Gita Govinda* of the twelfth century, tell of the loves of the god Krishna. He is shown scandalizing young women, dancing deliriously, and bathing with scores of admirers. Krishna's erotic appeal is a testament to his charisma. He is "divine in proportion to his superiority as a great lover."

> Worshippers were encouraged to commit excesses during festivals as the surest way to achieve. . . . ecstasy, the purging climax of the orgiastic feast, the surmounting of duality.[3]

Among the most popular forms of medieval Hindu worship were the *bhakti* cults, which originated in devotion to Krishna in the *Bhagavad Gita*. *Bhakti* cults underline the difference between Indian and European devotion. While the Christian church discouraged spiritual love that might easily lead to "carnal love," the Indian *bhakti* sects encouraged rituals of ecstasy and sensual love precisely because they obliterated moral distinctions. The ecstatic union with the divine Krishna, Vishnu, or Shiva enabled the worshiper to transcend the limitations of self and confining definitions of good and evil.

Thus, Indian ecstatic religion sought sexual expression as a path to spiritual fulfillment. It is interesting that the word *bhakti* meant sex as well as worship, while we use the word "devotion" to mean worship and love. Hindu eroticism had nothing to do with the private expression of romantic love. In fact, it was the opposite. While romantic love depended on the development of the individual personality and the cultivation of individual feelings, *bhakti* depended on the loss of self in the sexual act.

Bhakti cults differed from the European courtly love tradition in one other important respect. They were not expressions of upper-class control. They were popular expressions of religious feeling. In essence they were directed against the dominating *brahman* and *kshatriya* castes because they challenged the importance of caste distinctions altogether. The ecstatic communion with the deity that they preached was open to all, regardless of caste. They appealed even to women and untouchables, as well as to farmers and artisans.

As Christianity did in Europe, popular Hinduism of the Middle Ages replaced a classical formal tradition with a spiritual passion. Ovid's *Art of Love* and the *Kama Sutra* were mechanical, passionless exercises for tired ruling classes. Both India and Europe turned to more emotionally intense religious experiences in the Middle Ages. Perhaps the classical ideals seemed sterile after the spread of salvation religions like Christianity, Buddhism, and revived Hinduism. The similarity between Christian and Hindu emotionalism may be a product of

---

[3]Richard Lannoy, *The Speaking Tree: A Study of Indian Cultural and Society* (Oxford: Oxford University Press, 1971), 64.

uncertain times, barbarian threats, and diseases that stalked the Eurasian continent. But the differences between Christian courtly love and *bhakti* cults were also profound. In India, sexual passion was an avenue to spiritual salvation. In Christian Europe sexual passion was at best a dead end, and at worst a road to hell.

Polygamy, Sexuality, and Style: A Japanese Alternative

At the same time that feudal Europe was developing a code of chivalry that romanticized love and almost desexualized marriage, the aristocracy of feudal Japan was evolving a code of polygamous sexuality without chivalry and almost without passion. We know about the sexual lives of Japanese aristocrats between 950 and 1050—the apex of the Heian period—through a series of remarkable novels and diaries, almost all of which were written by women. These first classics of Japanese literature, like *The Tale of Genji* and *The Pillow Book,* were written by women because Japanese men were still writing the "more important" but less-informative laws and theological studies in Chinese (just as Europeans still wrote in a Latin that was very different from the everyday spoken language).

When well-born Japanese in the Heian court spoke of "the world" they were referring to a love affair, and the novels that aristocratic women like Murasaki Shikibu or Sei Shonagon had time to compose in the spoken language were full of stories of "the world."

In *The World of the Shining Prince* Ivan Morris distinguishes three types of sexual relationships between men and women of the Heian aristocracy. (Homosexuality among the court ladies was "probably quite common," he writes, "as in any society where women were obliged to live in continuous and close proximity," but male homosexuality among "warriors, priests, and actors" probably became prevalent in later centuries.) The first type of heterosexual relationship was between the male aristocrat and his "principal wife." She was often several years older than her boy-husband and frequently served more as a guardian than as a bride. She was always chosen for her social standing, usually to cement a political alliance between ruling families. Although the match must frequently have been loveless, her status was inviolate; it was strictly forbidden, for instance, for a prince to exalt a secondary wife to principal wife. Upon marriage the principal wife would normally continue to live with her family, visited by her husband at night, until he became the head of his own household on the death or retirement of his father. Then the principal wife would be installed with all of her servants and aides as the head of the north wing of her husband's residence. An aristocratic woman (but never a peasant woman) might also become a secondary wife or official concubine. If she were officially recognized as such (much to the pleasure of her family), she might be moved into another wing of the official residence (leading to inevitable conflicts with the principal wife and other past and future secondary wives), or she might be set up in her own house. The arrangements were virtually limitless. The third and most frequent type of sexual relationship between men and women was the simple (or complex) affair—with a lady at court, another man's wife or concubine, but usually with a woman of a far lower class than the man. Ivan Morris writes of this kind of relationship:

> Few cultured societies in history can have been as tolerant about sexual relations as was the world of *The Tale of Genji*. Whether or not a gentleman was married, it redounded to his prestige to have as many affairs as possible; and the palaces and great mansions were full of ladies who were only too ready to accommodate him if approached in the proper style. From reading the *Pillow Book* we can tell how extremely commonplace these casual affairs had become in court circles, the man usually visiting the girl at night behind her screen of state and leaving her at the crack of dawn.[4]

That emphasis on "the proper style" is what distinguishes the sexuality of medieval Japan from that of ancient Rome, and reminds us of the medieval European's display of form—the aristocracy's mark of "class." Perhaps because the sexuality of the Heian aristocracy was potentially more explosive than the repressed rituals of European chivalry, style was that much more important. Polygamous sexuality could be practiced without tearing the society apart (and destroying aristocratic dominance in the process) only if every attention were given to style. Listen, for instance, to what the lady of *The Pillow Book* expected from a good lover:

> A good lover will behave as elegantly at dawn as at any other time. He drags himself out of bed with a look of dismay on his face. The lady urges him on: "Come, my friend, it's getting light. You don't want anyone to find you here." He gives a deep sigh, as if to say that the night has not been nearly long enough and that it is agony to leave. Once up, he does not instantly pull on his trousers. Instead he comes close to the lady and whispers whatever was left unsaid during the night. Even when he is dressed, he still lingers, vaguely pretending to be fastening his sash.
>
> Presently he raises the lattice, and the two lovers stand together by the side door while he tells her how he dreads the coming day, which will keep them apart; then he slips away. The lady watches him go,

---

[4]Ivan Morris, *The World of the Shining Prince: Court Life in Ancient Japan* (Baltimore: Penguin Books, 1969), 237.

and this moment of parting will remain among her most charming memories.

Indeed, one's attachment to a man depends largely on the elegance of his leave-taking. When he jumps out of bed, scurries about the room, tightly fastens his trouser-sash, rolls up the sleeves of his Court cloak, over-robe, or hunting costume, stuffs his belongings into the breast of his robe and then briskly secures the outer sash—one really begins to hate him.[5]

The stylistic elegance of the lover's departure was one of the principal themes of Heian literature. Perhaps no situation better expressed the mood of the Japanese word *aware* (a word that was used over a thousand times in *The Tale of Genji*), which meant the poignant or the stylishly, even artistically, sorrowful—a style of elegant resignation. The word also suggests the mood of "the lady in waiting" and even the underlying anguish and jealousy of a precariously polygamous existence for the women consorts and writers of the Japanese feudal age. The ladies of the court were trained in calligraphy, poetry, and music; they were dressed in elaborate, colorful silks, painted with white faces and black teeth, and rewarded by sexual attention that always had to be justified by its cultured style. . . .

Aristocracies have behaved in similar ways throughout the world, and throughout history. They demonstrate their "class" or "good breeding" with elaborate rituals that differentiate their world from the ordinary. But the example of aristocratic Heian Japan a thousand years ago points to some of the differences between Japanese and Christian culture. The Japanese developed rituals of courtship and seduction for the leisured few that were sexually satisfying and posed no threat to marriage. They were rituals that showed artistic refinement rather than sexual "purity" or chastity. They could be sexual because Japanese culture did not disparage sexuality. Rather it disparaged lack of "taste." The affair did not threaten marriage because the culture did not insist on monogamy. The new sexual interest could be carried on outside or inside the polygamous estate of the Japanese aristocrat. Perhaps the main difference, then, is that the Japanese aristocrat invented stylized sex rather than romantic love.

[5]*The Pillow Book of Sei Shonagon,* trans. Ivan Morris (Baltimore: Penguin Books, 1971), 49–50.

54

JACK GOODY

Love, Lust, and Literacy

Jack Goody, a professor of cultural history and anthropology, is an African specialist who has argued that differences between Western and Eastern cultures are not nearly as significant as the differences between these two and the cultures of sub-Saharan Africa. For Goody, it is technology—specifically the invention of writing and the spread of literacy—that has historically separated some African societies (although not all) from most Eurasian cultures. In this selection he argues that romantic love was common in all literate societies, because it was actually created by writing. What do you think of his argument? How convincing is his evidence?

Thinking Historically

Notice that Goody is particularly interested in dismissing the argument that romantic love is a creation of European culture. He challenges the idea that cultures from different areas of Eurasia or cultures with different religious traditions have different ideas of love. Is he challenging the argument of the preceding selection or criticizing another view? Does he argue that there are no culturally different ideas of love or that these differences are a result of other factors?

A number of historians especially of the French *mentalité* school, as well as many sociologists, see modern Europe as marked by a particular constellation of sentiments, including love, that characterised, even promoted, the contemporary world in ways that were more difficult for others to accomplish. As with other features of domestic and personal relations, there are those who see this European exceptionalism as going back to the eighteenth century, to the period of the Enlightenment, or sometimes to the Reformation or Renaissance; others regard it as going yet further back, not (as with some claims about rationality) to the Greeks, but at least to the troubadours and to medieval poetry. There is no doubt this perception exists, both at the level of folk concepts and of scholarship, sometimes on a European basis (for example, in the work of de Rougement), sometimes on a more nationalistic one.

Jack Goody, *Food and Love: A Cultural History of East and West* (London: Verso, 1999), 96–97, 110–14, 120–23.

It is especially English historians who have considered love, between husband and wife, between parents and children, as well as romantic love, as being unique features of the modern affective family in which that country, the First Industrial Nation, is seen as leading the way in the process of "modernization." While that particular view is not likely to commend itself except to an Anglo-Saxon audience, there is a much more widespread belief that a unique attitude to love is characteristic of Europe, either ancient or modern.

Although the existence of this belief is indisputable, I want to question its basis. In doing so, I am not concerned to deny that contemporary (modern or post-modern) or European relationships may not have their identifiable profiles, connected in part to wider socio-economic features, but rather to suggest that the analytic descriptions are often unacceptable because they fail to take fully into account the comparative and longer-term historical dimensions. That questioning will lead to a criticism of certain sociological treatments of the concept of modernisation, which again seem to me too ego- and ethnocentric.

Some have even gone so far as to see other cultures, especially those of Black Africa, as being marked by lust or desire rather than love. Others, less obviously racist, see romantic love, if it exists at all in other parts, as being characteristic of relationships outside the family (in other words as "adulterous") or as displaying a yearning for the unattainable. Questionable as these hypotheses are in their general form, I want to suggest that we may be able to discover some more acceptable way of·accounting for differences and similarities. . . .

I would suggest that this elaboration of the discourse of love, this idealization of the beloved, occurs in societies with writing and is therefore not only earlier than the eighteenth century and even the troubadours, but is found in all cultures which developed literary traditions.

Let us first look at one example from the written poetry of romantic love, that of a trobaritz, one of the most famous of the female troubadours, Na Castelosa, from the Auvergne, wife of Turc de Meyronne, who loved Armand of Bréon and composed songs for him at the beginning of the thirteenth century. She wrote a poem which ran

> You have let pass a very long time since you left me:
> and that pains me because you swore with your life that you would have no other.
> And if it is another who preoccupies you, you have betrayed and killed me,
> for I hoped you would love me without the slightest doubt.

The lover and the loved one are separated in space; the poetry elaborates reflections about their situation, one of parting. This is not entirely Wordsworth's "emotion recollected in tranquility," but a parallel process, one that is encouraged by writing about rather than speaking to. Emotions are re-presented rather than presented; the written poem separates condition and reflection. I do not wish to assert that such separation is impossible in the spoken tongue; indeed, it is a feature of all or most language use, but it is definitely promoted by writing, which creates an object outside oneself in a way that speech cannot do, at least in the same clear-cut fashion.

This context seems to be one in which idealisation can flourish. As Lantz . . . notes, "their wishes and fantasies about the man–woman relationships [were] expressed in romantic love-tales," that is, essentially as text. Indeed, the love of the troubadour may be a purely literary phenomenon, for some have queried whether it existed at all outside the text. . . . These texts were also models. Writing of the twelfth-century romances, Duby . . . remarks that the "men and women who were enthused with this literature tended to copy their ways of thinking, of feeling and of acting."

That same element of distance and idealisation is found in the extensive tradition of love poetry which the Chinese developed dating back to *The Book of Songs* from the ninth to the seventh century B.C.E. Subsequently a corpus of erotic and elegiac rhapsodies known as *The Songs of Ch'u* was composed between the fourth century B.C.E. and the second century C.E. However, there was much ambivalence about this type of poetry, some believing it to be distinctly decadent. So that exegetical scholars were sometimes led to interpret the poems in a political or moralising way, just as Christian apologists did with *The Song of Songs*. In the years 534–45 a court poet, Hsü Ling, put together an anthology of love poems which he called *New Songs from a Jade Terrace*. This consisted largely of love poetry belonging to the aristocratic court tradition of southern China. The "Palace Style Poetry" took on a standardised rhetorical form that bristled with conventions. One of those was that "the woman's lover must be absent from the love scenario". . . . As a consequence there is throughout a pervasive sense of obligatory melancholy, a frustration of desire. Once again love poetry is founded on absence. In the earlier poems an "image of divine eroticism develops into an idealized portrayal of palace ladies," . . . a claim similar to that made for Christianity. . . . Later the focus shifts more to unhappy love. It is usually a woman who is the subject of the poem, often a wife whose husband has gone off on a long journey, for the love expressed is mainly conjugal. Women are "victims of love's desire" and inevitably remain behind while the man moves on. She looks back towards the past; "nostalgia reigns in the boudoir poems." The following poem by Fu Hsü is typical of the shorter poems.

Autumn orchid shades a jade pool,
Pool water clear and fragrant.

Lotus blooms to the wind unfold,
Among them is a pair of mandarin ducks.
And paired fish impulsive leap and dart,
And two birds capricious wheel and glide.
You promised nine autumns past
To share with me your robe in bed.

Or from a poem by the Emperor Wen of the Wei Dynasty:

Day to part so easy! day to meet so hard!
Mountains and rivers far away, the road is lost to sight.
My full cup of love for you I dare not confide.
I send words to floating clouds; they move on, never come back.
Tears fall, rain down my face, spoiling my appearance,
Who can endure despair alone with never a sigh?

This anthology of Hsü Ling consists of 656 poems; like others before and after, it bears ample witness to the cultivation of love, including romantic love, in China, especially within aristocratic conjugal relationships. As the current editor remarks, "The idea that Chinese poetry does not deal with love is a myth." . . .

We need to discount the division between Europe and Asia regarding love, especially "romantic love"; indeed, there is even a counter-current in European thought that sees love (not just desire or lust) as being a feature of the East rather than the West (think for example of Scheherazade, of Antony and Cleopatra, of Omar Khayyám, even of the Kama Sutra). Such a notion is clear in eighteenth- and nineteenth-century discussions of the origin of the language of flowers, especially in the context of love relationships. That language was attributed to the undefined east, referring at times to an account of emblematic communication in the Topkapi palace of the Turkish rulers, where it was said to have been a means of conveying secret messages between members of the harem and attractive slave boys but may rather have served the same purpose between the women themselves (that is, romantic lesbian love). . . .

One constant element of love, romantic love, in the Western as in the Chinese perspective involves the idealisation of the loved object. The paradigmatic case is that of the troubadour poet and *la grand dame,* who is not only indealised but distant, superior in rank. That feature is held to differentiate courtly (*fin'amor*) within a more generalised concept of romantic love. Difference in rank was clearly not altogether essential either to romantic love or to marriage itself, since many unions were not in fact hypogamous in this way. In the imagination courtly love involved an unattainable hierarchical relationship, which is part of the idealisation. But idealisation, as Lantz suggests, may take other forms in these societies. In fact, Duby . . . notes that courtly love acted "as a decoration, as a veil, but inadequately concealing the reality, that is the sexual appetite." Bodily pleasure did not die, as in courtly love, with marriage.

Do we find this idealisation more widely, in Africa for example? I have earlier remarked that we need to reject that grossly racist view of Africans as having lust rather than love, which I now examine in the context of my own field material. Nevertheless I do not find the same idealisation in the oral cultures of Africa.

Among the LoDagaa of Birifu in northern Ghana, who were "tribal," hoe agriculturists, local speakers of English translate certain words by "love" and "lover." We have seen that there is a general word *none* which can be translated as "like," "be fond of," and can be used of women or men, as well as of one's children. The neighbouring Gonja of northern Ghana use the word "want" (*fa*) both for the male and the female affect; "I love you" is the same as "I want you." I do not see much idealisation here. What one finds is attraction, and attraction involves desire and pleasure.

I have no entries in my field index for "love" but many for "lover," a term which I employ to translate the word *sen,* although the associated verb is better interpreted as "to court." *Sen* often designates a friend of the opposite sex and is the equivalent of *ba,* same-sex friend, male speaking. Both could be translated "friend," but *sen* is used for women or men to whom you might possibly make love. . . . If I went to a house where they were brewing beer and found there was none left, I might say to the brewer, if I knew her at all, "Have you not got something for your *sen?*" She might then bring me a small pot saying, "That's your lover's beer," meaning that I would not have to pay. Among the neighbouring LoDagaba of Nandom, a woman might gather together a number of her female friends and take them to her "lover's" farm in *sen kob,* to harvest groundnuts or even to hoe between the rows. Whether a relationship known by this term has a specifically sexual connotation is rarely clear (as appears to have been the case with the troubadours). Sometimes such an implication is present, as when Naabiere ran off with a girl without paying any bridewealth to her family. He wanted her to live in his house as his "lover" although the children would then be *sensenbie,* attached to the mother's patrilineage. . . .

I did not collect many songs among the LoDagaa—that was before the days of portable tape-recorders. But I have nothing in my notes that could be called a love song. The public situations in which the xylophone is played and songs are sung do not altogether lend themselves to such a theme. A number of the songs I did write down are about food (or hunger), others about death; in addition I recorded some praise songs. However, when I was visiting Birifu much later in 1978, a young woman called Akwei was staying with her baby at the bungalow attached to the chief's house, with which she had a connection. She had been a pupil teacher at Nandom before she became pregnant. Seeing my tape-recorder she asked to record some "love-songs" in English she had learnt at school. I tried to persuade her to sing the local equivalent, but significantly that proved difficult. The first two songs she sang in LoDagaa were about suffering and death, so too were the last two. The middle one did refer to the search for a husband, incorporating a protest against plural marriages.

> I hear it is difficult to get a husband,
> I will share him with no one.
> If somebody wants to play,
> I will shut the door and beat her,
> I will shut the door and beat her.
> A husband is not for sharing.
> I will not share with anybody.

The sentiments in this song may have been influenced by the Christian and modernising background of Nandom, a centre of the Roman Catholic mission where she had been teaching. But the desire for attachment to one man, which is perhaps one interpretation of Western "love," is not foreign to polygynous societies, any more than the opposite is to monogamous ones. . . .

Some love songs, lyrics, are known from that continent, especially among the Hausa, the Somali, and the peoples of the East African coast who have been influenced by the Arabs, with their developed written tradition of love poetry. But like nature poetry, songs of this kind are not at all common. In her comprehensive survey of the oral arts in Africa, Finnegan . . . gives a number of examples and provides some references. It cannot be said that much deeply passionate love poetry emerges, nothing like Ovid or *The Song of Songs*. But a Somali poem does approach this type of sentiment:

> Woman, lovely as lightening at dawn,
> Speak to me, even once.
> I long for you, as one
> Whose dhow in summer winds
> Is blown adrift and lost,
> Longs for land, and finds—
> Again the compass tells—
> A grey and empty sea.

Here there is both separation and idealisation. The Somali are of course literate, Muslim, and much influenced by the Near East. I certainly found no equivalent among the LoDagaa who were distant from and rejected such currents.

My discussion of love in the cultures of Africa has been based on first-hand data. We find a different but consistent picture in the fictional writings of the 1960s published in the *African Writer Series,* edited by Chinua Achebe. For example, the work of the Senegalese writer, Sembene Ousmane, and his short stories, *Voltaique* . . . tells the story of a young girl whose father shows her a photograph of an old migrant to France who is looking for a bride. She is attracted by the prospects of travel, by her father's sponsorship, and by an old photograph of the migrant when young. When she arrives in France she realises she has made an appalling mistake and falls for a younger man. Another story, entitled *Love in Sandy Lane* tells of a young kora player and the daughter of an administrator who were clearly in love but gave each other few signs. She is whisked away by a minister in his large automobile. It is not that love does not exist. It does, but it does not necessarily form the basis of marriage, as recent Western ideology insists.

How would we account for this difference in the idealisation of the loved one? I have maintained that there is not the great gulf in sentiments, attitudes, and structures between Europe and Asia, the West and the East, which many Eurocentred theories assume, except in relation to shifts of emphasis in the way that partners are chosen. That is particularly true of those notions that see the existence of romantic love as related to modernisation. On the other hand, there does seem to be a certain gap between Eurasia and Africa, the reasons for which have been partly indicated, namely differences in what we might call language use, between written and oral cultures. Connected with this difference is one of the nature of stratification, since the Bronze Age — that gave birth to writing and never reached Africa — also gave birth to a "leisure class." But let me concentrate upon literacy.

Few would dispute that the invention of language enabled human beings to acquire a measure of self-awareness, to advance oral communication (which is necessarily self-monitoring), to extend representation, and to develop role-playing. Writing introduces a further technique for expanding this process, and one of its functions is precisely to make the implicit explicit. As we have seen, historians have discussed the relationship between love and literacy. We must distinguish the problem of expansion and elaboration from that of creation. The view that romantic love has been handed down from the affluent classes to the poor . . . seems mistaken, as Thompson . . . has remarked. If we are looking at romantic love as a mechanism for the selection of a spouse, then there is evidence to suggest that in Europe "free choice" rather than arranged marriage was always more important among the poor. But everywhere there was some element of choice, as Hufton has noted. On the other hand, if we are thinking of romantic love as a developed form of address and response, then there is a case for saying that we borrow our expressions from literature, which has in earlier times often been more closely associated with the upper (educated) classes. Lantz . . . claims it has been suggested that "People have to be able to read and discuss feelings before feelings can become part of their experience." Because of the reflexive nature of the process, writing and reading encourages an elaboration of sentiment, a heightening of emotion. In writing a love poem one is rarely addressing directly the loved object; she or he is almost by definition at a distance—again communication at a distance is one of the attributes of writing. For the troubadours, courtly love, in retrospect called "romantic," was "l'amoor de lonh," distant love in both a physical and a social sense. The object addressed, usually feminine, is absent at the moment of composition and hence liable to be idealised in words. One is more likely to say, "My love is like a red, red rose" in her absence rather than in her presence, although these written phrases may subsequently become incorporated as words of immediate address in speech. In most Western societies, love discourse involves idealisation, often of a standardised kind, which one often borrows from expressions that others have developed, frequently in literature. One quotes rather than invents the discourse of love. It seems significant, as in the case of the troubadours, that such a developed discourse occurred in text rather than utterance, in written societies rather than in purely oral ones. That is not to say love discourse cannot take a spoken form in written societies; it can, but by way of feedback. Love poetry seems to me largely a development of writing. If the emotion of love is developed by the representation of a relationship, above all by a representation in written form, then it is understandable that "love" should be different in literate Europe and Asia than in oral Africa, except where that continent has been influenced by Islam and by Arabic texts.

In conclusion I suggest then that one major factor in the differences between Europe and Africa, and in the similarities between Europe and Asia, is that of language use, related to the means and mode of communication, which of course has some relationship in turn with relationships of production. That suggestion clearly links with the development and in some cases the revival of secular literacy in twelfth-century Europe, epitomised in the work of the troubadours. The tradition was developed in later literary forms. Chaucer's *Roman de la Rose* "purports to be a text based on love, an uncontrovertible vision of what happens in the garden of love." . . . How does this relate—if at all—to the attributions of romantic love to the "modern" period, that is, from the eighteenth century, and to the notion that this can be seen as a mark of (Western) modernity?

Literacy was the key to the mode of representation of love. Today modelling of love (and sex) in representation has been pushed

much further with the huge expansion of the journals that fill the
newsstands of airports and railway stations and, above all, with
the advent of television and electronic media. Such representations
encourage a certain reflexivity, a feedback on behaviour which occurs with any form of "narrative" but is especially marked in its
written form and, to a lesser extent, with graphic representation.
Such representation in itself emphasises the distance from the loved
object. In this sense the stress on love, especially romantic love and
the elaboration of its discourse, is linked with what is loosely called
modernity in no exclusive way and through the mediation of the
growth of literacy and the circulation of print. Love, even romantic
love, is neither exclusively European nor modern, but the discourse
of love, and hence in a sense its practice, has been promoted by
changes in communicative systems.

55

ANDREAS CAPELLANUS

From *The Art of Courtly Love*

Andreas Capellanus (Andreas the Chaplain) compiled this guide to
courtly love between 1184 and 1186. He probably intended his book
to update Ovid's *Art of Love*, as discussed in selection 53, but his approach reflects many of the new ideas of love circulating among the
upper classes of Europe in the twelfth century. Andreas says that love
is suffering, but also that it is wonderful. What does he mean? Compare his ideas to those of Ulrich von Lichtenstein. What are his ideas
about sex and marriage? Some of Andreas's ideas might seem strange
coming from a churchman, and the bishop of Paris condemned them
in 1277, but do they seem religious or Christian in any way? Notice
the author's attention to passion and proper behavior. How does he
combine or balance the two?

Andreas Capellanus, *The Art of Courtly Love*, trans. John J. Parry (New York: Columbia
University Press, 1990), 28–32, 159–86.

Thinking Historically

How unusual are these ideas about love? Do you think that most people in most societies would agree with these ideas or are they unique? Might these ideas be considered European? How might they be seen as products of literary culture?

Introduction to the Treatise on Love

We must first consider what love is, whence it gets its name, what the effect of love is, between what persons love may exist, how it may be acquired, retained, increased, decreased, and ended, what are the signs that one's love is returned, and what one of the lovers ought to do if the other is unfaithful.

What Love Is

Love is a certain inborn suffering derived from the sight of and excessive meditation upon the beauty of the opposite sex, which causes each one to wish above all things the embraces of the other and by common desire to carry out all of love's precepts in the other's embrace.

That love is suffering is easy to see, for before the love becomes equally balanced on both sides there is no torment greater, since the lover is always in fear that his love may not gain its desire and that he is wasting his efforts. He fears, too, that rumors of it may get abroad, and he fears everything that might harm it in any way, for before things are perfected a slight disturbance often spoils them. If he is a poor man, he also fears that the woman may scorn his poverty; if he is ugly, he fears that she may despise his lack of beauty or may give her love to a more handsome man; if he is rich, he fears that his parsimony in the past may stand in his way. To tell the truth, no one can number the fears of one single lover. This kind of love, then, is a suffering which is felt by only one of the persons and may be called "single love." But even after both are in love the fears that arise are just as great, for each of the lovers fears that what he has acquired with so much effort may be lost through the effort of someone else, which is certainly much worse for a man than if, having no hope, he sees that his efforts are accomplishing nothing, for it is worse to lose the things you are seeking than to be deprived of a gain you merely hope for. The lover fears, too, that he may offend his loved one in some way; indeed he fears so many things that it would be difficult to tell them.

That this suffering is inborn I shall show you clearly, because if you will look at the truth and distinguish carefully you will see that it does not arise out of any action; only from the reflection of the mind upon what it sees does this suffering come. For when a man sees some woman fit for love and shaped according to his taste, he begins at once to lust after her in his heart; then the more he thinks about her the more he burns with love, until he comes to a fuller meditation. Presently he begins to think about the fashioning of the woman and to differentiate her limbs, to think about what she does, and to pry into the secrets of her body, and he desires to put each part of it to the fullest use. Then after he has come to this complete meditation, love cannot hold the reins, but he proceeds at once to action; straightway he strives to get a helper to find an intermediary. He begins to plan how he may find favor with her, and he begins to seek a place and a time opportune for talking; he looks upon a brief hour as a very long year, because he cannot do anything fast enough to suit his eager mind. It is well known that many things happen to him in this manner. This inborn suffering comes, therefore, from seeing and meditating. Not every kind of meditation can be the cause of love, an excessive one is required; for a restrained thought does not, as a rule, return to the mind, and so love cannot arise from it.

Between What Persons Love May Exist

Now, in love you should note first of all that love cannot exist except between persons of opposite sexes. Between two men or two women love can find no place, for we see that two persons of the same sex are not at all fitted for giving each other the exchanges of love or for practicing the acts natural to it. Whatever nature forbids, love is ashamed to accept.

What the Effect of Love Is

Now it is the effect of love that a true lover cannot be degraded with any avarice. Love causes a rough and uncouth man to be distinguished for his handsomeness; it can endow a man even of the humblest birth with nobility of character; it blesses the proud with humility; and the man in love becomes accustomed to performing many services gracefully for everyone. O what a wonderful thing is love, which makes a man shine with so many virtues and teaches everyone, no matter who he is, so many good traits of character! There is another thing about love that we should not praise in few words: it adorns a man, so to speak, with the virtue of chastity, because he who shines with the light of one love can hardly think of embracing another woman, even a beautiful one. For when he thinks deeply of his beloved the sight of any other woman seems to his mind rough and rude.

If One of the Lovers Is Unfaithful to the Other

If one of the lovers should be unfaithful to the other, and the offender is the man, and he has an eye to a new love affair, he renders himself wholly unworthy of his former love, and she ought to deprive him completely of her embraces.

But what if he should be unfaithful to his beloved—not with the idea of finding a new love, but because he has been driven to it by an irresistible passion for another woman? What, for instance, if chance should present to him an unknown woman in a convenient place or what if at a time when Venus is urging him on to that which I am talking about he should meet with a little strumpet or somebody's servant girl? Should he, just because he played with her in the grass, lose the love of his beloved? We can say without fear of contradiction that just for this a lover is not considered unworthy of the love of his beloved unless he indulges in so many excesses with a number of women that we may conclude that he is overpassionate. But if whenever he becomes acquainted with a woman he pesters her to gain his end, or if he attains his object as a result of his efforts, then rightly he does deserve to be deprived of his former love, because there is strong presumption that he has acted in this way with an eye toward a new one, especially where he has strayed with a woman of the nobility or otherwise of an honorable estate.

I know that once when I sought advice I got the answer that a true lover can never desire a new love unless he knows that for some definite and sufficient reason the old love is dead; we know from our own experience that this rule is very true. We have fallen in love with a woman of the most admirable character, although we have never had, or hope to have, any fruit of this love. For we are compelled to pine away for love of a woman of such lofty station that we dare not say one word about it, nor dare we throw ourself upon her mercy, and so at length we are forced to find our body shipwrecked. But although rashly and without foresight we have fallen into such great waves in this tempest, still we cannot think about a new love or look for any other way to free ourself.

But since you are making a special study of the subject of love, you may well ask whether a man can have a pure love for one woman and a mixed or common love with another. We will show you, by an unanswerable argument, that no one can feel affection for two women in this fashion. For although pure love and mixed love may seem to be very different things, if you will look at the matter properly you will see that pure love, so far as its substance goes, is the same as mixed love and comes from the same feeling of the heart. The substance of the love is the same in each case, and only the manner and form of loving are different, as this illustration will make clear to you. Sometimes we see a man with a desire to drink his wine unmixed, and at another time his appetite prompts him to drink only water or wine and water mixed; although his appetite manifests itself differently, the substance of it is the same and unchanged. So likewise when two people have long been united by pure love and afterwards desire to practice mixed love, the substance of the love remains the same in them, although the manner and form and the way of practicing it are different.

Various Decisions in Love Cases

Now then, let us come to various decisions in cases of love:

I. A certain knight loved his lady beyond all measure and enjoyed her full embrace, but she did not love him with equal ardor. He sought to leave her, but she, desiring to retain him in his former status, opposed his wish. In this affair the Countess of Champagne gave this response: "It is considered very unseemly for a woman to seek to be loved and yet to refuse to love. It is silly for anybody disrespectfully to ask of others what she herself wholly refuses to give to others."

II. A certain man asked the Lady Ermengarde of Narbonne to make clear where there was the greater affection — between lovers or between married people. The lady gave him a logical answer. She said: "We consider that marital affection and the true love of lovers are wholly different and arise from entirely different sources, and so the ambiguous nature of the word prevents the comparison of the things and we have to place them in different classes. Comparisons of more or less are not valid when things are grouped together under an ambiguous heading and the comparison is made in regard to that ambiguous term. It is no true comparison to say that a name is simpler than a body or that the outline of a speech is better arranged than the delivery."

III. The same man asked the same lady this question. A certain woman had been married, but was now separated from her husband by a divorce, and her former husband sought eagerly for her love. In this case the lady replied: "If any two people have been married and afterwards separate in any way, we consider love between them wholly wicked."

IV. A certain knight was in love with a woman who had given her love to another man, but he got from her this much hope of her love — that if it should ever happen that she lost the love of her beloved, then without a doubt her love would go to this man. A little while after this the woman married her lover. The other knight then demanded that she give him the fruit of the hope she had granted him, but this she absolutely refused to do, saying that she had not lost the love of her lover. In this affair the Queen gave her decision as follows: "We dare not oppose the opinion of the Countess of Champagne, who ruled that love can exert no power between husband and wife. Therefore we recommend that the lady should grant the love she has promised."

V. The Queen was also asked which was preferable: the love of a young man or of one advanced in years. She answered this question with wonderful subtlety by saying, "We distinguish between a good and a better love by the man's knowledge and his character and his praiseworthy manners, not by his age. But as regards that natural instinct of passion, young men are usually more eager to gratify it with older women than with young ones of their own age; those who are older prefer to receive the embraces and kisses of young women rather than of the older ones. But on the other hand a woman whether young or somewhat older likes the embraces and solaces of young men better than those of older ones. The explanation of this fact seems to be a physiological one. . . . "

The Rules of Love

Let us come now to the rules of love, and I shall try to present to you very briefly those rules which the King of Love[1] is said to have proclaimed with his own mouth and to have given in writing to all lovers. . . .

I. Marriage is no real excuse for not loving.
II. He who is not jealous cannot love.
III. No one can be bound by a double love.
IV. It is well known that love is always increasing or decreasing.
V. That which a lover takes against the will of his beloved has no relish.
VI. Boys do not love until they arrive at the age of maturity.
VII. When one lover dies, a widowhood of two years is required of the survivor.
VIII. No one should be deprived of love without the very best of reasons.
IX. No one can love unless he is impelled by the persuasion of love.
X. Love is always a stranger in the home of avarice.
XI. It is not proper to love any woman whom one should be ashamed to seek to marry.
XII. A true lover does not desire to embrace in love anyone except his beloved.
XIII. When made public love rarely endures.
XIV. The easy attainment of love makes it of little value; difficulty of attainment makes it prized.
XV. Every lover regularly turns pale in the presence of his beloved.
XVI. When a lover suddenly catches sight of his beloved his heart palpitates.
XVII. A new love puts to flight an old one.
XVIII. Good character alone makes any man worthy of love.
XIX. If love diminishes, it quickly fails and rarely revives.
XX. A man in love is always apprehensive.

[1]King Arthur of Britain. [Ed.]

XXI.　　Real jealousy always increases the feeling of love.

XXII.　　Jealousy, and therefore love, are increased when one suspects his beloved.

XXIII.　　He whom the thought of love vexes, eats and sleeps very little.

XXIV.　　Every act of a lover ends in the thought of his beloved.

XXV.　　A true lover considers nothing good except what he thinks will please his beloved.

XXVI.　　Love can deny nothing to love.

XXVII.　　A lover can never have enough of the solaces of his beloved.

XXVIII.　　A slight presumption causes a lover to suspect his beloved.

XXIX.　　A man who is vexed by too much passion usually does not love.

XXX.　　A true lover is constantly and without intermission possessed by the thought of his beloved.

XXXI.　　Nothing forbids one woman being loved by two men or one man by two women.

56

MURASAKI SHIKIBU

From *The Tale of Genji*

The Tale of Genji is, by some measures, the world's first novel. It was written by Murasaki Shikibu, a woman at the Japanese court, probably in the first decade after the year 1000. During the Heian period (794–1185) of Japanese history, women in the Japanese aristocracy differentiated their culture from the Chinese one that had dominated it since the seventh century.

While Japanese men were still using a dated form of Chinese for official documents, women like Lady Murasaki were fashioning the Japanese language into an effective and contemporary medium of communication. As ladies of the court, they also had the experience and leisure for writing intriguing, richly evocative stories.

The Tale of Genji is about Prince Genji—an attractive, talented, and sensitive son of the emperor—and his love interests. This chapter,

Murasaki Shikibu, *The Tale of Genji*, trans. Arthur Waley (1929; reprint, Garden City, NY: Anchor Books, 1955), 201–10.

occurring near the end of the novel, tells of one of Prince Genji's many flirtations. It also reveals much about the culture of the Japanese court. Notice the cultivation of music, dance, and poetry among the court nobility. What, if anything, does this display of sensitivity have to do with ideas of love and marriage? What signs do you see here of the persistence of Chinese culture in Heian Japan?

Also, notice the absence of monogamy in the court. The emperor is married but has taken in turn three consorts: Kokiden, Kiritsubo, and now Fujitsubo. What is the relationship between marriage and sex in this society? What does that tell you about the mores of the time?

Thinking Historically

Would you call this a story of romantic love? In what ways is the love Lady Murasaki describes similar to or different from the love Andreas Capellanus describes in the previous selection? What aspects of Heian Japanese culture are different from the culture of medieval Europe? Is the dominant-upper class idea of love in Japan during this period different from that of Europe? Notice the role of writing in this Japanese culture. How might writing affect peoples' attitudes or ideas about love?

About the twentieth day of the second month the Emperor gave a Chinese banquet under the great cherry-tree of the Southern Court. Both Fujitsubo and the Heir Apparent were to be there. Kokiden, although she knew that the mere presence of the Empress was sufficient to spoil her pleasure, could not bring herself to forgo so delightful an entertainment. After some promise of rain the day turned out magnificent; and in full sunshine, with the birds singing in every tree, the guests (royal princes, noblemen, and professional poets alike) were handed the rhyme words which the Emperor had drawn by lot, and set to work to compose their poems. It was with a clear and ringing voice that Genji read out the word "Spring" which he had received as the rhyme-sound of his poem. Next came To no Chujo who, feeling that all eyes were upon him and determined to impress himself favourably on his audience, moved with the greatest possible elegance and grace; and when on receiving his rhyme he announced his name, rank, and titles, he took great pains to speak pleasantly as well as audibly. Many of the other gentlemen were rather nervous and looked quite pale as they came forward, yet they acquitted themselves well enough. But the professional poets, particularly owing to the high standard of accomplishment which the Emperor's and Heir Apparent's lively interest in Chinese poetry had at that time diffused through the Court, were very ill at ease; as they crossed the long space of the garden on their way to receive their rhymes they felt utterly helpless. A simple Chinese verse is surely not much to ask of a professional poet; but they all wore an expression of the deepest gloom. One expects elderly scholars to be somewhat odd in their movements and behaviour, and it was amusing to see the lively concern with which the Emperor watched their various but always uncouth and erratic methods of approaching the Throne. Needless to say a great deal of music had been arranged for. Towards dusk the delightful dance known as the Warbling of Spring Nightingales was performed, and when it was over the Heir Apparent, remembering the Festival of Red Leaves, placed a wreath on Genji's head and pressed him so urgently that it was impossible for him to refuse. Rising to his feet he danced very quietly a fragment of the sleeve-turning passage in the Wave Dance. In a few moments he was seated again, but even into this brief extract from a long dance he managed to import an unrivalled charm and grace. Even his father-in-law who was not in the best of humour with him was deeply moved and found himself wiping away a tear.

"And why have we not seen To no Chujo?" said the Heir Apparent. Whereupon Chujo danced the Park of Willow Flowers, giving a far more complete performance than Genji, for no doubt he knew that he would be called upon and had taken trouble to prepare his dance. It was a great success and the Emperor presented him with a cloak, which everyone said was a most unusual honour. After this the other young noblemen who were present danced in no particular order, but it was now so dark that it was impossible to discriminate between their performances.

Then the poems were opened and read aloud. The reading of Genji's verses was continually interrupted by loud murmurs of applause. Even the professional poets were deeply impressed, and it may well be imagined with what pride the Emperor, to whom at times Genji was a source of consolation and delight, watched him upon such an occasion as this. Fujitsubo, when she allowed herself to glance in his direction, marvelled that even Kokiden could find it in her heart to hate him. "It is because he is fond of me; there can be no other reason," she decided at last, and the verse, "Were I but a common mortal who now am gazing at the beauty of this flower, from its sweet petals not long should I withhold the dew of love," framed itself on her lips, though she dared not utter it aloud.

It was now very late and the banquet was over. The guests had scattered. The Empress and the Heir Apparent had both returned to the Palace—all was still. The moon had risen very bright and clear, and Genji, heated with wine, could not bear to quit so lovely a scene. The people at the Palace were probably all plunged in a heavy sleep. On such a night it was not impossible that some careless person might have left some door unfastened, some shutter unbarred. Cautiously and stealthily he crept towards Fujitsubo's apartments and inspected them. Every bolt was fast. He sighed; here there was evidently nothing to be done. He was passing the loggia of Kokiden's palace when he noted that the shutters of the third arch were not drawn. After the banquet Kokiden herself had gone straight to the Emperor's rooms. There did not seem to be anyone about. A door leading from the loggia into the house was standing open, but he could hear no sound within. "It is under just such circumstances as this that one is apt to drift into compromising situations," thought Genji. Nevertheless he climbed quietly on to the balustrade and peeped. Everyone must be asleep. But no; a very agreeable young voice with an intonation which was certainly not that of any waiting-woman or common person was softly humming the last two lines of the *Oborozuki-yo*.[1] Was not the voice coming towards him? It seemed so, and stretching out his hand he suddenly found that he was grasping a lady's sleeve. "Oh, how you frightened me!" she cried. "Who is it?" "Do not be alarmed," he whispered. "That both of us were not content to miss the beauty of this departing night is proof more clear than the half-clouded moon that we were meant to meet," and as he recited the words he took her gently by the hand and led her into the house, closing the door behind them. Her surprised and puzzled air fascinated him. "There is someone there," she whispered tremulously, pointing to the inner room. "Child," he answered, "I am allowed to go wherever I please and if you send for your friends they will only tell you that I have every right to be here. But if you will stay quietly here. . . . " It was Genji. She knew his voice and the discovery somewhat reassured her. She thought his conduct rather strange, but she was determined that he should not think her prudish or stiff. And so because he on his side was still somewhat excited after the doings of the evening, while she was far too young and pliant to offer any serious resistance, he soon got his own way with her.

Suddenly they saw to their discomfiture that dawn was creeping into the sky. She looked, thought Genji, as though many disquieting reflections were crowding into her mind. "Tell me your name" he said. "How can I write you unless you do? Surely this is not going to be our only meeting?" She answered with a poem in which she said that names are of this world only and he would not care to know hers if he were resolved that their love should last till worlds to come. It was a mere quip and Genji, amused at her quickness, answered, "You are quite right. It was a mistake on my part to ask." And he recited the poem: "While still I seek to find on which blade dwells the dew, a great wind shakes the grasses of the level land." "If you did not repent of this

---

[1] A famous poem by Oye no Chisato (ninth century): "What so lovely as a night when the moon though dimly clouded is never wholly lost to sight!"

meeting," he continued, "you would surely tell me who you are. I do not believe that you want. . . . " But here he was interrupted by the noise of people stirring in the next room. There was a great bustle and it was clear that they would soon be starting out to fetch Princess Kokiden back from the palace. There was just time to exchange fans in token of their new friendship before Genji was forced to fly precipitately from the room. In his own apartments he found many of his gentlemen waiting for him. Some were awake, and these nudged one another when he entered the room as though to say, "Will he never cease these disreputable excursions?" But discretion forbad them to show that they had seen him and they all pretended to be fast asleep. Genji too lay down, but he could not rest. He tried to recall the features of the lady with whom he had just spent so agreeable a time. Certainly she must be one of Kokiden's sisters. Perhaps the fifth or sixth daughter, both of whom were still unmarried. The handsomest of them (or so he had always heard) were Prince Sochi's wife and the fourth daughter, the one with whom To no Chujo got on so badly. It would really be rather amusing if it did turn out to be Chujo's wife. The sixth was shortly to be married to the Heir Apparent. How tiresome if it were she! But at present he could think of no way to make sure. She had not behaved at all as though she did not want to see him again. Why then had she refused to give him any chance of communicating with her? In fact he worried about the matter so much and turned it over in his mind with such endless persistency that it soon became evident he had fallen deeply in love with her. Nevertheless no sooner did the recollection of Fujitsubo's serious and reticent demeanour come back to his mind than he realized how incomparably more she meant to him than this light-hearted lady.

That day the after-banquet kept him occupied till late at night. At the Emperor's command he performed on the thirteen-stringed zither and had an even greater success than with his dancing on the day before. At dawn Fujitsubo retired to the Emperor's rooms. Disappointed in his hope that the lady of last night would somewhere or somehow make her appearance on the scene, he sent for Yoshikiyo and Koremitsu with whom all his secrets were shared and bade them keep watch upon the lady's family. When he returned next day from duty at the Palace they reported that they had just witnessed the departure of several coaches which had been drawn up under shelter in the Courtyard of the Watch. "Among a group of persons who seemed to be the domestic attendants of those for whom the coaches were waiting two gentlemen came threading their way in a great hurry. These we recognized as Shii no Shosho and Uchuben, so there is little doubt that the carriages belonged to Princess Kokiden. For the rest we noted that the ladies were by no means ill-looking and that the whole party drove away in three carriages." Genji's heart beat fast. But he was no nearer than before to finding out which of the sisters it had been. Supposing her father, the Minister of the Right, should hear anything of this, what a to-do there would be! It would indeed mean his absolute ruin. It was a pity that while he was about it he did not stay with her till it was a little lighter. But there it was! He did not know her face, but yet he was determined to recognize her. How? He lay on his bed devising and rejecting endless schemes. Murasaki too must be growing impatient. Days had passed since he had visited her and he remembered with tenderness how low-spirited she became when he was not able to be with her. But in a moment his thoughts had returned to the unknown lady. He still had her fan. It was a folding fan with ribs of hinoki-wood and tassels tied in a splice-knot. One side was covered with silverleaf on which was painted a dim moon, giving the impression of a moon reflected in water. It was a device which he had seen many times before, but it had agreeable associations for him, and continuing the metaphor of the "grass on the moor" which she had used in her poem, he wrote on the fan—"Has mortal man ever puzzled his head with such a question before as to ask where the moon goes to when she leaves the sky at dawn?" And he put the fan safely away. It was on his conscience that he had not for a long while been to the Great Hall; but fearing that Murasaki too might be feeling very unhappy, he first went home to give her her lessons. Every day she was improving not only in looks, but also in amiability of character. The beauty of her disposition was indeed quite out of the common. The idea that so perfect a nature was in his hands, to train and cultivate as he thought best, was very attractive to Genji. It might however have been objected that to receive all her education from a young man is likely to make a girl somewhat forward in her manner.

First there was a great deal to tell about what happened at the Court entertainments of the last few days. Then followed her music lesson, and already it was time to go. "Oh, why must he always go away so soon?" she wondered sadly, but by now she was so used to it that she no longer fretted as she had done a little while ago.

At the Great Hall he could, as usual, scarcely get a word out of Aoi. The moment that he sat idle a thousand doubts and puzzles began to revolve in his mind. He took up his zithern and began to sing:

Not softlier pillowed is my head
That rests by thine, unloving bride,
Than were those jagged stones my bed
Through which the falls of Nuki stride.

At this moment Aoi's father came by and began to discuss the unusual success of the recent festivities. "Old as I am," he said—"and I may say that I have lived to see four illustrious sovereigns occupy the

Throne, I have never taken part in a banquet which produced verses so spirited or dancing and music so admirably performed. Talent of every description seems at present to exist in abundance; but it is creditable to those in authority that they knew how to make good use of it. For my part I enjoyed myself so much that had I but been a few years younger I would positively have joined in the dancing!" "No special steps were taken to discover the musicians," answered Genji. "We merely used those who were known to the government in one part of the country and another as capable performers. If I may say so, it was Chujo's Willow Dance that made the deepest impression and is likely always to be remembered as a remarkable performance. But if you, Sir, had indeed honoured us, a new lustre would have been added to my Father's reign." Aoi's brothers now arrived and leaning against the balustrade gave a little concert, their various instruments blending delightfully.

Fugitive as their meeting had been, it had sufficed to plunge the lady whose identity Prince Genji was now seeking to establish into the depths of despair; for in the fourth month she was to become the Heir Apparent's wife. Turmoil filled her brain. Why had not Genji visited her again? He must surely know whose daughter she was. But how should he know which daughter? Besides, her sister Kokiden's house was not a place where, save under very strange circumstances, he was likely to feel at all at his ease. And so she waited in great impatience and distress; but of Genji there was no news.

About the twentieth day of the third month her father, the Minister of the Right, held an archery meeting in which most of the young noblemen and princes were present. It was followed by a wistaria feast. The cherry blossom was for the most part over, but two trees, which the Minister seemed somehow to have persuaded to flower later than all the rest, were still an enchanting sight. He had had his house rebuilt only a short time ago when celebrating the initiation of his granddaughters, the children of Kokiden. It was now a magnificent building and not a thing in it but was of the very latest fashion. He had invited Genji when he had met him at the Palace only a few days before and was extremely annoyed when he did not appear. Feeling that the party would be a failure if Genji did not come, he sent his son Shii no Shosho to fetch him, with the poem: "Were my flowers as those of other gardens never should I have ventured to summon you." Genji was in attendance upon the Emperor and at once showed him the message. "He seems very pleased with himself and his flowers," said His Majesty with a smile; adding, "as he has sent for you like this, I think you had better go. After all, your half-sisters are being brought up at his house, and you ought not to treat him quite as a stranger." He went to his apartments and dressed. It was very late indeed when at last he made his appearance at the party. He was dressed in a cloak of thin Chinese fabric, white outside but lined with yellow. His robe was of a deep wine-red colour with a very long train. The dignity and grace with which he carried this fancifully regal attire in a company where all were dressed in plain official robes were indeed remarkable, and in the end his presence perhaps contributed more to the success of the party than did the fragrance of the Minister's boasted flowers. His entry was followed by some very agreeable music. It was already fairly late when Genji, on the plea that the wine had given him a headache, left his seat and went for a walk. He knew that his two stepsisters, the daughters of Kokiden, were in the inner apartments of the palace. He went to the eastern portico and rested there. It was on this side of the house that the wistaria grew. The wooden blinds were raised and a number of ladies were leaning out of the window to enjoy the blossoms. They had hung bright-coloured robes and shawls over the windowsill just as is done at the time of the New Year dancing and other gala days and were behaving with a freedom of allure which contrasted very oddly with the sober decorum of Fujitsubo's household. "I am feeling rather overpowered by all the noise and bustle of the flower-party," Genji explained. "I am very sorry to disturb my sisters, but I can think of nowhere else to seek refuge . . . " and advancing towards the main door of the women's apartments, he pushed back the curtain with his shoulder. "Refuge indeed!" cried one of the ladies, laughing at him. "You ought to know by now that it is only poor relations who come to seek refuge with the more successful members of their family. What pray have you come to bother us for?" "Impertinent creatures!" he thought, but nevertheless there was something in their manner which convinced him they were persons of some consequence in the house and not, as he at first supposed, mere waiting-women. A scent of costly perfumes pervaded the room; silken skirts rustled in the darkness. There could be little doubt that these were Kokiden's sisters and their friends. Deeply absorbed, as indeed was the whole of his family, in the fashionable gaieties of the moment, they had flouted decorum and posted themselves at the window that they might see what little they could of the banquet which was proceeding outside. Little thinking that his plan could succeed, yet led on by delightful recollections of his previous encounter, he advanced towards them chanting in a careless undertone the song:

At Ishikawa, Ishikawa
A man from Koma [Korea] took my belt away . . .

But for "belt" he substituted "fan" and by this means he sought to discover which of the ladies was his friend. "Why, you have got it wrong! I never heard of *that* Korean," one of them cried. Certainly it was not she. But there was another who though she remained silent seemed to him to be sighing softly to herself. He stole towards the curtain-of-state behind which she was sitting and taking her hand in his at a venture he whispered the poem: "If on this day of shooting my arrow went astray, 'twas that in dim morning twilight only the mark had glimmered in my view." And she, unable any longer to hide that she knew him, answered with the verse: "Had it been with the arrows of the heart that you had shot, though from the moon's slim bow no brightness came, would you have missed your mark?" Yes, it was her voice. He was delighted, and yet . . .

REFLECTIONS

Cultural comparisons, formerly a staple of historical studies, have come under harsh criticism in recent years, and for good reason. The ambitious general histories and philosophical anthropologies written at the beginning of the twentieth century were full of gross generalizations about the "essence" of various cultures and the advantages of one civilization over another. These grand overviews, predating serious empirical studies of African, Asian, and Latin American societies, invariably argued that such "pre-modern," or "traditional," societies lacked some critical cultural attribute honed in Europe that enabled Europeans to conquer the world after 1500. It goes without saying that these sweeping interpretations were written by Europeans and their North American descendants.

The comparative history of love got caught up in the whirlwind. Denis de Rougemont's classic *Love in the Western World*, published in 1940, first explored the peculiar mix of the Western love myth—more passion than sexuality, ill suited for marriage, rooted in the troubadour tradition of southern France—but de Rougemont said very little about countries other than France and less about other cultures. Later, other historians and anthropologists, seeking to explain European expansion, industrialization, and modernization, argued that conjugal love—the nonromantic familial variety—created family units in Europe and America that were different from those in other parts of the world. They saw the Western family as the stimulus of modern society. Still others found the Western practices of dating, mate choosing, and individual decision making unique.

Toward the end of the twentieth century, in a postcolonial age that had grown skeptical of Western claims of objectivity, cultural comparisons were seen for what they often were—thinly veiled exercises in boasting, gloating, or self-aggrandizement, and implicit rationales for Western domination. For example, Western scientific racism, in which the reigning Western anthropologists and scientists divided the world by cranial sizes, nose width, or culture-bound intelligence tests (always putting themselves on top), came crashing down, after its rationale was exposed as the foundation for the horrific genocides of World War II. `

There is a growing debate about the strategy of explaining Western growth and dominance by looking for Western traits that non-Western cultures lacked. But whether or not such a strategy is wise, we would be foolish to stop trying to compare cultures. To reject cultural comparison completely is to embrace ignorance. Cultures are rich repositories of human thought and behavior; they differ over time and across the globe; and the process of comparison is essential to learning and creating knowledge. The best response to faulty comparisons is criticism and good comparisons, not no comparisons at all.

10

The First Crusade

Muslims, Christians, and Jews during the First Crusade, 1095–1102 C.E.

HISTORICAL CONTEXT

In the eleventh century the Seljuk Turks, recently converted to Islam, emerged from the grasslands of central Asia to conquer much of the land held by the weakened Caliphate at Baghdad, the Egyptian Fatimid Caliphate, and the Byzantine Empire. By 1095 the Seljuks controlled the important cities of Baghdad and Jerusalem and threatened to take Constantinople.

Alexius, the Byzantine emperor, appealed to the Roman pope for help and found a receptive audience. Pope Urban II was continuing recent papal efforts to strengthen the Roman church's power over the scattered nobles and princes of European feudal society. He sought to reform the church of abuses such as the sale of church offices, and to bring peace to the fractious countryside, riddled with private armies of knights that fought each other or preyed on Christian peasants. Urban II's efforts to revitalize Christendom found a mission in the Seljuk occupation of Jerusalem, and in 1095 the First Crusade began with his urgent call for Christians to rout the new Muslim occupiers of the Holy Land.

The Crusades were an important chapter in the religious and military history—or more broadly, the cultural and political history—of both European and Islamic civilizations. They brought large numbers of European Christians and Muslims into contact with each other in a struggle and dialogue that would last for centuries.

THINKING HISTORICALLY
Analyzing and Writing Narrative

When most people think of history, they think of narrative—the story itself. It is what the average person has come to expect from historians, not social science chapters on subjects like love and marriage—we will try to make amends.

Narrative settles on specific details—one at a time—neither indiscriminately nor as examples of general laws, but usually chronologically, as they happen, woven in a chain of cause and effect. The "truth" of narrative is different from that of social science, which aspires to generality. The social scientist writes, "Holy wars among states are a dime a dozen." The narrative historian immerses us in the specific details of the battle: "The Duke's trumpets sounded, the shimmering line swayed forward, the long lances came down to point at the foe, their pennons shadowing the ground before them." A good narrative has the appeal of a good story: It places the reader on the scene, enables us to feel the drama of the moment, to experience what happened as it happened.

In this chapter you will read a number of brief narratives about the Crusades. You will analyze each narrative in order to understand how it works, and then you will be encouraged to write your own.

57

FULCHER OF CHARTRES

Pope Urban at Clermont

The Chronicle of Fulcher of Chartres is one of the few firsthand accounts of the First Crusade. Born in 1059, Fulcher was present at the Council of Clermont, where Pope Urban II issued his call for the First Crusade in 1095. In response to Urban's plea, Fulcher joined the army of Robert of Normandy, Stephen of Blois, and Robert of Flanders. He then joined Baldwin of Boulogne in Edessa (see Map 10.1, p. 330),

The First Crusade: The Chronicle of Fulcher of Chartres and Other Source Materials, 2nd ed., ed. Edward Peters (Philadelphia: University of Pennsylvania Press, 1998), 49–55.

the first Crusader state, and later visited Jerusalem after its capture by the Crusaders. In 1100 when Baldwin became King of Jerusalem, Fulcher returned to the Holy City to become his chaplain. There he wrote his history from 1101 until about 1128. The reliability of Fulcher's Chronicles, therefore, depends on his important contacts as well as his own observations.

Why, according to Fulcher, did Pope Urban II call the Council of Clermont? What did he hope to accomplish? How important among the pope's concerns was the capture of Jerusalem? How important was strengthening the Church?

Thinking Historically

What indications do you see in Urban's speech that the call to capture Jerusalem was only part of his agenda, perhaps even an afterthought? Fulcher's introductory section before the speech and his section on "events after the council" address only the issue of Jerusalem. That emphasis is appropriate in a history of the crusade. A historical narrative must follow a particular thread. If Fulcher was writing a history of church reforms rather than of the First Crusade, what kind of "events after the council" might he have included?

A narrative, or story, is different from an explanation. What do you think were the causes of the First Crusade, based on what you have read so far. How is your answer an explanation rather than a narrative? How would you make your answer more of a narrative?

I. The Council of Clermont

1. In the year 1095 from the Lord's Incarnation, with Henry reigning in Germany as so-called emperor,[1] and with Philip as king in France, manifold evils were growing in all parts of Europe because of wavering faith. In Rome ruled Pope Urban II, a man distinguished in life and character, who always strove wisely and actively to raise the status of the Holy Church above all things.

2. He saw that the faith of Christianity was being destroyed to excess by everybody, by the clergy as well as by the laity. He saw that peace was altogether discarded by the princes of the world, who were engaged in incessant warlike contention and quarreling among themselves.

---

[1]Henry IV (1056–1106). Fulcher uses the term "so-called emperor," since Henry was not recognized as rightful emperor by adherents of Gregory VII and Urban II.

He saw the wealth of the land being pillaged continuously. He saw many of the vanquished, wrongfully taken prisoner and very cruelly thrown into foulest dungeons, either ransomed for a high price or, tortured by the triple torments of hunger, thirst, and cold, blotted out by a death hidden from the world. He saw holy places violated; monasteries and villas burned. He saw that no one was spared of any human suffering, and that things divine and human alike were held in derision.

3. He heard, too, that the interior regions of Romania, where the Turks ruled over the Christians, had been perniciously subjected in a savage attack.[2] Moved by long-suffering compassion and by love of God's will, he descended the mountains to Gaul, and in Auvergne he called for a council to congregate from all sides at a suitable time at a city called Clermont. Three hundred and ten bishops and abbots, who had been advised beforehand by messengers, were present.

4. Then, on the day set aside for it, he called them together to himself and, in an eloquent address, carefully made the cause of the meeting known to them. In the plaintive voice of an aggrieved Church, he expressed great lamentation, and held a long discourse with them about the raging tempests of the world, which have been mentioned, because faith was undermined.

5. One after another, he beseechingly exhorted them all, with renewed faith, to spur themselves in great earnestness to overcome the Devil's devices and to try to restore the Holy Church, most unmercifully weakened by the wicked, to its former honorable status.

II. *The Decree of Pope Urban in the Council*

1. "Most beloved brethren," he said, "by God's permission placed over the whole world with the papal crown, I, Urban, as the messenger of divine admonition, have been compelled by an unavoidable occasion to come here to you servants of God. I desired those whom I judged to be stewards of God's ministries to be true stewards and faithful, with all hypocrisy rejected.[3]

2. "But with temperance in reason and justice being remote, I, with divine aid, shall strive carefully to root out any crookedness or distortion which might obstruct God's law. For the Lord appointed you temporarily as stewards over His family to serve it nourishment seasoned with a modest savor. Moreover, blessed will you be if at last the Overseer find you faithful.[4]

---

[2]This refers to the Seljuk conquest of Anatolia, probably to Manzikert, 1071.
[3]Reference to I Corinthians 4:I, 2.
[4]Reference to Matthew 24:45, 46.

3. "You are also called shepherds; see that you are not occupied after the manner of mercenaries. Be true shepherds, always holding your crooks in your hands; and sleeping not, guard on every side the flock entrusted to you.

4. "For if through your carelessness or negligence, some wolf seizes a sheep, you doubtless will lose the reward prepared for you by our Lord.[5] Nay, first most cruelly beaten by the whips of the lictors, you afterwards will be angrily cast into the keeping of a deadly place.

5. "Likewise, according to the evangelical sermon, you are the 'salt of the earth.'[6] But if you fail, it will be disputed wherewith it was salted. O how much saltiness, indeed, is necessary for you to salt the people in correcting them with the salt of wisdom, people who are ignorant and panting with desire after the wantonness of the world; so that, unsalted, they might not be rotten with sins and stink whenever the Lord might wish to exhort them.

6. "For if because of the sloth of your management, He should find in them worms, that is, sin, straightway, He will order that they, despised, be cast into the dungheap. And because you could not make restoration for such a great loss, He will banish you, utterly condemned in judgment, from the familiarity of His love.

7. "It behooves saltiness of this kind to be wise, provident, temperate, learned, peace-making, truth-seeking, pious, just, equitable, pure. For how will the unlearned be able to make men learned, the intemperate make temperate, the impure make them pure? If one despises peace, how will he appease? Or if one has dirty hands, how will he be able to wipe the filth off another one defiled? For it is read, 'If the blind lead the blind, both shall fall into a ditch.'[7]

8. "Set yourselves right before you do others, so that you can blamelessly correct your subjects. If you wish to be friends of God, gladly practice those things which you feel will please Him.

9. "Especially establish ecclesiastical affairs firm in their own right, so that no simoniac heresy will take root among you. Take care lest the vendors and moneychangers, flayed by the scourges of the Lord, be miserably driven out into the narrow streets of destruction.[8]

10. "Uphold the Church in its own ranks altogether free from all secular power. See that the tithes of all those who cultivate the earth are given faithfully to God; let them not be sold or held back.

11. "Let him who has seized a bishop be considered an outlaw. Let him who has seized or robbed monks, clerics, nuns and their servants,

[5]Reference to John 10:12–16.
[6]Matthew 5:13.
[7]Matthew 15:14.
[8]Reference to John 2:15.

pilgrims, or merchants, be excommunicated. Let the robbers and burners of homes and their accomplices, banished from the Church, be smitten with excommunication.

12. "It must be considered very carefully, as Gregory says, by what penalty he must be punished who seizes other men's property, if he who does not bestow his own liberally is condemned to Hell. For so it happened to the rich man in the well-known Gospel, who on that account was not punished because he had taken away the property of others, but because he had misused that which he had received.

13. "And so by these iniquities, most beloved, you have seen the world disturbed too long; so long, as it was told to us by those reporting, that perhaps because of the weakness of your justice in some parts of your provinces, no one dares to walk in the streets with safety, lest he be kidnapped by robbers by day or thieves by night, either by force or trickery, at home or outside.

14. "Wherefore the Truce,[9] as it is commonly called, now for a long time established by the Holy Fathers, must be renewed. In admonition, I entreat you to adhere to it most firmly in your own bishopric. But if anyone affected by avarice or pride breaks it of his own free will, let him be excommunicated by God's authority and by the sanction of the decrees of this Holy Council."

III. The Pope's Exhortation Concerning the Expedition to Jerusalem

1. These and many other things having been suitably disposed of, all those present, both clergy and people, at the words of Lord Urban, the Pope, voluntarily gave thanks to God and confirmed by a faithful promise that his decrees would be well kept. But straightway he added that another thing not less than the tribulation already spoken of, but even greater and more oppressive, was injuring Christianity in another part of the world, saying:

2. "Now that you, O sons of God, have consecrated yourselves to God to maintain peace among yourselves more vigorously and to uphold the laws of the Church faithfully, there is work to do, for you must turn the strength of your sincerity, now that you are aroused by divine correction, to another affair that concerns you and God. Hastening to the way, you must help your brothers living in the Orient, who need your aid for which they have already cried out many times.

---

[9]Truce of God—Cessation of all feuds from Wednesday evening to Monday morning in every week and during church festivals, ordered by the Church in 1041. This was proclaimed anew at the Council of Clermont.

3. "For, as most of you have been told, the Turks, a race of Persians,[10] who have penetrated within the boundaries of Romania[11] even to the Mediterranean to that point which they call the Arm of Saint George, in occupying more and more of the lands of the Christians, have overcome them, already victims of seven battles, and have killed and captured them, have overthrown churches, and have laid waste God's kingdom. If you permit this supinely for very long, God's faithful ones will be still further subjected.

4. "Concerning this affair, I, with suppliant prayer—not I, but the Lord—exhort you, heralds of Christ, to persuade all of whatever class, both knights and footmen, both rich and poor, in numerous edicts, to strive to help expel that wicked race from our Christian lands before it is too late.

5. "I speak to those present, I send word to those not here; moreover, Christ commands it. Remission of sins will be granted for those going thither, if they end a shackled life either on land or in crossing the sea, or in struggling against the heathen. I, being vested with that gift from God, grant this to those who go.

6. "O what a shame, if a people, so despised, degenerate, and enslaved by demons would thus overcome a people endowed with the trust of almighty God, and shining in the name of Christ! O how many evils will be imputed to you by the Lord Himself, if you do not help those who, like you, profess Christianity!

7. "Let those," he said, "who are accustomed to wage private wars wastefully even against Believers, go forth against the Infidels in a battle worthy to be undertaken now and to be finished in victory. Now, let those, who until recently existed as plunderers, be soldiers of Christ; now, let those, who formerly contended against brothers and relations, rightly fight barbarians; now, let those, who recently were hired for a few pieces of silver, win their eternal reward. Let those, who wearied themselves to the detriment of body and soul, labor for a twofold honor. Nay, more, the sorrowful here will be glad there, the poor here will be rich there, and the enemies of the Lord here will be His friends there.

8. "Let no delay postpone the journey of those about to go, but when they have collected the money owed to them and the expenses for the journey, and when winter has ended and spring has come, let them enter the crossroads courageously with the Lord going on before."

---

[10]Really Seljuk Turks who conquered lands from east to west by way of Persia.

[11]Fulcher uses the term *Romania* to refer to the Anatolian as well as to the European provinces of the Byzantine Empire, but here, of course, he means the Anatolian. The Seljuks called the state which they founded here *Rum*.

IV. The Bishop of Puy and the Events after the Council

1. After these words were spoken, the hearers were fervently inspired. Thinking nothing more worthy than such an undertaking, many in the audience solemnly promised to go, and to urge diligently those who were absent. There was among them one Bishop of Puy, Ademar by name, who afterwards, acting as vicar-apostolic, ruled the whole army of God wisely and thoughtfully, and spurred them to complete their undertaking vigorously.

2. So, the things that we have told you were well established and confirmed by everybody in the Council. With the blessing of absolution given, they departed; and after returning to their homes, they disclosed to those not knowing, what had taken place. As it was decreed far and wide throughout the provinces, they established the peace, which they call the Truce, to be upheld mutually by oath.

3. Many, one after another, of any and every occupation, after confession of their sins and with purified spirits, consecrated themselves to go where they were bidden.

4. Oh, how worthy and delightful to all of us who saw those beautiful crosses, either silken or woven of gold, or of any material, which the pilgrims sewed on the shoulders of their woolen cloaks or cassocks by the command of the Pope, after taking the vow to go. To be sure, God's soldiers, who were making themselves ready to battle for His honor, ought to have been marked and fortified with a sign of victory. And so by embroidering the symbol [of the cross] on their clothing in recognition of their faith, in the end they won the True Cross itself. They imprinted the ideal so that they might attain the reality of the ideal.

5. It is plain that good meditation leads to doing good work and that good work wins salvation of the soul. But, if it is good to mean well, it is better, after reflection, to carry out the good intention. So, it is best to win salvation through action worthy of the soul to be saved. Let each and everyone, therefore, reflect upon the good, that he makes better in fulfillment, so that, deserving it, he might finally receive the best, which does not diminish in eternity.

6. In such a manner Urban, a wise man and reverenced,
Meditated a labor, whereby the world florescenced.

For he renewed peace and restored the laws of the Church to their former standards; also he tried with vigorous instigation to expel the heathen from the lands of the Christians. And since he strove to exalt all things of God in every way, almost everyone gladly surrendered in obedience to his paternal care. . . .

58

Chronicle of Solomon bar Simson

Solomon bar Simson (who is known only from this chronicle) provides the most complete of the Hebrew chronicles of the First Crusade. He takes up the story after Pope Urban II's appeal. Franks and Germans have organized their armies of knights, suppliers, aides, and followers, and have set off for Jerusalem by way of Constantinople. Why did these Crusaders stop at Mainz and other German cities to murder Jews?

Thinking Historically

This narrative, like the previous selection, includes quotations from speeches. How can you tell that some of these quotations do not contain the exact words that were spoken?

Solomon bar Simson's narrative contains another element that, while absent from modern histories, is found in other narratives of the Crusades and is especially pronounced here. This is not just a narrative of human action and intention, but it interprets divine action and intention as well. Why is this narrative strategy necessary for this author? If you were writing a narrative of the Crusades today, would you want to tell both of these stories, or only the human one? Why?

I will now recount the event of this persecution in other martyred communities as well—the extent to which they clung to the Lord, God of their fathers, bearing witness to His Oneness to their last breath.

In the year four thousand eight hundred and fifty-six, the year one thousand twenty-eight of our exile, in the eleventh year of the cycle Ranu, the year in which we anticipated salvation and solace, in accordance with the prophecy of Jeremiah: "Sing with gladness for Jacob, and shout at the head of the nations," etc.—this year turned instead to sorrow and groaning, weeping and outcry. Inflicted upon the Jewish People were the many evils related in all the admonitions; those enumerated in Scripture as well as those unwritten were visited upon us.

"Chronicle of Solomon bar Simson," in *The Jews and the Crusaders: The Hebrew Chronicles of the First and Second Crusades,* ed. and trans. Shlomo Eidelberg (Madison: The University of Wisconsin Press, 1977), 21–26.

At this time arrogant people, a people of strange speech, a nation bitter and impetuous, Frenchmen and Germans, set out for the Holy City, which had been desecrated by barbaric nations, there to seek their house of idolatry and banish the Ishmaelites and other denizens of the land and conquer the land for themselves. They decorated themselves prominently with their signs, placing a profane symbol—a horizontal line over a vertical one—on the vestments of every man and woman whose heart yearned to go on the stray path to the grave of their Messiah. Their ranks swelled until the number of men, women, and children exceeded a locust horde covering the earth; of them it was said: "The locusts have no king [yet go they forth all of them by bands]." Now it came to pass that as they passed through the towns where Jews dwelled, they said to one another: "Look now, we are going a long way to seek out the profane shrine and to avenge ourselves on the Ishmaelites, when here, in our very midst, are the Jews—they whose forefathers murdered and crucified him for no reason. Let us first avenge ourselves on them and exterminate them from among the nations so that the name of Israel will no longer be remembered, or let them adopt our faith and acknowledge the offspring of promiscuity."

When the Jewish communities became aware of their intentions, they resorted to the custom of our ancestors, repentance, prayer, and charity. The hands of the Holy Nation turned faint at this time, their hearts melted, and their strength flagged. They hid in their innermost rooms to escape the swirling sword. They subjected themselves to great endurance, abstaining from food and drink for three consecutive days and nights, and then fasting many days from sunrise to sunset, until their skin was shriveled and dry as wood upon their bones. And they cried out loudly and bitterly to God.

But their Father did not answer them; He obstructed their prayers, concealing Himself in a cloud through which their prayers could not pass, and He abhorred their tent, and He removed them out of His sight—all of this having been decreed by Him to take place "in the day when I visit"; and this was the generation that had been chosen by Him to be His portion, for they had the strength and the fortitude to stand in His Sanctuary, and fulfill His word, and sanctify His Great Name in His world. It is of such as these that King David said: "Bless the Lord, ye angels of His, ye almighty in strength, that fulfil His word," etc.

That year, Passover fell on Thursday, and the New Moon of the following month, Iyar, fell on Friday and the Sabbath. On the eighth day of Iyar, on the Sabbath, the foe attacked the community of Speyer and murdered eleven holy souls who sanctified their Creator on the holy Sabbath and refused to defile themselves by adopting the faith of their foe. There was a distinguished, pious woman there who slaughtered herself in sanctification of God's Name. She was the first among all the communities of those who were slaughtered. The remainder were saved by the local bishop without defilement [i.e., baptism], as described above.

On the twenty-third of Iyar they attacked the community of Worms.[1] The community was then divided into two groups; some remained in their homes and others fled to the local bishop seeking refuge. Those who remained in their homes were set upon by the steppe-wolves who pillaged men, women, and infants, children and old people. They pulled down the stairways and destroyed the houses, looting and plundering; and they took the Torah Scroll, trampled it in the mud, and tore and burned it. The enemy devoured the children of Israel with open maw.

Seven days later, on the New Moon of Sivan—the very day on which the Children of Israel arrived at Mount Sinai to receive the Torah—those Jews who were still in the court of the bishop were subjected to great anguish. The enemy dealt them the same cruelty as the first group and put them to the sword. The Jews, inspired by the valor of their brethren, similarly chose to be slain in order to sanctify the Name before the eyes of all, and exposed their throats for their heads to be severed for the glory of the Creator. There were also those who took their own lives, thus fulfilling the verse: "The mother was dashed in pieces with her children." Fathers fell upon their sons, being slaughtered upon one another, and they slew one another—each man his kin, his wife and children; bridegrooms slew their betrothed, and merciful women their only children. They all accepted the divine decree wholeheartedly and, as they yielded up their souls to the Creator, cried out: "Hear, O Israel, the Lord is our God, the Lord is One." The enemy stripped them naked, dragged them along, and then cast them off, sparing only a small number whom they forcibly baptized in their profane waters. The number of those slain during the two days was approximately eight hundred—and they were all buried naked. It is of these that the Prophet Jeremiah lamented: "They that were brought up in scarlet embrace dunghills." I have already cited their names above. May God remember them for good.

When the saints, the pious ones of the Most High, the holy community of Mainz, whose merit served as shield and protection for all the communities and whose fame had spread throughout the many provinces, heard that some of the community of Speyer had been slain and that the community of Worms had been attacked a second time, and that the sword would soon reach them, their hands became faint and their hearts melted and became as water. They cried out to the Lord with all their hearts, saying: "O Lord, God of Israel, will You completely annihilate the remnant of Israel? Where are all your wonders

---

[1]Town in the Holy Roman Empire (now Germany). [Ed.]

which our forefathers related to us, saying: 'Did You not bring us up from Egypt and from Babylonia and rescue us on numerous occasions?' How, then, have You now forsaken and abandoned us, O Lord, giving us over into the hands of evil Edom so that they may destroy us? Do not remove Yourself from us, for adversity is almost upon us and there is no one to aid us."

The leaders of the Jews gathered together and discussed various ways of saving themselves. They said: "Let us elect elders so that we may know how to act, for we are consumed by this great evil." The elders decided to ransom the community by generously giving of their money and bribing the various princes and deputies and bishops and governors. Then, the community leaders who were respected by the local bishop approached him and his officers and servants to negotiate this matter. They asked: "What shall we do about the news we have received regarding the slaughter of our brethren in Speyer and Worms?" They [the Gentiles] replied: "Heed our advice and bring all your money into our treasury. You, your wives, and your children, and all your belongings shall come into the courtyard of the bishop until the hordes have passed by. Thus will you be saved from the errant ones."

Actually, they gave this advice so as to herd us together and hold us like fish that are caught in an evil net, and then to turn us over to the enemy, while taking our money. This is what actually happened in the end, and "the outcome is proof of the intentions." The bishop assembled his ministers and courtiers—mighty ministers, the noblest in the land—for the purpose of helping us; for at first it had been his desire to save us with all his might, since we had given him and his ministers and servants a large bribe in return for their promise to help us. Ultimately, however, all the bribes and entreaties were of no avail to protect us on the day of wrath and misfortune.

It was at this time that Duke Godfrey [of Bouillon], may his bones be ground to dust, arose in the hardness of his spirit, driven by a spirit of wantonness to go with those journeying to the profane shrine, vowing to go on this journey only after avenging the blood of the crucified one by shedding Jewish blood and completely eradicating any trace of those bearing the name "Jew," thus assuaging his own burning wrath. To be sure, there arose someone to repair the breach—a God-fearing man who had been bound to the most holy of altars—called Rabbi Kalonymos, the *Parnass* of the community of Mainz. He dispatched a messenger to King Henry in the kingdom of Pula, where the king had been dwelling during the past nine years, and related all that had happened.

The king was enraged and dispatched letters to all the ministers, bishops, and governors of all the provinces of his realm, as well as to Duke Godfrey, containing words of greeting and commanding them to do no bodily harm to the Jews and to provide them with help and refuge. The evil duke then swore that he had never intended to do them harm. The Jews of Cologne nevertheless bribed him with five hundred *zekukim* of silver, as did the Jews of Mainz. The duke assured them of his support and promised them peace.

However, God, the maker of peace, turned aside and averted His eyes from His people, and consigned them to the sword. No prophet, seer, or man of wise heart was able to comprehend how the sin of the people infinite in number was deemed so great as to cause the destruction of so many lives in the various Jewish communities. The martyrs endured the extreme penalty normally inflicted only upon one guilty of murder. Yet, it must be stated with certainty that God is a righteous judge, and we are to blame.

Then the evil waters prevailed. The enemy unjustly accused them of evil acts they did not do, declaring: "You are the children of those who killed our object of veneration, hanging him on a tree, and he himself had said: 'There will yet come a day when my children will come and avenge my blood.' We are his children and it is therefore obligatory for us to avenge him since you are the ones who rebel and disbelieve in him. Your God has never been at peace with you. Although He intended to deal kindly with you, you have conducted yourselves improperly before Him. God has forgotten you and is no longer desirous of you since you are a stubborn nation. Instead, He has departed from you and has taken us for His portion, casting His radiance upon us."

When we heard these words, our hearts trembled and moved out of their places. We were dumb with silence, abiding in darkness, like those long dead, waiting for the Lord to look forth and behold from heaven.

And Satan—the Pope of evil Rome—also came and proclaimed to all the nations believing in that stock of adultery—these are the stock of Seir[2]—that they should assemble and ascend to Jerusalem so as to conquer the city, and journey to the tomb of the superstition whom they call their god. Satan came and mingled with the nations, and they gathered as one man to fulfill the command, coming in great numbers like the grains of sand upon the seashore, the noise of them clamorous as a whirlwind and a storm. When the drops of the bucket had assembled, they took evil counsel against the people of the Lord and said: "Why should we concern ourselves with going to war against the Ishmaelites dwelling about Jerusalem, when in our midst is a people who disrespect our god—indeed, their ancestors are those who crucified him. Why should we let them live and tolerate their dwelling among us? Let us commence by using our swords against them and then proceed upon our stray path."

[2]An enemy of ancient Israel.

The heart of the people of our God grew faint and their spirit flagged, for many sore injuries had been inflicted upon them and they had been smitten repeatedly. They now came supplicating to God and fasting, and their hearts melted within them. But the Lord did as He declared, for we had sinned before Him, and He forsook the sanctuary of Shiloh—the Temple-in-Miniature—which He had placed among His people who dwelt in the midst of alien nations. His wrath was kindled and He drew the sword against them, until they remained but as the flagstaff upon the mountaintop and as the ensign on the hill, and He gave over His nation into captivity and trampled them underfoot. See, O Lord, and consider to whom Thou hast done thus: to Israel, a nation despised and pillaged, Your chosen portion! Why have You uplifted the shield of its enemies, and why have they gained in strength? Let all hear, for I cry out in anguish; the ears of all that hear me shall be seared: How has the staff of might been broken, the rod of glory—the sainted community comparable to fine gold, the community of Mainz! It was caused by the Lord to test those that fear Him, to have them endure the yoke of His pure fear. . . .

59

ANNA COMNENA

From *The Alexiad*

Anna Comnena was the daughter of Emperor Alexius (r. 1081–1118) of Byzantium. Threatened on three sides—by the Seljuk Turks to the east, the Norman Kingdom of southern Italy to the west, and rebellions to the north—Alexius appealed for aid to Pope Urban II of Rome in 1095. He expected a mercenary army, but because the Pope saw a chance to send a massive force against Muslim occupiers of Jerusalem as well as against those threatening Istanbul, Alexius instead received an uncontrollable ragtag force of Christians and Crusaders that included his Norman enemies, led by Bohemond.

Anna Comnena, *The Alexiad of the Princess Anna Comnena,* trans. Elizabeth A. S. Dawes (London: Routledge & Kegan Paul Ltd., 1967), 247–52. Reprinted in William H. McNeill and Schuyler O. Houser, *Medieval Europe* (Oxford: Oxford University Press, 1971), 135–40.

Princess Anna, the emperor's daughter, recalled the story of the first Crusader's appearance in Byzantium some forty years later in her history called, *The Alexiad*, after her father. According to Anna, how did Alexius respond to the approach of the Crusader army? Did Alexius fear the Franks more than he feared the Turks?

Thinking Historically

This is a third perspective on the history of the First Crusade—the view of a Christian ally of Rome, more directly threatened than the Roman church by the Muslim armies. Yet, Byzantium and Rome were also at odds. Since 1054, they had accepted a parting of ways, theologically and institutionally. And with the advancing Frankish armies, Anna and Alexius were not sure whether they were facing friend or foe. How does Anna's critical perspective change our idea of the Crusaders? How might her idea of the Franks change our narrative of the early stage of the crusade?

Notice how this narrative combines a sequence of events with generalizations (often about the "race" or nature of the Franks) to explain specific events. Does a narrative history have to include generalizations as well as a sequence of specific events? Can the events alone provide sufficient explanation?

Before he had enjoyed even a short rest, he heard a report of the approach of innumerable Frankish armies. Now he dreaded their arrival for he knew their irresistible manner of attack, their unstable and mobile character and all the peculiar natural and concomitant characteristics which the Frank retains throughout; and he also knew that they were always agape for money, and seemed to disregard their truces readily for any reason that cropped up. For he had always heard this reported of them, and found it very true. However, he did not lose heart, but prepared himself in every way so that, when the occasion called, he would be ready for battle. And indeed the actual facts were far greater and more terrible than rumour made them. For the whole of the West and all the barbarian tribes which dwell between the further side of the Adriatic and the pillars of Heracles, had all migrated in a body and were marching into Asia through the intervening Europe, and were making the journey with all their household. The reason of this upheaval was more or less the following. A certain Frank, Peter by name, nicknamed Cucupeter, had gone to worship at the Holy Sepulchre and after suffering many things at the hands of the Turks and Saracens who were ravaging Asia, he got back to his own country with difficulty. But he was angry at having failed in his object, and wanted

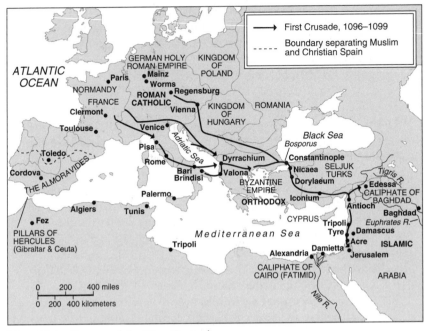

Map 10.1   Routes of the First Crusade.

Source: From *Medieval Europe* by William H. McNeill and Schuyler O. Houser (New York: Oxford University Press, 1971), 120.

to undertake the same journey again. However, he saw that he ought not to make the journey to the Holy Sepulchre alone again, lest worse things befall him, so he worked out a cunning plan. This was to preach in all the Latin countries that "the voice of God bids me announce to all the Counts in France" that they should all leave their homes and set out to worship at the Holy Sepulchre, and to endeavour wholeheartedly with hand and mind to deliver Jerusalem from the hand of Hagarenes.[1] And he really succeeded. For after inspiring the souls of all with this quasi-divine command he contrived to assemble the Franks from all sides, one after the other, with arms, horses and all the other paraphernalia of war. And they were all so zealous and eager that every highroad was full of them. And those Frankish soldiers were accompanied by an unarmed host more numerous than the sand or the stars, carrying palms and crosses on their shoulders, women and children, too, came away from their countries and the sight of them was like many rivers streaming from all sides, and they were advancing towards us through Dacia generally with all their hosts. Now the coming of

---

[1]Saracens, who were considered "children of Hagar" (cf. Gen. 16). [Ed.]

these many peoples was preceded by a locust which did not touch the wheat, but made a terrible attack on the vines. This was really a presage as the diviners of the time interpreted it, and meant that this enormous Frankish army would, when it came, refrain from interference in Christian affairs, but fall very heavily upon the barbarian Ishmaelites who were slaves to drunkenness, wine, and Dionysus.[2] For this race is under the sway of Dionysus and Eros,[3] rushes headlong into all kind of sexual intercourse, and is not circumcised either in the flesh or in their passions. It is nothing but a slave, nay triply enslaved, to the ills wrought by Aphrodite. For this reason they worship and adore Astarte and Ashtaroth[4] too and value above all the image of the moon, and the golden figure of Hobar[5] in their country. Now in these symbols Christianity was taken to be the corn because of its wineless and very nutritive qualities; in this manner the diviners interpreted the vines and the wheat. However let the matter of the prophecy rest.

The incidents of the barbarians' approach followed in the order I have described, and persons of intelligence could feel that they were witnessing a strange occurrence. The arrival of these multitudes did not take place at the same time nor by the same road (for how indeed could such masses starting from different places have crossed the straits of Lombardy all together?). Some first, some next, others after them and thus successively all accomplished the transit, and then marched through the Continent. Each army was preceded, as we said, by an unspeakable number of locusts; and all who saw this more than once recognized them as forerunners of the Frankish armies. When the first of them began crossing the straits of Lombardy sporadically the Emperor summoned certain leaders of the Roman forces, and sent them to the parts of Dyrrachium and Valona[6] with instructions to offer a courteous welcome to the Franks who had crossed, and to collect abundant supplies from all the countries along their route; then to follow and watch them covertly all the time, and if they saw them making any foraging-excursions, they were to come out from under cover and check them by light skirmishing. These captains were accompanied by some men who knew the Latin tongue, so that they might settle any disputes that arose between them.

---

[2]Anna's account of the beliefs of the Muslims was highly biased. Muhammad forbade his followers to drink intoxicating liquors.

[3]Dionysus was the Greek god associated with wine and revelry; Eros was the patron of lovers, and son of Aphrodite, goddess of love.

[4]Names of the Semitic goddess of fertility.

[5]I.e., Hathor, the Egyptian goddess of love, usually depicted with the head of a cow. (N.B. Idol worship was strictly forbidden by Islamic law.)

[6]Ports on the Adriatic, directly opposite the heel of Italy in modern Albania.

Let me, however, give an account of this subject more clearly and in due order. According to universal rumour Godfrey,[7] who sold his country, was the first to start on the appointed road; this man was very rich and very proud of his bravery, courage and conspicuous lineage; for every Frank is anxious to outdo the others. And such an upheaval of both men and women took place then as had never occurred within human memory, the simpler-minded were urged on by the real desire of worshipping at our Lord's Sepulchre, and visiting the sacred places; but the more astute, especially men like Bohemund and those of like mind, had another secret reason, namely, the hope that while on their travels they might by some means be able to seize the capital itself, looking upon this as a kind of corollary. And Bohemund disturbed the minds of many nobler men by thus cherishing his old grudge against the Emperor. Meanwhile Peter, after he had delivered his message, crossed the straits of Lombardy before anybody else with eighty thousand men on foot, and one hundred thousand on horseback, and reached the capital by way of Hungary.[8] For the Frankish race, as one may conjecture, is always very hotheaded and eager, but when once it has espoused a cause, it is uncontrollable.

The Emperor, knowing what Peter had suffered before from the Turks, advised him to wait for the arrival of the other Counts, but Peter would not listen for he trusted the multitude of his followers, so he crossed and pitched his camp near a small town called Helenopolis.[9] After him followed the Normans numbering ten thousand, who separated themselves from the rest of the army and devastated the country round Nicaea, and behaved most cruelly to all. For they dismembered some of the children and fixed others on wooden spits and roasted them at the fire, and on persons advanced in age they inflicted every kind of torture. But when the inhabitants of Nicaea became aware of these doings, they threw open their gates and marched out upon them, and after a violent conflict had taken place they had to dash back inside their citadel as the Normans fought so bravely. And thus the latter recovered all the booty and returned to Helenopolis. Then a dispute arose between them and the others who had not gone out with them, as is usual in such cases, for the minds of those who stayed behind were aflame with envy, and thus caused a skirmish after which the headstrong Normans drew apart again, marched to Xerigordus[10] and took it by assault. When the Sultan[11] heard what had happened, he dis-

---

[7]Godfrey of Bouillon, the duke of Lower Lorraine (c. 1060–1100). To raise money for the Crusade, he sold two of his estates, and pledged his castle at Bouillon to the bishop of Liège.

[8]Peter's contingent probably numbered about twenty thousand including noncombatants.

[9]I.e., Peter moved his forces across the Bosphorus and into Asia Minor.

[10]A castle held by the Turks.

[11]Qilij Arslan I, ruled 1092–1106.

patched Elchanes[12] against them with a substantial force. He came, and recaptured Xerigordus and sacrificed some of the Normans to the sword, and took others captive, at the same time laid plans to catch those who had remained behind with Cucupeter. He placed ambushes in suitable spots so that any coming from the camp in the direction of Nicaea would fall into them unexpectedly and be killed. Besides this, as he knew the Franks' love of money, he sent for two active-minded men and ordered them to go to Cucupeter's camp and proclaim there that the Normans had gained possession of Nicaea, and were now dividing everything in it. When this report was circulated among Peter's followers, it upset them terribly. Directly [When] they heard the words "partition" and "money" they started in a disorderly crowd along the road to Nicaea, all but unmindful of their military experience and the discipline which is essential for those starting out to battle. For, as I remarked above, the Latin race is always very fond of money, but more especially when it is bent on raiding a country; it then loses its reason and gets beyond control. As they journeyed neither in ranks nor in squadrons, they fell foul of the Turkish ambuscades near the river Dracon and perished miserably. And such a large number of Franks and Normans were the victims of the Ishmaelite sword, that when they piled up the corpses of the slaughtered men which were lying on either side they formed, I say, not a very large hill or mound or a peak, but a high mountain as it were, of very considerable depth and breadth—so great was the pyramid of bones. And later men of the same tribe as the slaughtered barbarians built a wall and used the bones of the dead to fill the interstices as if they were pebbles, and thus made the city their tomb in a way. This fortified city is still standing today with its walls built of a mixture of stones and bones. When they had all in this way fallen a prey to the sword, Peter alone with a few others escaped and reentered Helenopolis,[13] and the Turks who wanted to capture him, set fresh ambushes for him. But when the Emperor received reliable information of all this, and the terrible massacre, he was very worried lest Peter should have been captured. He therefore summoned Constantine Catacalon Euphorbenus (who has already been mentioned many times in this history), and gave him a large force which was embarked on ships of war and sent him across the straits to Peter's succour. Directly the Turks saw him land they fled. Constantine, without the slightest delay, picked up Peter and his followers, who were but few, and brought them safe and sound to the Emperor. On the Emperor's reminding him of his original thoughtlessness and saying that it was due to his not having obeyed his, the Emperor's, advice that he had incurred such disasters,

[12]An important Turkish military commander.
[13]According to other accounts of the battle, Peter was in Constantinople at the time.

Peter, being a haughty Latin, would not admit that he himself was the cause of the trouble, but said it was the others who did not listen to him, but followed their own will, and he denounced them as robbers and plunderers who, for that reason, were not allowed by the Saviour to worship at His Holy Sepulchre. Others of the Latins, such as Bohemund and men of like mind, who had long cherished a desire for the Roman Empire, and wished to win it for themselves, found a pretext in Peter's preaching, as I have said, deceived the more single-minded, caused this great upheaval and were selling their own estates under the pretence that they were marching against the Turks to redeem the Holy Sepulchre.

60

FULCHER OF CHARTRES

The Siege of Antioch

We return here to Fulcher's Chronicles (Book I, Chapters 16 and 17). Antioch, in northern Syria, was the largest and most formidable Muslim-controlled city on the Crusaders' route to Jerusalem. After laying siege to the city for more than two years, the Crusader forces had suffered losses that seriously reduced their strength and morale. After their initial success, what events seem to have caused these reversals? What were the strengths and weaknesses of the Crusader armies? What sorts of weapons did the Crusaders and Turks use?

Thinking Historically

Like the narrative of Solomon bar Simson, this narrative operates on two levels: the human and the divine. Notice how Fulcher attempts to interpret both of these narrative lines, separately and in their interaction. How much of Fulcher's narrative recounts God's work? How much recounts the work of the Crusaders? How does he combine these two threads? Of course, modern historians are normally limited to the human thread. Try to write a narrative that shows how the human Crusaders conquered Antioch.

The First Crusade: The Chronicle of Fulcher of Chartres and Other Source Materials, 2nd ed., ed. Edward Peters (Philadelphia: University of Pennsylvania Press, 1998), 73–75.

XVI. The Wretched Poverty of the Christians and the Flight of the Count of Blois

1. In the year of the Lord 1098, after the region all around Antioch had been wholly devastated by the multitude of our people, the strong as well as the weak were more and more harassed by famine.

2. At that time, the famished ate the shoots of beanseeds growing in the fields and many kinds of herbs unseasoned with salt; also thistles, which, being not well cooked because of the deficiency of firewood, pricked the tongues of those eating them; also horses, asses, and camels, and dogs and rats. The poorer ones ate even the skins of the beasts and seeds of grain found in manure.

3. They endured winter's cold, summer's heat, and heavy rains for God. Their tents became old and torn and rotten from the continuation of rains. Because of this, many of them were covered by only the sky.

4. So like gold thrice proved and purified sevenfold by fire, long predestined by God, I believe, and weighed by such a great calamity, they were cleansed of their sins. For even if the assassin's sword had not failed, many, long agonizing, would have voluntarily completed a martyr's course. Perhaps they borrowed the grace of such a great example from Saint Job, who, purifying his soul by the torments of his body, ever held God fast in mind. Those who fight with the heathen, labor because of God.

5. Granting that God—who creates everything, regulates everything created, sustains everything regulated, and rules by virtue—can destroy or renew whatsoever He wishes, I feel that He assented to the destruction of the heathen after the scourging of the Christians. He permitted it, and the people deserved it, because so many times they cheaply destroyed all things of God. He permitted the Christians to be killed by the Turks, so that the Christians would have the assurance of salvation; the Turks, the perdition of their souls. It pleased God that certain Turks, already predestined for salvation, were baptized by priests. "For those whom He predestined, He also called and glorified."

6. So what then? There were some of our men, as you heard before, who left the siege because it brought so much anguish; others, because of poverty; others, because of cowardice; others, because of fear of death; first the poor and then the rich.

7. Stephen, Count of Blois, withdrew from the siege and returned home to France by sea. Therefore all of us grieved, since he was a very noble man and valiant in arms. On the day following his departure, the city of Antioch was surrendered to the Franks. If he had persevered, he would have rejoiced much in the victory with the rest. This act disgraced him. For a good beginning is not beneficial to anyone unless it be well consummated. I shall cut short many things in the Lord's affairs lest I wander from the truth, because lying about them must be especially guarded against.

8. The siege lasted continuously from this same month of October, as it was mentioned, through the following winter and spring until June. The Turks and Franks alternately staged many attacks and counter-attacks; they overcame and were overcome. Our men, however, triumphed more often than theirs. Once it happened that many of the fleeing Turks fell into the Fernus River, and being submerged in it, they drowned. On the near side of the river, and on the far side, both forces often waged war alternately.

9. Our leaders constructed castles before the city, from which they often rushed forth vigorously to keep the Turks from coming out [of the city]. By this means, the Franks took the pastures from their animals. Nor did they get any help from Armenians outside the city, although these Armenians often did injury to our men.

XVII. *The Surrender of the City of Antioch*

1. When it pleased God that the labor of His people should be consummated, perhaps pleased by the prayers of those who daily poured out supplications and entreaties to Him, out of His compassion He granted that through a fraud of the Turks the city be returned to the Christians in a secret surrender. Hear, therefore, of a fraud, and yet not a fraud.

2. Our Lord appeared to a certain Turk, chosen beforehand by His grace, and said to him: "Arise, thou who sleepest! I command thee to return the city to the Christians." The astonished man concealed that vision in silence.

3. However, a second time, the Lord appeared to him: "Return the city to the Christians," He said, "for I am Christ who command this of thee." Meditating what to do, he went away to his ruler, the prince of Antioch, and made that vision known to him. To him the ruler responded: "You do not wish to obey the phantom, do you, stupid?" Returning, he was afterwards silent.

4. The Lord again appeared to him, saying: "Why hast thou not fulfilled what I ordered thee? Thou must not hesitate, for I, who command this, am Lord of all." No longer doubting, he discreetly negotiated with our men, so that by his zealous plotting they might receive the city.

5. He finished speaking, and gave his son as hostage to Lord Bohemond, to whom he first directed that discourse, and whom he first persuaded. On a certain night, he sent twenty of our men over the wall by means of ladders made of ropes. Without delay, the gate was opened. The Franks, already prepared, entered the city. Forty of our soldiers, who had previously entered by ropes, killed sixty Turks found there, guards of the tower. In a loud voice, altogether the Franks shouted: "God wills it! God wills it!" For this was our signal cry, when we were about to press forward on any enterprise.

6. After hearing this, all the Turks were extremely terrified. Then, when the redness of dawn had paled, the Franks began to go forward to attack the city. When the Turks had first seen Bohemond's red banner on high, furling and unfurling, and the great tumult aroused on all sides, and the Franks running far and wide through the streets with their naked swords and wildly killing people, and had heard their horns sounding on the top of the wall, they began to flee here and there, bewildered. From this scene, many who were able fled into the citadel situated on a cliff.

7. Our rabble wildly seized everything that they found in the streets and houses. But the proved soldiers kept to warfare, in following and killing the Turks.

61

RAYMOND OF ST. GILES, COUNT OF TOULOUSE

The Capture of Jerusalem by the Crusaders

The author of this letter or proclamation was the secular military leader chosen by Pope Urban II to lead the crusade. By the time of the capture of Jerusalem in 1099, he was certainly—with the Norman Bohemond and a couple other nobles—among the top military leaders. How does he account for their capture of Jerusalem? How would you explain it? Raymond tells how immediately after conquering Jerusalem, the Crusaders went to meet an Egyptian army (mistakenly identified as Babylonian) at Ascalon (modern Ashquelon, Israel). How does Raymond explain their success? How might you explain it?

Thinking Historically

A letter can read much like a historical narrative, as does this one by Raymond of St. Giles. The author clearly wants to tell his readers what has happened. But this letter addressed to the pope, his bishops,

Raymond of St. Giles, Count of Toulouse, "The Capture of Jerusalem by the Crusaders," in D. C. Munro, ed., *Translations and Reprints from the Original Sources of European History,* 4th ed., vol. I, bk. 4 (New York: AMC Press, Inc., 1971) 8–12.

and "the whole Christian people" is as much a testament to God's work as it is a history. Raymond is so intent on describing the acts of God that he practically ignores human motivation and strength. In fact, he declares that some Crusaders were punished for taking credit for their victories. This makes it very difficult to construct the human narrative. Which events could you confidently include in your history of the crusade?

To lord Paschal, pope of the Roman church, to all the bishops, and to the whole Christian people, from the archbishop of Pisa, duke Godfrey, now, by the grace of God, defender of the church of the Holy Sepulchre, Raymond, count of St. Giles, and the whole army of God, which is in the land of Israel, greeting.

Multiply your supplications and prayers in the sight of God with joy and thanksgiving, since God has manifested His mercy in fulfilling by our hands what He had promised in ancient times. For after the capture of Nicaea, the whole army, made up of more than three hundred thousand soldiers, departed thence. And, although this army was so great that it could have in a single day covered all Romania and drunk up all the rivers and eaten up all the growing things, yet the Lord conducted them amid so great abundance that a ram was sold for a penny and an ox for twelve pennies or less. Moreover, although the princes and kings of the Saracens rose up against us, yet, by God's will, they were easily conquered and overcome. Because, indeed, some were puffed up by these successes, God opposed to us Antioch, impregnable to human strength. And there He detained us for nine months and so humbled us in the siege that there were scarcely a hundred good horses in our whole army. God opened to us the abundance of His blessing and mercy and led us into the city, and delivered the Turks and all of their possessions into our power.

Inasmuch as we thought that these had been acquired by our own strength and did not worthily magnify God who had done this, we were beset by so great a multitude of Turks that no one dared to venture forth at any point from the city. Moreover, hunger so weakened us that some could scarcely refrain from eating human flesh. It would be tedious to narrate all the miseries which we suffered in that city. But God looked down upon His people whom He had so long chastised and mercifully consoled them. Therefore, He at first revealed to us, as a recompense for our tribulation and as a pledge of victory, His lance which had lain hidden since the days of the apostles. Next, He so fortified the hearts of the men, that they who from sickness or hunger had been unable to walk, now were endued with strength to seize their weapons and manfully to fight against the enemy.

After we had triumphed over the enemy, as our army was wasting away at Antioch from sickness and weariness and was especially hindered by the dissensions among the leaders, we proceeded into Syria, stormed Barra and Marra, cities of the Saracens, and captured the fortresses in that country. And while we were delaying there, there was so great a famine in the army that the Christian people now ate the putrid bodies of the Saracens. Finally, by the divine admonition, we entered into the interior of Hispania, and the most bountiful, merciful and victorious hand of the omnipotent Father was with us. For the cities and fortresses of the country through which we were proceeding sent ambassadors to us with many gifts and offered to aid us and to surrender their walled places. But because our army was not large and it was the unanimous wish to hasten to Jerusalem, we accepted their pledges and made them tributaries. One of the cities forsooth, which was on the sea-coast, had more men than there were in our whole army. And when those at Antioch and Laodicea and Archas heard how the hand of the Lord was with us, many from the army who had remained in those cities followed us to Tyre. Therefore, with the Lord's companionship and aid, we proceeded thus as far as Jerusalem.

And after the army had suffered greatly in the siege, especially on account of the lack of water, a council was held and the bishops and princes ordered that all with bare feet should march around the walls of the city, in order that He who entered it humbly in our behalf might be moved by our humility to open it to us and to exercise judgment upon His enemies. God was appeased by this humility and on the eighth day after the humiliation He delivered the city and His enemies to us. It was the day indeed on which the primitive church was driven thence, and on which the festival of the dispersion of the apostles is celebrated. And if you desire to know what was done with the enemy who were found there, know that in Solomon's Porch and in his temple our men rode in the blood of the Saracens up to the knees of their horses.

Then, when we were considering who ought to hold the city, and some moved by love for their country and kinsmen wished to return home, it was announced to us that the king of Babylon had come to Ascalon with an innumerable multitude of soldiers. His purpose was, as he said, to lead the Franks, who were in Jerusalem, into captivity, and to take Antioch by storm. But God had determined otherwise in regard to us.

Therefore, when we learned that the army of the Babylonians was at Ascalon, we went down to meet them, leaving our baggage and the sick in Jerusalem with a garrison. When our army was in sight of the enemy, upon our knees we invoked the aid of the Lord, that He who in our other adversities had strengthened the Christian faith, might in the present battle break the strength of the Saracens and of the devil and extend the kingdom of the church of Christ from sea to sea, over the whole world. There was no delay; God was present when we cried for His aid, and furnished us with so great boldness, that one who saw us rush upon the enemy would have taken us for a herd of deer hastening to quench their thirst in running water. It was wonderful, indeed, since there were in our army not more than 5,000 horsemen and 15,000 foot-soldiers, and there were probably in the enemy's army 100,000 horsemen and 400,000 foot-soldiers. Then God appeared wonderful to His servants. For before we engaged in fighting, by our very onset alone, He turned this multitude in flight and scattered all their weapons, so that if they wished afterwards to attack us, they did not have the weapons in which they trusted. There can be no question how great the spoils were, since the treasures of the king of Babylon were captured. More than 100,000 Moors perished there by the sword. Moreover, their panic was so great that about 2,000 were suffocated at the gate of the city. Those who perished in the sea were innumerable. Many were entangled in the thickets. The whole world was certainly fighting for us, and if many of ours had not been detained in plundering the camp, few of the great multitude of the enemy would have been able to escape from the battle.

And although it may be tedious, the following must not be omitted: On the day preceding the battle the army captured many thousands of camels, oxen, and sheep. By the command of the princes these were divided among the people. When we advanced to battle, wonderful to relate, the camels formed in many squadrons and the sheep and oxen did the same. Moreover, these animals accompanied us, halting when we halted, advancing when we advanced, and charging when we charged. The clouds protected us from the heat of the sun and cooled us.

Accordingly, after celebrating the victory, the army returned to Jerusalem. Duke Godfrey remained there; the count of St. Giles, Robert, count of Normandy, and Robert, count of Flanders, returned to Laodicea. There they found the fleet belonging to the Pisans and to Bohemond. After the archbishop of Pisa had established peace between Bohemond and our leaders, Raymond prepared to return to Jerusalem for the sake of God and his brethren.

Therefore, we call upon you of the Catholic Church of Christ and of the whole Latin church to exult in the so admirable bravery and devotion of your brethren, in the so glorious and very desirable retribution of the omnipotent God, and in the so devoutly hoped-for remission of all our sins through the grace of God. And we pray that He may make you—namely, all bishops, clerks, and monks who are leading devout lives, and all the laity—to sit down at the right hand of God, who liveth and reigneth God for ever and ever. And we ask and beseech you in the name of our Lord Jesus, who has ever been with us and aided us and freed us from all our tribulations, to be mindful of your brethren who return to you, by doing them kindnesses and by paying their debts, in order that God may recompense you and absolve you from all your sins and grant you a share in all the blessings which either we or they have deserved in the sight of the Lord. Amen.

62

IBN AL-ATHIR

The Conquest of Jerusalem

Ibn al-Athir (1160–1233) was an influential Arab historian who wrote a history of the first three crusades, having witnessed the third himself. The following selection, taken from his work *The Perfect History,* is one of the most authoritative, roughly contemporaneous histories of the First Crusade from the Muslim perspective. What reason does al-Athir give for the Egyptian capture of Jerusalem from the Turks? Why were the Franks successful in wresting Jerusalem and other lands from Muslim control? What is the significance of the poem at the end of the selection?

Thinking Historically

There are always more than two sides to a story, but it is certainly useful to have battle descriptions from two sides of a conflict. In constructing your own narrative of the battle of Jerusalem, you might first look for points of agreement. On what points does Ibn al-Athir agree with other accounts you have read? How else would you decide which elements from each account to include in your narrative?

Francesco Gabrieli, ed., *Arab Historians of the Crusades: Selected and Translated from the Arabic Sources,* ed. and trans. E. J. Costello. Islamic World Series. (Berkeley: University of California Press, 1969), 10–12.

Taj ad-Daula Tutūsh was the Lord of Jerusalem but had given it as a feoff to the amīr Suqmān ibn Artūq the Turcoman. When the Franks defeated the Turks at Antioch the massacre demoralized them, and the Egyptians, who saw that the Turkish armies were being weakened by desertion, besieged Jerusalem under the command of al-Afdal ibn Badr al-Jamali. Inside the city were Artūq's sons, Suqmān and Ilghazi, their cousin Sunij and their nephew Yaquti. The Egyptians brought more than forty siege engines to attack Jerusalem and broke down the walls at several points. The inhabitants put up a defense, and the siege and fighting went on for more than six weeks. In the end the Egyptians forced the city to capitulate, in Sha'bān 489/August 1096. Suqmān, Ilghazi, and their friends were well treated by al-Afdal, who gave them large gifts of money and let them go free. They made for Damascus and then crossed the Euphrates. Suqmān settled in Edessa and Ilghazi went on into Iraq. The Egyptian governor of Jerusalem was a certain Iftikhār ad-Daula, who was still there at the time of which we are speaking.

After their vain attempt to take Acre by siege, the Franks moved on to Jerusalem and besieged it for more than six weeks. They built two towers, one of which, near Sion, the Muslims burnt down, killing everyone inside it. It had scarcely ceased to burn before a messenger arrived to ask for help and to bring the news that the other side of the city had fallen. In fact Jerusalem was taken from the north on the morning of Friday 22 Sha'bān 492/July 15, 1099. The population was put to the sword by the Franks, who pillaged the area for a week. A band of Muslims barricaded themselves into the Oratory of David and fought on for several days. They were granted their lives in return for surrendering. The Franks honoured their word, and the group left by night for Ascalon. In the Masjid al-Aqsa the Franks slaughtered more than 70,000 people, among them a large number of Imams and Muslim scholars, devout and ascetic men who had left their homelands to live lives of pious seclusion in the Holy Place. The Franks stripped the Dome of the Rock of more than forty silver candelabra, each of them weighing 3,600 drams, and a great silver lamp weighing forty-four Syrian pounds, as well as a hundred and fifty smaller silver candelabra and more than twenty gold ones, and a great deal more booty. Refugees from Syria reached Baghdād in Ramadan, among them the qadi Abu Sa'd al-Hárawi. They told the Caliph's ministers a story that wrung their hearts and brought tears to their eyes. On Friday they went to the Cathedral Mosque and begged for help, weeping so that their hearers wept with them as they described the sufferings of the Muslims in that Holy City: the men killed, the women and children taken prisoner, the homes pillaged. Because of the terrible hardships they had suffered, they were allowed to break the fast. . . .

It was the discord between the Muslim princes, as we shall describe, that enabled the Franks to overrun the country. Abu l-Muzaffar al-Abiwardi composed several poems on this subject, in one of which he says:

We have mingled blood with flowing tears, and there is no room left in us for pity[?]

To shed tears is a man's worst weapon when the swords stir up the embers of war.

Sons of Islām, behind you are battles in which heads rolled at your feet.

Dare you slumber in the blessed shade of safety, where life is as soft as an orchard flower?

How can the eye sleep between the lids at a time of disasters that would waken any sleeper?

While your Syrian brothers can only sleep on the backs of their chargers, or in vultures' bellies!

Must the foreigners feed on our ignominy, while you trail behind you the train of a pleasant life, like men whose world is at peace?

When blood has been spilt, when sweet girls must for shame hide their lovely faces in their hands!

When the white swords' points are red with blood, and the iron of the brown lances is stained with gore!

At the sound of sword hammering on lance young children's hair turns white.

This is war, and the man who shuns the whirlpool to save his life shall grind his teeth in penitence.

This is war, and the infidel's sword is naked in his hand, ready to be sheathed again in men's necks and skulls.

This is war, and he who lies in the tomb at Medina seems to raise his voice and cry: "O sons of Hashim!

I see my people slow to raise the lance against the enemy: I see the Faith resting on feeble pillars.

For fear of death the Muslims are evading the fire of battle, refusing to believe that death will surely strike them."

Must the Arab champions then suffer with resignation, while the gallant Persians shut their eyes to their dishonour?

63

Letter from a Jewish Pilgrim in Egypt

The following letter was written in 1100 by an anonymous Jewish pilgrim from Alexandria, unable to make his pilgrimage to Jerusalem because of the ongoing war. How does the letter's author regard the Egyptian Sultan? How does he view the struggle between the Sultan and the Franks? What does this suggest about the lives of Jews under Muslim rule during this time period?

Thinking Historically

What does this letter add to your understanding of the Crusaders' capture of Jerusalem? How would you write a narrative of the First Crusade that took advantage of Christian, Muslim, and Jewish sources?

In Your name, You Merciful.

If I attempted to describe my longing for you, my Lord, my brother *and cousin,*—may God prolong your days and make permanent your honour, success, happiness, health, and welfare; and ... subdue your enemies—all the paper in the world would not suffice. My longing will but increase and double, just as the days will grow and double. May *the Creator of the World* presently make us meet together in joy when I return under His guidance to my homeland *and to the inheritance of my Fathers* in complete happiness, *so that we rejoice and be happy through His great mercy and His vast bounty; and thus may be His will!*

You may remember, my Lord, that many years ago I left our country to seek God's mercy and help in my poverty, to behold Jerusalem and return thereupon. However, when I was in Alexandria God brought about circumstances which caused a slight delay. Afterwards, however, "the sea grew stormy," and many armed bands made their appearance in Palestine; *"and he who went forth and he who came had no peace,"* so that hardly one survivor out of a whole group came back to us from Palestine and told us that scarcely anyone could save himself

---

"Contemporary Letters on the Capture of Jerusalem by the Crusaders," trans. S. D. Goitein, *Journal of Jewish Studies*, vol. 3, no. 4 (London: Jewish Chronicle Publications, 1952), 162–77.

from those armed bands, since they were so numerous and were gathered round . . . every town. There was further the journey through the desert, among [the bedouins] and whoever escaped from the one, fell into the hands of the other. Moreover, mutinies [spread throughout the country and reached] even Alexandria, so that we ourselves were besieged several times and the city was ruined; . . . the end however *was good,* for the Sultan—may God bestow glory upon his victories—conquered the city and caused justice to abound in it in a manner unprecedented in the history of any king in the world; not even a dirham was looted from anyone. Thus I had come to hope that because of his justice and strength God would give the land into his hands, and I should thereupon go to Jerusalem in safety and tranquility. For this reason I proceeded from Alexandria to Cairo, in order to start [my journey] from there.

When, however, God had given Jerusalem, the blessed, into his hands this state of affairs continued for too short a time to allow for making a journey there. The Franks arrived and killed everybody in the city, whether of *Ishmael or of Israel;* and the few who survived the slaughter were made prisoners. Some of these have been ransomed since, while others are still in captivity in all parts of the world.

Now, all of us had anticipated that our Sultan—may God bestow glory upon his victories—would set out against them [the Franks] with his troops and chase them away. But time after time our hope failed. Yet, to this very present moment we do hope that God will give his [the Sultan's] enemies into his hands. For it is inevitable that the armies will join in battle this year; and, if God grants us victory through him [the Sultan] and he conquers Jerusalem—and so it may be, with God's will—I for one shall not be amongst those who will linger, but shall go there to behold the city; and shall afterwards return straight to you—if God wills it. My salvation is in God, for this [is unlike] the other previous occasions [of making a pilgrimage to Jerusalem]. God, indeed, will exonerate me, since at my age I cannot afford to delay and wait any longer; I want to return home under any circumstances, if I still remain alive—whether I shall have seen Jerusalem or have given up the hope of doing it—both of which are possible.

You know, of course, my Lord, what has happened to us in the course of the last five years: the plague, the illnesses, and ailments have continued unabated for four successive years. As a result of this the wealthy became impoverished and a great number of people died *of the plague,* so that entire families perished in it. I, too, was affected with a grave illness, from which I recovered only about a year ago; then I was taken ill the following year so that (on the margin) for four years I have remained. . . . He who has said: *The evil diseases of Egypt* . . . he who hiccups does not live . . . ailments and will die . . . otherwise . . . will remain alive.

64

FULCHER OF CHARTRES

The Latins in the Levant

Fulcher wrote this part of his Chronicles later in his life after living for some decades in Jerusalem. He is writing of himself (as well as many others) when he says "We who were Occidentals. . . . " This poignant selection mixes nostalgia for Europe with an embrace of the East, including its people, languages, and customs. But does Fulcher's embrace of the East include the acceptance of non-Christians? And do his comments about servants, coins, and villas suggest a more unsettling relationship between newcomers and natives?

Thinking Historically

Every narrative must have a beginning and an end. The historian's choice of beginning and end shapes the theme and message of the story. How would a narrative of the First Crusade that ended in 1099 tell a different story than one that ended with Fulcher's Latins in the Levant?

Consider, I pray, and reflect how in our time God has transferred the West into the East. For we who were Occidentals now have been made Orientals. He who was a Roman or a Frank is now a Galilaean, or an inhabitant of Palestine. One who was a citizen of Rheims or of Chartres now has been made a citizen of Tyre or of Antioch. We have already forgotten the places of our birth; already they have become unknown to many of us, or, at least, are unmentioned. Some already possess here homes and servants which they have received through inheritance. Some have taken wives not merely of their own people, but Syrians, or Armenians, or even Saracens who have received the grace of baptism. Some have with them father-in-law, or daughter-in-law, or son-in-law, or step-son, or step-father. There are here, too, grandchildren and great-grandchildren. One cultivates vines, another the fields. The one and the other use mutually the speech and the idioms of

The First Crusade: The Chronicle of Fulcher of Chartres and Other Source Materials, 2nd ed., ed. Edward Peters (Philadelphia: University of Pennsylvania Press, 1998), 281–82.

the different languages. Different languages, now made common, become known to both races, and faith unites those whose forefathers were strangers. As it is written, "The lion and the ox shall eat straw together." Those who were strangers are now natives; and he who was a sojourner now has become a resident. Our parents and relatives from day to day come to join us, abandoning, even though reluctantly, all that they possess. For those who were poor there, here God makes rich. Those who had few coins, here possess countless besants; and those who had not had a villa, here, by the gift of God, already possess a city. Therefore, why should one who has found the East so favorable return to the West? God does not wish those to suffer want who, carrying their crosses, have vowed to follow Him, nay even unto the end. You see, therefore, that this is a great miracle, and one which must greatly astonish the whole world. Who has ever heard anything like it? Therefore, God wishes to enrich us all and to draw us to Himself as His most dear friends. And because He wishes it, we also freely desire the same; and what is pleasing to Him we do with a loving and submissive heart, that with Him we may reign happily throughout eternity.

REFLECTIONS

The First Crusade (1095–1102) only marks the beginning of a protracted conflict between Christians and Muslims that continued until, perhaps, the eighteenth century. In the Holy Land there were crusades in 1107–1108, 1120–1125, 1128–1129, and 1139–1140. Another in 1147–1149 was called the Second Crusade. Meanwhile, the conquest of Muslims in Spain, which had been equated with the crusade by Pope Urban II, continued, as did frequent crusades into Eastern Europe.

The establishment of Latin kingdoms in Palestine could not be maintained without continual reinforcements, and they were vulnerable to Muslim attack. In 1187 Saladin reconquered most of Palestine, including Jerusalem, for the Muslims, a trauma for the Christians that led to the Third Crusade (1189–1192) and German Crusade (1197–1198) by which Christians retook settlements on the coast. Popular enthusiasm continued in the Children's Crusade (1212) and the Crusade of the Shepherds (1251). The armies of the Fourth Crusade (1202–1204) were diverted to Constantinople, which they sacked in 1204, and the conquest of Greece. A Fifth Crusade (1217–1229) recovered Jerusalem, which was retaken by the Muslims in 1244, leading to crusades initiated by King Louis IX of France. Other crusading armies invaded Egypt, Tunisia, Muslim Spain, northwest Africa, southern France, Poland, Latvia, Germany, Russia, the Mongols, Finland, Bosnia, and Italy, against papal enemies and Eastern Orthodox Christians as well as Muslims. Recent histories of the Crusades have ended their narratives in 1521, 1560, 1588, and 1798, according to Jonathan Riley-Smith who ends the recent *Oxford Illustrated History of the Crusades* with images of the crusades in twentieth-century wars. Does the imagery of the Crusades still animate our wars?

11

Ecology, Technology, and Science

Europe, Asia, and Africa, 500–1500 C.E.

HISTORICAL CONTEXT

Everyone knows that the world has changed drastically since the Middle Ages. And, most people would agree that the most important and far-reaching changes have occurred in the fields of ecology, technology, and science. Global population has grown tenfold. The world has become a single ecological unit where microbes, migrants, and money travel everywhere at jet speed. In most parts of the world, average life expectancy has doubled; cities have mushroomed, replacing farm and pasture. Machines have replaced the labor of humans and animals. Powers that were only imagined in the Middle Ages — elixirs to cure disease, energy to harness rivers, machines that would fly — are now commonplace. Other aspects of life — among them religion, political behavior, music, and art — have also evolved, but even these were affected significantly by advances in modern science and technology.

Precisely what change or changes occurred? When did the cycle of change begin and what caused it? We will examine these questions here. You will read two substantial answers, the first two selections in the chapter. Lynn White Jr. defines the transformation to modernity in largely technological and ecological terms, but emphasizes the role of cultural causes. Lynda Shaffer, on the other hand, discusses technological and scientific changes as spreading through contact and trade.

These two explanations of long-term change differ most markedly in how they explain the roots of the transformation. White, a historian of medieval European technology, focuses on the role of medieval European religion: Christianity. Shaffer, a world historian, underscores the role of India and South Asia.

THINKING HISTORICALLY
Understanding and Evaluating Large-Scale Interpretations

In examining White's and Shaffer's contrasting interpretations of the global history of technology, ecology, and science, we evaluate possible answers to one of the biggest questions historians ask: "How did the West (Western Europe and North America) rise to prominence in the world in the last five hundred years?" Westernization, the modern spread of Western power — political, economic, cultural, scientific, and technological — is understood by both authors to have mainly technological and scientific roots. Although both White and Shaffer date the culmination of Western dominance to the nineteenth century industrial revolution, they both find the roots of this transformation in the medieval period, and even earlier.

As you read these two selections, you will be asked to weigh the evidence of each argument. You will need to draw on your understanding of how new religions reshaped the world, what role trade and commerce played in global histories, and how different types of medieval societies functioned. After reading the entire chapter, you will have understood and evaluated both of these grand interpretations. If you have not concluded that one is right and the other wrong, you will at least know where you agree and disagree with each. You will also develop your own interpretation of global technological history.

Using Pictorial Evidence

This chapter also introduces another historical skill or habit of mind: interpreting pictorial evidence. Images from the past, like writings from the past, are primary sources. They can add depth to historical inquiry by filling in gaps in the written record, and by demonstrating visually what writings convey with words. When examining a visual primary source it is important to ask who created it, for what purpose and audience, and with what means. Once you have learned how to "read" pictures as evidence, you will be able to glean important information from them and better understand how historians use them.

65

LYNN WHITE JR.

The Historical Roots of Our Ecological Crisis

This classic essay first appeared in the magazine *Science* in 1967 and has since been reprinted and commented on many times. What do you think of White's linkage of ecological crisis and Christianity? Which of White's arguments and evidence do you find most persuasive? Which do you find least convincing? Imagine a continuum that includes all of the world's people, from the most ecologically-minded "tree-huggers" on the left to the most damaging polluters and destroyers of the environment on the right. Where on that continuum would you place the historical majority of Christians? Buddhists? Why?

Thinking Historically

A grand theory like this — that Christianity is responsible for our environmental problems — argues far more than can be proven in such a brief essay. White concentrates on making certain kinds of connections and marshaling certain kinds of evidence. In addition to weighing the arguments he makes, consider the gaps in his argument. What sorts of evidence would you seek to make White's theory more convincing?

A conversation with Aldous Huxley[1] not infrequently put one at the receiving end of an unforgettable monologue. About a year before his lamented death he was discoursing on a favorite topic: man's unnatural treatment of nature and its sad results. To illustrate his point he told how, during the previous summer, he had returned to a little valley in England where he had spent many happy months as a child. Once it had been composed of delightful grassy glades; now it was becoming overgrown with unsightly brush because the rabbits that formerly kept such growth under control had largely succumbed to a disease, myxomatosis, that was deliberately introduced by the local farmers to reduce

---

[1] Aldous Huxley (1894–1963), British author of novels, short stories, travel books, biography, and essays. Best known for *Brave New World* (1932). [Ed.]

Lynn White Jr., "The Historical Roots of Our Ecologic Crisis," *Science* 155 (March 1967): 1203–7.

the rabbits' destruction of crops. Being something of a Philistine,[2] I could be silent no longer, even in the interests of great rhetoric. I interrupted to point out that the rabbit itself had been brought as a domestic animal to England in 1176, presumably to improve the protein diet of the peasantry.

All forms of life modify their contexts. The most spectacular and benign instance is doubtless the coral polyp. By serving its own ends, it has created a vast undersea world favorable to thousands of other kinds of animals and plants. Ever since man became a numerous species he has affected his environment notably. The hypothesis that his fire-drive[3] method of hunting created the world's great grasslands and helped to exterminate the monster mammals of the Pleistocene from much of the globe is plausible, if not proved. For six millennia at least, the banks of the lower Nile have been a human artifact rather than the swampy African jungle which nature, apart from man, would have made it. The Aswan Dam, flooding five thousand square miles, is only the latest stage in a long process. In many regions terracing or irrigation, overgrazing, and the cutting of forests by Romans to build ships to fight Carthaginians or by Crusaders to solve the logistics problems of their expeditions have profoundly changed some ecologies. Observation that the French landscape falls into two basic types, the open fields of the north and the *bocage*[4] of the south and west, inspired Marc Bloch to undertake his classic study of medieval agricultural methods. Quite unintentionally, changes in human ways often affect nonhuman nature. It has been noted, for example, that the advent of the automobile eliminated huge flocks of sparrows that once fed on the horse manure littering every street.

The history of ecologic change is still so rudimentary that we know little about what really happened, or what the results were. The extinction of the European aurochs[5] as late as 1627 would seem to have been a simple case of overenthusiastic hunting. On more intricate matters it often is impossible to find solid information. For a thousand years or more the Frisians and Hollanders have been pushing back the North Sea, and the process is culminating in our own time in the reclamation

---

[2] An anti-intellectual (though obviously White is not; he was only impatient with Huxley's pedantry). [Ed.]

[3] Paleolithic hunters used fires to drive animals to their deaths. [Ed.]

[4] Full of groves or woodlands. Marc Bloch reasoned that the open fields north of the Loire River in France must have been plowed by teams of oxen and heavy plows because of the hard soil. In the south farmers could use scratch plows on the softer soil and therefore did not clear large fields, preserving more woodlands. [Ed.]

[5] A now extinct European wild ox believed to be the ancestor of European domestic cattle. [Ed.]

of the Zuider Zee.[6] What, if any, species of animals, birds, fish, shore life, or plants have died out in the process? In their epic combat with Neptune have the Netherlanders overlooked ecological values in such a way that the quality of human life in the Netherlands has suffered? I cannot discover that the questions have ever been asked, much less answered.

People, then, have often been a dynamic element in their own environment, but in the present state of historical scholarship we usually do not know exactly when, where, or with what effects man-induced changes came. As we enter the last third of the twentieth century, however, concern for the problem of ecologic backlash is mounting feverishly. Natural science, conceived as the effort to understand the nature of things, had flourished in several eras and among several peoples. Similarly there had been an age-old accumulation of technological skills, sometimes growing rapidly, sometimes slowly. But it was not until about four generations ago that Western Europe and North America arranged a marriage between science and technology, a union of the theoretical and the empirical approaches to our natural environment. The emergence in widespread practice of the Baconian creed that scientific knowledge means technological power over nature can scarcely be dated before about 1850, save in the chemical industries, where it is anticipated in the eighteenth century. Its acceptance as a normal pattern of action may mark the greatest event in human history since the invention of agriculture, and perhaps in nonhuman terrestrial history as well.

Almost at once the new situation forced the crystallization of the novel concept of ecology; indeed, the word *ecology* first appeared in the English language in 1873. Today, less than a century later, the impact of our race upon the environment has so increased in force that it has changed in essence. When the first cannons were fired, in the early fourteenth century, they affected ecology by sending workers scrambling to the forests and mountains for more potash, sulfur, iron ore, and charcoal, with some resulting erosion and deforestation. Hydrogen bombs are of a different order: A war fought with them might alter the genetics of all life on this planet. By 1285 London had a smog problem arising from the burning of soft coal, but our present combustion of fossil fuels threatens to change the chemistry of the globe's atmosphere as a whole, with consequences which we are only beginning to guess. With the population explosion, the carcinoma of planless urbanism, the now geological deposits of sewage and garbage, surely no creature other than man has ever managed to foul its nest in such short order.

---

[6] Once a Dutch lake, it was joined to the North Sea by a flood in the thirteenth century but has since been reclaimed by the building of a dam. [Ed.]

There are many calls to action, but specific proposals, however worthy as individual items, seem too partial, palliative, negative: Ban the bomb, tear down the billboards, give the Hindus contraceptives and tell them to eat their sacred cows. The simplest solution to any suspect change is, of course, to stop it, or, better yet, to revert to a romanticized past: Make those ugly gasoline stations look like Anne Hathaway's cottage or (in the Far West) like ghost-town saloons. The "wilderness area" mentality invariably advocates deep-freezing an ecology, whether San Gimignano or the High Sierra, as it was before the first Kleenex was dropped. But neither atavism nor prettification will cope with the ecologic crisis of our time.

What shall we do? No one yet knows. Unless we think about fundamentals, our specific measures may produce new backlashes more serious than those they are designed to remedy.

As a beginning we should try to clarify our thinking by looking, in some historical depth, at the presuppositions that underlie modern technology and science. Science was traditionally aristocratic, speculative, intellectual in intent; technology was lower-class, empirical, action-oriented. The quite sudden fusion of these two, toward the middle of the nineteenth century, is surely related to the slightly prior and contemporary democratic revolutions which, by reducing social barriers, tended to assert a functional unity of brain and hand. Our ecologic crisis is the product of an emerging, entirely novel, democratic culture. The issue is whether a democratized world can survive its own implications. Presumably we cannot unless we rethink our axioms.

The Western Traditions of Technology and Science

One thing is so certain that it seems stupid to verbalize it: Both modern technology and modern science are distinctively *Occidental*. Our technology has absorbed elements from all over the world, notably from China; yet everywhere today, whether in Japan or in Nigeria, successful technology is Western. Our science is the heir to all the sciences of the past, especially perhaps to the work of the great Islamic scientists of the Middle Ages, who so often outdid the ancient Greeks in skill and perspicacity: al-Rāzī in medicine, for example; or ibn-al-Haytham in optics; or Omar Khayyám in mathematics. Indeed, not a few works of such geniuses seem to have vanished in the original Arabic and to survive only in medieval Latin translations that helped to lay the foundations for later Western developments. Today, around the globe, all significant science is Western in style and method, whatever the pigmentation or language of the scientists.

A second pair of facts is less well recognized because they result from quite recent historical scholarship. The leadership of the West, both in technology and in science, is far older than the so-called Scientific Revolution of the seventeenth century or the so-called Industrial Revolution of the eighteenth century. These terms are in fact outmoded and obscure the true nature of what they try to describe — significant stages in two long and separate developments. By A.D. 1000 at the latest — and perhaps, feebly, as much as two hundred years earlier — the West began to apply water power to industrial processes other than milling grain. This was followed in the late twelfth century by the harnessing of wind power. From simple beginnings, but with remarkable consistency of style, the West rapidly expanded its skills in the development of power machinery, labor-saving devices, and automation. Those who doubt should contemplate that most monumental achievement in the history of automation: the weight-driven mechanical clock, which appeared in two forms in the early fourteenth century. Not in craftsmanship but in basic technological capacity, the Latin West of the later Middle Ages far outstripped its elaborate, sophisticated, and esthetically magnificent sister cultures, Byzantium and Islam. In 1444 a great Greek ecclesiastic, Bessarion, who had gone to Italy, wrote a letter to a prince in Greece. He is amazed by the superiority of Western ships, arms, textiles, glass. But above all he is astonished by the spectacle of waterwheels sawing timbers and pumping the bellows of blast furnaces. Clearly, he had seen nothing of the sort in the Near East.

By the end of the fifteenth century the technological superiority of Europe was such that its small, mutually hostile nations could spill out over all the rest of the world, conquering, looting, and colonizing. The symbol of this technological superiority is the fact that Portugal, one of the weakest states of the Occident, was able to become, and to remain for a century, mistress of the East Indies. And we must remember that the technology of Vasco da Gama and Albuquerque was built by pure empiricism, drawing remarkably little support or inspiration from science.

In the present-day vernacular understanding, modern science is supposed to have begun in 1543, when both Copernicus and Vesalius published their great works. It is no derogation of their accomplishments, however, to point out that such structures as the *Fabrica*[7] and the *De revolutionibus*[8] do not appear overnight. The distinctive Western tradition of science, in fact, began in the late eleventh century with a massive movement of translation of Arabic and Greek scientific works into Latin. A

---

[7] *De Humani Corporis Fabrica* (1543), an illustrated work on human anatomy based on dissections, was produced by Andreas Vesalius (1514–1564), a Flemish anatomist, at the University of Padua in Italy. [Ed.]

[8] *De revolutionibus orbium coelestium* (1543; On the Revolutions of Heavenly Bodies) was published by Nicolas Copernicus (1473–1543); it showed the sun as the center of a system around which the Earth revolved. [Ed.]

few notable books — Theophrastus, for example — escaped the West's avid new appetite for science, but within less than two hundred years effectively the entire corpus of Greek and Muslim science was available in Latin, and was being eagerly read and criticized in the new European universities. Out of criticism arose new observation, speculation, and increasing distrust of ancient authorities. By the late thirteenth century Europe had seized global scientific leadership from the faltering hands of Islam. It would be as absurd to deny the profound originality of Newton, Galileo, or Copernicus as to deny that of the fourteenth-century scholastic scientists like Buridan or Oresme on whose work they built. Before the eleventh century, science scarcely existed in the Latin West, even in Roman times. From the eleventh century onward, the scientific sector of Occidental culture has increased in a steady crescendo.

Since both our technological and our scientific movements got their start, acquired their character, and achieved world dominance in the Middle Ages, it would seem that we cannot understand their nature or their present impact upon ecology without examining fundamental medieval assumptions and developments.

Medieval View of Man and Nature

Until recently, agriculture has been the chief occupation even in "advanced" societies; hence, any change in methods of tillage has much importance. Early plows, drawn by two oxen, did not normally turn the sod but merely scratched it. Thus, cross-plowing was needed and fields tended to be squarish. In the fairly light soils and semiarid climates of the Near East and Mediterranean, this worked well. But such a plow was inappropriate to the wet climate and often sticky soils of northern Europe. By the latter part of the seventh century after Christ, however, following obscure beginnings, certain northern peasants were using an entirely new kind of plow, equipped with a vertical knife to cut the line of the furrow, a horizontal share to slice under the sod, and a mold-board to turn it over. The friction of this plow with the soil was so great that it normally required not two but eight oxen. It attacked the land with such violence that cross-plowing was not needed, and fields tended to be shaped in long strips.

In the days of the scratch-plow, fields were distributed generally in units capable of supporting a single family. Subsistence farming was the presupposition. But no peasant owned eight oxen: to use the new and more efficient plow, peasants pooled their oxen to form large plow-teams, originally receiving (it would appear) plowed strips in proportion to their contribution. Thus, distribution of land was based no longer on the needs of a family but, rather, on the capacity of a power machine to till the earth. Man's relation to the soil was profoundly changed. Formerly man had been part of nature; now he was the exploiter of nature. Nowhere else in the world did farmers develop any analogous agricultural implement. Is it coincidence that modern technology, with its ruthlessness toward nature, has so largely been produced by descendants of these peasants of northern Europe?

This same exploitive attitude appears slightly before A.D. 830 in Western illustrated calendars. In older calendars the months were shown as passive personifications. The new Frankish calendars, which set the style for the Middle Ages, are very different: They show men coercing the world around them — plowing, harvesting, chopping trees, butchering pigs. Man and nature are two things, and man is master.

These novelties seem to be in harmony with larger intellectual patterns. What people do about their ecology depends on what they think about themselves in relation to things around them. Human ecology is deeply conditioned by beliefs about our nature and destiny — that is, by religion. To Western eyes this is very evident in, say, India or Ceylon. It is equally true of ourselves and of our medieval ancestors.

The victory of Christianity over paganism was the greatest psychic revolution in the history of our culture. It has become fashionable today to say that, for better or worse, we live in "the post-Christian age." Certainly the forms of our thinking and language have largely ceased to be Christian, but to my eye the substance often remains amazingly akin to that of the past. Our daily habits of action, for example, are dominated by an implicit faith in perpetual progress which was unknown either to Greco-Roman antiquity or to the Orient. It is rooted in, and is indefensible apart from, Judeo-Christian teleology.[9] The fact that Communists share it merely helps to show what can be demonstrated on many other grounds: that Marxism, like Islam, is a Judeo-Christian heresy. We continue today to live, as we have lived for about seventeen hundred years, very largely in a context of Christian axioms.

What did Christianity tell people about their relations with the environment?

While many of the world's mythologies provide stories of creation, Greco-Roman mythology was singularly incoherent in this respect. Like Aristotle, the intellectuals of the ancient West denied that the visible world had had a beginning. Indeed, the idea of a beginning was impossible in the framework of their cyclical notion of time. In sharp contrast, Christianity inherited from Judaism not only a concept of time as nonrepetitive and linear but also a striking story of creation. By gradual stages a loving and all-powerful God had created light and darkness, the heavenly bodies, the earth and all its plants, animals, birds, and fishes. Finally, God had created Adam and, as an afterthought,

---

[9] The Biblical idea that God's purpose is revealed in his creation, that human history can be seen as the result of God's intentions. [Ed.]

Eve to keep man from being lonely. Man named all the animals, thus establishing his dominance over them. God planned all of this explicitly for man's benefit and rule: No item in the physical creation had any purpose save to serve man's purposes. And, although man's body is made of clay, he is not simply part of nature: He is made in God's image.

Especially in its Western form, Christianity is the most anthropocentric religion the world has seen. As early as the second century both Tertullian and Saint Irenaeus of Lyons were insisting that when God shaped Adam he was foreshadowing the image of the incarnate Christ, the Second Adam. Man shares, in great measure, God's transcendence of nature. Christianity, in absolute contrast to ancient paganism and Asia's religions (except, perhaps, Zoroastrianism), not only established a dualism of man and nature but also insisted that it is God's will that man exploit nature for his proper ends.

At the level of the common people this worked out in an interesting way. In Antiquity every tree, every spring, every stream, every hill had its own *genius loci,* its guardian spirit. These spirits were accessible to men, but were very unlike men; centaurs, fauns, and mermaids show their ambivalence. Before one cut a tree, mined a mountain, or dammed a brook, it was important to placate the spirit in charge of that particular situation, and to keep it placated. By destroying pagan animism, Christianity made it possible to exploit nature in a mood of indifference to the feelings of natural objects.

It is often said that for animism the Church substituted the cult of saints. True; but the cult of saints is functionally quite different from animism. The saint is not *in* natural objects; he may have special shrines, but his citizenship is in heaven. Moreover, a saint is entirely a man; he can be approached in human terms. In addition to saints, Christianity of course also had angels and demons inherited from Judaism and perhaps, at one remove, from Zoroastrianism. But these were all as mobile as the saints themselves. The spirits *in* natural objects, which formerly had protected nature from man, evaporated. Man's effective monopoly on spirit in this world was confirmed, and the old inhibitions to the exploitation of nature crumbled.

When one speaks in such sweeping terms, a note of caution is in order. Christianity is a complex faith, and its consequences differ in differing contexts. What I have said may well apply to the medieval West, where in fact technology made spectacular advances. But the Greek East, a highly civilized realm of equal Christian devotion, seems to have produced no marked technological innovation after the late seventh century, when Greek fire was invented. The key to the contrast may perhaps be found in a difference in the tonality of piety and thought which students of comparative theology find between the Greek and the Latin Churches. The Greeks believed that sin was intellectual blindness, and that salvation was found in illumination, orthodoxy — that is, clear thinking. The Latins, on the other hand, felt that sin was moral evil, and that salvation was to be found in right conduct. Eastern theology has been intellectualist. Western theology has been voluntarist. The Greek saint contemplates; the Western saint acts. The implications of Christianity for the conquest of nature would emerge more easily in the Western atmosphere.

The Christian dogma of creation, which is found in the first clause of all the Creeds, has another meaning for our comprehension of today's ecologic crisis. By revelation, God had given man the Bible, the Book of Scripture. But since God had made nature, nature also must reveal the divine mentality. The religious study of nature for the better understanding of God was known as natural theology. In the early Church, and always in the Greek East, nature was conceived primarily as a symbolic system through which God speaks to men: The ant is a sermon to sluggards; rising flames are the symbol of the soul's aspiration. This view of nature was essentially artistic rather than scientific. While Byzantium preserved and copied great numbers of ancient Greek scientific texts, science as we conceive it could scarcely flourish in such an ambience.

However, in the Latin West by the early thirteenth century natural theology was following a very different bent. It was ceasing to be the decoding of the physical symbols of God's communication with man and was becoming the effort to understand God's mind by discovering how his creation operates. The rainbow was no longer simply a symbol of hope first sent to Noah after the Deluge: Robert Grosseteste, Friar Roger Bacon, and Theodoric of Freiberg produced startlingly sophisticated work on the optics of the rainbow, but they did it as a venture in religious understanding. From the thirteenth century onward, up to and including Leibnitz and Newton, every major scientist, in effect, explained his motivations in religious terms. Indeed, if Galileo had not been so expert an amateur theologian he would have got into far less trouble: The professionals resented his intrusion. And Newton seems to have regarded himself more as a theologian than as a scientist. It was not until the late eighteenth century that the hypothesis of God became unnecessary to many scientists.

It is often hard for the historian to judge, when men explain why they are doing what they want to do, whether they are offering real reasons or merely culturally acceptable reasons. The consistency with which scientists during the long formative centuries of Western science said that the task and the reward of the scientist was "to think God's thoughts after him" leads one to believe that this was their real motivation. If so, then modern Western science was cast in a matrix of Christian theology. The dynamism of religious devotion, shaped by the Judeo-Christian dogma of creation, gave it impetus.

An Alternative Christian View

We would seem to be headed toward conclusions unpalatable to many Christians. Since both *science* and *technology* are blessed words in our contemporary vocabulary, some may be happy at the notions, first, that, viewed historically, modern science is an extrapolation of natural theology and, second, that modern technology is at least partly to be explained as an Occidental, voluntarist realization of the Christian dogma of man's transcendence of, and rightful mastery over, nature. But, as we now recognize, somewhat over a century ago science and technology — hitherto quite separate activities — joined to give mankind powers which, to judge by many of the ecologic effects, are out of control. If so, Christianity bears a huge burden of guilt.

I personally doubt that disastrous ecologic backlash can be avoided simply by applying to our problems more science and more technology. Our science and technology have grown out of Christian attitudes toward man's relation to nature which are almost universally held not only by Christians and neo-Christians but also by those who fondly regard themselves as post-Christians. Despite Copernicus, all the cosmos rotates around our little globe. Despite Darwin, we are *not,* in our hearts, part of the natural process. We are superior to nature, contemptuous of it, willing to use it for our slightest whim. The newly elected Governor of California,[10] like myself a churchman but less troubled than I, spoke for the Christian tradition when he said (as is alleged), "when you've seen one redwood tree, you've seen them all." To a Christian a tree can be no more than a physical fact. The whole concept of the sacred grove is alien to Christianity and to the ethos of the West. For nearly two millennia Christian missionaries have been chopping down sacred groves, which are idolatrous because they assume spirit in nature.

What we do about ecology depends on our ideas of the man-nature relationship. More science and more technology are not going to get us out of the present ecologic crisis until we find a new religion, or rethink our old one. The beatniks, who are the basic revolutionaries of our time, show a sound instinct in their affinity for Zen Buddhism, which conceives of the man-nature relationship as very nearly the mirror image of the Christian view. Zen, however, is as deeply conditioned by Asian history as Christianity is by the experience of the West, and I am dubious of its viability among us.

Possibly we should ponder the greatest radical in Christian history since Christ: Saint Francis of Assisi. The prime miracle of Saint Francis is the fact that he did not end at the stake, as many of his left-wing fol-

---

[10] Ronald Reagan, governor from 1967 to 1975.

lowers did. He was so clearly heretical that a General of the Franciscan Order, Saint Bonaventura, a great and perceptive Christian, tried to suppress the early accounts of Franciscanism. The key to an understanding of Francis is his belief in the virtue of humility — not merely for the individual but for man as a species. Francis tried to depose man from his monarchy over creation and set up a democracy of all God's creatures. With him the ant is no longer simply a homily for the lazy, flames a sign of the thrust of the soul toward union with God; now they are Brother Ant and Sister Fire, praising the Creator in their own ways as Brother Man does in his.

Later commentators have said that Francis preached to the birds as a rebuke to men who would not listen. The records do not read so: He urged the little birds to praise God, and in spiritual ecstasy they flapped their wings and chirped rejoicing. Legends of saints, especially the Irish saints, had long told of their dealings with animals but always, I believe, to show their human dominance over creatures. With Francis it is different. The land around Gubbio in the Apennines was being ravaged by a fierce wolf. Saint Francis, says the legend, talked to the wolf and persuaded him of the error of his ways. The wolf repented, died in the odor of sanctity, and was buried in consecrated ground.

What Sir Steven Ruciman calls "the Franciscan doctrine of the animal soul" was quickly stamped out. Quite possibly it was in part inspired, consciously or unconsciously, by the belief in reincarnation held by the Cathar heretics who at that time teemed in Italy and southern France, and who presumably had got it originally from India. It is significant that at just the same moment, about 1200, traces of metempsychosis are found also in Western Judaism, in the Provençal *Cabbala*. But Francis held neither to transmigration of souls nor to pantheism. His view of nature and of man rested on a unique sort of pan-psychism of all things animate and inanimate, designed for the glorification of their transcendent Creator, who, in the ultimate gesture of cosmic humility, assumed flesh, lay helpless in a manger, and hung dying on a scaffold.

I am not suggesting that many contemporary Americans who are concerned about our ecologic crisis will be either able or willing to counsel with wolves or exhort birds. However, the present increasing disruption of the global environment is the product of a dynamic technology and science which were originating in the Western medieval world against which Saint Francis was rebelling in so original a way. Their growth cannot be understood historically apart from distinctive attitudes toward nature which are deeply grounded in Christian dogma. The fact that most people do not think of these attitudes as Christian is irrelevant. No new set of basic values has been accepted in our society to displace those of Christianity. Hence we shall continue to have a worsening ecologic crisis until we reject the Christian axiom that nature has no reason for existence save to serve man.

The greatest spiritual revolutionary in Western history, Saint Francis, proposed what he thought was an alternative Christian view of nature and man's relation to it: He tried to substitute the idea of the equality of all creatures, including man, for the idea of man's limitless rule of creation. He failed. Both our present science and our present technology are so tinctured with orthodox Christian arrogance toward nature that no solution for our ecologic crisis can be expected from them alone. Since the roots of our trouble are so largely religious, the remedy must also be essentially religious, whether we call it that or not. We must rethink and refeel our nature and destiny. The profoundly religious, but heretical, sense of the primitive Franciscans for the spiritual autonomy of all parts of nature may point a direction. I propose Francis as a patron saint for ecologists.

66

LYNDA NORENE SHAFFER

Southernization

The author of this selection began her career as a historian of China, but she is currently a world historian, having published books on Native American, Southeast Asian, and Chinese history. Shaffer coins the term *Southernization* to challenge the significance of *Westernization*. What are the elements of Southernization? Do you think she would say that Westernization never occurred, or only that it was preceded by an earlier "southern" process of technological expansion that eventually made it possible? Which of her examples of Southernization do you find most far-reaching? Which least far-reaching? Did India and Indian Ocean societies of the early Middle Ages play a role like that of the West today?

Thinking Historically

Shaffer did not write this essay to criticize Lynn White Jr., nor does her essay address precisely the same issues. Our exercise here is not the relatively simple task of weighing two debaters on a single issue. Rather, Shaffer's essay challenges some of the assumptions and arguments

Lynda Norene Shaffer, "Southernization," *Journal of World History* 5 (Spring 1994): 1–21.

made by White and many other historians when they discuss the history of technology. What are some of the assumptions and arguments of White that Shaffer challenges? Which essay provides a more satisfying explanation of the origins of modern science and technology?

The term *Southernization* is a new one. It is used here to refer to a multifaceted process that began in Southern Asia and spread from there to various other places around the globe. The process included so many interrelated strands of development that it is impossible to do more here than sketch out the general outlines of a few of them. Among the most important that will be omitted from this discussion are the metallurgical, the medical, and the literary. Those included are the development of mathematics; the production and marketing of subtropical or tropical spices; the pioneering of new trade routes; the cultivation, processing, and marketing of southern crops such as sugar and cotton; and the development of various related technologies.

The term *Southernization* is meant to be analogous to *Westernization*. Westernization refers to certain developments that first occurred in western Europe. Those developments changed Europe and eventually spread to other places and changed them as well. In the same way, southernization changed Southern Asia and later spread to other areas, which then underwent a process of change.

Southernization was well under way in Southern Asia by the fifth century C.E., during the reign of India's Gupta kings (320–535 C.E.). It was by that time already spreading to China. In the eighth century various elements characteristic of Southernization began spreading through the lands of the Muslim caliphates. Both in China and in the lands of the caliphate, the process led to dramatic changes, and by the year 1200 it was beginning to have an impact on the Christian Mediterranean. One could argue that within the Northern Hemisphere, by this time the process of Southernization had created an Eastern Hemisphere characterized by a rich south and a north that was poor in comparison. And one might even go so far as to suggest that in Europe and its colonies, the process of Southernization laid the foundation for Westernization.

The Indian Beginning

Southernization was the result of developments that took place in many parts of southern Asia, both on the Indian subcontinent and in Southeast Asia. By the time of the Gupta kings, several of its constituent parts already had a long history in India. Perhaps the oldest strand in the process was the cultivation of cotton and the production of cotton textiles for export. Cotton was first domesticated in the Indus River valley some time between 2300 and 1760 B.C.E., and by the second millennium B.C.E., the Indians had begun to develop sophisticated dyeing techniques. During these early millennia Indus River valley merchants are known to have lived in Mesopotamia, where they sold cotton textiles.

In the first century C.E. Egypt became an important overseas market for Indian cottons. By the next century there was a strong demand for these textiles both in the Mediterranean and in East Africa, and by the fifth century they were being traded in Southeast Asia. The Indian textile trade continued to grow throughout the next millennium. Even after the arrival of European ships in Asian ports at the turn of the sixteenth century, it continued unscathed. According to one textile expert, "India virtually clothed the world" by the mid-eighteenth century. The subcontinent's position was not undermined until Britain's Industrial Revolution, when steam engines began to power the production of cotton textiles.

Another strand in the process of Southernization, the search for new sources of bullion, can be traced back in India to the end of the Mauryan Empire (321–185 B.C.E.). During Mauryan rule Siberia had been India's main source of gold, but nomadic disturbances in Central Asia disrupted the traffic between Siberia and India at about the time that the Mauryans fell. Indian sailors then began to travel to the Malay peninsula and the islands of Indonesia in search of an alternative source, which they most likely "discovered" with the help of local peoples who knew the sites. (This is generally the case with bullion discoveries, including those made by Arabs and Europeans.) What the Indians (and others later on) did do was introduce this gold to international trade routes.

The Indians' search for gold may also have led them to the shores of Africa. Although its interpretation is controversial, some archaeological evidence suggests the existence of Indian influence on parts of East Africa as early as 300 C.E. There is also one report that gold was being sought in East Africa by Ethiopian merchants, who were among India's most important trading partners.

The sixth-century Byzantine geographer Cosmas Indicopleustes described Ethiopian merchants who went to some location inland from the East African coast to obtain gold. "Every other year they would sail far to the south, then march inland, and in return for various made-up articles they would come back laden with ingots of gold." The fact that the expeditions left every other year suggests that it took two years to get to their destination and return. If so, their destination, even at this early date, may have been Zimbabwe. The wind patterns are such that sailors who ride the monsoon south as far as Kilwa can catch the return monsoon to the Red Sea area within the same year. But if they go be-

yond Kilwa to the Zambezi River, from which they might go inland to Zimbabwe, they cannot return until the following year.

Indian voyages on the Indian Ocean were part of a more general development, more or less contemporary with the Mauryan Empire, in which sailors of various nationalities began to knit together the shores of the "Southern Ocean," a Chinese term referring to all the waters from the South China Sea to the eastern coast of Africa. During this period there is no doubt that the most intrepid sailors were the Malays, peoples who lived in what is now Malaysia, Indonesia, the southeastern coast of Vietnam, and the Philippines.

Sometime before 300 B.C.E. Malay sailors began to ride the monsoons, the seasonal winds that blow off the continent of Asia in the colder months and onto its shores in the warmer months. Chinese records indicate that by the third century B.C.E. "Kunlun" sailors, the Chinese term for the Malay seamen, were sailing north to the southern coasts of China. They may also have been sailing east to India, through the straits now called Malacca and Sunda. If so they may have been the first to establish contact between India and Southeast Asia.

Malay sailors had reached the eastern coast of Africa at least by the first century B.C.E., if not earlier. Their presence in East African waters is testified to by the peoples of Madagascar, who still speak a Malayo-Polynesian language. Some evidence also suggests that Malay sailors had settled in the Red Sea area. Indeed, it appears that they were the first to develop a long-distance trade in a southern spice. In the last centuries B.C.E., if not earlier, Malay sailors were delivering cinnamon from South China Sea ports to East Africa and the Red Sea.

By about 400 C.E. Malay sailors could be found two-thirds of the way around the world, from Easter Island to East Africa. They rode the monsoons without a compass, out of sight of land, and often at latitudes below the equator where the northern pole star cannot be seen. They navigated by the wind and the stars, by cloud formations, the color of the water, and swell and wave patterns on the ocean's surface. They could discern the presence of an island some thirty miles from its shores by noting the behavior of birds, the animal and plant life in the water, and the swell and wave patterns. Given their manner of sailing, their most likely route to Africa and the Red Sea would have been by way of the island clusters, the Maldives, the Chagos, the Seychelles, and the Comoros.

Malay ships used balance lug sails, which were square in shape and mounted so that they could pivot. This made it possible for sailors to tack against the wind, that is, to sail into the wind by going diagonally against it, first one way and then the other. Due to the way the sails were mounted, they appeared somewhat triangular in shape, and thus the Malays' balance lug sail may well be the prototype of the triangular lateen, which can also be used to tack against the wind. The latter was

invented by both the Polynesians to the Malays' east and by the Arabs to their west, both of whom had ample opportunity to see the Malays' ships in action.

It appears that the pepper trade developed after the cinnamon trade. In the first century C.E. southern India began supplying the Mediterranean with large quantities of pepper. Thereafter, Indian merchants could be found living on the island of Socotra, near the mouth of the Red Sea, and Greek-speaking sailors, including the anonymous author of the *Periplus of the Erythraean Sea,* could be found sailing in the Red Sea and riding the monsoons from there to India.

Indian traders and shippers and Malay sailors were also responsible for opening up an all-sea route to China. The traders' desire for silk drew them out into dangerous waters in search of a more direct way to its source. By the second century C.E. Indian merchants could make the trip by sea, but the route was slow, and it took at least two years to make a round trip. Merchants leaving from India's eastern coast rounded the shores of the Bay of Bengal. When they came to the Isthmus of Kra, the narrowest part of the Malay peninsula, the ships were unloaded, and the goods were portaged across to the Gulf of Thailand. The cargo was then reloaded on ships that rounded the gulf until they reached Funan, a kingdom on what is now the Kampuchea-Vietnam border. There they had to wait for the winds to shift, before embarking upon a ship that rode the monsoon to China.

Some time before 400 C.E. travelers began to use a new all-sea route to China, a route that went around the Malay peninsula and thus avoided the Isthmus of Kra portage. The ships left from Sri Lanka and sailed before the monsoon, far from any coasts, through either the Strait of Malacca or the Strait of Sunda into the Java Sea. After waiting in the Java Sea port for the winds to shift, they rode the monsoon to southern China. The most likely developers of this route were Malay sailors, since the new stopover ports were located within their territories.

Not until the latter part of the fourth century, at about the same time as the new all-sea route began to direct commercial traffic through the Java Sea, did the fine spices — cloves, nutmeg, and mace — begin to assume importance on international markets. These rare and expensive spices came from the Moluccas, several island groups about a thousand miles east of Java. Cloves were produced on about five minuscule islands off the western coast of Halmahera; nutmeg and mace came from only a few of the Banda Islands, some ten islands with a total area of seventeen square miles, located in the middle of the Banda Sea. Until 1621 these Moluccan islands were the only places in the world able to produce cloves, nutmeg, and mace in commercial quantities. The Moluccan producers themselves brought their spices to the international markets of the Java Sea ports and created the market for them.

It was also during the time of the Gupta kings, around 350 C.E., that the Indians discovered how to crystallize sugar. There is considerable disagreement about where sugar was first domesticated. Some believe that the plant was native to New Guinea and domesticated there, and others argue that it was domesticated by Southeast Asian peoples living in what is now southern China. In any case, sugar cultivation spread to the Indian subcontinent. Sugar, however, did not become an important item of trade until the Indians discovered how to turn sugarcane juice into granulated crystals that could be easily stored and transported. This was a momentous development, and it may have been encouraged by Indian sailing, for sugar and clarified butter (ghee) were among the dietary mainstays of Indian sailors.

The Indians also laid the foundation for modern mathematics during the time of the Guptas. Western numerals, which the Europeans called Arabic since they acquired them from the Arabs, actually come from India. (The Arabs call them Hindi numbers.) The most significant feature of the Indian system was the invention of the zero as a number concept. The oldest extant treatise that uses the zero in the modern way is a mathematical appendix attached to Aryabhata's text on astronomy, which is dated 499 C.E.

The Indian zero made the place-value system of writing numbers superior to all others. Without it, the use of this system, base ten or otherwise, was fraught with difficulties and did not seem any better than alternative systems. With the zero the Indians were able to perform calculations rapidly and accurately, to perform much more complicated calculations, and to discern mathematical relationships more aptly. These numerals and the mathematics that the Indians developed with them are now universal — just one indication of the global significance of Southernization.

As a result of these developments India acquired a reputation as a place of marvels, a reputation that was maintained for many centuries after the Gupta dynasty fell. As late as the ninth century Amr ibn Bahr al Jahiz (c. 776–868), one of the most influential writers of Arabic, had the following to say about India:

> As regards the Indians, they are among the leaders in astronomy, mathematics — in particular, they have Indian numerals — and medicine; they alone possess the secrets of the latter, and use them to practice some remarkable forms of treatment. They have the art of carving statues and painted figures. They possess the game of chess, which is the noblest of games and requires more judgment and intelligence than any other. They make Kedah swords, and excel in their use. They have splendid music. . . . They possess a script capable of expressing the sounds of all languages, as well as many numerals. They have a great deal of poetry, many long treatises, and a deep understanding of

philosophy and letters; the book *Kalila wa-Dimna* originated with them. They are intelligent and courageous. . . . Their sound judgment and sensible habits led them to invent pins, cork, toothpicks, the drape of clothes, and the dyeing of hair. They are handsome, attractive, and forbearing; their women are proverbial; and their country produces the matchless Indian aloes which are supplied to kings. They were the originators of the science of *fikr,* by which a poison can be counteracted after it has been used, and of astronomical reckoning, subsequently adopted by the rest of the world. When Adam descended from Paradise, it was to their land that he made his way.

The Southernization of China

These Southern Asian developments began to have a significant impact on China after 350 C.E. The Han dynasty had fallen in 221 C.E., and for more than 350 years thereafter China was ruled by an ever-changing collection of regional kingdoms. During these centuries Buddhism became increasingly important in China, Buddhist monasteries spread throughout the disunited realm, and cultural exchange between India and China grew accordingly. By 581, when the Sui dynasty reunited the empire, processes associated with Southernization had already had a major impact on China. The influence of Southernization continued during the T'ang (618–906) and Sung (960–1279) dynasties. One might even go so far as to suggest that the process of Southernization underlay the revolutionary social, political, economic, and technological developments of the T'ang and Sung.

The Chinese reformed their mathematics, incorporating the advantages of the Indian system, even though they did not adopt the Indian numerals at that time. They then went on to develop an advanced mathematics, which was flourishing by the time of the Sung dynasty. Cotton and indigo became well established, giving rise to the blue-black peasant garb that is still omnipresent in China. Also in the Sung period the Chinese first developed cotton canvas, which they used to make a more efficient sail for ocean-going ships.

Although sugar had long been grown in some parts of southern China it did not become an important crop in this region until the process of Southernization was well under way. The process also introduced new varieties of rice. The most important of these was what the Chinese called Champa rice, since it came to China from Champa, a Malay kingdom located on what is now the southeastern coast of Vietnam. Champa rice was a drought-resistant, early ripening variety that made it possible to extend cultivation up well-watered hillsides, thereby doubling the area of rice cultivation in China. . . .

In southern China the further development of rice production brought significant changes in the landscape. Before the introduction of Champa rice, rice cultivation had been confined to lowlands, deltas, basins, and river valleys. Once Champa rice was introduced and rice cultivation spread up the hillsides, the Chinese began systematic terracing and made use of sophisticated techniques of water control on mountain slopes. Between the mid-eighth and the early twelfth century the population of southern China tripled, and the total Chinese population doubled. According to Sung dynasty household registration figures for 1102 and 1110 — figures that Sung dynasty specialists have shown to be reliable — there were 100 million people in China by the first decade of the twelfth century.

Before the process of Southernization, northern China had always been predominant, intellectually, socially, and politically. The imperial center of gravity was clearly in the north, and the southern part of China was perceived as a frontier area. But Southernization changed this situation dramatically. By 600, southern China was well on its way to becoming the most prosperous and most commercial part of the empire. The most telling evidence for this is the construction of the Grand Canal, which was completed around 610, during the Sui dynasty. Even though the rulers of the Sui had managed to put the pieces of the empire back together in 581 and rule the whole of China again from a single northern capital, they were dependent on the new southern crops. Thus it is no coincidence that this dynasty felt the need to build a canal that could deliver southern rice to northern cities.

The T'ang dynasty, when Buddhist influence in China was especially strong, saw two exceedingly important technological innovations — the invention of printing and gunpowder. These developments may also be linked to Southernization. Printing seems to have developed within the walls of Buddhist monasteries between 700 and 750, and subtropical Sichuan was one of the earliest centers of the art. The invention of gunpowder in China by Taoist alchemists in the ninth century may also be related to the linkages between India and China created by Buddhism. In 644 an Indian monk identified soils in China that contained saltpeter and demonstrated the purple flame that results from its ignition. As early as 919 C.E. gunpowder was used as an igniter in a flamethrower, and the tenth century also saw the use of flaming arrows, rockets, and bombs thrown by catapults. The earliest evidence of a cannon or bombard (1127) has been found in Sichuan, quite near the Tibetan border, across the Himalayas from India.

By the time of the Sung the Chinese also had perfected the "south-pointing needle," otherwise known as the compass. Various prototypes of the compass had existed in China from the third century B.C.E., but the new version developed during the Sung was particularly well suited for navigation. Soon Chinese mariners were using the south-pointing needle on the oceans, publishing "needle charts" for the benefit of sea captains, and following "needle routes" on the Southern Ocean.

Once the Chinese had the compass they, like Columbus, set out to find a direct route to the spice markets of Java and ultimately to the Spice Islands in the Moluccas. Unlike Columbus, they found them. They did not bump into an obstacle, now known as the Western Hemisphere, on their way, since it was not located between China and the Spice Islands. If it had been so situated, the Chinese would have found it some 500 years before Columbus.

Cities on China's southern coasts became centers of overseas commerce. Silk remained an important export, and by the T'ang dynasty it had been joined by a true porcelain, which was developed in China sometime before 400 C.E. China and its East Asian neighbors had a monopoly on the manufacture of true porcelain until the early eighteenth century. Many attempts were made to imitate it, and some of the resulting imitations were economically and stylistically important. China's southern ports were also exporting to Southeast Asia large quantities of ordinary consumer goods, including iron hardware, such as needles, scissors, and cooking pots. Although iron manufacturing was concentrated in the north, the large quantity of goods produced was a direct result of the size of the market in southern China and overseas. Until the British Industrial Revolution of the eighteenth century, no other place ever equaled the iron production of Sung China.

The Muslim Caliphates

In the seventh century C.E., Arab cavalries, recently converted to the new religion of Islam, conquered eastern and southern Mediterranean shores that had been Byzantine (and Christian), as well as the Sassanian empire (Zoroastrian) in what is now Iraq and Iran. In the eighth century they went on to conquer Spain and Turko-Iranian areas of Central Asia, as well as northwestern India. Once established on the Indian frontier, they became acquainted with many of the elements of Southernization.

The Arabs were responsible for the spread of many important crops, developed or improved in India, to the Middle East, North Africa, and Islamic Spain. Among the most important were sugar, cotton, and citrus fruits. Although sugarcane and cotton cultivation may have spread to Iraq and Ethiopia before the Arab conquests, only after the establishment of the caliphates did these southern crops have a major impact throughout the Middle East and North Africa.

The Arabs were the first to import large numbers of enslaved Africans in order to produce sugar. Fields in the vicinity of Basra, at the northern end of the Persian Gulf, were the most important sugar-producing areas within the caliphates, but before this land could be used, it had to be desalinated. To accomplish this task, the Arabs imported East African (Zanj) slaves. This African community remained in the area, where they worked as agricultural laborers. The famous writer al Jahiz, whose essay on India was quoted earlier, was a descendant of Zanj slaves. In 869, one year after his death, the Zanj slaves in Iraq rebelled. It took the caliphate fifteen years of hard fighting to defeat them, and thereafter Muslim owners rarely used slaves for purposes that would require their concentration in large numbers.

The Arabs were responsible for moving sugarcane cultivation and sugar manufacturing westward from southern Iraq into other relatively arid lands. Growers had to adapt the plant to new conditions, and they had to develop more efficient irrigation technologies. By 1000 or so sugarcane had become an important crop in the Yemen; in Arabian oases; in irrigated areas of Syria, Lebanon, Palestine, Egypt, and the Mahgrib; in Spain; and on Mediterranean islands controlled by Muslims. By the tenth century cotton also had become a major crop in the lands of the caliphate, from Iran and Central Asia to Spain and the Mediterranean islands. Cotton industries sprang up wherever the plant was cultivated, producing for both local and distant markets. . . .

Under Arab auspices, Indian mathematics followed the same routes as the crops. Al-Kharazmi (c. 780–847) introduced Indian mathematics to the Arabic-reading world in his *Treatise on Calculation with the Hindu Numerals,* written around 825. Mathematicians within the caliphates then could draw upon the Indian tradition, as well as the Greek and Persian. On this foundation Muslim scientists of many nationalities, including al-Battani (d. 929), who came from the northern reaches of the Mesopotamian plain, and the Persian Omar Khayyám (d. 1123), made remarkable advances in both algebra and trigonometry.

The Arab conquests also led to an increase in long-distance commerce and the "discovery" of new sources of bullion. Soon after the Abbasid caliphate established its capital at Baghdad, the caliph al-Mansur (r. 745–75) reportedly remarked, "This is the Tigris; there is no obstacle between us and China; everything on the sea can come to us." By this time Arab ships were plying the maritime routes from the Persian Gulf to China, and they soon outnumbered all others using these routes. By the ninth century they had acquired the compass (in China, most likely), and they may well have been the first to use it for marine navigation, since the Chinese do not seem to have used it for this purpose until after the tenth century.

. . . Thus it was that the Arabs "pioneered" or improved an existing long-distance route across the Sahara, an ocean of sand rather than water. Routes across this desert had always existed, and trade and other contacts between West Africa and the Mediterranean date back at least to the Phoenician period. Still, the numbers of people and animals crossing this great ocean of sand were limited until the eighth century when Arabs, desiring to go directly to the source of the gold, prompted an expansion of trade across the Sahara. Also during the eighth century Abdul al-Rahman, an Arab ruler of Morocco, sponsored the construction of wells on the trans-Saharan route from Sijilmasa to Wadidara to facilitate this traffic. This Arab "discovery" of West African gold eventually doubled the amount of gold in international circulation. East Africa, too, became a source of gold for the Arabs. By the tenth century Kilwa had become an important source of Zimbabwean gold.

Developments after 1200: The Mongolian Conquest and the Southernization of the European Mediterranean

By 1200 the process of Southernization had created a prosperous south from China to the Muslim Mediterranean. Although mathematics, the pioneering of new ocean routes, and "discoveries" of bullion are not inextricably connected to locations within forty degrees of the equator, several crucial elements in the process of Southernization were closely linked to latitude. Cotton generally does not grow above the fortieth parallel. Sugar, cinnamon, and pepper are tropical or subtropical crops, and the fine spices will grow only on particular tropical islands. Thus for many centuries the more southern parts of Asia and the Muslim Mediterranean enjoyed the profits that these developments brought, while locations that were too far north to grow these southern crops were unable to participate in such lucrative agricultural enterprises.

The process of Southernization reached its zenith after 1200, in large part because of the tumultuous events of the thirteenth century. During that century in both hemispheres there were major transformations in the distribution of power, wealth, and prestige. In the Western Hemisphere several great powers went down. Cahokia (near East St. Louis, Illinois), which for three centuries had been the largest and most influential of the Mississippian mound-building centers, declined after 1200, and in Mexico Toltec power collapsed. In the Mediterranean the prestige of the Byzantine empire was destroyed when Venetians seized its capital in 1204. From 1212 to 1270 the Christians conquered southern Spain, except for Granada. In West Africa, Ghana fell to Sosso, and so did Mali, one of Ghana's allies. But by about 1230 Mali, in the process of seeking its own revenge, had created an empire even larger than Ghana's. At the same time Zimbabwe was also becoming a major power in southern Africa.

The grandest conquerors of the thirteenth century were the Central Asians. Turkish invaders established the Delhi sultanate in India. Mongolian cavalries devastated Baghdad, the seat of the Abbasid caliphate since the eighth century, and they captured Kiev, further weakening Byzantium. By the end of the century they had captured China, Korea, and parts of mainland Southeast Asia as well.

Because the Mongols were pagans at the time of their conquests, the western Europeans cheered them on as they laid waste to one after another Muslim center of power in the Middle East. The Mongols were stopped only when they encountered the Mamluks of Egypt at Damascus. In East Asia and Southeast Asia only the Japanese and the Javanese were able to defeat them. The victors in Java went on to found Majapahit, whose power and prestige then spread through maritime Southeast Asia.

Both hemispheres were reorganized profoundly during this turmoil. Many places that had flourished were toppled, and power gravitated to new locales. In the Eastern Hemisphere the Central Asian conquerors had done great damage to traditional southern centers just about everywhere, except in Africa, southern China, southern India, and maritime Southeast Asia. At the same time the Mongols' control of overland routes between Europe and Asia in the thirteenth and early fourteenth centuries fostered unprecedented contacts between Europeans and peoples from those areas that had long been southernized. Marco Polo's long sojourn in Yüan Dynasty China is just one example of such interaction.

Under the Mongols overland trade routes in Asia shifted north and converged on the Black Sea. After the Genoese helped the Byzantines to retake Constantinople from the Venetians in 1261, the Genoese were granted special privileges of trade in the Black Sea. Italy then became directly linked to the Mongolian routes. Genoese traders were among the first and were certainly the most numerous to open up trade with the Mongolian states in southern Russia and Iran. In the words of one Western historian, in their Black Sea colonies they "admitted to citizenship" people of many nationalities, including those of "strange background and questionable belief," and they "wound up christening children of the best ancestry with such uncanny names as Saladin, Hethum, or Hulugu."

Such contacts contributed to the Southernization of the Christian Mediterranean during this period of Mongolian hegemony. Although European conquerors sometimes had taken over sugar and cotton lands in the Middle East during the Crusades, not until some time after 1200 did the European-held Mediterranean islands become important exporters. Also after 1200 Indian mathematics began to have a significant impact in Europe. Before that time a few western European scholars had become acquainted with Indian numerals in Spain, where the works of al-Kharazmi, al-Battani, and other mathematicians had been translated into Latin. Nevertheless, Indian numerals and mathematics did not become important in western Europe until the thirteenth century after the book *Liber abaci* (1202), written by Leonardo Fibonacci of Pisa (c. 1170–1250), introduced them to the commercial centers of Italy. Leonardo had grown up in North Africa (in what is now Bejala, Algeria), where his father, consul over the Pisan merchants in that port, had sent him to study calculation with an Arab master.

In the seventeenth century, when Francis Bacon observed the "force and virtue and consequences of discoveries," he singled out three technologies in particular that "have changed the whole face and state of things throughout the world." These were all Chinese inventions — the compass, printing, and gunpowder. All three were first acquired by Europeans during this time of hemispheric reorganization.

It was most likely the Arabs who introduced the compass to Mediterranean waters, either at the end of the twelfth or in the thirteenth century. Block printing, gunpowder, and cannon appeared first in Italy in the fourteenth century, apparently after making a single great leap from Mongolian-held regions of East Asia to Italy. How this great leap was accomplished is not known, but the most likely scenario is one suggested by Lynn White Jr., in an article concerning how various other Southern (rather than Eastern) Asian technologies reached western Europe at about this time. He thought it most likely that they were introduced by "Tatar" slaves, Lama Buddhists from the frontiers of China whom the Genoese purchased in Black Sea marts and delivered to Italy. By 1450 when this trade reached its peak, there were thousands of these Asian slaves in every major Italian city.

Yet another consequence of the increased traffic and communication on the more northern trade routes traversing the Eurasian steppe was the transmission of the bubonic plague from China to the Black Sea. The plague had broken out first in China in 1331, and apparently rats and lice infected with the disease rode westward in the saddlebags of Mongolian post messengers, horsemen who were capable of traveling one hundred miles per day. By 1346 it had reached a Black Sea port, whence it made its way to the Middle East and Europe.

During the latter part of the fourteenth century the unity of the Mongolian empire began to disintegrate, and new regional powers began to emerge in its wake. Throughout much of Asia the chief beneficiaries of imperial disintegration were Turkic or Turko-Mongolian powers of the Muslim faith. The importance of Islam in Africa was also growing at this time, and the peoples of Southeast Asia, from the Malay peninsula to the southern Philippines, were converting to the faith.

Indeed, the world's most obvious dynamic in the centuries before Columbus was the expansion of the Islamic faith. Under Turkish auspices Islam was even spreading into eastern Europe, a development marked by the Ottoman conquest of Constantinople in 1453. This traumatic event lent a special urgency to Iberian expansion. The Iberians came to see themselves as the chosen defenders of Christendom.

Ever since the twelfth century, while Christian Byzantium had been losing Anatolia and parts of southeastern Europe to Islam, they had been retaking the Iberian peninsula for Christendom.

One way to weaken the Ottomans and Islam was to go around the North African Muslims and find a new oceanic route to the source of West African gold. Before the Portuguese efforts, sailing routes had never developed off the western shore of Africa, since the winds there blow in the same direction all year long, from north to south. (Earlier European sailors could have gone to West Africa, but they would not have been able to return home.)

The Portuguese success would have been impossible without the Chinese compass, Arabic tables indicating the declination of the noonday sun at various latitudes, and the lateen sail, which was also an Arab innovation. The Portuguese caravels were of mixed, or multiple, ancestry, with a traditional Atlantic hull and a rigging that combined the traditional Atlantic square sail with the lateen sail of Southern Ocean provenance. With the lateen sail the Portuguese could tack against the wind for the trip homeward.

The new route to West Africa led to Portugal's rounding of Africa and direct participation in Southern Ocean trade. While making the voyages to West Africa, European sailors learned the wind patterns and ocean currents west of Africa, knowledge that made the Columbian voyages possible. The Portuguese moved the sugarcane plant from Sicily to Madeira, in the Atlantic, and they found new sources of gold, first in West Africa and then in East Africa. Given that there was little demand in Southern Ocean ports for European trade goods, they would not have been able to sustain their Asian trade without this African gold.

The Rise of Europe's North

The rise of the north, or more precisely, the rise of Europe's northwest, began with the appropriation of those elements of Southernization that were not confined by geography. In the wake of their southern European neighbors, they became partially southernized, but they could not engage in all aspects of the process due to their distance from the equator. Full Southernization and the wealth that we now associate with northwestern Europe came about only after their outright seizure of tropical and subtropical territories and their rounding of Africa and participation in Southern Ocean trade. . . .

Even though the significance of indigenous developments in the rise of northwestern Europe should not be minimized, it should be emphasized that many of the most important causes of the rise of the West are not to be found within the bounds of Europe. Rather, they are the result of the transformation of western Europe's relationships with other regions of the Eastern Hemisphere. Europe began its rise only after the thirteenth-century reorganization of the Eastern Hemisphere facilitated its Southernization, and Europe's northwest did not rise until it too was reaping the profits of Southernization. Thus the rise of the North Atlantic powers should not be oversimplified so that it appears to be an isolated and solely European phenomenon, with roots that spread no farther afield than Greece. Rather, it should be portrayed as one part of a hemisphere-wide process, in which a northwestern Europe ran to catch up with a more developed south — a race not completed until the eighteenth century.

67

Image from a Cistercian Manuscript, Twelfth Century

Monk Chopping Tree

This image of a monk chopping down a tree while his lay servant prunes the branches is from a manuscript of the Cistercian order of monks, from the twelfth century. The Cistercians, more than other orders, spoke out in favor of conserving forest resources, but they also celebrated manual labor. Does this image indicate that the monks were in favor of forest clearance?

Thinking Historically

Does this image lend support to White's argument in selection 65? Why or why not? If there were many such images, would visual evidence like this convince you of White's argument? Would it be more convincing if almost all European images of trees showed someone chopping them down and virtually no Chinese tree images showed that? In other words, how much visual evidence would convince you of White's interpretation?

Image from a Cistercian manuscript, 12th c., monk chopping tree (Dijon, Bibliothèque municipale, MS 173), duplicated in *Cambridge Illustrated History of the Middle Ages*, Robert Fossier, ed. (Cambridge: Cambridge University Press, 1997), 72.

ad indaganda myſti
fortaſſe opiſ uacuare

ſacri eloqu
rium tam
ut utriuſc
hunc neq: r
deprimat
riç uacuit t
pe euiſ ſen
conceptioni
eas ad ſola
earu notit
Nonnulle r
tiſ inſeruit
luiſ penetr
nil inuenia
foriſ locum
ne quoq: n
ſignificatio
uirgaſ pop
linaſ· & ex
ticauit eaſ
hiſ que exp
apparuit·
uiridia pin
modū· colo
& ſubditur

Figure 11.1 Twelfth-Century Manuscript.
Source: Courtesy of Tresorier Principal
Municipal, Dijon.

68

Image from a French Calendar, Fifteenth Century

This French calendar scene for March is from the early fifteenth century. What sorts of activities does it show? How does it relate specifically to White's argument about the changing images of European calendars? (See p. 357.) The top half of the calendar shows a zodiac. In what ways are these images of nature different from those in the bottom half?

Thinking Historically

What technologies are shown here? Were any of these technologies particularly recent or European? Does this image merely illustrate White's argument, or does it support it to some extent? What other visual evidence would you want to see in order to be persuaded by White's argument?

___

From *Les trés riches heures du duc de Berry*, Giraudon, Musée de Condé.

Figure 11.2 French Calendar Scene.

Source: Bridgeman-Giraudon/Art Resource, NY.

69

FAN KUAN

Image of a Chinese Landscape

Travelers amid Mountains and Streams

Landscape was a frequent subject for Chinese painters. This painting is by Fan Kuan (c. 990–1020). What signs of human habitation can you see? What, if anything, does this image suggest to you about the view of the natural world in Chinese art and culture?

Thinking Historically

Does the popularity and prestige of this kind of landscape painting in China lend support to White's thesis? Does this sort of painting together with naturalist philosophies like Taoism persuade us of White's thesis? Does the relative absence of this sort of painting from Europe lend credence to White's argument?

Fan Kuan, *Travelers amid Mountains and Streams,* National Palace Museum, Taiwan, People's Republic of China; from *Cambridge Illustrated History of China,* Patricia Buckley Ebrey, ed. (Cambridge: Cambridge University Press, 1996), 162.

Figure 11.3 Travelers Amid Mountains and Streams.

Source: The National Palace Museum, Taipei, Taiwan, Republic of China.

$$\boxed{70}$$

Image of a Chinese *Feng-Shui* Master

Although the Chinese celebrated the natural landscape in their paintings, they also created drawings that showcased their advanced technologies. The Chinese made and used the compass (as well as paper, printing, and gunpowder) long before Europeans. Instead of using it to subdue the natural world, however, they used it to find harmony with nature, specifically through the practice of *feng-shui*. *Feng-shui*, which literally means wind over water, is the Chinese art of determining the best position and placement of structures such as houses within the natural environment. In the following image we see a type of compass used in the work of a Chinese *feng-shui* master. Before building, the *feng-shui* master would use instruments like this to ascertain the flow of energy (*chi*) on the site, resulting in new buildings that would be in harmony with, rather than obstruct, this flow. How might a compass detect energy? How was the Chinese use of a compass-like device different from the modern scientific use of the compass?

Thinking Historically

An image has many elements to read. What information is revealed about Chinese society in this image, in addition to the scientific devices? What significance do you attach to the artist's depiction of humans and the natural setting? In what ways does this image support Lynn White Jr.'s argument? In what ways does it challenge his interpretation? On balance, do you find it more supportive or critical of White's position?

Joseph Needham, *Science and Civilization in China,* vol. 2 (Cambridge: Cambridge University Press, 1956), 362.

Figure 11.4 Chinese *Feng-Shui* Master.

REFLECTIONS

The differing approaches to explaining the roots of modernity, represented in this chapter by White and Shaffer, reflect generational differences between the historians. White, whose training before 1960 emphasized the homogeneity and importance of Western Civilization (largely Europe and North America), represents an earlier generation of historians; Shaffer became an historian more recently in a world made both smaller by transportation and communication technologies and more knowable by the amount of research in the last few decades.

This difference in approach is, in part, the legacy of different wars. The idea of "Western Civilization" developed after World War I — first in American universities — as a way to explain and understand the new leadership role of the United States in an Atlantic alliance. (The first version of the civilization course, "War Aims," was taught at Columbia University in 1919.) Western civilization was the standard introduction to history for most college students from the 1930s to the 1960s.

The Cold War that developed between the United States (allied with Europe) and the Soviet Union (now Russia) after World War II prompted studies of specific areas and "non-Western" studies at universities in the United States. America's assumption of global leadership, combined with an influx of students and citizens from a new group of Asian and Latin American immigrants, brought to the fore interest in and knowledge of the histories of Asia, Africa, and Latin America. These areas of the world were virtually omitted from history, geography, and other courses in the United States prior to 1960.

The differences between the selections by White and Shaffer might be attributed to new knowledge. Today, world history is something that can be readily understood and taught. We can recognize global connections that simply were not obvious even thirty years ago thanks to satellite photos, coordinated research, instantaneous global communication, and the fading of national boundaries.

This new awareness has led some world historians to dismiss a "Western Civilization" approach as dated and Eurocentric. E. L. Jones, for example, in *Recurring Growth* (Oxford, 1988) criticizes the great economist John Maynard Keynes for having "a 'Western Civ' conception of history." He adds: "There was no room in it for the profound changes being made in China nor for the evidence of a progressive drift of ideas from China right across Eurasia, until at length they were embodied in the techniques of the red-haired barbarians of Europe." In the same book, Jones is expressly critical of White's thesis as a manifestation of this approach:

The assumption that there is something preternaturally malign about Christian attitudes toward nature is an aberrant opinion of the 1960s and 1970s. It has more to do with the self-abnegation of Western intellectuals than with real historical differences between cultures or religions. The evidence tends to be philosophical statements in the Christian literature rather than comparative data on how Christian and other societies actually treated the environment (pp. 60–61).

What do you make of this criticism? Does Jones overreact? Has the pendulum swung too far in rejecting European origins of modern science and the industrial revolution?

Our discussion of images was fairly elementary and inconclusive, but this might be a good time to reflect on the historical value of images of all kinds. Do you think that in research, for instance, you would find photographs more useful than paintings or drawings? Why? Of course, there were no photographs until the middle of the nineteenth century, but European painters of the Renaissance and seventeenth-century scientific revolution often painted with mirror-like naturalism. The Dutch painter Jan Vermeer (1632–1675) would often use a camera obscura (a darkened room-sized box with a small hole facing the subject that let in light and cast a reversed image of the subject on the back wall of the box), so the picture could be practically traced. Would a Vermeer be as useful historically as a photograph? Is it significant that Vermeer sought a mirror image and Fan Kuan did not?

12

"Barbarians" and Mongols

Mongol Eurasia, 1200–1350 C.E.

HISTORICAL CONTEXT

The ancient Greeks called any people who did not speak Greek "barbarians." For the Greeks, this term was both descriptive (foreign languages sounded to the Greeks like "barbar") and critical (foreigners were not Greek). In time, the term *barbarian* was applied with increasing criticism by the settled peoples of the Mediterranean to all of the nomadic peoples who came out of the enormous stretch of grasslands or steppe that stretched from eastern Europe to northern China. Periodic migrations or invasions of these nomads into the settled societies of China, India, and the Mediterranean fueled the stories and myths of their prowess and brutality. Successive waves of these barbarians were blamed for the fall of the Roman Empire, the Han dynasty, and (as we saw in Chapter 10) the Seljuk invasions of the Byzantine Empire and Muslim caliphate.

The Mongol[1] invasions of the thirteenth century (see Map 12.1) were simply another stage in the conflict between the pastoral people of the great Eurasian steppe and the settled people of farms and cities. But this time was different. In previous eras, population or grazing pressures forced one group of people to bump another, setting off chain reactions of expansion that eventually reached the great cities of China, the Middle East, India, and the Mediterranean. The Mongols organized a massive confederacy of peoples that, at least for a few generations, united the entire steppe under a single ruler. Mongols systematically conquered settlements from China to Europe, and ruled the largest empire the world had ever known.

---

[1] The term *Mongol* generally refers to the peoples of Mongolia in central Asia, whose language is Mongolian.

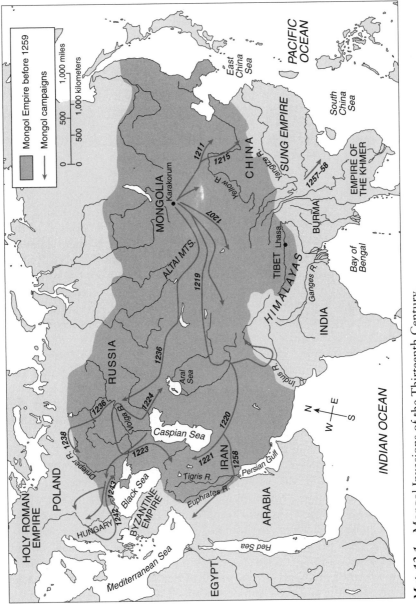

Map 12.1   Mongol Invasions of the Thirteenth Century.

In this chapter we ask: Who were the Mongols? While we pay some attention to the history of other nomadic peoples from the Eurasian grasslands, we do not focus on comparing the Mongols with other peoples. Rather, we examine how the Mongols viewed themselves and how other people saw them. Perhaps somewhere between these two accounts, we will discover who and what they were.

THINKING HISTORICALLY
Making Moral Judgments about History

While not all outside observers and non-Mongol historians have been critical of the Mongols, the Mongols were widely condemned in their heyday (1206–1348) and have been since. And yet, as their defenders are quick to point out, there are reasons to question the objectivity of all of this bad press. Initial criticism of course came from the settled, literate, wealthy, urban societies that the Mongols conquered. These city observers and historians were not good losers. Try to imagine, if you were conquered, how you would write about your conqueror. Would you be biased? Would you be right?

The role of moral or ethical judgments in history is a thorny issue. For the most part, historians believe they should not let their own sense of what is right and wrong intrude on the way they describe and explain the past. This may remain an elusive goal, but it is especially difficult to achieve when the historian believes that the facts demonstrate that one side was the aggressor, the other the victim. Even if we try to be objective, the language we use tends to be full of moral judgment, explicitly or implicitly. Do we call it a migration or an invasion? Do we speak of the dead or the slaughtered? And even if the historian can find a neutral vocabulary, there are some who would say that she should not. Perhaps outrageous acts require outrage, and bland description dulls their impact. These are some of the questions you will consider as you read these selections. What role does moral judgment play in a particular description or interpretation? What role should it play? Can historians be morally neutral? Should they be? Does the audience matter? Do the Mongols and their subjects need the same or different histories?

71

GREGORY GUZMAN

Were the Barbarians
a Negative or Positive Factor
in Ancient and Medieval History?

Gregory Guzman is a modern world historian, specializing in the
Middle Ages and the Mongols. In this essay he sets the treatment of
Mongol history within the context of "barbarian history."

How did the horse shape life on the steppe? How effective were
these herders as rulers of settled societies? What were the achievements of the pastoral nomads, including the Mongols?

Thinking Historically

Why, according to Guzman, have most histories of the barbarians
made them look bad? Have city people or historians let their own
judgments block an appreciation of the achievements of pastoralists in
general and the Mongols in particular?

According to the general surveys of ancient and medieval history found
in most textbooks, barbarian peoples and/or primitive savages repeatedly invaded the early Eurasian civilized centers in Europe, the Middle
East, India, and China. All accounts of the early history of these four
civilizations contain recurrent references to attacks by such familiar and
famous barbarians as the Hittites, Hyksos, Kassites, Aryans, Scythians,
Sarmatians, Hsiung-nu, Huns, Germans, Turks, and Mongols, and they
also record the absorption and assimilation of these Inner Asian barbarian hordes into the respective cultures and lifestyles of the more advanced coastal civilizations. The early sources generally equate the barbarians with chaos and destruction. The barbarians are presented as evil
and despicable intruders, associated only with burning, pillaging, and
slaughtering, while the civilized peoples are portrayed as the good and
righteous forces of stability, order, and progress.

But it must be remembered that most of these early sources are not
objective; they are blatantly one-sided, biased accounts written by
members of the civilized societies. Thus, throughout recorded history,

Gregory Guzman, "Were the Barbarians a Negative or Positive Factor in Ancient and Medieval History?" *The Historian* L (August 1988): 558–72.

barbarians have consistently received bad press — bad PR to use the modern terminology. By definition, barbarians were illiterate, and thus they could not write their own version of events. All written records covering barbarian-civilized interaction came from the civilized peoples at war with the barbarians — often the sedentary peoples recently defeated and overwhelmed by those same barbarians. Irritated and angered coastal historians tended to record and emphasize only the negative aspects of their recent interaction with the barbarians. The following quotations clearly illustrate the tendency of the authors to condemn and denigrate the way their barbarian opponents looked and to associate them with the devil and evil, rather than to report with objectivity what actually happened.

> The Roman historian Ammianus Marcellinus, whose description is distorted by hatred and fear, described the barbarians as "two-footed beasts, seemingly chained to their horses from which they take their meat and drink, never touching a plough and having no houses."

> While living in Jerusalem, St. Jerome also left a vivid description of the Huns who " . . . filled the whole earth with slaughter and panic alike as they flittered hither and thither on their swift horses. . . . They were at hand everywhere before they were expected; by their speed they outstripped rumor, and they took pity neither upon religion nor rank nor age nor wailing childhood. Those who had just begun to live were compelled to die. . . ."

Such reports obviously made the barbarians look bad, while their nomadic habits and practices, which differed from those of the sedentary coastal peoples, were clearly portrayed as inferior and less advanced: the incarnation of evil itself. These horror-filled and biased descriptions were not the accounts of weak and defenseless peoples. Rather, they were written by the citizens of the most advanced and powerful states and empires in Europe, the Middle East, India, and China. The individual barbarian tribes were, nevertheless, able to attack and invade these strong and well-organized civilized states with relative impunity — pillaging and killing almost at will.

Several important questions, not addressed by the ancient and medieval historians, need to be answered here. Who were these barbarians? Why and how did they manage to repeatedly defeat and overwhelm so easily the wealthiest and most advanced civilizations of the day? And why were they so vehemently condemned and hated in recorded history, if these barbarian Davids were able to consistently defeat such mighty Goliath civilized centers? Since the rich and populous civilized states enjoyed tremendous advantages in the confrontations, why have the barbarians so often been denied the popular role of the underdog?

In the process of answering those questions, this study would like to suggest that maybe the barbarians were not really the "bad guys." While they may not deserve to be called the "good guys," they made a much more positive contribution to human civilization than presented in the grossly distorted written sources. The barbarians deserve much more credit than they have been given, for they created a complex pastoral lifestyle as an alternative to sedentary agriculture, and in that achievement they were not subhuman savages only out to loot, pillage, and destroy. As this study will show, the barbarians played a much more positive and constructive role in the development and diffusion of early human history than that with which they are usually credited.

Before proceeding further, it is necessary to identify these much-maligned barbarians and describe how their way of life and their basic practices differed from those of the sedentary coastal peoples in order to better evaluate the barbarian role and its impact on the history of humanity.

In terms of identity, the barbarians were the steppe nomads of Inner Asia or Central Eurasia. This area represents one of the toughest and most inhospitable places in the world in which to survive. The climate of the interior of the large Eurasian landmass is not moderated by the distant seas, resulting in extremes of climate, of hot and cold, wet and dry. It is an area of ice, forest, desert, and mountains — with bitter winds, dust, and poor soil. Unlike the coastal regions with their dependable moisture and warmth, the soil of Inner Asia was too cold, poor, and dry for agriculture; thus the sedentary urban lifestyle of the coastal civilized centers was not an option in the Eurasian heartland. The people living there had to be tough to endure such a hostile environment, where they constantly fought both nature and other people for survival.

Due to necessity, the people of Inner Asia were nomads, wandering in search of food and pasture, and they became herdsmen, shepherds, and warriors. These steppe nomads, the barbarians of recorded history, were frequently nothing more than migrants looking for new homes; these people needed little encouragement to seek safety, security, and better living conditions in the warm, rich, and fertile coastal civilization centers. Thus the steppe barbarians were not always savage marauders coming only to loot and pillage. Many of the so-called barbarian invaders constituted a surplus population which harsh Inner Asia could not support, or they represented whole tribes being pushed out of their ancestral homeland by stronger tribes behind them. At any rate, these repeated waves of nomadic peoples leaving the steppes soon encountered the coastal civilizations.

These Inner Asian barbarians were more or less harmless outsiders until the horse dramatically changed their lifestyle on the vast steppes. They adopted the pastoral system as the best way of providing for basic needs. The natural pasture provided by the steppe grassland proved ideal for grazing large herds and flocks of animals. Soon their whole life revolved around their animals; they became shepherds, herders, and keepers of beasts. . . .

The dominant feature of this emerging barbarian pastoralism was its mounted nature; it was essentially a horse culture by 1000 B.C. At first small horses were kept only for food and milk, but bigger horses eventually led to riding. Once an accomplished fact, mounted practices dramatically changed the lifestyle of the barbarian steppe peoples. Horseback riding made the tending of scattered herds faster and less tiring, and it enlarged the size of herds while increasing the range of pastoral movement. It also made possible, when necessary, the total migration of entire tribes and clans. Mastery of the horse reduced the vast expanses of steppe pasturage to more manageable proportions. Steppe nomads moved twice a year between traditional winter and summer pastures; the spring and fall were spent moving between the necessary grazing grounds. All peoples and possessions moved with regularity; the nomads became used to living in the saddle, so to speak.

The horse thus became the center of pastoral life on the steppes. The barbarian nomads could literally live off their animals which provided meat, milk, and hides for clothing, coverings, boots, etc. Tools and weapons were made from the bones and sinews, and dried dung was used as fuel. The barbarians ate, sold, negotiated, slept, and took care of body functions in the saddle as indicated in the following quotations: "From their horses, by day and night every one of that nation buys and sells, eats and drinks, and bowed over the narrow neck of the animal relaxes in a sleep so deep as to be accompanied by many dreams." "All the time they let themselves be carried by their horses. In that way they fight wars, participate in banquets, attend public and private business. On their back, they move, stand still, carry on trade, and converse." These mounted practices led to the emergence of the centaur motif in Middle Eastern art, as the civilized people tended to view the horse and rider as one inseparable unit.

Military action also became an integral part of nomadic steppe life. Warfare was simply cavalry action by the pastoral herdsmen who served as soldiers for the duration of the conflict. Steppe military service differed little from the normal, on-the-move pastoral life. Large-scale steppe alliances were hard to organize and even harder to hold together among the independent nomads. Such temporary alliances, called hordes, rose swiftly to great strength and power, but they usually declined and disintegrated just as quickly.

At any rate, these barbarian nomads were tough and hardy warriors. The horse gave them speed and mobility over both the light and heavily armed infantry of the civilized centers, but for this speed and mobility the barbarians gave up any type of defensive armor. They learned to guide their horses with their knees, since both arms needed to be free for the bow and arrow, their primary offensive weapon. By

1000 B.C. the compound bow was in common use by barbarians. This shorter bow could be handled with ease from horseback, and arrows could be shot up to three hundred yards with accuracy. As steppe hunters, all barbarians made excellent archers.

Early civilized armies had no cavalry. The famous Macedonian phalanx and the formidable Roman legions contained only light and heavily armed infantry. At first these brave foot soldiers had no tactical maneuvers to face and contain a barbarian cavalry charge. Even more devastating was the storm of arrows raining down upon them long before they could engage in the traditional hand-to-hand combat. The formidable steppe cavalry thus subjected civilized defenses to continuous pressure. Every nomad with a horse and bow was a potential frontline soldier who was tough, resourceful, and ferocious, whereas only a small percentage of the civilized population was equipped and trained for war. The nomadic lifestyle and the speed of the horse eliminated the need for expensive and heavy metal armor and its accompanying technological skills. Cavalry tactics gave an initial military advantage to the barbarians and the mounted horsemen won most of the early battles. The best defense against barbarian cavalry was an insurmountable obstacle, a wall. Ten- to twenty-foot-high walls of dirt, wood, or stone were built around cities and along some frontiers, i.e., the Great Wall of China. The old statement that Rome fell because China built a wall may not be such a simple overstatement after all.

Since they had the military advantage of cavalry tactics, the steppe nomads attacked and conquered various coastal civilizations with regularity. In a typical conquest, the victorious barbarians were the new military/political rulers. These new rulers possessed strengths obvious to all. The barbarians had vigorous and dynamic leadership; good, able, and charismatic leadership had been needed to organize the independent nomads into an effective horde in the first place. The new rulers had the complete loyalty of their followers; their group identity based on common blood and ancestors resulted in an intense personal and individual allegiance and commitment.

The first century after the initial conquest was usually an era of dynamic leadership, good government, and economic prosperity, as nomadic strengths mixed with the local advances and practices of that civilization. The new ruling family was often a fusion of the best of both sides as the barbarian victors married into the previous ruling dynasty. This brought forth an age of powerful and successful rulers, and produced an era of energetic leadership, good government, low taxes, agricultural revival, and peace. . . .

After this early period of revitalized and dynamic rule, slow decline usually set in. Royal vigor and ability sank as the rulers became soft, both mentally and physically. Without physical exercise and self-discipline, the rulers became overindulgent, instantly acquiring everything they wanted — excessive amounts of food or drink, harems, puppets, and yes-men as advisers. At the same time court rivalries and internal divisiveness began to emerge once the strong unity required for the conquest was no longer needed. A rivalry that often arose was between the ruler and various groups of his followers — his military, his bureaucracy, his harem (especially the queen mothers), his conquered subjects, and his old nomadic supporters. His steppe horsemen began to give first loyalty to their new family land rather than to their individual leader who was now weak, impaired, and soft. Such internal rivalries weakened the central government and led to chaos and civil wars. Thus, a civilized center was ripe for the next series of invasions and conquest by the next group of unified, tough, and well-led barbarians who would, in turn, be assimilated and absorbed in this process of ongoing revitalization of stagnant civilizations.

Despite the usual negative view and definition of barbarians provided by the sedentary civilized peoples, the steppe nomads had developed a complex pastoral and nomadic society. They were tough and hardy horsemen whose cavalry tactics gave them the military advantage for several centuries. The barbarians used this advantage, and their periodic attacks on civilization centers caused destruction, sometimes severe destruction. But the barbarian role in mankind's history was not always negative. The barbarians can and should be viewed as representing a dynamic and vital element in human history for they periodically revived many stagnating coastal civilizations. Many of these sedentary centers flourished, growing rich and powerful. In the process they also became conservative, settled into a fixed routine. Preferring the status quo, they tended to use old answers and ways to face new problems and issues, and as a consequence they lost the vitality and flexibility required for healthy and progressive growth.

The barbarians were active and dynamic. In their conquests of civilized centers, they frequently destroyed and eliminated the old and outdated and preserved and passed on only the good and useful elements. Sometimes, the mounted invaders also introduced new ideas and practices. Some of these new barbarian innovations (horseback riding, archery, trousers, and boots, etc.) fused with the good and useful practices of the sedentary peoples. Old and new practices and processes merged, and provided viable alternatives to the old, outdated civilized ways which had failed or outlived their usefulness. This fusion brought forth dynamic creativity and development. The ongoing encounters with barbarian strangers inevitably fostered innovation and progress in the civilized centers — due to their need to adjust in order to survive. . . .

It can be argued that barbarians also played a positive role in the spread and diffusion of civilization itself. The four major Eurasian civilization centers were separated from each other by deserts, mountains, and the vast expanses of the steppe heartland of Inner Asia. In its early stages each civilization was somewhat isolated from the others. Overland trade and contact was possible only through the barbarian steppe highway which stretched over five thousand miles across Eurasia, from Hungary to Manchuria. There was little early sea contact between the four sedentary centers, as naval travel was longer and more dangerous than the overland routes.

Thus the steppe barbarians were the chief agency through which the ideas and practices of one civilization were spread to another before 1500 A.D. According to [historian] William H. McNeill, there was much conceptual diffusion carried along the steppe highway by the barbarians. Writing originated in the ancient Middle East. The concept, not the form, of writing then spread eastward from the Middle East, as the Indian and Chinese forms and characters were significantly different than Middle Eastern cuneiform. The making and use of bronze and chariots also spread from the Middle East to Europe, India, and China. Chariots were introduced to China, on the eastern end of the steppe highway, a few centuries after their appearance in the Middle East. Needless to say, this type of early cultural diffusion is difficult to document with any degree of certainty, but enough evidence exists to make it highly probable, even if not scientifically provable.

The late medieval period provides even more examples of cultural diffusion via the movement of barbarians along the Inner Asian steppe highway. The great Eurasian *Pax Mongolica* opened the way for much cultural cross-fertilization in the late-thirteenth and early-fourteenth centuries. Chinese inventions like gunpowder and printing made their way to the Middle East and Europe in this period. Records show that Chinese artillerymen accompanied the Mongol armies into the Middle East. Papal envoys like John of Plano Carpini and William of Rubruck traveled to the Mongol capital of Karakorum in the 1240s and 1250s. In the 1280s, Marco Polo brought with him from Kublai Khan's court in China a Mongol princess to be the bride of the Mongol Khan of Persia. . . .

This cultural interaction and exchange between Eurasian coastal civilizations ended with the collapse of the Mongol Khanates in Persia and China in the mid-fourteenth century. The barbarian Mongols, therefore, provided the last period of great cultural cross-fertilization before the modern age.

Historical evidence that exists enables one to argue that the barbarian nomads played an active and positive role in the history of mankind. The barbarian invaders revitalized stagnant and decaying civilizations and were responsible for a certain amount of cultural diffusion between emerging ancient and medieval civilizations. The traditional portrayal of barbarians as mere marauders and destroyers is misleading and incorrect. Unfortunately this is the usual role they are given when historians center their study of the past narrowly on the civilized centers and the biased written sources produced by those peoples. All too often historians tend to adopt and reflect the biases and values of their subjects under study, and thus continue to denigrate and condemn all barbarians without objectively evaluating their real contributions to human development. The study of the steppe nomads, the barbarians, is just as valid a topic for historical analysis as the traditional study of coastal sedentary civilizations. Only by knowing and understanding the pastoral barbarian can historians accurately evaluate the constant interaction between the two lifestyles and come to understand the full picture of humanity's early growth and development in the ancient and medieval periods of Eurasian history.

72

DAVID MORGAN

From *The Mongols*

In this selection, another modern historian of the Mongols examines the military aspects of Mongol society. Judging from the reading, would you consider the Mongols a warrior society? What accounts for their success at conquest and governing? Why is it difficult to determine the size of Mongol armies? What were the limitations of Mongol expansion?

Thinking Historically

Underline the language in this selection that you would classify as moral or judgmental. What other phrasing or words might Morgan have used? Does Morgan's writing suggest or support a particular moral judgment about the Mongols? How would you characterize that judgment? How is Morgan's opinion and interpretation of the Mongols similar to or different from that of Guzman's in the preceding selection?

David Morgan, *The Mongols* (Oxford: Blackwell, 1986), 73–94, passim.

The immediate effects of Chingiz Khān's[1] conquests, seen from the point of view of those who bore the brunt of them, were undeniably catastrophic, though this has not prevented some modern historians from arguing that the destruction and loss of life have been greatly exaggerated. But one should not be distracted by admiration for the later achievements of Qubilai in China, or by respect for the attempts of Ghazan to put matters right in Persia, from recognising that the Mongol conquests were a disaster on a grand and unparalleled scale. North China was subjected to a series of destructive campaigns over a period of twenty-five years. According to one oft-repeated if possibly apocryphal story, the Mongols seriously considered wiping out the whole population of the former Chin Empire so as to turn the land over to pasture: They were only dissuaded when their Khitan adviser Yeh-lü Ch'u-ts'ai pointed out to them how much income in taxation they could expect to extract from an unmassacred Chinese people. To the west, Transoxania and more particularly eastern Persia had to endure something that must have seemed to approximate very nearly to attempted genocide.

Contemporary historians were unanimous when they wrote about the horrors that accompanied the Mongol invasion of the Khwārazm-shāh's empire. Ibn al-Athīr . . . is perhaps the best known and the most vivid of them. Jūzjānī wrote a similar account in his Delhi sanctuary. Jalāl al-Dīn's secretary, Nasawī, who accompanied that last of the Khwārazm-shāhs in his campaigns and wanderings, conveys much the same impression, as do such sources as the local history of Harāt, Sayfī's *Ta'rīkh-nāma-i Harāt*. The figures that these writers quote for the numbers of people massacred are beyond belief. Sayfī tells us that 1,600,000 were killed at the sack of Harāt, and 1,747,000 at Nīshāpūr. Jūzjānī puts the Harāt death toll even higher, at 2,400,000.

What are we to make of such figures? One difficulty is that no one has a clear idea of what size the population of a great Islamic city may have been in the early thirteenth century. It does not seem likely, however, that Khurāsān possessed so many cities with more inhabitants than the Sung Chinese capital, Hang-chou, which as we saw is estimated at about one million people. Moreover, not enough Islamic archaeology has been comprehensively undertaken to enable us to estimate population from the remains now on or under the ground. . . .

It is possible, indeed likely, that the great walled cities of Khurāsān had to find room at the last minute for large numbers of refugees from the countryside. This may be part of the explanation for the

---

[1] The Mongol sound for Great Khan has been spelled a number of different ways, using the Latin alphabet: Chingiz Khān (as here), Chinggis or Chingis Khan, Jenghiz Khan, and Genghis Khan. [Ed.]

chroniclers' huge numbers. But it is no more a total solution than the glib assertion that "chroniclers always exaggerate." Very similar chroniclers reported the Saljūq invasions of the eleventh century, and if they indulged in exaggeration of its (admittedly much lesser) horrors, that exaggeration was kept within strict limits. On the other hand, the sorts of figures just quoted cannot be reproduced as though they were reliable statistics. Even if our chroniclers had been present at the massacres, how would they have been in a position to calculate the numbers involved? It seems more reasonable to regard these figures not as statistical information but as evidence of the state of mind created by the character of the Mongol invasion. The shock induced by the scale of the catastrophe had no precedent: hence these enormous figures. This must imply that the death and destruction which produced that shock had no precedent either. . . .

The Mongol Army

The Mongol Empire was the creation of military conquest, and it was military supremacy that sustained it. There may have been truth in the old Chinese saw that Yeh-lü Ch'u-ts'ai is said to have repeated to the Great Khān Ögedei: that although the empire had been conquered on horseback, it could not be ruled from horseback. But without the Mongol army, no amount of efficient administration would have kept the Mongol Empire in being. The army must therefore be regarded as the basic and most essential of imperial institutions.

The nature of nomadic society on the steppe was such that to speak of the Mongol army is really no more than to speak of the Mongol people in one of its natural aspects. For the whole of life was a process of military training. The same techniques that were necessary for survival in a herding and hunting environment were, with very little adaptation, those used in warfare.

This was particularly true of hunting. The Mongols mounted an annual expedition for the acquisition of meat to tide them through the hard Mongolian winter. This took the form of a *nerge,* a vast ring of hunters, which gradually contracted, driving the game before it. Any hunter who allowed an animal to escape from the ring, or who killed one before the appointed time, was punished. At the end the khān would loose the first arrow, and the slaughter would commence. A few "emaciated stragglers" would ultimately be spared. Juwaynī remarks that "war — with its killing, counting of the slain, and sparing of the survivors — is after the same fashion, and indeed analogous in every detail." . . .

Mongols learned to ride very young indeed; and a Mongol who could ride was a potential soldier. All male Mongol adults below the age of sixty were liable for military service. There was no such thing as a civilian. Juwaynī says that the Mongol army "is a peasantry in the dress of an army, of which, in time of need, all, from small to great, from those of high rank to those of low estate, are swordsmen, archers, or spearmen." The Mongol rulers therefore had available to them a cavalry force which could be speedily mobilised, was highly trained, and consisted in theory — and even to some extent in practice — of the entire adult male population.

Can this be part of the explanation of the enormous size — if we are to believe our sources — of the Mongol armies? It must certainly have been of great significance that the Mongols could mobilise so much greater a proportion of their manpower than was possible in the sedentary states that they invaded. Other explanations have been offered. Marco Polo took the view that more men were to hand because of the Asiatic custom of polygamy. According to him the result of this was that more children would be born than under a monogamous system — a somewhat dubious proposition if the ratio between the sexes was more or less equal. More plausibly it might be pointed out that the very manoeuvrability of the Mongol forces would incline their enemies to overestimate the numbers involved. The Mongols themselves were not above employing tricks to suggest that they were present in overwhelming strength. Each Mongol went on campaign with a string of several horses. The number quoted varies, but something of the order of five horses per man would seem not to have been unusual. The mounting of dummies on spare horses, a device sometimes used, could have the effect, on the battlefield, of multiplying the apparent size of the army and increasing the terror in the hearts of the enemy soldiers.

It is probably impossible to arrive at a really accurate estimate of the size of the Mongol army. The two most valuable figures in the sources are those that can be extracted from the *Secret History* and from the *Altan Debter*, via Rashīd al-Dīn. Both sources offer a detailed breakdown of the Mongol military formations at their respective dates, and it is possible that the totals may have some relation to reality. The *Secret History*'s figures refer to the army at the time of the *quriltai*[2] of 1206, and seem to suggest an army of around 105,000 men. Rashīd al-Dīn is concerned with the forces inherited by Chingiz Khān's sons at his death in 1227. According to him the size of the army in Mongolia proper was 129,000 men.

Chroniclers writing from outside the Mongol Empire tend to quote much higher figures. Jūzjānī variously reports Chingiz Khān's army

---

[2] An assembly of Mongol princes or tribal leaders; the *quriltai* of 1206 elected or acclaimed Temujin (sometimes written as Temuchin) as Chingiz Khān and set on a plan to conquer China. [Ed.]

that attacked the Khwārazm-shāh as being 700,000 or 800,000 strong. The Mamlūk fourteenth-century writer al-'Umarī estimated the number of soldiers on the registers of the Ilkhanate in his day at 200,000 to 300,000. He says that an army from the Golden Horde that invaded Transoxania around the end of the thirteenth century consisted of 250,000 men, each having not only five horses but also two slaves, a weapon wagon, and thirty head of sheep and goats.

It does not seem likely that such figures should be treated literally, though it is only fair to point out that some scholars think that they should. If Chingiz Khān's army in around 1220 was indeed 800,000 strong, and if for the sake of argument al-'Umari's remarks are taken as representing some kind of norm, then theoretically some four million horses, to say nothing of twenty-four million sheep and goats, may have been on the move through Transoxania and Khurāsān. The Mongols certainly developed considerable expertise in solving logistical problems, as Juwaynī's account of the elaborate arrangements made by Hülegü for the supply of his army shows. But however efficient the sturdy Mongol horse may have been at feeding itself in the most unpromising circumstances, it is hard to believe that eastern Persia could have sustained an influx of animals on anything remotely approaching this scale. . . . It is the character rather than the size of the Mongol army that is crucial.

The best-known fact about the Mongols' military administration is that they organised their forces according to a decimal system, with units of ten, one hundred, one thousand, and ten thousand. Of these the *tümen* of ten thousand was the major fighting unit, but the individual Mongol trooper would probably identify most readily with his thousand. This may be illustrated in the name "Hazāra," that of a people of central Afghanistan, Persian-speaking but with a very Mongolian look about it, and which is thought to descend from Mongol military settlers. *Hazāra* is Persian for one thousand. . . .

Although the succession to the Mongol Great Khanate and to the various successor khanates was contested frequently and more often than not bloodily, there is one very striking fact about such contests: No candidates appear to have been considered except for properly authenticated descendants of Chingiz Khān. There was no attempt to set up an alternative ruling house of, say, Kerait or Tatar origin. This is presumably to be explained partly in terms of the almost sacred prestige that accrued to the house of the founder of the empire. But it may be suspected that there was more to it than this, and that Chingiz Khān's radical reconstruction of the old tribal pattern in Mongolia provides the main explanation.

Chingiz Khān reorganised the whole Turko-Mongolian manpower of Mongolia into his new decimal military structure. Old tribal identities were not wholly ignored, and tribes which had been allies of the rising Chingiz retained at least some of their integrity as groupings: Hence there were Önggüt and Qonggirat thousand formations. But the "enemy" tribes — Tatars, Merkits, Keraits, Naimans, and so forth — were broken up, and such of their men as had not been killed during the process of tribal unification were distributed among other units. So there were no Kerait *tümens* in existence that might have posed a threat to Mongol and Chingizid supremacy. Instead, Chingiz seems to have created what might be described as an artificial tribal system, in which old tribal loyalties were superseded by loyalty to the individual soldier's new military unit. Beyond that the Mongol royal house became the ultimate focus of obedience and allegiance.

Over and above the ordinary fighting formations, Chingiz Khān created an imperial guard (*keshig*). Its nucleus was his original and most faithful followers, the *nökers* of his early days of struggle. As time passed its functions multiplied, as did its numbers. By 1206 it was ten thousand strong. It was recruited across tribal boundaries, and membership was regarded as a supreme honour. The enlistment of highborn guards from all the tribes of Mongolia enabled Chingiz to treat his imperial guard corps as a useful form of honourable hostage taking. The guard in effect constituted Chingiz's household too, and as such provided the machinery and personnel through which the empire was administered in its early stages. Any trooper in the imperial guard took precedence, if necessary, even over a commander of a thousand in the army proper. The imperial guard formed the nursery of the new empire's ruling class.

Originally the Mongol soldier received no pay other than booty, which was divided up according to fixed principles. Military service was not regarded as a job. Indeed, the Mongol soldiers themselves paid contributions in kind, called *qūbchūr*, to their commanders for such purposes as the maintenance of poor or disabled troopers. However, this did not prove to be a workable system once the empire had ceased its rapid expansion and when plunder was no longer so readily available. Ultimately the Mongol troops in China were salaried, at least so far as the officers were concerned; and they were able to pass on their military offices to their heirs. In Persia the reforming Ilkhān Ghazan, after trying out various methods of providing for the Mongols' needs, attempted to meet the problem by utilising a traditional Persian device, the *iqtā'*, whereby the soldiers were allotted assignments of agricultural land, receiving the produce in lieu of salary.

In the first instance a cavalry force, the army consisted essentially of light cavalry archers, using the standard compound bow of the steppes, which was made of layers of horn and sinew on a wooden frame. This bow required a pull much stiffer than the English longbow, even though it was fired from horseback. It had impressive range and power of penetration. It was a very long time indeed before the handgun could match the compound bow in range, penetration, or rate of fire; we should be wary of assuming that the invention of gunpowder immediately made the steppe archer obsolete. The Tatar archers of the Crimea were still campaigning successfully in eastern Europe in the seventeenth century. In addition to their light cavalry the Mongols also used some armoured heavy cavalry, equipped with lances. Both the Chinese and the Middle Easterners provided units of siege engineers.

It would not have been possible to conquer such enormous areas if the Mongol army proper had alone been available. From very early days, Chinese troops were used in large numbers, and the Sung Empire, with its vast walled cities, its numerous waterways, and its rice paddy fields, could hardly have been taken by any number of cavalry manoeuvres. Chinese forces were used mainly as infantry and as garrison troops once the conquest was completed. In Persia, similarly, native Persian troops were utilised for garrison duty and to guard passes. Ghazan is said to have organised them decimally.

A further use of non-Mongols was as a rather disagreeable tactical device. When prisoners were taken at the fall of a city they were compelled to undertake dangerous siege works, or were driven in front of the Mongol assault troops at the storming of the next city. The expectation was that the defenders would be reluctant to slaughter their own compatriots, or at least that casualties among the Mongols themselves would be minimised. Other tactics included encirclement (after the pattern of the hunt); the use of surprise, especially through appearing by an unexpected (sometimes a supposedly impossible) route; the efficient synchronisation of forces that were far apart; the ancient steppe device of the feigned flight, which could usually be counted on to work; and terror. Unlike many other Asiatic conquerors the Mongols did not generally indulge in wanton cruelty as such. Countless thousands of innocent people were killed, but normally this was done as quickly and efficiently as possible, without the use of torture.

Chingiz's principle seems to have been much the same as President Truman's over Hiroshima and Nagasaki. The apparent rationale was that if the population of one city was subjected to a frightful massacre, the next city would be more likely to surrender without resistance, thus avoiding unnecessary Mongol casualties. The morality of this approach to warfare is no doubt open to discussion, but there can be no disputing that it worked. The Mongols' policy was that any city which surrendered without fighting would be spared, but that those who caused the Mongol army to suffer casualties could expect no mercy. The Mongols usually kept their word, and the message, to judge from the number of cities that did surrender on demand, seems speedily to have spread. . . .

73

From *The Secret History*
of the Mongols

This Mongol account records the early years of Mongol expansion under Chingis Khan, the founder of the empire. Born Temujin in 1155 or 1167, the young son of a minor tribal chieftain attracted the support of Mongol princes in the years between 1187 and 1206 through a series of decisive military victories over other tribes and competing Mongol claimants to the title of Great Khan.

The Mongols were illiterate before the time of Chingis Khan, who adopted the script of the Uighurs, one of the more literate peoples of the steppe. Thus the *Secret History* was written in Mongolian with Uighur letters. The only surviving version is a fourteenth-century Chinese translation. The author is unknown, but the book provides detailed accounts of the early years of Temujin and ends with the reign of his son and successor, Ogodai, in 1228 — only a year after his father's death.

Because so much about the Mongols was written by their literate enemies, *The Secret History* is an invaluable resource: It is clearly an "insider's" account of the early years of Mongol expansion. While it includes mythic elements — it begins with the augury of the birth of a blue wolf to introduce Chingis Khan — *The Secret History* is, without doubt, an authentic representation of a Mongol point of view.

In this selection, you will read three passages. The first describes a meeting in about 1187 of several tribal leaders who agree that the twenty-year-old Temujin should become Great Khan (Chingis Khan). What do these tribal leaders expect to gain from this alliance under Temujin? What do they offer in return?

The second passage deals with an early Mongol victory in 1202 over the neighboring Tatars, a tribe that Europeans often confused with the Mongols. How merciful or harsh does Chingis Khan seem?

The third passage recounts the story of an important Mongol victory over the Naiman in 1204. What does this section tell you about the sources of Mongol military strength?

Adapted by K. Reilly from R. P. Lister, *Genghis Khan* (New York: Barnes & Noble, 1993), 99–100, 136–39, 166–76, 191–93. While this volume is a retelling of the almost indecipherable *The Secret History of the Mongols* in Lister's own words, the selections that follow simplify without contextualizing or explaining the original work. More scholarly editions, trans. and ed. Francis Woodman Cleaves (Cambridge: Harvard University Press, 1982) and Paul Kahn (San Francisco: North Point Press, 1984) are less accessible.

How does this "insider's" view of the Mongols provide unique information or a perspective that would be unattainable from non-Mongols?

Thinking Historically

What moral values does this selection reveal? Do the Mongols think of themselves as "moral" people? Is the author-historian interested in describing what happened objectively, or in presenting an unblemished, sanitized view?

In what ways does this written Mongol history make you more sympathetic to the Mongols? Notice that the "Mongols Conquer the Naiman" passage begins with a Naiman account of the Mongols. How fair does the Mongol author seem to be toward the Naiman? Would this be a good source for understanding the Naiman? Do you think the Mongol authors described the Naiman more accurately than Chinese or Europeans described the Mongols?

The Choosing of the Khan

. . . A general council of all the chieftains was called, and the three most notable men among them, Prince Altan, Khuchar, and Sacha Beki, came forward. They addressed Temujin formally, in the following manner:

> We will make you Khan; you shall ride at our head, against our foes.
> We will throw ourselves like lightning on your enemies;
> We will bring you their finest women and girls, their rich tents like palaces.
> From all the peoples and nations we will bring you the fair girls and the high-stepping horses;
> When you hunt wild beasts, we will drive them towards you; we will encircle them, pressing hard at their heels.

> If on the day of battle we disobey you,
> Take our flocks from us, our women and children, and cast our worthless heads on the steppe.
> If in times of peace we disobey you,
> Part us from our men and our servants, our wives and our sons;
> Abandon us and cast us out, masterless, on the forsaken earth. . . .

Mongol Conquest of Tatars

. . . Temujin came up against the Tatars at Dalan Namurgas, on the Khalkha, east of Buir Nor, and defeated them in battle. They fell back; the Mongol armies pursued them, slaying and capturing them in large numbers.

The princes, Altan, Khuchar, and Daritai, were less assiduous in the pursuit. Finding a great number of animals roaming the steppes in the absence of their Tatar owners, they followed the usual custom of rounding them up, and collecting anything that took their fancy in the abandoned Tatar camps.

Temujin, having issued a clear order [against looting], could not tolerate their disobedience. He detached portions of his army, placed them under the command of Jebe and Khubilai, and sent them off after the disobedient princes, with orders to take away from them everything they had captured. The outcome was what might have been expected. Prince Altan and Khuchar, retiring in haste with as much of their booty as they could take with them, departed from their allegiance to him. They re-established themselves as independent chieftains, entering into such arrangements with Ong Khan, Jamukha, and other rulers as seemed desirable.

Daritai, however, seeing a little more clearly than the others, submitted to having his booty taken away from him.

Owing to his determined pursuit of the Tatars, Temujin found that he had a very considerable number of Tatar prisoners. They were kept under guard in the Mongol camp, and for the most part they were not greatly perturbed by their situation. Some of the chieftains might expect to be executed, but the lesser men had a reasonable hope of surviving. Some might have to serve as warriors under the Mongols, or even be enslaved, but a slave of talents could always hope to become a warrior again.

Temujin held a council to decide what to do with them. It was a great matter, and nobody was present at this council but his own family. The Khan's intention [was] to wipe out his enemies on a large scale. . . .

Belgutai had . . . made friends among the Tatar prisoners. One of these was Yeke Charan, the principal Tatar leader. . . . When Yeke Charan asked him what decision the family council had come to, Belgutai did not hesitate to tell him.

"We agreed to measure you against the linchpin,"[1] he said.

Yeke Charan told his fellow prisoners of the Khan's decision. Having nothing to lose, they rose up against their guards and fought their way out of the camp, taking with them what weapons they could seize. They gathered themselves together on a hilltop in a tight formation of fierce warriors. Men who are going to be killed whatever happens, and

---

[1] This was a not unknown procedure, though it had never been applied on quite such a vast scale. Prisoners were led past the wheel of a wagon. Those who were taller than the linchpin were beheaded; the children, who were smaller, survived to be taken into the Mongol armies when they grew up.

know it, fight well. The destruction of the Tatars, which was in due course accomplished, cost many Mongol lives.

Temujin was remarkably lenient towards Belgutai.

"Because Belgutai revealed the decision of the family council," he said, "Our army suffered great losses. From now on, Belgutai will take no part in the council. While it is being held, he will remain outside, keeping order in the camp, and he will sit in judgment during that time over the quarrelsome, the thieves, and the liars. When the council is finished and the wine is all drunk, then Belgutai can come in."

He ordered at the same time that Daritai should be banned from the family councils, for disobeying his *yasakh*.[2] . . .

Mongols Conquer the Naiman

When the news was brought to Tayang Khan that someone claiming to be Ong Khan had been slain at the Neikun watercourse, his mother, Gurbesu, said: "Ong Khan was the great Khan of former days. Bring his head here! If it is really he, we will sacrifice to him."

She sent a message to Khorisu, commanding him to cut the head off and bring it in. When it was brought to her, she recognised it as that of Ong Khan. She placed it on a white cloth, and her daughter-in-law carried out the appropriate rites. . . . A wine-feast was held and stringed instruments were played. Gurbesu, taking up a drinking-bowl, made an offering to the head of Ong Khan.

When the sacrifice was made to it, the head grinned.

"He laughs!" Tayang Khan cried. Overcome by religious awe, he flung the head on the floor and trampled on it until it was mangled beyond recognition.

The great general Kokse'u Sabrakh was present at these ceremonies, and observed them without enthusiasm. It was he who had been the only Naiman general to offer resistance to Temujin and Ong Khan on their expedition against Tayang Khan's brother Buyiruk.

"First of all," he remarked, "you cut off the head of a dead ruler, and then you trample it into the dust. What kind of behaviour is this? Listen to the baying of those dogs: It has an evil sound. The Khan your father, Inancha Bilgei, once said: 'My wife is young, and I, her husband, am old. Only the power of prayer has enabled me to beget my son, this same Tayang. But will my son, born a weakling, be able to guard and hold fast my common and evil-minded people?'

"Now the baying of the dogs seems to announce that some disaster is at hand. The rule of our queen, Gurbesu, is firm; but you, my Khan,

---

[2] Order, law.

Torlukh Tayang, are weak. It is truly said of you that you have no thought for anything but the two activities of hawking and driving game, and no capacity for anything but these."

Tayang Khan was accustomed to the disrespect of his powerful general, but he was stung into making a rash decision.

"There are a few Mongols in the east. From the earliest days this old and great Ong Khan feared them, with their quivers; now they have made war on him and driven him to death. No doubt they would like to be rulers themselves. There are indeed in Heaven two shining lights, the sun and the moon, and both can exist there; but how can there be two rulers here on earth? Let us go and gather those Mongols in."

His mother Gurbesu said: "Why should we start making trouble with them? The Mongols have a bad smell; they wear black clothes. They are far away, out there; let them stay there. Though it is true," she added, "that we could have the daughters of their chieftains brought here; when we had washed their hands and feet, they could milk our cows and sheep for us."

Tayang Khan said: "What is there so terrible about them? Let us go to these Mongols and take away their quivers."

"What big words you are speaking," Kokse'u Sabrakh said. "Is Tayang Khan the right man for it? Let us keep the peace."

Despite these warnings, Tayang Khan decided to attack the Mongols. It was a justifiable decision; his armies were stronger, but time was on Temujin's side. Tayang sought allies, sending a messenger to Alakhu Shidigichuri of the Onggut, in the south, the guardians of the ramparts between Qashin and the Khingan. "I am told that there are a few Mongols in the east," he said. "Be my right hand! I will ride against them from here, and we will take their quivers away from them."

[Alakhu Shidigichuri's] reply was brief: "I cannot be your right hand." He in his turn sent a message to Temujin. "Tayang Khan of the Naiman wants to come and take away your quivers. He sent to me and asked me to be his right hand. I refused. I make you aware of this, so that when he comes your quivers will not be taken away."[3]

When he received Alakhu's message Temujin, having wintered near Guralgu, was holding one of his . . . roundups of game on the camel-steppes of Tulkinche'ut, in the east. The beasts had been encircled by the clansmen and warriors; the chieftains were gathered together, about to begin the great hunt.

---

[3] Temujin, grateful for this warning, sent him five hundred horses and a thousand sheep. His friendship with Alakhu was valuable to him at a later time.

"What shall we do now?" some of them said to each other. "Our horses are lean at this season."

. . . The snow had only lately left the steppe; the horses had found nothing to graze on during these recent months. Their ribs stuck out and they lacked strength.

The Khan's youngest brother, Temuga, spoke up. . . .

"How can that serve as an excuse," he said, "that the horses are lean? My horses are quite fat enough. How can we stay sitting here, when we receive a message like that?"

Prince Belgutai spoke. . . .

"If a man allows his quivers to be taken away during his lifetime, what kind of an existence does he have? For a man who is born a man, it is a good enough end to be slain by another man, and lie on the steppe with his quiver and bow beside him. The Naiman make fine speeches, with their many men and their great kingdom. But suppose, having heard their fine speeches, we ride against them, would it be so difficult to take their quivers away from them? We must mount and ride; it is the only thing to do."

Temujin was wholly disposed to agree with these sentiments. He broke off the hunt, set the army in motion, and camped near Ornu'u on the Khalkha. Here he paused for a time while he carried out a swift re-organisation of the army. A count was held of the people; they were divided up into thousands, hundreds, and tens, and commanders of these units were appointed. Also at this time he chose his personal body-guards, the seventy day-guards and eighty night-guards. . . .

Having reorganised the army, he marched away from the mountainside of Ornu'u on the Khalkha, and took the way of war against the Naiman.

The spring of the Year of the Rat [1204] was by now well advanced. During this westward march came the Day of the Red Disc, the sixteenth day of the first moon of summer. On this day, the moon being at the full, the Khan caused the great yak's-tail banner to be consecrated, letting it be sprinkled with fermented mare's milk, with the proper observances.

They continued the march up the Kerulen, with Jebe and Khubilai in the van. When they came on to the Saari steppes, they met with the first scouts of the Naiman. There were a few skirmishes between the Naiman and Mongol scouts; in one of these, a Mongol scout was captured, a man riding a grey horse with a worn saddle. The Naiman studied this horse with critical eyes, and thought little of it. "The Mongols' horses are inordinately lean," they said to each other.

The Mongol army rode out on to the Saari steppes, and began to deploy themselves for the forthcoming battle. . . . Dodai Cherbi, one of the newly appointed captains, put a proposal before the Khan.

"We are short in numbers compared to the enemy; besides this, we are exhausted after the long march, our horses in particular. It would be a good idea to settle in this camp, so that our horses can graze on the steppe, until they have had as much to eat as they need. Meanwhile, we can deceive the enemy by making puppets and lighting innumerable fires. For every man, we will make at least one puppet, and we will burn fires in five places. It is said that the Naiman people are very numerous, but it is rumoured also that their king is a weakling, who has never left his tents. If we keep them in a state of uncertainty about our numbers, with our puppets and our fires, our geldings can stuff themselves till they are fat."

The suggestion pleased Temujin, who had the order passed on to the soldiers to light fires immediately. Puppets were constructed and placed all over the steppe, some sitting or lying by the fires, some of them even mounted on horses.

At night, the watchers of the Naiman saw, from the flanks of the mountain, fires twinkling all over the steppe. They said to each other: "Did they not say that the Mongols were very few? Yet they have more fires than there are stars in Heaven."

Having previously sent to Tayang Khan news of the lean grey horse with the shabby saddle, they now sent him the message: "The warriors of the Mongols are camped out all over the Saari steppes. They seem to grow more numerous every day; their fires outnumber the stars."

When this news was brought to him from the scouts, Tayang Khan was at the watercourse of Khachir. He sent a message to his son Guchuluk.

"I am told that the geldings of the Mongols are lean, but the Mongols are, it seems, numerous. Once we start fighting them, it will be difficult to draw back. They are such hard warriors that when several men at once come up against one of them, he does not move an eyelid; even if he is wounded, so that the black blood flows out, he does not flinch. I do not know whether it is a good thing to come up against such men.

"I suggest that we should assemble our people and lead them back to the west, across the Altai; and all the time, during this retreat, we will fight off the Mongols as dogs do, by running in on them from either side as they advance. Our geldings are too fat; in this march we shall make them lean and fit. But the Mongols' lean geldings will be brought to such a state of exhaustion they will vomit in the Mongols' faces."

On receiving this message, Guchuluk Khan, who was more warlike than his father, said: "That woman Tayang has lost all his courage, to speak such words. Where does this great multitude of Mongols come from? Most of the Mongols are with Jamukha, who is here with us. Tayang speaks like this because fear has overcome him. He has never been farther from his tent than his pregnant wife goes to urinate. He has never dared to go so far as the inner pastures where the knee-high calves are kept." So he expressed himself on the subject of his father, in the most injurious and wounding terms.

When he heard these words, Tayang Khan said: "I hope the pride of this powerful Guchuluk will not weaken on the day when the clash of arms is heard and the slaughter begins. Because once we are committed to battle against the foe, it will be hard to disengage again."

Khorisu Beki, a general who commanded under Tayang Khan, said: "Your father, Inancha Bilgei, never showed the back of a man or the haunch of a horse to opponents who were just as worthy as these. How can you lose your courage so early in the day? We would have done better to summon your mother Gurbesu to command over us. It is a pity that Kokse'u Sabrakh has grown too old to lead us. Our army's discipline has become lax. For the Mongols, their hour has come. It is finished! Tayang, you have failed us." He belted on his quiver and galloped off.

Tayang Khan grew angry. "All men must die," he said. "Their bodies must suffer. It is the same for all men. Let us fight, then."

So, having created doubt and dismay, and lost the support of some of his best leaders, he decided to give battle. He broke away from the watercourse of Khachir, marched down the Tamir, crossed the Orkhon and skirted the eastern flanks of the mountain Nakhu. When they came to Chakirma'ut, Temujin's scouts caught sight of them and brought back the message: "The Naiman are coming!"

The Battle of Chakirma'ut

When the news was brought to Temujin he said: "Sometimes too many men are just as big a handicap as too few."

Then he issued his general battle orders. "We will march in the order 'thick grass,' take up positions in the 'lake' battle order, and fight in the manner called 'gimlet.'"[4] He gave Kasar the command of the main army, and appointed Prince Otchigin to the command of the reserve horses, a special formation of great importance in Mongol warfare.

The Naiman, having advanced as far as Chakirma'ut, drew themselves up in a defensive position on the foothills of Nakhu, with the mountain behind them. . . . The Mongols forced their scouts back on to the forward lines, and then their forward lines back on to the main army, and drove tightly knit formations of horsemen again and again into the Naiman ranks. The Naiman, pressed back on themselves, could do nothing but retreat gradually up the mountain. Many of their

---

[4] These were the names of various tactical disciplines in which he had drilled his army.

men . . . hardly had the chance to fight at all, but were cut down in an immobile mass of men as soon as the Mongols reached them.

Tayang Khan, with his advisers, also retreated up the mountain as the day advanced. From the successive spurs to which they climbed, each one higher than the last, they could see the whole of this dreadful disaster as it took place below them.

Jamukha was with Tayang Khan. . . .

"Who are those people over there," Tayang Khan asked him, "who throw my warriors back as if they were sheep frightened by a wolf, who come huddling back to the sheepfold?"

Jamukha said: "My *anda*[5] Temujin has four hounds whom he brought up on human flesh, and kept in chains. They have brows of copper, snouts like chisels, tongues like bradawls, hearts of iron, and tails that cut like swords. They can live on dew, and ride like the wind. On the day of battle they eat the flesh of men. You see how, being set loose, they come forward slavering for joy. Those two are Jebe and Khubilai; those two are Jelmei and Subetai. That is who those four hounds are."

He pointed out to him also the Uru'ut and the Mangqut, who, as Tayang Khan remarked, seemed to bound like foals set loose in the morning, when, after their dams have suckled them, they frisk around her on the steppe. "They hunt down men who carry lances and swords," he said. "Having struck them down, they slay them, and rob them of all they possess. How joyful and boisterous they look, as they ride forward!"

"Who is it coming up there in the rear," Tayang Khan asked him, "who swoops down on our troops like a ravening falcon?"

"That is my *anda* Temujin. His entire body is made of sounding copper; there is no gap through which even a bodkin could penetrate. There he is, you see him? He advances like an eagle about to seize his prey. You said formerly that if you once set eyes on the Mongols you would not leave so much of them as the skin of a lamb's foot. What do you think of them now?"

By this time the chieftains were standing on a high spur. Below them, the great army of the Naiman, Jamukha's men with them, were retreating in confusion, fighting desperately as the Mongols hemmed them in.

"Who is that other chieftain," Tayang asked Jamukha, "who draws ever nearer us, in a dense crowd of men?"

"Mother Hoelun brought up one of her own sons on human flesh. He is nine feet tall; he eats a three-year-old cow every day. If he swallows an armed man whole, it makes no difference to his appetite. When

---

5 Sworn brother, blood brother, declared ally.

he is roused to anger, and lets fly with one of his *angqu'a* [forked] arrows, it will go through ten or twenty men. His normal range is a thousand yards; when he draws his bow to its fullest extent, he shoots over eighteen hundred yards. He is mortal, but he is not like other mortals; he is more than a match for the serpents of Guralgu. He is called Kasar."

They were climbing high up the mountain now, to regroup below its summit. Tayang Khan saw a new figure among the Mongols.

"Who is that coming up from the rear?" he asked Jamukha.

"That is the youngest son of Mother Hoelun. He is called Otchigin [Odeigin] the Phlegmatic. He is one of those people who go to bed early and get up late. But when he is behind the army, with the reserves, he does not linger; he never comes too late to the battle lines."

"We will climb to the peak of the mountain," Tayang Khan said.

Jamukha, seeing that the battle was lost, slipped away to the rear and descended the mountain, with a small body of men. One of these he sent to Temujin with a message. "Say this to my *anda*. Tayang Khan, terrified by what I have told him, has completely lost his senses. He has retreated up the mountain as far as he can. He could be killed by one harsh word. Let my *anda* take note of this: They have climbed to the top of the mountain, and are in no state to defend themselves any more. I myself have left the Naiman."

Since the evening was drawing on, Temujin commanded his troops in the forefront of the attack to draw back. Bodies of men were sent forward on the wings, east and west, to encircle the summit of Mount Nakhu. There they stood to arms during the night. During the night, the Naiman army tried to break out of the encircling ring. Bodies of horsemen plunged down the mountainside in desperate charges; many fell and were trampled to death, the others were slain. In the first light they were seen lying about the mountain in droves, like fallen trees. Few were left defending the peak; they put up little resistance to the force sent up against them.

74

JOHN OF PLANO CARPINI
History of the Mongols

Chingis Khan united the tribes of the steppe and conquered northern China, capturing Peking by 1215. He then turned his armies against the West, conquering the tribes of Turkestan and the Khorezmian Empire, the great Muslim power of central Asia, by 1222. The following year he chased Khorezmian troops into northern India, while sending an army around the Caspian Sea into Russia. In 1226, he turned again to the East, subduing and destroying the kingdom of Tibet before he died in 1227. One historian, Christopher Dawson, summarizes the career of Chingis Khan this way:

> In spite of the primitive means at his disposal, it is possible that [Chingis Khan] succeeded in destroying a larger portion of the human race than any modern expert in total warfare. Within a dozen years from the opening of his campaign against China, the Mongol armies had reached the Pacific, the Indus, and the Black Sea, and had destroyed many of the great cities in India. For Europe especially, the shock was overwhelming.

European fears intensified in 1237 as the principal Mongol armies under Batu Khan systematically destroyed one Russian city after another. In April 1241, one Mongol army destroyed a combined force of Polish and German armies, while another defeated the Hungarian army and threatened Austria. Only the death and funeral of Ogedai (r. 1229–41), the second Great Khan, provided relief, because Batu Khan returned to Mongolia for the funeral, leaving his troops at their headquarters in Russia.

At the time no one could have known that future Mongol pressure would be brought against the Muslim Middle East rather than the Christian West. Pope Innocent IV sent a mission to the Mongols in 1245, trying to accomplish such a shift and to learn as much as possible about Mongol intentions. For this important task, he sent two Franciscan monks — one of whom was John of Plano Carpini — with two letters addressed to the Emperor of the Tartars (a compounded error that changed the Tatars, the Mongols' enemy, into the denizens

---

John of Plano Carpini, "History of the Mongols," in *Mission to Asia: Narratives and Letters of the Franciscan Missionaries in Mongolia and China in the Thirteenth and Fourteenth Centuries*, trans. a nun of Stanbrook Abbey, ed. Christopher Dawson (1955; reprint, New York: Harper & Row, 1966), 60–69.

of Tartarus, or Hell). In May, the barefoot sixty-five-year-old Friar John reached Batu's camp on the Volga River, from which he was relayed to Mongolia by five fresh horses a day in order to reach the capital at Karakorum in time for the installation of the third Great Khan, Guyuk (r. 1246–48) in July and August.

In this selection from his *History of the Mongols,* John writes of his arrival in Mongolia for the installation of Guyuk (here written as Cuyuk). In what ways does John's account change or expand your understanding of the Mongols? Was John a good observer? How does he compensate for his ignorance (as an outside observer) of Mongol society and culture? In what ways does he remain a victim of his outsider status?

Thinking Historically

What explicit moral judgments does John make about the Mongols? What moral judgments does he merely assume? Does his account change your own opinion of the Mongols? If so, how? Is your own moral judgment of the Mongols important to you? How is it related to your historical understanding?

. . . On our arrival Cuyuc had us given a tent and provisions, such as it is the custom for the Tartars to give, but they treated us better than other envoys. Nevertheless we were not invited to visit him for he had not yet been elected, nor did he yet concern himself with the government. The translation of the Lord Pope's letter, however, and the things I had said had been sent to him by Bati. After we had stayed there for five or six days he sent us to his mother where the solemn court was assembling. By the time we got there a large pavilion had already been put up made of white velvet, and in my opinion it was so big that more than two thousand men could have got into it. Around it had been erected a wooden palisade, on which various designs were painted. On the second or third day we went with the Tartars who had been appointed to look after us and there all the chiefs were assembled and each one was riding with his followers among the hills and over the plains round about.

On the first day they were all clothed in white velvet, on the second in red — that day Cuyuc came to the tent — on the third day they were all in blue velvet, and on the fourth in the finest brocade. In the palisade round the pavilion were two large gates, through one of which the Emperor alone had the right to enter and there were no guards placed at it although it was open, for no one dare enter or leave by it; through the other gate all those who were granted admittance entered and there were guards there with swords and bows and arrows. If any-one approached the tent beyond the fixed limits, he was beaten if caught; if he ran away he was shot at, but with arrows however which had no heads. The horses were, I suppose, two arrow-flights away. The chiefs went about everywhere armed and accompanied by a number of their men, but none, unless their group of ten was complete, could go as far as the horses; indeed those who attempted to do so were severely beaten. There were many of them who had, as far as I could judge, about twenty marks' worth of gold on their bits, breastplates, saddles, and cruppers. The chiefs held their conference inside the tent and, so I believe, conducted the election. All the other people however were a long way away outside the aforementioned palisade. There they re-mained until almost midday and then they began to drink mare's milk and they drank until the evening, so much that it was amazing to see. We were invited inside and they gave us mead as we would not take mare's milk. They did this to show us great honour, but they kept on plying us with drinks to such an extent that we could not possibly stand it, not being used to it, so we gave them to understand that it was disagreeable to us and they left off pressing us.

Outside were Duke Jerozlaus of Susdal in Russia and several chiefs of the Kitayans and Solangi, also two sons of the King of Georgia, the ambassador of the Caliph of Baghdad, who was a Sultan, and more than ten other Sultans of the Saracens, so I believe and so we were told by the stewards. There were more than four thousand envoys there, counting those who were carrying tribute, those who were bringing gifts, the Sultans and other chiefs who were coming to submit to them, those summoned by the Tartars and the governors of territories. All these were put together outside the palisade and they were given drinks at the same time, but when we were outside with them we and Duke Jerozlaus were always given the best places. I think, if I remember rightly, that we had been there a good four weeks when, as I believe, the election took place; the result however was not made public at that time; the chief ground for my supposition was that whenever Cuyuc left the tent they sang before him and as long as he remained outside they dipped to him beautiful rods on the top of which was scarlet wool, which they did not do for any of the other chiefs. They call this court the Sira Orda.

Leaving there we rode all together for three or four leagues to an-other place, where on a pleasant plain near a river among the moun-tains another tent had been set up, which is called by them the Golden Orda, it was here that Cuyuc was to be enthroned on the feast of the Assumption of Our Lady. . . .

At that place we were summoned into the presence of the Emperor, and Chingay the protonotary wrote down our names and the names of those who had sent us, also the names of the chief of the Solangi and of others, and then calling out in a loud voice he recited them before the Emperor and all the chiefs. When this was finished each one of us genuflected four times on the left knee and they warned us not to touch the lower part of the threshold. After we had been most thoroughly searched for knives and they had found nothing at all, we entered by a door on the east side, for no one dare enter from the west with the sole exception of the Emperor or, if it is a chief's tent, the chief; those of lower rank do not pay much attention to such things. This was the first time since Cuyuc had been made Emperor that we had entered his tent in his presence. He also received all the envoys in that place, but very few entered his tent.

So many gifts were bestowed by the envoys there that it was marvellous to behold — gifts of silk, samite, velvet, brocade, girdles of silk threaded with gold, choice furs, and other presents. The Emperor was also given a sunshade or little awning such as is carried over his head, and it was all decorated with precious stones. . . .

Leaving there we went to another place where a wonderful tent had been set up all of red velvet, and this had been given by the Kitayans; there also we were taken inside. Whenever we went in we were given mead and wine to drink, and cooked meat was offered us if we wished to have it. A lofty platform of boards had been erected, on which the Emperor's throne was placed. The throne, which was of ivory, was wonderfully carved and there was also gold on it, and precious stones, if I remember rightly, and pearls. Steps led up to it and it was rounded behind. Benches were also placed round the throne, and here the ladies sat in their seats on the left; nobody, however, sat on the right, but the chiefs were on benches in the middle and the rest of the people sat beyond them. Every day a great crowd of ladies came.

The three tents of which I have spoken were very large. The Emperor's wives however had other tents of white felt, which were quite big and beautiful. At that place they separated, the Emperor's mother going in one direction and the Emperor in another to administer justice. The mistress of the Emperor had been arrested; she had murdered his father with poison at the time when their army was in Hungary and as a result the army in these parts retreated. Judgment was passed on her along with a number of others and they were put to death. . . .

After the death of Jerozlaus, if I remember the time correctly, our Tartars took us to the Emperor. When he heard from them that we had come to him he ordered us to go back to his mother, the reason being that he wished on the following day to raise his banner against the whole of the Western world — we were told this definitely by men who knew . . . — and he wanted us to be kept in ignorance of this. On our return we stayed for a few days, then we went back to him again and remained with him for a good month, enduring such hunger and thirst that we could scarcely keep alive, for the food provided for four was barely sufficient for one, moreover, we were unable to find anything to buy, for the market was a very long way off. If the Lord had not sent us a certain Russian, by name Cosmas, a goldsmith and a great favourite of the Emperor, who supported us to some extent, we would, I believe, have died, unless the Lord had helped us in some other way.

Before the enthronement Cosmas showed us the Emperor's throne which he himself had made and his seal which he had fashioned, and he also told us what the inscription was on the seal. We picked up many other bits of private information about the Emperor from men who had come with other chiefs, a number of Russians and Hungarians knowing Latin and French, and Russian clerics and others, who had been among the Tartars, some for thirty years, through wars and other happenings, and who knew all about them, for they knew the language and had lived with them continually some twenty years, others ten, some more, some less. With the help of these men we were able to gain a thorough knowledge of everything. They told us about everything willingly and sometimes without being asked, for they knew what we wanted.

After this the Emperor sent for us, and through Chingay his protonotary told us to write down what we had to say and our business, and give it to him, We did this and wrote out for him all that we said earlier to Bati. . . . A few days passed by; then he had us summoned again and told us through Kadac, the procurator of the whole empire, in the presence of Bala and Chingay his protonotaries and many other scribes, to say all we had to say: We did this willingly and gladly. Our interpreter on this as on the previous occasion was Temer, a knight of Jerozlaus': and there were also present a cleric who was with him and another cleric who was with the Emperor. On this occasion we were asked if there were any people with the Lord Pope who understood the writing of the Russians or Saracens or even of the Tartars. We gave answer that we used neither the Ruthenian nor Saracen writing; there were however Saracens in the country but they were a long way from the Lord Pope; but we said that it seemed to us that the most expedient course would be for them to write in Tartar and translate it for us, and we would write it down carefully in our own script and we would take both the letter and the translation to the Lord Pope. Thereupon they left us to go to the Emperor.

On St. Martin's day we were again summoned, and Kadac, Chingay, and Bala, the aforementioned secretaries, came to us and translated the letter for us word by word. When we had written it in Latin, they had it translated so that they might hear a phrase at a time, for they wanted to know if we had made a mistake in any word. When both letters were written, they made us read it once and a second time in case we had left out anything, and they said to us: "See that you clearly understand everything, for it would be inconvenient if you did not understand everything, seeing you have to travel to such far-distant lands." When we replied "We understand everything clearly," they wrote the letter once again in Saracenic, in case anyone should be found in those parts who could read it, if the Lord Pope so wished.

It is the custom for the Emperor of the Tartars never to speak to a foreigner, however important he may be, except through an intermediary, and he listens and gives his answer, also through the intermediary. Whenever his subjects have any business to bring before Kadac, or while they are listening to the Emperor's reply, they stay on their knees until the end of the conversation, however important they may be. It is not possible nor indeed is it the custom for anyone to say anything about any matter after the Emperor has declared his decision. This Emperor not only has a procurator and protonotaries and secretaries, but all officials for dealing with both public and private matters, except that he has no advocates, for everything is settled according to the decision of the Emperor without the turmoil of legal trials. The other princes of the Tartars do the same in those matters concerning them.

The present Emperor may be forty or forty-five years old or more; he is of medium height, very intelligent, and extremely shrewd, and most serious and grave in his manner. He is never seen to laugh for a slight cause nor to indulge in any frivolity, so we were told by the Christians who are constantly with him. The Christians of his household also told us that they firmly believed he was about to become a Christian, and they have clear evidence of this, for he maintains Christian clerics and provides them with supplies of Christian things; in addition he always has a chapel before his chief tent and they sing openly and in public and beat the board for services after the Greek fashion like other Christians, however big a crowd of Tartars or other men be there. The other chiefs do not behave like this.

According to our Tartars the Emperor proposed sending ambassadors with us, to accompany us. I think, however, that they wanted us to request him to do this, for one of our Tartars, the eldest, advised us to make this petition. But since it did not seem good to us that they should come, we told him it was not for us to do the asking, but if the Emperor by his own desire should send them, we would by the help of God conduct them safely. There were several reasons why it did not seem expedient to us that they should come. In the first place we were afraid lest, seeing the dissensions and wars which are rife among us, they might be all the more encouraged to attack us. The second reason was that we feared that their real purpose might be to spy out the land. The third reason was that we were apprehensive that they might be killed, for our people are for the most part arrogant and proud. When at the request of the Cardinal, who is legate in Germany, the servants with us went to him wearing Tartar costume, they were very nearly stoned by the Germans on the way and obliged to take off the costume.

Now it is the custom of the Tartars never to make peace with men who kill their envoys, until they have taken vengeance on them.

The fourth reason is that we were afraid they might be taken from us by force, as happened on one occasion to a Saracen prince, who is still in captivity if he has not died. The fifth reason is that no good purpose would be served by their coming, since they would have no other mandate or authority than that of taking to the Lord Pope and to the other princes the letters which we had; and we believed that this might have harmful consequences. For these reasons we were not in favour of their coming.

Two days later, that is to say on the feast of St. Brice [November 13th], they gave us a permit to depart and a letter sealed with the Emperor's seal, and sent us to the Emperor's mother. She gave each of us a fox-skin cloak, which had the fur outside and was lined inside, and a length of velvet; our Tartars stole a good yard from each of the pieces of velvet and from the piece given to our servant they stole more than half. This did not escape our notice, but we preferred not to make a fuss about it.

We then set out on the return journey. . . .

GUYUK KHAN

Letter to Pope Innocent IV

This is the letter to Pope Innocent IV that John of Plano Carpini refers to in the previous selection. This version of the letter comes from a brief narrative of the same trip by John's Polish companion, Brother Benedict the Pole. What is Guyuk Khan's message? Judging from this letter and the previous selection, what is the religion of the Mongols, and what is the status of Christianity among the Mongols?

From "Narrative of Brother Benedict the Pole," in *Mission to Asia: Narratives and Letters of the Franciscan Missionaries in Mongolia and China in the Thirteenth and Fourteenth Centuries*, trans. by a nun of Stanbrook Abbey and ed. Christopher Dawson (1955; reprint, New York: Harper & Row, 1966), 83–84.

Thinking Historically

How would you describe the moral tone of Guyuk's letter? In what ways does Guyuk's moral tone differ from or resemble John's tone in the previous selection? Do moral issues prevent either Guyuk or Pope Innocent IV from understanding each other?

The Strength of God, the Emperor of All Men, to the Great Pope, Authentic and True Letters

Having taken counsel for making peace with us, You Pope and all Christians have sent an envoy to us, as we have heard from him and as your letters declare. Wherefore, if you wish to have peace with us, You Pope and all kings and potentates, in no way delay to come to me to make terms of peace and then you shall hear alike our answer and our will. The contents of your letters stated that we ought to be baptized and become Christians. To this we answer briefly that we do not understand in what way we ought to do this. To the rest of the contents of your letters, viz: that you wonder at so great a slaughter of men, especially of Christians and in particular Poles, Moravians, and Hungarians, we reply likewise that this also we do not understand. However, lest we may seem to pass it over in silence altogether, we give you this for our answer.

Because they did not obey the word of God and the command of Chingis Chan and the Chan, but took council to slay our envoys, therefore God ordered us to destroy them and gave them up into our hands. For otherwise if God had not done this, what could man do to man? But you men of the West believe that you alone are Christians and despise others. But how can you know to whom God deigns to confer His grace? But we worshipping God have destroyed the whole earth from the East to the West in the power of God. And if this were not the power of God, what could men have done? Therefore if you accept peace and are willing to surrender your fortresses to us, You Pope and Christian princes, in no way delay coming to me to conclude peace and then we shall know that you wish to have peace with us. But if you should not believe our letters and the command of God nor hearken to our counsel then we shall know for certain that you wish to have war. After that we do not know what will happen: God alone knows.

Chingis Chan, first Emperor, second Ochoday Chan, third Cuiuch Chan.

The Journey of William of Rubrick

William of Rubrick, who is known only from this account of his travels to Mongolia eight years after John of Plano Carpini, was a younger man than John, probably a native of Flanders, and also a Franciscan friar.

In two main respects, William's mission was different from John's: First, in addition to having information about the earlier mission, William — as a resident of the Crusaders' city of Acre — was more in touch with Asia, more knowledgeable about the Mongols, and was able to have his letters of introduction translated into Persian and Syrian. Second, his mission was more religious than political, despite the fact that he went in the service of King Louis IX of France (called St. Louis) and not the Pope. The Crusading King Louis had learned that Batu Khan's son was a Christian, so he sent William to establish relations with Mongol Christians. William's journey proceeded much like John's, beginning with an overland trip to Batu Khan's camp on the Volga and then long days of horse relays to the Mongolian capital of Karakorum where he met Monke (r. 1251–59) (here written as Mangu), the fourth Great Khan.

In this selection, William has arrived at the palace of Monke where a goldsmith named Master William of Paris has completed an unusual work of sculpture. Notice the number of Europeans and other foreigners at the court of Monke. How have they adapted to Mongol rule?

William is interested, as John was, in Mongol religion. Notice William's conflicted attitude toward Nestorian Christianity, an Eastern Christianity that was practiced by, among others, much of the Kerait tribe — a source of intermarriage for the Mongols. Many Kerait wives of Mongol princes exerted great influence on their husbands and sons.

Thinking Historically

What sorts of moral struggles does William experience in the court of the Great Khan? Compare William's attitude toward the Nestorian Christians with Monke's. How do the moral and religious commitments of these two men affect their behavior? How do William's moral and religious attitudes affect his account? Would William's history have been more accurate if he had no moral or religious ideas of his own?

"The Journey of William of Rubrick," in *Mission to Asia: Narratives and Letters of the Franciscan Missionaries in Mongolia and China in the Thirteenth and Fourteenth Centuries*, trans. a nun of Stanbrook Abbey, ed. Christopher Dawson (1955; reprint, New York: Harper & Row, 1966), 175–78.

At Caracorum, Mangu has a large orda[1] close by the city walls; it is surrounded by a brick wall as are our priories of monks. There is a large palace there in which he holds his drinking festival twice in the year, once round about Easter when he passes by that way and once in the summer on his return. The second is the more important for on that occasion there assemble at his court all the nobles anywhere within a two months' journey; and then he bestows on them garments and presents and displays his great glory. There are many other buildings there, long like barns, and in these are stored his provisions and treasures.

At the entrance to this palace, seeing it would have been unseemly to put skins of milk and other drinks there, Master William of Paris has made for him a large silver tree, at the foot of which are four silver lions each having a pipe and all belching forth white mares' milk. Inside the trunk four pipes lead up to the top of the tree and the ends of the pipes are bent downward and over each of them is a gilded serpent, the tail of which twines round the trunk of the tree. One of these pipes pours out wine, another caracosmos, that is the refined milk of mares, another *boal*, which is a honey drink, and another rice mead, which is called *terracina*. Each of these has its silver basin ready to receive it at the foot of the tree between the other four pipes. At the very top he fashioned an angel holding a trumpet; underneath the tree he made a crypt in which a man can be secreted, and a pipe goes up to the angel through the middle of the heart of the tree. At first he had made bellows but they did not give enough wind. Outside the palace there is a chamber in which the drinks are stored, and servants stand there ready to pour them out when they hear the angel sounding the trumpet. The tree has branches, leaves, and fruit of silver.

And so when the drinks are getting low the chief butler calls out to the angel to sound his trumpet. Then, hearing this, the man who is hidden in the crypt blows the pipe going up to the angel with all his strength, and the angel, placing the trumpet to his mouth, sounds it very loudly. When the servants in the chamber hear this each one of them pours out his drink into its proper pipe, and the pipes pour them out from above and below into the basins prepared for this, and then the cup-bearers draw the drinks and carry them round the palace to the men and women.

The palace is like a church with a middle nave and two side aisles beyond two rows of pillars, and there are three doors on the south side; inside before the middle door stands the tree, and the Chan himself sits at the northern end high up so that he can be seen by everyone; and there are two stairways leading up to him, and the man bringing him his cup goes up by the one and comes down by the other. The space in

---

[1] A tent-palace compound.

the middle between the tree and the steps up to him is empty, and there the cup-bearer stands and also envoys who are bringing gifts. The Chan sits up there like a god. On his right-hand side, that is to the west, are the men, on the left the women, for the palace extends from the north southward. To the south, next to the pillars on the right, are rows of seats raised up like a balcony, on which sit his son and brothers. It is the same on the left where his wives and daughters sit. Only one wife sits up there beside him; she however is not as high up as he is.

When the Chan heard that the work was finished he gave orders to the master to place it in position and get it in working order, and he himself about Passion Sunday went ahead with the small dwellings leaving the large ones behind. The monk and we followed him and he sent us another bottle of wine. He journeyed through mountainous districts, and there was a strong wind and severe cold and a heavy fall of snow. Consequently about midnight the Chan sent to the monk and us asking us to pray to God to lessen the cold and the wind, for all the animals accompanying them were in danger, especially because at that season they were with young and bringing forth. Thereupon the monk sent him some incense, bidding him put it on the coals as an offering to God. I do not know if he did this, but the storm, which had lasted for two days and was already entering on its third, did abate.

On Palm Sunday we were near Caracorum. At dawn we blessed branches of willow, which as yet bore no sign of buds, and about three o'clock we entered the city, the cross raised on high with the banner, and passing the Saracen quarters, where the bazaar and market are, we went to the church. The Nestorians came to meet us in procession. On entering the church we found them ready to celebrate Mass; when this had been celebrated they all received Holy Communion and asked me if I wished to communicate. I replied that I had had a drink and it is not lawful to receive the Sacrament except fasting.

Mass having been said, it was now evening and Master William took us with great joy to his lodging to have supper with him. His wife, who was born in Hungary, was the daughter of a man from Lorraine and she knew French and Coman well. We also came across another man there, Basil by name, the son of an Englishman, who had been born in Hungary and knew the same languages. After supper they accompanied us with great rejoicing to our hut, which the Tartars had set up for us in a square near the church along with the monk's oratory.

The following day the Chan entered his palace and the monk and I and the priests went to him. My companion was not allowed to go because he had trodden on the threshold. I deliberated a great deal about my own case, what I ought to do, whether to go or not to go, and, fearing to give scandal by dissociating myself from the other Christians, and seeing that it pleased the Chan, and fearing lest the good I was hoping to be able to bring about might be hindered, I decided to go even though it meant that I should witness their acts of sorcery and idolatry. And there I did nothing but pray aloud for the whole Church and also for the Chan that God would direct him into the way of eternal salvation.

And so we made our entrance into that orda, which is very well laid out and in summer they convey streams of water in all directions to irrigate it. We next entered the palace, which was full of men and women, and we stood before the Chan having at our backs the tree I have mentioned which together with its basins occupied a large part of the palace; the priests brought two little blessed cakes of bread and fruit on a dish which they presented to the Chan after they had pronounced a blessing, and a butler took them to him as he sat there in a place very high and lifted up. He immediately began to eat one of the cakes and sent the other to his son and his younger brother, who is being brought up by a Nestorian and knows the Gospel, and he also sent for my Bible so that he could look at it. After the priests the monk said his prayer, and I after the monk. Then the Chan promised that the following day he would come to the church, which is quite large and beautiful, and the roof above is all covered with silk interwoven with gold. The following day he went on his way, sending a message of excuse to the priests saying he dared not come to the church for he had learned that the dead were carried there. . . .

REFLECTIONS

The great Chinese artist Cheng Ssu-hsaio (1241–1318) continued to paint his delicate Chinese orchids in the years after the Mongol defeat of the Sung dynasty, under the alien rule of Khubilai Khan (r. 1260–94), the fifth Great Khan and the founder of the Mongol Yuan Dynasty of China. But when Cheng was asked why he always painted the orchids without earth around their roots, he replied that the earth had been stolen by the barbarians.

Just as it would be a mistake to see a fifth generation Mongol ruler like Khubilai as a barbarian, it would also be a mistake to assume that Cheng's hardened resistance remained the norm. In fact, a younger generation of artists found opportunity and even freedom in Khubilai's China. Khubilai appointed some of the most famous Chinese painters of his era to positions of government — Ministries of War, Public Works, Justice, Personnel, Imperial Sacrifices — actively recruiting the bright young men, artists and intellectuals, for his government. While some painters catered to the Mongol elite's inclination for paintings of horses, others relished the wider range of subjects allowed by a regime free of highly cultivated prejudices.

If conquest invariably brings charges of barbarism, it also eventually turns to issues of government and administration. Administrators need officials. Though Khubilai abolished the Chinese civil service examination system because it would have forced him to rely on Chinese officials, the Chinese language, and an educational system based on the Chinese classics, he actively sought ways of governing that were neither too Chinese nor too Mongolian. Typically, he promulgated a Chinese alphabet that was based on Tibetan, hoping that its phonetic symbols would make communication easier and less classical. Many of his achievements were unintended. While his officials continued to use Chinese characters and the Uighur script, the Yüan dynasty witnessed a flowering of literary culture, including theater and novels. For some, no doubt, the wind from the steppe blew away the dust and cobwebs that had accumulated for too long.

Our judgment of the Mongols depends to a great extent on the period of Mongol history we consider. But while it is easy to condemn the initial conquests and praise the later enlightened governance, two considerations come to mind. First, in the great sweep of history, many "barbarians" became benign, even indulgent, administrators. Second, the Mongols were not unique in making that transition.

This raises an interesting moral question: Namely, what is the relation between historical memory and forgiveness? In recent years, we have pondered this when commemorating the fiftieth anniversary of World War II, the five-hundredth anniversary of the European settlement of the Americas, and the history of slavery.

At some point, it seems, former "barbarians" should be judged in terms of what they have become rather than what they once were. Even if forgiveness is not possible or desirable, old wounds fester, and the better course is to move forward with hope.

On the other hand, as Cheng's orchids remind us, people need to remember the past in order not to repeat it. Judgments about the past set guidelines, norms for the future.

Have you ever had an experience in your own life when you felt memory was a moral act? Was there ever a time when you thought it was better to forget? Does forgiveness require forgetting?

13

On Cities

European, Chinese, and Islamic Cities,
1000–1550 C.E.

HISTORICAL CONTEXT

During the last five thousand years, cities have grown and multiplied, the world becoming increasingly urbanized. There have been interruptions in this process, however: the period of the Mongol invasions in the first half of the thirteenth century and the era of the Black Death, a plague that wiped out urban populations in the middle of the fourteenth century, for instance. But, by and large, the general course of world history has promoted the rise and expansion of cities and of urban over rural populations.

In this chapter, we ask what this increasing urbanization meant for those who lived in the cities and for those who did not. We compare cities in various parts of the world between 1000 and 1550. We will study primary and secondary sources, and you will be asked to note the ways in which these cities are similar and different.

THINKING HISTORICALLY
Evaluating Alternate Theses

As you compare and contrast various cities in this chapter, you will consider two alternate theses (or perhaps, more broadly, two different approaches) to understanding the history of cities. The first thesis considers the differences or contrasting characteristics between cities to be more important and more telling than similarities. Sometimes the contrast is cultural, as if cities are microcosms of their particular cultures. In this view, Paris is an extreme version of "Frenchness" — more a magnification of its own culture than a sister city to New York. Defin-

ing what a culture is can be difficult, though. Is Cairo extremely Egyptian, or is it Arab, Muslim, or Middle Eastern? Is Calcutta a distillation
of things Indian? Or, is it more Bengal, South Asian, or Hindu? Cultural characterizations are always disputable, but clearly cities do concentrate local cultural tendencies. They produce newspapers, gather
writers and artists, and serve as cultural hothouses.

The alternative approach might be called "convergence" or coming
together. Cities have a way of assimilating people, so regardless of local
variations in culture or traditions, we are able to identify certain urban
universals. For instance, city inhabitants are less concerned with the immediate tasks of growing food and are more devoted to such secondary
activities as trade, arts and crafts, and government. As well, all cities
must find ways of dealing with population density, the close contact of
strangers, and protecting concentrated stores of wealth. This idea seems
especially convincing in light of today's modern globalization: City
people the world over seem to imitate each other, communicate with
each other, and share more of the same values than they do with people
in the more rural areas of their countries.

In addition, we might compare and contrast types of cities: rich versus poor, big versus small, inland versus port, administrative versus
commercial, and capital versus lesser cities, for instance.

FERNAND BRAUDEL

Towns and Cities

Fernand Braudel was one of the great historians of the twentieth century, and the following selection, which provides a broad overview of
medieval towns and cities throughout the world, is from one of his in-
terpretative works of world history. According to Braudel, what were
some of the distinctive characteristics of Western, or European,
towns? Why did Western towns acquire these characteristics? How
does Braudel describe Chinese and Islamic cities? Why and how did
these towns develop differently?

Fernand Braudel, *The Structures of Everyday Life: The Limits of the Possible* (London:
Collins, 1983), 509–15, 518–25.

Thinking Historically

Braudel's piece begins with an emphasis on contrast, arguing that Western towns were original, vastly different from those of other cultures. It was not European *culture*, however, that made Western towns different, according to Braudel; it was the accidents of European history, geography, and social life.

Notice also that Braudel sees some similarities or convergence among the world's cities. Throughout the selection he describes a historic running battle between cities and states. How did this conflict encourage the development of different kinds of cities? Braudel also describes an evolutionary pattern of normal urban development—from open to closed to dominated—that was repeated everywhere, although in some places (e.g., the Americas) stages were aborted or skipped. Thus Braudel defines the two approaches one could take to understanding cities—that they reflect their different cultures, and that they are the same everywhere or becoming similar. As you read this, are you more impressed with the differences or similarities among the world's cities?

The Originality of Western Towns

... What were Europe's differences and original features? Its towns were marked by an unparalleled freedom. They had developed as autonomous worlds and according to their own propensities. They had outwitted the territorial state, which was established slowly and then only grew with their interested co-operation—and was moreover only an enlarged and often insipid copy of their development. They ruled their countrysides autocratically, regarding them exactly as later powers regarded their colonies, and treating them as such. They pursued an economic policy of their own via their satellites and the nervous system of urban relay points; they were capable of breaking down obstacles and creating or recreating protective privileges. Imagine what would happen if modern states were suppressed so that the Chambers of Commerce of the large towns were free to act as they pleased!

Even without resort to doubtful comparisons these long-standing realities leap to the eye. And they lead us to a key problem which can be formulated in two or three different ways: What stopped the other cities of the world from enjoying the same relative freedom? Or to take another aspect of the same problem, why was change a striking feature of the destiny of Western towns (even their physical existence was transformed) while the other cities have no history by comparison and seem to have been shut in long periods of immobility? Why were some cities like steam-engines while the others were like clocks, to parody Lévi-Strauss? Comparative history compels us to look for the reason for these differences and to attempt to establish a dynamic "model" of the turbulent urban evolution of the West, whereas a model representing city life in the rest of the world would run in a straight and scarcely broken line across time.

Free Worlds

Urban freedom in Europe is a classic and fairly well documented subject; let us start with it.

In a simplified form we can say:

1. The West well and truly lost its urban framework with the end of the Roman Empire. Moreover the towns in the Empire had been gradually declining since before the arrival of the barbarians. The very relative animation of the Merovingian period was followed, slightly earlier in some places, slightly later in others, by a complete halt.

2. The urban renaissance from the eleventh century was precipitated by and superimposed on a rise in rural vigour, a growth of fields, vineyards, and orchards. Towns grew in harmony with villages and clearly outlined urban law often emerged from the communal privileges of village groups. The town was often simply the country revived and remodeled. The names of a number of streets in Frankfurt (which remained very rural until the sixteenth century) recall the woods, clumps of trees, and marshland amid which the town grew up.

This rural rearrangement naturally brought to the nascent city the representatives of political and social authority: nobles, lay princes, and ecclesiastics.

3. None of this would have been possible without a general return to health and a growing monetary economy. Money, a traveler from perhaps distant lands (from Islam, according to Maurice Lombard), was the active and decisive force. Two centuries before Saint Thomas Aquinas, Alain de Lille said: "Money, not Caesar, is everything now." And money meant towns.

Thousands of towns were founded at this time, but few of them went on to brilliant futures. Only certain regions, therefore, were urbanized in depth, thus distinguishing themselves from the rest and playing a vitalizing role: such was the region between the Loire and the Rhine, for instance, or northern and central Italy, and certain key points on Mediterranean coasts. Merchants, craft guilds, industries, long-distance trade, and banks were quick to appear there, as well as a certain kind of bourgeoisie and even some sort of capitalism. The destinies of these very special cities were linked not only to the progress of the surrounding countryside but to international trade. Indeed, they often broke free of rural society and former political ties. The break might be achieved violently or amicably, but it was always a sign of strength, plentiful money, and real power.

Soon there were no states around these privileged towns. This was the case in Italy and Germany, with the political collapses of the thirteenth century. The hare beat the tortoise for once. Elsewhere—in France, England, Castile, even in Aragon—the earlier rebirth of the territorial state restricted the development of the towns, which in addition were not situated in particularly lively economic areas. They grew less rapidly than elsewhere.

But the main, the unpredictable thing was that certain towns made themselves into autonomous worlds, city-states, buttressed with privileges (acquired or extorted) like so many juridical ramparts. Perhaps in the past historians have insisted too much on the legal factors involved, for if such considerations were indeed sometimes more important than, or of equal importance to, geographical, sociological, and economic factors, the latter did count to a large extent. What is privilege without material substance?

In fact the miracle in the West was not so much that everything sprang up again from the eleventh century, after having been almost annihilated with the disaster of the fifth. History is full of examples of secular revivals, of urban expansion, of births and rebirths: Greece from the fifth to the second century B.C.E.; Rome perhaps; Islam from the ninth century; China under the Sungs. But these revivals always featured two runners, the state and the city. The state usually won and the city then remained subject and under a heavy yoke. The miracle of the first great urban centuries in Europe was that the city won hands down, at least in Italy, Flanders, and Germany. It was able to try the experiment of leading a completely separate life for quite a long time. This was a colossal event. Its genesis cannot be pinpointed with certainty, but its enormous consequences are visible.

Towns as Outposts of Modernity

It was on the basis of this liberty that the great Western cities, and other towns they influenced and to which they served as examples, built up a distinctive civilization and spread techniques which were new, or had been revived or rediscovered after centuries—it matters little which. The important thing is that these cities had the rare privilege of following through an unusual political, social, and economic experience.

In the financial sphere, the towns organized taxation, finances, public credit, customs, and excise. They invented public loans: the first issues of the Monte Vecchio in Venice could be said to go back to 1167, the first formulation of the Casa di San Giorgio to 1407. One after another, they reinvented gold money, following Genoa which may have minted the *genovino* as early as the late twelfth century. They organized industry and the guilds; they invented long-distance trade, bills of exchange, the first forms of trading companies and accountancy. They also quickly became the scene of class struggles. For if the towns were "communities" as has been said, they were also "societies" in the modern sense of the word, with their tensions and civil struggles: nobles against bourgeois; poor against rich ("thin people" *popolo magro* against "fat people" *popolo grosso*). The struggles in Florence were already more deeply akin to those of the industrial early nineteenth century than to the faction-fights of ancient Rome, as the drama of the Ciompi (1378) demonstrates.

This society divided from within also faced enemies from without—the worlds of the noble, prince, or peasant, of everybody who was not a citizen. The cities were the West's first focus for patriotism—and the patriotism they inspired was long to be more coherent and much more conscious than the territorial kind, which emerged only slowly in the first states. One can reflect upon this by looking at a curious painting representing the battle on 19 June 1502 between the citizens of Nuremberg and the Margrave Casimir of Brandenburg-Ansbach who was attacking the town. One does not have to ask who commissioned the picture. Most of the townspeople are depicted on foot, without armour, in their everyday clothes. Their leader, on horseback and dressed in a black suit, is talking to the humanist Willibald Pirckheimer, who is wearing one of the enormous ostrich-feather hats of the period and who is, significantly, leading a band of men to assist the rightful cause of the town under attack. The Brandenburg assailants are heavily armed and on horseback, their faces hidden by the visors of their helmets. One group of three men in the picture could be taken as a symbol of the freedom of the towns against the authority of princes and noblemen: two burghers with unshielded faces stand proudly one each side of an armoured horseman they are escorting away as their shamefaced prisoner.

"Bourgeois," "burghers," in their little city strongholds: These are convenient terms but highly imprecise. Werner Sombart has placed a good deal of emphasis on this birth of a society, and more still of a new state of mind. "It is in Florence towards the end of the fourteenth century, if I am not mistaken," he wrote, "that we meet the perfect bourgeois for the first time." Perhaps. In fact the assumption of power (1293) by the *Arti Maggiori*—those of wool and of the *Arte di Calimala*—marked the victory of the old and new rich and the spirit of enterprise in Florence. Sombart, as usual, preferred to place the problem on the level of mentalities and the development of the rational spirit, rather than on the plane of societies, or even of the economy, where he was afraid of following in Marx's footsteps.

A new state of mind was established, broadly that of an early, still faltering, Western capitalism—a collection of rules, possibilities, calculations, the art both of getting rich and of living. It also included gambling and risk: the key words of commercial language, *fortuna, ventura, ragione, prudenza, sicurta,* define the risks to be guarded against. No question now of living from day to day as noblemen did, always putting up their revenues to try to meet the level of their expenditure, which invariably came first—and letting the future take care of itself. The merchant was economical with his money, calculated his expenditure according to his returns, his investments according to their yield. The hour-glass had turned back the right way. He would also be economical with his time: A merchant could already say that *chi tempo ha e tempo aspetta tempo perde,* which means much the same thing as "time is money."

Capitalism and towns were basically the same thing in the West. Lewis Mumford humorously claimed that capitalism was the cuckoo's egg laid in the confined nests of the medieval towns. By this he meant to convey that the bird was destined to grow inordinately and burst its tight framework (which was true), and then link up with the state, the conqueror of towns but heir to their institutions and way of thinking and completely incapable of dispensing with them. The important thing was that even when it had declined as a city the town continued to rule the roost all the time it was passing into the actual or apparent service of the prince. The wealth of the state would still be the wealth of the town: Portugal converged on Lisbon, the Netherlands on Amsterdam, and English primacy was London's primacy (the capital modelled England in its own image after the peaceful revolution of 1688). The latent defect in the Spanish imperial economy was that it was based on Seville—a controlled town rotten with dishonest officials and long dominated by foreign capitalists—and not on a powerful free town capable of producing and carrying through a really individual economic policy. Likewise, if Louis XIV did not succeed in founding a "royal bank," despite various projects (1703, 1706, 1709), it was because faced with the power of the monarch, Paris did not offer the protection of a town free to do what it wanted and accountable to no one.

Urban Patterns

Let us imagine we are looking at a comprehensive history of the towns of Europe covering the complete series of their forms from the Greek city-state to an eighteenth-century town—everything Europe was able to build at home and overseas, from Muscovy in the East to America in the West. How is one to classify such a wealth of material? One might begin with political, economic, or social characteristics. Politically a differentiation would be made between capitals, fortresses, and administrative towns in the full meaning of "administrative." Economically, one would distinguish between ports, caravan towns, market towns, industrial towns, and money markets. Socially, a list could be drawn up of *rentier*[1] towns, and Church, Court, or craftsmen's towns. This is to adopt a series of fairly obvious categories, divisible into sub-categories and capable of absorbing all sorts of local varieties. Such a classification has advantages, not so much for the question of the town in itself as for the study of particular economies limited in time and space.

On the other hand, some more general distinctions arising out of the very process of town development offer a more useful classification for our purpose. Simplifying, one could say that the West has had three basic types of town in the course of its evolution: open towns, that is to say not differentiated from their hinterland, even blending into it (A); towns closed in on themselves in every sense, their walls marking the boundaries of an individual way of life more than a territory (B); finally towns held in subjection, by which is meant the whole range of known controls by prince or state (C).

Roughly, A preceded B, and B preceded C. But there is no suggestion of strict succession about this order. It is rather a question of directions and dimensions shaping the complicated careers of the Western towns. They did not all develop at the same time or in the same way. Later we will see if this "grid" is valid for classifying all the towns of the world.

Type A: the ancient Greek or Roman city was open to the surrounding countryside and on terms of equality with it. Athens accepted inside its walls as rightful citizens the Eupatrid horse-breeders as well as the vine-growing peasants so dear to Aristophanes. As soon as the smoke rose above the Pnyx, the peasant responded to the signal and attended the Assembly of the People, where he sat among his equals. At the beginning of the Peloponnesian war, the entire population of the Attic countryside evacuated itself to Athens where it took refuge while the Spartans ravaged the fields, olive groves, and houses. When the Spartans fell back at the approach of winter, the country people returned to their homes. The Greek city was in fact the sum of the town and its surrounding countryside. . . . Likewise, if one explores the ruins of Roman cities, one is in open country immediately outside the gates: There are no suburbs, which is as good as saying no industry or active and organized trades in their duly allotted place.

Type B: the closed city: the medieval town was the classic example of a closed city, a self-sufficient unit, an exclusive, Lilliputian empire. Entering its gates was like crossing one of the serious frontiers of the world today. You were free to thumb your nose at your neighbour from the other side of the barrier. He could not touch you. The peasant who uprooted himself from his land and arrived in the town was immediately

---

[1] Based on real estate investment and development. [Ed.]

another man. He was free—or rather he had abandoned a known and hated servitude for another, not always guessing the extent of it beforehand. But this mattered little. If the town had adopted him, he could snap his fingers when his lord called for him. And though obsolete elsewhere, such calls were still frequently to be heard in Silesia in the eighteenth century and in Muscovy up to the nineteenth.

Though the towns opened their gates easily it was not enough to walk through them to be immediately and really part of them. Full citizens were a jealous minority, a small town inside the town itself. A citadel of the rich was built up in Venice in 1297 thanks to the *serrata,* the closing of the Great Council to new members. The *nobili* of Venice became a closed class for centuries. Very rarely did anyone force its gates. The category of ordinary *cittadini*—at a lower level—was probably more hospitable. But the Signoria very soon created two types of citizen, one *de intus,* the other *de intus et extra,* the latter full, the former partial. Fifteen years' residence were still required to be allowed to apply for the first, twenty-five years for the second. A decree by the Senate in 1386 even forbade new citizens (including those who were full citizens) from trading directly in Venice with German merchants at the Fondego dei Todeschi or outside it. The ordinary townspeople were no less mistrustful or hostile to newcomers. According to Marin Sanudo, in June 1520, the street people attacked the peasants who had arrived from the mainland as recruits for the galleys or the army, crying *"Poltroni ande arar!"* "Back to the plough, shirkers!"

Of course Venice was an extreme example. Moreover, it owed the preservation of its own constitution until 1797 to an aristocratic and extremely reactionary regime, as well as to the conquest at the beginning of the fifteenth century of the Terra Firma, which extended its authority as far as the Alps and Brescia. It was the last *polis* in the West. But citizenship was also parisimoniously granted in Marseilles in the sixteenth century; it was necessary to have "ten years of domicile, to possess property, to have married a local girl." Otherwise the man remained amongst the masses of non-citizens of the town. This limited conception of citizenship was the general rule everywhere.

The main source of contention can be glimpsed throughout this vast process: to whom did industry and craft, their privileges and profits, belong? In fact they belonged to the town, to its authorities and to its merchant entrepreneurs. They decided if it were necessary to deprive, or to try to deprive, the rural area of the city of the right to spin, weave, and dye, or if on the contrary it would be advantageous to grant it these rights. Everything was possible in these interchanges, as the history of each individual town shows.

As far as work inside the walls was concerned (we can hardly call it industry without qualification), everything was arranged for the benefit of the craft guilds. They enjoyed exclusive contiguous monopolies, fiercely defended along the imprecise frontiers that so easily led to absurd conflicts. The urban authorities did not always have the situation under control. Sooner or later, with the help of money, they were to allow obvious, acknowledged, honorary superiorities, consecrated by money or power, to become apparent. The "Six Corps" (drapers, grocers, haberdashers, furriers, hosiers, goldsmiths) were the commercial aristocracy of Paris from 1625. In Florence it was the *arte dela lana* and the *Arte di Calimala* (engaged in dyeing fabric imported from the north, unbleached). But town museums in Germany supply the best evidence of these old situations. In Ulm, for example, each guild owned a picture hinged in triptych form. The side panels represented characteristic scenes of the craft. The centre, like a treasured family album, showed innumerable small portraits recalling the successive generations of masters of the guild over the centuries.

An even more telling example was the City of London and its annexes (running along its walls) in the eighteenth century, still the domain of fussy, obsolete, and powerful guilds. If Westminster and the suburbs were growing continually, noted a well-informed economist (1754), it was for obvious reasons: "These suburbs are free and present a clear field for every industrious citizen, while in its bosom London nourishes ninety-two of all sorts of those exclusive companies [guilds], whose numerous members can be seen adorning the Lord Mayor's Show every year with immoderate pomp." Let us come to a halt here before this colourful scene. And for the moment let us also pass over the free crafts, around London and elsewhere, which kept outside the guild-masterships and their regulations, outside their constraint and protection.

Type C: subjugated towns, of early modern times. Everywhere in Europe, as soon as the state was firmly established it disciplined the towns with instinctive relentlessness, whether or not it used violence. The Habsburgs did so just as much as the Popes, the German princes as much as the Medicis or the kings of France. Except in the Netherlands and England, obedience was imposed.

Take Florence as an example: The Medicis had slowly subjugated it, almost elegantly in Lorenzo's time. But after 1532 and the return of the Medicis to power the process accelerated. Florence in the seventeenth century was no more than the Grand Duke's court. He had seized everything—money, the right to govern, and to distribute honours. From the Pitti Palace, on the left bank of the Arno, a gallery—a secret passage in fact—allowed the prince to cross the river and reach the Uffizi. This elegant gallery, still in existence today on the Ponte Vecchio, was the thread from which the spider at the extremity of his web supervised the imprisoned town. . . .

Different Types of Development

But we know, of course, that urban development does not happen of its own accord: It is not an endogenous phenomenon produced under a bell-jar. It is always the expression of a society which controls it from within, but also from without, and in this respect, our classification is, I repeat, too simple. That said, how does it work when applied outside the narrow confines of Western Europe?

1. *Towns in colonial America.* We should say "in Latin America," because the English towns remained a separate case. They had to live by their own resources and emerge from their wilderness to find a place in the vast world; the real parallel for them is the medieval city. The towns in Iberian America had a much simpler and more limited career. Built like Roman camps inside four earth walls, they were garrisons lost in the midst of vast hostile expanses, linked together by communications which were slow because they stretched across enormous empty spaces. Curiously, at a period when the privileged medieval town had spread over practically the whole of Europe, the ancient rule prevailed in all Hispano-Portuguese America, apart from the large towns of the viceroys: Mexico City, Lima, Santiago de Chile, San Salvador (Bahia) — that is to say the official, already parasitical organisms.

There were scarcely any purely commercial towns in this part of America, or if there were they were of minor importance. For example, Recife — the merchants' town — stood next to aristocratic Olinda, town of great plantation owners, *senhores de engenbos,*[2] and slave owners. It was rather like Piraeus or Phalera in relation to Pericles' Athens. Buenos Aires after its second foundation (the successful one on 1580) was still a small market village — like Megara or Aegina. It had the misfortune to have nothing but Indian *bravos* round about, and its inhabitants complained of being forced to earn "their bread by the sweat of their brow" in this America where the whites were *rentiers.*[3] But caravans of mules or large wooden carts arrived there from the Andes, from Lima, which was a way of acquiring Potosi silver. Sugar, and soon gold, came by sailing ship from Brazil. And contact with Portugal and Africa was maintained through the smuggling carried on by sailing ships bringing black slaves. But Buenos Aires remained an exception amidst the "barbarism" of nascent Argentina.

The American town was generally tiny, without these gifts from abroad. It governed itself. No one was really concerned with its fate. Its masters were the landowners who had their houses in the town, with rings for tethering their horses fixed on the front walls overlooking the

[2]Men of talent. [Ed.]
[3]Property owners. [Ed.]

street. These were the "men of property," *os homes bons* of the munici-palities of Brazil, or the *hacendados* of the Spanish *cabildos*.[4] These towns were so many miniature versions of Sparta or of Thebes in the time of Epaminondas. It could safely be said that the history of the Western towns in America began again from zero. Naturally there was no separation between the towns and the hinterland and there was no industry to be shared out. Wherever industry appeared—in Mexico city, for example—it was carried on by slaves or semi-slaves. The me-dieval European town would not have been conceivable if its artisans had been serfs.

2. *How should Russian towns be classified?* One can tell at a glance that the towns that survived or grew up again in Muscovy after the terrible catastrophes of the Mongol invasion no longer lived according to the Western pattern. Although there were great cities among them, like Moscow or Novgorod, they were kept in hand sometimes brutally. In the sixteenth century a proverb still asked: "Who can set his face against God and the mighty Novgorod?" But the proverb was wrong. The town was harshly brought to heel in 1427 and again in 1477 (it had to deliver 300 cartloads of gold). Executions, deportations, confis-cations followed in quick succession. Above all, these towns were caught up in the slow circulation of traffic over an immense, already Asiatic, still wild expanse. In 1650, as in the past, transport on the rivers or overland by sledge or by convoys of carts moved with an enor-mous loss of time. It was often dangerous even to go near villages, and a halt had to be called every evening in open country—as on the Balkan roads—deploying the carriages in a circle, with everyone on the alert to defend himself.

For all these reasons the Muscovy towns did not impose themselves on the vast surrounding countryside; quite the reverse. They were un-able to dictate their wishes to a peasant world which was biologically extraordinarily strong, although poverty-stricken, restless, and perpetu-ally on the move. The important fact was that "harvests per hectare in the European countries of the East remained constant on average, from the sixteenth to the nineteenth century"—at a low level. There was no healthy rural surplus and therefore no really prosperous town. Nor did the Russian towns have serving them those secondary towns that were a characteristic of the West and its lively trade.

Consequently, there were innumerable peasant serfs practically without land, insolvent in the eyes of their lords and even the state. It was of no importance whether they went to towns or to work in the houses of rich peasants. In the town they became beggars, porters,

---

[4]Town councils. [Ed.]

craftsmen, poor tradesmen, or very rarely merchants who got rich quickly. They might also stay put and become craftsmen in their own villages, or seek the necessary supplement to their earnings by becoming carriers or travelling pedlars. This irresistible tide of mendicancy could not be stemmed, and indeed it often served the interests of the landlord who gave it his blessing: All such artisans and traders remained his serfs whatever they did and however great their social success; they still owed him their dues.

These examples and others indicate a fate resembling what may after all have happened at the beginning of Western urbanization. Though a clearer case, it is comparable to the caesura[5] between the eleventh and thirteenth centuries, that interlude when almost everything was born of the villages and peasant vitality. We might call it an intermediate position between A and C, without the B type (the independent city) ever having arisen. The prince appeared too quickly, like the ogre in a fairy tale.

3. *Imperial towns in the East and Far East.* The same problems and ambiguities—only deeper—arise when we leave Europe and move east.

Towns similar to those in medieval Europe—masters of their fate for a brief moment—only arose in Islam when the empires collapsed. They marked some outstanding moments in Islamic civilization. But they only lasted for a time and the main beneficiaries were certain marginal towns like Cordoba, or the cities which were urban republics by the fifteenth century, like Ceuta before the Portuguese occupation in 1415, or Oran before the Spanish occupation in 1509. The usual pattern was the huge city under the rule of a prince or a Caliph: a Baghdad or a Cairo.

Towns in distant Asia were of the same type: imperial or royal cities, enormous, parasitical, soft, and luxurious—Delhi and Vijnayanagar, Peking and to some extent Nanking, though this was rather different. The great prestige enjoyed by the prince comes as no surprise to us. And if one ruler was swallowed up by the city or more likely by his palace, another immediately took his place and the subjection continued. Neither will it surprise us to learn that these towns were incapable of taking over the artisanal trades from the countryside: They were both open towns and subject towns simultaneously. Besides, in India as in China, social structures already existing hampered the free movement of the towns. If the town did not win its independence, it was not only because of the bastinadoes[6] ordered by the mandarins or the cru-

---

[5]Pause. [Ed.]
[6]Beatings (often on soles of the feet). [Ed.]

elty of the prince to merchants and ordinary citizens. It was because society was prematurely fixed, crystallized in a certain mould.

In India, the caste system automatically divided and broke up every urban community. In China, the cult of the *gentes*[7] on the one hand was confronted on the other by a mixture comparable to that which created the Western town: Like the latter it acted as a melting-pot, breaking old bonds and placing individuals on the same level. The arrival of immigrants created an "American" environment, where those already settled set the tone and the way of life. In addition, there was no independent authority representing the Chinese town as a unit, in its dealings with the State or with the very powerful countryside. The rural areas were the real heart of living, active, and thinking China.

The town, residence of officials and nobles, was not the property of either guilds or merchants. There was no gradual "rise of the bourgeoisie" here. No sooner did a bourgeoisie appear than it was tempted by class betrayal, fascinated by the luxurious life of the mandarins. The towns might have lived their own lives, filled in the contours of their own destiny, if individual initiative and capitalism had had a clear field. But the tutelary State hardly lent itself to this. It did occasionally nod, intentionally or not: At the end of the sixteenth century a bourgeoisie seems to have emerged with a taste for business enterprise, and we can guess what part it played in the large iron-works near Peking, in the private porcelain workshops that developed in King-te-chen, and even more in the rise of the silk trade in Su-Chu, the capital of Kiang-tsu. But this was no more than a flash in the pan. With the Manchu conquest, the Chinese crisis was resolved in the seventeenth century in a direction completely opposed to urban freedoms.

Only the West swung completely over in favour of its towns. The towns caused the West to advance. It was, let us repeat, an enormous event, but the deep-seated reasons behind it are still inadequately explained. What would the Chinese towns have become if the junks had discovered the Cape of Good Hope at the beginning of the fifteenth century, and had made full use of such a chance of world conquest?

[7]People. [Ed.]

78

European Guilds and Urban Autonomy

The following primary source documents, two from England and one from Italy, illuminate the influence of guilds and city government in medieval Europe. The first document is a decree by King Henry II of England, establishing a guild for the cordwainers, or shoemakers, of Oxford. The second is a charter granted by King John of England to the citizens of Dunwich. The third document records a meeting of the Florentine cloth-makers guild, working together with other guild members to collect taxes. According to these primary sources, what connections existed between guilds and city government? Why did kings and princes give guilds and towns such freedoms, privileges, and independence? Which of these towns had the greatest autonomy? Which had the least?

Thinking Historically

How do these documents support Braudel's history of medieval European towns? If Braudel's interpretation were valid, where in the world would you expect to find similar documents? What sort of primary sources documenting city governance would you expect to find in the Islamic world or in China?

Henry II of England: Grant of a Guild to the Oxford Cordwainers, 1175

Know ye that I have granted and confirmed to the corvesars of Oxford all the liberties and customs which they had in the time of King Henry, my grandfather, and that they have their guild, so that none carry on their trade in the town of Oxford, except he be of that guild.

A Source Book for Medieval Economic History, ed. Roy C. Cave and Herbert H. Coulson (Milwaukee: The Bruce Publishing Co., 1936; reprint, New York: Biblo & Tannen, 1965), 237–38.

Select Charters of English Constitutional History, ed. William Stubbs and H. W. C. Davis. (Oxford: Clarendon Press, 1913), 308, reprinted in *A Source Book for Medieval Economic History,* ed. Roy C. Cave and Herbert H. Coulson (Milwaukee: The Bruce Publishing Co., 1936; reprint, New York: Biblo & Tannen, 1965), 208–9.

P. Santini, ed., *Documenti dell'Antica Costituzione del Comune di Firenze,* vol. I, p. 386, in *Documenti di Storia Italiana,* Tome X (Florence, 1895); reprinted in *A Source Book for Medieval Economic History,* ed. Roy C. Cave and Herbert H. Coulson (Milwaukee: The Bruce Publishing Co., 1936; reprint, New York: Biblo & Tannen, 1965), 211–12.

I grant also that the cordwainers who afterwards may come into the town of Oxford shall be of the same guild and shall have the same liberties and customs which the corvesars had or ought to have.

For this grant and confirmation, however, the corvesars and cordwainers ought to pay me every year an ounce of gold.

John, King of England: Charter of Privileges Granted to Men of Dunwich, 1200

John, by the grace of God, etc. Know that we have conceded, and confirmed by this charter, to our citizens of Dunwich, that the borough of Dunwich be our free borough, and have *soc* and *sac*[1] and *toll*[2] and *team*[3] and *infangentheof*,[4] and that they be quit of[5] thelony[6] the lestage[7] and passage and pontage[8] and stallage[9] and of *leve*[10] and of Danegeld[11] and of ewage,[12] of wreck[13] and *lagan*,[14] and of all other customs throughout all our land, saving the liberties of our citizens of London, and that they pay the lawful and customary farm[15] at our exchequer by their own hand; and that they make no plea before the shire court or the hundred court except in the presence of our justices; and when they are summoned into the presence of our justices let them send twelve lawful men from their borough to answer for all of them; and if, by chance, they ought to be amerced,[16] let them be amerced by six honest men of their own borough and six honest men from outside their borough.

We have also conceded to them that they may marry their sons and daughters freely wherever they wish throughout our whole land, and widows likewise on the advice of their friends, and that they may give

[1]Power to hold court and administer justice. [Ed.]

[2]The right to collect tolls or duties. [Ed.]

[3]The right to compel a person with stolen property to name the person from whom he received it. [Ed.]

[4]Jurisdiction over a thief caught within the limit of the estate to which the right belonged. [Ed.]

[5]Free of. [Ed.]

[6]Toll levied on imports and exports. [Ed.]

[7]Tax on weight of goods. [Ed.]

[8]Transportation and bridge tolls. [Ed.]

[9]Fee on market location. [Ed.]

[10]Required assembly on call of the king. [Ed.]

[11]Tribute originally paid to the Danes (Dane Gold); later the system of personal taxation used to finance the king's activities. [Ed.]

[12]Obligation of military service. [Ed.]

[13]Right to wreckage. [Ed.]

[14]Right to retrieved goods from shipwreck (flotsam and jetsam). [Ed.]

[15]Fixed annual rent of town land. [Ed.]

[16]Fined (by the "mercy" of the court). [Ed.]

or sell or do as they wish with their possessions in lands and buildings, and whenever they wish. We have also conceded to them a hanse and gild merchant just as they have been accustomed to have. Therefore we wish and firmly command that our said burgesses may have and hold the said liberties and free customs freely, peacefully, and wholly, without hindrance.

Witnesses, etc.

The Arte della Lana *and the Government of Florence, 1224*

In the name of God, amen. We, Albert de Corsino, Astoldo Iochi, Gerard Giraldi, Astancollo Astancolli, Alioto Rodighieri, Pelacane Arrighi, Abbate Erbolotti, Gualterotto Bardi, Buono Vernacci, Odarigo Davanzi, Buonaiunta Cambiati, and Reniero Montancollo, elected and appointed by the common council of the Commune of Florence, in the time of the lordship of Inghirrami de Magreto, by the grace of God, Podestà of Florence according to the mandate of the same Council gathered, according to custom, at the sound of the bell on March 20th in the palace of the Commune of Florence; at which council there were also present at the wish and command of the said Podestà the consuls of the merchants, bankers, of the Arte della Lana, the priors of the crafts, and also twenty men from every *sestiere*[17] of the city, in which Council it was said, confirmed, and agreed that twelve men should be elected, two from each *sestiere,* who ought to have full power and authority over all the consuls who were in office when the tower of Semifonte was destroyed, and over all other greater consuls of the city, and over all court officials, castellans, syndics, procurators, and prefects who have been in office from the time of the said consuls up to the first of last January, and over those who have and hold the new and old walls of the city of Florence, and who keep them, and also over those who have and hold the public squares of the Commune wherever they are and who keep them; and over all and each they should have full and free authority to speak, pronounce, and impose (their commands) for clearing the debt of the Commune of Florence; wherefore we, etc., impose, etc. The greater abbey, of Florence, i.e., St. Mary's for 166 fathoms of wall:, 191. 17 solidi. 6 denarii.

[17]District. [Ed.]

79

AIDAN SOUTHALL

Guilds and the Chinese City

Aidan Southall, a distinguished urban anthropologist, begins this selection with a discussion of Chinese economic growth in the tenth century. He then explores the role of guilds in medieval Chinese society, emphasizing their prevalence and long history in the region. The previous two selections showed how guilds were a critical source of urban autonomy in European cities. How might guilds reduce the power of kinship groups, the king, or the central state, thus allowing a town or city to prosper? Why didn't Chinese guilds have the same effect?

Thinking Historically

Does Southall's study of China support Braudel's emphasis on European uniqueness? Does the political weakness of Chinese guilds explain why China, despite its economic development, did not undergo an industrial revolution hundreds of years before the West? How was the weakness of Chinese guilds tied to China's social structure, which differed greatly from Europe's?

... The first century of Song rule, from about 980, witnessed the most rapid economic growth in the history of China. All known economic indicators showed an extraordinary burst of expansion. The acreage of arable land rose from 2.9 to 4.6 million, despite the exclusion of the far north.

It is claimed that the consumption of coal and iron during this period rose faster than in the first two centuries of the industrial revolution in Britain. The production of pig iron in the mid-eleventh century was fourteen times what it had been under the T'ang in A.D. 800; that of silver thirteen times and copper eight times as great. Such increased production of currency metals inevitably led to price inflation, but the rise in price was actually less than the rise in production, for the national budget only rose seven times, from 20 million strings in A.D. 1004 to 150 million in A.D. 1021, against the rise of eight times in copper production, which provided the bulk of the currency, while the

Aidan Southall, *The City in Time and Space* (New York: Cambridge University Press, 1998), 147–51.

luxury and overseas trading currency in silver rose thirteen times. At the same time the monetization of the economy probably proceeded even faster, since in the eighth century only 4% of revenue was received in money, as against over 50% by the mid-eleventh century. In fact, production seems to have more than caught up with price inflation, for the budget of A.D. 1065 was only 116 million strings as against 150.8 million in 1021. In paper currency there were 10 million strings in circulation by A.D. 1166. Although the currency was not unified, the capacity to print paper money added greatly to the speed and volume of transactions and the importance of banking. The Song administration also established pawnshops which made loans to peasants.

The annual supply of grain to the capital from the main producing areas of the Yangtze valley averaged 6 million piculs[1] in the eleventh century, reaching 8 million in some years, as against 2 million to T'ang Chang'an 400 years before, 2 to 5 million to Yüan Peking in the fourteenth century and an average of 4 million to Peking throughout the Ming and Qing dynasties.

The Song capital at Kaifeng was easier to provision by the waterways from the south than any other northern capital. The Song did not attempt to reconquer the far north, much of which was devastated, but paid off its Khitan Liao dynasty with an ample tribute which was far cheaper than maintaining huge armies like the T'ang. The number of mandarins administering the empire almost doubled in a few decades from 9,785 in 1016 to 17,300 in 1049.

In the Song era, if ever, China might have taken off into the self-sustaining growth of an industrial revolution. But the powerful intellectual and potentially innovative interests of the urban elite were too narrowly focused in other directions: the acquisition of higher rank and more land. Furthermore, no autonomous urban community capable of promoting energetic and co-ordinated economic development existed. The Song merchant class seemed to be bursting with energy, but dissipated it in diverse personal concerns and never made any attempt to claim civic rights or autonomy and to organize for corporate advance. If they had they would surely have been suppressed. Failure to industrialize was due to the "indifferent unity of town and country," emphasized by both Marx and Weber. The cities were not discrete, exclusive territorial units, even for bureaucratic administration. "The Chinese urban dweller legally belonged to his family and native village, in which the temples of his ancestors stood and to which he conscientiously maintained affiliation." He was like a temporary sojourner, without effective identification with the city, inhibiting development of an urban class to fight for autonomy and economic transformation.

---

[1] 1 picul = 133 pounds.

Guilds

Here it might be thought that the guilds could have made a strategic contribution. They were certainly very numerous and ancient in Chinese cities. They had great potential, but it could not be realized in classical China. Only in late imperial Hankow did Rowe find "the rise of a guild-centred, sub-rosa municipal government apparatus, which reached full development only in the political crisis of 1911." Hankow had 179 guilds with halls, and far larger numbers without. Some were vast, containing several temples, assembly halls, courtyards, fish ponds, pleasure gardens, and theatres. They were religious brotherhoods, dedicated to their patron deities. They staged operatic and theatrical performances to vast crowds. Their magnificent lantern processions and festivals were a "public burning off of profits" in the economic rivalry between guilds as well as the personal assertion of major benefactors and ritual propitiation. They organized schools to prepare their sons for civil service examinations which were, of course, an escape from merchant status.

Guilds had traditionally had nothing to do with city government, which was monopolized by the mandarins, who endeavoured to suppress any resources which could pose the threat of alternative sources of power. There was no chance for guilds, any more than cities, to acquire official charters.

Guilds were always local, to one city and its immediate hinterland at most, for any wider combination would clearly have been a threat, which is doubtless the reason why secret societies have been such a characteristic Chinese product.

Marco Polo found guilds flourishing in thirteenth-century Hangchow. A few of the twentieth-century guilds in Peking seem to date as far back as T'ang, in the eighth or ninth century, but all have been constantly reorganized. Korean guilds, derived from those of China, have retained constitutions more than 1,000 years old. T'ang Chang'an is said to have had 220 guilds, Loyang 120, while Song Hangchow had 414.

Burgess' study of Peking in 1928 estimates that it had 128 guilds then, with at least 128,000 members and probably another 50,000 apprentices, controlling over 5,000 shops. This suggests that virtually all crafts and commerce were under guild control and there are strong reasons for assuming that such had been the case in all Chinese cities for many centuries, so that we are justified in taking this late study as some indication of much earlier institutions.

Guilds were characterized by face-to-face intimacy and high solidarity, with both a kinship and a religious element. Not only in the countryside, but even in small towns with populations of several thousand, there were often considerable and frequently dominant

concentrations of persons of the same surname, regarding one another
as at least distant fellow clansmen. Sometimes such towns also concentrated on a particular craft or occupation. Thus came about the combination of common occupation and common residence with some sense
of common descent, which was reproduced in the wards of the larger
cities. Such guilds cannot clearly be distinguished from regional associations, since if rural–urban migrants from the same region settled in the
same ward of a city and tended to concentrate on the same occupation
all distinctions disappear. It seems that this was usually the case, although at least in the nineteenth-century Treaty Ports there evidently
were some regional associations which were not craft or commercial
guilds at the same time.

The basic motive for guild formation was protection from exploitation by the bureaucracy. The latter tolerated guilds as convenient and
orderly institutions which could in fact be used by officials to collect
tax and special levies from members. But the guilds were effective and
could usually make a successful stand against an official who tried to
exploit them beyond what had come to be recognized as customary
limits. Guilds could also strike against employers for higher pay, or
boycott intruders, as they even did foreign traders successfully on occasion. Peking guilds were also called upon to serve the imperial court in
various customary ways, as when six groups of eight porters were
called to take turns carrying the coffin of a royal concubine. The
absence of any consistent common law in China made guild self-
regulation all the more important, including matters such as insolvency,
for which there was no recourse to any court of law.

Whether membership was explicitly regarded as compulsory or not,
it seems to have been virtually impossible for anyone to practise a craft
or trade without belonging to its guild, in view of the boycott as well as
violence to which he would have been subjected. Thus guilds exercised
local monopolies. Their strength and policy was bound to vary with the
state of the economy. In good times they would be more open, in bad
times they could simply restrict membership to sons or brothers of those
already belonging. They collected dues from all members regularly and
effectively, they made comprehensive rules to regulate prices and practices, they organized apprenticeships, usually for three years, and fed,
clothed, and housed members in need and found jobs for them if necessary. Apprentices were general servants to their masters, having to cook
and make their beds for them as well as work at the trade from dawn
to dusk. All guilds had appropriate mythical patrons, regarded as
ancient ancestors and culture heroes or deities, for whom they performed regular rituals. They also maintained burial grounds, which
provided one of their most highly valued services. Their names were
not always obvious, thus, Peking Porters' Guild was called the Public
Welfare Enduring Righteous Holy Tea Association. The Actors' Guild

was called Pear Garden Public Welfare Association, after the garden where a T'ang emperor had called upon their services. The Guild of the Blind was called Three Kings Association and that of Barbers, Beautify the Face Association. Others were more descriptive. Many were highly specialized, thus, there were separate guilds for shoe repairers, sole makers, shoe fastening makers and for those who assembled the different parts of a shoe. An extraordinary range of occupations and socioeconomic status seems to have been covered, from the Guild of Bankers to the Guild of Coolies. Guild bonds must also have been highly significant in some, where the range of wealth within the guild could have been very wide. This was partly provided for where only the head of a shop would belong to the guild and not any others of those involved or employed in it.

80

MARCO POLO
From *The Travels of Marco Polo*

According to *The Travels of Marco Polo*, by the time the Venetian merchant had come to Hangchow (which he calls Kinsay) he had been to Karakorum, the Mongol capital; Peking; Changan, the T'ang dynasty capital; and a number of other cities in China (which he calls Manzi); other parts of Asia; and, of course, his native Venice. Why does he say that this city is the "finest and noblest of the world"? How does his description support that characterization?

Thinking Historically

In what ways does the Hangchow that emerges from this document resemble London or Florence? In what ways was Hangchow significantly different? Does Marco Polo's description show signs that Chinese cities were autonomous or that they were not?

Marco Polo, *The Travels of Marco Polo*, the Complete Yule-Currier ed., vol. 2 (New York: Dover, 1993), 185–93, 200–206.

When you have left the city of Changan and have travelled for three days through a splendid country, passing a number of towns and villages, you arrive at the most noble city of Kinsay, a name which is as much as to say in our tongue "The City of Heaven," as I told you before.

And since we have got thither I will enter into particulars about its magnificence; and these are well worth the telling, for the city is beyond dispute the finest and the noblest in the world. In this we shall speak according to the written statement which the Queen of this Realm sent to Bayan the conqueror of the country for transmission to the Great Kaan, in order that he might be aware of the surpassing grandeur of the city and might be moved to save it from destruction or injury. I will tell you all the truth as it was set down in that document. For truth it was, as the said Messer Marco Polo at a later date was able to witness with his own eyes. And now we shall rehearse those particulars.

First and foremost, then, the document stated the city of Kinsay to be so great that it hath an hundred miles of compass. And there are in it twelve thousand bridges of stone,[1] for the most part so lofty that a great fleet could pass beneath them. And let no man marvel that there are so many bridges, for you see the whole city stands as it were in the water and surrounded by water, so that a great many bridges are required to give free passage about it. [And though the bridges be so high, the approaches are so well contrived that carts and horses do cross them.]

The document aforesaid also went on to state that there were in this city twelve guilds of the different crafts, and that each guild had twelve thousand houses in the occupation of its workmen. Each of these houses contains at least twelve men, whilst some contain twenty and some forty,—not that these are all masters, but inclusive of the journeymen who work under the masters. And yet all these craftsmen had full occupation, for many other cities of the kingdom are supplied from this city with what they require.

The document aforesaid also stated that the number and wealth of the merchants, and the amount of goods that passed through their hands, was so enormous that no man could form a just estimate thereof. And I should have told you with regard to those masters of the different crafts who are at the head of such houses as I have mentioned, that neither they nor their wives ever touch a piece of work with their own hands, but live as nicely and delicately as if they were kings and queens. The wives indeed are most dainty and angelical creatures! Moreover it was an ordinance laid down by the King that every man should follow his father's business and no other, no matter if he possessed 100,000 bezants.[2]

---

[1] Generally assumed to be an exaggeration; one thousand would have been a lot. [Ed.]

[2] A gold coin struck at Byzantium (or Constantinople) and used throughout Europe from the ninth century. [Ed.]

Inside the city there is a Lake which has a compass of some thirty miles:[3] and all round it are erected beautiful palaces and mansions, of the richest and most exquisite structure that you can imagine, belonging to the nobles of the city. There are also on its shores many abbeys and churches of the Idolaters. In the middle of the Lake are two Islands, on each of which stands a rich, beautiful and spacious edifice, furnished in such style as to seem fit for the palace of an Emperor. And when any one of the citizens desired to hold a marriage feast, or to give any other entertainment, it used to be done at one of these palaces. And everything would be found there ready to order, such as silver plate, trenchers, and dishes [napkins and tablecloths], and whatever else was needful. The King made this provision for the gratification of his people, and the place was open to every one who desired to give an entertainment. . . .

The people are Idolaters; and since they were conquered by the Great Kaan they use paper money. [Both men and women are fair and comely, and for the most part clothe themselves in silk, so vast is the supply of that material, both from the whole district of Kinsay, and from the imports by traders from other provinces.] And you must know they eat every kind of flesh, even that of dogs and other unclean beasts, which nothing would induce a Christian to eat.

Since the Great Kaan occupied the city he has ordained that each of the twelve thousand bridges should be provided with a guard of ten men, in case of any disturbance, or of any being so rash as to plot treason or insurrection against him. [Each guard is provided with a hollow instrument of wood and with a metal basin, and with a timekeeper to enable them to know the hour of the day or night. . . .

Part of the watch patrols the quarter, to see if any light or fire is burning after the lawful hours; if they find any they mark the door, and in the morning the owner is summoned before the magistrates, and unless he can plead a good excuse he is punished. Also if they find any one going about the streets at unlawful hours they arrest him, and in the morning they bring him before the magistrates. Likewise if in the daytime they find any poor cripple unable to work for his livelihood, they take him to one of the hospitals, of which there are many, founded by the ancient kings, and endowed with great revenues. Or if he be capable of work they oblige him to take up some trade. If they see that any house has caught fire they immediately beat upon that wooden instrument to give the alarm, and this brings together the watchmen from the other bridges to help to extinguish it, and to save the goods of the merchants or others, either by removing them to the towers above

---

[3]The circumference of the lake was more probably 30 li. A li was about a third of a mile, but it was sometimes used to mean a hundredth of a day's march. The entire circumference of the city could not have been more than 100 li. [Ed.]

mentioned, or by putting them in boats and transporting them to the islands in the lake. For no citizen dares leave his house at night, or to come near the fire; only those who own the property, and those watchmen who flock to help, of whom there shall come one or two thousand at the least.] . . .

The Kaan watches this city with especial diligence because it forms the head of all Manzi;[4] and because he has an immense revenue from the duties levied on the transactions of trade therein, the amount of which is such that no one would credit it on mere hearsay.

All the streets of the city are paved with stone or brick, as indeed are all the highways throughout Manzi, so that you ride and travel in every direction without inconvenience. Were it not for this pavement you could not do so, for the country is very low and flat, and after rain 'tis deep in mire and water. [But as the Great Kaan's couriers could not gallop their horses over the pavement, the side of the road is left unpaved for their convenience. The pavement of the main street of the city also is laid out in two parallel ways of ten paces in width on either side, leaving a space in the middle laid with fine gravel, under which are vaulted drains which convey the rain water into the canals; and thus the road is kept ever dry.]

You must know also that the city of Kinsay has some three thousand baths, the water of which is supplied by springs. They are hot baths, and the people take great delight in them, frequenting them several times a month, for they are very cleanly in their persons. They are the finest and largest baths in the world; large enough for one hundred persons to bathe together.

And the Ocean Sea comes within twenty-five miles of the city at a place called Ganfu, where there is a town and an excellent haven, with a vast amount of shipping which is engaged in the traffic to and from India and other foreign parts, exporting and importing many kinds of wares, by which the city benefits. And a great river flows from the city of Kinsay to that sea-haven, by which vessels can come up to the city itself. This river extends also to other places further inland.

Know also that the Great Kaan hath distributed the territory of Manzi into nine parts, which he hath constituted into nine kingdoms. To each of these kingdoms a king is appointed who is subordinate to the Great Kaan, and every year renders the accounts of his kingdom to the fiscal office at the capital. This city of Kinsay is the seat of one of these kings, who rules over one hundred forty great and wealthy cities. For in the whole of this vast country of Manzi there are more than twelve hundred great and wealthy cities, without counting the towns and villages, which are in great numbers. And you may receive it for

[4]China. [Ed.]

certain that in each of those twelve hundred cities the Great Kaan has a garrison, and that the smallest of such garrisons musters one thousand men; whilst there are some of ten thousand, twenty thousand, and thirty thousand; so that the total number of troops is something scarcely calculable. The troops forming these garrisons are not all Tartars. Many are from the province of Cathay, and good soldiers too. But you must not suppose they are by any means all of them cavalry; a very large proportion of them are foot soldiers, according to the special requirements of each city. And all of them belong to the army of the Great Kaan.

I repeat that everything appertaining to this city is on so vast a scale, and the Great Kaan's yearly revenues therefrom are so immense, that it is not easy even to put it in writing, and it seems past belief to one who merely hears it told. But I *will* write it down for you.

First, however, I must mention another thing. The people of this country have a custom, that as soon as a child is born they write down the day and hour and the planet and sign under which its birth has taken place; so that every one among them knows the day of his birth. And when any one intends a journey he goes to the astrologers, and gives the particulars of his nativity in order to learn whether he shall have good luck or no. Sometimes they will say *no*, and in that case the journey is put off till such day as the astrologer may recommend. These astrologers are very skilful at their business, and often their words come to pass, so the people have great faith in them.

They burn the bodies of the dead. And when any one dies the friends and relations make a great mourning for the deceased, and clothe themselves in hempen garments, and follow the corpse playing on a variety of instruments and singing hymns to their idols. And when they come to the burning place, they take representations of things cut out of parchment, such as caparisoned horses, male and female slaves, camels, armour suits of cloth of gold (and money), in great quantities, and these things they put on the fire along with the corpse, so that they are all burnt with it. And they tell you that the dead man shall have all these slaves and animals of which the effigies are burnt, alive in flesh and blood, and the money in gold, at his disposal in the next world; and that the instruments which they have caused to be played at his funeral, and the idol hymns that have been chaunted, shall also be produced again to welcome him in the next world; and that the idols themselves will come to do him honour.

Furthermore there exists in this city the palace of the king who fled, him who was Emperor of Manzi, and that is the greatest palace in the world, as I shall tell you more particularly. For you must know its demesne[5] hath a compass of ten miles, all enclosed with lofty

[5]Size. [Ed.]

battlemented walls; and inside the walls are the finest and most delectable gardens upon earth, and filled too with the finest fruits. There are numerous fountains in it also, and lakes full of fish. In the middle is the palace itself, a great and splendid building. It contains twenty great and handsome halls, one of which is more spacious than the rest, and affords room for a vast multitude to dine. It is all painted in gold, with many histories and representations of beasts and birds, of knights and dames, and many marvellous things. It forms a really magnificent spectacle, for over all the walls and all the ceiling you see nothing but paintings in gold. And besides these halls the palace contains one thousand large and handsome chambers, all painted in gold and divers colours.

Moreover, I must tell you that in this city there are 160 *tomans*[6] of fires, or in other words 160 *tomans* of houses. Now I should tell you that the *toman* is 10,000, so that you can reckon the total as altogether 1,600,000 houses, among which are a great number of rich palaces. There is one church only, belonging to the Nestorian Christians.

There is another thing I must tell you. It is the custom for every burgess of this city, and in fact for every description of person in it, to write over his door his own name, the name of his wife, and those of his children, his slaves, and all the inmates of his house, and also the number of animals that he keeps. And if any one dies in the house then the name of that person is erased, and if any child is born its name is added. So in this way the sovereign is able to know exactly the population of the city. And this is the practice also throughout all Manzi and Cathay.

And I must tell you that every hosteler who keeps an hostel for travellers is bound to register their names and surnames, as well as the day and month of their arrival and departure. And thus the sovereign hath the means of knowing, whenever it pleases him, who come and go throughout his dominions. And certes this is a wise order and a provident. . . .

[The position of the city is such that it has on one side a lake of fresh and exquisitely clear water (already spoken of), and on the other a very large river. The waters of the latter fill a number of canals of all sizes which run through the different quarters of the city, carry away all impurities, and then enter the Lake; whence they issue again and flow to the Ocean, thus producing a most excellent atmosphere. By means of these channels, as well as by the streets, you can go all about the city. Both streets and canals are so wide and spacious that carts on the one and boats on the other can readily pass to and fro, conveying necessary supplies to the inhabitants.

At the opposite side the city is shut in by a channel, perhaps forty miles in length, very wide, and full of water derived from the river

---

[6]A *toman* is a Mongol measurement of ten thousand. [Ed.]

aforesaid, which was made by the ancient kings of the country in order to relieve the river when flooding its banks. This serves also as a defence to the city, and the earth dug from it has been thrown inward, forming a kind of mound enclosing the city.

In this part are the ten principal markets, though besides these there are a vast number of others in the different parts of the town. The former are all squares of half a mile to the side, and along their front passes the main street, which is forty paces in width, and runs straight from end to end of the city, crossing many bridges of easy and commodious approach. At every four miles of its length comes one of those great squares of two miles (as we have mentioned) in compass. So also parallel to this great street, but at the back of the marketplaces, there runs a very large canal, on the bank of which toward the squares are built great houses of stone, in which the merchants from India and other foreign parts store their wares, to be handy for the markets. In each of the squares is held a market three days in the week, frequented by forty thousand or fifty thousand persons, who bring thither for sale every possible necessary of life, so that there is always an ample supply of every kind of meat and game, as of roebuck, red-deer, fallow-deer, hares, rabbits, partridges, pheasants, francolins, quails, fowls, capons, and of ducks and geese an infinite quantity; for so many are bred on the Lake that for a Venice groat of silver you can have a couple of geese and two couple of ducks. Then there are the shambles where the larger animals are slaughtered, such as calves, beeves, kids, and lambs, the flesh of which is eaten by the rich and the great dignitaries.

Those markets make a daily display of every kind of vegetables and fruits; and among the latter there are in particular certain pears of enormous size, weighing as much as ten pounds apiece, and the pulp of which is white and fragrant like a confection; besides peaches in their season both yellow and white, of every delicate flavour.

Neither grapes nor wine are produced there, but very good raisins are brought from abroad, and wine likewise. The natives, however, do not much care about wine, being used to that kind of their own made from rice and spices. From the Ocean Sea also come daily supplies of fish in great quantity, brought twenty-five miles up the river, and there is also great store of fish from the lake, which is the constant resort of fishermen, who have no other business. Their fish is of sundry kinds, changing with the season; and, owing to the impurities of the city which pass into the lake, it is remarkably fat and savoury. Any one who should see the supply of fish in the market would suppose it impossible that such a quantity could ever be sold; and yet in a few hours the whole shall be cleared away; so great is the number of inhabitants who are accustomed to delicate living. Indeed they eat fish and flesh at the same meal.

All the ten marketplaces are encompassed by lofty houses, and below these are shops where all sorts of crafts are carried on, and all sorts of wares are on sale, including spices and jewels and pearls. Some of these shops are entirely devoted to the sale of wine made from rice and spices, which is constantly made fresh, and is sold very cheap.

Certain of the streets are occupied by the women of the town, who are in such a number that I dare not say what it is. They are found not only in the vicinity of the marketplaces, where usually a quarter is assigned to them, but all over the city. They exhibit themselves splendidly attired and abundantly perfumed, in finely garnished houses, with trains of waiting-women. These women are extremely accomplished in all the arts of allurement, and readily adapt their conversation to all sorts of persons, insomuch that strangers who have once tasted their attractions seem to get bewitched, and are so taken with their blandishments and their fascinating ways that they never can get these out of their heads. Hence it comes to pass that when they return home they say they have been to Kinsay or the City of Heaven, and their only desire is to get back thither as soon as possible.

Other streets are occupied by the Physicians, and by the Astrologers, who are also teachers of reading and writing; and an infinity of other professions have their places round about those squares. In each of the squares there are two great palaces facing one another, in which are established the officers appointed by the King to decide differences arising between merchants, or other inhabitants of the quarter. It is the daily duty of these officers to see that the guards are at their posts on the neighbouring bridges, and to punish them at their discretion if they are absent. . . .

The natives of the city are men of peaceful character, both from education and from the example of their kings, whose disposition was the same. They know nothing of handling arms, and keep none in their houses. You hear of no feuds or noisy quarrels or dissensions of any kind among them. Both in their commercial dealings and in their manufactures they are thoroughly honest and truthful, and there is such a degree of good will and neighbourly attachment among both men and women that you would take the people who live in the same street to be all one family.

And this familiar intimacy is free from all jealousy or suspicion of the conduct of their women. These they treat with the greatest respect, and a man who should presume to make loose proposals to a married woman would be regarded as an infamous rascal. They also treat the foreigners who visit them for the sake of trade with great cordiality, and entertain them in the most winning manner, affording them every help and advice on their business. But on the other hand they hate to see soldiers, and not least those of the Great Kaan's garrisons, regarding them as the cause of their having lost their native kings and lords.

81

S. D. GOITEIN

Cairo: An Islamic City
in Light of the Geniza

The author of this selection provides an especially detailed picture of medieval Cairo due to an unusual discovery of documents. "The Geniza" refers to a treasure trove of documents maintained by a Jewish synagogue in Cairo from the tenth to thirteenth centuries. Because it was considered sacrilegious for Jews to destroy the word of God or the word "God," the synagogue maintained a room where all written records could be deposited. Since anything might contain a word that should not be destroyed, virtually anything that had writing on it was brought to the synagogue for safe deposit. The Geniza contains correspondence, legal documents, receipts, inventories, prescriptions, and notes—written in Hebrew characters in the Arabic language—and offers a rare opportunity to review virtually everything a community wrote over a long period of time. It is an extremely valuable resource that can answer most questions about medieval society in Cairo.

In this selection, S. D. Goitein studies the documents for the insight they provide into city life in Cairo. What do the Geniza documents tell us about city life in Cairo? What possible inferences can we draw from the author's first sentence? What meaning does he draw? What would it have been like to live in medieval Cairo?

Thinking Historically

In what ways would life in medieval Cairo have been similar to or different from life in a city of medieval Europe? What is the significance of the lack of public buildings and guilds in Cairo? In what ways was the Muslim identity larger or more cosmopolitan than European urban identities?

. . . It is astounding how rarely government buildings are mentioned in the Geniza documents. There were the local police stations and prisons, as well as the offices where one received the licenses occasionally needed, but even these are seldom referred to. The Mint and the

S. D. Goitein, "Cairo: An Islamic City in Light of the Geniza," in *Middle Eastern Cities*, ed. Ira M. Lapidus (Berkeley and Los Angeles: University of California Press, 1969), 90–95.

Exchange are frequently referred to, but at least the latter was only semi-public in character, since the persons working there were not on the government payroll. Taxes were normally collected by tax farmers. Thus there was little direct contact between the government and the populace and consequently not much need for public buildings. The imperial palace and its barracks formed a city by itself, occasionally mentioned in Ayyūbid times, but almost never in the Fāṭimid period.

Government, although not conspicuous by many public buildings, was present in the city in many other ways. A city was governed by a military commander called *amīr,* who was assisted by the *wālī* or superintendent of the police. Smaller towns had only a *wālī* and no *amīr.* Very powerful, sometimes more powerful than the *amīr,* was the *qāḍī,* or judge, who had administrative duties in addition to his substantial judicial functions. The chief *qāḍī* often held other functions such as the control of the taxes or of a port, as we read with regard to Alexandria or Tyre. The city was divided into small administrative units called *rab'* (which is not the classical *rub',* meaning quarter, but instead designates an area, or rather a compound). Each *rab'* had a superintendent called *ṣāḥib rab'* (pronounced rub'), very often referred to in the Geniza papers. In addition to regular and mounted police there were plain clothesmen, or secret service men, called *aṣḥāb al-khabar,* "informants" who formed a government agency independent even of the *qāḍī,* a state of affairs for which there seem to exist parallels in more modern times.

An ancient source tells us that the vizier[1] al-Ma'mūn, mentioned above, instructed the two superintendents of the police of Fusṭāṭ and Cairo, respectively, to draw up exact lists of the inhabitants showing their occupations and other circumstances and to permit no one to move from one house to another without notification of the police. This is described as an extraordinary measure aimed at locating any would-be assassins who might have been sent to the Egyptian capital by the Bāṭiniyya, an Ismā'īlī group using murder as a political weapon. Such lists, probably with fewer details, no doubt were in regular use for the needs of taxation. In a letter from Sicily, either from its capital Palermo or from Mazara on its southwestern tip, the writer, an immigrant from Tunisia around 1063, informs his business friend in Egypt that he is going to buy a house and that he has already registered for the purpose in the *qānūn* (Greek *canon*) which must have designated an official list of inhabitants. With regard to non-Muslims, a differentiation was made between permanent residents and newcomers. Whether the same practice existed with respect to Muslims is not evident from the Geniza papers.

---

[1]Prime minister. [Ed.]

What were the dues that a town dweller had to pay to the government in his capacity as the inhabitant of a city, and what were the benefits that he derived from such payments? By right of conquest, the ground on which Fusṭāṭ stood belonged to the Muslims, that is, to the government (the same was the case in many other Islamic cities), and a ground rent, called ḥikr, had to be paid for each building. A great many deeds of sale, gift, and rent refer to this imposition. . . .

Besides the ground rent, every month a ḥarāsa, or "due for protection," had to be paid to the government. The protection was partly in the hands of a police force, partly in those of the superintendents of the compounds, and partly was entrusted to nightwatchmen, usually referred to as ṭawwāfūn, literally, "those that make the round," but known also by other designations. As we learn expressly from a Geniza source, the nightwatchmen, like the regular police, were appointed by the government (and not by a municipality or local body which did not exist). The amounts of the ḥarāsa in the communal accounts cannot be related to the value of the properties for which they were paid, but it is evident that they were moderate.

In a responsum written around 1165, Rabbi Maimon, the father of Moses Maimonides, states that the markets of Fusṭāṭ used to remain open during the nights, in contrast of course to what the writer was accustomed from having lived in other Islamic cities. In Fusṭāṭ, too, this had not been always the case. In a description of the festival of Epiphany from the year 941 in which all parts of the population took part, it is mentioned as exceptional that the streets were not closed during that particular night.

Sanitation must have been another great concern of the government, for the items "removal of rubbish" (called "throwing out of dust") and "cleaning of pipes" appear with great regularity in the monthly accounts preserved in the Geniza. One gets the impression that these hygienic measures were not left to the discretion of each individual proprietor of a house. The clay tubes bringing water (for washing purposes) to a house and those connecting it with a cesspool constantly needed clearing, and there are also many references to their construction. The amounts paid for both operations were considerable. The Geniza has preserved an autograph note by Maimonides permitting a beadle to spend a certain sum on "throwing out of dust" (presumably from a synagogue). This may serve as an illustration for the fact that landlords may have found the payment of these dues not always easy.

In this context we may also draw attention to the new insights gained through the study of the documents from the Geniza about the social life of Cairo. Massignon had asserted, and he was followed by many, that the life-unit in the Islamic city was the professional corporation, the guilds of the merchants, artisans, and scholars which had professional, as well as social and religious functions. No one would deny that this was true to a large extent for the sixteenth through the nineteenth centuries. However, there is not a shred of evidence that this was true for the ninth through the thirteenth centuries. . . .

The term "guild" designates a medieval union of craftsmen or traders which supervised the work of its members in order to uphold standards, and made arrangements for the education of apprentices and their initiation into the union. The guild protected its members against competition, and in Christian countries was closely connected with religion.

Scrutinizing the records of the Cairo Geniza or the Muslim handbooks of market supervision contemporary with them, one looks in vain for an Arabic equivalent of the term "guild." There was no such word because there was no such institution. The supervision of the quality of the artisans' work was in the hands of the state police, which availed itself of the services of trustworthy and expert assistants.

Regarding apprenticeship and admission to a profession, no formalities and no rigid rules are to be discovered in our sources. Parents were expected to have their sons learn a craft and to pay for their instruction, and the Geniza has preserved several contracts to this effect.

The protection of the local industries from the competition of newcomers and outsiders is richly documented by the Geniza records, but nowhere do we hear about a professional corporation fulfilling this task. It was the Jewish local community, the central Jewish authorities, the state police, or influential notables, Muslim and Jewish, who were active in these matters.

As to the religious aspect of professional corporation, the associations of artisans and traders in imperial Rome, or at least a part of them, bore a religious character and were often connected with the local cult of the town from which the founders of an association had originated. Similarly, the Christian guilds of the late Middle Ages had their patron saints and special rites. The fourteenth century was the heyday of Muslim corporations, especially in Anatolia (the present day Turkey), which adopted the doctrines and ceremonies of Muslim mystic brotherhoods. One looks in vain for similar combinations of artisanship and religious cult in the period and the countries under discussion. On the other hand, we find partnerships of Muslims and Jews both in workshops and in mercantile undertakings, for free partnerships were the normal form of industrial cooperation, and were common as well in commercial ventures. The classical Islamic city was a free enterprise society, the very opposite of a community organized in rigid guilds and tight professional corporations.

Further, we have stated before that no formal citizenship existed. The question is, however, how far did people feel a personal attachment to their native towns. "Homesickness," says Professor Gibb in his translation of the famous traveler Ibn Baṭṭūṭa "was hardly to be expected in a society so cosmopolitan as that of medieval Islam." Indeed the extent of travel and migration reflected in the Geniza is astounding. No less remarkable, however, is the frequency of expressions of longing for one's native city and the wish to return to it, as well as the fervor with which compatriots stuck together when they were abroad. On the other hand, I cannot find much of neighborhood factionalism or professional *esprit de corps,* both of which were so prominent in the later Middle Ages. Under an ever more oppressive military feudalism and government-regimented economy, life became miserable and insecure, and people looked for protection and assistance in their immediate neighborhood. In an earlier period, in a free-enterprise, competitive society, there was no place for such factionalism. A man felt himself to be the son of a city which provided him with the security, the economic possibilities, and the spiritual amenities which he needed.

82

AL OMARI

Cairo and Niane

The world of Islam extended across the Indian Ocean and the Sahara desert. In 1324 while making a pilgrimage to Mecca, the king of Mali, Mansa Musa, stopped in Cairo. The presence of his five-hundred member entourage, each carrying a four-pound staff of gold, was vividly recalled by Cairenes for years after his departure. One of those witnesses was the sultan's welcoming official, who here tells the historian Al Omari about that memorable visit. Al Omari also writes about Mansa Musa's Mali and its capital city, Niane.

Why was Mansa Musa reluctant to see the Sultan of Egypt? Why did the price of gold decline after Mansa Musa's visit to Egypt? Who were the pagans, and why did the king of Mali not convert them? What was the importance of the horse to Mali?

Al Omari, "Cairo and Niane," in *The African Past*, trans. and ed. Basil Davidson (Boston: Atlantic, Little Brown, 1964), 75–79.

Thinking Historically

In what ways was Cairo a different kind of city from Mansa Musa's Niane? Sociologists distinguish between administrative capital cities that are usually large and contain a bureaucracy and "regal" ceremonial cities that are marked more by importance than size. Which of these would you call Niane?

Traveling through Cairo

During my first journey to Cairo and sojourn there I heard talk of the arrival of the Sultan Musa [*Mansa* Musa, emperor of Mali], and I found the Cairenes very glad to talk of the large expenditures of those people. I questioned the Emir Abu'l 'Abbas Ahmed ben Abi'l Haki, el Mehmendar, who spoke of the sultan's noble appearance, dignity, and trustworthiness. "When I went out to greet him in the name of the glorious Sultan el Malik en Nasir [of Egypt]," he told me, "he gave me the warmest of welcomes and treated me with the most careful politeness. But he would talk to me only through an interpreter [that is, his spokesman or linguist], although he could speak perfect Arabic. He carried his imperial treasure in many pieces of gold, worked or otherwise.

"I suggested that he should go up to the palace and meet the Sultan [of Egypt]. But he refused, saying: 'I came for the pilgrimage, and for nothing else, and I do not wish to mix up my pilgrimage with anything else.' He argued about this. However, I well understood that the meeting was repugnant to him because he was loath to kiss the ground [before the Sultan] or to kiss his hand. I went on insisting, and he went on making excuses. But imperial protocol obliged me to present him, and I did not leave him until he had agreed. When he came into the Sultan's presence we asked him to kiss the ground. But he refused and continued to refuse, saying: 'However can this be?' Then a wise man of his suite whispered several words to him that I could not understand. 'Very well,' he thereupon declared, 'I will prostrate myself before Allah who created me and brought me into the world.' Having done so he moved toward the Sultan. The latter rose for a moment to welcome him and asked him to sit beside him; then they had a long conversation. After Sultan Musa had left the palace the Sultan of Cairo sent him gifts of clothing for himself, his courtiers, and all those who were with him; saddled and bridled horses for himself and his chief officers . . .

"When the time of pilgrimage arrived, [the Sultan of Egypt] sent him a large quantity of drachmas, baggage camels, and choice riding camels with saddles and harness. [The Sultan of Egypt] caused abundant quantities of foodstuffs to be bought for his suite and his followers, established posting-stations for the feeding of the animals, and gave to the emirs of the pilgrimage a written order to look after and respect [the Emperor of Mali]. When the latter returned it was I who went to greet him and settle him into his quarters . . . "

"This man," el Mehmendar also told me, "spread upon Cairo the flood of his generosity: There was no person, officer of the [Cairo] court or holder of any office of the [Cairo] sultanate who did not receive a sum in gold from him. The people of Cairo earned incalculable sums from him, whether by buying and selling or by gifts. So much gold was current in Cairo that it ruined the value of money." . . .

Let me add [continues Omari] that gold in Egypt had enjoyed a high rate of exchange up to the moment of their arrival. The gold *mitqal* that year had not fallen below twenty-five drachmas. But from that day [of their arrival] onward, its value dwindled; the exchange was ruined, and even now it has not recovered. The *mitqal* scarcely touches twenty-two drachmas. That is how it has been for twelve years from that time, because of the great amounts of gold they brought to Egypt and spent there.

The Empire of Mali

The king of this country is known to the people of Egypt as the king of Tekrur [roughly, inland Senegal]; but he himself becomes indignant when he is called thus, since Tekrur is only one of the countries of his empire. The title he prefers is that of lord of Mali, the largest of his states; it is the name by which he is most known. He is the most important of the Muslim Negro kings; his land is the largest, his army the most numerous; he is the king who is the most powerful, the richest, the most fortunate, the most feared by his enemies, and the most able to do good to those around him.

His kingdom consists of the lands of Gana, Zagun, Tirakka, Tekrur, Bambugu, Zarquatabana, Darmura, Zara, Kabora, Bara-guri, Gao-gao. The inhabitants of Gao-gao are of the tribes of Yarten. The region of Mali is that where the residence of the king is situated [in] the town of Niane, and all the other regions are dependent on it; it has the official name of Mali because it is the capital of this kingdom which also includes towns, villages, and centers of population to the number of fourteen.

The honorable and truthful Sheikh Abu Sa'id Otman ed Dukkali, who has lived in the town of Niane for thirty-five years and traveled throughout the kingdom, has told me that this is square in shape, being four months [of travel] in length and at least as much in breadth. . . .

The sultan of this country has sway over the land of the "desert of native gold," whence they bring him gold every year. The inhabitants of that land are savage pagans whom the sultan would subject to him if he wished. But the sovereigns of this kingdom have learned by experience that whenever one of them has conquered one of these gold towns, established Islam there, and sounded the call to prayer, the harvest of gold dwindles and falls to nothing, meanwhile it grows and expands in neighboring pagan countries. When experience had confirmed them in this observation, they left the gold country in the hands of its pagan inhabitants, and contented themselves with assuring their obedience and paying tribute.

Reception at Court

The sultan of this kingdom presides in his palace on a great balcony called *bembe,* where he has a great seat of ebony that is like a throne fit for a large and tall person: On either side it is flanked by elephant tusks turned toward each other. His arms stand near him, being all of gold, saber, lance, quiver, bow, and arrows. He wears wide trousers made of about twenty pieces [of stuff] of a kind which he alone may wear. Behind him there stand about a score of Turkish or other pages which are bought for him in Cairo. One of them, at his left, holds a silk umbrella surmounted by a dome and a bird of gold: The bird has the figure of a falcon. His officers are seated in a circle about him, in two rows, one to the right and one to the left; beyond them sit the chief commanders of his cavalry. In front of him there is a person who never leaves him and who is his executioner; also another who serves as intermediary [that is, official spokesman] between the sovereign and his subjects, and who is named the herald. In front of them again, there are drummers. Others dance before their sovereign, who enjoys this, and make him laugh. Two banners are spread behind him. Before him they keep two saddled and bridled horses in case he should wish to ride.

The Importance of Horses

Arab horses are brought for sale to the kings of this country, who spend considerable sums in this way. Their army numbers one hundred thousand men, of whom there are about ten thousand horse-mounted cavalry: The others are infantry, having neither horses nor any other mounts. They have camels in this country but do not know the art of riding them with a saddle . . .

The officers of this king, his soldiers, and his guard receive gifts of land and presents. Some among the greatest of them receive as much as fifty thousand *mitqals* of gold a year, besides which the king provides them with horses and clothing. He is much concerned with giving them fine garments and making his cities into capitals.

REFLECTIONS

In the debate between cities as contrasting and converging worlds, this chapter has emphasized the case for contrasting types, focusing on the differences between European autonomous and communal cities and Chinese and Muslim administrative ones. Now let us qualify those judgments.

First, we should not assume that autonomous or communal cities were limited to Europe. Rather, they were a product of a feudal, or politically weak and decentralized society, where urban populations could bargain for special privileges. We could find similar examples of urban autonomy among, for example, Japanese port cities during the Japanese feudal era of the fourteenth to sixteenth centuries. One of these, Sakai, was called the Venice of Japan. Sakai's wealthy commercial elite—whose prosperity resulted from commerce in textiles, lacquer ware, metal castings, rice, and lumber—staffed and ran their own municipal governments. The Japanese cities of Nara and Amagasaki also used commercial prosperity to gain political independence. Not until after 1600 and the re-centralization of Japan under the Tokugawa administration were these independent cities brought to heel. In many ways, Tokugawa developments paralleled those of Europe, where centralized states also subordinated the independence of commercial cities after 1700.

Second, the absence of a movement for urban autonomy in Islamic and Chinese cities—important as it was in the time and places discussed in this chapter—was not universal. Chinese cities before the Mongol Yüan dynasty, especially in the earlier Sung dynasty, had developed an extremely prosperous commercial class. And while it is true that they did not gain (or seek) urban independence, they were content to exercise sufficient influence on the local representatives of the emperor. No appointed mayor could think lightly of ignoring the advice of the many Chinese guilds (one of the more important forces for self-government in Europe) or of the uniquely Chinese class of civil-service exam graduates, active and retired. Chinese merchants did not create democratic voting councils to govern their cities. Most distrusted the judgments of the uneducated people. But governors always sought the wisdom and advice of the well educated, and the urban elite always got their way.

Third, while medieval Muslim cities encouraged little urban autonomy or identity, a prosperous class of merchants—always at the core of Islam—were nourished by more enlightened sultans and emirs. The Turkish historian Halil Inalcik writes that it was "the deliberate policy" of the Ottoman government, as it founded its successive capitals at Bursa in 1326, Edirne in 1402, and Istanbul in 1453, to create commercial and industrial centers, and that it consequently used every means—from tax exemptions to force—to attract and settle merchants and artisans in the new capitals. With the same end in view, Mehmed II encouraged the Jews of Europe to migrate to his new capital at Istanbul as they were being expelled from Spain and Portugal.

Fourth, there are many forces of convergence in the history of urbanization that the selections in this chapter have not addressed. Almost all of our sources celebrate the magnificence and magnification of urban, as opposed to rural or village, life. Each city is the largest or richest of its kind; the authors of these sources, especially the visitors, are overwhelmed.

Are there certain pressures that all cities exert? If so, what are they? In Chapters 1 and 2, you read about ancient cities. Did those cities have certain tendencies that continued in medieval cities? Chapter 1, for example, asked if ancient cities created patriarchies. Did medieval urbanization continue this trend? The cities, after all, were the places where men came together. Patriarchs must protect their wives and daughters in cities. In China, foot-binding, which crippled women's feet and restricted their movement, developed in the cities of the T'ang and Sung. While Berber and Muslim women traveled freely in the countryside, cities exposed them to the glances of men who were strangers, so they had to be veiled. No doubt cities provided opportunities as well as patriarchal traps for women, but it is likely that the opportunities came at considerable cost.

Finally, we have limited our survey in the interest of coherence to a few great societies—European, Chinese, and Muslim. We said little of Africa and nothing of the Americas. The Americas will be the subject of the next chapter, and we will begin with a survey of one of its great cities, the Aztec capital of Mexico. While we will read about the Americas for other purposes, think about cities as well: Broaden the range of your knowledge to encompass more of the world.

The Spanish Conquest
of Mexico

Mexico and "The Indies," 1500–1550 C.E.

HISTORICAL CONTEXT

In the last five hundred years, Europeans colonized, conquered, and converted much of the world. European expansion began with the crusades almost five hundred years earlier. Later, European sailors traded blows with Muslim navies as merchants from Venice, Genoa, Portugal, and Spain sought shortcuts through the Muslim trade routes with the Spice Islands of east Asia.

Christopher Columbus sailed across the Atlantic because he believed he could reach the Spice Islands of modern Indonesia more quickly by sailing west. The new Spanish monarchs, Ferdinand and Isabella, supported his voyage as part of their effort to extend their power beyond the Mediterranean. In 1492, they not only funded Columbus, but also expelled Jews and Muslims from the Iberian peninsula. Columbus had previously asked the Portuguese king for funding, but Portuguese navigators used better maps to predict that sailing eastward around Africa was shorter.

Of course, no Europeans knew that a vast continent, the huge Western Hemisphere, stood between Europe and Asia, but the lesser Spanish knowledge proved to be an unexpected boon. Columbus made four trips between 1492 and 1504, touching on the coasts of South America and Central America as well as the islands of the Bahamas and the Caribbean. Despite the fact that he found no Asian spices, he died believing that he had traveled through the islands of Asia.

Fortuitous or not, Spain rapidly established, in Santo Domingo on Hispaniola, an imperial administration that sought out every opportunity to trade and profit, to conquer and convert — all for God and gold.

In many ways, Spain's expansionism was a continuation of the Crusades — the next step after the defeat of Granada, the last Muslim stronghold on the Iberian Peninsula in 1492. Its consequences, however, would create a new world that was more integrated than Columbus ever could have imagined.

The conquest of Mexico was the first financially successful strike for the Spanish. On the Caribbean islands, the Spanish failed to find the gold, spices, or fabled cities Columbus had imagined. The chief economic advantage of the islands was land, which the Spanish claimed with due ceremony, and Indian labor, which they seized without hesitation. The land remained but the Indians died off, requiring the Spanish to look further afield for new opportunities. Then came the discovery of Mexico. Mexico provided opportunities beyond the Spaniards' wildest dreams, but the conquest had consequences that even today are profound and tragic.

While in retrospect historians can easily see how the Spanish experience in the Indies and Mexico bore certain similarities to other colonial endeavors (e.g., Crusader states in Jerusalem, earlier Muslim expansion), the experience for those involved was one of continual shock and surprise. Little could be expected of a world not previously known to exist.

Observe what the Spanish and Indians see and think of each other in this far-reaching encounter. What were each group's motives, their strategies, their successes and failures? What drove the Spanish in their conquest, especially because they were on foreign ground? What, ultimately, do you think these two peoples understood of each other?

THINKING HISTORICALLY

Understanding How and Why Events Are Reinterpreted

Not only are there two sides to every story, but the context of the story changes over time. In this chapter, we examine the encounter between the Spanish and the Indians of Mexico when it occurred, as it was understood within a generation or two of the conquest, and as it is interpreted by present-day historians at the end of the twentieth century. Our goal here is to understand how and why an event — particularly such a consequential event about which much is known — is remembered and reinterpreted, and then remembered and reinterpreted once again. What, this chapter asks, is the relationship between the truth of the past and each generation's need to ask its own questions and develop its own understanding?

83

BERNAL DÍAZ

From *The Conquest of New Spain*

Bernal Díaz del Castillo was born in Spain in 1492, the year Columbus sailed to America. After participating in two explorations of the Mexican coast, Díaz joined the expedition of Hernán Cortés in 1519. He wrote this history of the conquest much later, in his seventies, and he died around 1580, a municipal official with a small estate in Guatemala.

The conquest of Mexico did not automatically follow from the first Spanish settlements in the West Indies (first in Santo Domingo, Hispaniola, and then Cuba). The Spanish crown had given permission for trade and exploration, not colonization. But the fortune-seeking peasant-soldiers whose fathers had fought to rid Spain of Muslims and Jews were not easily dissuaded from conquering their own lands and gaining their own populations of dependent Indians.

Hernán Cortés, of minor noble descent and a failed student at the University of Salamanca, at the age of nineteen sailed to the Indies, where he enjoyed a sizeable estate on the island of Hispaniola. When he heard stories of Montezuma's gold from an Indian woman who had been given to him in tribute, he determined to find the fabled capital of the Aztec Empire, Tenochtitlán (modern Mexico City). Cortés gathered more than five hundred amateur soldiers, eleven ships, sixteen horses, and several pieces of artillery, sailed across the Caribbean and Gulf of Mexico to a settlement he christened Veracruz, and then began the long march from the coast up to the high central plateau of Mexico.

The Aztecs were new to central Mexico, arriving from the North American desert only about two hundred years before the Spanish, around 1325. They settled on an island in the middle of the large lake on the central plain, shunned by the peoples of other cities who considered themselves more sophisticated and cultured than the newcomers. In less than two hundred years, this band of uncouth foreigners established control over almost all the other city-states of Mexico, by 1500 ruling an empire that stretched as far south as Guatemala and as far east as the Mayan lands of the Yucatan Peninsula.

Bernal Díaz, *The Conquest of New Spain*, trans. J. M. Cohen (London: Penguin Books), 220–45. Map of Mexico City, published with the Second Letter of Hernán Cortés, in *Praeclara Ferdinandi Cortesii De Nova Maris Oceani Hispanica Narratio* (Nuremberg, 1524).

Aztec power relied on a combination of old and new religious ideas and a military system that conquered through terrorism. The older religious traditions that the Aztecs adopted were those of the classical Toltec culture, at the center of which stood the god Quetzalcoatl — the feathered serpent, god of creation and brotherhood. The nurturing forces of Quetzalcoatl continued in Aztec society in a system of universal and obligatory education and in festivals dedicated to life, creativity, and procreation. But the Aztecs also celebrated a god they had brought with them from the north, Huitzilopochtli — a warrior god, primed for death and sacrifice.

Huitzilopochtli (rendered as Huichilobos in this selection) was given dominant status in the Aztec pantheon by Tlacaelel, an adviser to Montezuma's predecessor, Itzcoatl (r. 1428–1440). Tlacaelel envisioned Huitzilopochtli as a force for building a powerful Aztec Empire. Drawing on the god's need for human sacrifice — a need not unknown among the religions of central Mexico (or Christians) — Tlacaelel built altars to Huitzilopochtli at Tenochtitlán, Cholula, and other sites. According to the tenets of the religion, the war god required a neverending supply of human hearts, which compelled Aztec armies to seek out sacrificial victims in ever more remote sections of Central America, necessarily creating an endless supply of enemies for the Aztecs. Among these, the Tlaxcalans — whom the Aztecs left independent so they could be conquered at will for war captives — proved to be an eager ally of Cortés and the Spanish. Other Mexican peoples eagerly joined the Spanish-Tlaxcalan alliance.

The eclipse of Quetzalcoatl by Huitzilopochtli was never complete. In 1519, people still remembered the stories of Quetzalcoatl's departure. He had been given a mirror by his enemies. When he looked into it, he saw that his image was like his creation — and thus might be subject to the same mortality. Despondent, he left his people, promising to return on a fixed day in the future, Ce Acatl, the Day of the Reed.

As that day approached in 1519, the Aztec seers recorded various unnatural disturbances: Fires streaked across the sky; the waters of the lake around Tenochtitlán boiled with rage; and a woman was heard crying for people to leave the city. In addition, an unusual gray bird was found in the nets of fishermen — a bird with a mirror in its head; in the mirror Montezuma could see strange people coming forward quickly over a distant plain. When Montezuma was informed of the two great towers (ships) that moved over the waters, when he heard of the white-faced fishermen sitting on giant deer (horses), he knew Quetzalcoatl had returned.

With the help of his Indian captive and companion, Doña Marina, called La Malinche by some of the Indians (Montezuma thus sometimes calls Cortés "Lord Malinche" in the selection), Cortés was able to communicate with the Tlaxcalans and other Indians who were frustrated with Aztec domination. On his march toward Tenochtitlán,

Cortés stopped to join forces with the Tlaxcalans, perhaps cementing the relationship and demonstrating his resolve with a brutal massacre of the people of Cholula, an Aztec ally and arch enemy of the Tlaxcalans. By the time Cortés arrived at Tenochtitlán, Montezuma knew of the defeat of his allies at Cholula.

This selection from Bernal Díaz begins with the Spanish entry into Tenochtitlán. What impresses Díaz, and presumably other Spanish conquistadors, about the Mexican capital city? What parts of the city most attract his attention? What conclusions does he draw about Mexican (or Aztec) civilization? Does he think Spanish civilization is equal, inferior, or superior to that of Mexico?

Map of Tenochtitlán (Mexico City) from Cortés's Letter

Notice the map of Tenochtitlán included here (see Figure 14.1). Cortez drew this map as part of a letter to the Spanish king. This rendition was the engraving made for the published edition of the letter in Nuremberg in 1524. You can trace the route of Cortés from the southern city of Iztalpalapa up the causeway to Tenochtitlán. Notice that the central square within the main temple is at the center of the city. Notice also the number of other cities shown on the map. This map was a popular introduction to Mexico for readers in Europe. What does a map like this tell Europeans who believe that cities are the mark of a civilized people? The Latin inscription on the central square that shows both the great temple (called Teocali) and Montezuma's palace reads, "A temple where human sacrifice was carried out" (see Figure 14.2). Beneath the great temple stands a headless figure, and racks of heads with hair appear both under the figure and to the left of the great temple. What message does this imagery convey about Aztec civilization?

Thinking Historically

In this chapter we examine the ways in which the encounter between Spaniards and Mexicans has been understood and debated over the centuries. What does the history of Díaz tell you about the ways in which Spaniards and Aztecs viewed each other in 1519? Díaz, of course, is a Spanish conquistador, but does he, intentionally or not, help us understand the Aztec view of this encounter?

Díaz gives us a dramatic account of the meeting of Cortés and Montezuma. What do you think each is thinking and feeling? Do you detect any signs of tension in their elaborate greetings? Why are both behaving so politely? What do they want from each other?

What causes the initial hospitality to turn tense? Is either side more to blame for what happens next? Was conflict inevitable? Could the encounter have ended in some sort of peaceful resolution?

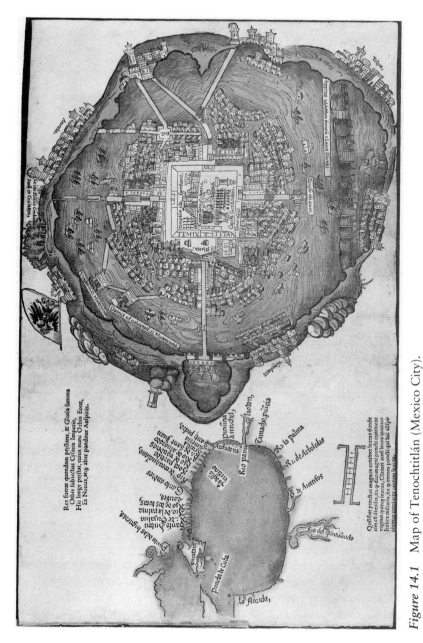

Figure 14.1 Map of Tenochtitlán (Mexico City).

Source: Courtesy of Edward E. Ayer, The Newberry Library, Chicago.

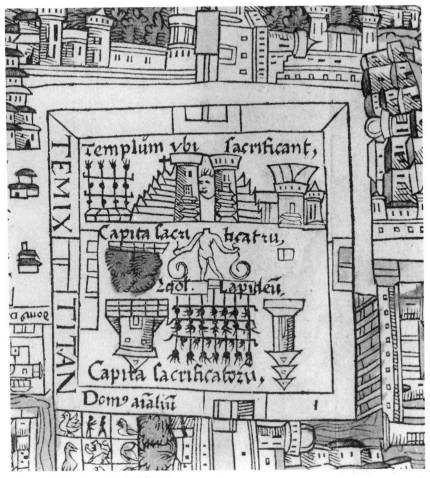

Figure 14.2   Detail of Central Square.

Source: Courtesy of Edward E. Ayer, The Newberry Library, Chicago.

Cortés's map can also be studied for clues about Spanish and Mexican perceptions of each other. The map renders the main causeways, streets, and canals with a fair degree of accuracy. The houses, however, are European rather than Mexican, as is the monumental architecture. Only the inset with the Teocali temple features Aztec pyramid architecture. That, too, is surrounded by European-style towers and palaces, including that of Montezuma. Why does the artist turn Mexican dwellings into European ones? Why does he translate the pyramid towers, except for Teocali, into European-style towers? Why, in short, does the artist prefer European icons for house, temple, and palace, instead of images that show what these buildings actually looked like? Is it possible that Tenochtitlán looked too foreign for Spanish eyes? Might European icons have made the city more Spanish?

When Cortes saw, heard, and was told that the great Montezuma was approaching, he dismounted from his horse, and when he came near to Montezuma each bowed deeply to the other. Montezuma welcomed our Captain, and Cortes, speaking through Doña Marina, answered by wishing him very good health. Cortes, I think, offered Montezuma his right hand, but Montezuma refused it and extended his own. Then Cortes brought out a necklace which he had been holding. It was made of those elaborately worked and coloured glass beads called *margaritas* . . . and was strung on a gold cord and dipped in musk to give it a good odour. This he hung round the great Montezuma's neck, and as he did so attempted to embrace him. But the great princes who stood round Montezuma grasped Cortes's arm to prevent him, for they considered this an indignity.

Then Cortes told Montezuma that it rejoiced his heart to have seen such a great prince, and that he took his coming in person to receive him and the repeated favours he had done him as a high honour. After this Montezuma made him another complimentary speech, and ordered two of his nephews who were supporting him, the lords of Texcoco and Coyoacan, to go with us and show us our quarters. Montezuma returned to the city with the other two kinsmen of his escort, the lords of Cuitlahuac and Tacuba; and all those grand companies of *Caciques*[1] and dignitaries who had come with him returned also in his train. And as they accompanied their lord we observe them marching with their eyes downcast so that they should not see him, and keeping close to the wall as they followed him with great reverence. Thus space was made for us to enter the streets of Mexico without being pressed by the crowd. . . .

They led us to our quarters, which were in some large houses capable of accommodating us all and had formerly belonged to the great Montezuma's father, who was called Axayacatl. Here Montezuma now kept the great shrines of his gods, and a secret chamber containing gold bars and jewels. This was the treasure he had inherited from his father, which he never touched. Perhaps their reason for lodging us here was that, since they called us *Teules*[2] and considered us as such, they wished to have us near their idols. In any case they took us to this place, where there were many great halls, and a dais hung with the cloth of their country for our Captain, and matting beds with canopies over them for each of us.

On our arrival we entered the large court, where the great Montezuma was awaiting our Captain. Taking him by the hand, the prince led him to his apartment in the hall where he was to lodge, which was

[1] Chiefs. [Ed.]
[2] Gods. [Ed.]

very richly furnished in their manner. Montezuma had ready for him a very rich necklace, made of golden crabs, a marvellous piece of work, which he hung round Cortes's neck. His captains were greatly astonished at this sign of honour.

After this ceremony, for which Cortes thanked him through our interpreters, Montezuma said: "Malinche, you and your brothers are in your own house. Rest awhile." He then returned to his palace, which was not far off. . . .

So, with luck on our side, we boldly entered the city of Tenochtitlán or Mexico on 8 November in the year of our Lord 1519.

The Stay in Mexico

When the great Montezuma had dined and was told that our Captain and all of us had finished our meal some time ago, he came to our quarters in the grandest state with a great number of princes, all of them his kinsmen. On being told of his approach, Cortes came into the middle of the hall to receive him. Montezuma then took him by the hand, and they brought chairs made in their fashion and very richly decorated in various ways with gold. Montezuma requested our Captain to sit down, and both of them sat, each on his own chair.

Then Montezuma began a very good speech, saying that he was delighted to have such valiant gentlemen as Cortes and the rest of us in his house and his kingdom. That two years ago he had received news of a Captain who had come to Champoton, and that last year also he had received a report of another Captain who had come with four ships. Each time he had wished to see them, and now that he had us with him he was not only at our service but would share all that he possessed with us. He ended by saying that we must truly be the men about whom his ancestors had long ago prophesied, saying that they would come from the direction of the sunrise to rule over these lands, and that he was confirmed in this belief by the valour with which we had fought at Champoton and Tabasco and against the Tlascalans, for lifelike pictures of these battles had been brought to him.

Cortes replied through our interpreters that we did not know how to repay the daily favours we received from him, and that indeed we did come from the direction of the sunrise, and were vassals and servants of a great king called the Emperor Charles, who was ruler over many great princes. Having heard news of Montezuma and what a great prince he was, the Emperor, he said, had sent us to this country to visit him, and to beg them to become Christians, like our Emperor and all of us, so that his soul and those of all his vassals might be saved. Cortes promised to explain to him later how this could be, and how we worship the one true God and who He is, also many other good things which he had already communicated to his ambassadors Tendile, Pitalpitoque, and Quintalbor. . . .

Next day Cortes decided to go to Montezuma's palace. . . .

Cortes began to make a speech through our interpreters, saying that we were all now rested, and that in coming to see and speak with such a great prince we had fulfilled the purpose of our voyage and the orders of our lord the King. The principal things he had come to say on behalf of our Lord God had already been communicated to Montezuma through his three ambassadors,[3] on that occasion in the sandhills when he did us the favour of sending us the golden moon and sun. We had then told him that we were Christians and worshipped one God alone, named Jesus Christ, who had suffered His passion and death to save us; and that what they worshipped as gods were not gods but devils, which were evil things, and if they were ugly to look at, their deeds were uglier. But he had proved to them how evil and ineffectual their gods were, as both the prince and his people would observe in the course of time, since, where we had put up crosses such as their ambassadors had seen, they had been too frightened to appear before them.

The favour he now begged of the great Montezuma was that he should listen to the words he now wished to speak. Then he very carefully expounded the creation of the world, how we are all brothers, the children of one mother and father called Adam and Eve; and how such a brother as our great Emperor, grieving for the perdition of so many souls as their idols were leading to hell, where they burnt in living flame, had sent us to tell him this, so that he might put a stop to it, and so that they might give up the worship of idols and make no more human sacrifices — for all men are brothers — and commit no more robbery or sodomy. He also promised that in the course of time the King would send some men who lead holy lives among us, much better than our own, to explain this more fully, for we had only come to give them warning. Therefore he begged Montezuma to do as he was asked.

As Montezuma seemed about to reply, Cortes broke off his speech, saying to those of us who were with him: "Since this is only the first attempt, we have now done our duty."

"My lord Malinche," Montezuma replied, "these arguments of yours have been familiar to me for some time. I understand what you said to my ambassadors on the sandhills about the three gods and the cross, also what you preached in the various towns through which you passed. We have given you no answer, since we have worshipped our own gods here from the beginning and know them to be good. No doubt yours are good also, but do not trouble to tell us any more about them at present. Regarding the creation of the world, we have held the same belief for many

---

[3] A meeting on the coast of the Gulf of Mexico with Montezuma's ambassadors on the prior Easter Sunday (1519). [Ed.]

ages, and for this reason are certain that you are those who our ancestors predicted would come from the direction of the sunrise. As for your great King, I am in his debt and will give him of what I possess. For, as I have already said, two years ago I had news of the Captains who came in ships, by the road that you came, and said they were servants of this great king of yours. I should like to know if you are all the same people."

Cortes answered that we were all brothers and servants of the Emperor, and that they had come to discover a route and explore the seas and ports, so that when they knew them well we could follow, as we had done. Montezuma was referring to the expeditions of Francisco Hernandez de Cordoba and of Grijalva, the first voyages of discovery. He said that ever since that time he had wanted to invite some of these men to visit the cities of his kingdom, where he would receive them and do them honour, and that now his gods had fulfilled his desire, for we were in his house, which we might call our own. Here we might rest and enjoy ourselves, for we should receive good treatment. . . .

We all thanked him heartily for his . . . good will, and Montezuma replied with a laugh, because in his princely manner he spoke very gaily: "Malinche, I know that these people of Tlascala with whom you are so friendly have told you that I am a sort of god or *Teule,* and keep nothing in any of my houses that is not made of silver and gold and precious stones. But I know very well that you are too intelligent to believe this and will take it as a joke. See now, Malinche, my body is made of flesh and blood like yours, and my houses and palaces are of stone, wood, and plaster. It is true that I am a great king, and have inherited the riches of my ancestors, but the lies and nonsense you have heard of us are not true. You must take them as a joke, as I take the story of your thunders and lightnings." . . .

The great Montezuma was about forty years old, of good height, well proportioned, spare and slight, and not very dark, though of the usual Indian complexion. He did not wear his hair long but just over his ears, and he had a short black beard, well-shaped and thin. His face was rather long and cheerful, he had fine eyes, and in his appearance and manner could express geniality or, when necessary, a serious composure. He was very neat and clean, and took a bath every afternoon. He had many women as his mistresses, the daughters of chieftains, but two legitimate wives who were *Caciques* in their own right, and when he had intercourse with any of them it was so secret that only some of his servants knew of it. He was quite free from sodomy. The clothes he wore one day he did not wear again till three or four days later. He had a guard of two hundred chieftains lodged in rooms beside his own, only some of whom were permitted to speak to him. When they entered his presence they were compelled to take off their rich cloaks and put on others of little value. They had to be clean and walk barefoot, with their eyes downcast, for they were not allowed to look him in the face, and as they approached they had to make three obeisances, saying as they did so, "Lord, my lord, my great lord!" Then, when they had said what they had come to say, he would dismiss them with a few words. They did not turn their backs on him as they went out, but kept their faces toward him and their eyes downcast, only turning round when they had left the room. Another thing I noticed was that when other great chiefs came from distant lands about disputes or on business, they too had to take off their shoes and put on poor cloaks before entering Montezuma's apartments; and they were not allowed to enter the palace immediately but had to linger for a while near the door, since to enter hurriedly was considered disrespectful. . . .

Montezuma had two houses stocked with every sort of weapon; many of them were richly adorned with gold and precious stones. There were shields large and small, and a sort of broadsword, and two-handed swords set with flint blades that cut much better than our swords, and lances longer than ours, with five-foot blades consisting of many knives. Even when these are driven at a buckler or a shield they are not deflected. In fact they cut like razors, and the Indians can shave their heads with them. They had very good bows and arrows, and double and single-pointed javelins as well as their throwing-sticks and many slings and round stones shaped by hand, and another sort of shield that can be rolled up when they are not fighting, so that it does not get in the way, but which can be opened when they need it in battle and covers their bodies from head to foot. . . .

I have already described the manner of their sacrifices. They strike open the wretched Indian's chest with flint knives and hastily tear out the palpitating heart which, with the blood, they present to the idols in whose name they have performed the sacrifice. Then they cut off the arms, thighs, and head, eating the arms and thighs at their ceremonial banquets. The head they hang up on a beam, and the body of the sacrificed man is not eaten but given to the beasts of prey. They also had many vipers in this accursed house, and poisonous snakes which have something that sounds like a bell in their tails. These, which are the deadliest snakes of all, they kept in jars and great pottery vessels full of feathers, in which they laid their eggs and reared their young. They were fed on the bodies of sacrificed Indians and the flesh of the dogs that they bred. We know for certain, too, that when they drove us out of Mexico and killed over eight hundred and fifty of our soldiers, they fed those beasts and snakes on their bodies for many days, as I shall relate in due course. These snakes and wild beasts were dedicated to their fierce idols, and kept them company. As for the horrible noise when the lions and tigers roared, and the jackals and foxes howled, and the serpents hissed, it was so appalling that one seemed to be in hell.

I must now speak of the skilled workmen whom Montezuma employed in all the crafts they practised, beginning with the jewellers and workers in silver and gold and various kinds of hollowed objects, which excited the admiration of our great silversmiths at home. Many of the best of them lived in a town called Atzcapotzalco, three miles from Mexico. There were other skilled craftsmen who worked with precious stones and *chalchihuites,* and specialists in feather-work, and very fine painters and carvers. We can form some judgment of what they did then from what we can see of their work today. . . .

Let us go on to the women, the weavers and sempstresses, who made such a huge quantity of fine robes with very elaborate feather designs. These things were generally brought from some towns in the province of Cotaxtla, which is on the north coast, quite near San Juan de Ulua. In Montezuma's own palaces very fine cloths were woven by those chieftains' daughters whom he kept as mistresses; and the daughters of other dignitaries, who lived in a kind of retirement like nuns in some houses close to the great *cue*[4] of Huichilobos, wore robes entirely of feather-work. Out of devotion for that god and a female deity who was said to preside over marriage, their fathers would place them in religious retirement until they found husbands. They would then take them out to be married.

Now to speak of the great number of performers whom Montezuma kept to entertain him. There were dancers and stilt-walkers, and some who seemed to fly as they leapt through the air, and men rather like clowns to make him laugh. There was a whole quarter full of these people who had no other occupation. He had as many workmen as he needed, too — stonecutters, masons, and carpenters — to keep his houses in repair. . . .

We carried our weapons, as was our custom, both by night and day. Indeed, Montezuma was so used to our visiting him armed that he did not think it strange. I say this because our Captain and those of us who had horses went to Tlatelolco mounted, and the majority of our men were fully equipped. On reaching the marketplace, escorted by the many *Caciques* whom Montezuma had assigned to us, we were astounded at the great number of people and the quantities of merchandise, and at the orderliness and good arrangements that prevailed, for we had never seen such a thing before. The chieftains who accompanied us pointed everything out. Every kind of merchandise was kept separate and had its fixed place marked for it. . . .

Now let us leave the market . . . and come to the courts and enclosures in which their great *cue* stood. Before reaching it you passed through a series of large courts, bigger I think than the Plaza at Salamanca. These courts were surrounded by a double masonry wall and paved, like the whole place, with very large smooth white flagstones.

4 Pyramid or temple. [Ed.]

Where these stones were absent everything was whitened and polished, indeed the whole place was so clean that there was not a straw or a grain of dust to be found there.

When we arrived near the great temple and before we had climbed a single step, the great Montezuma sent six *papas* and two chieftains down from the top, where he was making his sacrifices, to escort our Captain; and as he climbed the steps, of which there were one hundred and fourteen, they tried to take him by the arms to help him up in the same way as they helped Montezuma, thinking he might be tired, but he would not let them near him.

The top of the *cue* formed an open square on which stood something like a platform, and it was here that the great stones stood on which they placed the poor Indians for sacrifice. Here also was a massive image like a dragon, and other hideous figures, and a great deal of blood that had been spilled that day. Emerging in the company of two *papas* from the shrine which houses his accursed images, Montezuma made a deep bow to us all and said: "My lord Malinche, you must be tired after climbing this great *cue* of ours." And Cortes replied that none of us was ever exhausted by anything. Then Montezuma took him by the hand, and told him to look at his great city and all the other cities standing in the water, and the many others on the land round the lake; and he said that if Cortes had not had a good view of the great marketplace he could see it better from where he now was. So we stood there looking, because that huge accursed *cue* stood so high that it dominated everything. We saw the three causeways that led into Mexico: the causeway of Iztapalapa by which we had entered four days before, and that of Tacuba along which we were afterward to flee on the night of our great defeat, when the new prince Cuitlahuac drove us out of the city (as I shall tell in due course), and that of Tepeaquilla.[5] We saw the fresh water which came from Chapultepec to supply the city, and the bridges that were constructed at intervals on the causeways so that the water could flow in and out from one part of the lake to another. We saw a great number of canoes, some coming with provisions and others returning with cargo and merchandise; and we saw too that one could not pass from one house to another of that great city and the other cities that were built on the water except over wooden drawbridges or by canoe. We saw *cues* and shrines in these cities that looked like gleaming white towers and castles: a marvellous sight. All the houses had flat roofs, and on the causeways were other small towers and shrines built like fortresses.

Having examined and considered all that we had seen, we turned back to the great market and the swarm of people buying and selling. The mere murmur of their voices talking was loud enough to be heard

[5] Guadalupe.

more than three miles away. Some of our soldiers who had been in many parts of the world, in Constantinople, in Rome, and all over Italy, said that they had never seen a market so well laid out, so large, so orderly, and so full of people. . . .

It being our habit to examine and inquire into everything, when we were all assembled in our lodging and considering which was the best place for an altar, two of our men, one of whom was the carpenter Alonso Yañez, called attention to some marks on one of the walls which showed that there had once been a door, though it had been well plastered up and painted. Now as we had heard that Montezuma kept his father's treasure in this building, we immediately suspected that it must be in this room, which had been closed up only a few days before. Yañez made the suggestion to Juan Velazquez de Leon and Francisco de Lugo, both relatives of mine, to whom he had attached himself as a servant; and they mentioned the matter to Cortes. So the door was secretly opened, and Cortes went in first with certain captains. When they saw the quantity of golden objects — jewels and plates and ingots — which lay in that chamber they were quite transported. They did not know what to think of such riches. The news soon spread to the other captains and soldiers, and very secretly we all went in to see. The sight of all that wealth dumbfounded me. Being only a youth at the time and never having seen such riches before, I felt certain that there could not be a store like it in the whole world. We unanimously decided that we could not think of touching a particle of it, and that the stones should immediately be replaced in the doorway, which should be blocked again and cemented just as we had found it. We resolved also that not a word should be said about this until times changed, for fear Montezuma might hear of our discovery.

Let us leave this subject of the treasure and tell how four of our most valiant captains took Cortes aside in the church, with a dozen soldiers who were in his trust and confidence, myself among them, and asked him to consider the net or trap in which we were caught, to look at the great strength of the city and observe the causeways and bridges, and remember the warnings we had received in every town we had passed through that Huichilobos had counselled Montezuma to let us into the city and kill us there. We reminded him that the hearts of men are very fickle, especially among the Indians, and begged him not to trust the good will and affection that Montezuma was showing us, because from one hour to another it might change. If he should take it into his head to attack us, we said, the stoppage of our supplies of food and water, or the raising of any of the bridges, would render us helpless. Then, considering the vast army of warriors he possessed, we should be incapable of attacking or defending ourselves. And since all the houses stood in the water, how could our Tlascalan allies come in to help us? We asked him to think over all that we had said, for if we wanted to preserve our lives we must seize Montezuma immediately, without even a day's delay. We pointed out that all the gold Montezuma had given us, and all that we had seen in the treasury of his father Axayacatl, and all the food we ate was turning to poison in our bodies, for we could not sleep by night or day or take any rest while these thoughts were in our minds. If any of our soldiers gave him less drastic advice, we concluded, they would be senseless beasts charmed by the gold and incapable of looking death in the eye.

When he had heard our opinion, Cortes answered: "Do not imagine, gentlemen, that I am asleep or that I do not share your anxiety. You must have seen that I do. But what strength have we got for so bold a course as to take this great lord in his own palace, surrounded as he is by warriors and guards? What scheme or trick can we devise to prevent him from summoning his soldiers to attack us at once?"

Our captains (Juan Velazquez de Leon, Diego de Ordaz, Gonzalo de Sandoval, and Pedro de Alvarado) replied that Montezuma must be got out of his palace by smooth words and brought to our quarters. Once there, he must be told that he must remain as a prisoner, and that if he called out or made any disturbance he would pay for it with his life. If Cortes was unwilling to take this course at once, they begged him for permission to do it themselves. With two very dangerous alternatives before us, the better and more profitable thing, they said, would be to seize Montezuma rather than wait for him to attack us. Once he did so, what chance would we have? Some of us soldiers also remarked that Montezuma's stewards who brought us our food seemed to be growing insolent, and did not serve us as politely as they had at first. Two of our Tlascalan allies had, moreover, secretly observed to Jeronimo de Aguilar that for the last two days the Mexicans had appeared less well disposed to us. We spent a good hour discussing whether or not to take Montezuma prisoner, and how it should be done. But our final advice, that at all costs we should take him prisoner, was approved by our Captain, and we then left the matter till next day. All night we prayed God to direct events in the interests of His holy service. . . .

84

From *The Broken Spears: The Aztec Account of the Conquest of Mexico*

This Aztec account of the encounter between the Spanish and Indians of Mexico was written some years after the events described. Spanish Christian monks helped a postconquest generation of Aztec Nahuatl speakers translate the illustrated manuscripts of the conquest period. According to this account, how did Montezuma (Motecuhzoma in this account) respond to Cortés? Did other Aztecs share Montezuma's attitude toward the Spanish? How reliable do you find this account, in describing Montezuma's thoughts, motives, and behavior?

Thinking Historically

How does the Aztec account of the conquest differ from that of the Spanish, written by Díaz? Does the Aztec account contradict the Spanish account in some areas? How? If you find contradictions, how will you decide which account to believe and accept?

In some areas, the Aztec account is merely different from that of Díaz. For one thing, it tells us about a later period. Overall, how different is the Aztec account from that of Díaz?

Speeches of Motecuhzoma and Cortes

When Motecuhzoma had given necklaces to each one, Cortes asked him: "Are you Motecuhzoma? Are you the king? Is it true that you are the king Motecuhzoma?"

And the king said: "Yes, I am Motecuhzoma." Then he stood up to welcome Cortes; he came forward, bowed his head low and addressed him in these words: "Our lord, you are weary. The journey has tired you, but now you have arrived on the earth. You have come to your city, Mexico. You have come here to sit on your throne, to sit under its canopy.

"The kings who have gone before, your representatives, guarded it and preserved it for your coming. The kings Itzcoatl, Motecuhzoma the Elder, Axayacatl, Tizoc, and Ahuitzol ruled for you in the City of Mexico. The people were protected by their swords and sheltered by their shields.

"Do the kings know the destiny of those they left behind, their posterity? If only they are watching! If only they can see what I see!

The Broken Spears: The Aztec Account of the Conquest of Mexico, ed. Miguel Leon-Portilla (Boston: Beacon Press, 1990), 64–76.

"No, it is not a dream. I am not walking in my sleep. I am not seeing you in my dreams. . . . I have seen you at last! I have met you face to face! I was in agony for five days, for ten days, with my eyes fixed on the Region of the Mystery. And now you have come out of the clouds and mists to sit on your throne again.

"This was foretold by the kings who governed your city, and now it has taken place. You have come back to us; you have come down from the sky. Rest now, and take possession of your royal houses. Welcome to your land, my lords!"

When Motecuhzoma had finished, La Malinche translated his address into Spanish so that the Captain could understand it. Cortes replied in his strange and savage tongue, speaking first to La Malinche: "Tell Motecuhzoma that we are his friends. There is nothing to fear. We have wanted to see him for a long time, and now we have seen his face and heard his words. Tell him that we love him well and that our hearts are contented."

Then he said to Motecuhzoma: "We have come to your house in Mexico as friends. There is nothing to fear."

La Malinche translated this speech and the Spaniards grasped Motecuhzoma's hands and patted his back to show their affection for him. . . .

The Spaniards Take Possession of the City

When the Spaniards entered the Royal House, they placed Motecuhzoma under guard and kept him under their vigilance. They also placed a guard over Itzcuauhtzin, but the other lords were permitted to depart.

Then the Spaniards fired one of their cannons, and this caused great confusion in the city. The people scattered in every direction; they fled without rhyme or reason; they ran off as if they were being pursued. It was as if they had eaten the mushrooms that confuse the mind, or had seen some dreadful apparition. They were all overcome by terror, as if their hearts had fainted. And when night fell, the panic spread through the city and their fears would not let them sleep.

In the morning the Spaniards told Motecuhzoma what they needed in the way of supplies: tortillas, fried chickens, hens' eggs, pure water, firewood, and charcoal. Also: large, clean cooking pots; water jars; pitchers; dishes; and other pottery. Motecuhzoma ordered that it be sent to them. The chiefs who received this order were angry with the king and no longer revered or respected him. But they furnished the Spaniards with all the provisions they needed — food, beverages and water, and fodder for the horses.

The Spaniards Reveal Their Greed

When the Spaniards were installed in the palace, they asked Motecuhzoma about the city's resources and reserves and about the warriors' ensigns and shields. They questioned him closely and then demanded gold.

Motecuhzoma guided them to it. They surrounded him and crowded close with their weapons. He walked in the center, while they formed a circle around him.

When they arrived at the treasure house called Teucalco, the riches of gold and feathers were brought out to them: ornaments made of quetzal feathers, richly worked shields, disks of gold, the necklaces of the idols, gold nose plugs, gold greaves, and bracelets, and crowns.

The Spaniards immediately stripped the feathers from the gold shields and ensigns. They gathered all the gold into a great mound and set fire to everything else, regardless of its value. Then they melted down the gold into ingots. As for the precious green stones, they took only the best of them; the rest were snatched up by the Tlaxcaltecas. The Spaniards searched through the whole treasure house, questioning and quarreling, and seized every object they thought was beautiful.

The Seizure of Motecuhzoma's Treasures

Next they went to Motecuhzoma's storehouse, in the place called Totocalco [Place of the Palace of the Birds],[1] where his personal treasures were kept. The Spaniards grinned like little beasts and patted each other with delight.

When they entered the hall of treasures, it was as if they had arrived in Paradise. They searched everywhere and coveted everything; they were slaves to their own greed. All of Motecuhzoma's possessions were brought out: fine bracelets, necklaces with large stones, ankle rings with little gold bells, the royal crowns and all the royal finery — everything that belonged to the king and was reserved to him only. They seized these treasures as if they were their own, as if this plunder were merely a stroke of good luck. And when they had taken all the gold, they heaped up everything else in the middle of the patio.

La Malinche called the nobles together. She climbed up to the palace roof and cried: "Mexicanos, come forward! The Spaniards need your help! Bring them food and pure water. They are tired and hungry; they are almost fainting from exhaustion! Why do you not come forward? Are you angry with them?"

---

[1] The zoological garden attached to the royal palaces.

The Mexicans were too frightened to approach. They were crushed by terror and would not risk coming forward. They shied away as if the Spaniards were wild beasts, as if the hour were midnight on the blackest night of the year. Yet they did not abandon the Spaniards to hunger and thirst. They brought them whatever they needed, but shook with fear as they did so. They delivered the supplies to the Spaniards with trembling hands, then turned and hurried away. . . .

The Statue of Huitzilopochtli

On the evening before the fiesta of Toxcatl, the celebrants began to model a statue of Huitzilopochtli. They gave it such a human appearance that it seemed the body of a living man. Yet they made the statue with nothing but a paste made of the ground seeds of the chicalote, which they shaped over an armature of sticks. . . .

The Beginning of the Fiesta

Early the next morning, the statue's face was uncovered by those who had been chosen for that ceremony. They gathered in front of the idol in single file and offered it gifts of food, such as round seedcakes or perhaps human flesh. But they did not carry it up to its temple on top of the pyramid.

All the young warriors were eager for the fiesta to begin. They had sworn to dance and sing with all their hearts, so that the Spaniards would marvel at the beauty of the rituals.

The procession began, and the celebrants filed into the temple patio to dance the Dance of the Serpent. When they were all together in the patio, the songs and the dance began. . . .

The great captains, the bravest warriors, danced at the head of the files to guide the others. The youths followed at a slight distance. Some of the youths wore their hair gathered into large locks, a sign that they had never taken any captives. Others carried their headdresses on their shoulders; they had taken captives, but only with help.

Then came the recruits, who were called "the young warriors." They had each captured an enemy or two. The others called to them: "Come, comrades, show us how brave you are! Dance with all your hearts!"

The Spaniards Attack the Celebrants

At this moment in the fiesta, when the dance was loveliest and when song was linked to song, the Spaniards were seized with an urge to kill the celebrants. They all ran forward, armed as if for battle. They closed the entrances and passageways, all the gates of the patio: the Eagle Gate in the lesser palace, the Gate of the Canestalk and the Gate of the Serpent of Mirrors. They posted guards so that no one could escape, and then rushed into the Sacred Patio to slaughter the celebrants. They came on foot, carrying their swords and their wooden or metal shields.

They ran in among the dancers, forcing their way to the place where the drums were played. They attacked the man who was drumming and cut off his arms. Then they cut off his head, and it rolled across the floor.

They attacked all the celebrants, stabbing them, spearing them, striking them with their swords. They attacked some of them from behind, and these fell instantly to the ground with their entrails hanging out. Others they beheaded: they cut off their heads, or split their heads to pieces.

They struck others in the shoulders, and their arms were torn from their bodies. They wounded some in the thigh and some in the calf. They slashed others in the abdomen, and their entrails all spilled to the ground. Some attempted to run away, but their intestines dragged as they ran; they seemed to tangle their feet in their own entrails. No matter how they tried to save themselves, they could find no escape.

Some attempted to force their way out, but the Spaniards murdered them at the gates. Others climbed the walls, but they could not save themselves. Those who ran into the communal houses were safe there for a while; so were those who lay down among the victims and pretended to be dead. But if they stood up again, the Spaniards saw them and killed them.

The blood of the warriors flowed like water and gathered into pools. The pools widened, and the stench of blood and entrails filled the air. The Spaniards ran into the communal houses to kill those who were hiding. They ran everywhere and searched everywhere; they invaded every room, hunting and killing.

85

BARTOLOMÉ DE LAS CASAS

From *The History of the Indies*

Spanish and Aztec chroniclers presented different views of the Spanish conquest of Mexico, but they did not engage in historical debate. History was among the spoils that went to the victor.

Still, as Spanish dominion in the Americas extended throughout the Caribbean and Mexico, spilling over into the Inca Empire in Peru, voices were raised that questioned the Spanish treatment of conquered peoples throughout the New World. Often these voices belonged to members of the Spanish clergy living in the Americas.

One of the most effective of these critics was Bartolomé de Las Casas (1474–1566). Las Casas was nineteen years old when he witnessed Columbus's triumphal return to Spain in 1493 and twenty-eight when he sailed to Hispaniola in 1502. As a Spaniard, he was entitled to and received an *encomienda,* a grant from the king of all the Indians within a village or territory. In return for their protection and instruction in Christian doctrine, the encomienda holder received indian labor. As he learned in Hispaniola and during his participation in the conquest of Cuba between 1511 and 1515, this arrangement usually amounted to a system of indifferent slavery. In 1515 Las Casas renounced his *encomienda* and sailed for Spain to speak out against the brutal treatment of the Indians in the Indies. He dedicated his life to this cause, becoming a Dominican priest in 1524 and returning to Mexico.

This selection from Las Casas's personal and passionate *History of the Indies* — written between 1527 and 1564 and left unfinished at his death — describes an episode of the conquest of Cuba and a Christmas sermon delivered by a Dominican priest Fray Antonio de Montesinos, in Hispaniola in 1511. How was the Spanish conquest of Caribbean islands like Hispaniola and Cuba different from their conquest of Mexico? What accounts for these differences? What was the impact of the Catholic Church in Spain's colonization of the Americas? How typical do you think Fray Antonio de Montesinos was?

Bartolomé de Las Casas, from *The History of the Indies,* in *Bartolomé de Las Casas: A Selection of His Writings,* ed. and trans. George Sanderlin (New York: Knopf, 1971), 61–66, 80–85. Reproduced in *The Borzoi Anthology of Latin American Literature,* vol. I, ed. Emir Rodriquez Monegal (New York: Knopf, 1987), 24–30.

Thinking Historically

Las Casas's history offers an insight into the debates that were going on among settlers in the first decades of Spanish colonization. In addition to pointing out the role an independent clergy could sometimes play, this selection lays bare the economic interests underlying an emerging debate. What kind of people were these settlers? What was the basis of their disagreements about Indian slavery? What sorts of objections did the colonialists of Hispaniola have to the defense of the Indians by Fray Antonio de Montesinos?

The controversy over Spanish treatment of the Indians came to a head in 1550 when King Charles commanded Las Casas and one of his chief opponents, Juan Ginés de Sepúlveda, to come to the city of Valadoid and debate the issue of Spanish responsibility to the Indians in the colonies.

Sepúlveda (1490–1573) — a scholar who had translated Aristotle — like the ancient Greek philosopher believed in a hierarchy of natural superiors and inferiors and considered the benefits of slavery to the inferiors: "It is with perfect right that the Spanish dominate these barbarians of the New World . . . who are so inferior to the Spanish in prudence, intelligence, virtue, and humanity, as children are to adults, as women to men, that I am tempted to say that there is between us both as much difference as between . . . monkeys and men."[1] For Sepúlveda, the rightness of enslavement could be seen in the conquest itself and in the different characters of Montezuma and Cortés:

> Cortés, though aided by such a small number of Spanish and so few natives, was able to hold [the Aztecs], oppressed and fearful at the beginning, for many days. They were so immense a multitude that he seemed entirely lacking not only in prudence but in common sense. Could there be a better or clearer testimony of the superiority that some men have over others in talent, skill, strength of spirit, and virtue? Is it not proof that the Mexicans are slaves by nature?

Drawing on this selection from Las Casas and your previous readings on the conquest, write a reply to Sepúlveda that Las Casas might have delivered. How might your own reply to Sepúlveda differ from that which Las Casas would have delivered in 1550?

---

1 Adapted by Kevin Reilly from Juan Ginés de Sepúlveda, *Democrates Secundus, or the Treatise on the Just Causes of War Against the Indians* (1547) in Charles Gibson, ed., *The Spanish Tradition in America* (New York: Harper & Row, 1968), 113.

The Spaniards entered the province of Camagüey, which is large and densely populated . . . and when they reached the villages, the inhabitants had prepared as well as they could cassava bread from their food; what they called *guaminiquinajes* from their hunting; and also fish, if they had caught any.

Immediately upon arriving at a village, the cleric Casas would have all the little children band together; taking two or three Spaniards to help him, along with some sagacious Indians of this island of Hispaniola, whom he had brought with him, and a certain servant of his, he would baptize the children he found in the village. He did this throughout the island . . . and there were many for whom God provided holy baptism because He had predestined them to glory. God provided it at a fitting time, for none or almost none of those children remained alive after a few months. . . .

When the Spaniards arrived at a village and found the Indians at peace in their houses, they did not fail to injure and scandalize them. Not content with what the Indians freely gave, they took their wretched subsistence from them, and some, going further, chased after their wives and daughters, for this is and always has been the Spaniards' common custom in these Indies. Because of this and at the urging of the said father, Captain Narváez ordered that after the father had separated all the inhabitants of the village in half the houses, leaving the other half empty for the Spaniards' lodging, no one should dare go to the Indians' section. For this purpose, the father would go ahead with three or four men and reach a village early; by the time the Spaniards came, he had already gathered the Indians in one part and cleared the other.

Thus, because the Indians saw that the father did things for them, defending and comforting them, and also baptizing their children, in which affairs he seemed to have more command and authority than others, he received much respect and credit throughout the island among the Indians. Further, they honored him as they did their priests, magicians, prophets, or physicians, who were all one and the same.

Because of this . . . it became unnecessary to go ahead of the Spaniards. He had only to send an Indian with an old piece of paper on a stick, informing them through the messenger that those letters said thus and so. That is, that they should all be calm, that no one should absent himself because he would do them no harm, that they should have food prepared for the Christians and their children ready for baptism, or that they should gather in one part of the village, and anything else that it seemed good to counsel them — and that if they did not carry these things out, the father would be angry, which was the greatest threat that could be sent them. . . .

They [Spaniards] arrived at the town of Caonao in the evening. Here they found many people, who had prepared a great deal of food consisting of cassava bread and fish, because they had a large river close by and also were near the sea. In a little square were two thousand Indians, all squatting because they have this custom, all staring, frightened, at the mares. Nearby was a large *bohio*, or large house, in which were more than five hundred other Indians, close-packed and fearful, who did not dare come out.

When some of the domestic Indians the Spaniards were taking with them as servants (who were more than one thousand souls . . .) wished to enter the large house, the Cuban Indians had chickens ready and said to them: "Take these — do not enter here." For they already knew that the Indians who served the Spaniards were not apt to perform any other deeds than those of their masters.

There was a custom among the Spaniards that one person, appointed by the captain, should be in charge of distributing to each Spaniard the food and other things the Indians gave. And while the captain was thus on his mare and the others mounted on theirs, and the father himself was observing how the bread and fish were distributed, a Spaniard, in whom the devil is thought to have clothed himself, suddenly drew his sword. Then the whole hundred drew theirs and began to rip open the bellies, to cut and kill those lambs — men, women, children, and old folk, all of whom were seated, off guard and frightened, watching the mares and the Spaniards. And within two credos, not a man of all of them there remains alive.

The Spaniards enter the large house nearby, for this was happening at its door, and in the same way, with cuts and stabs, begin to kill as many as they found there, so that a stream of blood was running, as if a great number of cows had perished. Some of the Indians who could make haste climbed up the poles and woodwork of the house to the top, and thus escaped.

The cleric had withdrawn shortly before this massacre to where another small square of the town was formed, near where they had lodged him. This was in a large house where all the Spaniards also had to stay, and here about forty of the Indians who had carried the Spaniards' baggage from the provinces farther back were stretched out on the ground, resting. And five Spaniards chanced to be with the cleric. When these heard the blows of the swords and knew that the Spaniards were killing the Indians — without seeing anything, because there were certain houses between — they put hands to their swords and are about to kill the forty Indians . . . to pay them their commission.

The cleric, moved to wrath, opposes and rebukes them harshly to prevent them, and having some respect for him, they stopped what they were going to do, so the forty were left alive. The five go to kill where the others were killing. And as the cleric had been detained in hindering the slaying of the forty carriers, when he went he found a heap of dead, which the Spaniards had made among the Indians, which was certainly a horrible sight.

When Narváez, the captain, saw him he said: "How does your Honor like what these our Spaniards have done?"

Seeing so many cut to pieces before him, and very upset at such a cruel event, the cleric replied: "That I commend you and them to the devil!"

The heedless Narváez remained, still watching the slaughter as it took place, without speaking, acting, or moving any more than if he had been marble. For if he had wished, being on horseback and with a lance in his hands, he could have prevented the Spaniards from killing even ten persons.

Then the cleric leaves him, and goes elsewhere through some groves seeking Spaniards to stop them from killing. For they were passing through the groves looking for someone to kill, sparing neither boy, child, woman, nor old person. And they did more, in that certain Spaniards went to the road to the river, which was nearby. Then all the Indians who had escaped with wounds, stabs, and cuts — all who could flee to throw themselves into the river to save themselves — met with the Spaniards who finished them.

Another outrage occurred which should not be left untold, so that the deeds of our Christians in these regions may be observed. When the cleric entered the large house where I said there were about five hundred souls — or whatever the number, which was great — and saw with horror the dead there and those who had escaped above by the poles or woodwork, he said to them:

"No more, no more. Do not be afraid. There will be no more, there will be no more."

With this assurance, believing that it would be thus, an Indian descended, a well-disposed young man of twenty-five or thirty years, weeping. And as the cleric did not rest but went everywhere to stop the killing, the cleric then left the house. And just as the young man came down, a Spaniard who was there drew a cutlass or half sword and gives him a cut through the loins, so that his intestines fall out. . . .

The Indian, moaning, takes his intestines in his hands and comes fleeing out of the house. He encounters the cleric . . . and the cleric tells him some things about the faith, as much as the time and anguish permitted, explaining to him that if he wished to be baptized he would go to heaven to live with God. The sad one, weeping and showing pain as if he were burning in flames, said yes, and with this the cleric baptized him. He then fell dead on the ground. . . .

Of all that has been said, I am a witness. I was present and saw it; and I omit many other particulars in order to shorten the account.

"Are Not the Indians Men?"

When Sunday and the hour to preach arrived . . . Father Fray Antonio de Montesinos ascended the pulpit and took as the text and foundation of his sermon, which he carried written out and signed by the other friars: "I am the voice of one crying in the desert." After he completed his introduction and said something concerning the subject of Advent, he began to emphasize the aridity in the desert of Spanish consciences in this island, and the ignorance in which they lived; also, in what danger of eternal damnation they were, from taking no notice of the grave sins in which, with such apathy, they were immersed and dying.

Then he returns to his text, speaking thus: "I have ascended here to cause you to know those sins, I who am the voice of Christ in the desert of this island. Therefore it is fitting that you listen to this voice, not with careless attention, but with all your heart and senses. For this voice will be the strangest you ever heard, the harshest and hardest, most fearful and most dangerous you ever thought to hear."

This voice cried out for some time, with very combative and terrible words, so that it made their flesh tremble, and they seemed already standing before the divine judgment. Then, in a grand manner, the voice . . . declared what it was, or what that divine inspiration consisted of: "This voice," he said, "declares that you are all in mortal sin, and live and die in it, because of the cruelty and tyranny you practice among these innocent peoples.

"Tell me, by what right or justice do you hold these Indians in such a cruel and horrible servitude? On what authority have you waged such detestable wars against these peoples, who dwelt quietly and peacefully on their own land? Wars in which you have destroyed such infinite numbers of them by homicides and slaughters never before heard of? Why do you keep them so oppressed and exhausted, without giving them enough to eat or curing them of the sicknesses they incur from the excessive labor you give them, and they die, or rather, you kill them, in order to extract and acquire gold every day?

"And what care do you take that they should be instructed in religion, so that they may know their God and creator, may be baptized, may hear Mass, and may keep Sundays and feast days? Are these not men? Do they not have rational souls? Are you not bound to love them as you love yourselves? Don't you understand this? Don't you feel this? Why are you sleeping in such a profound and lethargic slumber? Be assured that in your present state you can no more be saved than the Moors or Turks, who lack the faith of Jesus Christ and do not desire it."

In brief, the voice explained what it had emphasized before in such a way that it left them astonished — many numb as if without feeling, others more hardened than before, some somewhat penitent, but none, as I afterward understood, converted.

When the sermon was concluded, Antonio de Montesinos descended from the pulpit with his head not at all low, for he was not a man who would want to show fear — as he felt none — if he displeased his hearers by doing and saying what seemed fitting to him, according to God. With his companion he goes to his thatch house where, perhaps, they had nothing to eat but cabbage broth without olive oil, as sometimes happened. But after he departed, the church remains full of murmurs so that, as I believe, they scarcely permitted the mass to be finished. . . .

Seeing how little God's servants feared all kinds of threats made against them, the officials softened, beseeching them to reconsider the matter and, having carefully done so, to emend what had been said in another sermon — this to satisfy the community, which had been, and was, greatly scandalized. At last . . . in order to rid themselves of the officials and to put an end to their frivolous importunities, the fathers conceded that at a seasonable time it would be thus: the same Father Fray Antonio de Montesinos would return to preach the next Sunday and would go back to the subject and say what seemed best to him about it, and, as much as possible, would try to satisfy them and explain everything he had said. This having been agreed upon, the officials departed, happy in this hope.

They then proclaimed, or some of them did, that they had left with an agreement with the vicar and the others that on the following Sunday that friar would retract everything he had said. And to hear this second sermon no invitations were needed, for there was not a person in the whole city who was not found in the church on that day. . . .

When the hour for the sermon came, after Antonio de Montesinos ascended the pulpit, the text given as the basis of his retraction was a saying from Job, Chapter 36, which commences: "I will go back over my knowledge from the beginning, and I will prove that my discourse is without falsehood." That is, "I will go back to rehearse from the beginning my knowledge and the truths which I preached to you last Sunday, and I will show that those words of mine which embittered you are true."

Upon hearing this text of his, the most clear-sighted saw immediately where he was going to end, and it was misery enough to allow him to go on from there. He began to . . . corroborate with more arguments and texts what he had affirmed before, that those oppressed and exhausted peoples were held unjustly and tyrannically. He repeated his understanding that the Spaniards could certainly not be saved in the state they were in, and that therefore they should in time heal themselves. He made them know that the friars would not confess a man of them, any more than they would confess highway robbers, and that the Spaniards might proclaim and write that to whomever they wished in Castile. In all this, the friars considered it certain that they were serving God and doing the king no small favor.

After the sermon was finished, Antonio de Montesinos went to his house. And all the people in the church remained agitated, grumbling, and much angrier at the friars than before, finding themselves de-

frauded of their vain and wicked hope that what had been said would
be unsaid — as if, after the friar made his retraction, the law of God
which they disobeyed by oppressing and exterminating these peoples
would be changed.

86

CARLOS FUENTES

From *The Buried Mirror*

In this selection from a recent history of Mexico, Carlos Fuentes, one
of Mexico's great writers, explores some of the connections between
Mexico and Spain and between the past and present. In the first part
of this selection, "The Indies Are Being Destroyed!" Fuentes recalls
Father Antonio and Las Casas. In what ways did Las Casas serve the
interests of the Spanish monarchy as opposed to "feudal pretension"?
Was the *encomienda* system a continuation or revival of European
feudalism? Why would the crown want to leave the conquistadors and
their descendants in legal ambiguity regarding their holdings?

Fuentes also discusses the development of the Black Legend — the
"legend," spread especially by Protestant Northern European powers,
that Catholic Spanish colonialism was "blackest" or most brutal of
all. Las Casas was often blamed for providing ammunition for the
Black Legend. Do you think this is a fair charge? Often, published images like those of Theodor de Bry, which other European publishers
used to illustrate Las Casas's text, were more instrumental than words
in spreading the Black Legend. How would the images (see Figures
14.3, 14.4, and 14.5) spread the idea that Spanish colonialism was the
most brutal? What does Fuentes say about criticisms of Spanish colonialism? How is his judgment different from that of Las Casas?

In the second part of the selection, "Father and Mother," Fuentes
examines the religious impact of the Spanish conquest of Mexico.
What, according to Fuentes, was that impact? Was it what Las Casas
would have wanted?

Carlos Fuentes, *The Buried Mirror* (Boston: Houghton Mifflin, 1992), 130–35, 144–47.

Thinking Historically

Fuentes says in the second part of this selection that after the conquest Las Casas saw hope for Mexicans in "denunciation" — denouncing the injustices, the atrocities, slavery, and exploitation. What do you think Fuentes thinks about denunciation as a path to hope today, almost five hundred years later? How does Fuentes's approach to the Spanish conquest differ from Las Casas's? How would you characterize his approach, and how does it provide hope for Mexicans?

"The Indies Are Being Destroyed!"

This was the cry of Father Bartolomé de Las Casas, who picked up Father Montesinos's Christmas sermon of 1511 and his question about the Indians: "Are these not men? Have they not rational souls?" — "the first cry for justice in the Americas," wrote the modern Dominican writer Pedro Henríquez Ureña.

Bartolomé de Las Casas was a slave owner in Cuba who renounced his holdings and joined the Dominicans in 1524, accusing the conquistadors of "endless crimes and offenses against the Indians who were the

Figure 14.3 Indians Mining Silver.
Source: Bridgeman-Giraudon/Art Resource, NY.

Figure 14.4 Three Native Americans.
Source: Bridgeman-Giraudon/Art Resource, NY.

Figure 14.5 Indians Retaliating.
Source: Bridgeman-Giraudon/Art Resource, NY.

king's subjects. "Over a period of fifty years, from the moment he forsook his *encomienda* in 1515 to his death in 1566, Father Las Casas denounced the "destruction of the Indies" by the conquistadors, accusing them of "the torts and offenses that they do to the kings of Castile, destroying their kingdoms . . . in the Indies." He went so far as to praise the Indians for the religiosity that they displayed, even if they were pagans. Had not the Greeks, the Romans, and the Hebrews been idolaters too? And had this pagan religiosity excluded them from the human race, or rather, nicely predisposed them for conversion?

Las Casas denied the rights of conquest, especially the institution of the *encomienda,* which he considered "more unjust and cruel than Pharaoh's oppression of the Jews," and which deprived "both masters and subjects of their freedom and of their lives." These modern ideas on the master-slave relationship, along with Las Casas's principal demands, were incorporated into the Laws of the Indies in 1542. The *encomienda* was legally abolished, although it remained, disguised as *repartimientos,* or provisional allotments of Indian laborers, as a self-perpetuating fact within the real economic system in the New World. The Crown went on combatting it, substituting administrative systems and royalist controls for it, refusing the conquistadors and their descendants property rights to their lands, and endlessly postponing decisions that would grant them feudal domination, titles of nobility, or hereditary rights.

In this sense, it can be said, with all due respect to Father Bartolomé de Las Casas, that he was the Crown's most useful tool in attacking feudal pretensions while defending humanitarian values. But in the final analysis, this struggle left a wide margin for the de facto powers of the conquistadors while preserving the eminent domain of Spanish royalty. The conquistadors and their descendants were purposely left by the Crown in the legal light of usurpers. But the Laws of the Indies, it was said, were like a spider's web, which caught only the smaller criminals and let the big ones get off scot free.

Many sixteenth-century testimonies depict the actual brutality of the *encomienda* and its even more severe form, work in the mine (*la mita*). In his marvelous line drawings of the life of Peru before and after the conquest, Guamán Poma de Ayala, a descendant of the Inca nobility, depicted the absolute impunity of the *encomendero* and his henchmen. The drawings of Theodor de Bry, which accompanied the best-selling volume by Father Las Casas, *The Destruction of the Indies,* fathered the so-called Black Legend of a brutal, sanguinary, and sadistic Spain, torturing and killing wherever she went — in tacit contrast, no doubt, to the lily-white colonialists from France, England, and the Netherlands. Yet while the latter piously disguised their own cruelties and inhumanities, they never did what Spain permitted. A debate on the nature of the conquered peoples and the rights of conquest raged through the Hispanic world for a full century, becoming the first full-fledged modern debate on human rights. This was hardly anything that the other colonial powers worried about.

There were even notes of humor in the debate, from both the Indian and the Spanish sides. During the conquest of Chile, the Araucanian chieftain Caupolicán was impaled by the conquistadors, yet as he was dying, he said, "I wish I had invaded and conquered Spain." The same idea, from the other side of the water, was expressed by a defender of human rights just as important as Las Casas, Father Francisco de Vitoria. A Jesuit teaching at Salamanca in 1539, he asked his students if they would like to see Spaniards treated by Indians in Spain the way Spaniards treated Indians in America. Discovery and conquest, he said, gave Spain no more right to American territory than the Indians would have if they discovered and conquered Spain. No doubt the same thing could have been said of the English colonization of North America. But what Father Vitoria did in his books and teachings was to internationalize the problem of power over the colonies and of the human rights of the conquered peoples. He attempted to set down rules limiting colonial power through international law, then called *jus gentium*, or the rights of people. His nemesis was the aforementioned Juan Ginés de Sepúlveda, who accused the Indians of cannibalism and human sacrifice in a society not very different from a colony of ants. As the Indians were presocial, they could legitimately be conquered by "civil men" from Europe, and all their goods could be put to civilized use, argued Sepúlveda. But were not the Spaniards, Vitoria argued right back, also guilty of crimes against nature? Were not all European nations culpable of acts of destruction and war? If this was so, no one had the moral right to conquer the Indians. . . .

Father and Mother

Whether the conquest was right or wrong, the church knew that its primary mission was to evangelize. Its missionaries met a population torn between the desire to revolt and the desire to find protection. The church offered the latter as abundantly as it could. Many Indian groups, including the Coras in Mexico, the Quechuas in Peru, and the Araucanians in Chile, resisted the Spanish for a long time. Others thronged to the church, asking for baptism in the streets and roads. The Franciscan priest Toribio de Benavente, who arrived in Mexico in 1524, was called Motolinia by the Indians, which means "the poor and humble one." He wrote, "Many come to be baptized, not only on Sundays or feast days, but even on weekdays, children and adults, healthy and sick, and from all the regions; and when the friars travel, the Indians come out to the roads with their children in their arms, and with their sick on their backs, and even decrepit old people come out, demanding to be baptized. . . . And as they go to baptism, some pray, others complain, others implore on their knees, others lift their arms, moaning and twisting, and others receive it crying and sighing."

Motolinia affirmed that in this way, fifteen years after the fall of the Aztecs in 1521, "more than four million souls had been baptized." Even if this is church propaganda, the fact remains that the formal events of Catholicism, from baptism to death rites, became a permanent fixture of popular life throughout Spanish America, and that church architecture displayed a practical imagination in uniting two vital factors of the new societies of the Americas: the need for a sense of parenthood, a father and mother, and the need for a protective physical space where the old gods might be admitted in disguise, behind the altars of the new gods.

Most mestizos did not know their fathers. They knew only their Indian mothers, the common-law wives of the Spanish. Miscegenation was certainly the rule in the Iberian colonies, as opposed to racial purity and puritanical hypocrisy in the English colonies. But this did not soften the sensation of orphanhood that many offspring of Spaniards and Indian women must have felt. La Malinche had a child by Cortés, who recognized him and had him baptized Martín. Cortés had another son, also named Martín, by his not yet strangled wife, Catalina Juárez. In time the brothers met, and in 1565 staged the first rebellion of Mexican Creole and mestizo nationalism against Spanish rule. The legitimation of the bastard, the identification of the orphan, became one of the central, if at times unspoken, problems of Latin American culture. It was dealt with by the Spaniards through religious and legal means.

The flight of the gods, who had abandoned their people; the destruction of the temples; the razing of the cities; the wholesale pillage and destruction of Indian culture; the devastation of the Indian economy by the mine and the *encomienda;* plus the almost paralyzing sense of amazement, of sheer wonder at what had happened — where was hope to be found? The subjugated Indians could hardly see a glimmer anywhere. How were despair and insurrection to be avoided? This was the question raised by the humanists of the colonies, but also by their wiser (and wilier) politicians. One answer had been Las Casas's denunciation. But it was truly the second viceroy and first archbishop of Mexico City, Juan de Zumárraga, who found the lasting solution: Give a mother to the orphaned children of the New World.

In early December 1531, on Tepeyac Hill near Mexico City, a site previously dedicated to the worship of the Aztec goddess Tonantzin, the Virgin of Guadalupe appeared, bearing roses in winter and choosing a lowly *tameme,* or Indian bearer, Juan Diego, as the object of her love and recognition. In one fabulous stroke, the Spanish authorities transformed the Indian people from children of violated women to children of the pure Virgin. From Babylon to Bethlehem, in one flash of political genius, whore became virgin and Malinche became Guadalupe. Nothing has proved as consoling, unifying, and worthy of fierce respect since then as the figure of the Virgin of Guadalupe in Mexico, the Virgin of La Caridad del Cobre in Cuba, and the Virgin of Coromoto in Venezuela. The conquered people now had a mother.

They also found a father. Mexico imposed on Cortés the mask of Quetzalcoatl. Cortés refused it and instead imposed on Mexico the mask of Christ. Ever since, it has been impossible to know who is worshipped at the baroque altars of Puebla, Oaxaca, and Tlaxcala: Christ or Quetzalcoatl? In a universe accustomed to seeing men sacrificed to the gods, nothing amazed the Indians more than the sight of a god who had sacrificed himself to men. It was the redemption of humankind by Christ that fascinated and really defeated the Indians of the New World. The true return of the gods was the arrival of Christ. Christ was the recovered memory that in the beginning it *was* the gods who sacrificed themselves for the benefit of humankind. This misty memory, engulfed by the somber human sacrifices ordained by Aztec power, was now rescued by the Christian church. The result was flagrant syncretism, the blending of Christian and aboriginal faiths, one of the cultural foundations of the Spanish American world.

Yet a striking fact remains: All the Mexican Christs are dead, or at the very least in agony. Whether in Calvary, on the cross, or laid out in a glass bier, the Christ that one sees in Mexico's village churches is bleeding, prostrate, and lonely. By contrast, the Virgin, as in Spain, is surrounded by perpetual glory, celebration, flowers, and processions. And the decor itself, the great baroque architecture of Latin America, is both a celebration of the new religion and a risky celebration of the survival of the old one.

The marvelous chapel at Tonantzintla near Cholula is one of the most startling confirmations of syncretism as the dynamic basis of postconquest culture. What happened here happened throughout Latin America. The Indian artisans were given engravings of the saints and other religious motifs by the Christian evangelizers and asked to reproduce them inside the churches. But the artisans and masons of the temples had something more than a copy in mind. They wished to celebrate their old gods as well as the new ones, but they had to mask this intention by blending a praise of nature with a praise of heaven and making them indistinguishable. Tonantzintla is in effect a re-creation of the Indian paradise. White and gold, it overflows with plenty as all the fruits and the flowers of the tropics climb up to its dome, a dream of infinite abundance. Religious syncretism triumphed as, somehow, the conquerors were conquered.

In Tonantzintla, the Indians depicted themselves as innocent angels on the way to heaven, while the Spanish conquistadors were shown as ferocious, fork-tongued, bearded devils. Paradise can be regained after all.

87

ALFRED CROSBY

From *Germs, Seeds, and Animals*

The modern historian Alfred Crosby takes us back to Aztec Mexico, even if the names and dates at first do not seem familiar. Why, according to Crosby, were the Spanish able to conquer the Aztecs? What were the major consequences of the conquest? What would have most surprised Lord Ahuitzotl if he could have returned one hundred years later?

Thinking Historically

What does the Spanish conquest mean for this modern historian? Is his interpretation better, more modern, or merely different from the earlier interpretations you have read? To what extent do his interpretations come from just asking different questions? Does he pose "modern" questions that could not have been asked in the sixteenth century?

Chimalpahin Cuauhlehuanitzin, one of our best sources of information on Mexico in the years immediately before and after the Spanish conquest, was an Indian historian whom the invaders trained in the reading and writing of the Roman alphabet in the sixteenth century. His writings (in Nahuatl) inform us that the year 13-Flint before the invasion was a grim one in the Valley of Mexico. There was sickness, hunger, and an eclipse of the sun; an eruption of some sort between the volcanoes Iztaccíhuatl and Popocatépetl; "and many ferocious beasts devoured the children." But 13-Flint, Chimalpahin makes clear, was an exception in what was an era of triumph for the Aztecs. They, who within recorded memory had been wanderers from the savage north, now exacted tributes of food, gold, quetzal feathers, and human hearts from vassal states all the way from the remote dry lands from which they had emerged to the rain forests of the south and east. The stiff-necked Tarascos, at the cost of perennial war, retained their independence, as did — precariously — the anciently civilized Mayas, and

Alfred W. Crosby, "The Biological Metamorphosis of the Americas," in *Germs, Seeds, and Animals: Studies in Ecological History*, ed. Alfred W. Crosby (Armonk: M. E. Sharpe, 1994), 45–49, 60.

there were a few others who survived in the chinks of the Aztec Empire. Otherwise, central Mexico lay under the hegemony of the Aztecs.

Lord Ahuitzotl, who was ruler of the Aztecs in 13-Flint, used the legions and wealth under his command to improve and adorn his capital, the incomparable Tenochtitlán. He built a new aqueduct to bring fresh water to its scores of thousands of inhabitants. He rebuilt and reconsecrated the gigantic temple to the Aztec tribal deities, Huitzilopochtli and Tezcatlipoca. He did not — how could he have? — see in the strange events of 13-Flint portents of the end of his empire and of his world.

A decade later, in 10-Rabbit, his nephew Motecuhzoma Xocoyotzin, known to us as Montezuma, succeeded him as leader of the Aztecs. Montezuma's subjects numbered in the millions, and, so far as he or they knew, the empire had no equal in power and riches under the sky. Montezuma made plans to rebuild the great temple once more, higher and more extravagantly than any of his predecessors.

Reports drifted in from the eastern coast of pale, hairy visitors in boats "like towers or small mountains." There were only a few of them, and invaders traditionally came from the north, as had the Aztecs themselves, not from the east and never from the sea. Gods, however, might come from the sea.

The Onslaught

In the year 1-Reed the visitors came to invade and to stay forever. The invaders proved to be humans, not gods, but they were incomprehensibly alien and powerful. . . .

Most hideous of all the invaders' allies was a pestilence, a *hueyzahuatl*, that swept all the land immediately after the Aztecs, quickened by atrocities, turned on the invaders, killing half of them as they fought their way out of Tenochtitlán. The pestilence spared the invaders but was a thing of agony, disfigurement, and death for the peoples of Mexico. There was no defense against it nor cure for it. Bernardino de Sahagún learned how it struck in the month of Tepeilhuitl and

> spread over the people as great destruction. Some it quite covered on all parts — their faces, their heads, their breasts, and so on. There was a great havoc. Very many died of it. They could not walk; they only lay in their resting places and beds. They could not move; they could not stir; they could not change position, nor lie on one side; nor face down, nor on their backs. And if they stirred, much did they cry out. Great was its destruction. Covered, mantled with pustules, very many people died of them.

One-third, one-half — no one knows how many — of the Aztecs and the other peoples of Mexico died. . . .

The invaders' chief, Hernán Cortés, ordered that stones from the temple of which Lord Ahuitzotl had been so proud should be gathered up, and that a Christian cathedral should be made of them in the center of what had become, by his victory, Mexico City. The vanquished learned that the ominous year 13-Flint was more properly designated as the year 1492 of a deity both more imperialistic and more merciful than Huitzilopochtli or Tezcatlipoca, and that Tenochtitlán had fallen in the year 1521, not 3-House.

The fall of Tenochtitlán in the year 3-House was the worst discrete event in the Aztecs' history. Worse, however, was this: 3-House was the beginning of the most tragic century of their history. Their civilization suffered massive amputations and survived at the root only by accepting alien graftings in the branch, as the conquistadores and the friars replaced their ancient noble and priestly classes. There were advantages that came with the defeat: an alphabet, a more supple instrument for expression than their own logo-syllabic system of writing; the true arch to replace the corbel; tools with an iron edge that did not shatter like an obsidian edge when it struck the rock hidden in the leaves. But the magnitude of the change, good and bad, was almost greater than the mind could encompass or the heart endure. The metamorphosis was more than political or religious or intellectual or technological; it was biological. The biota of Mexico — its *life* — and, in time, that of the entire Western Hemisphere changed.

The Change

If Lord Ahuitzotl had returned to Mexico (now New Spain) a hundred years after 13-Flint he would have found much the same as in his lifetime. He would have recognized the profiles of the mountains, all the wild birds, and most of the plants. The basic and holy food of his people was still maize. But he would have been stunned by the sight of plants and creatures he had never seen or dreamed of during his days on earth. Alien plants grew alongside the old plants in Mexico, and its 1592 fauna, in its large animals, was as different from that of 1492 as the native fauna of Zimbabwe is from that of Spain.

The invaders had brought in wheat and other Eurasian and African grains; peach, pear, orange, and lemon trees; chick-peas, grape vines, melons, onions, radishes, and much more. A Spanish nobleman come to America could require his *indios* to furnish his table with the foods of his ancestors. Along with the Old World crops had come Old World weeds. European clover was by now so common that the Aztecs had a word of their own for it. They called it Castilian *ocoxochitl,* naming it after a low native plant that also prefers shade and moisture.

Of all the new sights of 1592 — the cathedrals, the fields of wheat, wheeled vehicles, brigantines with sails and lounging sailors on Lake Texcoco where there had once been only canoes and sweating paddlers — nothing could have amazed Ahuitzotl more than the new animals: pigs, sheep, goats, burros, and others. Now there were cattle everywhere, and ranches with more than a hundred thousand each in the north. Now there were thousands upon thousands of horses, and they were available to any European (and, despite the law, the Indian, too) with a few coins or the skill to rope them. The horsemanship of the Mexican *vaquero* was already legendary on both sides of the Atlantic.

During Lord Ahuitzotl's lifetime the best way to move four hundred ears of maize in Mexico was on the bent back of a man, and the fastest means to deliver a message was by a runner. Now the bent man loaded four thousand ears onto a wheeled wagon pulled by a burro, and the messenger vaulted onto a horse and set off at several times the fastest pace of the fastest sprinter.

But Lord Ahuitzotl was an Aztec, an *indio,* and what would have put a catch in his breath a century after 13-Flint was not so much the new animals, for all their number, but his own kind of people, in their meager number. War, brutality, hunger, social and family disarray, loss of farmland to the invading humans and their flocks, and exploitation in general had taken their toll, but disease was the worst enemy. The *hueyzahuatl* of 1520–21, like the fall of Tenochtitlán, may have been the worst of its kind, but, more important, it was the beginning of a series of pestilential onslaughts. The worst of the worst of the times of *cocoliztli* were 1545–48, a time of bleeding from the nose and eyes, and 1576–81, when, again, many bled from the nose and windrows of Indians fell, but few Spaniards. If Lord Ahuitzotl had returned a century after his death, he would have found one for every ten or even twenty *indios* who had lived in his time.

Some of the survivors were *mestizos,* children of European men and Indian women. The mestizo, with his Indian skin and Visigothic eyes, proffering a cup of cocoa, a mixture of *chocolatl* and Old World sugar; the wild Chichimec on his Berber mare; the Zapotec herder with his sheep; the Aztec, perhaps the last of the line of Ahuitzotl, receiving the final rites of the Christian faith as he slipped into the terminal coma of an infection newly arrived from Seville — in so many ways New Spain was *new,* a combination, crossing, and concoction of entities that had never before existed on the same continent. . . .

And on and on to the present day. Alaska's and Canada's most remote Eskimos and Indians and South America's last tribes of hunter-gatherers and horticulturists have been decimated by tuberculosis, measles, and influenza within living memory. In 1990 the Yanomamö of the borderland of Brazil and Venezuela were decreasing rapidly under the attack not only or even primarily of the encroaching gold miners, but of malaria, influenza, measles, and chicken pox. The best ally of the invaders continues to be disease. . . .

Native Americans often object to the name "New World," a European term for the lands of the Western Hemisphere. They point out that those lands were familiar to them long before Christopher Columbus was born, and their argument is one the rest of us owe respectful consideration. But we all are justified in the use of the title for the Americas since 1492. Until Columbus found his way across the Atlantic, the biota of the two sets of continents on either side were markedly different, the products of what, through time, had usually been divergent evolution. Since then the biota of both, most undeniably of the Americas, have in significant part been the product of revolution, that is, the abrupt addition and explosive propagation of exotic species from the lands on the other side of the waters that Columbus crossed in 1492. The great Genovese navigated, administered, crusaded, enslaved, but above all he mixed, mingled, jumbled, and homogenized the biota of our planet.

REFLECTIONS

Truth and change are concepts we sometimes have difficulty reconciling. If something is true, how can it change? How can new truths replace old truths without making the old truths false? These questions become even more perplexing when it comes to historical writing, because history is the study of the past. It would seem that because the past does not change, a new interpretation of it would simply supercede the older one, and, yet, this is not necessarily so.

Las Casas's *The History of the Indies,* with its grand comparative sweep and its great political mission, could not have been written in the heat of battle. We might say that it is a wonder that it was written at all, and a wonder that it found an audience — especially a Spanish audience — and a king, who were willing to listen, read, and debate the issues it raised. The Protestant Reformation might have ensured its publication by Spain's enemies, but, as Fuentes observes, the Spanish debate over Indian rights was unique in Europe. It was also a debate that the Spanish could not have held before 1550. The language of the initial contact, in Díaz's and the Aztec accounts, expressed wonder, surprise, revulsion, fear, remorse perhaps, but not self-analysis, cultural criticism, or political reform. The year 1550 was, in fact, too early for tolerance or equality. Slavery did not end in European colonies for another three hundred years. It took three hundred years to build a consensus around the rights of life, liberty, and property — a consensus nourished by history books perceived as moral tales, stories of outrageous acts in the tradition of Las Casas.

Good guys and bad guys were out of style at the end of the twentieth century. Historians in former colonies that have been self-governing for generations or centuries find no benefit in blaming the colonizers or in feeling victimized. What is needed for renewal are stories that highlight old abilities and new hopes. In a world of hyphenated identities, five hundred years after the beginning of a "new race" in Mexico, what is needed is no race, no division. Fuentes looks for a Mexico that is both Spanish and Indian, Christian and pagan, beyond blame and schism. Like many of today's historians of the Spanish conquest, Fuentes emphasizes the continuity between preconquest and postconquest Mexican culture, Malinche and Guadalupe, Quetzalcoatl and Christ. Does the desire for solidarity make for a history that is less true? Or is it more true because it answers questions that are relevant to peoples' needs today?

Alfred Crosby is a founder of ecological history in the United States, probably one of the most rapidly developing subfields in the discipline. Like world history, its approach answers recent questions and concerns. Much of our knowledge of species, microbes, and climate comes from a postsatellite age. If postsatellite ecological history glosses over heroes and villains (as postmodern history forsakes morals and heroics for irony and nuance), every generation gets what it needs. Old narrative styles do not disappear.

In choices of history, like everything else, our age tries to "have it all." In one sense we can: Bookstores — new, used, and virtual — offer abundant possibilities. It's a free country: People can read whatever they want. But when writing a history, a common goal is to get it right. Readers want something accurate, informed, and truthful. On all such levels, historians must make choices. Even if we only want to tell a story, we must choose whose story to tell. Reading the accounts by Díaz and the Aztec account and Alfred Crosby reminds us that observations of the same event are as unique as the individual who communicates them; indeed, the tellings may seem to record different events altogether.

One of the most useful lessons history teaches us, then, is the partiality of any interpretation and, by inference, the possibility of so many other interpretations. Perhaps that realization will allow us to tolerate the eccentric, grow from disagreements, and expand our own possibilities, asking our own questions, yielding our own answers. And if we can do that without losing sight of the obdurate, unchanging reality of the past, we will have learned to think historically.

ACKNOWLEDGMENTS

Al-Muttaqi. Excerpts from "Kanz al-'Ummal" iii (Lewis translation), pp. 150–51, in *Islam: From the Prophet Muhammad to the Capture of Constantinople, Volume 1: Politics and War*, edited by Bernard Lewis, translated by Bernard Lewis. Copyright © 1974 by Bernard Lewis. Used by permission of Oxford University Press.

Natalie Angier. "Furs for Evening, But Cloth Was the Stone Age Standby." From *The New York Times*, December 15, 1999. Copyright © 1999 The New York Times. Reprinted by permission.

Anonymous. "Brahman and Atman. From Chandogya Upanishad." in *The Upanishads: Breath of the Eternal*, translated by Juan Mascaro. Copyright © by 1965 by Juan Mascaro. Reprinted with permission of Penguin Books, Ltd.

Anonymous. Excerpt from the *Bhagavad Gita: Caste and Self*, translated by Barbara Stoler Miller. Copyright © 1986 by Barbara Stoler Miller. Used by permission of Bantam Books, a division of Random House, Inc.

Anonymous. Excerpt from *The Epic of Gilgamesh*, translated by N. K. Sanders. Copyright © 1972 by N. K. Sanders. Reprinted with the permission of Penguin Books, Ltd.

Anonymous. "The Rig-Veda: Sacrifice as Creation." Excerpt from *Sources of Indian Tradition*, Second Edition, edited by Ainslie T. Embree. Copyright © 1988 by Columbia University Press. Reprinted with permission of the publisher.

Anonymous. "*Svetasvatara* Upanishad." From *The Upanishads: Breath of the Eternal*, translated by Swami Prabhavananda and Frederick Manchester. Copyright © 1948, 1957 by The Vedanta Society of Southern California. Reprinted with permission.

Anonymous. "The Upanishads: Karma and Reincarnation." Excerpt from *The Hindu Tradition: Readings in Oriental Thought*, edited by Ainslie T. Embree. Copyright ©1966 by Random House, Inc. Used by permission of Random House, Inc.

Aristotle. "The Athenian Constitution." From *Aristotle, Politics, and the Athenian Constitution*, translated by John Warrington. Copyright © 1959 by John Warrington. Reprinted with the permission of David Campbell Publishers, Ltd.

"Aztec Account of the Conquest." From *The Broken Spears: The Aztec Account of the Conquest of Mexico*, by Miguel Leon-Portilla. Copyright 1962, 1990 by Miguel Leon-Portilla. Expanded and Updated Edition © 1992 by Miguel Leon-Portilla. Reprinted by permission of Beacon Press, Boston.

J. P. V. D. Balsdon. Excerpts from *Roman Women: Their History and Habits*, by J. P. V. D. Balsdon. Barnes & Noble, 1962. Reprinted by permission.

Ban Zhao. "Lessons for Women." From *Pan Chao: Foremost Woman Scholar of China*, translated by Nancy Lee Swann. Copyright © The East Asian Library and the Gest Collection, Princeton University. Reprinted by permission of Princeton University.

Bartolomé de Las Casas. Excerpt from *Bartolomé de Las Casas: A Selection of His Writings* by Bartolomé de Las Casas, translated by George Sanderlin. Copyright © 1971 by Alfred A. Knopf, a division of Random House, Inc. Used by permission of Alfred A. Knopf, a division of Random House, Inc.

Jerry H. Bentley. "The Spread of World Religions." From *Old World Encounters: Cross-Cultural Contacts and Exchanges in Pre-Modern Times.* Copyright © 1993 by Oxford University Press, Inc. Used by permission of Oxford University Press, Inc.

Elise Boulding. "Women and the Agricultural Revolution." From *The Underside of History: A View of Women Through Time* (Boulder: Westview Press, 1976). Copyright © 1976 by Elise Boulding. Reprinted by permission of the author.

Fernand Braudel. "Towns and Cities." Excerpt from *The Structures of Everyday Life: The Limits of the Possible* by Fernand Braudel. (London: Collins, 1983). Copyright © 1983. Reprinted by permission of Armand Colin Foreign Rights.

"Buddhism and Caste," "Buddha's First Sermon," and "Buddhism in China" (Hung-ming chi, in Taisho daizokyo, LII, 1-7) from *The Buddhist Tradition in India, China, and Japan* by William Theodore de Bary. Copyright © 1969. Used by permission of Random House, Inc.

Richard W. Bulliet. "Religious Conversion and the Spread of Innovation." Excerpt from *Conversion to Islam in the Medieval Period* by Richard W. Bulliet. Copyright © 1979. Published by Harvard University Press. Reprinted by permission of the author.

Andreas Capellanus. Excerpt from *The Art of Courtly Love,* translated by John J. Parry. Copyright © 1990 by Columbia University Press. Reprinted with the permission of the publisher.

"Chronicle of Solomon bar Simson." From *The Jews and the Crusaders: The Hebrew Chronicles of the First and Second Crusades* by Shlomo Eidelberg, editor and translator (The University of Wisconsin Press, 1977). © 1977. Reprinted with the permission of Shlomo Eidelberg.

Thomas B. Coburn. "The Devi-Mahatmya." Excerpt from *Encountering the Goddess: A Translation of the Devi-Mahatmya and a Study of Its Interpretation* by Thomas B. Coburn. Copyright © 1991 State University of New York Press. Reprinted by permission. All rights reserved.

Anna Comnena. Excerpt from *The Alexiad of Princess Anna Comnena,* translated by Elizabeth A. S. Dawes. Reprinted with the permission of Barnes and Noble Books, Totowa, New Jersey, 07512.

Alfred Crosby. "The Columbian Exchange." From *Germs, Seeds, and Animals: Studies in Ecological History,* by Alfred Crosby. Copyright © 1994 by M. E. Sharpe, Inc. Reprinted with permission.

Bernal Díaz. Excerpt from *The Conquest of New Spain*, translated by J. M. Cohen. Copyright © 1963 J. M. Cohen. Reprinted with the permission of Penguin Books, Ltd.

Fan Zhongyan. "Rules for the Fan Lineage's Charitable Estate." From *Chinese Civilization: A Sourcebook*, Second Edition, by Patricia Buckley Ebrey. Copyright © 1993 by Patricia Buckley Ebrey. Reprinted with the permission of The Free Press, A Division of Simon & Schuster Adult Publishing Group. All rights reserved.

Richard C. Foltz. "The Islamization of the Silk Road." Excerpts from *Religions of the Silk Road: Overland Trade and Cultural Exchange from Antiquity to the Fifteenth Century* by Richard C. Foltz. Copyright © Richard C. Foltz. Reprinted by permission of Palgrave Macmillan.

Carlos Fuentes. Excerpt from *The Buried Mirror* by Carlos Fuentes. Copyright © 1992 by Carlos Fuentes. Reprinted by permission of Houghton Mifflin Company. All rights reserved.

Fulcher of Chartres. "Pope Urban at Clermont," "The Siege of Antioch," and "The Latins in the Levant." From *The First Crusade: The Chronicle of Fulcher of Chartres and Other Source Materials*, Second Edition, by Edward Peters, editor. Copyright © 1998. Reprinted by permission of the University of Pennsylvania Press.

Jack Goody. "Love, Lust, and Literacy." Excerpts from *Food and Love: A Cultural History of the East and West*. Copyright © 1999. Reprinted by permission of Verso.

S. D. Goitein. "Cairo: An Islamic City in Light of the Geniza." From *Middle Eastern Cities*, edited by Ira M. Lapidus. Copyright © 1969 by the Regents of the University of California. Reprinted with the permission of the University of California Press.

Gregory Guzman. "Were the Barbarians a Negative or Positive Factor in Ancient and Medieval History?" From *The Historian*, August 1988. Reprinted with the permission of the author.

Valerie Hansen. "The Creation of the Chinese Empire." From *The Open Empire: A History of China to 1600*, by Valerie Hansen. Copyright © 2000 by W. W. Norton & Company. Used by permission of W. W. Norton & Company, Inc.

Zahi Hawass. "Love and Marriage in Ancient Egypt." Excerpt reprinted from *Silent Images: Women in Pharaonic Egypt*. Copyright © 2000 Harry N. Abrams, Inc. Reprinted by permission.

Morton Hunt. Quotes and paraphrased text from Morton Hunt's *The Natural History of Love*, 1959, 1987, are reprinted by permission of Morton Hunt. Copyright © 1987 by Morton Hunt.

Ibn al-Athir. "The Conquest of Jerusalem." Excerpt from *Arab Historians of the Crusades: Selected and Translated from the Arabic Sources,* edited and translated by E. J. Costello. Islamic World Series, 1969. Copyright © 1969 Routledge & Kegan Paul, Ltd. Reprinted by permission of the University of California Press.

"Image from Cistercian Manuscript, 12th Century, Monk Choppng Tree." Courtesy of Tresorier Principal Municipal–Dijon.

John of Plano Carpini. Excerpt from *History of the Mongols;* Guyuk Khan, "Letter to Pope Innocent IV"; excerpt from "Narrative of Brother Benedict the Pole"; and excerpt from *The Journey of William of Rubrick* from *Mission to Asia: Narratives and Letters of the Franciscan Missionaries to Mongolia and China in the Thirteenth and Fourteenth Centuries,* translated by a nun of Stanbrook Abbey, edited by Christopher Dawson. Copyright © 1955. Reprinted with permission of Rowman & Littlefield.

The Koran. Excerpts from *The Glorious Koran,* translated by Muhammad Marmaduke Pickthall (Mecca: Muslim World League, 1977). Reprinted with permission.

Gerda Lerner. "The Urban Revolution: Origins of Patriarchy." From *The Creation of Patriarchy.* Copyright © 1986, 1987 by Gerda Lerner. Used by permission of Oxford University Press, Inc.

"Letter from a Jewish Pilgrim in Egypt." Translated by S. D. Goitein, *Journal of Jewish Studies,* vol. 3, no. 4 (Jewish Chronicle Publications, 1952). The Oxford Centre for Hebrew and Jewish Studies.

Liu Tsung-yuan. "Camel Kuo the Gardener." From *An Anthology of Chinese Literature: From Early Times to the Fourteenth Century,* edited and translated by Cyril Birch. Copyright © 1965 by Grove Press, Inc. Used by permission of Grove/Atlantic, Inc.

Marco Polo. Excerpt from *Marco Polo: The Travels,* translated by Ronald Latham. Copyright © 1958 by Ronald Latham. Reprinted with the permission of Penguin Books, Ltd.

William H. McNeill. "Greek and Indian Civilization." From *A World History*, Second Edition. Copyright © 1971 by Oxford University Press. Reprinted by permission of the author.

Ichisada Miyazaki. "The Chinese Civil Service Exam System." From *China's Examination Hell,* translated by Conrad Schirokauer. Copyright © 1976. Reprinted by permission of the publishers, Weatherhill, Inc.

David Morgan. Excerpt from *The Mongols.* Copyright © 1986 by David Morgan. Reprinted with the permission of Basil Blackwell.

R. K. Nararyan. Excerpt from *The Ramayama* by R. K. Narayan. Copyright R. K. Narayan 1972. Used by permission of the Wallace Literary Agency, Inc.

Al Omari. "Cairo and Niane." Excerpt from "Mali in the Fourteenth Century" in *The African Past,* translated and edited by Basil Davidson. Copyright © 1964 Basil Davidson. Reprinted by permission of Curtis Brown Ltd.

Pliny. From *Pliny the Younger: Volume II,* Loeb Classical Library Volume 59, translated by Betty Radice. Copyright © 1969 by the President and Fellows of Harvard College. The Loeb Classical Library® is a registered trademark of the President and Fellows of Harvard College. Reprinted by permission of the Publishers and Trustees of the Loeb Classical Library.

Plutarch. "Cicero." From *Fall of the Roman Empire*, translated by Rex Warner. Copyright © 1958 by Rex Warner, renewed 1986 by Frances C. Warner. Reprinted with the permission of Penguin Books, Ltd.

Roxann Prazniak. "Ban Zhao and the End of Chinese Feudalism." From *Dialogues across Civilizations* by Roxann Prazniak. Copyright © 1996 Westview Press. Reprinted by permission.

Nicholas Purcell. "Rome: The Arts of Government." From *Oxford History of the Classical World: The Roman World*, edited by John Boardman, Jasper Griffin, and Oswyn Murray. Copyright © 1988. Reprinted by permission of Oxford University Press.

Kevin Reilly. "Cities and Civilizations," and "Love in Medieval Europe, India, and Japan." From *The West and the World: A History of Civilization,* Second Edition. Copyright © 1989 by Kevin Reilly. Reprinted with the permission of HarperCollins Publishers, Inc.

J. J. Saunders. Excerpt from "Civilization of Medieval Islam." From *A History of Medieval Islam.* Copyright © 1978. Reprinted with the permission of Routledge UK.

Lynda Norene Shaffer. "Southernization." From *Journal of World History 5*, no. 1, Spring 1994. Copyright © 1994 by the University of Hawaii Press. Reprinted with the permission of the publishers. All rights reserved.

Murasaki Shikibu. Excerpts from *The Tale of Genji,* translated by Arthur Waley. Copyright © 1929 by Houghton Mifflin Company. Reprinted with the permission of Houghton Mifflin Company and Unwin Hyman/HarperCollins Publishers, Ltd., London. All rights reserved.

Marjorie Shostak. "Memories of a !Kung Girlhood." From *Nisa: The Life and Words of a !Kung Woman.* Copyright © 1981 by Marjorie Shostak. Reprinted with the permission of Harvard University Press.

Sima Qian. "The Annals of Qin." From *Historical Records*, translated by Raymond Dawson. Copyright © 1994 by Raymond Dawson. Reprinted by permission of Oxford University Press.

Aidan Southall. "Guilds and the Chinese City." Excerpt from *The City in Time and Space* by Aidan Southall. Copyright © 1998. Reprinted by permission of Cambridge University Press.

Travelers Amid Mountains and Streams by K'uan, Sung Dynasty, Courtesy of National Palace Museum, Taipei, Taiwan, Republic of China.

Paul Veyne. "The Roman Empire: Where Public Life Was Private." From *A History of Private Life: Volume 1: From Pagan Rome to Byzantium*, by Paul Veyne. Copyright © 1987 by the President and Fellows of Harvard College. Reprinted by permission of the publisher, The Belknap Press of Harvard University Press.

Lynn White Jr. "The Historical Roots of Our Ecological Crisis." From *Science* 155: 1203–7 (1967). Copyright © 1967 AAAS. Reprinted by permission.